———— Stanley Gibbons ————

GREAT BRITAIN
CONCISE
STAMP CATALOGUE

1994 Edition

GW00506278

Stanley Gibbons Ltd
London and Ringwood

By Appointment to Her Majesty The Queen
Stanley Gibbons Ltd., London
Philatelists

Published by **Stanley Gibbons Publications**
Editorial, Sales Offices and Distribution Centre:
5 Parkside, Christchurch Road, Ringwood,
Hants BH24 3SH

First Edition — May 1986
Second Edition — May 1987
Third Edition — May 1988
Fourth Edition — May 1989
Fifth Edition — May 1990
Sixth Edition—May 1991
Seventh Edition—May 1992
Eighth Edition—April 1993
Ninth Edition—April 1994

© Stanley Gibbons Ltd 1994

ISBN:0-85259-368-6

Item No. 2887 (94)

Made and Printed in Great Britain by
Black Bear Press Limited, Cambridge

THE GREAT BRITAIN CONCISE CATALOGUE

1994 Edition

The *Concise Catalogue,* now in its ninth year of publication, has rapidly established itself as an essential guide for the "one-country" collector of Great Britain.

The popularity of Great Britain stamps continues to grow — the *Concise Catalogue* supplies the information to enhance your collection.

The *Concise* listings are based on the Great Britain section of our *Part 1 (British Commonwealth) Catalogue,* but there is much more additional material within its pages:

- All issues from the Penny Black of 1840 to March 1994 including Regional, Postage Due, Official and Postal Fiscal stamps.
- All different stamp designs are illustrated.
- Every basic stamp listed, including those with different watermarks or perforations and those showing graphite lines or phosphor bands.
- Unmounted mint and mounted mint prices quoted for King Edward VII and King George V issues.
- Missing colours, missing embossing, watermark errors, imperforate errors and phosphor omitted varieties from those stamps normally issued with phosphor bands.
- Gutter Pairs and "Traffic light" Gutter Pairs listed in mint sets.
- First Day Covers for all Special Issues, definitives, Sponsored Booklet definitive panes and Regionals, of the present reign. All British Post Office special First Day of Issue postmarks are illustrated and priced on cover.
- Post Office Picture Cards (PHQ cards) are priced as sets, both mint and used with First Day of Issue postmarks.
- Presentation, Collector and Gift Packs, including the scarce versions with foreign inscriptions.
- Quick-reference diagrams for listed Machin decimal booklet panes.
- Design Index for Commemorative and Special Stamps after the Philatelic Information Section.
- Machin and commemorative underprints given separate catalogue numbers.
- Post Office Yearbooks.
- Royal Mail Postage Labels priced in mint or used sets and on British Post Office First Day Covers.
- Wartime issues for the Channel Islands.
- Separate section for Post Office Stamp Booklets with dated editions of King George VI listed separately.
- Helpful Introductory section providing definitions and guidance for the collector and including all watermark illustrations shown together to assist identification.
- Separate section for Postmaster and U.P.U. Specimen overprints.
- Addresses for specialist philatelic societies covering Great Britain stamps.
- Recently discovered errors and varieties listed. See Nos. 164b, 626a, 774Ec, 796ab, X972a, X977a, X994a, 894Eb, 903Ed, 1199Ea, 1201Eb, 1582a, 1625a, 1659a, 1665Ey, 1666Ey, 1790a, D39Wi, D41Wi.

David J. Aggersberg

Stanley Gibbons Holdings Plc.

STANLEY GIBBONS LTD, STANLEY GIBBONS AUCTIONS

399 STRAND, LONDON WC2R 0LX

Auction Room and Specialist Departments. Open Monday–Friday, 9.30 a.m. to 5 p.m.

Shop: Open Monday–Friday 8.30 a.m. to 6 p.m. and Saturday 10 a.m. to 4 p.m.
Telephone 071-836 8444 and Fax 071 836 7342 for all departments.

STANLEY GIBBONS PUBLICATIONS

5 PARKSIDE, CHRISTCHURCH ROAD, RINGWOOD, HANTS BH24 3SH

Telephone 0425 472363 (24 hour answer phone service) and **Fax 0425 470247**
Publications Shop (at above address). Open Monday-Friday 9 a.m. to 3 p.m.
Publications Mail Order. FREEPHONE 0800 611622 Monday-Friday 8.30 a.m. to 5 p.m.

For the Great Britain specialist collector . . .

Stanley Gibbons Great Britain Specialised Catalogue in five volumes. Recognised as leading publications of their kind, and spanning British stamp issues from the 1840s to the 1980s.

Item 0285 Volume 1 (Queen Victoria)
Item 0286 Volume 2 (King Edward VII to King George VI)
Item 2810 Volume 3 (Queen Elizabeth II Pre-decimal issues)
Item 2820 Volume 4 (Queen Elizabeth II Decimal Definitive issues)
Item 2891 Volume 5 (Queen Elizabeth II Decimal Special issues)

Great Britain Checklist

Printed in colour, published annually, this handy size checklist provides a clear update on GB stamp prices.

Item 0289 Collect British Stamps

For details of these and other S.G. Publications write to the Ringwood address for free Mail Order catalogue.

Great Britain Philatelic Societies

The Great Britain Philatelic Society. Hon. Membership Secretary: D. Glover, 10 Rockwood Park, Saint Hill, East Grinstead, West Sussex, RH19 4JX.

The British Decimal Stamps Study Circle. The Secretary: P. Daniels, 70 Moor Park Close, Rainham, Gillingham, Kent, ME8 8QT.

The Great Britain Decimal Stamp Book Study Circle. Hon. Membership Secretary: A. J. Wilkins, 3 Buttermere Close, Brierley Hill, West Midlands, DY5 3SD.

STANLEY GIBBONS PUBLICATIONS

OVERSEAS REPRESENTATION

Stanley Gibbons Publications are represented overseas by the following sole distributors (*), distributors (**) or licensees (***)

Australia
Lighthouse Philatelic (Aust.) Pty Ltd*
PO Box 763
Strawberry Hills
New South Wales 2012
Australia

Stanley Gibbons (Australia) Pty Ltd***
PO Box 863J
Melbourne 3001
Australia

Belgium and Luxembourg
Davo c/o Philac
Rue du Midi 48
Bruxelles 1000
Belgium

Canada*
Lighthouse Publications (Canada) Ltd
255 Duke Street
Montreal
Quebec
Canada H3C 2M2

Denmark**
Davo
c/o Lindner Falzlos
Gl Randersvej 28
8450 Hammel
Denmark

Finland**
Davo
c/o Suomen Postimerkkeily
Ludvingkatu 5
SF-00130 Helsinki
Finland

France*
Davo France
25 Rue Monge
7500 5 Paris
France

Germany and Austria*
Leuchtturm Albenverlag
Paul Koch KG
Am Spakenberg 45
Postfach 1340
D-2054 Geesthacht
Germany

Hong Kong**
Po-on Stamp Service
GPO Box 2498
Hong Kong

Israel**
Capital Stamps
PO Box 3769
Jerusalem 91036
Israel

Italy*
Secrian Srl
Via Pantelleria 2
I-20156 Milano
Italy

Japan**
Japan Philatelic Co Ltd
PO Box 2
Suginami-Minami
Tokyo
Japan

Netherlands*
Davo Publications
PO Box 411
7400 AK Deventer
Netherlands

New Zealand**
Stanley Gibbons (New Zealand) Ltd
PO Box 80
Wellington
New Zealand

Norway**
Davo Norge A/S
PO Box 738 Sentrum
N-01 05 Oslo
Norway

Singapore**
Stanley Gibbons (Singapore)
Pte Ltd
Raffles City
P.O. Box 1689
Singapore 9117

South Africa*
Philatelic Holdings (Pty) Ltd***
P.O. Box 930
Parklands
RSA 2121

Republic Coin and Stamp
Accessories (Pty) Ltd**
P.O. Box 260325
Excom 2023
Johannesburg
RSA

Sweden*
Chr Winther Sorensen AB
Box 43
S-310 Knaered
Sweden

Switzerland**
Phila Service
Burgstrasse 160
CH4125 Riehen
Switzerland

USA*
Lighthouse Publications Inc.
P.O. Box 705
274 Washington Avenue
Hackensack
New Jersey 07602-0705
USA

West Indies/Caribbean**
Hugh Dunphy
PO Box 413
Kingston 10
Jamaica
West Indies

Contents

PRICES

The prices quoted in this catalogue are the estimated selling prices of Stanley Gibbons Ltd at the time of publication. They are, *unless it is specifically stated otherwise*, for examples in fine condition for the issue concerned. Superb examples are worth more; those of a lower quality considerably less.

All prices are subject to change without prior notice and Stanley Gibbons Ltd may from time to time offer stamps below catalogue price in consequence of special purchases or particular promotions.

No guarantee is given to supply all stamps priced, since it is not possible to keep every catalogued item in stock.

Quotation of prices. The prices in the left-hand column are for unused stamps and those in the right-hand column are for used.

A dagger (†) denotes that the item listed does not exist in that condition and a blank, or dash, that it exists, or may exist, but no market price is known.

Prices are expressed in pounds and pence sterling. One pound comprises 100 pence (£1 = 100p).

The method of notation is as follows: pence in numerals (e.g. 5 denotes five pence); pounds and pence up to £100, in numerals (e.g. 4.25 denotes four pounds and twenty-five pence); prices above £100 expressed in whole pounds with the "£" sign shown.

Unused and Used stamps. The prices for unused stamps of Queen Victoria are for lightly hinged examples. Unused stamps of King Edward VII and King George V are priced in both unmounted and mounted condition. Unused prices for Edward VIII to Queen Elizabeth II issues are for unmounted mint (though when not available, mounted mint stamps are often supplied at a lower price). Prices for used stamps are for postally used examples.

Prices quoted for bisects on cover or on large piece are for those dated during the period officially authorised.

Minimum price. The minimum price quoted is ten pence. This represents a handling charge rather than a basis for valuing common stamps, for which the 10p price should not be reckoned automatically, since it covers a variation in real scarcity.

Set prices. Set prices are generally for one of each value, excluding shades and varieties, but including major colour changes. Where there are alternative shades, etc., the cheapest is usually included. The number of stamps in the set is always stated for clarity.

The mint prices for sets containing *se-tenant* pieces are based on the prices quoted for such combinations, and not on those for the individual stamps. The used set price is for single stamps.

Gutter Pairs. These, and traffic light gutter pairs, are priced as complete sets.

Used on Cover prices. To assist collectors, cover prices are quoted in a third column for postage and Official stamps issued in the reign of Queen Victoria and in boxed notes for King Edward VII and King George V stamps.

The cover should be of non-philatelic origin, bearing the correct postal rate for the period and distance involved and cancelled with the markings normal to the offices concerned. Purely philatelic items have a cover value only slightly greater than the catalogue value for the corresponding used stamps. This applies generally to those high-value stamps used philatelically rather than in the normal course of commerce.

Oversized covers, difficult to accommodate on an album page, should be reckoned as worth little more than the corresponding value of the used stamps. The condition of a cover affects its value. Except for "wreck covers", serious damage or soiling reduce the value where the postal markings and stamps are ordinary ones. Conversely, visual appeal adds to the value and this can include freshness of appearance, important addresses, old-fashioned but legible handwriting, historic town-names, etc. The prices quoted are a base on which further value would be added to take account of the cover's postal historical importance in demonstrating such things as unusual, scarce or emergency cancels, interesting routes, significant postal markings, combination usage, the development of postal rates, and so on.

First Day Cover prices. Prices are quoted for commemorative first day covers from 1924 British Empire Exhibition pair onwards. These prices are for special covers (from 1937) franked with complete sets and cancelled by ordinary operational postmarks to the end of 1962 or the various standard "First Day of Issue" markings from 1963.

The Philatelic Bureau and other special "First Day of Issue" postmarks provided by the Post Office since 1963 are listed under each issue. Prices quoted are for these postmarks used on illustrated covers (from 1964 those produced by the Post Office), franked with complete sets.

The British Post Office did not introduce special First Day of Issue postmarks for definitive issues until the first instalment of the Machin £sd series, issued 5 June 1967, although "First Day" treatment had been provided for some Regional stamps from 8 June 1964 onwards. Prices for the First Day Covers from 1952 to 1966, showing definitive stamps are for the stamps indicated, used on illustrated envelopes and postmarked with operational cancellations.

From 1967 onwards the prices quoted are for stamps as indicated, used on illustrated envelopes and postmarked with special First Day of Issue handstamps. Other definitives issued during this period were not accepted for "First Day" treatment by the British Post Office.

Guarantee

All stamps are guaranteed genuine originals in the following terms:

If not as described, and returned by the purchaser, we undertake to refund the price paid to us in the original transaction. If any stamp is certified as genuine by the Expert Committee of the Royal Philatelic Society, London, or by B.P.A. Expertising Ltd, the purchaser shall not be entitled to make any claim against us for any error, omission or mistake in such certificate.

Consumers' statutory rights are not affected by the above guarantee.

The recognised Expert Committees in this country are those of the Royal Philatelic Society, 41 Devonshire Place, London W1N 1PE, and B.P.A. Expertising Ltd, P.O. Box 137, Leatherhead, Surrey KT22 0RG. They do not undertake valuations under any circumstances and fees are payable for their services.

CONTACTING THE CATALOGUE EDITOR

The Editor is always interested in hearing from people who have new information which will improve or correct the Catalogue. As a general rule he must see and examine the actual stamps before they can be considered for listing; photographs or photocopies are insufficient evidence.

Submissions should be made in writing to the Catalogue Editor, Stanley Gibbons Publications. The cost of return postage for items submitted is appreciated, and this should include the registration fee if required.

Where information is solicited purely for the benefit of the enquirer, the editor cannot undertake to reply if the answer is already contained in these published notes or if return postage is omitted. Written communications are greatly preferred to enquiries by telephone and the editor regrets that he or his staff cannot see personal callers without a prior appointment being made. Correspondence may be subject to delay during the production period of each new edition.

Please note that the following classes of material are outside the scope of this Catalogue:

(a) Non-postal revenue or fiscal stamps.
(b) Postage stamps used fiscally.
(c) Local carriage labels and private local issues.
(d) Punctured postage stamps (perfins).
(e) Telegraph stamps.
(f) Bogus or phantom stamps.
(g) Railway or airline letter fee stamps, bus or road transport company labels.
(h) Postal stationery cut-outs.
(i) All types of non-postal labels and souvenirs.
(j) Documentary labels for the postal service, e.g. registration, recorded delivery, airmail etiquettes, etc.
(k) Privately applied embellishments to official issues and privately commissioned items generally.
(l) Stamps for training postal staff.

We regret we do not give opinions as to the genuineness of stamps, nor do we identify stamps or number them by our Catalogue.

Stanley Gibbons Stamp Collecting Series

A well illustrated series of handbooks, packed with essential information for all collectors.

Item 2760 Stamp Collecting: How to Start – Especially for the beginner. A clear outline of the basic elements.

Item 2762 Stamp Collecting: Collecting by Theme – Sound practical advice on how to form and develop a thematic collection, including an A–Z of collecting subjects.

Item 2766 The Stanley Gibbons Guide to Stamp Collecting – Based on the classic work by Stanley Phillips, thoroughly revised and updated by John Holman. Everything you need to know about stamp collecting.

GENERAL ABBREVIATIONS

Alph	Alphabet
Anniv	Anniversary
Brt	Bright (colour)
C, c	Chalky paper
C.	Overprinted in carmine
Des	Designer; designed
Dp	Deep (colour)
Eng	Engraver; engraved
Horiz	Horizontal; horizontally
Imp, Imperf	Imperforate
Inscr	Inscribed
L	Left
Litho	Lithographed
Lt	Light (colour)
mm	Millimetres
MS	Miniature sheet
O, o	Ordinary paper
Opt(d)	Overprint(ed)
P, Pf or Perf	Perforated
Photo	Photogravure
Pl	Plate
Pr	Pair
Ptd	Printed
Ptg	Printing
PVA	Polyvinyl alcohol (gum)
R	Right
R.	Row
Recess	Recess-printed
T	Type
Typo	Typographed
Un	Unused
Us	Used
Vert	Vertical; vertically
W or wmk	Watermark
Wmk s	Watermark sideways

(†) = Does not exist.

(—) (or blank price column) = Exists, or may exist, but no market price is known.

/ between colours means "on" and the colour following is that of the paper on which the stamp is printed.

PRINTERS

B.W.	Bradbury Wilkinson & Co, Ltd.
D.L.R.	De La Rue & Co, Ltd, London, and (from 1961) Bogota, Colombia.
Enschedé	Joh. Enschedé en Zonen, Haarlem, Netherlands.
Harrison	Harrison & Sons, Ltd, High Wycombe.
J.W.	John Waddington Security Print, Ltd, Leeds
P.B.	Perkins Bacon Ltd, London.
Questa	Questa Colour Security Printers, Ltd.
Waterlow	Waterlow & Sons, Ltd, London.
Walsall	Walsall Security Printers, Ltd.

PHILATELIC INFORMATION

Catalogue Numbers

The catalogue number appears in the extreme left column. The boldface Type numbers in the next column are merely cross-reference to illustrations. Catalogue numbers in the Gibbons *Stamp Monthly* Supplement are provisional only and may need to be altered when the lists are consolidated.

Our catalogue numbers are universally recognised in specifying stamps and as a hallmark of status.

Inverted and other watermark varieties incorporate "Wi", etc., within the number. Other items which appear in this Catalogue but not *Part 1 (British Commonwealth) Catalogue*, incorporate "Ea", etc.

Catalogue Illustrations

Stamps and first day postmarks are illustrated at three-quarters linear size. Stamps not illustrated are the same size and format as the value shown, unless otherwise indicated. Overprints, surcharges and watermarks are normally actual size. Illustrations of varieties are often enlarged to show the detail. Illustrations of miniature sheets are half linear size and their dimensions, in millimetres, are stated with the width given first.

Designers

Designers' names are quoted where known, though space precludes naming every individual concerned in the production of a set. In particular, photographers supplying material are usually named only when they also make an active contribution in the design stage; posed photographs of reigning monarchs are, however, an exception to this rule.

Printing Errors

Errors in printing are of major interest to the Catalogue. Authenticated items meriting consideration would include: background, centre or frame inverted or omitted; centre or subject transposed; error of colour; error or omission of value; double prints and impressions; printed both sides; and so on. Designs *tête-bêche*, whether intentionally or by accident, are listable. Colours only partially omitted are not listed. However, stamps with embossing, phosphor or both omitted and stamps printed on the gummed side are included.

Printing technology has radically improved over the years, during which time photogravure and lithography have become predominant. Varieties nowadays are more in the nature of flaws which are almost always outside the scope of this book.

In no catalogue, however, do we list such items as: dry prints, kiss prints, doctor-blade flaws, colour shifts or registration flaws (unless they lead to the complete omission of a colour from an individual stamp), lithographic ring flaws, and so on. Neither do we recognise fortuitous happenings like paper creases or confetti flaws.

Paper Types

All stamps listed are deemed to be on "ordinary" paper of the wove type and white in colour; only departures from this are normally mentioned.

A coloured paper is one that is coloured right through (front and back of the stamp). In the Catalogue the colour of the paper is given in *italics*, thus:

purple/*yellow* = purple design on yellow paper.

Papers have been made specially white in recent years by, for example, a very heavy coating of chalk. We do not classify shades of whiteness of paper as distinct varieties.

The availability of many postage stamps for revenue purposes made necessary some safeguard against the illegitimate re-use of stamps with removable cancellations. This was at first secured by using fugitive inks and later by printing on chalky (chalk-surfaced) paper, both of which made it difficult to remove any form of obliteration without also damaging the stamp design. We have indicated the existence of the papers by the letters "O" (ordinary) and "C" (chalky) after the description of all stamps where the chalky paper may be found. Where no indication is given the paper is "ordinary".

Our chalky paper is specifically one which shows a black mark when touched with a silver wire. Stamps on chalk-surfaced paper can easily lose this coating through immersion in water.

Perforation Measurement

The gauge of a perforation is the number of holes in a length of 2 cm.

Philatelic Information

The Gibbons *Instanta* gauge is the standard for measuring perforations. The stamp is viewed against a dark background with the transparent gauge put on top of it. Though the gauge measures to decimal accuracy, perforations read from it are generally quoted in the Catalogue to the nearest half. For example:

Just over perf 12¾ to just under 13¼ = perf 13
Perf 13¼ exactly, rounded up = perf 13½
Just over perf 13¼ to just under 13¾ = perf 13½
Perf 13¾ exactly, rounded up = perf 14

However, where classification depends on it, actual quarter-perforations are quoted. Perforations are usually abbreviated (and spoken) as follows, though sometimes they may be spelled out for clarity.

P 14: perforated alike on all sides (read: "perf 14").

P 14 × 15: the first figure refers to top and bottom, the second to left and right sides (read: "perf 14 by 15"). This is a compound perforation.

Such headings as "*P* 13 × 14 (*vert*) and *P* 14 × 13 (*horiz*)" indicate which perforations apply to which stamp format—vertical or horizontal.

From 1992 onwards most definitive and greetings stamps from both sheets and booklets occur with a large elliptical (oval) hole inserted in each line of vertical perforations as a security measure. The £10 definitive, No. 1658, is unique in having two such holes in the horizontal perforations.

Elliptical Perforations

Perforation Errors

Authenticated errors, where a stamp normally perforated is accidentally issued imperforate, are listed provided no traces of perforation (blind holes or indentations) remain. They must be provided as pairs, both stamps wholly imperforate, and are only priced in that form.

Numerous part-perforated stamps have arisen from the introduction of the Jumelle Press. This has a rotary perforator with rows of pins on one drum engaging with holes on another. Engagement is only gradual when the perforating unit is started up or stopped, giving rise to perforations "fading out", a variety mentioned above as not listed.

Stamps from the Jumelle printings sometimes occur imperforate between stamp and sheet margin. Such errors are not listed in this catalogue, but are covered by the fourth volume of the *Great Britain Specialised Catalogue*.

Pairs described as "imperforate between" have the line of perforations between the two stamps omitted.

Imperf between (*horiz pair*): a horizontal pair of stamps with perfs all around the edges but none between the stamps.

Imperf between (*vert pair*): a vertical pair of stamps with perfs all around the edges but none between the stamps.

Imperf between
(vertical pair)

Imperf horizontally
(vertical pair)

Where several of the rows have escaped perforation the resulting varieties are listable. Thus:

Imperf vert (*horiz pair*): a horizontal pair of stamps perforated at top and bottom; all three vertical directions are imperf—the two outer edges and between the stamps.

Imperf horiz (*vert pair*): a vertical pair perforated at left and right edges; all three horizontal directions are imperf—the top, bottom and between the stamps.

Varieties of double, misplaced or partial perforation caused by error or machine malfunction are not listable, neither are freaks, such as perforations placed diagonally from paper folds, nor missing holes caused by broken pins.

Phosphor Issues

Machines which sort mail electronically have been introduced progressively and the British Post Office issued the first stamps specially marked for electronic sorting in 1957. This first issue had easily visible graphite lines printed on the back beneath the gum (see Nos. 561/6). They were issued in the Southampton area where the experiment was carried out.

The graphite lines were replaced by phosphor bands, activated by ultra-violet light. The bands are printed on the front of the stamps and show as a matt surface against the usual smooth or shiny appearance of the untreated surface of the paper. The bands show clearly in the top or bottom horizontal margins of the sheet.

The first phosphor issues appeared in 1959 (see Nos. 599/609) and these stamps also had graphite lines on the back. Further details will be found in the listings above Nos. 599 and 619. From 1962 onwards most commemoratives were issued in versions with or without bands. From 1967 all commemorative stamps had phosphor bands, but from 1972 they were replaced by "all-over" phosphor covering the entire area of the stamp.

After a considerable period of development a special paper was produced in which the phosphor had been incorporated into the coating. From 15 August 1979 phosphorised paper was accepted for use generally, this paper replacing phosphor bands on most issues for all values except the second class letter rate. Phosphorised paper can only be identified by ultra-violet light. The Stanley Gibbons Uvitec Micro ultra-violet lamp is firmly recommended for use in identifying the phosphor stamps listed in this Catalogue. *Warning*. Never stare at the lighted lamp but follow the manufacturer's instructions.

During the years, 1967 to 1972, when all issues, except the high values, should have shown phosphor bands, a number of stamps appeared with them omitted in error. These varieties are listed in this Catalogue. Stamps with "all-over" phosphor omitted can only be detected by the use of an ultra-violet lamp and these varieties are listed in the Stanley Gibbons *Great Britain Specialised Catalogue*. Note that prices are for unmounted mint examples only. Varieties such as double bands, misplaced or printed on the back are not listed in this Catalogue.

Gum Description

All stamps listed are assumed to have gum of some kind and original gum (o.g.) means that which was present on the stamp as issued to the public. Deleterious climates and the presence of certain chemicals can cause gum to crack and, with early stamps, even make the paper deteriorate. Unscrupulous fakers are adept in removing it and regumming the stamp to meet the unreasoning demand often made for "full o.g." in cases where such a thing is virtually impossible.

The gum normally used on stamps has been gum arabic until the late 1960s when synthetic adhesives were introduced. Harrison and Sons Ltd for instance use *polyvinyl alcohol*, known to philatelists as PVA (see note above SG723).

Colour Identification

The 100 colours most used for stamp identification are given in the Stanley Gibbons Colour Guide; these, plus a further 100 variations for more specialised use, are included in the Stanley Gibbons Stamp Colour Key. The Catalogue has used the Guide and Key as standards for describing new issues for some years. The names are also introduced as lists are rewritten, though exceptions are made for those early issues where traditional names have become universally established.

In compound colour names the second is the predominant one, thus:

orange-red = a red tending towards orange;

red-orange = an orange containing more red than usual.

When comparing actual stamps with colour samples in the Guide or Key, view in a good north daylight (or its best substitute: fluorescent "colour-matching" light). Sunshine is not recommended. Choose a solid portion of the stamp design; if available, marginal markings such as solid bars of colour or colour check dots are helpful. Shading lines in the design can be misleading as they appear lighter than solid colour. Furthermore, the listings refer to colours as issued: they may deteriorate into something different through the passage of time.

Shades are particularly significant when they can be linked to specific printings. In general, shades need to be quite marked to fall within the scope of this Catalogue.

Modern colour printing by lithography is prone to marked differences of shade, even within a single run, and variations can occur within the same sheet. Such shades are not listed.

Errors of Colour

Major colour errors in stamps or overprints which qualify for listing are: wrong colours; albinos (colourless impressions), where these have Expert Committee certificates; colours completely omitted, but only on unused stamps (if found on used stamps the information is usually footnoted) and with good credentials, missing colours being frequently faked.

Colours only partially omitted are not recognised. Colour shifts, however spectacular, are not listed.

Booklet Stamps

Single stamps from booklets are listed if they are distinguishable in some way (such as watermark or phosphor bands) from similar sheet stamps.

Booklet Pane with Printed Labels   *Se-tenant* Pane of Four

Booklet panes are listed where they contain stamps of different denominations *se-tenant*, where stamp-size printed labels are included, or where such panes are otherwise identifiable. Booklet panes are placed in the listing under the lowest denomination present.

In the listing of complete booklets the numbers and prefix letters are the same as used in the Stanley Gibbons *Great Britain Specialised Catalogue*.

Coil Stamps

Stamps only issued in coil form are given full listing. If stamps are issued in both sheets and coils, the coil stamps are listed separately only where there is some feature (e.g. watermark sideways or gum change) by which single stamps can be distinguished. Coil strips containing different values *se-tenant* are also listed.

Multi-value Coil Strip

Coil join pairs are generally too random and easily faked to permit listing; similarly ignored are coil stamps which have accidentally suffered an extra row of perforations from the claw mechanism in a malfunctioning vending machine.

Gutter Pairs

In 1988 the recess-printed Castle high value definitives were issued in sheets containing four panes separated by a gutter margin. All modern Great Britain commemoratives and special stamps are produced in sheets containing two panes separated by a blank horizontal or vertical margin known as a gutter. This feature first made its appearance on some supplies of the 1972 Royal Silver Wedding 3p and marked the introduction of Harrison & Sons' new "Jumelle" stamp-printing press. There are advantages for both the printer and the Post Office in such a layout which has now been used for all commemorative issues since 1974.

The term "gutter pair" is used for a pair of stamps separated by part of the blank gutter margin as illustrated below.

Most printers include some form of colour check device on the sheet margins, in addition to the cylinder or plate numbers. Harrison & Sons use round "dabs", or spots of colour, resembling traffic lights. For the period from the 1972 Royal Silver Wedding until the end of 1979 these colour dabs appeared in the gutter margin. There was always one example to every double pane sheet of stamps. Although they no longer appear in the commemorative issues they can be found in the high value Machin issue printed in photogravure. Gutter pairs showing these "traffic lights" are worth considerably more than the normal version.

Gutter Pair

Traffic Light Gutter Pair

Miniature Sheets

A miniature sheet contains a single stamp or set with wide inscribed or decorated margins. The stamps usually also exist in normal sheet format. This Catalogue lists, with **MS** prefix, complete miniature sheets which have been issued by the Post Office and which are valid for postal purposes.

Miniature Sheet containing a set of stamps

Se-tenant Combinations

Se-tenant means "joined together". Some sets include stamps of different design arranged *se-tenant* as blocks or strips and, in mint condition, these are usually collected unsevered as issued. Such *se-tenant* combinations can often be supplied in used condition at a premium over the used prices of the individual stamps. See also the note on Set Prices.

Specimen Stamps

Stamps of Great Britain overprinted "SPECIMEN" for circulation to postmasters and the Universal Postal Union are listed in a special section following the Postal Fiscal stamps. For other "SPECIMEN" overprints see Stanley Gibbons *Great Britain Specialised Catalogue.*

Presentation and Souvenir Books

Special Packs comprising slip-in cards with printed commemorative inscriptions and notes on the back and with protective covering, were introduced in 1964 for the Shakespeare issue. Definitive issues first appeared in Presentation Packs in 1960. Notes will be found in the listings to describe souvenir books issued on special occasions.

    Issues of 1968–69 (British Paintings to the Prince of ᵥVales Investiture) were also issued in packs with text in German for sale through the Post Office's German Agency and these are also included.

13 August 1975 Public Railways Presentation Pack

    Collectors packs, first called gift packs, containing commemoratives issued in the preceeding twelve months, first appeared in 1967. These are listed and priced.

Yearbooks

Special Post Office Yearbooks were first available in 1984. They contain all of the commemorative issues for one year in a hardbound book, illustrated in colour complete with slip case. These are listed and priced.

Commemorative First Day Covers

Until 1963 the Post Office did not provide any special first day of issue postmark facilities for collectors. Several philatelic organisations and stamp dealers did produce pictorial covers for the various commemorative issues and collectors serviced these to receive ordinary operational postmarks. Occasionally a special handstamp was produced which coincided with a new stamp issue, or relevant slogan postmarks, like the 1953 'Long Live the Queen' type, were in general use at the time.

On 21 March 1963 the Post Office installed special posting boxes at eleven main offices so that collectors could obtain 'uniformly high standard' impressions, from normal operational postmarks, for their first day covers. From 7 May 1963 special 'First Day of Issue' slogans (Type A) were applied to mail posted in these special boxes, whose number had, by then, risen to thirty. The Philatelic Bureau accepted orders by post for such covers from the issue of 16 May 1963 onwards.

The slogan type was replaced on 23 April 1964 by "First Day of Issue" handstamps (Type B). These were, initiallly, of considerable size, but were later replaced by smaller versions (Type C) which remain in service today at nearly 200 principal offices. From 1970 the Bureau postmarks as Type C were inscribed "British Philatelic Bureau".

Since 1972 the Post Office has provided pictorial cancellations at the Philatelic Bureau and, often, at one or more towns connected with each issue.

From time to time "First Day of Issue" handstamps in the standard type have been provided on a temporary basis for offices which had a link with a particular stamp issue. Such postmarks could not be ordered through the Philatelic Bureau.

Other special handstamps sponsored by organisations or individuals also exist, but are not listed.

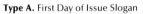

Type A. First Day of Issue Slogan

Type B. Large Handstamp

Type C. Small Handstamp

Type D. Maltese Cross

Type E

Type F. £ Sign

Type G. Three Lions

Type H. Four Castles

Type I. Windsor Keep

PHQ Cards

From 1973 the Post Office produced sets of picture cards to accompany commemorative issues which can be sent through the post as postcards. Each card shows an enlarged colour reproduction of one stamp, initially of a single value from one set and subsequently of all values. The Post Office gives each card a "PHQ" serial number, hence the term. The cards are usually on sale shortly before the date of issue of the stamps, but there is no officially designated "first day".

PHQ Card cancelled on First Day of Issue

Cards are priced in fine mint condition for complete sets as issued. Used prices are for cards franked with the stamp affixed, on the obverse, as illustrated above, or reverse; the stamp being cancelled with an official postmark for first day of issue.

Watermark Types

Stamps are on unwatermarked paper except where the heading to the set states otherwise.

Watermarks are detected for Catalogue description by one of four methods: (1) holding stamps to the light; (2) laying stamps face down on a dark background; (3) by use of the Morley-Bright Detector, which works by revealing the thinning of the paper at the watermark; or (4) by the more complex electric watermark detectors such as the Signoscope.

The diagram below shows how watermark position is described in the Catalogue. Watermarks are usually impressed so that they read normally when looked through from the printed side. However, since philatelists customarily detect watermarks by looking at the back of the stamp, the watermark diagram also makes clear what is actually seen. Note that "G v R" is only an example and illustrations of the different watermarks employed are shown in the listings. The illustrations are actual size and shown in normal positions (from the front of the stamps).

AS DESCRIBED (Read through front of stamp)		AS SEEN DURING WATERMARK DETECTION (Stamp face down and back examined)
GvR	Normal	ꓤvꓳ
ꓤ∧ꓜ	Inverted	ꓛ∧ꓤ
ꓤvꓳ	Reversed	GvR
ꓛ∧ꓤ	Reversed and inverted	ꓤ∧ꓜ
GvR (sideways)	Sideways	ꓛvꓳ (sideways)
GvR (sideways inverted)	Sideways inverted	ꓤvꓳ (sideways inverted)

Philatelic Information

General Types of watermark as seen through the front side of the stamp.

2 Small Crown

4 Large Crown

9 (Extends over three stamps)

13 V R

15 Small Garter

16 Medium Garter

17 Large Garter

20 Emblems

33 Spray of Rose

39 Maltese Cross

40 Large Anchor

47 Small Anchor

48 Orb

49 Imperial Crown

100 Simple Cypher

103 Multiple Cypher

110 Single Cypher

111 Block Cypher

117 PUC £1

125 E8R

127

133

153 Tudor Crown

Postal Fiscals

165 St. Edward's Crown

179 Multiple Crowns

F5 Double-lined Anchor

F6 Single-lined Anchor

Watermark Errors and Varieties

Watermark errors are recognised as of major importance. They comprise stamps showing the wrong watermark devices or stamps printed on paper with the wrong watermark. Stamps printed on paper showing broken or deformed bits on the dandy roll, are not listable.

Underprints

From 1982 various values appeared with underprints, printed on the reverse, in blue, over the gum. These were usually from special stamp booklets, sold at a discount by the Post Office, but in 1985 surplus stocks of such underprinted paper were used for other purposes.

In this Catalogue stamps showing underprints are priced mint only. Used examples can be obtained, but care has to be taken in floating the stamps since the ink employed to print the device is solvent in water.

Underprint Types

1 Star with central dot

2 Double-lined Star

3 Double-lined "D"

4 Multiple double-lined Stars

5 Multiple double-lined "D"

*(Types **4/5** are shown ¾ actual size)*

Note: Types **4/5** are arranged in a random pattern so that stamps from the same sheet or booklet pane will show the underprint in a slightly different position to the above. Stamps, when inspected, should be placed the correct way up, face down, when comparing with the illustrations.

COMMEMORATIVE DESIGN INDEX

This index gives an easy reference to the inscriptions and designs of the Special Stamps 1953 to March 1993. Where a complete set shares an inscription or type of design, then only the catalogue number of the first stamp is given in addition to separate entries for stamps depicting popular thematic subjects. Paintings, inventions, etc., are indexed under the name of the artist or inventor, where this is shown on the stamp.

Commemorative Design Index

Commemorative Design Index

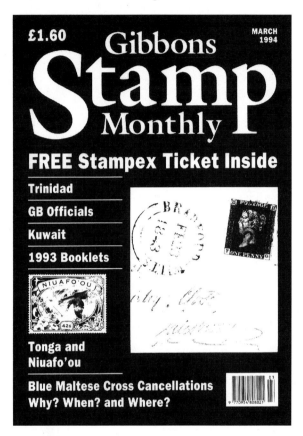

QUEEN VICTORIA
20 June 1837—22 January 1901

MULREADY ENVELOPES AND LETTER SHEETS, so called from the name of the designer, William Mulready, were issued concurrently with the first British adhesive stamps.

1d. black

Envelopes:......... £125 *unused;* £175 *used.*
Letter Sheets: ..... £110 *unused;* £145 *used.*

2d. blue

Envelopes: ....£200 *unused;* £600 *used.*
Letter Sheets: ......£175 *unused;* £575 *used.*

LINE–ENGRAVED ISSUES

GENERAL NOTES

Brief notes on some aspects of the line-engraved stamps follow, but for further information and a full specialist treatment of these issues collectors are recommended to consult Volume I of the Stanley Gibbons *Great Britain Specialised Catalogue.*

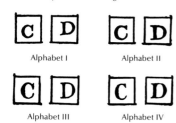

| Alphabet I | Alphabet II |
| Alphabet III | Alphabet IV |

Typical Corner Letters of the four Alphabets

Alphabets. Four different letterings were used for the corner letters on stamps prior to the issue with letters in all four corners, these being known to collectors as:
Alphabet I. Used for all plates made from 1840 to the end of 1851. Letters small.
Alphabet II. Plates from 1852 to mid-1855. Letters larger, heavier and broader.
Alphabet III. Plates from mid-1855 to end of period. Letters tall and more slender.
Alphabet IV. 1861. 1d. Die II, Plates 50 and 51 only. Letters were hand-engraved instead of being punched on the plate. They are therefore inconsistent in shape and size but generally larger and outstanding.
While the general discriptions and the illustrations of typical letters given above may be of some assistance, only long experience and published aids can enable every stamp to be allocated to its particular Alphabet without hesitation, as certain letters in each are similar to those in one of the others.

Blued Paper. The blueing of the paper of the earlier issues is believed to be due to the presence of prussiate of potash in the printing ink, or in the paper, which, under certain conditions, tended to colour the paper when the sheets were damped for printing. An alternative term is bleuté paper.

Corner Letters. The corner letters on the early British stamps were intended as a safeguard against forgery, each stamp in the sheet having

a different combination of letters. Taking the first 1d. stamp, printed in 20 horizontal rows of 12. as an example, the lettering is as follows:

Row. 1.   A A, A B, A C, etc. to A L.

Row. 2.   B A, B B, B C, etc. to B L.

and so on to

Row. 20.   T A, T B, T C, etc. to T L.

On the stamps with four corner letters, those in the upper corners are in the reverse positions to those in the lower corners. Thus in a sheet of 240 (12 ×20) the sequence is:

Row 1. $\begin{matrix} A A & B A & C A \\ A A & A B & A C \end{matrix}$ etc. to $\begin{matrix} L A \\ A L \end{matrix}$

Row 2. $\begin{matrix} A B & B B & C B \\ B A & B B & B C \end{matrix}$ etc. to $\begin{matrix} L B \\ B L \end{matrix}$

and so on to

Row 20. $\begin{matrix} A T & B T & C T \\ T A & T B & T C \end{matrix}$ etc. to $\begin{matrix} L T \\ T L \end{matrix}$

Placing letters in all four corners was not only an added precaution against forgery but was meant to deter unmarked parts of used stamps being pieced together and passed off as an unused whole.

Dies. The first die of the 1d. was used for making the original die of the 2d., both the No Lines and White Lines issues. In 1855 the 1d. Die I was amended by retouching the head and deepening the lines on a transferred impression of the original. This later version, known to collectors as Die II, was used for making the dies for the 1d. and 2d. with letters in all four corners and also for the 1½d.

The two dies are illustrated above No. 17 in the catalogue.

Double letter

Guide line in corner

Guide line through value

Double Corner Letters. These are due to the workman placing his letter-punch in the wrong position at the first attempt, when lettering the plate, and then correcting the mistake; or to a slight shifting of the punch when struck. If a wrong letter was struck in the first instance, traces of a wrong letter may appear in a corner in addition to the correct one. A typical example is illustrated.

Guide Lines and Dots. When laying down the impressions of the design on the early plates, fine vertical and horizontal guide lines were marked on the plates to assist the operative. These were usually removed from the gutter margins, but could not be removed from the stamp impressions without damage to the plate, so that in such cases they appear on the printed stamps, sometimes in the corners, sometimes through "POSTAGE" or the value. Typical examples are illustrated.

Guide dots or cuts were similarly made to indicate the spacing of the guide lines. These too sometimes appear on the stamps.

Ivory Head

"Ivory Head". The so-called "ivory head" variety is one in which the Queen's Head shows white on the back of the stamp. It arises from the comparative absence of ink in the head portion of the design, with consequent absence of blueing. (*See* "Blued Paper", on page 1).

Line-engraving. In this context "line-engraved" is synonymous with recess-printing, in which the engraver cuts recesses in a plate and printing (the coloured areas) is from these recesses. "Line-engraved" is the traditional philatelic description for these stamps; other equivalent terms found are "engraving in *taille-douce*" (French) or "in *intaglio*" (Italian).

Plates. Until the introduction of the stamps with letters in all four corners, the number of the plate was not indicated in the design of the stamp, but was printed on the sheet margin. By long study of indentifiable blocks and the minor variation in the design, coupled with the position of the corner letters, philatelists are now able to allot many of these stamps to their respective plates. Specialist collectors often endeavour to obtain examples of a given stamp printed from its different plates and our catalogue accordingly reflects this depth of detail.

Postmarks. The so-called "Maltese Cross" design was the first employed for obliterating British postage stamps and was in use from 1840 to 1844. Being hand-cut, the obliterating stamps varied greatly in detail and some distinctive types can be allotted to particular towns or offices. Local types, such as those used at Manchester, Norwich, Leeds, etc., are keenly sought. A red ink was first employed, but was superseded by black, after some earlier experiments, in February 1841. Maltese Cross obliterations in other colours are rare.

Obliterations of this type, numbered 1 to 12 in the centre, were used at the London Chief Office in 1843 and 1844.

Some straight-line cancellations were in use in 1840 at the Penny Post receiving offices, normally applied on the envelope, the adhesives then being obliterated at the Head Office. They are nevertheless known, with or without Maltese Cross, on the early postage stamps.

In 1842 some offices in S.W. England used dated postmarks in place of the Maltese Cross, usually on the back of the letter since they were not originally intended as obliterators. These town postmarks have likewise been found on adhesives.

In 1844 the Maltese Cross design was superseded by numbered obliterators of varied type, one of which is illustrated. They are naturally comparatively scarce on the first 1d. and 2d. stamps. Like the Maltese Cross they are found in various colours, some of which are rare.

Re-entry

"Union Jack" re-entry

Re-entries. Re-entries on the plate show as a doubling of part of the design of the stamp generally at top or bottom. Many re-entries are very slight while others are most marked. A typical one is illustrated.

The *"Union Jack"* re-entry, so-called owing to the effect of the re-entry on the appearance of the corner stars (*see illustration*) occurs on stamp L K of Plate 75 of the 1d. red, Die I.

Maltese Cross   Type of Town postmark

Type of Penny Post cancellation

Example of 1844 type postmark

T A (T L)   M A (M L)
Varieties of Large Crown Watermark

I   Two states of Large Crown Watermark   II

Watermarks. Two watermark varieties, as illustrated, consisting of crowns of entirely different shape, are found in sheets of the Large Crown paper and fall on stamps lettered M A and T A (or M L and T L when the paper is printed on the wrong side). Both varieties are found on the 1d. rose-red of 1857, while the M A (M L) variety comes also on some plates of the 1d. of 1864 (Nos. 43, 44) up to about Plate 96. On the 2d. the T A (T L) variety is known on plates 8 and 9, and the M A (M L) on later prints of plate 9. These varieties may exist inverted, or inverted reversed on stamps lettered A A and A L and H A and H L, and some are known.

In 1861 a minor alteration was made in the Large Crown watermark by the removal of the two vertical strokes, representing *fleurs-de-lis*, which projected upwards from the uppermost of the three horizontal curves at the base of the Crown. Hence two states are distinguishable, as illustrated.

CONDITION—IMPERFORATE LINE–ENGRAVED ISSUES

The prices quoted for the 1840 and 1841 imperforate Line-engraved issues are for "fine" examples. As condition is most important in assessing the value of a stamp, the following definitions will assist collectors in the evaluation of individual examples.

Four main factors are relevant when considering quality.

(a) **Impression.** This should be clean and the surface free of any rubbing or unnatural blurring which would detract from the appearance.

(b) **Margins.** This is perhaps the most difficult factor to evaluate. Stamps described as "fine", the standard adopted in this catalogue for pricing purposes, should have margins of the recognised width, defined as approximately one half of the distance between two adjoining unsevered stamps. Stamps described as "very fine" or "superb" should have margins which are proportionately larger than those of a "fine" stamp. Examples with close margins should not, generally, be classified as "fine".

(c) **Cancellation.** On a "fine" stamp this should be reasonably clear and not noticeably smudged. A stamp described as "superb" should have a neat cancellation, preferably centrally placed or to the right.

(d) **Appearance.** Stamps, at the prices quoted, should always be without any tears, creases, bends or thins and should not be toned on either the front or back. Stamps with such defects are worth only a proportion of the catalogue price.

Good

Fine

Very Fine

Superb

The actual size illustrations of 1840 1d. blacks show the various grades of quality. When comparing these illustrations it should be assumed that they are all from the same plate and that they are free of any hidden defects.

PRINTERS. Nos. 1/53a were recess-printed by Perkins, Bacon & Petch, known from 1852 as Perkins, Bacon & Co.

> **STAMPS ON COVER.** Prices are quoted, as a third price column, for those Victorian and Edwardian issues usually found used on cover. In general these prices refer to the cheapest version of each basic stamp with other shades, plates or varieties, together with unusual frankings and postmarks, being worth more.

| 1 | 1a | 2 Small Crown |

(Eng Charles and Frederick Heath)

1840 (6–8 May). *Letters in lower corners. Wmk Small Crown. W 2. Imperf.*

No.	Type		Un	Used	Used on cover
1	1	1d. intense black	£3500	£200	
2		1d. black	£3000	£150	£250
		Wi. Watermark inverted	£3750	£350	
3		1d. grey-black (worn plate)	£3000	£200	
4	1a	2d. dp full blue (8.5.40)	£7000	£400	
5		2d. blue	£5500	£300	£650
		Wi. Watermark inverted	£7000	£675	
6		2d. pale blue	£7000	£375	

The 1d. stamp in black was printed from Plates 1 to 11. Plate 1 exists in two states (known to collectors as 1a and 1b), the latter being the result of extensive repairs.

Repairs were also made to plates 2, 5, 6, 8, 9, 10 and 11, and certain impressions exist in two or more states.

The so-called "Royal reprint" of the 1d. black was made in 1864, from Plate 66, Die II, on paper with Large Crown watermark, inverted. A printing was also made in carmine, on paper with the same watermark, normal.

For 1d. black with "VR" in upper corners see No. V1 under Official Stamps.

The 2d. stamps were printed from Plates 1 and 2.

Plates of 1d. black

Plate	Un	Used	Used on Cover
1a	£4500	£180	£300
1b	£3000	£150	£250
2	£3000	£150	£250
3	£3500	£190	£325
4	£3000	£160	£250
5	£3000	£150	£250
6	£3000	£150	£250
7	£3250	£180	£325
8	£3500	£200	£350
9	£4000	£250	£400
10	£4500	£325	£600
11	£4500	£1600	£3000

Varieties of 1d. black

	Un	Used
On *bleuté* paper (Plates 1 to 8) ....*from*	—	£200
Double letter in corner ....*from*	£3000	£180
Re-entry ....*from*	£3250	£200
"PB" re-entry (Plate 5, 3rd state)	—	£4000
Guide line in corner	£3000	£180
Large letters in each corner (E J, I L, J C and P A) (Plate 1*b*) ....*from*	£3500	£325
Guide line through value	£3000	£180

Obliterated by Maltese Cross

In red	—	£160
In black	—	£150
In blue	—	£1500
In magenta	—	£600
In yellow	—	£4000

Obliterated by Maltese Cross with number in centre

No. 1	—	£2250
No. 2	—	£1250
No. 3	—	£1250
No. 4	—	£1250
No. 5	—	£1250
No. 6	—	£1250
No. 7	—	£1250
No. 8	—	£1250
No. 9	—	£1250
No. 10	—	£1250
No. 11	—	—
No. 12	—	£1250

Obliterated "Penny Post" in black ....*from*	—	£1200

Obliterated by town postmark (without Maltese Cross)

In black ....*from*	—	£1000
In yellow ....*from*	—	£5000
In red ....*from*	—	£1200
Obliterated by 1844 type postmark in black *from*	—	£475

Plates of 2d. blue

Plate	Un	Used	Used on Cover
1 ....*Shades from*	£5500	£300	£650
2 ....*Shades from*	£6500	£375	£650

Varieties of 2d. blue

	Un	Used
Double letter in corner	—	£425
Re-entry	—	£475
Guide line in corner	—	£375
Guide line through value	—	£375

Obliterated by Maltese Cross

In red	—	£325
In black	—	£300
In blue	—	£2500
In magenta	—	£2000

Obliterated by Maltese Cross with number in centre

No. 1	—	£2500
No. 2	—	£2500
No. 3	—	—
No. 4	—	£2500
No. 5	—	£2500
No. 6	—	£2750
No. 7	—	£2500
No. 8	—	£2500
No. 9	—	£3000
No. 10	—	£2750
No. 11	—	£2500
No. 12	—	£2500
Obliterated "Penny Post" in black ....*from*	—	£1400

h. Obliterated by town postmark (without Maltese Cross) in black ....*from* — £1200

i. Obliterated by 1844 type postmark

In black ....*from*	—	£750
In blue ....*from*	—	£2000

1841 (10 Feb). *Printed from "black" plates. Wmk W **2**. Paper more or less blued. Imperf.*

No.	Type		Un	Used	Used on cover
7	**1**	1d. red-brown (shades)	£450	40.00	70.00
		a. "PB" re-entry (Plate 5, 3rd state)	—	£1200	
		Wi. Watermark inverted (Plates 1b and 8)...........................	—	£850	

The first printings of the 1d. in red-brown were made from Plates 1*b*, 2, 5 and 8 to 11 used for the 1d. black.

1d. red-brown from "black" plates

Plate	Un	Used	Used on cover
1*b*....................................	£3000	£150	£250
2....................................	£1750	£100	£150
5....................................	£650	50.00	85.00
8....................................	£500	40.00	80.00
9....................................	£450	40.00	75.00
10....................................	£475	40.00	80.00
11....................................	£500	40.00	75.00

1841 (late Feb). *Plate 12 onwards. Wmk W **2**. Paper more or less blued. Imperf.*

			Un	Used	Used on cover
8	**1**	1d. red-brown	£130	3.50	8.00
		Wi. Watermark inverted.............	£350	38.00	
8a		1d. red-brown on very blue paper	£150	3.50	
9		1d. pale red-brown (worn plates)	£200	10.00	
10		1d. deep red-brown..................	£150	7.00	
11		1d. lake-red	£650	£225	
12		1d. orange-brown	£300	50.00	

Error. No letter "A" in right lower corner (Stamp B (A), Plate 77)

12a	**1**	1d. red-brown	—	£5000	

The error "No letter A in right corner" was due to the omission to insert this letter on stamp B A of Plate 77. The error was discovered some months after the plate was registered and was then corrected.

There are innumerable variations in the colour and shade of the 1d. "red" and those given in the above list represent colour groups each covering a wide range.

Varieties of 1d. red-brown, etc.

		Un	Used
b.	Re-entry ....*from*	—	22.00
c.	Double letter in corner ....*from*	—	12.00
d.	Double Star (Plate 75) "Union Jack" re-entry	—	£475
e.	Guide line in corner	—	6.00
f.	Guide line through value	—	12.00
g.	Thick outer frame to stamp	—	12.00
h.	Ivory head	£180	6.00
j.	Left corner letter "S" inverted (Plates 78, 105, 107)......................................*from*	—	40.00
k.	P converted to R (Plates 30, 33, 83, 86) ......*from*	—	30.00
l.	Obliterated by Maltese Cross		
	In red	—	£800
	In black	—	8.00
	In blue	—	£110
m.	Obliterated by Maltese Cross with number in centre.		
	No. 1	—	30.00
	No. 2	—	30.00
	No. 3	—	40.00

No. 4	—	£100			
No. 5	—	30.00			
No. 6	—	25.00			
No. 7	—	22.00			
No. 8	—	22.00			
No. 9	—	30.00			
No. 10	—	40.00			
No. 11	—	50.00			
No. 12	—	70.00			

n. Obliterated "Penny Post" in black .... — £200
o. Obliterated by town postmark (without Maltese Cross)

In black .... from	—	£100
In blue .... from	—	£225
In green .... from	—	£375
In yellow .... from	—	£3500
In red .... from	—	£2000

p. Obliterated by 1844 type postmark

In blue .... from	—	30.00
In red .... from	—	£850
In green .... from	—	£150
In violet .... from	—	£500
In black .... from	—	3.50

Stamps with thick outer frame to the design are from plates on which the frame-lines have been straightened or recut, particularly Plates 76 and 90.

For "Union Jack" re-entry see General Notes to Line-engraved Issues.

In "P converted to R" the corner letter "R" is formed from the "P", the distinctive long tail having been hand-cut.

KEY TO LINE–ENGRAVED ISSUES

S.G. Nos.	Description	Date	Wmk	Perf	Die	Alphabet
	THE IMPERFORATE ISSUES					
1/3	1d. black	6.5.40	SC	Imp	I	I
4/6	2d. no lines	8.5.40	SC	Imp	I	I
	PAPER MORE OR LESS BLUED					
7	1d. red-brown	Feb 1841	SC	Imp	I	I
8/12	1d. red-brown	Feb 1841	SC	Imp	I	I
8/12	1d. red-brown	6.2.52	SC	Imp	I	II
13/15	2d. white lines	13.3.41	SC	Imp	I	I
	THE PERFORATED ISSUES					
	ONE PENNY VALUE					
16a	1d. red-brown	1848	SC	Roul	I	I
16b	1d. red-brown	1850	SC	16	I	I
16c	1d. red-brown	1853	SC	16	I	II
16d	1d. red-brown	1854	SC	14	I	I
17/18	1d. red-brown	Feb 1854	SC	16	I	II
22	1d. red-brown	Jan 1855	SC	14	I	II
24/5	1d. red-brown	28.2.55	SC	14	II	II
21	1d. red-brown	1.3.55	SC	16	II	II
26	1d. red-brown	15.5.55	LC	16	II	II
29/33	1d. red-brown	Aug 1855	LC	14	II	III
	NEW COLOURS ON WHITE PAPER					
37/41	1d. rose-red	Nov 1856	LC	14	II	III
36	1d. rose-red	26.12.57	LC	16	II	III
42	1d. rose-red	1861	LC	14	II	IV
	TWO PENCE VALUE					
19, 20	2d. blue	1.3.54	SC	16	I	I
23	2d. blue	22.2.55	SC	14	I	I
23a	2d. blue	5.7.55	SC	14	I	II
20a	2d. blue	18.8.55	SC	16	I	II
27	2d. blue	20.7.55	LC	16	I	II
34	2d. blue	20.7.55	LC	14	I	II
35	2d. blue	2.7.57	LC	14	I	III
36a	2d. blue	1.2.58	LC	16	I	III
	LETTERS IN ALL FOUR CORNERS					
48/9	½d. rose-red	1.10.70	W **9**	14	—	
43/4	1d. rose-red	1.4.64	LC	14	II	
53a	1½d. rosy mauve	1860	LC	14	II	
51/3	1½d. rose-red	1.10.70	LC	14	II	
45	2d. blue	July 1858	LC	14	II	
46/7	2d. thinner lines	7.7.69	LC	14	II	

Watermarks: SC = Small Crown, T **2**. LC = Large Crown, T **4**.
   Dies: See notes above No. 17 in the catalogue.
   Alphabets: See General Notes to this section.

3 White lines added

1841 (13 Mar)–**51**. *White lines added. Wmk W* **2**. *Paper more or less blued. Imperf.*

				Un	Used	Used on cover
13	**3**	2d. pale blue		£1300	45.00	
14		2d. blue		£1000	35.00	£150
		Wi. Watermark inverted		£2250	£200	
15		2d. dp full blue		£1400	50.00	
15aa		2d. violet-blue (1851)		£7000	£500	

The 2d. stamp with white lines was printed from Plates 3 and 4.

No. 15aa came from Plate 4 and the quoted price is for examples in thicker, lavender tinted paper.

Plates of 2d. blue

Plate		Un	Used
3 .... Shades from		£1000	40.00
4 .... Shades from		£1300	35.00

Varieties of 2d. blue

		Un	Used
a.	Guide line in corner	—	38.00
b.	Guide line through value	£1500	38.00
bb.	Double letter in corner	—	45.00
be.	Re-entry	£1800	60.00
c.	Ivory head	£1600	40.00
e.	Obliterated by Maltese Cross		
	In red	—	£4000
	In black	—	55.00
	In blue	—	£800
f.	Obliterated by Maltese Cross with number in centre		
	No. 1	—	£160
	No. 2	—	£160
	No. 3	—	£160
	No. 4	—	£150
	No. 5	—	£200
	No. 6	—	£150
	No. 7	—	£300
	No. 8	—	£200
	No. 9	—	£300
	No. 10	—	£350
	No. 11	—	£200
	No. 12	—	£110
g.	Obliterated by town postmark (without Maltese Cross)		
	In black .... from	—	£350
	In blue .... from	—	£600

Obliterated by 1844 type postmark

	Un	Used
In black .... from	—	35.00
In blue .... from	—	£350
In red .... from	—	£4000
In green .... from	—	£500

1841 (April). *Trial printing (unissued) on Dickinson silk-thread paper. Imperf.*

| 6 | 1 | 1d. red-brown (Plate 11)............... | £1500 | |

Eight sheets were printed on this paper, six being gummed, two ungummed, but we have only seen examples without gum.

1848. *Wmk W 2. Rouletted approx 11½ by Henry Archer.*

| 16a | 1 | 1d. red-brown (Plates 70, 71)............ | £4000 | |

1850. *Wmk W 2. P 16 by Henry Archer.*

| 16b | 1 | 1d. red-brown (Alph 1) (from Plates 71, 79, 90–101, 105 & 107. Also Plate 8, unused only) .. from | £500 | £150 |
| | | bWi. Watermark inverted................ | — | £300 |

1853. *Wmk W 2. Government Trial Perforations.*

| 16c | 1 | 1d. red-brown (p 16) (Alph II) (on cover)......... | † | £4750 |
| 16d | | 1d. red-brown (p 14) (Alph I) .... | £3750 | |

SEPARATION TRIALS. Although the various trials of machines for rouletting and perforating were unofficial, Archer had the consent of the authorities in making his experiments, and sheets so experimented upon were afterwards used by the Post Office.

As Archer ended his experiments in 1850 and plates with corner letters Alphabet II did not come into issue until 1852, perforated stamps with corner letters of Alphabet I may safely be assumed to be Archer productions, if genuine.

The Government trial perforations were done on Napier machines in 1853. As Alphabet II was by that time in use, the trials can be distinguished from the perforated stamps listed below by being dated prior to 28 January 1854, the date when the perforated stamps were officially issued.

Die I   Die II   **4** Large Crown

Die I: The features of the portrait are lightly shaded and consequently lack emphasis.

Die II (Die I retouched): The lines of the features have been deepened and appear stronger.

The eye is deeply shaded and made more lifelike. The nostril and lips are more clearly defined, the latter appearing much thicker. A strong downward stroke of colour marks the corner of the mouth. There is a deep indentation of colour between lower lip and chin. The band running from the back of the ear to the chignon has a bolder horizontal line below it than in Die I.

1854-57. *Paper more or less blued. (a) Wmk Small Crown, W 2. P 16.*

			Un	Used	★ Used on cover
17	1	1d. red-brown (Die I) (2.54)........	£125	3.50	10.00
		Wi. Watermark inverted.............	—	25.00	
18		1d. yellow-brown (Die I)............	£175	10.00	
19	3	2d. dp blue (Plate 4) (1.3.54).......	£1300	35.00	55.00
		a. Imperf three sides (horiz pair)	†	—	
		Wi. Watermark inverted.............	—	70.00	
20		2d. pale blue (Plate 4).................	£1300	45.00	
20a		2d. blue (Plate 5) (18.8.55)..........	£1800	£130	£200
		aWi. Watermark inverted............	£2000	£250	
21	1	1d. red-brown (Die II) (1.3.55).....	£175	12.00	22.00
		a. Imperf (Plates 2, 14)..........			
		Wi. Watermark inverted.............	£400	35.00	

(b) Wmk Small Crown, W 2. P 14

22	1	1d. red-brown (Die I) (1.55)........	£275	18.00	35.00
		Wi. Watermark inverted.............	—	65.00	
23	3	2d. blue (Plate 4) (22.2.55).........	£1800	£120	£160
		Wi. Watermark inverted.............	—	£200	
23a		2d. blue (Plate 5) (5.7.55)	£1800	£120	£150
		b. Imperf (Plate 5)			
		aWi. Watermark inverted.............	—	£225	
24	1	1d. red-brown (Die II) (28.2.55)...	£250	16.00	25.00
		Wi. Watermark inverted.............	£400	40.00	
24a		1d. dp red-brown (very blue paper) (Die II)................	£275	20.00	
25		1d. orange-brown (Die II)	£650	45.00	

(c) Wmk Large Crown, W 4, P 16

26	1	1d. red-brown (Die II) (15.5.55)...	£500	35.00	50.00
		a. Imperf (Plate 7)			
		Wi. Watermark inverted.............	—	75.00	
27	3	2d. blue (Plate 5) (20.7.55)	£2000	£130	£200
		a. Imperf	—	£2500	
		Wi. Watermark inverted.............	—	£275	

(d) Wmk Large Crown, W 4. P 14

29	1	1d. red-brown (Die II) (18.8.55) ...	£100	1.00	5.50
		a. Imperf (shades) (Plates 22, 24, 25, 32, 43)..............	£950	£750	
		Wi. Watermark inverted.............	£350	16.00	
30		1d. brick-red (Die II)	£160	12.00	
31		1d. plum (Die II) (2.56)	£850	£275	
32		1d. brown-rose (Die II)	£180	14.00	
33		1d. orange-brown (Die II) (3.57)..	£275	17.00	
34	3	2d. blue (Plate 5) (20.7.55)	£1000	25.00	70.00
		Wi. Watermark inverted.............	—	90.00	
35		2d. blue (Plate 6) (2.7.57)	£1100	22.00	60.00
		a. Imperf...............................	—	£2750	
		b. Imperf horiz (vert pair)	†	—	
		Wi. Watermark inverted.............	—	60.00	
★17/35a		**For well-centred, lightly used**		+125%	

1856-58. *Paper no longer blued. (a) Wmk Large Crown, W 4. P 16.*

36	1	1d. rose-red (Die II) (26.12.57)	£600	22.00	40.00
36a	3	2d. blue (Plate 6) (1.2.58)	£3000	£130	£200
		aWi. Watermark inverted.............	—	£300	

(b) (Die II) Wmk Large Crown, W 4. P 14

37	1	1d. red-brown (11.56)................	£250	50.00	
38		1d. pale red (9.4.57)	40.00	2.00	
		a. Imperf	£500	£425	
39		1d. pale rose (3.57)	40.00	6.00	
40		1d. rose-red (9.57)	25.00	1.00	2.00
		a. Imperf	£550	£425	
		Wi. Watermark inverted.............	40.00	18.00	
41		1d. dp rose-red (7.57)..............	40.00	2.00	

1861. *Letters engraved on plate instead of punched (Alphabet IV).*

42	1	1d. rose-red (Die II) (Plates 50 & 51)...............	£125	8.00	22.00
		a. Imperf	—	£1800	
		Wi. Watermark inverted.............	£180	12.00	
★36/42a		**For well-centred, lightly used**		+125%	

The original die (Die I) was used to provide roller dies for the laying down of all the line-engraved stamps from 1840 to 1855. In that year a

GREAT BRITAIN COLLECTORS

FOR EVERYTHING IN GREAT BRITAIN CONTACT US

ALL ASPECTS INCLUDED IN OUR EXTENSIVE STOCK

REGULAR ILLUSTRATED LISTS

WORLDWIDE APPROVAL SERVICE

WANTS LISTS SERVICED

INTERNATIONAL MAIL ORDER SERVICE

BUYING – ALWAYS INTERESTED IN QUALITY
COLLECTIONS & SINGLE ITEMS

As leaders since 1856 – our reputation is your guarantee.
Whatever aspect of Great Britain you collect consult:

THE 'PRECISE' SERVICE FOR THE 'CONCISE' USER

STANLEY GIBBONS LIMITED
399 STRAND
LONDON WC2R 0LX
Telephone: 071 836 8444   Fax: 071 836 7342

new master die was laid down (by means of a Die I roller die) and the impression was retouched by hand engraving by William Humphrys. This retouched die, always known to philatelists as Die II, was from that time used for preparing all new roller dies.

One Penny. The numbering of the 1d. plates recommenced at 1 on the introduction of Die II. Plates 1 to 21 were Alphabet II from which a scarce plum shade exists. Corner letters of Alphabet III appear on Plate 22 and onwards.

As an experiment, the corner letters were engraved by hand on Plates 50 and 51 in 1856, instead of being punched (Alphabet IV), but punching was again resorted to from Plate 52 onwards. Plates 50 and 51 were not put into use until 1861.

Two Pence. Unlike the 1d. the old sequence of plate numbers continued. Plates 3 and 4 of the 2d. had corner letters of Alphabet I, Plate 5 Alphabet II and Plate 6 Alphabet III. In Plate 6 the white lines are thinner than before.

In both values, varieties may be found as described in the preceding issues—ivory heads, inverted watermarks, re-entries, and double letters in corners.

The change of perforation from 16 to 14 was decided upon late in 1854 since the closer holes of the former gauge tended to cause the sheets of stamps to break up when handled, but for a time both gauges were in concurrent use. Owing to faulty alignment of the impressions on the plates and to shrinkage of the paper when damped, badly perforated stamps are plentiful in the line-engraved issues.

| 5 | 6 | Showing position of the plate number on the 1d. and 2d. values. (Plate 170 shown) |

1858–79. *Letters in all four corners. Wmk Large Crown, W* **4**. *Die* II (1d. *and* 2d.). P 14.

			Un	Used	★ Used on cover
43	5	1d. rose-red (1.4.64)	4.50	50	1.50
44		1d. lake-red	4.50	50	
		a. Imperf ....*from*	£750	£600	
		Wi. Watermark inverted	22.00	3.00	
★43/4a		**For well-centred, lightly used**		**+125%**	

Plate		Un	Used	Plate		Un	Used
71		12.00	2.00	88		80.00	5.50
72		18.00	2.50	89		20.00	50
73		12.00	2.00	90		14.00	50
74		10.00	50	91		20.00	3.50
76		20.00	50	92		7.00	50
77		£50000	£30000	93		20.00	50
78		50.00	50	94		20.00	3.00
79		15.00	50	95		12.00	50
80		10.00	75	96		14.00	50
81		30.00	1.00	97		8.00	1.75
82		60.00	2.50	98		8.00	3.50
83		70.00	4.00	99		12.00	3.00
84		30.00	1.00	100		18.00	1.25
85		12.00	1.00	101		25.00	6.00
86		15.00	2.50	102		10.00	55
87		4.50	50	103		10.00	1.50

Plate		Un	Used	Plate		Un	Used
104		14.00	3.00	166		7.50	3.50
105		35.00	4.00	167		5.00	50
106		15.00	55	168		6.00	5.50
107		20.00	3.75	169		15.00	4.00
108		15.00	1.00	170		6.00	50
109		38.00	1.75	171		4.50	50
110		10.00	6.00	172		4.50	90
111		18.00	1.00	173		25.00	6.00
112		30.00	1.00	174		4.50	40
113		8.00	7.50	175		18.00	1.75
114		£175	8.00	176		13.00	90
115		50.00	1.00	177		5.00	50
116		38.00	6.00	178		7.50	2.00
117		8.00	50	179		8.00	1.00
118		12.00	50	180		8.00	3.00
119		5.00	75	181		7.50	50
120		4.50	50	182		50.00	3.00
121		20.00	6.00	183		13.00	1.50
122		4.50	50	184		4.50	75
123		6.00	75	185		7.50	1.50
124		6.00	50	186		15.00	1.00
125		8.00	1.00	187		6.00	50
127		17.00	1.00	188		10.00	7.00
129		6.00	5.00	189		18.00	4.00
130		9.00	1.00	190		7.00	3.50
131		38.00	11.00	191		4.50	4.00
132		50.00	16.00	192		13.00	50
133		45.00	6.00	193		4.50	50
134		4.50	50	194		7.50	5.00
135		50.00	20.00	195		7.50	5.00
136		50.00	15.00	196		5.00	3.00
137		8.00	90	197		8.00	6.00
138		6.00	50	198		4.50	3.50
139		16.00	11.00	199		10.00	3.50
140		6.00	50	200		10.00	50
141		75.00	6.00	201		4.50	3.00
142		25.00	18.00	202		7.50	5.00
143		15.00	10.00	203		4.50	10.00
144		50.00	15.00	204		6.00	75
145		4.50	1.00	205		6.00	2.00
146		5.00	3.50	206		6.00	6.00
147		9.00	2.00	207		6.00	6.00
148		10.00	1.50	208		6.00	10.00
149		7.50	3.50	209		7.50	6.00
150		4.50	50	210		10.00	8.00
151		13.00	6.00	211		22.00	15.00
152		9.00	3.25	212		7.50	7.50
153		35.00	6.00	213		7.50	7.50
154		7.50	50	214		13.00	13.00
155		8.00	75	215		13.00	13.00
156		7.50	50	216		13.00	13.00
157		7.50	50	217		10.00	4.00
158		4.50	50	218		6.00	5.00
159		4.50	50	219		30.00	50.00
160		4.50	50	220		4.50	3.50
161		15.00	4.00	221		15.00	10.00
162		8.00	4.00	222		25.00	25.00
163		7.50	1.50	223		30.00	40.00
164		7.50	2.00	224		35.00	35.00
165		10.00	50	225		£1000	£300

Error. Imperf. Issued at Cardiff (Plate 116)

			Un	Used
44b	5	1d. rose-red (18.1.70)	£1750	£1000

The following plate numbers are also known imperf and used (No. 44a): 72, 79, 80, 81, 82, 83, 84, 85, 86, 87, 88, 90, 91, 92, 93, 96, 97, 100, 101, 102, 103, 104, 105, 107, 108, 109, 112, 113, 114, 116, 117, 120, 121, 122, 136, 137, 142, 146, 148, 158, 162, 164, 166, 171, 174, 191 and 202.

The numbering of this series of 1d. red plates follows after that of the previous 1d. stamp, last printed from Plate 68.

Plates 69, 70, 75, 126 and 128 were prepared for this issue but rejected owing to defects, and stamps from these plates do not exist, so that specimens which appear to be from these plates (like many of those which optimistic collectors believe to be from Plate 77) bear other plate numbers. Owing to faulty engraving or printing it is not always easy to identify the plate number. Plate 77 was also rejected but some stamps printed from it were used. One specimen is in the Tapling Collection and six or seven others are known. Plates 226 to 228 were made but not used.

Specimens from most of the plates are known with inverted watermark. The variety of watermark described in the General Notes to this section occurs on stamp M A (or M L) on plates up to about 96 (*Prices from £85 used*).

Re-entries in this issue are few, the best being on stamps M K and T K of Plate 71 and on S L and T L, Plate 83.

				Un	Used	★ Used on cover
45	**6**	2d. blue (thick lines) (7.58)		£160	4.00	15.00
		a. Imperf (Plate 9)		—	£3000	
		Wi. Watermark inverted		£250	50.00	
		Plate				
			7	£400	18.00	
			8	£450	14.00	
			9	£160	4.00	
			12	£700	40.00	
46		2d. blue (thin lines) (1.7.69)		£150	6.00	16.00
		Wi. Watermark inverted		£225	50.00	
47		2d. dp blue (thin lines)		£150	6.00	
		a. Imperf (Plate 13)		£2000		
		Plate				
			13	£180	6.00	
			14	£200	8.00	
			15	£150	8.00	
★45/7		**For well-centred, lightly used**				**+125**%

Plates 10 and 11 of the 2d. were prepared but rejected. Plates 13 to 15 were laid down from a new roller impression on which the white lines were thinner.

There are some marked re-entries and repairs, particularly on Plates 7, 8, 9 and 12.

Stamps with inverted watermark may be found and also the T A (T L) and M A (M L) watermark varieties (see General Notes to this section).

Though the paper is normally white, some printings showed blueing and stamps showing the "ivory head" may therefore be found.

7 | Showing the plate number (9)

9

1870 (1 Oct). *Wmk W **9**, extending over three stamps. P* 14.

			Un	Used	★ Used on cover
48	**7**	½d. rose-red	45.00	6.00	24.00
49		½d. rose	45.00	6.00	
		a. Imperf (Plates 1, 4, 5, 6, 8, 14) .... *from*	£950	£600	
		Wi. Watermark inverted	—	55.00	
		Wj. Watermark reversed	—	45.00	

(49)		Wk. Watermark inverted & reversed	£120	35.00
		Plate		
		1	95.00	45.00
		3	60.00	14.00
		4	75.00	8.00
		5	55.00	6.00
		6	45.00	6.00
		8	85.00	45.00
		9	£2250	£300
		10	75.00	6.00
		11	45.00	6.00
		12	45.00	6.00
		13	45.00	6.00
		14	45.00	6.00
		15	60.00	9.00
		19	90.00	20.00
		20	95.00	32.00
★48/9a		**For well-centred, lightly used**		**+200%**

The ½d. was printed in sheets of 480 (24 × 20) so that the check letters run from

$$\begin{matrix} A\ A \\ A\ A \end{matrix} \text{ to } \begin{matrix} X\ T \\ T\ X \end{matrix}$$

Plates 2, 7, 16, 17 and 18 were not completed while plates 21 and 22 though made, were not used.

Owing to the method of perforating, the outer side of stamps in either the A or X row (ie the left or right side of the sheet) is imperf.

Stamps may be found with watermark inverted or reversed, or without watermark, the latter due to misplacement of the paper when printing.

8 | Position of plate Number

1870 (1 Oct). *Wmk W **4**. P* 14.

			Un	Used	★ Used or cove
51	**8**	1½d. rose-red	£150	18.00	£14●
52		1½d. lake-red	£150	18.00	
		a. Imperf (Plates 1 & 3) *from*	£1900	†	
		Wi. Watermark inverted	—	£100	
		Plate			
		(1)	£350	25.00	
		3	£150	18.00	

Error of lettering. OP–PC for CP–PC (*Plate 1*)

53	**8**	1½d. rose-red	£4000	£650
★51/3		**For well-centred, lightly used**		**+125%**

1860. *Prepared for use but not issued; blued paper. Wmk W **4**. P* 14.

			Un	Used
53a	**8**	1½d. rosy mauve (Plate 1)	£2000	
		b. Error of lettering, OP–PC for CP–PC		

Owing to a proposed change in the postal rates, 1½d. stamps were first printed in 1860, in rosy mauve, No. 53a, but the change was not approved and the greater part of the stock was destroyed.

In 1870 a 1½d. stamp was required and was issued in rose-red.

Plate 1 did not have the plate number in the design of the stamps, but on stamps from Plate 3 the number will be found in the frame as shown above.

Plate 2 was defective and was not used.

The error of lettering OP–PC on Plate 1 was apparently not noticed by the printer, and therefore not corrected.

EMBOSSED ISSUES

Volume 1 of the Stanley Gibbons *Great Britain Specialised Catalogue* gives further detailed information on the embossed issues.

PRICES. The prices quoted are for cut-square stamps with average to fine embossing. Stamps with exceptionally clear embossing are worth more.

| 10 | 11 | 12 |

13   Position of die number

(Primary die engraved at the Royal Mint by William Wyon. Stamps printed at Somerset House)

1847–54. *Imperf* (For paper and wmk see footnote.)

				Un	Used	Used on cover
54	**10**	1s.	pale green (11.9.47)	£2750	£350	£450
55		1s.	green	£2750	£400	
56		1s.	dp green	£3250	£450	
			Die I (1847)	£2750	£350	
			Die 2 (1854)	£3250	£400	
57	**11**	10d.	brown (6.11.48)	£2250	£575	£900
			Die I (1848)	£2500	£625	
			Die 2 (1850)	£2250	£575	
			Die 3 (1853)	£2250	£575	
			Die 4 (1854)	£2500	£625	
			Die 5	£16000		
58	**12**	6d.	mauve (1.3.54)	£2500	£425	
59		6d.	dull lilac	£2500	£400	£500
60		6d.	purple	£2500	£400	
		Wi.	Watermark inverted	—	£400	
		Wj.	Watermark reversed	£2500	£425	
		Wk.	Watermark inverted & reversed	£2500	£400	
61		6d.	violet	£3500	£750	

The 1s. and 10d. are on "Dickinson" paper with "silk" threads. The 6d. is on paper watermarked V R in single-lined letters, W **13**, which may be found in four ways—upright, inverted, upright, reversed, and inverted reversed; upright reversed being the commonest.

The die numbers are indicated on the base of the bust. Only Die 1 (1 W W) of the 6d. was used for the adhesive stamps. The 10d. is from Die 1 (W.W.1 on stamps), and Dies 2 to 5 (2W.W., 3W.W., 4W.W. and 5W.W.) but the number and letters on stamps from Die 1 are seldom clear and many specimens are known without any trace of them. Because of this the stamp we previously listed as "No die number" has been deleted. That they are from Die 1 is proved by the existence of blocks showing stamps with and without the die number. The 1s. is from Dies 1 and 2 (W.W.1, W.W.2).

The normal arrangement of the "silk" threads in the paper was in pairs running down each vertical row of the sheet, the space between the threads of each pair being approximately 5 mm and between pairs of threads 20 mm. Varieties due to misplacement of the paper in printing show a single thread on the first stamp from the sheet margin and two threads 20 mm apart on the other stamps of the row. Faulty manufacture is the cause of stamps with a single thread in the middle.

Through bad spacing of the impressions, which were handstruck, all values may be found with two impressions more or less overlapping. Owing to the small margin allowed for variation of spacing, specimens with good margins on all sides are not common.

Double impressions are known of all values.

Later printings of the 6d. had the gum tinted green to enable the printer to distinguish the gummed side of the paper.

SURFACE–PRINTED ISSUES

GENERAL NOTES

Volume 1 of the Stanley Gibbons *Great Britain Specialised Catalogue* gives further detailed information on the surface-printed issues.

"Abnormals". The majority of the great rarities in the surface-printed group of issues are the so-called "abnormals", whose existence is due to the practice of printing six sheets from every plate as soon as made, one of which was kept for record purposes at Somerset House, while the others were perforated and usually issued. If such plates were not used for general production or if, before they came into full use, a change of watermark or colour took place, the six sheets originally printed would differ from the main issue in plate, colour or watermark and, if issued, would be extremely rare.

The abnormal stamps of this class listed in this Catalogue and distinguished, where not priced, by an asterisk (*) are:

No.		
78	3d.	Plate 3 (with white dots)
152	4d.	vermilion, Plate 16
153	4d.	sage-green, Plate 17
109	6d.	mauve, Plate 10
122/4	6d.	pale chestnut & 6d. chestnut, Plate 12
145	6d.	pale buff, Plate 13
88	9d.	Plate 3 (hair lines)
98	9d.	Plate 5 (see footnote to No. 98)
113	10d.	Plate 2
91	1s.	Plate 3 ("Plate 2")
148/50	1s.	green, Plate 14
120	2s.	blue, Plate 3

Those which may have been issued, but of which no specimens are known, are 2½d. wmk. Anchor, Plates 4 and 5; 3d. wmk Emblems, Plate 5; 3d. wmk Spray, Plate 21; 6d. grey, wmk Spray, Plate 18; 8d. orange, Plate 2; 1s. wmk Emblems, Plate 5. 5s. wmk Maltese Cross, Plate 4.

The 10d. Plate 1, wmk Emblems (No. 99), is sometimes reckoned among the abnormals, but was an error, due to the use of the wrong paper.

Corner Letters. With the exception of the 4d., 6d. and 1s. of 1855–57, the ½d., 1½d., 2d. and 5d. of 1880, the 1d. lilac of 1881 and the £5 (which had letters in lower corners only, and in the reverse order to the normal), all the surface-printed stamps issued prior to 1887 had letters in all four corners, as in the later line-engraved stamps. The arrangement is the same, the letters running in sequence right across and down the sheets, whether these were divided into panes or not. The corner letters existing naturally depend on the number of stamps in the sheet and their arrangement.

Imprimaturs and Imperforate Stamps. The Post Office retained in their records (now in the National Postal Museum) one imperforate sheet from each plate, known as the Imprimatur (or officially approved) sheet. Some stamps were removed from time to time for presentation purposes and have come on to the market, but these imperforates are not listed as they were not issued. Full details can be found in Volume I of the *Great Britain Specialised Catalogue*.

However, other imperforate stamps are known to have been issued and these are listed where it has been possible to prove that they do not come from the Imprimatur sheets. It is therefore advisable to purchase these only when accompanied by an Expert Committee certificate of genuineness.

Plate Numbers. All stamps from No. 75 to No. 163 bear in their designs either the plate number or, in one or two earlier instances, some other indication by which one plate can be distinguished from another. With the aid of these and of the corner letters it is thus possible to "reconstruct" a sheet of stamps from any plate of any issue or denomination.

Surface-printing. In this context the traditional designation "surface-printing" is synonymous with typo(graphy)—a philatelic term—or letterpress—the printers' term—as meaning printing from (the surface of) raised type. It is also called relief-printing, as the image is in relief (in French, *en épargne*), unwanted parts of the design having been cut away. Duplicate impressions can be electrotyped or stereotyped from an original die, the resulting *clichés* being locked together to form the printing plate.

Wing Margins. As the vertical gutters (spaces) between the panes, into which sheets of stamps of most values were divided until the introduction of the Imperial Crown watermark, were perforated through the centre with a single row of holes, instead of each vertical row of stamps on the inner side of the panes having its own line of perforation as is now usual, a proportion of the stamps in each sheet have what is called a "wing margin" about 5 mm wide on one or other side.

The stamps with "wing margins" are the watermark Emblems and Spray of Rose series (3d., 6d., 9d., 10d., 1s. and 2s.) with letters D, E, H or I in S.E. corner, and the watermark Garter series (4d. and 8d.) with letters F or G in S.E. corner. Knowledge of this lettering will enable collectors to guard against stamps with wing margin cut down and re-perforated, but note that wing margin stamps of Nos. 62 to 73 are also to be found re-perforated.

PRINTERS. The issues of Queen Victoria, Nos. 62/214, were typo by Thomas De La Rue & Co.

PERFORATIONS. All the surface-printed issues of Queen Victoria are Perf 14, with the exception of Nos. 126/9.

1855–57. *No corner letters.*
(a) *Wmk Small Garter, W* **15.** *Highly glazed, deeply blued paper* (31 July 1855)

			Un	Used	★ Used or cover
62	14	4d. carmine (*shades*)	£2250	£170	£275
		a. Paper slightly blued	£2500	£160	
		b. White paper	£3000	£350	
		Wi. Watermark inverted	—	£250	

(b) *Wmk Medium Garter, W* **16**

(i) *Thick, blued highly glazed paper* (25 February 1856)

			Un	Used	
63	14	4d. carmine (*shades*)	£2750	£160	£250
		a. White paper	£2500		
		Wi. Watermark inverted	—	£250	

(ii) *Ordinary thin white paper* (September 1856)

			Un	Used	
64	14	4d. pale carmine	£1800	£150	£225
		a. Stamp printed double	†	—	
		Wi. Watermark inverted	—	£180	

(iii) *Ordinary white paper, specially prepared ink* (1 November 1856)

			Un	Used	
65	14	4d. rose or dp rose	£1800	£160	£250

(c) *Wmk Large Garter, W* **17.** *Ordinary white paper* (January 1857)

			Un	Used	
66	14	4d. rose-carmine	£700	40.00	75.00
		a. Rose	£600	40.00	
		b. Thick glazed paper	£1700	95.00	
		Wi. Watermark inverted	—	55.00	
		Wj. Watermark inverted & reversed			
★62/6b		**For well-centred, lightly used**		+125%	

18

19

20 Emblems wmk (normal)

20a Watermark error, three roses and shamrock

20b Watermark error, three roses and thistle

(d) *Wmk Emblems, W* **20**

			Un	Used	★ Used or cover
69	18	6d. dp lilac (21.10.56)	£550	55.00	
70		6d. pale lilac	£500	40.00	75.00
		a. Azure paper	£2500	£350	
		b. Thick paper	£750	£130	
		c. Error. Watermark. W **20a**			
		Wi. Watermark inverted	—	75.00	
		Wj. Watermark reversed			
		Wk. Watermark inverted & reversed			
71	19	1s. dp green (1.11.56)	£1200	£150	
72		1s. green	£650	£140	£160

14

15 Small Garter

16 Medium Garter

17 Large Garter

73	**19**	1s. pale green............................	£650	£140
		a. Azure paper	—	£500
		b. Thick paper	—	£160
		c. Imperf.................................		
		Wi. Watermark inverted.............	—	£160
		Wj. Watermark reversed	—	£650
		Wk. Watermark inverted and reversed............................		
★69/73b		**For well-centred, lightly used**		+125%

146/7	6d. grey	Spray	20.3.74
161	6d. grey	Crown	1.1.81
162	6d. on 6d. lilac	Crown	1.1.83
156a	8d. purple-brown	Large Garter	July 1876
156	8d. orange	Large Garter	11.9.76
148/50	1s. green	Spray	1.9.73
151	1s. brown	Spray	14.10.80
163	1s. brown	Crown	29.5.81

Watermarks:	Anchor	W **40, 47**
	Cross	W **39**
	Crown	W **49**
	Emblems	W **20**
	Large Garter	W **17**
	Medium Garter	W **16**
	Orb	W **48**
	Small Garter	W **15**
	Spray	W **33**

KEY TO SURFACE-PRINTED ISSUES 1855–83

S.G. Nos.	Description	Watermark	Date of Issue
NO CORNER LETTERS			
62	4d. carmine	Small Garter	31.7.55
63/5	4d. carmine	Medium Garter	25.2.56
66/a	4d. carmine	Large Garter	Jan 1857
69/70	6d. lilac	Emblems	21.10.56
71/3	1s. green	Emblems	1.11.56
SMALL WHITE CORNER LETTERS			
75/7	3d. carmine	Emblems	1.5.62
78	3d. carmine (dots)	Emblems	Aug 1862
79/82	4d. red	Large Garter	15.1.62
83/5	6d. lilac	Emblems	1.12.62
86/8	9d. bistre	Emblems	15.1.62
89/91	1s. green	Emblems	1.12.62
LARGE WHITE CORNER LETTERS			
92	3d. rose	Emblems	1.3.65
102/3	3d. rose	Spray	July 1867
93/5	4d. vermilion	Large Garter	4.7.65
96/7	6d. lilac	Emblems	7.3.65
104/7	6d. lilac	Spray	21.6.67
108/9	6d. lilac	Spray	8.3.69
122/4	6d. chestnut	Spray	12.4.72
125	6d. grey	Spray	24.4.73
98	9d. straw	Emblems	30.10.65
110/11	9d. straw	Spray	3.10.67
99	10d. brown	Emblems	11.11.67
112/14	10d. brown	Spray	1.7.67
101	1s. green	Emblems	Feb 1865
115/17	1s. green	Spray	13.7.67
118/20b	2s. blue	Spray	1.7.67
121	2s. brown	Spray	27.2.80
126/7	5s. rose	Cross	1.7.67
128	10s. grey	Cross	26.9.78
129	£1 brown-lilac	Cross	26.9.78
130, 134	5s. rose	Anchor	25.11.82
131, 135	10s. grey-green	Anchor	Feb 1883
132, 136	£1 brown-lilac	Anchor	Dec 1882
133, 137	£5 orange	Anchor	21.3.82
LARGE COLOURED CORNER LETTERS			
138/9	2½d. rosy mauve	Anchor	1.7.75
141	2½d. rosy mauve	Orb	1.5.76
142	2½d. blue	Orb	5.2.80
157	2½d. blue	Crown	23.3.81
143/4	3d. rose	Spray	5.7.73
158	3d. rose	Crown	Jan 1881
159	3d. on 3d. lilac	Crown	1.1.83
152	4d. vermilion	Large Garter	1.3.76
153	4d. sage-green	Large Garter	12.3.77
154	4d. brown	Large Garter	15.8.80
160	4d. brown	Crown	9.12.80
145	6d. buff	Spray	15.3.73

21 22

23 24 25 Plate 2

A. White dots added

B. Hair lines

1862–64. *A small uncoloured letter in each corner, the 4d. wmk Large Garter. W* **17**, *the others Emblems, W* **20**.

			Un	★ Used	Used on cover
75	**21**	3d. dp carmine-rose (Plate 2) (1.5.62)............................	£1200	£130	
76		3d. brt carmine-rose	£700	£110	£225
		Wi. Watermark inverted.............	—	£160	
77		3d. pale carmine-rose	£700	£100	
		b. Thick paper......................	—	£175	
		Wj. Watermark reversed			
78		3d. rose (with white dots, Type A, Plate 3) (8.62).....................	*	£2500	
		a. Imperf (Plate 3)..................	£2000		
79	**22**	4d. brt red (Plate 3) (15.1.62)	£750	50.00	
80		4d. pale red............................	£500	35.00	85.00
		Wi. Watermark inverted	—	75.00	

81	22	4d. brt red (Hair lines, Type B, Plate 4) (16.10.63)	£650	38.00	
82		4d. pale red (Hair lines, Type B, Plate 4)	£550	28.00	75.00
		a. Imperf (Plate 4)	£1500		
		Wi. Watermark inverted		50.00	
83	23	6d. dp lilac (Plate 3) (1.12.62)	£750	50.00	
84		6d. lilac	£650	30.00	65.00
		a. Azure paper	—	£300	
		b. Thick paper	—	65.00	
		c. Error. Watermark W **20**b (stamp TF)			
		Wi. Watermark inverted	—	50.00	
		Wj. Watermark inverted and reversed			
85		6d. lilac (Hair lines, Plate 4) (20.4.64)	£800	50.00	£120
		a. Imperf (watermark inverted)	£1100		
		Eb. Imperf and watermark upright			
		c. Thick paper	£1200	80.00	
		Wi. Watermark inverted	—	80.00	
		Wj. Watermark inverted and reversed			
86	24	9d. bistre (Plate 2) (15.1.62)	£1100	£140	£250
		Wi. Watermark inverted	—	£175	
		Wj. Watermark reversed	—	£200	
87		9d. straw	£1100	£130	
		a. On azure paper			
		b. Thick paper	£1700	£200	
88		9d. bistre (Hair lines, Plate 3) (5.62)	£6000	£1800	
89	25	1s. dp green (Plate No. 1 = Plate 2) (1.12.62)	£800	£110	
90		1s. green (Plate No. 1 = Plate 2)	£700	65.00	£130
		a. "K" in lower left corner in white circle (stamp KD)	£4250	£500	
		aa. "K" normal (stamp KD)	—	£750	
		b. On azure paper			
		c. Thick paper	—	£160	
		ca. Thick paper, "K" in circle as No. 90a	—	£1000	
		Wi. Watermark inverted	—	90.00	
		Wj. Watermark inverted and reversed			
91		1s. dp green (Plate No. 2 = Plate 3)	£11000		
		a. Imperf	£1500		
		aWi. Watermark inverted	£1000		

★75/91   **For well-centred, lightly used** .....   +125%

The 3d. as Type **21**, but with network background in the spandrels which is found overprinted SPECIMEN, was never issued.

The plates of this issue may be distinguished as follows:

3d. Plate 2   No white dots
Plate 3   White dots as Illustration A.
4d. Plate 3   No hair lines. Roman I next to lower corner letters.
Plate 4.   Hair lines in corners. (Illustration B.). Roman II.
6d. Plate 3.   No hair lines.
Plate 4.   Hair lines in corners.
9d. Plate 2.   No hair lines
Plate 3.   Hair lines in corners. Beware of faked lines.
1s. Plate 2.   Numbered 1 on stamps.
Plate 3.   Numbered 2 on stamps & with hair lines.

The 9d. on azure paper (No. 87a) is very rare, only one confirmed example being known.

The variety "K" in circle, No. 90a, is believed to be due to a damaged letter having been cut out and replaced. It is probable that the punch was driven in too deeply, causing the flange to penetrate the surface, producing an indentation showing as an uncoloured circle.

The watermark variety "three roses and a shamrock" illustrated in W **20**a was evidently due to the substitution of an extra rose for the thistle in a faulty watermark bit. It is found on stamp T A of Plates 2 and 4

of the 3d., Plates 1 (No. 70c), 3, 5 and 6 of the 6d., Plate 4 of the 9d. and Plate 4 of the 1s.

A similar variety, W **20**b, but showing three roses and a thistle is found on stamp T F of the 6d. (No. 84) and 9d. (No. 98).

| 26 | 27 |

| 28 | 28a |
| (with hyphen) | (without hyphen) |

| 29 | 30 | 31 |

1865–67. *Large uncoloured corner letters. Wmk. Large Garter* (4d.); *others Emblems.*

| | | | | | ★ Used on |
			Un	Used	cover
92	26	3d. rose (Plate 4) (1.3.65)	£375	40.00	95.00
		a. Error. Watermark W **20**a	£900	£275	
		b. Thick paper	£500	50.00	
		Wi. Watermark inverted	—	75.00	
		Wj. Watermark reversed			
		Wk. Watermark inverted and reversed			
93	27	4d. dull vermilion (4.7.65)	£225	15.00	35.00
94		4d. vermilion	£225	15.00	
		a. Imperf (Plates 11, 12)	£500		
		Wi. Watermark inverted	£225	18.00	
95		4d. dp vermilion	£225	20.00	
		Plate			
		7 (1865)	£300	19.00	
		8 (1866)	£250	19.00	
		9 (1867)	£250	15.00	
		10 (1868)	£300	30.00	
		11 (1869)	£250	15.00	
		12 (1870)	£225	15.00	
		13 (1872)	£250	17.00	
		14 (1873)	£300	35.00	
96	28	6d. dp lilac (with hyphen) (7.3.65)	£400	38.00	
97		6d. lilac (with hyphen)	£350	28.00	65.00
		a. Thick paper	£450	55.00	
		b. Stamp doubly printed (Plate 6)	—	£4000	
		c. Error. Watermark W **20**a (Pl 5, 6)	from	—	£300
		Wi. Watermark inverted	—	55.00	
		Wj. Watermark reversed			
		Plate			
		5 (1865)	£350	28.00	
		6 (1867)	£1000	55.00	
98	29	9d. straw (Plate 4) (30.10.65)	£700	£200	£300
		a. Thick paper	£950	£325	
		b. Error. Watermark W **20**a	—	£375	

(98)	c.	Error. Watermark W **20**b (stamp TF)..........................			
		Wi. Watermark inverted.............	—	£250	
99	**30**	10d. red-brown (Plate 1) (11.11.67)	*	£12000	
101	**31**	1s. green (plate 4) (26.1.65)	£650	65.00	£110
		a. Error. Watermark W **20**a	—	£350	
		b. Thick paper.......................	£750	£120	
		c. Imperf between (vert pair)	—	£4000	
		Wi. Watermark inverted.............	—	90.00	
		Wj. Imperf watermark inverted ...			
★92/101c		**For well-centred, lightly used**		+**100**%	

From mid-1866 to about the end of 1871 4d. stamps of this issue appeared generally with watermark inverted.

Unused copies of No. 98 from Plate 5 exist, but this was never put to press and all evidence points to the existing copies being from a portion of the Imprimatur sheet which was perforated by De La Rue in 1887 for insertion in albums to be presented to members of the Stamp Committee (*Price* £10000 un).

The 10d. stamps, No. 99, were printed in *error* on paper watermarked "Emblems" instead of on "Spray of Rose".

32	**33** Spray of Rose	**34**

1867–80. *Wmk Spray of Rose, W* **33.**

				★ Used on
			Un	Used cover

102	**26**	3d. dp rose (12.7.67)	£225	18.00	
103		3d. rose	£200	12.00	38.00
		a. Imperf (Plates 5, 6, 8) .... from	£700		
		Wi. Watermark inverted.............	£350	45.00	
		Plate			
		4 (1867)	£300	50.00	
		5 (1868)	£200	14.00	
		6 (1870)	£225	12.00	
		7 (1871)	£275	15.00	
		8 (1872)	£250	14.00	
		9 (1872)	£250	20.00	
		10 (1873)	£275	42.00	
104	**28**	6d. lilac (with hyphen) (Plate 6) (21.6.67)	£550	30.00	90.00
		a. Imperf			
		Wi. Watermark inverted.............	—	60.00	
105		6d. dp lilac (with hyphen) (Plate 6)	£550	30.00	
106		6d. purple (with hyphen) (Pl 6) ...	£550	45.00	
107		6d. brt violet (with hyphen) (Plate 6) (22.7.68)	£550	32.00	
108	**28**a	6d. dull violet (without hyphen) (Plate 8) (18.3.69).................	£325	25.00	
		Wi. Watermark inverted.............	—	60.00	
109		6d. mauve (without hyphen)	£275	25.00	55.00
		a. Imperf (Plate Nos. 8 & 9) ...	£750	£650	
		Wi. Watermark inverted.............	—	60.00	
		Plate			
		8 (1869, mauve)	£275	25.00	
		9 (1870, mauve)	£275	25.00	
		10 (1869, mauve)	*	£12000	
110	**29**	9d. straw (Plate No. 4) (3.10.67)...	£600	£100	£200
111		Wi. Watermark inverted.............	—	£140	
		9d. pale straw (Plate No. 4)	£600	£100	
		a. Imperf (Plate 4)	£1900		

112	**30**	10d. red-brown (1.7.67).............	£1000	£130	£325
		Wi. Watermark inverted.............	—	£250	
113		10d. pale red-brown	£1000	£140	
114		10d. dp red-brown	£1200	£160	
		a. Imperf (Plate 1)	£1800		
		Plate			
		1 (1867)	£1000	£130	
		2 (1867)	£12000	£2500	
115	**31**	1s. dp green (13.7.67)...............	£425	10.00	
117		1s. green	£350	10.00	20.00
		a. Imperf between (horiz pair) (Pl 7)			
		b. Imperf (Plate 4)	£1000	£600	
		Wi. Watermark inverted.............	£450	35.00	
		Plate			
		4 (1867)	£350	15.00	
		5 (1871)	£400	12.00	
		6 (1872)	£550	10.00	
		7 (1873)	£550	30.00	
118	**32**	2s. dull blue (1.7.67)	£950	60.00	£325
		Wi. Watermark inverted.............	—	£150	
119		2s. dp blue	£950	60.00	
		a. Imperf (Plate 1)	£1900		
120		2s. pale blue	£1500	95.00	
		aa. Imperf (Plate 1)	£1800		
120a		2s. cobalt	£5000	£900	
120b		2s. milky blue........................	£3000	£400	
		Plate			
		1 (1867)	£950	60.00	
		3 (1868)	*	£3000	
121		2s. brown (Plate No. 1) (27.2.80) ...	£6000	£1000	
		a. Imperf...........................	£4000		
		b. No watermark	†	—	
		Wi. Watermark inverted.............			
★102/21		**For well-centred, lightly used**		+75%	

Examples of the 1s. from Plates 5 and 6 *without* watermark are postal forgeries used at the Stock Exchange Post Office in the early 1870s.

1872–73. *Uncoloured letters in corners. Wmk Spray, W* **33.**

				★ Used on
			Un	Used cover

122	**34**	6d. dp chestnut (12.4.72)	£425	18.00	50.00
123		6d. chestnut (22.5.72)	£350	18.00	
		Wi. Watermark inverted	—	65.00	
123a		6d. pale chestnut (1872)	*	£1300	
124		6d. pale buff (24.10.72)	£400	35.00	£130
		Wi. Watermark inverted.............	—	£100	
		Plate			
		11 (1872, dp chestnut)	£425	18.00	
		11 (1872, chestnut)	£350	18.00	
		11 (1872, pale buff)	£400	35.00	
		12 (1872, pale chestnut)	*	£1300	
		12 (1872, chestnut)	*	£1300	
		12 (1872, pale buff)	£750	55.00	
125		6d. grey (Plate No. 12) (24.4.73)...	£600	80.00	£130
		a. Imperf	£1300		
		Wi. Watermark inverted.............	£750	£100	
★122/5		**For well-centred, lightly used**		+50%	

35	**36**

37

38

41

42

43

44

45

46

39 Maltese Cross

40 Large Anchor

47 Small Anchor

48 Orb

1867–83. *Uncoloured letters in corners.*

(a) Wmk Maltese Cross, W **39.** *P* 15½ ×15

			Un	★ Used
126	**35**	5s. rose (1.7.67)	£2500	£250
127		5s. pale rose	£2750	£250
		a. Imperf (Plate 1)	£4000	
		Plate		
		1 (1867)	£2500	£250
		2 (1874)	£3500	£325
128	**36**	10s. greenish grey (Plate 1) (26.9.78)	£18000	£850
129	**37**	£1 brown-lilac (Plate 1) (26.9.78)	£22000	£1200

(b) Wmk Anchor, W **40.** *P* 14. (i) *Blued paper*

130	**35**	5s. rose (Plate 4) (25.11.82)	£5000	£850
		Wi. Watermark inverted	—	£2000
131	**36**	10s. grey-green (Plate 1) (2.83)	£20000	£1200
132	**37**	£1 brown-lilac (Plate 1) (12.82)	£27000	£2250
133	**38**	£5 orange (Plate 1) (21.3.82)	£15000	£3500

(ii) *White paper*

134	**35**	5s. rose (Plate 4)	£4500	£850
135	**36**	10s. greenish grey (Plate 1)	£22000	£1200
136	**37**	£1 brown-lilac (Plate 1)	£32000	£2000
137	**38**	£5 orange (Plate 1)	£4250	£1200
★126/37		**For well-centred, lightly used**		+75%

For full information on all future British issues, collectors should write to the British Post Office Philatelic Bureau, 20 Brandon Street, Edinburgh EH3 5TT

1873–80. *Large coloured letters in the corners.*

(a) Wmk Anchor, W **47**

			Un	★ Used	Used on cover
138	**41**	2½d. rosy mauve (*blued paper*) (1.7.75)	£375	35.00	
		a. Imperf			
		Wi. Watermark inverted	£500	75.00	
139		2½d. rosy mauve (*white paper*)	£225	25.00	50.00
		Wi. Watermark inverted	£350	40.00	
		Plate			
		1 (*blued paper*) (1875)	£375	35.00	
		1 (*white paper*) (1875)	£225	25.00	
		2 (*blued paper*) (1875)	£3000	£600	
		2 (*white paper*) (1875)	£225	25.00	
		3 (*white paper*) (1875)	£400	30.00	
		3 (*blued paper*) (1875)	—	£2250	

Error of Lettering L H—F L *for* L H—H L (*Plate 2*)

| 140 | **41** | 2½d. rosy mauve | £7000 | £700 | |

(b) Wmk Orb, W **48**

141	**41**	2½d. rosy mauve (1.5.76)	£225	14.00	35.00
		Wi. Watermark inverted	£325	30.00	
		Plate			
		3 (1876)	£500	30.00	
		4 (1876)	£225	14.00	
		5 (1876)	£225	18.00	
		6 (1876)	£225	14.00	
		7 (1877)	£225	14.00	
		8 (1877)	£225	18.00	
		9 (1877)	£225	14.00	
		10 (1878)	£250	20.00	
		11 (1878)	£225	14.00	
		12 (1878)	£225	18.00	
		13 (1878)	£225	18.00	

(141)		*Plate*				
		14 (1879)		£225	14.00	
		15 (1879)		£225	14.00	
		16 (1879)		£225	14.00	
		17 (1880)		£550	90.00	
142	**41**	2½d. blue (5.2.80)		£180	10.00	15.00
		Wi. Watermark inverted		£250	22.00	
		Plate				
		17 (1880)		£180	20.00	
		18 (1880)		£200	12.00	
		19 (1880)		£180	10.00	
		20 (1880)		£180	10.00	

*(c) Wmk Spray, W **33***

143	**42**	3d. rose (5.7.73)		£200	12.00	35.00
		Wi. Watermark inverted		£300	35.00	
144		3d. pale rose		£200	12.00	
		Plate				
		11 (1873)		£200	12.00	
		12 (1873)		£225	14.00	
		14 (1874)		£250	15.00	
		15 (1874)		£200	14.00	
		16 (1875)		£200	14.00	
		17 (1875)		£225	14.00	
		18 (1875)		£225	14.00	
		19 (1876)		£200	14.00	
		20 (1879)		£200	30.00	
145	**43**	6d. pale buff (Plate 13) (15.3.73) ..	*	£4500		
146		6d. dp grey (20.3.74)		£225	20.00	40.00
147		6d. grey		£225	20.00	
		Wi. Watermark inverted		£325	40.00	
		Plate				
		13 (1874)		£225	22.00	
		14 (1875)		£225	22.00	
		15 (1876)		£225	20.00	
		16 (1878)		£225	20.00	
		17 (1880)		£300	38.00	
148	**44**	1s. dp green (1.9.73)		£325	35.00	
150		1s. pale green		£250	28.00	50.00
		Wi. Watermark inverted		£300	45.00	
		Plate				
		8 (1873)		£325	35.00	
		9 (1874)		£325	35.00	
		10 (1874)		£300	35.00	
		11 (1875)		£300	35.00	
		12 (1875)		£250	28.00	
		13 (1876)		£250	28.00	
		14 (—)		*	£10000	
151		1s. orange-brown (Plate 13) (14.10.80)		£1100	£190	£300
		Wi. Watermark inverted		£1400	£225	

*(d) Wmk Large Garter, W **17***

152	**45**	4d. vermilion (1.3.76)		£600	£140	£275
		Wi. Watermark inverted		—	£180	
		Plate				
		15 (1876)		£600	£140	
		16 (1877)		*	£10000	
153		4d. sage-green (12.3.77)		£400	90.00	£180
		Wi. Watermark inverted		—	£110	
		Plate				
		15 (1877)		£450	95.00	
		16 (1877)		£400	90.00	
		17 (1877)		*	£6000	
154		4d. grey-brown (Plate 17) (15.8.80)		£600	£150	£250
		a. Imperf		£2000		
		Wi. Watermark inverted		—	£160	
156	**46**	8d. orange (Plate 1) (11.9.76)		£550	£110	£200
		Wi. Watermark inverted		—	£140	
★138/56		**For well-centred, lightly used**			**+100%**	

1876 (July). *Prepared for use but not issued.*

156a	**46**	8d. purple-brown (Plate 1)		£3000	

49 Imperial Crown   (**50**)

1880–83. *Wmk Imperial Crown, W **49**.*

				★	*Used on*
				Un	*Used* *cover*
157	**41**	2½d. blue (23.3.81)		£180	8.00 20.00
		Wi. Watermark inverted		£250	16.00
		Plate			
		21 (1881)		£225	9.00
		22 (1881)		£180	8.00
		23 (1881)		£180	8.00
158	**42**	3d. rose (3.81)		£200	30.00 38.00
		Wi. Watermark inverted		£500	45.00
		Plate			
		20 (1881)		£250	45.00
		21 (1881)		£200	30.00
159		3d. on 3d. lilac (T **50**) (C.) (Plate 21) (1.1.83)		£225	70.00 £225
		Wi. Watermark inverted			
160	**45**	4d. grey-brown (8.12.80)		£180	25.00 70.00
		Wi. Watermark inverted		—	75.00
		Plate			
		17 (1880)		£180	25.00
		18 (1882)		£180	25.00
161	**43**	6d. grey (1.1.81)		£150	25.00 45.00
		Wi. Watermark inverted		—	50.00
		Plate			
		17 (1881)		£180	22.00
		18 (1882)		£150	22.00
162		6d. on 6d. lilac (as T **50**) (C.) (Plate 18) (1.1.83)		£200	70.00 £140
		a. Slanting dots (various) ..*from*		£250	80.00
		b. Opt double		—	£4000
		Wi. Watermark inverted		£325	95.00
163	**44**	1s. orange-brown (29.5.81)		£225	45.00 90.00
		Wi. Watermark inverted		£300	60.00
		Plate			
		13 (1881)		£275	45.00
		14 (1881)		£225	45.00
★157/63		**For well-centred, lightly used**			**+75%**

The 1s. plate 14 (line perf 14) exists in purple but was not issued in this shade (*Price £2500 unused*). Examples were included in a few of the Souvenir Albums prepared for members of the "Stamp Committee of 1884".

52   53

54   **55**   **56**

The variety "frame broken at bottom" (No. 173b) shows a white space just inside the bottom frame-line from between the "N" and "E" of "ONE" to below the first "N" of "PENNY", breaking the pearls and cutting into the lower part of the oval below "PEN".

1880–81. *Wmk Imperial Crown,* W **49**.

				★ Used on	
			Un	Used	cover
164	52	½d. dp green (14.10.80)	15.00	3.00	6.00
		a. Imperf	£600		
		b. No watermark	£2500		
		Wi. Watermark inverted	—	25.00	
165		½d. pale green	17.00	5.00	
166	53	1d. Venetian red (1.1.80)	5.00	2.00	4.00
		a. Imperf	£600		
		Wi. Watermark inverted	—	30.00	
167	54	1½d. Venetian red (14.10.80)	80.00	14.00	60.00
168	55	2d. pale rose (8.12.80)	95.00	30.00	60.00
		Wi. Watermark inverted	£140	50.00	
168a		2d. dp rose	95.00	30.00	
169	56	5d. indigo (15.3.81)	£350	45.00	£125
		a. Imperf	£1100	£700	
		Wi. Watermark inverted	—	£750	
★164/9		**For well-centred, lightly used**		+75%	

57   Die I   Die II

1881. *Wmk Imperial Crown,* W **49**. (a) 14 *dots in each corner, Die* I (12 July).

				★ Used on	
			Un	Used	cover
170	**57**	1d. lilac	75.00	12.00	20.00
		Wi. Watermark inverted			
171		1d. pale lilac	75.00	12.00	

(b) 16 *dots in each corner, Die* II (13 December)

172	**57**	1d. lilac	1.00	40	1.10
		Wi. Watermark inverted	9.00	4.50	
172a		1d. bluish lilac	£180	45.00	
173		1d. dp purple	1.00	30	
		a. Printed both sides	£400	†	
		b. Frame broken at bottom	£475	£180	
		c. Printed on gummed side	£375	†	
		d. Imperf three sides (pair)	£2000	†	
		e. Printed both sides but impression on back inverted	£400	†	
		f. No watermark	£750	†	
		g. Blued paper	£1500		
174		1d. mauve	1.00	40	
		a. Imperf (pair)	£900		
★170/4		**For well-centred, lightly used**		+50%	

1d. stamps with the words "PEARS SOAP" printed on back in *orange*, *blue* or *mauve* price *from* £300, *unused*.

KEY TO SURFACE–PRINTED ISSUES 1880–1900

S.G. Nos.	Description	Date of Issue
164/5	½d. green	14.10.80
187	½d. slate-blue	1.4.84
197/d	½d. vermilion	1.1.87
213	½d. blue-green	17.4.1900
166	1d. Venetian red	1.1.80
170/1	1d. lilac, Die I	12.7.81
172/4	1d. lilac, Die II	12.12.81
167	1½d. Venetian red	14.10.80
188	1½d. lilac	1.4.84
198	1½d. purple & green	1.1.87
168/a	2d. rose	8.12.80
189	2d. lilac	1.4.84
199/200	2d. green & red	1.1.87
190	2½d. lilac	1.4.84
201	2½d. purple on blue paper	1.1.87
191	3d. lilac	1.4.84
202/4	3d. purple on yellow paper	1.1.87
192	4d. dull green	1.4.84
205/a	4d. green & brown	1.1.87
206	4½d. green & carmine	15.9.92
169	5d. indigo	15.3.81
193	5d. dull green	1.4.84
207	5d. purple & blue, Die I	1.1.87
207a	5d. purple & blue, Die II	1888
194	6d. dull green	1.4.84
208/a	6d. purple on rose-red paper	1.1.87
195	9d. dull green	1.8.83
209	9d. purple & blue	1.1.87
210	10d. purple & carmine	24.2.90
196	1s. dull green	1.4.84
211	1s. green	1.1.87
214	1s. green & carmine	11.7.1900
175	2s. 6d. lilac on blued paper	2.7.83
178/9	2s. 6d. lilac	1884
176	5s. rose on blued paper	1.4.84
180/1	5s. rose	1884
177/a	10s. ultramarine on blued paper	1.4.84
182/3a	10s. ultramarine	1884
185	£1 brown-lilac, wmk Crowns	1.4.84
186	£1 brown-lilac, wmk Orbs	1.2.88
212	£1 green	27.1.91

Note that the £5 value used with the above series is listed as Nos. 133 and 137.

58   **59**

60

1883–84. *Coloured letters in the corners. Wmk Anchor, W **40**.*

(a) Blued paper

			Un	★ Used
175	58	2s. 6d. lilac (2.7.83)	£2000	£475
176	59	5s. rose (1.4.84)	£3500	£950
177	60	10s. ultramarine (1.4.84)	£12000	£2750
177a		10s. cobalt (5.84)	£14000	£3750

(b) White paper

			Un	★ Used
178	58	2s. 6d. lilac	£200	60.00
179		2s. 6d. dp lilac	£200	60.00
		a. Error. On blued paper	£1600	£550
		Wi. Watermark inverted	—	£2500
180	59	5s. rose	£400	75.00
		Wi. Watermark inverted	†	
181		5s. crimson	£400	75.00
182	60	10s. cobalt	£13000	£3250
183		10s. ultramarine	£750	£225
183a		10s. pale ultramarine	£750	£225
★175/83a		**For well-centred, lightly used**		+50%

For No. 180 perf 12 see second note below No. 196.

61

Broken frames, Plate 2

1884 (1 April). *Wmk Three Imperial Crowns, W **49**.*

			Un	★ Used
185	61	£1 brown-lilac	£10000	£850
		a. Frame broken	£17500	£1500
		Wi. Watermark inverted	—	£3000

1888 (1 Feb). *Watermark Three Orbs, W **48**.*

			Un	★ Used
186	61	£1 brown-lilac	£16000	£1300
		a. Frame broken	£25000	£2250
★185/6a		**For well-centred, lightly used**		+50%

The broken-frame varieties, Nos. 185a and 186a, are on Plate 2 stamps JC and TA, as illustrated. *See also* No. 212a.

62

63

64

65

66

1883 (1 Aug) (9d.) *or* **1884** (1 April) (*others*). *Wmk Imperial Crown, W **49** (sideways on horiz designs).*

			Un	★ Used	Used on cover
187	52	½d. slate-blue	8.00	1.50	5.00
		a. Imperf	£450		
		Wi. Watermark inverted	—	35.00	
188	62	1½d. lilac	55.00	18.00	55.00
		a. Imperf	£450		
		Wi. Watermark inverted	—	60.00	
189	63	2d. lilac	70.00	30.00	60.00
		a. Imperf	£500		
		Wi. Watermark sideways-inverted	—		
190	64	2½d. lilac	40.00	5.00	12.00
		a. Imperf	£500		
		Wi. Watermark sideways-inverted	—		
191	65	3d. lilac	90.00	40.00	60.00
		a. Imperf	£500		
		Wi. Watermark inverted	†	—	
192	66	4d. dull green	£225	90.00	£130
		a. Imperf	£550		
193	62	5d. dull green	£225	90.00	£120
		a. Imperf	£550		
194	63	6d. dull green	£250	95.00	£140
		a. Imperf	£550		
		Wi. Watermark sideways-inverted	—		
195	64	9d. dull green (1.8.83)	£475	£225	£600
		Wi. Watermark sideways-inverted	£600	£350	
196	65	1s. dull green	£350	£130	£250
		a. Imperf	£1200		
		Wi. Watermark-inverted	—		
★187/96		**For well-centred, lightly used**		+100%	

The above prices are for stamps in the true dull green colour. Stamps which have been soaked, causing the colour to run, are virtually worthless.

Stamps of the above set and No. 180 are also found perf 12; these are official perforations, but were never issued. A second variety of the 5d. is known with a line instead of a stop under the "d" in the value; this was never issued and is therefore only known *unused* (*Price £5000*).

71

72

73

74 **75** **76**

77 **78** **79**

80 **81** **82**

Die I   Die II

Die I: Square dots to right of "d".
Die II: Thin vertical lines to right of "d".

1887 (1 Jan)–**1892.** *"Jubilee" issue. New types. The bicoloured stamps have the value tablets, or the frames including the value tablets, in the second colour. Wmk Imperial Crown, W **49** (Three Crowns on £1).*

			Un	★ Used	Used on cover
197	71	½d. vermilion	1.00	50	5.00
		a. Printed on gummed side	£800	†	
		b. Printed both sides			
		c. Doubly printed	£2750		
		d. Imperf	£750		
		Wi. Watermark inverted	12.00		
197e		½d. orange-vermilion	1.00	50	
198	72	1½d. dull purple & pale green	10.00	4.00	18.00
		a. Purple part of design double	—	£3000	
		Wi. Watermark inverted	£350	£140	
199	73	2d. green & scarlet	£275	£150	
200		2d. grey-green & carmine	15.00	6.00	18.00
		Wi. Watermark inverted	£450	£150	
201	74	2½d. purple/*blue*	10.00	75	5.00
		a. Printed on gummed side	£1000	†	
		b. Imperf three sides	£1200		
		c. imperf	£1500		
		Wi. Watermark inverted	£450		

			Un	Used	Used on cover
202	75	3d. purple/*yellow*	15.00	1.50	20.00
		a. Imperf	£3000		
		Wi. Watermark inverted	—	£170	
203		3d. dp purple/*yellow*	15.00	1.50	
204		3d. purple/*orange* (1891)	£400	£150	
205	76	4d. green & purple-brown	18.00	7.25	18.00
		aa. Imperf			
		Wi. Watermark inverted	£400	£130	
205a		4d. green & dp brown	18.00	7.25	
206	77	4½d. green & carmine (15.9.92)	5.00	20.00	55.00
		Wi. Watermark inverted			
206a		4½d. green & dp brt carmine	£450	£300	
207	78	5d. dull purple & blue (Die I)	£350	30.00	60.00
207a		5d. dull purple & blue (Die II) (1888)	18.00	6.00	22.00
		Wi. Watermark inverted	—	£150	
208	79	6d. purple/*rose-red*	18.00	7.50	15.00
		Wi. Watermark inverted	£475	£110	
208a		6d. dp purple/*rose-red*	18.00	7.50	
209	80	9d. dull purple & blue	40.00	25.00	50.00
		Wi. Watermark inverted	£500	£150	
210	81	10d. dull purple and carmine (*shades*) (24.2.90)	35.00	22.00	60.00
		aa. Imperf	£3250		
		Wi. Watermark inverted	£600	£250	
210a		10d. dull mauve & dp carmine	£350	£150	
210b		10d. dull purple and dull scarlet	45.00	28.00	
211	82	1s. dull green	£130	30.00	75.00
		Wi. Watermark inverted	£350	£150	
212	61	£1 green (28.1.91)	£2000	£350	
		a. Frame broken	£4500	£800	
		Wi. Watermark inverted	£18000	£1750	

★197/212a   **For well-centred, lightly used** .....   **+50%**

The broken-frame varieties, No. 212a, are on Plate 2 stamps JC or TA, as illustrated above No. 185.

½d. stamps with "PEARS SOAP" printed on the back in *orange*, *blue* or *mauve*, price *from* £300 each.

			Un	★ Used	Used on cover
213	71	½d. blue-green (17.4)	1.00	60	5.00
		a. Printed on gummed side	—	†	
		b. Imperf	£1500		
		Wi. Watermark inverted	10.00		
214	82	1s. green & carmine (11.7)	45.00	80.00	£225
		Wi. Watermark inverted	£500	£130	
		Set of 14	£325	£190	

★213/14   **For well-centred, lightly used** .....   **+50%**

The ½d. No. 213, in bright blue, is a colour changeling.

KING EDWARD VII

22 January 1901–6 May 1910

PRINTINGS. Distinguishing De La Rue printings from the provisional printings of the same values made by Harrison & Sons Ltd. or at Somerset House may prove difficult in some cases. For very full guidance Volume 2 of the Stanley Gibbons *Great Britain Specialised Catalogue* should prove helpful.

Note that stamps perforated 15 × 14 must be Harrison; the 2½d., 3d. and 4d. in this perforation are useful reference material, their shades and appearance in most cases matching the Harrison perf 14 printings.

Except for the 6d. value, all stamps on chalk-surfaced paper were printed by De La Rue.

Of the stamps on ordinary paper, the De La Rue impressions are usually clearer and of a higher finish than those of the other printers. The shades are markedly different except in some printings of the 4d., 6d. and 7d. and in the 5s., 10s. and £1.

Used stamps in good, clean, unrubbed condition and with dated postmarks can form the basis of a useful reference collection, the dates often assisting in the assignment to the printers.

PRICES. For Nos. 215/456a prices are quoted for unmounted mint, mounted mint and used stamps.

USED STAMPS. For well-centred, lightly used examples of King Edward VII stamps, add the following percentages to the used prices quoted below:

De La Rue printings (Nos. 215/66)—3d. values + 35%, 4d. orange +100%, 6d. +75%, 7d. & 1s. + 25%, all other values + 50%.

Harrison printings (Nos. 267/86)—all values and perforations +75%.

Somerset House printings (Nos. 287/320)—1s. values + 25%, all other values + 50%.

97

(Des E. Fuchs)

1902 (1 Jan)–**10**. *Printed by De La Rue & Co. Wmk Imperial Crown W* **49** (½d. to 1s. Three Crowns on £1); *Anchor, W* **40** (2s. 6d. to 10s.). *Ordinary paper. P* 14.

			Unmtd mint	Mtd mint	Used
215	83	½d. dull blue-green (1.1.02)	1.00	50	30
		Wi. Watermark inverted.............	£900	£750	£400
216		½d. blue-green	1.00	50	30
217		½d. pale yellowish green (26.11.04)	75	40	30
218		½d. yellowish green	75	40	30
		a. Booklet pane. Five stamps plus St. Andrew's Cross label (6.06)................................	£200	£150	
		b. Doubly printed (bottom row on one pane) (Control H9)	—	£9750	
		Wi. Watermark inverted.............	7.50	5.00	2.00
219		1d. scarlet (1.1.02)	75	40	30
220		1d. brt scarlet	75	40	30
		a. Imperf (pair).......................	—	£7500	
		Wi. Watermark inverted.............	2.00	1.50	1.25
221	84	1½d. dull purple and green (21.3.02)...........................	20.00	12.00	6.00
222		1½d. slate-purple and green	20.00	10.00	4.75
		Wi. Watermark inverted.............	—	—	£300
223		1½d. pale dull purple and green (*chalk-surfaced paper*) (8.05) .	25.00	15.00	5.50
224		1½d. slate-purple & bluish green (*chalk-surfaced paper*)..........	25.00	15.00	4.25
225	85	2d. yellowish green and carmine-red (25.3.02)	24.00	15.00	5.00
226		2d. grey-green and carmine-red (1904)	24.00	15.00	5.00
227		2d. pale grey-green & carmine-red (*chalk-surfaced paper*) (4.06)................................	25.00	15.00	7.00
		Wi. Watermark inverted.............			
228		2d. pale grey-green & scarlet (*chalk-surfaced paper*) (1909)	25.00	15.00	6.00
229		2d. dull blue-green & carmine (*chalk-surfaced paper*) (1907)	50.00	35.00	20.00
230	86	2½d. ultramarine (1.1.02)	5.50	4.00	2.50
231		2½d. pale ultramarine.................	5.50	4.00	2.50
		Wi. Watermark inverted.............	—		£600
232	87	3d. dull purple/*orange-yellow* (20.3.02)...........................	25.00	15.00	2.50
		Wi. Watermark inverted.............			
		a. Chalk-surfaced paper...........	£125	65.00	18.00
232*b*		3d. dp purple/*orange-yellow*	25.00	15.00	2.50
232*c*		3d. pale reddish purple/*orange-yellow* (*chalk-surfaced paper*) (3.06)................................	£110	60.00	15.00
233		3d. dull reddish purple/*yellow* (*lemon* back) (*chalk-surfaced paper*)	£110	60.00	28.00
233*b*		3d. pale purple/*lemon* (*chalk-surfaced paper*)	24.00	12.00	6.00
234		3d. purple/*lemon* (*chalk-surfaced paper*)	24.00	12.00	6.00

83

84

85

86

87

88

89

90

91

92

93

94

95

96

235	88	4d. green and grey-brown (27.3.02)	40.00	20.00	12.00
		Wi. Watermark inverted			
236		4d. green & chocolate- brown	40.00	20.00	12.00
		a. Chalk-surfaced paper (1.06)	25.00	15.00	7.00
238		4d. dp green and chocolate-brown (*chalk-surfaced paper*)	25.00	15.00	8.50
239		4d. brown-orange (1.11.09)	£140	90.00	80.00
240		4d. pale orange (12.09)	11.00	7.50	6.50
241		4d. orange-red (12.09)	10.00	7.50	7.00
242	89	5d. dull purple and ultramarine (14.5.02)	35.00	15.00	6.00
		a. Chalk-surfaced paper (5.06)	35.00	15.00	8.00
244		5d. slate-purple & ultramarine (*chalk-surfaced paper*)	35.00	15.00	8.00
		Wi. Watermark inverted	£650	£500	
245	83	6d. pale dull purple (1.1.02)	25.00	12.00	4.00
		a. Chalk-surfaced paper (1.06)	26.00	12.00	4.00
246		6d. slate-purple	25.00	12.00	4.00
248		6d. dull purple (*chalk-surfaced paper*)	28.00	15.00	4.00
		Wi. Watermark inverted	—	—	£750
249	90	7d. grey-black (4.5.10)	4.00	3.00	6.00
249*a*		7d. dp grey-black	75.00	60.00	60.00
250	91	9d. dull purple and ultramarine (7.4.02)	75.00	35.00	24.00
		a. Chalk-surfaced paper (6.05)	80.00	35.00	30.00
		aWi. Watermark inverted	—	—	£750
251		9d. slate-purple and ultramarine	75.00	35.00	24.00
		a. Chalk-surfaced paper (6.05)	75.00	35.00	30.00
254	92	10d. dull purple and carmine (3.7.02)	80.00	35.00	18.00
		a. No cross on crown	£225	£160	£100
		b. Chalk-surfaced paper (9.06)	80.00	35.00	24.00
255		10d. slate-purple and carmine (*chalk-surfaced paper*) (9.06)	75.00	35.00	28.00
		a. No cross on crown	£200	£140	90.00
256		10d. dull purple & scarlet (*chalk-surfaced paper*) (9.10)	80.00	35.00	35.00
		a. No cross on crown	£190	£125	80.00
257	93	1s. dull green and carmine (24.3.02)	75.00	35.00	8.50
		a. Chalk-surfaced paper (9.05)	80.00	35.00	12.00
259		1s. dull green & scarlet (*chalk-surfaced paper*) (9.10)	80.00	35.00	20.00
260	94	2s. 6d. lilac (5.4.02)	£200	£100	45.00
		Wi. Watermark inverted	£950	£750	£500
261		2s. 6d. pale dull purple (*chalk-surfaced paper*) (7.10.05)	£225	£100	80.00
		Wi. Watermark inverted	£950	£750	£500
262		2s. 6d. dull purple (*chalk-surfaced paper*)	£225	£100	55.00
263	95	5s. brt carmine (5.4.02)	£225	£100	55.00
		Wi. Watermark inverted	—	—	£750
264		5s. dp brt carmine	£225	£100	55.00
265	96	10s. ultramarine (5.4.02)	£500	£325	£200
266	97	£1 dull blue-green (16.6.02)	£1100	£750	£300
		Wi. Watermark inverted	—	£15000	£5000

97*a*

1910 (May).   *Prepared for use, but not issued.*

266*a*	**97***a*	2d. Tyrian plum	£12000	£10000

One example of this stamp is known used, but it was never issued to the public.

1911.   *Printed by Harrison & Sons. Ordinary paper. Wmk Imperial Crown. W* **49**. *(a) P* 14.

			Unmtd mint	Mtd mint	Used
267	**83**	½d. dull yellow-green (3.5.11)	1.75	90	40
		Wi. Watermark inverted	15.00	7.50	7.50
268		½d. dull green	2.25	1.25	40
269		½d. dp dull green	8.00	5.00	2.00
270		½d. pale bluish green	35.00	20.00	22.00
		a. Booklet pane. Five stamps plus St. Andrew's Cross label	£250	£195	
		b. Watermark sideways	†	†	£10000
		c. Imperf (pair)	—	£9500	†
271		½d. brt green (fine impression) (6.11)	£175	£150	£110
272		1d. rose-red (3.5.11)	2.50	1.75	5.00
		Wi. Watermark inverted	15.00	6.50	5.50
		a. No wmk	40.00	35.00	35.00
273		1d. dp rose-red	4.00	2.75	5.00
274		1d. rose-carmine	40.00	25.00	10.00
275		1d. aniline pink (5.11)	£350	£250	£110
275*a*		1d. aniline rose	£125	80.00	75.00
276	**86**	2½d. brt blue (10.7.11)	35.00	20.00	10.00
		Wi. Watermark inverted	£450	£350	
277	**87**	3d. purple/*lemon* (12.9.11)	50.00	30.00	£120
277*a*		3d. grey/*lemon*	£3750	£2750	
278	**88**	4d. brt orange (13.7.11)	50.00	30.00	30.00

(b) P 15 × 14

279	**83**	½d. dull green (30.10.11)	25.00	18.00	25.00
279*a*		½d. dp dull green	35.00	20.00	20.00
280		1d. rose-red (5.10.11)	18.00	15.00	10.00
281		1d. rose-carmine	10.00	6.50	5.00
282		1d. pale rose-carmine	12.00	8.00	3.00
283	**86**	2½d. bright blue (14.10.11)	15.00	10.00	5.00
284		2½d. dull blue	15.00	10.00	5.00
		Wi. Watermark inverted	—	—	£200
285	**87**	3d. purple/*lemon* (22.9.11)	25.00	15.00	4.00
285*a*		3d. grey/*lemon*	£3000	£2250	
286	**88**	4d. bright orange (11.11.11)	15.00	10.00	6.00
		Set of 5	90.00	55.00	40.00

1911–13. *Printed at Somerset House. Ordinary paper. Wmk as 1902–10. P 14.*

287	**84**	1½d. reddish purple and brt green (13.7.11)	30.00	20.00	12.00
288		1½d. dull purple and green	15.00	10.00	10.00
289		1½d. slate-purple & green (9.12)	20.00	12.00	12.00
290	**85**	2d. dp dull green & red (8.8.11)	15.00	10.00	5.00
291		2d. dp dull green and carmine	15.00	10.00	5.00
292		2d. grey-green and brt carmine (carmine shows clearly on back) (11.3.12)	15.00	10.00	7.00
293	**89**	5d. dull reddish purple and brt blue (7.8.11)	20.00	12.00	4.75
294		5d. dp dull reddish purple and brt blue	15.00	10.00	4.75
295	**83**	6d. royal purple (31.10.11)	35.00	25.00	40.00
296		6d. brt magenta (*chalk-surfaced paper*) (31.10.11)	£2750	£1750	
297		6d. dull purple	18.00	12.00	6.00
298		6d. reddish purple (11.11)	18.00	12.00	8.00
		a. No cross on crown (*various shades*)	£250	£175	
299		6d. very dp reddish purple (11.11)	35.00	20.00	18.00
300		6d. dark purple (3.12)	18.00	15.00	15.00
301		6d. dull purple "Dickinson" coated paper* (3.13)	£130	95.00	80.00
303		6d. dp plum (*chalk-surfaced paper*) (7.13)	18.00	10.00	35.00
		a. No cross on crown	£300	£200	
305	**90**	7d. slate-grey (1.8.12)	6.00	4.00	8.50
306	**91**	9d. reddish purple and lt blue (24.7.11)	75.00	45.00	30.00
306a		9d. dp dull reddish purple and dp brt blue (9.11)	75.00	45.00	32.00
307		9d. dull reddish purple and blue (10.11)	50.00	30.00	22.00
307a		9d. dp plum and blue (7.13)	50.00	30.00	30.00
308		9d. slate-purple and cobalt-blue (3.12)	80.00	60.00	35.00
309	**92**	10d. dull purple and scarlet (9.10.11)	60.00	35.00	25.00
310		10d. dull reddish purple and aniline pink	£200	£150	£110
311		10d. dull reddish purple and carmine (5.12)	45.00	30.00	20.00
		a. No cross on crown	£650	£450	
312	**93**	1s. dark green and scarlet (13.7.11)	80.00	55.00	25.00
313		1s. dp green & scarlet (9.10.11)	60.00	35.00	9.00
314		1s. green & carmine (15.4.12)	50.00	25.00	8.00
		Wi. Watermark inverted	90.00	75.00	†
315	**94**	2s. 6d. dull greyish purple (27.9.11)	£400	£275	£150
316		2s. 6d. dull reddish purple (10.11)	£175	£100	55.00
317		2s. 6d. dark purple	£175	£100	55.00
318	**95**	5s. carmine (29.2.12)	£250	£150	55.00
319	**96**	10s. blue (14.1.12)	£450	£300	£200
320	**97**	£1 dp green (3.9.11)	£1100	£750	£300
		Set of 15 (*to 1s incl. ½d. (2)*)	£325	£160	90.00

*No. 301 was on an experimental coated paper which does not respond to the silver test.

USED ON COVER PRICES:					
No. 288	£30	No. 290	£30	No. 293	£50
No. 297	£60	No. 305	£85	No. 307	£85
No. 311	£85	No. 313	£85		

KING GEORGE V
6 May 1910–20 January 1936

Further detailed information on the issues of King George V will be found in Volume 2 of the Stanley Gibbons *Great Britain Specialised Catalogue*.

PRINTERS. Types **98** to **102** were typographed by Harrison & Sons Ltd, with the exception of certain preliminary printings made at Somerset House and distinguishable by the controls "A.11", "B.11" or "B.12" (the Harrison printings do not have a full stop after the letter). The booklet stamps, Nos. 334/7, and 344/5 were printed by Harrison only.

WATERMARK VARIETIES. Many British stamps to 1967 exist without watermark owing to misplacement of the paper, and with either inverted, reversed, or inverted and reversed watermarks. A proportion of the low-value stamps issued in booklets have the watermark inverted in the normal course of printing.

Low values with *watermark sideways* are normally from stamp rolls used in machines with sideways delivery or, from June 1940, certain booklets.

STAMPS WITHOUT WATERMARK. Stamps found without watermark, due to misplacement of the sheet in relation to the dandy roll, are not listed here but will be found in the *Great Britain Specialised Catalogue*.

The 1½d. and 5d. 1912–22, and 2d. and 2½d., 1924–26, listed here, are from *whole* sheets completely without watermark.

98	99	**100** Simple Cypher

For type differences with T **101/2** see notes below the latter.

Die A	Die B

Dies of Halfpenny

Die A. The three upper scales on the body of the right hand dolphin form a triangle; the centre jewel of the cross inside the crown is suggested by a comma.

Die B. The three upper scales are incomplete; the centre jewel is suggested by a crescent.

Die A	Die B

Dies of One Penny

Die A. The second line of shading on the ribbon to the right of the crown extends right across the wreath; the line nearest to the crown on the right hand ribbon shows as a short line at the bottom of the ribbon.

Die B. The second line of shading is broken in the middle; the first line is little more than a dot.

(Des Bertram Mackennal and G. W. Eve. Head from photograph by W. and D. Downey. Die eng J. A. C. Harrison)

1911–12. *Wmk Imperial Crown, W* **49**. *P* 15 × 14.

			Unmtd mint	Mtd mint	Used
321	**98**	½d. pale green (Die A) (22.6.11) ..	4.50	3.00	1.00
322		½d. green (Die A) (22.6.11)	3.50	2.50	1.00
		a. Error. Perf 14 (8.11)	—	—	£250
		Wi. Watermark inverted	—	—	£500
323		½d. bluish green (Die A)	£300	£225	£130
324		½d. yellow-green (Die B)	7.50	4.00	60
325		½d. brt green (Die B)	7.50	4.00	60
		a. Watermark sideways............	—	—	£1700
		Wi. Watermark inverted	6.00	4.00	2.50
326		½d. bluish green (Die B)	£175	£140	70.00
327	**99**	1d. carmine-red (Die A) (22.6.11)	4.00	2.25	1.00
		c. Watermark sideways...........	†	†	—
		Wi Watermark inverted	£750	£500	£350
328		1d. pale carmine (Die A) (22.6.11)	12.00	8.00	1.25
		a. No cross on crown	£350	£250	£150
329		1d. carmine (Die B)	6.00	4.00	1.00
		Wi. Watermark inverted	6.00	4.00	2.25
330		1d. pale carmine (Die B)	6.00	4.00	1.00
		a. No cross on crown	£450	£350	£250
331		1d. rose-pink (Die B)	85.00	60.00	20.00
332		1d. scarlet (Die B) (6.12)...........	20.00	13.00	9.00
		Wi. Watermark inverted	20.00	13.00	6.00
333		1d. aniline scarlet (Die B)	£150	95.00	55.00

For note on the aniline scarlet No. 333 see below No. 343.

1912 (Aug). *Booklet stamps. Wmk Royal Cypher ("Simple"), W* **100**. *P* 15 × 14.

334	**98**	½d. pale green (Die B)..............	30.00	20.00	22.00
335		½d. green (Die B)	30.00	20.00	22.00
		Wi. Watermark inverted..............	30.00	20.00	22.00
		Wj. Watermark reversed.............	£325	£275	£150
		Wk. Watermark inverted and reversed	£325	£275	£150
336	**99**	1d. scarlet (Die B)	16.00	12.00	12.00
		Wi. Watermark inverted..............	16.00	12.00	12.00
		Wj. Watermark reversed.............	£300	£275	
		Wk. Watermark inverted and reversed	—	—	75.00
337		1d. brt scarlet (Die B)	16.00	12.00	12.00

1912 (1 Jan). *Wmk Imperial Crown, W* **49**. *P* 15 × 14.

338	**101**	½d. dp green	12.00	7.00	3.00
339		½d. green	6.00	3.00	50
340		½d. yellow-green	6.00	3.00	75
		a. No cross on crown.............	75.00	50.00	15.00
		Wi. Watermark inverted	£300	£250	£150
341	**102**	1d. brt scarlet.......................	2.25	1.25	50
		a. No cross on crown.............	60.00	40.00	15.00
		b. Printed double, one albino ..	£125	95.00	
		Wi. Watermark inverted	£150	£125	£100
342		1d. scarlet............................	2.25	1.50	50
343		1d. aniline scarlet*.................	£135	£100	55.00
		a. No cross on crown	£750	£600	

* Our prices for the aniline scarlet 1d. stamps, Nos. 333 and 343, are for the specimens in which the colour is suffused on the surface of the stamp and shows through clearly on the back. Specimens without these characteristics but which show "aniline" reactions under the quartz lamp are relatively common.

1912 (Aug). *Wmk Royal Cypher ("Simple"), W* **100**. *P* 15 × 14.

344	**101**	½d. green..............................	4.00	2.50	70
		a. No cross on crown	75.00	60.00	15.00
		Wi. Watermark inverted............	75.00	50.00	15.00
		Wj. Watermark reversed	70.00	40.00	15.00
		Wk. Watermark inverted and reversed	6.00	4.00	2.00
345	**102**	1d. scarlet	3.00	2.00	50
		a. No cross on crown	65.00	50.00	15.00
		Wi. Watermark inverted............	10.00	6.00	4.50
		Wj. Watermark reversed...........	20.00	10.00	6.00
		Wk. Watermark inverted and reversed	8.00	4.00	4.00

1912 (Sept-Oct). *Wmk Royal Cypher ("Multiple"), W* **103**. *P* 15 × 14.

346	**101**	½d. green (Oct)	7.00	6.00	4.00
		a. No cross on crown	75.00	60.00	20.00
		b. Imperf.............................	£110	75.00	
		c. Watermark sideways...........	†	†	£1000
		d. Printed on gummed side	—	—	†
		Wi. Watermark inverted............	8.00	5.00	4.00
		Wj. Watermark reversed...........	8.00	5.00	4.00
		Wk. Watermark inverted and reversed	18.00	10.00	
347		½d. yellow-green	8.00	6.00	4.50
348		½d. pale green	10.00	6.00	4.00
349	**102**	1d. brt scarlet	10.00	6.00	4.50
350		1d. scarlet	9.00	5.00	4.50
		a. No cross on crown	85.00	65.00	16.00
		b. Imperf.............................	95.00	65.00	
		c. Watermark sideways...........	95.00	65.00	75.00
		d. Watermark sideways. No cross on crown	£550	£450	
		Wi. Watermark inverted............	10.00	6.00	
		Wj. Watermark reversed...........	10.00	6.00	
		Wk. Watermark inverted and reversed	£350	£250	£150

101

102

103 Multiple Cypher

Type differences

½d. In T **98** the ornament above "P" of "HALFPENNY" has two thin lines of colour and the beard is undefined. In T **101** the ornament has one thick line and the beard is well defined.

1d. In T **99** the body of the lion is unshaded and in T **102** it is shaded.

104

105

106

107

108

No. 357ab

No. 357ac

No. 357a

Die I

Die II

Two Dies of the 2d.

Die I.—Inner frame-line at top and sides close to solid of background. *Four* complete lines of shading between top of head and oval frame-line. These four lines do *not* extend to the oval itself. White line round "TWOPENCE" thin.

Die II.—Inner frame-line farther from solid of background. *Three* lines between top of head and extending to the oval. White line round "TWOPENCE" thicker.

(Des Bertram Mackennal (heads) and G. W. Eve (frames). Coinage head (½, 1½, 2, 3 and 4d.); large medal head (1d., 2½d.); intermediate medal head (5d. to 1s.); small medal head used for fiscal stamps. Dies eng J. A. C. Harrison)

(Typo by Harrison & Sons Ltd., except the 6d. printed by the Stamping Department of the Board of Inland Revenue, Somerset House. The latter also made printings of the following which can only be distinguished by the controls: ½d. B.13; 1½d. A.12; 2d. C.13; 2½d. A.12; 3d. A.12, B.13, C.13; 4d. B.13; 5d. B.13; 7d. C.13; 8d. C.13; 9d. agate B.13; 10d. C.13; 1s. C.13)

1912-24. *Wmk Royal Cypher.* W **100.** *Chalk-surfaced paper* (6d.) *P* 15 × 14.

351	**105**	½d. green (1.13)	60	30	25
		a. Doubly printed (half of bottom row) (Control G15)....	—	£12500	†
		Wi. Watermark inverted	2.00	1.00	25
		Wj. Watermark reversed	12.00	8.00	5.00
		Wk. Watermark inverted and reversed	3.00	2.25	1.50
352		½d. brt green	60	30	25
353		½d. dp green	4.00	2.25	1.00
354		½d. yellow-green.....................	5.00	3.50	1.25
355		½d. very yellow (Cyprus) green (1914)	£2500	£1750	†
356	**105**	½d. blue-green	32.00	20.00	12.00
357	**104**	1d. brt scarlet (10.12)..............	60	30	25
		a. "Q" for "O" (R.1/4) (Control E14).................................	£150	£125	75.00
		ab. "Q" for "O" (R.4/11) (Control T22)	£225	£175	£100
		ac. Reversed "Q" for "O" (R.15/9) (Control T22)	£300	£225	£130
		ad. Inverted "Q" for "O" (R.20/3)...........................	£375	£300	£150
		b. *Tête-bêche* (pair).................	—	£45000	†
		Wi. Watermark inverted.............	2.00	1.00	25
		Wj. Watermark reversed	12.00	8.00	5.00
		Wk. Watermark inverted and reversed	2.00	1.00	50
358		1d. vermilion	3.00	1.50	60
359		1d. pale rose-red.....................	10.00	6.00	50
360		1d. carmine-red	7.00	4.00	2.50
361		1d. scarlet-vermilion	95.00	70.00	20.00
		a. Printed on back†	£225	£175	†
362	**105**	1½d. red-brown (10.12)..............	1.25	1.00	25
		a. "PENCF" (R.15/12)...............	£225	£180	£125
		b. Booklet pane. Four stamps plus two printed labels (2.24) .	£300	£250	
		Wi. Watermark inverted.............	3.50	2.00	65
		Wi. Watermark reversed	12.00	8.00	3.00
		Wk. Watermark inverted and reversed	6.00	4.50	2.25
363		1½d. chocolate-brown...............	3.50	2.00	35
		a. No watermark.....................	£120	90.00	
364		1½d. chestnut	2.50	1.50	25
		a. "PENCF" (R.15/12)..............	£125	95.00	75.00
365		1½d. yellow-brown	12.00	8.00	9.00
366	**106**	2d. orange-yellow (Die I) (8.12) ...	6.00	4.00	1.50
367		2d. reddish orange (Die I) (11.13)	2.50	1.25	50
368		2d. orange (Die I)	1.50	1.00	50
		Wi. Watermark inverted.............	10.00	6.50	3.00
		Wj. Watermark reversed	10.00	7.00	4.50
		Wk. Watermark inverted and reversed	7.00	5.00	2.50
369		2d. brt orange (Die I)...............	2.75	1.50	70
370		2d. orange (Die II) (9.21)	3.00	2.00	1.75
		Wi. Watermark inverted.............	12.00	8.00	4.50
		Wj. Watermark inverted and reversed	12.00	8.00	4.50
371	**104**	2½d. cobalt-blue (10.12).............	7.50	4.50	1.00
371a		2½d. brt blue (1914).................	7.50	4.50	1.00
372		2½d. blue	7.50	4.50	1.00
		Wi. Watermark inverted.............	28.00	18.00	12.00
		Wj. Watermark reversed	15.00	10.00	3.50
		Wk. Watermark inverted and reversed	15.00	10.00	4.00
373		2½d. indigo-blue* (1920)	£1100	£850	£550
373a		2½d. dull Prussian blue* (1921)......	£600	£475	£350
374	**106**	3d. dull reddish violet (10.12)......	9.00	6.00	1.00
375		3d. violet	3.00	2.00	75
		Wi. Watermark inverted.............	40.00	20.00	9.00
		Wj. Watermark reversed	70.00	50.00	15.00
		Wk. Watermark inverted and reversed	12.00	8.00	6.00
376		3d. bluish violet (11.13)............	5.00	2.75	90
377		3d. pale violet	6.00	4.00	90
378		4d. dp grey-green (1.13)............	25.00	15.00	3.50
379		4d. grey-green........................	7.00	4.00	75
		Wi. Watermark inverted.............	15.00	8.00	9.00
		Wj. Watermark reversed	40.00	25.00	6.00
		Wk. Watermark inverted and reversed	25.00	18.00	4.50
380		4d. pale grey-green.................	15.00	10.00	2.00

381	107	5d. brown (6.13)	7.50	3.50	3.00
		Wi. Watermark inverted	£350	£250	£150
		Wj. Watermark inverted and reversed	£110	90.00	40.00
		Wk. Watermark reversed	†	†	—
382		5d. yellow-brown	7.50	4.50	3.00
		a. No watermark	£500	£350	
383		5d. bistre-brown	90.00	65.00	25.00
384		6d. dull purple (8.13)	20.00	12.00	3.00
385		6d. reddish purple	12.00	6.00	1.50
		a. Perf 14 (10.20)	75.00	60.00	85.00
		Wi. Watermark inverted	25.00	15.00	9.00
		Wj. Watermark reversed	£550	£400	
		Wk. Watermark inverted and reversed	25.00	15.00	6.00
386		6d. dp reddish purple	25.00	12.00	1.50
387		7d. olive (8.13)	12.00	6.00	3.75
		Wi. Watermark inverted	25.00	20.00	15.00
		Wj. Watermark inverted and reversed	£1250	£900	
		Wk. Watermark reversed	†	†	—
388		7d. bronze-green (1915)	50.00	35.00	12.00
389		7d. sage-green (1917)	50.00	35.00	6.00
390		8d. black/yellow (8.13)	25.00	15.00	6.50
		Wi. Watermark inverted	50.00	35.00	35.00
		Wj. Watermark reversed	75.00	55.00	
		Wk. Watermark inverted and reversed	£1500	£1250	
391		8d. black/yellow-buff (granite) (5.17)	25.00	15.00	8.00
392	108	9d. agate (6.13)	10.00	5.00	2.50
		Wi. Watermark inverted	45.00	30.00	20.00
		Wj. Watermark inverted and reversed	40.00	28.00	14.00
393		9d. dp agate	16.00	10.00	2.75
393a		9d. olive-green (9.22)	£125	65.00	15.00
		aWi. Watermark inverted	£500	£400	£225
		aWj. Watermark inverted and reversed	£400	£300	£225
393b		9d. pale olive-green	£140	65.00	15.00
394		10d. turquoise-blue (8.13)	15.00	9.00	12.00
		Wi. Watermark inverted	£800	£600	£200
		Wj. Watermark inverted and reversed	£110	85.00	28.00
394a		10d. deep turquoise-blue	55.00	40.00	15.00
395		1s. bistre (8.13)	25.00	15.00	1.00
		Wi. Watermark inverted	95.00	65.00	15.00
		Wj. Watermark inverted and reversed	30.00	20.00	10.00
396		1s. bistre-brown	28.00	18.00	5.00
		Set of 15	£225	£125	45.00

Imperf stamps of this issue exist but may be war-time colour trials.
† The impression of No. 361a is set sideways and is very pale.
* No. 373 comes from Control O 20 and also exists on toned paper.
No. 373a comes from Control R 21 and also exists on toned paper, but both are unlike the rare Prussian blue shade of the 1935 2½d. Jubilee issue.

Examples of the 2d., T**106** which are in the hands of philatelists, are known bisected in Guernsey from 27 December 1940 to February 1941.

See also Nos. 418/29.

1913 (Aug). *Wmk Royal Cypher ("Multiple"), W* **103**. *P* 15 ×14.

397	**105**	½d. brt green	£125	50.00	95.00
		Wi. Watermark inverted	£300	£225	
398	**104**	1d. dull scarlet	£200	£110	£130
		Wi. Watermark inverted	£375	£300	

Both these stamps were originally issued in rolls only. Subsequently sheets were found, so that horizontal pairs and blocks are known but are of considerable rarity.

109

A

110 Single Cypher

Major Re-entries on 2s. 6d.

Nos. 400a and 408a

No. 415b

(Des Bertram Mackennal. Dies eng J. A. C. Harrison. Recess)

High values, so-called "Sea Horses" design: *T* **109**. *Background around portrait consists of horizontal lines, Type* A. *Wmk Single Cypher, W* **110**. *P* 11 × 12.

1913 (30 June–Aug). *Printed by Waterlow Bros & Layton.*

399	**109**	2s. 6d. dp sepia-brown	£180	95.00	65.00
400		2s. 6d. sepia-brown	£180	95.00	60.00
		a. Re-entry (R.2/1)	£900	£650	£400
401		5s. rose-carmine (4 July)	£300	£200	£150
402		10s. indigo-blue (1 Aug)	£600	£300	£225
403		£1 green (1 Aug)	£1500	£950	£600
404		£1 dull blue-green (1 Aug)	£1500	£950	£650
★399/404		**For well-centred, lightly used**			**+25%**

For full information on all future British issues, collectors should write to the British Post Office Philatelic Bureau, 20 Brandon Street, Edinburgh EH3 5TT

1915 (Nov–Dec). *Printed by De La Rue & Co.*

405	**109**	2s. 6d. dp yellow-brown............	£200	£125	70.00
		Wi. Watermark inverted.............	£450	£350	
406		2s. 6d. yellow-brown	£200	£125	65.00
		Wi. Watermark inverted............	£400	£300	
		Wj. Watermark reversed	£400	£300	
		Wk. Watermark inverted and reversed...........................	£900	£750	
407		2s. 6d. pale-brown (worn plate)..	£180	£110	65.00
		Wi. Watermark inverted............	£400	£300	
		Wj. Watermark reversed	£450	£350	
408		2s. 6d. sepia (seal-brown)	£200	£125	70.00
		a. Re-entry (R.2/1)	£700	£550	£400
		Wi. Watermark inverted............	£400	£300	
		Wj. Watermark reversed	£400	£300	
409		5s. brt carmine	£325	£200	£140
		Wi. Watermark inverted............	£950	£750	
		Wj. Watermark reversed	£850	£650	
		Wk. Watermark inverted and reversed...........................	£3000	£2500	†
410		5s. pale carmine (worn plate)....	£350	£225	£140
411		10s. dp blue (12.15)..................	£1200	£750	£300
412		10s. blue	£950	£550	£250
		Wi. Watermark inverted and reversed...........................	—	—	†
413		10s. pale blue	£950	£550	£250
★405/13		**For well-centred, lightly used**			**+25%**

1918 (Dec)–**19.** *Printed by Bradbury, Wilkinson & Co, Ltd.*

413a	**109**	2s. 6d. olive-brown	90.00	55.00	25.00
414		2s. 6d. chocolate-brown...........	95.00	70.00	30.00
415		2s. 6d. reddish-brown..............	£100	75.00	30.00
415a		2s. 6d. pale brown...................	95.00	75.00	25.00
		b. Major re-entry (R.1/2)..........	£600	£450	£250
416		5s. rose-red (1.19)	£180	£125	45.00
417		10s. dull grey-blue (1.19)............	£300	£200	80.00
		Set of 4	£1800	£1250	£700
★413a/17		**For well-centred, lightly used**			**+25%**

DISTINGUISHING PRINTINGS. Note that the £1 value was only printed by Waterlow.

Waterlow and De La Rue stamps measure exactly 22 mm vertically. In the De La Rue printings the gum is usually patchy and yellowish, and the colour of the stamp, particularly in the 5s., tends to show through the back. The holes of the perforation are smaller than those of the other two printers, but there is a thick perforation tooth at the top of each vertical side.

In the Bradbury Wilkinson printings the height of the stamp is 22¾ or 23 mm. On most of the 22¾ mm high stamps a minute coloured guide dot appears in the margin just above the middle of the upper frame-line.

For (1934) re-engraved Waterlow printings see Nos. 450/2.

111   Block Cypher   **111a**

The watermark Type **111a**, as compared with Type **111**, differs as follows: Closer spacing of horizontal rows (12½ mm instead of 14½ mm). Letters shorter and rounder. Watermark thicker.

(Typo by Waterlow & Sons, Ltd (all values except 6d.) and later, 1934–35, by Harrison & Sons, Ltd (all values). Until 1934 the 6d. was printed at Somerset House where a printing of the 1½d. was also made in 1926 (identifiable only by control E.26). Printings by Harrisons in 1934–35 can be identified, when in mint condition, by the fact that the gum shows a streaky appearance vertically, the Waterlow gum being uniformly applied, but Harrisons also used up the balance of the Waterlow "smooth gum" paper)

1924 (Feb)–**26.** *Wmk Block Cypher, W **111**. P 15 × 14.*

418	**105**	½d. green	25	15	25
		a. Watermark sideways (5.24)....	7.00	5.00	2.50
		b. Doubly printed	—	£6500	†
		Wi. Watermark inverted............	2.50	1.00	30
		Wj. Watermark sideways-inverted..............................			
419	**104**	1d. scarlet.............................	25	15	25
		a. Watermark sideways............	16.00	10.00	10.00
		b. Experimental paper, W **111a** (10.24)	25.00	20.00	
		c. Inverted "Q" for "O" (R.20/3)...........................	£375	£275	
		Wi. Watermark inverted............	2.00	1.00	45
420	**105**	1½d. red-brown	25	15	25
		a. Tête-bêche (pair).................	£375	£275	£500
		b. Watermark sideways (8.24)...	8.00	4.25	2.25
		c. Printed on the gummed side	£400	£300	†
		d. Booklet pane. Four stamps plus two printed labels (6.24)	£100	75.00	
		e. Ditto. Watermark sideways ...	£300	£2500	
		f. Experimental paper, W **111a** (10.24)	50.00	35.00	
		g. Double impression.............	—	£4500	†
		Wi. Watermark inverted............	1.00	50	30
		Wj. Watermark sideways-inverted..............................			
421	**106**	2d. orange (Die II) (9.24)	1.50	75	80
		a. No watermark....................	£500	£400	
		b. Watermark sideways (7.26)....	70.00	45.00	55.00
		c. Doubly printed	—	£10000	†
		Wi. Watermark inverted............	10.00	6.00	10.00
422	**104**	2½d. blue (10.24)	5.00	3.00	1.25
		a. No watermark....................	£750	£550	
		b. Watermark sideways............	†	†	†
		Wi. Watermark inverted............	20.00	15.00	15.00
423	**106**	3d. violet (10.24)......................	10.00	4.00	1.00
		Wi. Watermark inverted............	18.00	10.00	10.00
424		4d. grey-green (11.24)	12.00	6.00	1.00
		a. Printed on the gummed side	£1100	£850	†
		Wi. Watermark inverted............	50.00	30.00	10.00
425	**107**	5d. brown (11.24)	20.00	10.00	1.60
		Wi. Watermark inverted............	35.00	25.00	20.00
426		6d. reddish purple (*chalk-surfaced paper*) (9.24)...........	10.00	5.00	1.50
		Wi. Watermark inverted............	25.00	16.00	12.00
		Wj. Watermark inverted and reversed...........................	£125	75.00	
426a		6d. purple (6.26)......................	3.00	1.50	50
		aWi. Watermark inverted...........	25.00	16.00	12.00
427	**108**	9d. olive-green (12.24)..............	20.00	5.00	2.25
		Wi. Watermark inverted............	50.00	25.00	15.00
428		10d. turquoise-blue (11.24)	40.00	15.00	16.00
		Wi. Watermark inverted............	£600	£500	£250
429		1s. bistre-brown (10.24).............	25.00	10.00	1.00
		Wi. Watermark inverted............	£225	£175	£150
		Set of 12............................	£120	50.00	£30

There are numerous shades in this issue.

The 6d. on chalk-surfaced and ordinary papers was printed by both Somerset House and Harrisons. The Harrison printings have streaky gum, differ slightly in shade, and that on chalk-surfaced paper is printed in a highly fugitive ink. The prices quoted are for the commonest (Harrison) printing in each case.

112

(Des H. Nelson. Eng J. A. C. Harrison. Recess Waterlow)

1924–25. British Empire Exhibition. W 111. P 14.

(a) Dated "1924" (23.4.24)

430	**112**	1d. scarlet	8.00	5.00	6.00
431		1½d. brown	15.00	7.50	11.00
		Set of 2	23.00	12.00	17.00
		First Day Cover			£350

(b) Dated "1925" (9.5.25)

432	**112**	1d. scarlet	10.00	8.00	17.00
433		1½d. brown	40.00	25.00	50.00
		Set of 2	50.00	32.00	65.00
		First Day Cover			£1200

113

114

115

116 St. George and the Dragon

117

(Des J. Farleigh (T **113** and **115**), E. Linzell (T **114**) and H. Nelson (T **116**). Eng C. G. Lewis (T **113**), T. E. Storey (T **115**), both at the Royal Mint; J. A. C. Harrison, of Waterlow (T **114** & **116**). Typo by Waterlow from plates made at the Royal Mint, except T **116**, recess by Bradbury, Wilkinson from die and plate of their own manufacture)

1929 (10 May). **Ninth U.P.U. Congress, London.**

*(a) W **111**. P 15 × 14*

434	**113**	½d. green	2.25	1.50	1.50
		a. Watermark sideways...........	35.00	25.00	32.00
		Wi. Watermark inverted...........	20.00	9.00	7.00
435	**114**	1d. scarlet	2.25	1.50	1.50
		a. Watermark sideways...........	75.00	45.00	45.00
		Wi. Watermark inverted...........	20.00	9.00	7.00
436		1½d. purple-brown....................	1.50	1.00	1.00
		a. Watermark sideways...........	45.00	25.00	21.00
		b. Booklet pane. Four stamps plus two printed labels.........	£175	£150	
		Wi. Watermark inverted...........	7.50	2.50	4.50
437	**115**	2½d. blue...............................	15.00	7.50	9.00
		Wi. Watermark inverted...........	£950	£550	£350

*(b) W **117**. P 12*

438	**116**	£1 black................................	£750	£550	£400
		Set of 4 (to 2½d.)	23.00	10.00	11.50
		First Day Cover (4 vals.)........			£500
		First Day Cover (5 vals.)........			£2500

PRINTERS. All subsequent issues were printed in photogravure by Harrison & Sons, Ltd, *except where otherwise stated.*

118

119

120

121

122

1934–36. W 111. P 15 × 14.

439	**118**	½d. green (19.11.34)	25	10	25
		a. Watermark sideways...........	10.00	6.00	3.00
		b. Imperf three sides	£1100	£975	
		Wi. Watermark inverted...........	8.00	4.00	1.00
		Wj. Watermark sideways-inverted...........................	£175	£150	75.00
440	**119**	1d. scarlet (24.9.34)	25	10	25
		a. Imperf (pair)......................	£975	£750	
		b. Printed on gummed side	£500	£375	†
		c. Watermark sideways...........	10.00	8.00	3.25
		d. Double impression..............	†	†	£9500
		e. Imperf between (pair)	£1500	£1100	
		f. Imperf (three sides) (pair)	£975	£750	
		Wi. Watermark inverted...........	10.00	6.00	2.50
		Wj. Watermark sideways-inverted...........................	40.00	30.00	
441	**118**	1½d. red-brown (20.8.34)	25	10	25
		a. Imperf (pair)......................	£300	£250	
		b. Imperf (three sides) (lower stamp in vert. pair)	£550	£450	
		c. Imperf between (horiz. pair)			
		d. Watermark sideways...........	6.00	5.00	3.00
		e. Booklet pane. Four stamps plus two printed labels (1.35)	60.00	50.00	
		Wi. Watermark inverted...........	2.00	1.00	50
		Wj. Watermark sideways-inverted...........................			

442	**120**	2d. orange (21.1.35)	50	25	25
		a. Imperf (pair)	£1250	£950	
		b. Watermark sideways............	85.00	45.00	45.00
443	**119**	2½d. ultramarine (18.3.35)	1.50	75	60
444	**120**	3d. violet (18.3.35)	1.50	75	50
		Wi. Watermark inverted...........	—	—	£350
445		4d. deep grey-green (2.12.35)	2.50	1.00	55
		Wi. Watermark inverted...........	†	†	—
446	**121**	5d. yellow-brown (17.2.36)	8.00	4.00	1.50
447	**122**	9d. dp olive-green (2.12.35)	15.00	10.00	1.60
448		10d. turquoise-blue (24.2.36)	20.00	12.00	8.00
449		1s. bistre-brown (24.2.36)	28.00	12.00	50
		a. Double impression..............	—	—	†
		Set of 11..............................	65.00	35.00	11.00

Owing to the need for wider space for the perforations the size of the designs of the ½d. and 2d. were once, and the 1d. and 1½d. twice reduced from that of the first printings.

The format description, size in millimetres and S.G. catalogue number are given but further details will be found in the *Great Britain Specialised Catalogue, Volume 2*.

Description	Size	S.G. Nos.	Date of Issue
½d. intermediate format	18.4 × 22.2	–	19.11.34
½d. small format	17.9 × 21.7	439	1935
1d. large format	18.7 × 22.5	–	24.9.34
1d. intermediate format	18.4 × 22.2	–	1934
1d. small format	17.9 × 21.7	440	1935
1½d. large format	18.7 × 22.5	–	20.8.34
1½d. intermediate format	18.4 × 22.2	–	1934
1½d. small format	17.9 × 21.7	441	1935
2d. intermediate format	18.4 × 22.2	–	21.1.35
2d. small format	18.15 × 21.7	442	1935

There are also numerous minor variations, due to the photographic element in the process.

The ½d. imperf three sides, No. 439b, is known in a block of four, from a sheet, in which the bottom pair is imperf at top and sides.

Examples of 2d., T **120** which are in the hands of philatelists are known bisected in Guernsey from 27 December 1940 to February 1941.

B   **123**

(Eng J. A. C. Harrison. Recess Waterlow)

1934 (Oct.). T **109** (re-engraved). *Background around portrait consists of horizontal and diagonal lines, Type B, W* **110**. *P* 11 × 12.

450	**109**	2s. 6d. chocolate-brown	70.00	40.00	15.00
451		5s. brt rose-red	£200	90.00	50.00
452		10s. indigo	£300	£225	50.00
		Set of 3	£500	£300	£100

There are numerous other minor differences in the design of this issue.

(Des B. Freedman)

1935 (7 May). **Silver Jubilee**. W **111**. *P* 15 × 14.

453	**123**	½d. green	75	25	20
		Wi. Watermark inverted	10.00	4.00	1.25
454		1d. scarlet	2.00	1.00	1.00
		Wi. Watermark inverted	10.00	5.00	1.25
455		1½d. red-brown	75	25	20
		Wi. Watermark inverted	3.00	1.50	75
456		2½d. blue	4.00	3.00	5.50
456a		2½d. Prussian blue	£3750	£2750	£3000
		Set of 4	5.50	4.00	6.00
		First Day Cover			£400

The 1d., 1½d. and 2½d. values differ from T **123** in the emblem in the panel at right.

No. 456a, from three sheets printed with the wrong ink, was issued at a P.O. in Edmonton, North London.

KING EDWARD VIII

20 January–10 December 1936

Further detailed information on the stamps of King Edward VIII will be found in Volume 2 of the Stanley Gibbons *Great Britain Specialised Catalogue*.

PRICES. From S.G.457 prices quoted in the first column are for stamps in unmounted mint condition.

124   **125**

(Des from photo by Hugh Cecil)

			Unmtd mint	Used
1936.	W **125**. *P* 15 ×14.			
457	**124**	½d. green (1.9.36).............................	20	15
		a. Double impression		
		Wi. Watermark inverted	4.50	1.60
458		1d. scarlet (14.9.36)	50	20
		Wi. Watermark inverted	4.50	1.00
459		1½d. red-brown (1.9.36)	25	15
		a. Booklet pane. Four stamps plus two printed labels	40.00	
		Wi. Watermark inverted	1.00	1.00
460		2½d. brt blue (1.9.36)...........................	25	60
		Set of 4	1.00	1.00

KING GEORGE VI

11 December 1936–6 February 1952

Further detailed information on the stamps of King George VI will be found in Volume 2 of the Stanley Gibbons *Great Britain Specialised Catalogue*.

126 King George VI and Queen Elizabeth

(Des E. Dulac)

1937 (13 May). **Coronation**. W **127**. *P* 15 × 14.

461	**126**	1½d. maroon	40	25
		First Day Cover		24.00

127   **128**

129   **130**

King George VI and National Emblems

(Des T **128/9**, E. Dulac (head) and E. Gill (frames). T **130**, E. Dulac (whole stamp))

937–47. W **127**. P 15 × 14.

52	**128**	½d. green (10.5.37)	10	15
		a. Watermark sideways (1.38)	25	25
		ab. Booklet pane of 4	20.00	
		Wi. Watermark inverted	7.50	35
53		1d. scarlet (10.5.37)	10	15
		a. Watermark sideways (2.38)	17.00	4.00
		ab. Booklet pane of 4	45.00	
		Wi. Watermark inverted	30.00	1.75
54		1½d. red-brown (30.7.37)	20	15
		a. Watermark sideways (2.38)	90	70
		b. Booklet pane. Four stamps plus two printed labels	35.00	
		c. Imperf three sides (pair)		
		Wi. Watermark inverted	8.00	50
55		2d. orange (31.1.38)	1.25	45
		a. Watermark sideways (2.38)	60.00	25.00
		b. Bisected (on cover)	†	22.00
		Wi. Watermark inverted	40.00	3.00
56		2½d. ultramarine (10.5.37)	25	15
		a. Watermark sideways (6.40)	65.00	15.00
		b. Tête-bêche (horiz pair)		
		Wi. Watermark inverted	28.00	2.00
57		3d. violet (31.1.38).............................	4.50	60
58	**129**	4d. grey-green (21.11.38)......................	35	40
		a. Imperf (pair)	£1200	
		b. Imperf three sides (horiz pair)	£1500	
59		5d. brown (21.11.38)	3.00	35
		a. Imperf (pair)	£1300	
		b. Imperf three sides (horiz pair)	£1000	
70		6d. purple (30.1.39)	1.75	40
71	**130**	7d. emerald-green (27.2.39)	4.00	50
		a. Imperf three sides (horiz pair)	£1000	
72		8d. brt carmine (27.2.39)......................	5.00	50
73		9d. dp olive-green (1.5.39)	6.50	50
74		10d. turquoise-blue (1.5.39)	6.00	60
		aa. Imperf (pair)	£2000	
74a		11d. plum (29.12.47)...........................	3.00	1.50
75		1s. bistre-brown (1.5.39)	7.00	40
		Set of 15	39.00	6.00

For later printings of the lower values in apparently lighter shades nd different colours, see Nos. 485/90 and 503/8.

No. 465b was authorised for use in Guernsey from 27 December 1940 ntil February 1941.

Nos. 468b and 496b are perforated at foot only and each occurs in e same sheet as Nos. 468a and 469a.

No. 471a is also perforated at foot only, but occurs on the top row of a sheet.

131   **132**

133

(Des E. Dulac (T **131**) and Hon. G. R. Bellew (T **132**). Eng J. A. C. Harrison. Recess Waterlow)

1939–48. W **133**. P 14.

476	**131**	2s. 6d. brown (4.9.39).........................	40.00	7.00
476a		2s. 6d. yellow-green (9.3.42)	9.00	1.00
477		5s. red (21.8.39)	18.00	1.50
478	**132**	10s. dark blue (30.10.39)	£130	18.00
478a		10s. ultramarine (30.11.42)	40.00	4.50
478b		£1 brown (1.10.48)	15.00	19.00
		Set of 6	£225	45.00

134 Queen Victoria and King George VI

(Des H. L. Palmer)

1940 (6 May). **Centenary of First Adhesive Postage Stamps.** W **127** P 14½ × 14.

479	**134**	½d. green	30	20
480		1d. scarlet	90	40
481		1½d. red-brown	30	30
482		2d. orange	50	40
		a. Bisected (on cover)	†	16.00
483		2½d. ultramarine	1.90	80
484		3d. violet	4.00	4.00
		Set of 6	7.00	5.50
		First Day Cover		35.00

No. 482a was authorised for use in Guernsey from 27 December 1940 until February 1941.

1941–42. Head as Nos. 462/7, but lighter background. W **127** P 15 × 14.

485	**128**	½d. pale green (1.9.41)	15	10
		a. Tête-bêche (horiz pair)	£2500	
		b. Imperf (pair)	£1200	
		Wi. Watermark inverted	3.50	20

486	128	1d. pale scarlet (11.8.41)	15	10
		a. Watermark sideways (10.42)............	4.00	5.00
		b. Imperf (pair)	£1500	
		c. Imperf three sides (horiz pair)........	£1000	
		d. Imperf between (vert pair)..............		
487		1½d. pale red-brown (28.9.42)	75	45
488		2d. pale orange (6.10.41)	50	40
		a. Watermark sideways (6.42)	20.00	12.00
		b. Tête-bêche (horiz pair)	£1500	
		c. Imperf (pair)	£1500	
		d. Imperf pane*	£4000	
		Wi. Watermark inverted	2.75	20
489		2½d. light ultramarine (21.7.41)	15	10
		a. Watermark sideways (8.42)	12.00	8.00
		b. Tête-bêche (horiz pair)	£1300	
		c. Imperf (pair)	£2000	
		d. Imperf pane*	£2500	
		e. Imperf three sides (horiz pair)..........		
		Wi. Watermark inverted	1.00	40
490		3d. pale violet (3.11.41)	1.50	50
		Set of 6......................................	2.75	1.50

The *tête-bêche* varieties are from defectively made-up stamp booklets.

Nos. 486c and 489e are perforated at foot only and occur in the same sheets as Nos. 486b and 489c.

* BOOKLET ERRORS. Those listed as "imperf panes" show one row of perforations either at the top or at the bottom of the pane of 6.

135   **136**

(Des·H. L. Palmer (T **135**) and R. Stone (T **136**))

1946 (11 June). **Victory.** *W* **127**. *P* 15 × 14.
491	135	2½d. ultramarine	25	15
492	136	3d. violet..	25	15
		Set of 2	50	30
		First Day Cover		42.00

137   **138**

King George VI and Queen Elizabeth

(Des G. Knipe and Joan Hassall from photographs by Dorothy Wilding)

1948 (26 Apr). **Royal Silver Wedding.** *W* **127**. *P* 15 × 14 (2½d.) *or* 14 × 15 (£1).
493	137	2½d. ultramarine	30	30
494	138	£1 blue	32.00	32.00
		Set of 2	32.00	32.00
		First Day Cover		£375

1948 (10 May). Stamps of 1d. and 2½d. showing seaweed-gathering were on sale at eight Head Post Offices in Great Britain, but were primarily for use in the Channel Islands and are listed there (see Nos. C1/2, after Royal Mail Postage Labels).

139 Globe and Laurel Wreath   **140** "Speed"

141 Olympic Symbol   **142** Winged Victory

(Des P. Metcalfe (T **139**), A. Games (T **140**), S. D. Scott (T **141**) and E. Dulac (T **142**))

1948 (29 July). **Olympic Games.** *W* **127**. *P* 15 × 14.
495	139	2½d. ultramarine	10	10
496	140	3d. violet..	30	30
497	141	6d. brt purple...................................	60	30
498	142	1s. brown	1.25	1.50
		Set of 4	2.00	2.00
		First Day Cover		28.00

143 Two Hemispheres   **144** U.P.U. Monument, Berne

145 Goddess Concordia, Globe   **146** Posthorn & Globe
and Points of Compass

(Des Mary Adshead (T **143**), P. Metcalfe (T **144**), H. Fleury (T **145**) and Hon. G. R. Bellew (T **146**))

1949 (10 Oct). **75th Anniv of Universal Postal Union.** *W* **127**. *P* 15 × 14.
499	143	2½d. ultramarine	10	10
500	144	3d. violet..	30	40
501	145	6d. brt purple...................................	60	75
502	146	1s. brown	1.25	1.50
		Set of 4	2.00	2.75
		First Day Cover		50.00

1950–52. 4d. as No. 468 and others as Nos. 485/9, but colours changed. *W* **127**. *P* 15×14.
503	128	½d. pale orange (3.5.51)	10	15
		a. Imperf (pair)		
		b. Tête-bêche (horiz pair)	£2000	
		c. Imperf pane*	£3250	
		Wi. Watermark inverted	10	10

504	**128**	1d. lt ultramarine (3.5.51)	15	15
		a. Watermark sideways (5.51)	40	45
		b. Imperf (pair)	£1100	
		c. Imperf three sides (horiz pair)..........	£1000	
		d. Booklet pane. Three stamps plus three printed labels (3.52)...............	11.00	
		e. Ditto. Partial *téte-bêche* pane	£1750	
		Wi. Watermark inverted	2.00	1.00
505		1½d. pale green (3.5.51)	25	30
		a. Watermark sideways (9.51)..............	2.00	2.50
		Wi. Watermark inverted	2.00	60
506		2d. pale red-brown (3.5.51)	25	20
		a. Watermark sideways (5.51)..............	80	1.10
		b. *Téte-bêche* (horiz pair)	£2000	
		c. Imperf three sides (horiz pair)..........	£900	
		Wi. Watermark inverted	2.75	3.50
507		2½d. pale scarlet (3.5.51)	20	15
		a. Watermark sideways (5.51)..............	80	90
		b. *Téte-bêche* (horiz pair)		
		Wi. Watermark inverted	60	35
508	**129**	4d. lt ultramarine (2.10.50)...................	1.50	1.10
		a. Double impression	†	£3000
		Set of 6	2.25	1.75

* BOOKLET ERRORS. Those listed as "imperf panes" show one row of perforations either at the top or at the bottom of the pane of 6.

No. 504c is perforated at foot only and occurs in the same sheet as No. 504b.

No. 506c is also perforated at foot only.

147 H.M.S. *Victory*

148 White Cliffs of Dover

149 St. George and the Dragon

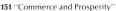

150 Royal Coat of Arms

(Des Mary Adshead (T **147/8**), P. Metcalfe (T **149/50**). Recess Waterlow)

1951 (3 May). W **133**. P 11 × 12.

509	**147**	2s. 6d. yellow-green	8.00	75
510	**148**	5s. red..	30.00	1.50
511	**149**	10s. ultramarine	18.00	10.00
512	**150**	£1 brown	40.00	14.00
		Set of 4	85.00	22.00

151 "Commerce and Prosperity"   **152** Festival Symbol

(Des E. Dulac (T **151**), A. Games (T **152**))

1951 (3 May). **Festival of Britain**. W **127**. P 15 × 14.

513	**151**	2½d. scarlet	25	15
514	**152**	4d. ultramarine	50	45
		Set of 2	75	60
		First Day Cover		16.00

QUEEN ELIZABETH II

6 February 1952

Further detailed information on the stamps of Queen Elizabeth II will be found in Volumes 3, 4 and 5 of the Stanley Gibbons *Great Britain Specialised Catalogue*.

153 Tudor Crown   **154**

155   **156**   **157**

158   **159**   **160**

Queen Elizabeth II and National Emblems

I   II

Two types of the 2½d.

Type I:—In the frontal cross of the diadem, the top line is only half the width of the cross.

Type II:—The top line extends to the full width of the cross and there are signs of strengthening in other parts of the diadem.

(Des Enid Marx (T **154**), M. Farrar-Bell (T **155/6**), G. Knipe (T **157**), Mary Adshead (T **158**), E. Dulac (T **159/60**). Portrait by Dorothy Wilding)

1952–54. W **153**. P 15 × 14.

515	**154**	½d. orange-red (31.8.53)	10	15
		Wi. Watermark inverted (3.54)..............	30	45
516		1d. ultramarine (31.8.53)	20	20
		a. Booklet pane. Three stamps plus three printed labels	18.00	
		Wi. Watermark inverted (3.54)..............	3.75	1.50

517	**154**	1½d. green (5.12.52)	10	15
		a. Watermark sideways (15.10.54)	35	60
		b. Imperf pane*		
		Wi. Watermark inverted (5.53)	25	40
518		2d. red-brown (31.8.53)........................	20	15
		a. Watermark sideways (8.10.54)	80	1.25
		Wi. Watermark inverted (3.54)	20.00	14.00
519	**155**	2½d. carmine-red (Type I) (5.12.52)	10	15
		a. Watermark sideways (15.11.54)	8.00	7.50
		b. Type II (Booklets) (5.53)	1.00	70
		bWi. Watermark inverted (5.53)..............	15	50
520		3d. dp lilac (18.1.54)	1.00	30
521	**156**	4d. ultramarine (2.11.53)	3.00	80
522	**157**	5d. brown (6.7.53).............................	90	2.00
523		6d. reddish purple (18.1.54)	3.00	60
		a. Imperf three sides (pair)		
524		7d. brt green (18.1.54)	9.00	3.50
525	**158**	8d. magenta (6.7.53)...........................	1.00	60
526		9d. bronze-green (8.2.54)	22.00	3.00
527		10d. Prussian blue (8.2.54)	18.00	3.00
528		11d. brown-purple (8.2.54).....................	30.00	16.00
529	**160**	1s. bistre-brown (6.7.53)......................	1.00	40
530	**159**	1s. 3d. green (2.11.53)	4.50	2.00
531	**160**	1s. 6d. grey-blue (2.11.53)	11.00	2.75
		Set of 17......................................	95.00	28.00

See also Nos. 540/56, 561/6, 570/94 and 599/618a.
* BOOKLET ERRORS.—This pane of 6 stamps is *completely* imperf (see No. 540a, etc.).
Stamps with *sideways watermark* come from left-side delivery coils and stamps with *inverted watermark* are from booklets.

First Day Covers

5.12.52	1½d., 2½d. (*517, 519*)	6.00
6.7.53	5d., 8d., 1s. (*522, 525, 529*)	25.00
31.8.53	½d., 1d., 2d. (*515/16, 518*)	20.00
2.11.53	4d., 1s. 3d., 1s. 6d. (*521, 530/1*)	50.00
18.1.54	3d., 6d., 7d. (*520, 523/4*)	30.00
8.2.54	9d., 10d., 11d. (*526/28*)	60.00

161

163

162

164

(Des E. Fuller (2½d.), M. Goaman (4d.), E. Dulac (1s. 3d.), M. Farrar-Bell (1s. 6d.), Portrait (except 1s. 3d.) by Dorothy Wilding)

1953 (3 June). **Coronation.** W 153. *P* 15 × 14.

532	**161**	2½d. carmine-red	10	25
533	**162**	4d. ultramarine	40	1.50
534	**163**	1s. 3d. dp yellow-green	3.50	2.50
535	**164**	1s. 6d. dp grey-blue	6.00	3.50
		Set of 4	9.00	7.00
		First Day Cover		40.00

165 St. Edward's Crown

166 Carrickfergus Castle

167 Caernarvon Castle

168 Edinburgh Castle

169 Windsor Castle

(Des L. Lamb. Portrait by Dorothy Wilding. Recess Waterlow (until 31.12.57) and De La Rue (subsequently))

1955–58. W **165**. *P* 11 × 12.

536	**166**	2s. 6d. black-brown (23.9.55)................	10.00	2.00
		a. De La Rue printing (17.7.58)..............	30.00	2.50
		Watermark inverted	†	
537	**167**	5s. rose-carmine (23.9.55)	35.00	3.50
		a. De La Rue printing (30.4.58).............	75.00	6.50
538	**168**	10s. ultramarine (1.9.55)........................	85.00	11.00
		a. De La Rue printing. *Dull ultramarine* (25.4.58)	£150	19.00
539	**169**	£1 black (1.9.55)	£150	28.00
		a. De La Rue printing (28.4.58).............	£275	50.00
		Set of 4 (Nos. 536/9)	£250	40.00
		Set of 4 (Nos. 536a/9a)	£475	70.00
		First Day Cover (538/9)		£400
		First Day Cover (536/7)		£175

See also Nos. 595/8a & 759/62.
On 1 January 1958, the contract for printing the high values, T **166** to **169** was transferred to De La Rue & Co, Ltd.
The work of the two printers is very similar, but the following notes will be helpful to those attempting to identify Waterlow and De La Rue stamps of the W **165** issue.
The De La Rue sheets are printed in pairs and have a ⊣ or ⊢ shaped guide-mark at the centre of one side-margin, opposite the middle row of perforations, indicating left- and right-hand sheets respectively.
The Waterlow sheets have a small circle (sometimes crossed) instead of a "⊢" and this is present in both side-margins opposite the 6th row of stamps, though one is sometimes trimmed off. Short dashes are also present in the perforation gutter between the marginal stamps marking the middle of the four sides and a cross is at the centre of the sheet. The four corners of the sheet have two lines forming a right-angle as trimming marks, but some are usually trimmed off. All these gutter marks and sheet-trimming marks are absent in the De La Rue printings.
De La Rue used the Waterlow die and no alterations were made to it, so that no difference exists in the design or its size, but the making of new plates at first resulted in slight but measurable variations in the width of the gutters between stamps, particularly the horizontal, as follows:

	Waterlow	De La Rue
Horiz gutters, mm	3.8 to 4.0	3.4 to 3.8

Later D.L.R. plates were however less distinguishable in this respect.

For a short time in 1959 the D.L.R. 2s. 6d. appeared with one dot in the bottom margin below the first stamp.

It is possible to sort singles with reasonable certainty by general characteristics. The individual lines of the D.L.R. impression are cleaner and devoid of the whiskers of colour of Waterlow's, and the whole impression lighter and softer.

Owing to the closer setting of the horizontal rows the strokes of the perforating comb are closer; this results in the topmost tooth on each side of De La Rue stamps being narrower than the corresponding teeth in Waterlow's which were more than normally broad.

Shades also help. The 2s. 6d. D.L.R. is a warmer, more chocolate shade than the blackish brown of Waterlow; the 5s. a lighter red with less carmine than Waterlow's; the 10s. more blue and less ultramarine; the £1 less intense black.

The paper of D.L.R. printings is uniformly white, identical with that of Waterlow printings from February 1957 onwards, but earlier Waterlow printings are on paper which is creamy by comparison.

In this and later issues of T **166/9** the dates of issue given for changes of watermark or paper are those on which supplies were first sent to the Supplies Department to Postmasters.

1955–58. W **165.** P 15 × 14.

540	154	½d. orange-red (booklets 8.55, sheets 12.12.55)	10	15
		a. Part perf pane*		
		Wi. Watermark inverted (9.55)	15	25
541		1d. ultramarine (19.9.55)	25	15
		a. Booklet pane. Three stamps plus three printed labels	10.00	
		b. Tête-bêche (horiz pair)		
		Wi. Watermark inverted (9.55)	40	30
542		1½d. green (booklets 8.55, sheets 11.10.55)	10	15
		a. Watermark sideways (7.3.56)	15	75
		b. Tête-bêche (horiz pair)	£900	
		Wi. Watermark inverted (8.55)	20	25
543		2d. red-brown (6.9.55)	20	20
		aa. Imperf between (vert pair)	£1500	
		a. Watermark sideways (31.7.56)	20	60
		ab. Imperf between (wmk sideways) (horiz pair)	£1500	
		Wi. Watermark inverted (9.55)	10.00	6.00
543b		2d. light red-brown (17.10.56)	20	15
		ba. Tête-bêche (horiz pair)	£600	
		bb. Imperf pane*		
		bc. Part perf pane*		
		bWi. Watermark inverted (1.57)	4.00	2.00
		d. Watermark sideways (5.3.57)	9.00	5.50
544	155	2½d. carmine-red (Type I) (28.9.55)	20	15
		a. Watermark sideways (Type I) (23.3.56)	1.25	1.10
		b. Type II (booklets 9.55, sheets 1957)	25	40
		ba. Tête-bêche (horiz pair)	£750	
		bb. Imperf pane*	£900	
		bc. Part perf pane*		
		bWi. Watermark inverted (9.55)	25	50
545		3d. dp lilac (17.7.56)	20	15
		aa. Tête-bêche (horiz pair)	£750	
		a. Imperf three sides (pair)	£500	
		b. Watermark sideways (22.11.57)	14.00	10.00
		Wi. Watermark inverted (1.10.57)	60	1.00
546	156	4d. ultramarine (14.11.55)	1.40	40
547	157	5d. brown (21.9.55)	5.00	3.50
548		6d. reddish purple (20.12.55)	4.00	75
		aa. Imperf three sides (pair)	£400	
		a. Deep claret (8.5.58)	3.50	80
		ab. Imperf three sides (pair)	£400	
549		7d. brt green (23.4.56)	48.00	7.50
550	158	8d. magenta (21.12.55)	6.00	1.00
551		9d. bronze-green (15.12.55)	18.00	2.25

552	158	10d. Prussian blue (22.9.55)	17.00	2.25
553		11d. brown-purple (28.10.55)	40	1.50
554	160	1s. bistre-brown (3.11.55)	18.00	40
555	159	1s. 3d. green (27.3.56)	24.00	1.50
556	160	1s. 6d. grey-blue (27.3.56)	17.00	1.25
		Set of 18	£140	22.00

The dates given for Nos. 540/556 are those on which they were first issued by the Supplies Dept to postmasters.

In December 1956 a completely imperforate sheet of No. 543b was noticed by clerks in a Kent post office, one of whom purchased it against P.O. regulations. In view of this irregularity we do not consider it properly issued.

Types of 2½d. In this issue, in 1957, Type II formerly only found in stamps from booklets, began to replace Type I on sheet stamps.

*BOOKLET ERRORS. Those listed as "imperf panes" show one row of perforations either at top or bottom of the booklet pane; those as "part perf panes" have one row of 3 stamps imperf on three sides.

For Nos. 542 and 553 in Presentation Pack, see after No. 586.

170 Scout Badge and "Rolling Hitch"

171 "Scouts coming to Britain"

172 Globe within a Compass

(Des Mary Adshead (2½d.), P. Keely (4d.), W. H. Brown (1s. 3d.))

1957 (1 Aug). **World Scout Jubilee Jamboree.** W **165.** P 15 × 14.

557	170	2½d. carmine-red	15	10
558	171	4d. ultramarine	50	1.00
559	172	1s. 3d. green	4.50	4.50
		Set of 3	4.50	4.50
		First Day Cover		12.00

173

½d. to 1½d., 2½d., 3d.   2d.
Graphite-line arrangements
(Stamps viewed from back)

1957 (12 Sept). **46th Inter-Parliamentary Union Conference.** W **165.** P 15 × 14.

560	173	4d. ultramarine	1.00	1.00
		First Day Cover		90.00

GRAPHITE–LINED ISSUES. These were used in connection with automatic sorting machinery, first introduced experimentally at Southampton.

The graphite lines were printed in black on the back, beneath the gum; two lines per stamp, except for the 2d.

In November 1959 phosphor bands were introduced (see notes after No. 598).

1957 (19 Nov). *Graphite-lined issue. Two graphite lines on the back, except 2d. value, which has one line.* W **165**. *P* 15 × 14.

561	**154**	½d. orange-red	20	30
562		1d. ultramarine	20	35
563		1½d. green	30	1.25
		a. Both lines at left	£750	£350
564		2d. light red-brown	2.50	1.50
		a. Line at left	£500	£175
565	**155**	2½d. carmine-red (Type II)	6.00	6.25
566		3d. dp lilac..................................	30	50
		Set of 6	8.50	9.00
		First Day Cover		60.00

No. 564a results from a misplacement of the line and horizontal pairs exist showing one stamp without line. No. 563a results from a similar misplacement.
See also Nos. 587/94.

176 Welsn Dragon

177 Flag and Games Emblem

178 Welsh Dragon

(Des R. Stone (3d.), W. H. Brown (6d.), P. Keely (1s. 3d.))

1958 (18 July). **Sixth British Empire and Commonwealth Games, Cardiff.** W **165**. *P* 15 × 14.

567	**176**	3d. dp lilac..................................	15	10
568	**177**	6d. reddish purple	25	45
569	**178**	1s. 3d. green	2.25	2.25
		Set of 3	2.25	2.25
		First Day Cover		55.00

179 Multiple Crowns

1958–65. W **179**. *P* 15 × 14.

570	**154**	½d. orange-red (25.11.58)	10	10
		a. Watermark sideways (26.5.61)...........	10	15
		c. Part perf pane*	£800	
		Wi. Watermark inverted (11.58)..............	30	25
		k. Chalk-surfaced paper (15.7.63)	2.00	2.25
		kWi. Watermark inverted..........	2.00	2.25
		l. Booklet pane. No. 570k × 3 *se-tenant*		
		with 574k	7.50	
		m. Booklet pane. No. 570a × 2 *se-tenant*		
		with 574l × 2 (1.7.64)	1.25	

571	**154**	1d. ultramarine (booklets 11.58, sheets		
		24.3.59)...	10	10
		aa. Imperf (vert pair from coil)...........		
		a. Watermark sideways (26.5.61)	60	40
		b. Part perf pane*		
		c. Imperf pane................................		
		Wi. Watermark inverted (11.58)	15	20
		l. Booklet pane. No 571i × 2 *se-tenant*		
		with 575a × 2† (16.8.65).................	7.50	
572		1½d. green (booklets 12.58, sheets 30.8.60)	10	15
		a. Imperf three sides (horiz strip of 3)...		
		b. Watermark sideways (26.5.61)	7.50	3.50
		Wi. Watermark inverted (12.58)	1.00	40
573		2d. light red-brown (4.12.58)..............	10	10
		a. Watermark sideways (3.4.59)	25	65
		Wi. Watermark inverted (10.4.61)...........	80.00	30.00
574	**155**	2½d. carmine-red (Type II) (booklets 11.58,		
		sheets 15.9.59)	10	10
		a. Imperf strip of 3		
		b. Tête-bêche (horiz pair)		
		c. Imperf pane	£1100	
		Wi. Watermark inverted (II) (11.58)	4.00	90
		d. Watermark sideways (Type I)		
		(10.11.60).................................	20	30
		da. Imperf strip of 6...........................		
		e. Type I (wmk upright) (4.10.61)	15	35
		k. Chalk-surfaced paper (Type II)		
		(15.7.63)	20	45
		kWi. Do. Watermark inverted (15.7.63)......	20	60
		l. Watermark sideways (Type II) Ord		
		paper (1.7.64)	40	75
575		3d. dp lilac (booklets 11.58, sheets		
		8.12.58)	10	10
		a. Watermark sideways (24.10.58)	15	25
		b. Imperf pane*	£850	
		c. Part perf pane*		
		d. Phantom "R" (Cyl 41 no dot)	£250	
		Eda. Do. First retouch	10.00	
		Edb. Do. Second retouch.........................	10.00	
		e. Phantom "R" (Cyl 37 no dot)	25.00	
		Eea. Do. Retouch	8.00	
		Wi. Watermark inverted (11.58)	15	20
576	**156**	4d. ultramarine (29.10.58).................	50	20
		a. Dp ultramarine†† (28.4.65)	15	10
		ab. Watermark sideways (31.5.65)	45	35
		ac. Imperf pane*		
		ad. Part perf pane*	£650	
		aWi. Watermark inverted (21.6.65)..........	30	30
577		4½d. chestnut (9.2.59)......................	10	15
		Ea. Phantom frame	5.00	
578	**157**	5d. brown (10.11.58)......................	25	20
579		6d. dp claret (23.12.58).....................	25	15
		a. Imperf three sides (pair)	£450	
		b. Imperf (pair).............................	£550	
580		7d. brt green (26.11.58)	40	20
581	**158**	8d. magenta (24.2.60)	40	15
582		9d. bronze-green (24.3.59)	40	15
583		10d. Prussian blue (18.11.58)	1.00	15
584	**160**	1s. bistre-brown (30.10.58)	40	15
585	**159**	1s. 3d. green (17.6.59)	25	15
586	**160**	1s. 6d. grey-blue (16.12.58)	5.00	40
		Set of 17 (one of each value)............	8.00	2.10
		First Day Cover (577)		45.00
		*Presentation Pack***.....................	80.00	

*BOOKLET ERRORS. See note after No. 556.

**This was issued in 1960 and comprises Nos. 542, 553, 570/1 and 573/86. It exists in two forms: (a) inscribed "10s 6d" for sale in the U.K.; and (b) inscribed "$1.80" for sale in the U.S.A.

†Booklet pane No. 571l comes in two forms, with the 1d. stamps on the left or on the right.

††This "shade" was brought about by making more deeply etched cylinders, resulting in apparent depth of colour in parts of the design. There is no difference in the colour of the ink.

Sideways watermark. The 2d., 2½d., 3d. and 4d. come from coils and the ½d., 1d., 1½d., 2½d., 3d. and 4d. come from booklets. In *coil* stamps the sideways watermark shows the top of the watermark to the left *as seen from the front of the stamp*. In the *booklet* stamps it comes equally to the left or right.

Nos. 570k and 574k only come from 2s. "Holiday Resort" Experimental undated booklets issued in 1963, in which one page contained 1 × 2½d. *se-tenant* with 3 × ½d. (See No. 570l).

No. 574l comes from coils, and the "Holiday Resort" Experimental booklets dated "1964" comprising four panes each containing two of these 2½d. stamps *se-tenant* vertically with two ½d. No. 570a. (See No. 570m.)

2½d. imperf. No. 574a comes from a booklet with watermark upright. No. 574da is from a coil with sideways watermark.

No. 574e comes from sheets bearing cylinder number 42 and is also known on vertical delivery coils.

In 1964 No. 575 was printed from cylinder number 70 no dot and dot on an experimental paper which is distinguished by an additional watermark letter "T" lying on its side, which occurs about four times in the sheet, usually in the side margins. 48,000 sheets were issued.

Phantom "R" varieties

Nos. 575d and 615a   No. 575Eda
(Cyl 41 no dot)

No. 575e (Cyl 37 no dot)

3d. An incomplete marginal rule revealed an "R" on cyls 37 and 41 no dot below R.20/12. It is more noticeable on cyl 41 because of the wider marginal rule. The "R" on cyl 41 was twice retouched, the first being as illustrated here (No. 575Eda) and traces of the "R" can still be seen in the second retouch.

The rare variety, No. 575d, is best collected in a block of 4 or 6 with full margins in order to be sure that it is not 615a with phosphor lines removed.

The retouch on cyl 37 is not easily identified: there is no trace of the "R" but the general appearance of that part of the marginal rule is uneven.

Phantom Frame variety

Nos. 577Ea and 616Eba

4½d. An incomplete marginal rule revealed a right-angled shaped frame-line on cyl 8 no dot below R.20/12. It occurs on ordinary and phosphor.

WHITER PAPER. On 18 May 1962 the Post Office announced that a whiter paper was being used for the current issue (including Nos. 595/8). This is beyond the scope of this catalogue, but the whiter papers are listed in Vol. 3 of the Stanley Gibbons *Great Britain Specialised Catalogue*.

1958 (24 Nov)–**61.** *Graphite-lined issue. Two graphite lines on the back, except 2d. value, which has one line. W* **179.** *P* 15 × 14.

587	154	½d. orange-red (15.6.59)		7.00	7.00
		Wi. Watermark inverted (4.8.59)		1.25	2.25
588		1d. ultramarine (18.12.58)		1.00	1.50
		a. Misplaced graphite lines (7.61)*		60	90
		Wi. Watermark inverted (4.8.59)		1.25	2.00
589		1½d. green (4.8.59)		95.00	60.00
		Wi. Watermark inverted (4.8.59)		40.00	40.00
590		2d. lt red-brown (24.11.58)		6.50	3.25
591	155	2½d. carmine-red (Type II) (9.6.59)		9.00	10.00
		Wi. Watermark inverted (21.8.59)		48.00	45.00
592		3d. dp lilac (24.11.58)		50	50
		a. Misplaced graphite lines (5.61)*		£375	£350
		Wi. Watermark inverted (4.8.59)		35	60
593	156	4d. ultramarine (29.4.59)		3.50	4.50
		a. Misplaced graphite lines (1961)*		£1400	
594		4½d. chestnut (3.6.59)		5.00	4.50
		Set of 8 (*cheapest*)		65.00	60.00

Nos. 587/9 were only issued in booklets or coils (587/8).

*No. 588a (in coils), and Nos. 592 and 593a (both in sheets) result from the use of a residual stock of graphite-lined paper. As the use of graphite lines had ceased, the register of the lines in relation to the stamps was of no importance and numerous misplacements occurred —two lines close together, one line only, etc. No. 588a refers to two lines at left or right; No. 592a refers to stamps with two lines only at left and both clear of the perforations and No. 593a to stamps with two lines at left (with left line down perforations) and traces of a third line down the opposite perforations.

(Recess D.L.R. (until 31.12.62), then B.W.)

1959–68. *W* **179.** *P* 11 × 12.

595	166	2s. 6d. black-brown (22.7.59)		10.00	75
		Wi. Watermark inverted			
		a. B.W. printing (1.7.63)		50	30
		aWi. Watermark inverted		£800	75.00
		k. Chalk-surfaced paper (30.5.68)		50	1.10
596	167	5s. scarlet-vermilion (15.6.59)		40.00	2.00
		Wi. Watermark inverted		—	£250
		a. B.W. ptg. *Red* (*shades*) (3.9.63)		1.00	60
		ab. Printed on the gummed side		£750	
		aWi. Watermark inverted		£225	50.00

37

597	**168**	10s. blue (21.7.59)	35.00	5.00
		a. B.W. ptg. *Bright ultramarine* (16.10.63)	2.50	3.00
		aWi. Watermark inverted	—	£650
598	**169**	£1 black (23.6.59)	85.00	12.00
		Wi. Watermark inverted	—	£1500
		a. B.W. printing (14.11.63)	10.00	5.00
		aWi. Watermark inverted	—	£2000
		Set of 4 (Nos. 595/8)	£150	17.00
		Set of 4 (Nos. 595a/8a)	13.00	8.00
		*Presentation Pack (1960)**	£450	

The B.W. printings have a marginal Plate Number. They are generally more deeply engraved than the D.L.R., showing more of the Diadem detail and heavier lines on Her Majesty's face. The vertical perf is 11.9 to 12 as against D.L.R. 11.8.

*This exists in two forms: (a) inscribed "$6.50" for sale in the U.S.A.; and (b) without price for sale in the U.K.

See also Nos. 759/62.

PHOSPHOR BAND ISSUES. These are printed on the front and are wider than graphite lines. They are not easy to see but show as broad vertical bands at certain angles to the light.

Values representing the rate for printed papers (and when this was abolished in 1968 for second class mail) have one band and others two, three or four bands as stated, according to the size and format.

In the small size stamps the bands are on each side with the single band at left (*except where otherwise stated*). In the large-size commemorative stamps the single band may be at left, centre or right, varying in different designs. The bands are vertical on both horizontal and vertical designs *except where otherwise stated*.

The phosphor was originally applied typographically but later usually by photogravure and sometimes using flexography, a typographical process using rubber cylinders.

Three different types of phosphor have been used, distinguishable by the colour emitted under an ultra-violet lamp, the first being green, then blue and now violet. Different sized bands are also known. All these are fully listed in Vol. 3 of the Stanley Gibbons *Great Britain Specialised Catalogue*.

Varieties. Misplaced and missing phosphor bands are known but such varieties are beyond the scope of this Catalogue.

1959 (18 Nov). *Phosphor-Graphite issue. Two phosphor bands on front and two graphite lines on back, except 2d. value, which has one band on front and one line on back.* P 15 × 14. (a) W **165**.

599	**154**	½d. orange-red	4.00	6.00
600		1d. ultramarine	6.00	6.00
601		1½d. green	2.50	5.00

(b) W **179**

605	**154**	2d. lt red-brown (1 band)	5.00	3.75
		a. Error. W **165**	£150	£150
606	**155**	2½d. carmine-red (Type II)	22.00	11.00
607		3d. dp lilac	11.00	8.00
608	**156**	4d. ultramarine	12.00	25.00
609		4½d. chestnut	28.00	15.00
		Set of 8	80.00	70.00
		*Presentation Pack**	£200	

*This was issued in 1960 and comprises two each of Nos. 599/609. It exists in two forms: (a) inscribed "3s 8d" for sale in the U.K. and (b) inscribed "50 c" for sale in the U.S.A.

1960 (22 June)–**67**. *Phosphor issue. Two phosphor bands on front, except where otherwise stated.* W **179**. P 15 × 14.

610	**154**	½d. orange-red	10	15
		a. Watermark sideways (26.5.61)	9.00	8.00
		Wi. Watermark inverted (14.8.60)	60	60
611		1d. ultramarine	10	10
		a. Watermark sideways (14.7.61)	35	40
		Wi. Watermark inverted (14.8.60)	20	30
		l. Booklet pane. No. 611a ×2 se-tenant with 615b × 2† (16.8.65)	10.00	
		m. Booklet pane. No. 611a × 2 se-tenant with 615b × 2†† (11.67)	4.75	

612	**154**	1½d. green	10	20
		a. Watermark sideways (14.7.61)	9.00	9.00
		Wi. Watermark inverted (14.8.60)	9.00	5.00
613		2d. lt red-brown (1 band)	20.00	20.00
613a		2d. lt red-brown (2 bands) (4.10.61)	10	10
		aa. Imperf three sides***		
		ab. Watermark sideways (6.4.67)	15	60
614	**155**	2½d. carmine-red (Type II) (2 bands)*	10	40
		Wi. Watermark inverted (14.8.60)	£140	80.00
614a		2½d. carmine-red (Type II) (1 band) (4.10.61)	40	75
		aWi. Watermark inverted (3.62)	30.00	18.00
614b		2½d. carmine-red (Type I) (1 band) (4.10.61)	35.00	27.00
615		3d. dp lilac (2 bands)	60	60
		a. Phantom "R" (Cyl 41 no dot)	20.00	
		Wi. Watermark inverted (14.8.60)	45	70
		b. Watermark sideways (14.7.61)	1.25	90
615c		3d. dp lilac (1 band at right) (29.4.65)	35	60
		cEa. Band at left	35	60
		cWi. Watermark inverted (band at right) (2.67)	60	60
		cWia. Watermark inverted (band at left) (2.67)	16.00	12.00
		d. Watermark sideways (band at right) (16.8.65)	4.50	3.50
		dEa. Watermark sideways (band at left)	4.50	3.50
		e. One centre band (8.12.66)	25	40
		eWi. Watermark inverted (8.67)	75	80
		ea. Wmk sideways (19.6.67)	25	60
616	**156**	4d. ultramarine	3.00	2.50
		a. Dp ultramarine (28.4.65)	15	15
		aa. Part perf pane**		
		ab. Watermark sideways (16.8.65)	15	25
		aWi. Watermark inverted (21.6.65)	25	20
616b		4½d. chestnut (13.9.61)	15	25
		Eba. Phantom frame	7.50	
616c	**157**	5d. brown (9.6.67)	20	25
617		6d. dp claret (27.6.60)	40	20
617a		7d. brt green (15.2.67)	60	20
617b	**158**	8d. magenta (28.6.67)	20	25
617c		9d. bronze-green (29.12.66)	60	25
617d		10d. Prussian blue (30.12.66)	80	35
617e	**160**	1s. bistre-brown (28.6.67)	40	20
618	**159**	1s. 3d. green	1.75	2.50
618a	**160**	1s. 6d. grey-blue (12.12.66)	2.00	1.00
		Set of 17 (one of each value)	7.00	6.00

The automatic facing equipment was brought into use on 6 July 1960 but the phosphor stamps may have been released a few days earlier.

The stamps with watermark sideways are from booklets except Nos. 613/a and 615ea which are from coils. No. 616ab comes from both booklets and coils.

No. 615a. See footnote after No. 586.

*No. 614 with two bands on the creamy paper was originally from cylinder 50 dot and no dot. When the change in postal rates took place in 1965 it was reissued from cylinder 57 dot and no dot on the whiter paper. Some of these latter were also released in error in districts of S.E. London in September 1964. The shade of the reissue is slightly more carmine.

**Booklet error. Two stamps at bottom left imperf on three sides and the third imperf on two sides.

***This comes from the bottom row of a sheet which is imperf at bottom and both sides.

†Booklet pane No. 611l comes in two forms, with the 1d. stamps on the left or on the right. This was printed in this manner to provide for 3d. stamps with only one band.

††Booklet pane No. 611m comes from 2s. booklets of January and March 1968. The two bands on the 3d. stamp thus created were intentional because of the technical difficulty of producing a single band on one stamp se-tenant with a two-banded stamp, as this requires perfect registration of the bands.

The Phosphor-Graphite stamps had the phosphor applied by typography but the Phosphor issue can be divided into those with the

hosphor applied typographically and others where it was applied by
hotogravure. Moreover the photogravure form can be further divided
to those which phosphoresce green and others which phosphoresce
ue under ultra-violet light. From 1965 violet phosphorescence was
troduced in place of the blue. All these are fully listed in Vol. 3 of the
anley Gibbons *Great Britain Specialised Catalogue.*
The Stanley Gibbons Uvitec Micro ultra-violet lamp will reveal these
fferences. See also Philatelic Information at the beginning of this
atalogue.
Unlike previous one-banded phosphor stamps, No. 615c has a broad
and extending over two stamps so that alternate stamps have the band
left or right (same prices either way). No. 615cWi comes from the 10s.
hosphor booklet of February 1967 and No. 615eWi comes from the
0s. phosphor booklets of August 1967 and February 1968.

arieties:
Nos. 615a (Phantom "R") and 616Eba (Phantom frame), see illus-
ations following No. 586.

184 "Growth of Savings"

183 Thrift Plant

185 Thrift Plant

180 Postboy of 1660   181 Posthorn of 1660

(Des R. Stone (3d.), Faith Jaques (1s. 3d.))

60 (7 July). **Tercentenary of Establishment of General Letter Office.**
W 179 (*sideways on* 1s. 3d.). P 15 × 14 (3d.) or 14 × 15 (1s. 3d.).

9	180	3d. dp lilac	20	10
0	181	1s. 3d. green	3.50	3.50
		Set of 2	3.50	3.50
		First Day Cover		40.00

182 Conference Emblem

(Des R. Stone (emblem, P. Rahikainen))

60 (19 Sept). **First Anniv of European Postal and Telecommunications Conference.** *Chalk-surfaced paper.* W 179. P 15 × 14.

1	182	6d. bronze-green and purple	40	60
2		1s. 6d. brown and blue	5.00	4.50
		Set of 2	5.00	4.50
		First Day Cover		28.00

CREENS. Up to this point all photogravure stamps were printed in a
0 screen (200 dots per linear inch), but all later commemorative
amps are a finer 250 screen. Exceptionally No. 622 has a 200 screen for
e portrait and a 250 screen for the background.

STAMP MONTHLY

inest and most informative magazine for all collectors.
btainable from your newsagent or by postal subscription –
etails on request

(Des P. Gauld (2½d.), M. Goaman (others))

1961 (28 Aug). **Centenary of Post Office Savings Bank.** *Chalk-surfaced
paper.* W 179 (*sideways on* 2½d.) P 14 × 15 (2½d.) or 15 × 14 (*others*).
I. "TIMSON" Machine
II. "THRISSELL" Machine

			I		II	
623	183	2½d. black and red	10	10	2.00	1.75
		a. Black omitted	£6000	—	†	
624	184	3d. orange-brown & violet	10	10	25	25
		a. Orange-brown omitted	£110	—	£250	—
		x. Perf through side sheet margin	26.00	23.00	†	
		xa. Orange-brown omitted	£400	—	†	
625	185	1s. 6d. red and blue	2.25	2.00	†	
		Set of 3	2.25	2.00		
		First Day Cover		60.00		

2½d. TIMSON. Cyls 1E–1F. Deeply shaded portrait (brownish black).
2½d. THRISSELL. Cyls 1D–1B or 1D (dot)–1B (dot). Lighter portrait (grey-
black).
3d. TIMSON. Cyls 3D–3E. Clear, well-defined portrait with deep shadows and bright highlights.
3d. THRISSELL. Cyls 3C–3B or 3C (dot)–3B (dot). Dull portrait, lacking in
contrast.

Sheet marginal examples *without* single extension perf hole on the
short side of the stamp are always "Timson", as are those with large
punch-hole *not* coincident with printed three-sided box guide mark.
The 3d. "Timson" perforated completely through the right-hand side
margin comes from a relatively small part of the printing perforated on
a sheet-fed machine.
Normally the "Timsons" were perforated in the reel, with three large
punch-holes in both long margins and the perforations completely
through both short margins. Only one punch-hole coincides with the
guide-mark.
The "Thrissells" have one large punch-hole in one long margin,
coinciding with guide-mark and one short margin imperf (except
sometimes for encroachments).

186 C.E.P.T. Emblem

187 Doves and Emblem

188 Doves and Emblem

(Des M. Goaman (doves T. Kurpershoek))

1961 (18 Sept). **European Postal and Telecommunications (C.E.P.T.) Conference, Torquay.** *Chalk-surfaced paper.* W **179**. P 15 × 14.

626	186	2d. orange, pink and brown	10	10
		a. Orange omitted................................		
627	187	4d. buff, mauve and ultramarine	20	10
628	188	10d. turquoise, pale green & Prussian blue	40	35
		a. Pale green omitted..........................	£3000	
		b. Turquoise omitted..........................	£1800	
		Set of 3	60	50
		First Day Cover		2.50

189 Hammer Beam Roof, Westminster Hall

190 Palace of Westminster

(Des Faith Jaques)

1961 (25 Sept). **Seventh Commonwealth Parliamentary Conference.** *Chalk-surfaced paper.* W **179** (*sideways on 1s. 3d.*). P 15 × 14 (6d.) *or* 14 × 15 (1s. 3d.).

629	189	6d. purple and gold	25	25
		a. Gold omitted	£300	
630	190	1s. 3d. green and blue........................	2.50	2.00
		a. Blue (Queen's head) omitted...........	£4000	
		Set of 2	2.50	2.00
		First Day Cover		26.00

191 "Units of Productivity"

192 "National Productivity"

193 "Unified Productivity"

(Des D. Gentleman)

1962 (14 Nov). **National Productivity Year.** *Chalk-surfaced pap* W **179** (*inverted on 2½d. and 3d.*). P 15 × 14.

631	191	2½d. myrtle-green & carmine-red (*shades*)	20	
		Ea. Blackish olive & carmine-red	25	
		p. One phosphor band. *Blackish olive &*		
		carmine-red	1.00	
632	192	3d. light blue and violet (*shades*)..........	25	
		a. Lt blue (Queen's head) omitted	£600	
		p. Three phosphor bands	1.00	
633	193	1s. 3d. carmine, lt blue & dp green.......	1.75	1.
		a. Lt blue (Queen's head) omitted	£3500	
		p. Three phosphor bands	21.00	18.
		Set of 3 (Ordinary)	2.00	1.
		Set of 3 (Phosphor)	21.00	18.
		First Day Cover (Ordinary)		30.
		First Day Cover (Phosphor)		95.

194 Campaign Emblem and Family

195 Children of Three Races

(Des M. Goaman)

1963 (21 Mar). **Freedom from Hunger.** *Chalk-surfaced paper.* W 1 (*inverted*). P 15 × 14.

634	194	2½d. crimson and pink	10	1
		p. One phosphor band	1.00	1.
635	195	1s. 3d. bistre-brown and yellow	2.00	1.7
		p. Three phosphor bands	21.00	18.
		Set of 2 (Ordinary)	2.00	1.7
		Set of 2 (Phosphor)	21.00	18.
		First Day Cover (Ordinary)		28.0
		First Day Cover (Phosphor)		30.0

196 "Paris Conference"

(Des R. Stone)

1963 (7 May). **Paris Postal Conference Centenary.** *Chalk-surface paper.* W **179** (*inverted*). P 15 × 14.

636	196	6d. green & mauve.............................	50	4
		a. Green omitted	£1200	
		p. Three phosphor bands	6.00	5.
		First Day Cover (Ordinary)		12.
		First Day Cover (Phosphor)		20.

197 Posy of Flowers

198 Woodland Life

(Des S. Scott (3d.), M. Goaman (4½d.))

1963 (16 May). **National Nature Week.** *Chalk-surfaced paper.* W **179.** P 15 × 14.

637	197	3d. yellow, green, brown and black	25	20
		p. Three phosphor bands	50	50
638	198	4½d. black, blue, yellow, magenta & brown-red	40	40
		p. Three phosphor bands	2.50	2.50
		Set of 2 (Ordinary)	60	60
		Set of 2 (Phosphor)	3.00	3.00
		First Day Cover (Ordinary)		14.00
		First Day Cover (Phosphor)		28.00

Special First Day of Issue Postmark

	Ordin- ary	Phos- phor
London E.C. (Type A)	15.00	30.00

This postmark was used on first day covers serviced by the Philatelic Bureau.

199 Rescue at Sea

200 19th-century Lifeboat

201 Lifeboatmen

(Des D. Gentleman)

1963 (31 May). **Ninth International Lifeboat Conference, Edinburgh.** *Chalk-surfaced paper.* W **179.** P 15 × 14.

639	199	2½d. blue, black and red	10	10
		p. One phosphor band	40	50
640	200	4d. red, yellow, brown, black and blue ..	40	30
		p. Three phosphor bands	20	50
641	201	1s. 6d. sepia, yellow and grey-blue........	2.50	2.50
		p. Three phosphor bands	25.00	24.00
		Set of 3 (Ordinary)	2.75	2.50
		Set of 3 (Phosphor)	26.00	24.00
		First Day Cover (Ordinary)		26.00
		First Day Cover (Phosphor)		38.00

Special First Day of Issue Postmark

	Ordin- ary	Phos- phor
London	32.00	40.00

This postmark was used on first day covers serviced by the Philatelic Bureau.

202 Red Cross

203

204

(Des H. Bartram)

1963 (15 Aug). **Red Cross Centenary Congress.** *Chalk-surfaced paper.* W **179.** P 15 × 14.

642	202	3d. red & dp lilac	10	10
		a. Red omitted..................................	£1750	
		p. Three phosphor bands	60	60
		pa. Red omitted................................	£5500	
643	203	1s. 3d. red, blue and grey	2.75	2.50
		p. Three phosphor bands	32.00	30.00
644	204	1s. 6d. red, blue & bistre	2.50	2.50
		p. Three phosphor bands	23.00	20.00
		Set of 3 (Ordinary)	5.00	4.50
		Set of 3 (Phosphor)	50.00	45.00
		First Day Cover (Ordinary)		28.00
		First Day Cover (Phosphor)		60.00

Special First Day of Issue Postmark

1863 RED CROSS CENTENARY A CENTURY OF SERVICE 1963

	Ordin- ary	Phos- phor
London E.C.	40.00	70.00

This postmark was used on first day covers serviced by the Philatelic Bureau.

205 Commonwealth Cable

(Des P. Gauld)

1963 (3 Dec). **Opening of COMPAC (Trans-Pacific Telephone Cable).** *Chalk-surfaced paper.* W **179.** P 15 × 14.

645	205	1s. 6d. blue and black	2.50	2.25
		a. Black omitted................................	£2000	
		p. Three phosphor bands	15.00	13.50
		First Day Cover (Ordinary)		22.00
		First Day Cover (Phosphor)		24.00

Special First Day of Issue Postmark

	Ordin- ary	Phos- phor
Philatelic Bureau, London E.C.1 (Type A)	26.00	28.00

PRESENTATION PACKS. Special Packs comprising slip-in cards with printed commemorative inscriptions and descriptive notes on the back and with protective covering, were introduced in 1964 with the Shakespeare issue. These are listed and priced.

Issues of 1968–69 (British Paintings to the Prince of Wales Investiture) were also issued in packs with text in German for sale through the Post Office's German Agency and these are also quoted. Subsequently, however, the packs sold in Germany were identical with the normal English version with the addition of a separate printed insert card with German text. These, as also English packs with Japanese and Dutch printed cards for sale in Japan and the Netherlands respectively, are listed in Vols. 3 and 4 of the Stanley Gibbons *Great Britain Specialised Catalogue.*

206 Puck and Bottom
(*A Midsummer Night's Dream*)

207 Feste (*Twelfth Night*)

208 Balcony Scene
(*Romeo and Juliet*)

209 "Eve of Agincourt" (*Henry V*)

210 Hamlet contemplating Yorick's
Skull (*Hamlet*) and Queen Elizabeth II

Des D. Gentleman. Photo Harrison & Sons (3d., 6d., 1s. 3d., 1s. 6d.). Des C. and R. Ironside. Recess B.W. (2s. 6d.))

1964 (23 April). **Shakespeare Festival.** *Chalk-surfaced paper.* W **179.** P 11 × 12 (2s. 6d.) or 15 × 14 (others).

646	206	3d. yellow-bistre, black & dp violet blue (shades)	10	10
		p. Three phosphor bands	20	30
647	207	6d. yellow, orange, black & yellow-olive (shades)	20	30
		p. Three phosphor bands	60	70
648	208	1s. 3d. cerise, blue-green, black & sepia (shades)	90	1.00
		Wi. Watermark inverted		
		p. Three phosphor bands	5.75	5.50
		pWi. Watermark inverted	£100	
649	209	1s. 6d. violet, turquoise, black & blue (shades)	1.25	1.00
		Wi. Watermark inverted		
		p. Three phosphor bands	9.00	5.75
650	210	2s. 6d. dp slate-purple (shades)	2.00	2.00
		Wi. Watermark inverted	£300	
		Set of 5 (Ordinary)	4.00	4.00
		Set of 5 (Phosphor)	13.00	11.00
		First Day Cover (Ordinary)		11.00
		First Day Cover (Phosphor)		11.00
		Presentation Pack (Ordinary)	10.00	

The 3d. is known with yellow-bistre missing in the top two-thirds of the figures of Puck and Bottom. This occurred in the top row only of a sheet.

Special First Day of Issue Postmark

	Ordin- ary	Phos- phor
Stratford-upon-Avon, Warwicks	13.00	13.00

This postmark was used on first day covers serviced by the Philatelic Bureau, as well as on covers posted at Stratford P.O.

211 Flats near Richmond Park ("Urban Development")

212 Shipbuilding Yards, Belfast ("Industrial Activity")

213 Beddgelert Forest Park, Snowdonia ("Forestry")

214 Nuclear Reactor, Dounreay ("Technological Development")

(Des D. Bailey)

1964 (1 July). **20th International Geographical Congress, London.** *Chalk-surfaced paper.* W **179.** P 15 × 14.

651	211	2½d. black, olive-yellow, olive-grey & turquoise-blue	10	10
		p. One phosphor band	50	40
652	212	4d. orange-brown, red-brown, rose, black & violet	25	25
		a. Violet omitted	£150	
		b. Red-brown omitted		
		c. Violet and red-brown omitted	£150	
		Wi. Watermark inverted	£500	
		p. Three phosphor bands	75	70
653	213	8d. yellow-brown, emerald, green & black	60	50
		a. Green (lawn) omitted	£3500	
		Wi. Watermark inverted	£250	
		p. Three phosphor bands	1.75	1.50
654	214	1s. 6d. yellow-brown, pale pink, black & brown	3.25	3.25
		Wi. Watermark inverted	19.00	
		p. Three phosphor bands	20.00	18.00
		Set of 4 (Ordinary)	4.00	4.00
		Set of 4 (Phosphor)	20.00	18.00
		First Day Cover (Ordinary)		18.00
		First Day Cover (Phosphor)		27.00
		Presentation Pack (Ordinary)	80.00	

Special First Day of Issue Postmark

	Ordin- ary	Phos- phor
G.P.O. Philatelic Bureau, London E.C.1 (Type B)	20.00	30.00

215 Spring Gentian

216 Dog Rose

217 Honeysuckle

218 Fringed Water Lily

(Des M. and Sylvia Goaman)

1964 (5 Aug). **Tenth International Botanical Congress, Edinburgh.** *Chalk-surfaced paper.* W **179**. P 15 × 14.

655	215	3d. violet, blue and sage-green	10	10
		a. Blue omitted	£3500	
		p. Three phosphor bands	20	20
656	216	6d. apple-green, rose, scarlet and green	20	20
		Wi. Watermark inverted		
		p. Three phosphor bands	1.25	1.00
657	217	9d. lemon, green, lake and rose-red	1.60	2.00
		a. Green (leaves) omitted	£3500	
		Wi. Watermark inverted	32.00	
		p. Three phosphor bands	3.75	3.00
658	218	1s. 3d. yellow, emerald, reddish violet & grey-green	2.50	1.90
		a. Yellow (flowers) omitted	£7500	
		Wi. Watermark inverted	£225	
		p. Three phosphor bands	20.00	16.00
		Set of 4 (Ordinary)	4.00	4.00
		Set of 4 (Phosphor)	22.00	18.00
		First Day Cover (Ordinary)		18.00
		First Day Cover (Phosphor)		28.00
		Presentation Pack (Ordinary)	80.00	

Special First Day of Issue Postmark

	Ordin-ary	Phos-phor
G.P.O. Philatelic Bureau, London E.C.1 (Type B)	22.00	30.00

219 Forth Road Bridge

220 Forth Road and Railway Bridges

(Des A. Restall)

1964 (4 Sept). **Opening of Forth Road Bridge.** *Chalk-surfaced paper.* W **179**. P 15 × 14.

659	219	3d. black, blue & reddish violet	15	10
		p. Three phosphor bands	50	50
660	220	6d. black, lt blue & carmine-red	45	40
		a. Lt blue omitted	£1500	£1500
		Wi. Watermark inverted	1.50	
		p. Three phosphor bands	4.50	4.50
		pWi. Watermark inverted	55.00	
		Set of 2 (Ordinary)	60	50
		Set of 2 (Phosphor)	5.00	5.00

First Day Cover (Ordinary)		5.⬛
First Day Cover (Phosphor)		10.⬛
Presentation Pack (Ordinary)	£180	

Special First Day of Issue Postmarks

	Ordin-ary	Phos-phor
G.P.O. Philatelic Bureau, London E.C.1 (Type B)	7.00	11.00
North Queensferry, Fife	20.00	85.00
South Queensferry, West Lothian	15.00	45.00

The Queensferry postmarks were applied to first day covers sent to a temporary Philatelic Bureau at Edinburgh.

221 Sir Winston Churchill

(Des D. Gentleman and Rosalind Dease, from photograph by Karsh

1965 (8 July). **Churchill Commemoration.** *Chalk-surfaced pape* W **179**. P 15 × 14.

I. "REMBRANDT" Machine

661	221	4d. black and olive-brown	15	⬛
		Wi. Watermark inverted	1.75	
		p. Three phosphor bands	30	⬛

II "TIMSON" Machine

661a	221	4d. black and olive-brown	25	⬛

III. "L. & M. 4" Machine

662	–	1s. 3d. black and grey	45	⬛
		Wi. Watermark inverted	65.00	
		p. Three phosphor bands	3.00	3.2⬛
		Set of 2 (Ordinary)	60	⬛
		Set of 2 (Phosphor)	3.00	3.2⬛
		First Day Cover (Ordinary)		2.⬛
		First Day Cover (Phosphor)		4.⬛
		Presentation Pack (Ordinary)	13.00	

The 1s. 3d. shows a closer view of Churchill's head.

4d. REMBRANDT, Cyls 1A-1B dot and no dot. Lack of shading detail c Churchill's portrait. Queen's portrait appears dull and coarse. This a rotary machine which is sheet-fed.

4d. TIMSON. Cyls 5A-6B no dot. More detail on Churchill's portra —furrow on forehead, his left eyebrow fully drawn and more shadin on cheek. Queen's portrait lighter and sharper. This is a reel-fe two-colour 12-in. wide rotary machine and the differences in impre sion are due to the greater pressure applied by this machine.

1s. 3d. Cyls 1A-1B no dot. The "Linotype and Machinery No. 4" machi is an ordinary sheet-fed rotary press machine. Besides being used f printing the 1s. 3d. stamps it was als employed for overprinting th phosphor bands on both values.

Two examples of the 4d. value exist with the Queen's head omitted, one due to something adhering to the cylinder and the other due to a paper fold. The stamp also exists with Churchill's head omitted, also due to a paper fold.

Special First Day of Issue Postmark

	Ordin-ary	Phos-phor
G.P.O. Philatelic Bureau, London E.C.1 (Type B)	3.50	5.50

A First Day of Issue handstamp was provided at Bladon, Oxford, for this issue.

222 Simon de Montfort's Seal

223 Parliament Buildings (after engraving by Hollar, 1647)

(Des S. Black (6d.), R. Guyatt (2s. 6d.))

1965 (19 July). **700th Anniv of Simon de Montfort's Parliament.** *Chalk-surfaced paper.* W **179**. P 15 × 14.

563	222	6d. olive-green	10	10
		p. Three phosphor bands	40	40
564	223	2s. 6d. black, grey and pale drab	1.25	1.25
		Wi. Watermark inverted	12.00	
		Set of 2 (Ordinary)	1.25	1.25
		First Day Cover (Ordinary)		12.00
		First Day Cover (Phosphor)		16.00
		Presentation Pack (Ordinary)	35.00	

Special First Day of Issue Postmark

	Ordin-ary
G.P.O. Philatelic Bureau, London E.C.1 (Type B)	14.00

A First Day of Issue handstamp was provided at Evesham, Worcs, for this issue.

224 Bandsmen and Banner

225 Three Salvationists

(Des M. Farrar-Bell (3d.), G. Trenaman (1s. 6d))

1965 (9 Aug). **Salvation Army Centenary.** *Chalk-surfaced paper.* W **179**. P 15 × 14.

665	224	3d. indigo, grey-blue, cerise, yellow & brown	10	10
		p. One phosphor band	40	40

666	225	1s. 6d. red, blue, yellow and brown	1.00	1.00
		p. Three phosphor bands	2.75	3.25
		Set of 2 (Ordinary)	1.10	1.10
		Set of 2 (Phosphor)	3.00	3.50
		First Day Cover (Ordinary)		20.00
		First Day Cover (Phosphor)		22.00

The Philatelic Bureau did not provide first day cover services for Nos. 665/70.

226 Lister's Carbolic Spray

227 Lister and Chemical Symbols

(Des P. Gauld (4d.), F. Ariss (1s.))

1965 (1 Sept). **Centenary of Joseph Lister's Discovery of Antiseptic Surgery.** *Chalk-surfaced paper.* W **179**. P 15 × 14.

667	226	4d. indigo, brown-red and grey-black	10	10
		a. Brown-red (tube) omitted	£150	75.00
		b. Indigo omitted	£1500	
		p. Three phosphor bands	15	20
		pa. Brown-red (tube) omitted	£1100	
668	227	1s. black, purple and new blue	1.00	1.25
		Wi. Watermark inverted	£140	
		p. Three phosphor bands	1.60	1.60
		pWi. Watermark inverted	£140	
		Set of 2 (Ordinary)	1.10	1.25
		Set of 2 (Phosphor)	1.75	1.75
		First Day Cover (Ordinary)		9.50
		First Day Cover (Phosphor)		8.50

228 Trinidad Carnival Dancers

229 Canadian Folk-dancers

(Des D. Gentleman and Rosalind Dease)

1965 (1 Sept). **Commonwealth Arts Festival.** *Chalk-surfaced paper.* W **179**. P 15 × 14.

669	228	6d. black and orange	10	10
		p. Three phosphor bands	30	30
670	229	1s. 6d. black & lt reddish violet	1.25	1.50
		p. Three phosphor bands	2.25	2.25
		Set of 2 (Ordinary)	1.25	1.50
		Set of 2 (Phosphor)	2.50	2.50
		First Day Cover (Ordinary)		10.00
		First Day Cover (Phosphor)		10.00

230 Flight of Spitfires

231 Pilot in Hurricane

232 Wing-tips of Spitfire and Messerschmitt "ME-109"

233 Spitfires attacking Heinkel "HE-111" Bomber

234 Spitfire attacking Stuka Dive-bomber

235 Hurricanes over Wreck of Dornier "DO-17z2" Bomber

238 Tower and Georgian Buildings

239 Tower and "Nash" Terrace, Regent's Park

236 Anti-aircraft Artillery in Action

237 Air-battle over St. Paul's Cathedral

(Des D. Gentleman and Rosalind Dease (4d. × 6 and 1s. 3d.), A. Restall (9d.))

1965 (13 Sept). **25th Anniv of Battle of Britain.** *Chalk-surfaced paper.* W **179**. *P* 15 ×14.

671	**230**	4d. yellow-olive and black....................	30	35
		a. Block of 6. Nos. 671/6	5.50	5.50
		p. Three phosphor bands	40	50
		pa. Block of 6. Nos. 671p/6p	10.00	9.00
672	**231**	4d. yellow-olive, olive-grey and black	30	35
		p. Three phosphor bands	40	50
673	**232**	4d. red, new blue, yellow-olive, olive-grey & black	30	35
		p. Three phosphor bands	40	50
674	**233**	4d. olive-grey, yellow-olive and black	30	35
		p. Three phosphor bands	40	50
675	**234**	4d. olive-grey, yellow-olive and black	30	35
		p. Three phosphor bands	40	50
676	**235**	4d. olive-grey, yellow-olive, new blue & black	30	35
		a. New blue omitted..........................	—	£3000
		p. Three phosphor bands	40	50
677	**236**	9d. bluish violet, orange & slate-purple ..	1.25	1.25
		Wi. Watermark inverted	25.00	
		p. Three phosphor bands	1.25	80
678	**237**	1s. 3d. lt grey, dp grey, black, lt blue and brt blue	1.25	1.25
		Wi. Watermark inverted	18.00	
		p. Three phosphor bands	1.25	80
		pWi. Watermark inverted	3.00	
		Set of 8 (Ordinary)	7.00	4.25
		Set of 8 (Phosphor)	12.00	4.25
		First Day Cover (Ordinary)		18.00
		First Day Cover (Phosphor)		18.00
		Presentation Pack (Ordinary)	48.00	

Nos. 671/6 were issued together *se-tenant* in blocks of 6 (3 ×2) within the sheet.

Special First Day of Issue Postmark

	Ordinary	Phosphor
G.P.O. Philatelic Bureau, London E.C.1 (Type C)	19.00	19.00

(Des C. Abbott)

1965 (8 Oct). **Opening of Post Office Tower.** *Chalk-surfaced paper.* W **179** *(sideways on 3d.). P* 14 × 15 (3d.) or 15 × 14 (1s. 3d.).

679	**238**	3d. olive-yellow, new blue & bronze-green....................................	10	10
		a. Olive-yellow (Tower) omitted	£500	
		p. One phosphor band at right	10	10
		pEa. Band at left	10	10
680	**239**	1s. 3d. bronze-green, yellow-green & blue	65	75
		Wi. Watermark inverted	38.00	
		p. Three phosphor bands	50	50
		pWi. Watermark inverted	35.00	
		Set of 2 (Ordinary)	75	85
		Set of 2 (Phosphor)	60	60
		First Day Cover (Ordinary)		6.00
		First Day Cover (Phosphor)		8.00
		Presentation Pack (Ordinary)	3.00	
		Presentation Pack (Phosphor)	3.00	

The one phosphor band on No. 679p was produced by printing broad phosphor bands across alternate vertical perforations. Individual stamps show the band at right or left.

Special First Day of Issue Postmark

	Ordinary	Phosphor
G.P.O. Philatelic Bureau, London E.C.1 (Type C)	6.50	8.50

240 U.N. Emblem

241 I.C.Y. Emblem

(Des J. Matthews)

1965 (25 Oct). **20th Anniv of U.N.O. and International Co-operation Year.** *Chalk-surfaced paper.* W **179**. *P* 15 ×14.

681	**240**	3d. black, yellow-orange & lt blue	15	20
		p. One phosphor band	25	25

682 **241** 1s. 6d. black, brt purple & lt blue 1.10 90
Wi. Watermark inverted 2.50 2.50
p. Three phosphor bands 2.50 2.50
Set of 2 (Ordinary) 1.25 1.10
Set of 2 (Phosphor) 2.75 2.75
First Day Cover (Ordinary) 11.00
First Day Cover (Phosphor) 9.50

The Philatelic Bureau did not provide first day cover services for Nos.
681/4.

242 Telecommunications
Network

243 Radio Waves and
Switchboard

(Des A. Restall)

1965 (15 Nov). **I.T.U. Centenary.** *Chalk-surfaced paper.* W 179.
P 15 × 14.
683 **242** 9d. red, ultramarine, dp slate, violet, black
& pink 20 20
Wi. Watermark inverted 12.00
p. Three phosphor bands 60 50
pWi. Watermark inverted 60.00
684 **243** 1s. 6d. red, greenish blue, indigo, black &
lt pink 1.40 1.10
a. Lt pink omitted £850
Wi. Watermark inverted 45.00
p. Three phosphor bands 4.50 4.50
Set of 2 (Ordinary) 1.50 1.25
Set of 2 (Phosphor) 5.00 5.00
First Day Cover (Ordinary) 11.00
First Day Cover (Phosphor) 11.50

Originally scheduled for issue on 17 May 1965, supplies from the
Philatelic Bureau were sent in error to reach a dealer on that date and
another dealer received his supply on 27 May.

244 Robert Burns (after Skirving
chalk drawing)

245 Robert Burns (after Nasmyth
portrait)

(Des G. Huntly)

1966 (25 Jan). **Burns Commemoration.** *Chalk-surfaced paper.* W 179.
P 15 × 14.
685 **244** 4d. black, dp violet-blue & new blue 15 15
p. Three phosphor bands 25 25
686 **245** 1s. 3d. black, slate-blue & yellow-orange 70 70
p. Three phosphor bands 1.00 1.00
Set of 2 (Ordinary) 85 85
Set of 2 (Phosphor) 1.25 1.25
First Day Cover (Ordinary) 2.50
First Day Cover (Phosphor) 3.50
Presentation Pack (Ordinary) 35.00

Special First Day of Issue Postmarks

(35 mm diameter)

	Ordin-ary	Phos-phor
Alloway, Ayrshire	5.00	5.00
Ayr	9.50	9.50
Dumfries	7.00	7.00
Edinburgh	7.50	7.50
Glasgow	7.50	7.50
Kilmarnock, Ayrshire..........................	9.50	9.50

A special Philatelic Bureau was set up in Edinburgh to deal
with first day covers of this issue. The Bureau serviced covers
to receive the above postmarks, and other versions were
applied locally. The locally applied handstamps were 38–
39mm in diameter, the Bureau postmarks, applied by
machine, 35mm. The Ayr, Edinburgh, Glasgow and Kilmar-
nock postmarks are similar in design to that for Alloway.
Similar handstamps were also provided at Greenock and
Mauchline, but the Bureau did not provide a service for
these.

246 Westminster Abbey

247 Fan Vaulting, Henry VII
Chapel

(Des Sheila Robinson. Photo Harrison (3d.). Des and eng Bradbury,
Wilkinson. Recess (2s. 6d.))

1966 (28 Feb). **900th Anniv of Westminster Abbey.** *Chalk-surfaced
paper (3d.).* W 179. P 15 × 14 (3d.) or 11 ×12 (2s. 6d.).
687 **246** 3d. black, red-brown & new blue 15 10
p. One phosphor band 30 30
688 **247** 2s. 6d. black 85 90
Set of 2 .... 1.00 1.00
First Day Cover (Ordinary) 4.50
First Day Cover (Phosphor) 7.50
Presentation Pack (Ordinary) 17.00

Special First Day of Issue Postmark

Ordin-
ary
G.P.O. Philatelic Bureau, London E.C.1 (Type B) .. 5.50
The Bureau did not provide a first day cover service for the
3d. phosphor stamp.

248 View near Hassocks, Sussex

249 Antrim, Northern Ireland

254 Goalkeeper saving Goal

250 Harlech Castle, Wales

251 Cairngorm Mountains, Scotland

(Des L. Rosoman. Queen's portrait, adapted by D. Gentleman from coinage)

1966 (2 May). **Landscapes.** *Chalk-surfaced paper. W* **179**. *P* 15 ×14.

689	**248**	4d. black, yellow-green & new blue	15	15
		p. Three phosphor bands	15	15
690	**249**	6d. black, emerald & new blue	15	15
		Wi. Watermark inverted	4.50	
		p. Three phosphor bands	25	25
		pWi. Watermark inverted	25.00	
691	**250**	1s. 3d. black, greenish yellow & greenish blue	35	35
		p. Three phosphor bands	35	35
692	**251**	1s. 6d. black, orange and Prussian blue .	50	50
		Wi. Watermark inverted	8.00	
		p. Three phosphor bands	50	50
		Set of 4 (Ordinary)	1.00	1.00
		Set of 4 (Phosphor)	1.00	1.00
		First Day Cover (Ordinary)		6.00
		First Day Cover (Phosphor)		6.00

Special First Day of Issue Postmark

	Ordin-ary	Phos-phor
G.P.O. Philatelic Bureau, London E.C.1 (Type B)	7.50	7.50

First Day of Issue handstamps were provided at Lewes, Sussex; Coleraine, Co. Londonderry; Harlech, Merioneth and Grantown-on-Spey, Morayshire, for this issue.

(Des D. Gentleman (4d.), W. Kempster (6d.), D. Caplan (1s. 3d.). Queen's portrait adapted by D. Gentleman)

1966 (1 June). **World Cup Football Competition.** *Chalk-surfaced paper. W* **179** (*sideways on* 4d.). *P* 14 ×15 (4d.) *or* 15 ×14 (*others*).

693	**252**	4d. red, reddish purple, brt blue, flesh & black	15	10
		p. Two phosphor bands	15	10
694	**253**	6d. black, sepia, red, apple-green & blue	20	20
		a. Black omitted	85.00	
		b. Apple-green omitted	£1800	
		c. Red omitted	£1800	
		Wi. Watermark inverted	1.25	
		p. Three phosphor bands	20	20
		pa. Black omitted	£300	
695	**254**	1s. 3d. black, blue, yellow, red & lt yellow-olive	50	50
		a. Blue omitted	£150	
		Wi. Watermark inverted	60.00	
		p. Three phosphor bands	50	50
		pWi. Watermark inverted	1.25	
		Set of 3 (Ordinary)	75	75
		Set of 3 (Phosphor)	75	75
		First Day Cover (Ordinary)		6.50
		First Day Cover (Phosphor)		6.50
		Presentation Pack (Ordinary)	14.00	

Special First Day of Issue Postmark

	Ordin-ary	Phos-phor
G.P.O. Philatelic Bureau, London E.C.1 (Type C)	7.50	7.50

A First Day of Issue handstamp was provided at Wembley, Middx, for this issue.

255 Black-headed Gull

256 Blue Tit

252 Players with Ball

253 Goalmouth Mêlée

257 European Robin

258 Blackbird

(Des J. Norris Wood)

)66 (8 Aug). **British Birds.** *Chalk-surfaced paper.* W **179**. *P* 15 ×14.

)6	**255**	4d. grey, black, red, emerald-green, brt blue, greenish yellow & bistre..........	10	15
		Wi. Watermark inverted........................	3.00	
		a. Block of 4. Nos. 696/9........................	1.00	1.00
		ab. Black (value), etc. omitted* (block of four)...	£4000	
		ac. Black only omitted*..........................		
		aWi. Watermark inverted (block of four)...	12.00	
		p. Three phosphor bands	10	15
		pWi. Watermark inverted........................	14.00	
		pa. Block of 4. Nos. 696p/9p	1.00	1.00
		paWi. Watermark inverted (block of four)...	60.00	
)7	**256**	4d. black, greenish yellow, grey, emerald-green, brt blue & bistre	10	15
		Wi. Watermark inverted........................	3.00	
		p. Three phosphor bands	10	15
		pWi. Watermark inverted........................	14.00	
)8	**257**	4d. red, greenish yellow, black, grey, bistre, reddish brown & emerald-green...	10	15
		Wi. Watermark inverted........................	3.00	
		p. Three phosphor bands	10	15
		pWi. Watermark inverted........................	14.00	
)9	**258**	4d. black, reddish brown, greenish yellow, grey & bistre**....................	10	15
		Wi. Watermark inverted........................	3.00	
		p. Three phosphor bands	10	15
		pWi. Watermark inverted........................	14.00	
		Set of 4 (Ordinary)..........................	1.00	50
		Set of 4 (Phosphor)........................	1.00	50
		First Day Cover (Ordinary)		6.50
		First Day Cover (Phosphor)		6.50
		Presentation Pack (Ordinary)...........	7.00	

Nos. 696/9 were issued together *se-tenant* in blocks of four within the sheet.

*In No. 696ab the blue, bistre and reddish brown are also omitted but in No. 696ac only the black is omitted.

**In No. 699 the black was printed over the bistre.

Other colours omitted, and the stamps affected:

d.	Greenish yellow (Nos. 696/9)	£400
e.	Red (Nos. 696 and 698)	£400
f.	Emerald-green (Nos. 696/8)	75.00
pf.	Emerald-green (Nos. 696p/8p)	75.00
g.	Brt blue (Nos. 696/7)...............................	£250
pg.	Brt blue (Nos. 696p and 697p)	£500
h.	Bistre (Nos. 696/9)	90.00
ph.	Bistre (Nos. 696p/9p)...............................	90.00
j.	Reddish brown (Nos. 698/9)	80.00
pj.	Reddish brown (Nos. 698p and 699p)	80.00

The prices quoted are for each stamp.

Special First Day of Issue Postmark

	Ordinary	Phosphor
G.P.O. Philatelic Bureau, London E.C.1 (Type C)..	9.00	9.00

STAMP MONTHLY

Finest and most informative magazine for all collectors. Obtainable from your newsagent or by postal subscription – details on request

259 Cup Winners

1966 (18 Aug). **England's World Cup Football Victory.** *Chalk-surfaced paper.* W **179** (*sideways*). *P* 14 ×15.

700	**259**	4d. red, reddish purple, brt blue, flesh & black	20	20
		First Day Cover		2.00

These stamps were only put on sale at post offices in England, the Channel Islands and the Isle of Man, and at the Philatelic Bureau in London and also, on 22 August, in Edinburgh on the occasion of the opening of the Edinburgh Festival as well as at Army post offices at home and abroad.

The Philatelic Bureau did not service first day covers for this stamp, but a First Day of Issue handstamp was provided inscribed 'Harrow & Wembley' to replace the 'Wembley, Middx.' postmark of the initial issue.

260 Jodrell Bank Radio Telescope

261 British Motor-cars

262 "SRN 6" Hovercraft

263 Windscale Reactor

(Des D. and A. Gillespie (4d., 6d.), A. Restall (others))

1966 (19 Sept). **British Technology.** *Chalk-surfaced paper.* W **179**. *P* 15 × 14.

701	**260**	4d. black & lemon...............................	15	15
		p. Three phosphor bands	15	15
702	**261**	6d. red, dp blue & orange	15	15
		a. Red (Mini-cars) omitted	£4000	
		b. Dp blue (Jaguar & inscr) omitted	£2500	
		p. Three phosphor bands	15	15
703	**262**	1s. 3d. black, orange-red, slate & lt greenish blue.................................	30	40
		p. Three phosphor bands	45	50
704	**263**	1s. 6d. black, yellow-green, bronze-green, lilac & dp blue	50	45
		p. Three phosphor bands	65	60
		Set of 4 (Ordinary)	1.00	1.00
		Set of 4 (Phosphor)	1.25	1.25
		First Day Cover (Ordinary)		3.00
		First Day Cover (Phosphor)		3.00
		Presentation Pack (Ordinary)	7.00	

Special First Day of Issue Postmark

	Ordin-ary	Phos-phor
G.P.O. Philatelic Bureau, Edinburgh 1 (Type C)	3.25	3.50

264 **265**

266 **267**

268 **269**

All the above show battle scenes and they were issued together se-tenant in horizontal strips of six within the sheet.

270 Norman Ship

271 Norman Horsemen attacking Harold's Troops

(All the above are scenes from the Bayeux Tapestry)

(Des D. Gentleman. Photo. Queen's head die-stamped (6d., 1s. 3d.))

1966 (14 Oct). **900th Anniv of Battle of Hastings.** *Chalk-surfaced paper.* W **179** (*sideways on* 1s. 3d.). P 15 × 14.

705	**264**	4d. black, olive-green, bistre, dp blue, orange, magenta, green, blue and grey	10	15
	a.	Strip of 6. Nos. 705/10	2.00	2.00
	aWi.	Strip of 6. Watermark inverted	35.00	
	Wi.	Watermark inverted	5.00	
	p.	Three phosphor bands	10	25
	pa.	Strip of 6. Nos. 705p/10p	2.00	2.00
	paWi.	Strip of 6. Watermark inverted	15.00	
	pWi.	Watermark inverted	2.00	

706	**265**	4d. black, olive-green, bistre, dp blue, orange, magenta, green, blue and grey	10	15
	Wi.	Watermark inverted	5.00	
	p.	Three phosphor bands	10	25
	pWi.	Watermark inverted	2.00	
707	**266**	4d. black, olive-green, bistre, dp blue, orange, magenta, green, blue and grey	10	15
	Wi.	Watermark inverted	5.00	
	p.	Three phosphor bands	10	25
	pWi.	Watermark inverted	2.00	
708	**267**	4d. black, olive-green, bistre, dp blue, magenta, green, blue & grey	10	15
	Wi.	Watermark inverted	5.00	
	p.	Three phosphor bands	10	25
	pWi.	Watermark inverted	2.00	
709	**268**	4d. black, olive-green, bistre, dp blue, orange, magenta, green, blue and grey	10	15
	Wi.	Watermark inverted	5.00	
	p.	Three phosphor bands	10	25
	pWi.	Watermark inverted	2.00	
710	**269**	4d. black, olive-green, bistre, dp blue, orange, magenta, green, blue & grey	10	15
	Wi.	Watermark inverted	5.00	
	p.	Three phosphor bands	10	25
	pWi.	Watermark inverted	2.00	
711	**270**	6d. black, olive-green, violet, blue, green & gold	10	10
	Wi.	Watermark inverted	35.00	
	p.	Three phosphor bands	10	10
	pWi.	Watermark inverted	45.00	
712	**271**	1s. 3d. black, lilac, bronze-green, rosine, bistre-brown & gold	20	20
	a.	Lilac omitted	£450	
	Wi.	Watermark sideways inverted (top of crown pointing to right)*	30.00	
	p.	Four phosphor bands	20	20
	pa.	Lilac omitted	£650	
	pWi.	Watermark sideways inverted (top of crown pointing to right)*	11.00	
		Set of 8 (Ordinary)	2.25	1.50
		Set of 8 (Phosphor)	2.25	1.90
		First Day Cover (Ordinary)		3.00
		First Day Cover (Phosphor)		3.00
		Presentation Pack (Ordinary)	7.00	

*The normal sideways watermark shows the tops of the Crowns pointing to the left, *as seen from the back of the stamp.*

Other colours omitted in the 4d. values and the stamps affected:

b.	Olive-green (Nos. 705/10)	25.00
pb.	Olive-green (Nos. 705p/10p)	25.00
c.	Bistre (Nos. 705/10)	25.00
pc.	Bistre (Nos. 705p/10p)	30.00
d.	Dp blue (Nos. 705/40)	35.00
pd.	Dp blue (Nos. 705p/10p)	35.00
e.	Orange (Nos. 705/7 and 709/10)	25.00
pe.	Orange (Nos. 705p/7p and 709p/10p)	20.00
f.	Magenta (Nos. 705/10)	30.00
pf.	Magenta (Nos. 705p/10p)	30.00
g.	Green (Nos. 705/10)	25.00
pg.	Green (Nos. 705p/10p)	25.00
h.	Blue (Nos. 705/10)	20.00
ph.	Blue (Nos. 705p/10p)	35.00
j.	Grey (Nos. 705/10)	20.00
pj.	Grey (Nos. 705p/10p)	20.00
pk.	Magenta and green (Nos. 705p/10p)	

The prices quoted are for each stamp.

Nos. 705 and 709, with grey and blue omitted, have been seen commercially used, posted from Middleton-in-Teesdale.

The 6d. phosphor is known in a yellowish gold as well as the reddish gold as used in the 1s. 3d.

Three examples of No. 712 in a right-hand top corner block of 10 (2 × 5) are known with the Queen's head omitted as a result of a double paper fold prior to die-stamping. The perforation is normal. Of the other seven stamps, four have the Queen's head misplaced and three are normal.

MISSING GOLD HEADS. The 6d. and 1s. 3d. were also issued with the die-stamped gold head omitted but as these can also be removed by chemical means we are not prepared to list them unless a way is found of distinguishing the genuine stamps from the fakes which will satisfy the Expert Committees.

The same remarks apply to Nos. 713/14.

Special First Day of Issue Postmark

	Ordinary	Phosphor
G.P.O. Philatelic Bureau, Edinburgh 1 (Type C)	5.00	5.50

A First Day of Issue handstamp was provided at Battle, Sussex, for this issue.

272 King of the Orient   **273** Snowman

(Des Tasveer Shemza (3d.), J. Berry (1s. 6d.) (winners of children's design competition). Photo, Queen's head die-stamped)

1966 (1 Dec). **Christmas.** *Chalk-surfaced paper.* W **179** (*sideways on 3d.*). P 14 × 15.

713	272	3d. black, blue, green, yellow, red & gold	10	10
		a. Queen's head double		
		b. Green omitted	—	£150
		p. One phosphor band at right	10	10
		pEa. Band at left	10	10
714	273	1s. 6d. blue, red, pink, black & gold	35	35
		a. Pink (hat) omitted	£750	
		Wi. Watermark inverted	9.00	
		p. Two phosphor bands	35	35
		pWi. Watermark inverted	38.00	
		Set of 2 (Ordinary)	45	45
		Set of 2 (Phosphor)	45	45
		First Day Cover (Ordinary)		1.50
		First Day Cover (Phosphor)		1.50
		Presentation Pack (Ordinary)	7.00	

Special First Day of Issue Postmarks

	Ordinary	Phosphor
G.P.O. Philatelic Bureau, Edinburgh 1 (Type C)	1.50	1.50
Bethlehem, Llandeilo, Carms (Type C)	1.50	1.50

274 Sea Freight   **275** Air Freight

(Des C. Abbot)

1967 (20 Feb). **European Free Trade Association (EFTA).** *Chalk-surfaced paper.* W **179**. P 15 × 14.

715	274	9d. dp blue, red, lilac, green, brown, new blue, yellow & black	15	15
		a. Black (Queen's head, etc.), brown, new blue & yellow omitted	£650	
		b. Lilac omitted	60.00	
		c. Green omitted	40.00	
		d. Brown omitted	45.00	
		e. New blue omitted	42.00	
		f. Yellow omitted	42.00	
		Wi. Watermark inverted	20.00	
		p. Three phosphor bands	15	15
		pb. Lilac omitted	75.00	
		pc. Green omitted	45.00	
		pd. Brown omitted	45.00	
		pe. New blue omitted	45.00	
		pf. Yellow omitted	75.00	
		pWi. Watermark inverted	10.00	
716	275	1s. 6d. violet, red, dp blue, brown, green, blue-grey, new blue, yellow & black	30	30
		a. Red omitted		
		b. Dp blue omitted	£225	
		c. Brown omitted	45.00	
		d. Blue-grey omitted	45.00	
		e. New blue omitted	45.00	
		f. Yellow omitted	45.00	
		p. Three phosphor bands	30	30
		pa. Red omitted		
		pb. Dp blue omitted	£200	
		pc. Brown omitted	45.00	
		pd. Blue-grey omitted	45.00	
		pf. New blue omitted	45.00	
		pWi. Watermark inverted	22.00	
		Set of 2 (Ordinary)	40	40
		Set of 2 (Phosphor)	40	40
		First Day Cover (Ordinary)		1.50
		First Day Cover (Phosphor)		1.50
		Presentation Pack (Ordinary)	1.50	

Special First Day of Issue Postmark

	Ordinary	Phosphor
G.P.O. Philatelic Bureau, Edinburgh 1 (Type C)	1.75	1.75

276 Hawthorn and Bramble   **277** Larger Bindweed and Viper's Bugloss

278 Ox-eye Daisy, Coltsfoot and Buttercup

279 Bluebell, Red Campion and Wood Anemone

T **276/9** were issued together *se*-tenant in blocks of four within the sheet.

280 Dog Violet

281 Primroses

(Des Rev. W. Keble Martin (T **276/9**), Mary Grierson (others))

1967 (24 Apr). **British Wild Flowers.** *Chalk-surfaced paper.* W **179**. P 15 × 14.

717	**276**	4d.	grey, lemon, myrtle-green, red, agate & slate-purple	15	10
		a.	Block of 4. Nos. 717/20	1.25	1.25
		aWi.	Block of 4. Watermark inverted	7.50	
		b.	Grey double*		
		c.	Red omitted	£1500	
		f.	Slate-purple omitted		
		Wi.	Watermark inverted	1.50	
		p.	Three phosphor bands	10	10
		pa.	Block of 4. Nos. 717p/20p	1.00	1.00
		paWi.	Block of 4. Watermark inverted	7.50	
		pd.	Agate omitted	£900	
		pf.	Slate-purple omitted	£150	
		pWi.	Watermark inverted	1.50	
718	**277**	4d.	grey, lemon, myrtle-green, red, agate & violet	15	10
		b.	Grey double*		
		Wi.	Watermark inverted	1.50	
		p.	Three phosphor bands	10	10
		pd.	Agate omitted	£450	
		pe.	Violet omitted	£1250	
		pWi.	Watermark inverted	1.50	
719	**278**	4d.	grey, lemon, myrtle-green, red & agate	15	10
		b.	Grey double*		
		Wi.	Watermark inverted	1.50	
		p.	Three phosphor bands	10	10
		pd.	Agate omitted	£450	
		pWi.	Watermark inverted	1.50	
720	**279**	4d.	grey, lemon, myrtle-green, reddish purple, agate & violet	15	10
		b.	Grey double*		
		c.	Reddish purple omitted	£950	
		Wi.	Watermark inverted	1.50	
		p.	Three phosphor bands	10	10
		pd.	Agate omitted	£450	
		pe.	Violet omitted	£1250	
		pWi.	Watermark inverted	1.50	
721	**280**	9d.	lavender-grey, green, reddish violet & orange-yellow	15	10
		Wi.	Watermark inverted	75	
		p.	Three phosphor bands	10	10

722	**281**	1s. 9d.	lavender-grey, green, greenish yellow & orange	20	20
		p.	Three phosphor bands	30	20
			Set of 6 (Ordinary)	1.40	65
			Set of 6 (Phosphor)	1.25	65
			First Day Cover (Ordinary)		2.50
			First Day Cover (Phosphor)		2.50
			Presentation Pack (Ordinary)	3.00	
			Presentation Pack (Phosphor)	3.00	

*The double impression of the grey printing affects the Queen's head, value and inscription.

Special First Day of Issue Postmark

	Ordin-ary	Phos-phor
G.P.O. Philatelic Bureau, Edinburgh 1 (Type C)	2.75	3.00

PHOSPHOR BANDS. Issues from No. 723 are normally with phosphor bands only, except for the high values but most stamps have appeared with the phosphor bands omitted in error. Such varieties are listed under "Ey" numbers and are priced unused only. See also further notes after 1971–92 Decimal Machin issue.

PHOSPHORISED PAPER. Following the adoption of phosphor bands the Post Office started a series of experiments involving the addition of the phosphor to the paper coating before the stamps were printed No. 743c. was the first of these experiments to be issued for normal postal use. See also notes after 1971–92 Decimal Machin issue.

PVA GUM. Polyvinyl alcohol was introduced by Harrisons in place of gum arabic in 1968. It is almost invisible except that a small amount of pale yellowish colouring matter was introduced to make it possible to see that the stamps had been gummed. Although this can be distinguished from gum arabic in unused stamps there is, of course, no means of detecting it in used examples. Where the two forms of gum exist on the same stamp, the PVA type are listed under "Ev" numbers, except in the case of the 1d. and 4d. (vermilion), both one centre band, which later appeared with gum arabic and these have "Eg" numbers. "Ev" and "Eg" numbers are priced unused only. All stamps printed from No. 763 onwards were issued with PVA gum only *except where otherwise stated.*

It should be further noted that gum arabic is shiny in appearance, and that, normally, PVA gum has a matt appearance. However, depending upon the qualities of the paper ingredients and the resultant absorption of the gum, occasionally, PVA gum has a shiny appearance. In such cases, especially in stamps from booklets, it is sometimes impossible to be absolutely sure which gum has been used except by testing the stamps chemically which destroys them. Therefore, whilst all gum arabic is shiny it does not follow that all shiny gum is gum arabic.

282   **282a**

I   II

Two types of the 2d.

I. Value spaced away from left side of stamp (cylinders 1 no dot and dot).

II. Value close to left side from new multipositive used for cylinders 5 no dot and dot onwards. The portrait appears in the centre, thus conforming to the other values.

Three types of the Machin head, known as Head A, B or C, are distinguished by specialists. These are illustrated in Vol. 3 of the *Great Britain Specialised Catalogue.*

(Des after plaster cast by Arnold Machin)

1967 (5 June)–**70.** *Chalk-surfaced paper. Two phosphor bands except where otherwise stated. No wmk. PVA gum except Nos. 725m, 728, 729, 731, 731Ea, 740, 742/Ea, 743/a and 744/Ea.*

723	**282**	½d. orange-brown (5.2.68)	10	20
		Ey. Phosphor omitted..........................	30.00	
724		1d. lt olive (*shades*) (2 bands) (5.2.68)	10	10
		a. Imperf (coil strip)†.........................	£750	
		b. Part perf pane*.............................		
		c. Imperf pane*...............................	£3750	
		d. Uncoated paper (1970)**.................	65.00	
		Ey. Phosphor omitted..........................	1.00	
		l. Booklet pane. No. 724 × 2 *se-tenant* with 730 × 2 (6.4.68)	2.75	
		lEy. Booklet pane. Phosphor omitted........	75.00	
		m. Booklet pane. No. 724 × 4 *se-tenant* with 734 × 2 (6.1.69)	3.25	
		mEy. Booklet pane. Phosphor omitted......	£100	
		n. Booklet pane. No. 724 × 6, 734 × 3, 734Eb × 3 & 735 × 3 *se-tenant* (1.12.69)	8.50	
		na. Booklet pane. Uncoated paper**......	£900	
		nEy. Booklet pane. Phosphor omitted	£150	
725		1d. yellowish olive (1 centre band) (16.9.68)	25	30
		Eg. Gum arabic (27.8.69)	25	
		l. Booklet pane. No. 725 × 4 *se-tenant* with 732 × 2	3.75	
		lEy. Booklet pane. Phosphor omitted......	30.00	
		m. Coil strip. No. 728 × 2 *se-tenant* with 729, 725Eg & 733Eg (27.8.69)	1.25	
726		2d. lake-brown (Type I) (2 bands) (5.2.68)	10	15
		Ey. Phosphor omitted..........................	25.00	
727		2d. lake-brown (Type II) (2 bands) (1969)	15	15
		Ey. Phosphor omitted..........................	1.00	
728		2d. lake-brown (Type II) (1 centre band) (27.8.69).....................................	40	50
729		3d. violet (*shades*) (1 centre band) (8.8.67)	10	10
		a. Imperf (pair)	£475	
		Ey. Phosphor omitted..........................	1.25	
		Ev. PVA gum (*shades*) (12.3.68)..............	10	
		Evy. Phosphor omitted..........................	1.25	
730		3d. violet (2 bands) (6.4.68)	30	30
		a. Uncoated paper**.........................	£900	
731		4d. dp sepia (*shades*) (2 bands)	10	10
		Ey. Phosphor omitted..........................	1.00	
		Ea. *Dp olive-brown*	10	15
		Eay. Phosphor omitted..........................	1.25	
		b. Part perf pane*.............................	£550	
		Ev. PVA gum (*shades*) (22.1.68)..............	10	
		Evy. Phosphor omitted..........................	1.00	
732		4d. dp olive-brown (*shades*) (1 centre band) (16.9.68)	10	10
		a. Part perf pane*.............................	£450	
		l. Booklet pane. Two stamps plus two printed labels..............................	75	
		lEy. Booklet pane. Phosphor omitted......	45.00	
733		4d. brt vermilion (1 centre band) (6.1.69)	10	10
		a. *Tête-bêche* (horiz pair)	£2500	
		b. Uncoated paper**.........................	6.00	
		Ey. Phosphor omitted..........................	1.25	
		Eg. Gum arabic (27.8.69)	10	
		Egy. Phosphor omitted..........................	£600	
		l. Booklet pane. Two stamps plus two printed labels (3.3.69)	80	
		lEy. Booklet pane. Phosphor omitted......	70.00	
734		4d. brt vermilion (1 band at left) (6.1.69) .	1.40	1.60
		a. Uncoated paper**.........................	£150	
		Eb. One band at right (1.12.69)	2.00	3.00
		Eba. Ditto. Uncoated paper**................	£150	

735	**282**	5d. royal blue (*shades*) (1.7.68)..............	10	10
		a. Imperf pane*...............................	£450	
		b. Part perf pane*.............................	£400	
		c. Imperf (pair)††	£100	
		d. Uncoated paper**.........................	13.00	
		Ey. Phosphor omitted..........................	1.25	
		Ee. *Dp blue*	10	15
		Eey. Phosphor omitted..........................	2.00	
736		6d. brt reddish purple (*shades*) (5.2.68) ..	20	20
		Ey. Phosphor omitted..........................	4.50	
		Ea. *Brt magenta*	2.00	50
		Eb. *Claret*	50	40
		Eby. Phosphor omitted..........................	10.00	
737	**282a**	7d. brt emerald (1.7.68).......................	40	30
		Ey. Phosphor omitted..........................	45.00	
738		8d. brt vermilion (1.7.68).....................	15	30
		Ey. Phosphor omitted..........................	£400	
739		8d. lt turquoise-blue (6.1.69).................	45	50
		Ey. Phosphor omitted..........................	50.00	
740		9d. myrtle-green (8.8.67)	50	30
		Ey. Phosphor omitted..........................	16.00	
		Ev. PVA gum (29.11.68)	50	
		Evy. Phosphor omitted..........................	18.00	
741	**282**	10d. drab (1.7.68)	45	50
		a. Uncoated paper**.........................	23.00	
		Ey. Phosphor omitted..........................	40.00	
742		1s. lt bluish violet (*shades*)..................	40	30
		Ey. Phosphor omitted..........................	60.00	
		Ea. *Pale bluish violet*	60	30
		Ev. Ditto. PVA gum (26.4.68)	50	
		Evy. Phosphor omitted..........................	3.50	
743		1s. 6d. greenish blue and deep blue (*shades*) (8.8.67)	50	30
		a. Greenish blue omitted	£100	
		Ey. Phosphor omitted	6.00	
		Ev. PVA gum. (28.8.68)	60	
		Eva. Greenish blue omitted	80.00	
		Evy. Phosphor omitted..........................	14.00	
		Evb. *Prussian blue & indigo*	1.50	75
		Evby. Phosphor omitted..........................	11.00	
		c. Phosphorised paper (Prussian blue & indigo) (10.12.69)	75	90
		ca. Prussian blue omitted	£225	
744		1s. 9d. dull orange & black (*shades*)	40	30
		Ey. Phosphor omitted..........................	25.00	
		Ea. *Brt orange & black*	1.50	50
		Ev. PVA gum (*brt orange & black*) (16.11.70)	40	
		Set of 16 (one of each value & colour)	3.00	3.25
		Presentation Pack (one of each value)	6.00	
		Presentation Pack (German)...........	45.00	

*BOOKLET ERRORS. See note after No. 556.

**Uncoated paper. This does not respond to the chalky test, and may be further distinguished from the normal chalk-surfaced paper by the fibres which clearly show on the surface, resulting in the printing impression being rougher, and by the screening dots which are not so evident. The 1d., 4d. and 5d. come from the £1 "Stamps for Cooks" Booklet (1970); the 3d. and 10d. from sheets (1969). The 20p. and 50p. high values (Nos. 830/1) exist with similar errors.

†No. 724a occurs in a vertical strip of four, top stamp perforated on three sides, bottom stamp imperf three sides and the two middle stamps completely imperf.

††No. 735c comes from the original state of cylinder 15 which is identifiable by the screening dots which extend through the gutters of the stamps and into the margins of the sheet. This must not be confused with imperforate stamps from cylinder 10, a large quantity of which was stolen from the printers early in 1970.

The 1d. with centre band and PVA gum (725) only came in the September 1968 10s. booklet (No. XP6). The 1d., 2d. and 4d. with centre band and gum arabic (725Eg, 728 and 733Eg respectively) only came in the coil strip (725m). The 3d. (No. 730) appeared in booklets on 6.4.68, from coils during Dec 68 and from sheets in Jan 1969. The 4d. with one side band at left (734) came from 10s. and £1 booklet se-tenant panes, and the 4d. with one side band at right (734Eb) came from the £1 booklet se-tenant panes only.

The 4d. (731) in shades of washed-out grey are colour changelings which we understand are caused by the concentrated solvents used in modern dry cleaning methods.

For decimal issue, see Nos. X841, etc

First Day Covers

5.6.67	4d., 1s., 1s. 9d. (731, 742, 744)	1.40
8.8.67	3d., 9d., 1s. 6d. (729, 740, 743)	1.40
5.2.68	½d., 1d., 2d., 6d. (723/4, 726, 736)	75
1.7.68	5d., 7d., 8d., 10d. (735, 737/8, 741)	1.10

283 "Master Lambton" (Sir Thomas Lawrence)   **284** "Mares and Foals in a Landscape" (George Stubbs)

285 "Children Coming Out of School" (L. S. Lowry)

(Des S. Rose)

1967 (10 July).   **British Paintings.** Chalk-surfaced paper. Two phosphor bands. No wmk. P 14×15 (4d.) or 15×14 (others).

748	**283**	4d. rose-red, lemon, brown, black, new blue & gold	10	10
		a. Gold (value & Queen's head) omitted	£180	
		b. New blue omitted	£2500	
		Ey. Phosphor omitted	5.00	
749	**284**	9d. Venetian red, ochre, grey-black, new blue, greenish yellow & black	20	20
		a. Black (Queen's head) omitted	£400	
		b. Greenish yellow omitted	£1200	
		Ey. Phosphor omitted	£450	
750	**285**	1s. 6d. greenish yellow, grey, rose, new blue, grey-black & gold	35	25
		a. Gold (Queen's head) omitted	£750	
		b. New blue omitted	£140	
		c. Grey omitted	85.00	
		Ey. Phosphor omitted	£300	
		Set of 3	50	50
		First Day Cover		1.50
		Presentation Pack	5.50	

Special First Day of Issue Postmark
G.P.O. Philatelic Bureau, Edinburgh 1 (Type C) 1.75
A First Day of Issue handstamp was provided at Bishop Auckland, Co. Durham, for this issue.

286 Gypsy Moth IV

(Des M. and Sylvia Goaman)

1967 (24 July).   **Sir Francis Chichester's World Voyage.** Chalk-surfaced paper. Three phosphor bands. No wmk. P 15 × 14.

751	**286**	1s. 9d. black, brown-red, lt emerald & blue	25	25
		First Day Cover		1.00

Special First Day of Issue Postmarks

G.P.O. Philatelic Bureau, Edinburgh 1	1.25
Greenwich, London SE10	2.00
Plymouth, Devon	2.00

The Philatelic Bureau and Greenwich postmarks are similar in design to that for Plymouth. A First Day of Issue handstamp was provided at Chichester, Sussex for this issue.

287 Radar Screen   **288** Penicillium notatum

289 "VC-10" Jet Engines   **290** Television Equipment

(Des C. Abbott (4d., 1s.), Negus-Sharland team (others))

1967 (19 Sept).   **British Discovery and Invention.** Chalk-surfaced paper. Three phosphor bands (4d.) or two phosphor bands (others). W **179** (sideways on 1s. 9d.). P 14 × 15 (1s. 9d.) or 15 × 14 (others).

752	**287**	4d. greenish yellow, black & vermilion	10	10
		Ey. Phosphor omitted	1.25	

753	**288**	1s. blue-green, lt greenish blue, slate-purple & bluish violet.....................	10	10
		Wi. Watermark inverted	10.00	
		Ey. Phosphor omitted.........................	7.00	
754	**289**	1s. 6d. black, grey, royal blue, ochre & turquoise-blue	25	15
		Wi. Watermark inverted	30.00	
		Ey. Phosphor omitted.........................	£500	
755	**290**	1s. 9d. black, grey-blue, pale olive-grey, violet & orange	30	20
		a. Grey-blue omitted	£500	
		Ey. Phosphor omitted.........................	£500	
		Set of 4	60	50
		First Day Cover		1.00
		Presentation Pack	2.00	

Special First Day of Issue Postmark
G.P.O. Philatelic Bureau, Edinburgh (Type C) 1.75

WATERMARK. All issues from this date are on unwatermarked paper.

291 "The Adoration of the Shepherds" (School of Seville)

292 "Madonna and Child" (Murillo)

293 "The Adoration of the Shepherds" (Louis le Nain)

(Des S. Rose)

1967. Christmas. *Chalk-surfaced paper. One phosphor band (3d.) or two phosphor bands (others). P 15×14 (1s. 6d.) or 14×15 (others).*

756	**291**	3d. olive-yellow, rose, blue, black & gold (27.11)	10	10
		a. Gold (value & Queen's head) omitted	60.00	
		b. Printed on the gummed side	£300	
		c. Rose omitted		
		Ey. Phosphor omitted......................,.......	50	
757	**292**	4d. brt purple, greenish yellow, new blue, grey-black & gold (18.10)	10	10
		a. Gold (value & Queen's head) omitted	60.00	
		b. Greenish yellow (Child, robe & Madonna's face) omitted		
		Ey. Phosphor omitted.........................	£100	
758	**293**	1s. 6d. brt purple, bistre, lemon, black, orange-red, ultramarine & gold (27.11)	35	35
		a. Gold (value & Queen's head) omitted	£2000	
		b. Ultramarine omitted	£300	
		Ey. Phosphor omitted.........................	10.00	
		Set of 3	50	50
		First Day Covers (2)		1.00

Distinct shades exist of the 4d. value but are not listable as there are intermediate shades. Stamps emanating from one machine show a darker background and give the appearance of the yellow colour being omitted but this is not so and these should not be confused with the true missing yellow No. 757b.

Special First Day of Issue Postmarks

G.P.O. Philatelic Bureau, Edinburgh, Edinburgh 1 (4d.) (18 Oct.) (Type C)	75
G.P.O. Philatelic Bureau, Edinburgh 1 (3d., 1s. 6d.) (27 Nov.) (Type C)...	75
Bethlehem, Llandeilo, Carms (4d.) (18 Oct.) (Type C)	1.25
Bethlehem, Llandeilo, Carms (3d., 1s. 6d.) (27 Nov.) (Type C)	1.25

Gift Pack 1967

1967 (27 Nov). *Comprises Nos. 715p/22p and 748/58.*
GP758c Gift Pack... 2.50

(Recess Bradbury, Wilkinson)

1967–68. *No wmk. White paper. P 11 × 12.*

759	**166**	2s. 6d. black-brown (1.7.68)	40	50
760	**167**	5s. red (10.4.68)................................	1.00	1.00
761	**168**	10s. brt ultramarine (10.4.68)	5.00	5.50
762	**169**	£1 black (4.12.67)	4.00	4.00
		Set of 4	9.00	10.00

PVA GUM. All the following issues from this date have PVA gum *except where footnotes state otherwise.*

294 Tarr Steps, Exmoor

295 Aberfeldy Bridge

296 Menai Bridge

297 M4 Viaduct

(Des A. Restall (9d.), L. Rosoman (1s. 6d.), J. Matthews (others))

1968 (29 Apr). **British Bridges.** *Chalk-surfaced paper. Two phosphor bands. P 15 × 14.*

763	**294**	4d. black, bluish violet, turquoise-blue & gold	10	10
		a. Printed on gummed side.................	25.00	
		Ey. Phosphor omitted.........................	1.25	
764	**295**	9d. red-brown, myrtle-green, ultramarine, olive-brown, black & gold........	10	10
		a. Gold (Queen's head) omitted..........	£100	
		b. Ultramarine omitted	†	£3000
		Ey. Phosphor omitted.........................	13.00	
765	**296**	1s. 6d. olive-brown, red-orange, brt green, turquoise-green & gold........	20	15
		a. Gold (Queen's head) omitted	£100	
		b. Red-orange omitted	£150	
		Ey. Phosphor omitted........................	40.00	

766	**297**	1s. 9d. olive-brown, greenish yellow, dull green, dp ultramarine & gold	25	30
		a. Gold (Queen's head) omitted..........	£150	
		Ey. Phosphor omitted.........................	7.00	
		Eya. Gold (Queen's head) & phosphor omitted	£300	
		Set of 4	60	60
		First Day Cover		1.10
		Presentation Pack..........................	2.00	

No. 764b is only known on first day covers posted from Canterbury, Kent, or the Philatelic Bureau, Edinburgh.

Special First Day of Issue Postmarks

G.P.O. Philatelic Bureau, Edinburgh 1.................	3.50
Bridge, Canterbury, Kent..................................	3.50
Aberfeldy, Perthshire (Type A) (9d. value only).....	27.00
Menai Bridge, Anglesey (Type A) (1s. 6d. value only)	27.00

The Bridge, Canterbury, postmark is similar in design to that for the Philatelic Bureau.

769	**300**	1s. olive-brown, blue, red, slate-blue & black	20	20
		Ey. Phosphor omitted.........................	8.00	
770	**301**	1s. 9d. yellow-ochre & blackish brown...	25	25
		Ey. Phosphor omitted.........................	£140	
		Set of 4	60	60
		First Day Cover		3.25
		Presentation Pack..........................	3.00	

Special First Day of Issue Postmarks

G.P.O. Philatelic Bureau, Edinburgh 1 (Type C)	3.50
Manchester	45.00
Aldeburgh, Suffolk	45.00
Hendon, London NW4	45.00
Whitby, Yorkshire..	45.00

298 "TUC" and Trades Unionists

299 Mrs. Emmeline Pankhurst (statue)

300 Sopwith "Camel" and "Lightning" Fighters

301 Captain Cook's *Endeavour* and Signature

(Des D. Gentleman (4d.), C. Abbott (others))

1968 (29 May). **British Anniversaries.** *Events described on stamps. Chalk-surfaced paper. Two phosphor bands. P 15 × 14.*

767	**298**	4d. emerald, olive, blue & black............	10	10
		Ey. Phosphor omitted	10.00	
768	**299**	9d. reddish violet, bluish grey & black ...	10	10
		Ey. Phosphor omitted.........................	5.50	

302 "Queen Elizabeth I" (unknown artist)

303 "Pinkie" (Lawrence)

304 "Ruins of St. Mary Le Port" (Piper)

305 "The Hay Wain" (Constable)

(Des S. Rose)

1968 (12 Aug). **British Paintings.** *Queen's head embossed. Chalk-surfaced paper. Two phosphor bands. P 15×14 (1s. 9d.) or 14×15 (others).*

771	**302**	4d. black, vermilion, greenish yellow, grey & gold..................................	10	10
		a. Gold (value & Queen's head) omitted	£100	
		b. Vermilion omitted*.........................	£200	
		Ec. Embossing omitted	80.00	
		Ey. Phosphor omitted..........................	1.00	
		Eya. Gold (value & Queen's head) & phosphor omitted	£180	
772	**303**	1s. mauve, new blue, greenish yellow, black, magenta & gold.................	15	15
		a. Gold (value & Queen's head) omitted	£180	
		Eb. Gold (value & Queen's head), embossing & phosphor omitted	£200	
		Ec. Embossing omitted		
		Ey. Phosphor omitted..........................	6.00	
773	**304**	1s. 6d. slate, orange, black, mauve, greenish yellow, ultramarine & gold .	20	20
		a. Gold (value & Queen's head) omitted	£100	
		Eb. Embossing omitted		
		Ey. Phosphor omitted..........................	6.00	
774	**305**	1s. 9d. greenish yellow, black, new blue, red & gold..................................	25	25
		a. Gold (value & Queen's head) & embossing omitted	£450	
		b. Red omitted..................................		
		Ec. Embossing omitted.........................		
		Ey. Phosphor omitted..........................	17.00	
		Set of 4	60	60
		First Day Cover		1.00
		Presentation Pack..........................	2.00	
		Presentation Pack (German).............	6.00	

No. 774a is only known with the phosphor also omitted.
*The effect of this is to leave the face and hands white and there is more yellow and olive in the costume.
The 4d. also exists with the value only omitted resulting from a colour shift.

Special First Day of Issue Postmark
G.P.O. Philatelic Bureau, Edinburgh 1 (Type C) 2.00

Gift Pack 1968

1968 (16 Sept). *Comprises Nos. 763/74.*
GP774c Gift Pack 6.00
GP774d Gift Pack (German) 24.00

Collectors Pack 1968

1968 (16 Sept). *Comprises Nos. 752/8 and 763/74.*
CP774e Collectors Pack 6.00

306 Boy and Girl with Rocking Horse

307 Girl with Doll's House   **308** Boy with Train Set
(Des Rosalind Dease. Head printed in gold and then embossed)

1968 (25 Nov). **Christmas.** *Chalk-surfaced paper. One centre phosphor band (4d.) or two phosphor bands (others). P 15 × 14 (4d.) or 14 × 15 (others).*

775	**306**	4d. black, orange, vermilion, ultramarine, bistre & gold..........................	10	10
		a. Gold omitted	£1500	
		b. Vermilion omitted*.........................	£140	
		c. Ultramarine omitted	£150	
		Ed. Embossing omitted	5.00	
		Ey. Phosphor omitted..........................	1.25	
776	**307**	9d. yellow-olive, black, brown, yellow, magenta, orange, turquoise-green & gold	15	15
		a. Yellow omitted.............................	60.00	
		Eb. Embossing omitted	5.00	
		Ey. Phosphor omitted..........................	8.00	
		Eya. Embossing & phosphor omitted	7.50	
777	**308**	1s. 6d. ultramarine, yellow-orange, brt purple, blue-green, black & gold	25	25
		Ea. Embossing omitted		
		Ey. Phosphor omitted..........................	13.00	
		Set of 3	50	50
		First Day Cover		1.00
		Presentation Pack..........................	2.00	
		Presentation Pack (German).............	5.00	

*The effect of the missing vermilion is shown on the rocking horse, saddle and faces which appear orange instead of red.
A single used example of the 4d. exists with the bistre omitted.
No. 775c is only known with phosphor also omitted.
Two machines were used for printing the 4d. value:
Stamps from cylinders 1A–1B–2C–1D–1E in combination with 1F, 2F or 3F (gold) were printed entirely on the Rembrandt sheet-fed machine. They invariably have the Queen's head level with the top of the boy's head and the sheets are perforated through the left side margin.
Stamps from cylinders 2A–2B–3C–2D–2E in combination with 1F, 2F, 3F or 4F (gold) were printed on the reel-fed Thrissell machine in five colours (its maximum colour capacity) and subsequently sheet-fed on the Rembrandt machine for the gold Queen's head and the embossing. The position of the Queen's head is generally lower than on the stamps printed at one operation but it varies in different parts of the sheet and is not, therefore, a sure indication for identifying single stamps. Another small difference is that the boy's grey pullover is noticeably "moth-eaten" in the Thrissell printings and is normal on the Rembrandt. The Thrissell printings are perforated through the top margin.

Special First Day of Issue Postmarks
G.P.O. Philatelic Bureau, Edinburgh 1 (Type C) 1.25
Bethlehem, Llandeilo, Carms (Type C) 3.50

309 R.M.S. *Queen Elizabeth 2*

310 Elizabethan Galleon

311 East Indiaman

312 *Cutty Sark*

313 S.S. *Great Britain*

314 R.M.S. *Mauretania I*

(Des D. Gentleman)

1969 (15 Jan). **British Ships.** *Chalk-surfaced paper. Two vertical phosphor bands at right* (1s.), *one horizontal phosphor band* (5d.) *or two phosphor bands* (9d.). P 15 × 14.

778	**309**	5d. black, grey, red & turquoise		10	10
		a. Black (Queen's head, value, hull & inscr) omitted		£600	
		b. Grey (decks, etc.) omitted		90.00	
		c. Red omitted		50.00	
		Ey. Phosphor omitted		1.50	
		Eya. Red & phosphor omitted		80.00	
779	**310**	9d. red, blue, ochre, brown, black & grey		10	15
		a. Strip of 3. Nos. 779/81		1.00	1.00
		ab. Red & blue omitted		£900	
		ac. Blue omitted		£1000	
		Ey. Phosphor omitted		10.00	
		Eya. Strip of 3. Nos. 779/81 phosphor omitted		35.00	
780	**311**	9d. ochre, brown, black & grey		10	15
		Ey. Phosphor omitted		10.00	
781	**312**	9d. ochre, brown, black & grey		10	15
		Ey. Phosphor omitted		10.00	
782	**313**	1s. brown, black, grey, green & greenish yellow		25	25
		a. Pair. Nos. 782/3		90	85
		ab. Greenish yellow omitted		£2000	
		Ey. Phosphor omitted		25.00	
		Eya. Pair. Nos. 782/3. Phosphor omitted		60.00	
783	**314**	1s. red, black, brown, carmine & grey		25	25
		a. Carmine (hull overlay) omitted		£7500	
		Ey. Phosphor omitted		25.00	
		Set of 6		1.75	90
		First Day Cover			3.25
		Presentation Pack		3.00	
		Presentation Pack (German)		22.00	

The 9d. and 1s. values were arranged in horizontal strips of three and pairs respectively throughout the sheet.

No. 779ab is known only with the phosphor also omitted.

Special First Day of Issue Postmark
G.P.O. Philatelic Bureau, Edinburgh 1 (Type C) 5.00

315 "Concorde" in Flight

316 Plan and Elevation Views

317 "Concorde's" Nose and Tail

(Des M. and Sylvia Goaman (4d.), D. Gentleman (9d., 1s. 6d.))

1969 (3 Mar). **First Flight of "Concorde".** *Chalk-surfaced paper. Two phosphor bands.* P 15 × 14.

784	**315**	4d. yellow-orange, violet, greenish blue, blue-green & pale-green		10	10
		a. Violet (value, etc.) omitted		£200	
		b. Yellow-orange omitted		90.00	
		Ey. Phosphor omitted		75	
		Eya. Yellow-orange & phosphor omitted		£100	
785	**316**	9d. ultramarine, emerald, red & grey-blue		20	20
		Ey. Phosphor omitted		£100	
786	**317**	1s. 6d. deep blue, silver-grey & lt blue		30	30
		a. Silver-grey omitted		£275	
		Ey. Phosphor omitted		7.00	
		Set of 3		50	50
		First Day Cover			1.25
		Presentation Pack		2.50	
		Presentation Pack (German)		18.00	

No. 786a affects the Queen's head which appears in the light blue colour.

Special First Day of Issue Postmarks
G.P.O. Philatelic Bureau, Edinburgh (Type C) 1.50
Filton, Bristol (Type C) 2.50

318 Queen Elizabeth II. (See also Type **357**)

(Des after plaster cast by Arnold Machin. Recess Bradbury, Wilkinson)

1969 (5 Mar). P 12.
787	**318**	2s. 6d. brown	50	30
788		5s. crimson-lake	2.25	60
789		10s. dp ultramarine	7.00	7.50
790		£1 bluish black	3.00	1.60
		Set of 4	11.50	9.00
		First Day Cover		15.00
		Presentation Pack	18.00	
		Presentation Pack (German)	45.00	

Special First Day of Issue Postmarks

G.P.O. Philatelic Bureau (Type C)	15.00
Windsor, Berks (Type C)	30.00

For decimal issue, see Nos. 829/31b and notes after No. 831b.

319 Page from *Daily Mail*, and Vickers "Vimy" Aircraft

320 Europa and CEPT Emblems

321 ILO Emblem

322 Flags of NATO Countries

323 Vickers "Vimy" Aircraft and Globe showing Flight

(Des P. Sharland (5d., 1s., 1s. 6d.), M. and Sylvia Goaman (9d., 1s. 9d.))

1969 (2 Apr). **Anniversaries.** *Events described on stamps. Chalk-surfaced paper. Two phosphor bands.* P 15 × 14.

791	**319**	5d. black, pale sage-green, chestnut & new blue	10	10
		Ey. Phosphor omitted		
792	**320**	9d. pale turquoise, dp blue, lt emerald-green & black	20	20
		Ey. Phosphor omitted	16.00	
793	**321**	1s. brt purple, dp blue & lilac	20	20
		Ey. Phosphor omitted	5.00	
794	**322**	1s. 6d. red, royal blue, yellow-green, black, lemon & new blue	20	20
		e. Black omitted	60.00	
		f. Yellow-green omitted	48.00	
		Ey. Phosphor omitted	7.00	
		Eya. Yellow-green & phosphor omitted	55.00	

795	**323**	1s. 9d. yellow-olive, greenish yellow & pale turquoise-green	25	25
		a. Uncoated paper*	£200	
		Ey. Phosphor omitted	4.00	
		Set of 5	85	85
		First Day Cover		1.50
		Presentation Pack	2.50	
		Presentation Pack (German)	40.00	

*Uncoated paper. The second note after No. 744 also applies here.

Special First Day of Issue Postmark
G.P.O. Philatelic Bureau, Edinburgh (Type C) 3.00

324 Durham Cathedral

325 York Minster

326 St. Giles' Cathedral, Edinburgh

327 Canterbury Cathedral

328 St. Paul's Cathedral

329 Liverpool Metropolitan Cathedral

(Des P. Gauld)

1969 (28 May). **British Architecture.** *Cathedrals. Chalk-surfaced paper. Two phosphor bands.* P 15 × 14.

796	**324**	5d. grey-black, orange, pale bluish violet & black	10	10
		a. Block of 4. Nos. 796/9	85	1.00
		ab. Block of 4. Uncoated paper†		
		b. Pale bluish violet omitted	£1750	
797	**325**	5d. grey-black, pale bluish violet, new blue & black	10	10
		b. Pale bluish violet omitted	£1750	
798	**326**	5d. grey-black, purple, green & black	10	10
		c. Green omitted*	40.00	
799	**327**	5d. grey-black, green, new blue & black	10	10
800	**328**	9d. grey-black, ochre, pale drab, violet & black	15	15
		a. Black (value) omitted	£100	
		Ey. Phosphor omitted	40.00	
801	**329**	1s. 6d. grey-black, pale turquoise, pale reddish violet, pale yellow-olive & black	15	15
		a. Black (value) omitted	£1850	
		b. Black (value) double		
		Ey. Phosphor omitted	18.00	
		Set of 6	1.00	55
		First Day Cover		2.00
		Presentation Pack	3.00	
		Presentation Pack (German)	22.00	

†Uncoated paper. The second note after No. 744 also applies here.

*The missing green on the roof top is known on R.2/5, R.8/5 and R.10/5 but all from different sheets and it only occurred in part of the printing, being "probably caused by a batter on the impression cylinder". Examples are also known with the green partly omitted.

The 5d. values were issued together *se-tenant* in blocks of four throughout the sheet.

Special First Day of Issue Postmark
G.P.O. Philatelic Bureau, Edinburgh (Type C) 3.25

330 The King's Gate, Caernarvon Castle

331 The Eagle Tower, Caernarvon Castle

332 Queen Eleanor's Gate, Caernarvon Castle

333 Celtic Cross, Margam Abbey

334 H.R.H. The Prince of Wales (after photo by G. Argent)

(Des D. Gentleman)

1969 (1 July). **Investiture of H.R.H. The Prince of Wales.** *Chalk-surfaced paper. Two phosphor bands. P* 14 × 15.

802	**330**	5d. dp olive-grey, lt olive-grey, dp grey, lt grey, red, pale turquoise-green, black & silver	10	10
		a. Strip of 3. Nos. 802/4	70	75
		b. Black (value & inscr) omitted	£150	
		c. Red omitted*	£250	
		d. Dp grey omitted*	90.00	
		e. Pale turquoise-green omitted	£250	
		Ey. Phosphor omitted	3.00	
		Eya. Strip of 3. Nos. 802/4. Phosphor omitted	10.00	

803	**331**	5d. dp olive-grey, lt olive-grey, dp grey, lt grey, red, pale turquoise-green, black & silver	10	10
		b. Black (value and inscr) omitted	£150	
		c. Red omitted**	£250	
		d. Dp grey omitted**	90.00	
		e. Pale turquoise-green omitted	£250	
		Ey. Phosphor omitted	3.00	
804	**332**	5d. dp olive-grey, lt olive-grey, dp grey, lt grey, red, pale turquoise-green, black & silver	10	10
		b. Black (value & inscr) omitted	£150	
		c. Red omitted**	£250	
		d. Dp grey omitted**	90.00	
		e. Pale turquoise-green omitted	£250	
		Ey. Phosphor omitted	3.00	
805	**333**	9d. dp grey, lt grey, black & gold	20	10
		Ey. Phosphor omitted	20.00	
806	**334**	1s. blackish yellow-olive & gold	20	10
		Ey. Phosphor omitted	11.00	
		Set of 5	1.00	45
		First Day Cover		1.25
		Presentation Pack†	1.40	
		Presentation Pack (German)	16.00	

The 5d. values were issued together *se-tenant* in strips of three throughout the sheet.

*The 5d. value is also known with the red misplaced downwards and where this occurs the red printing does not take very well on the silver background and in some cases is so faint that it could be mistaken for a missing red. However, the red can be seen under a magnifying glass and caution should therefore be exercised when purchasing copies of Nos. 802/4c.

**The deep grey affects the dark portions of the windows and doors.

†In addition to the generally issued Presentation Pack a further pack in different colours and with all texts printed in both English and Welsh was made available exclusively through Education Authorities for free distribution to all schoolchildren in Wales and Monmouthshire (*Price £4*).

Special First Day of Issue Postmarks

G.P.O. Philatelic Bureau, Edinburgh 1 (Type C) 3.00
Day of Investiture, Caernarvon 1.50

335 Mahatma Gandhi

(Des B. Mullick)

1969 (13 Aug). **Gandhi Centenary Year.** *Chalk-surfaced paper. Two phosphor bands. P* 15 × 14.

807	**335**	1s. 6d. black, green, red-orange & grey	30	30
		a. Printed on the gummed side	£300	
		Ey. Phosphor omitted	3.00	
		First Day Cover		1.00

Special First Day of Issue Postmark
G.P.O. Philatelic Bureau, Edinburgh (Type C) 1.00

Collectors Pack 1969

969 (15 Sept). *Comprises Nos. 775/86 and 791/807.*
CP807b Collectors Pack 20.00

336 National Giro "G" Symbol

337 Telecommunications-
International Subscriber Dialling

338 Telecommunications—
Pulse Code Modulation

339 Postal Mechanisation—
Automatic Sorting

(Des D. Gentleman. Litho De La Rue)

969 (1 Oct). **Post Office Technology Commemoration.** *Chalk-surfaced paper. Two phosphor bands.* P 13½ × 14.

808	336	5d. new blue, greenish blue, lavender & black	10	10
		Ey. Phosphor omitted........................	4.00	
809	337	9d. emerald, violet-blue & black...........	15	15
810	338	1s. emerald, lavender & black	15	15
		Ey. Phosphor omitted........................	£300	
811	339	1s. 6d. brt purple, lt blue, grey-blue & black	40	40
		Set of 4	70	70
		First Day Cover		1.00
		Presentation Pack........................	2.25	

Special First Day of Issue Postmark
G.P.O. Philatelic Bureau, Edinburgh (Type C) 2.00

(Des F. Wegner. Queen's head (and stars 4d., 5d. and scroll work 1s. 6d.) printed in gold and then embossed)

1969 (26 Nov). **Christmas.** *Chalk-surfaced paper. Two phosphor bands (5d., 1s. 6d.) or one centre band (4d.).* P 15 × 14.

812	340	4d. vermilion, new blue, orange, brt purple, lt green, bluish violet, blackish brown & gold................................	10	10
		a. Gold (Queen's head etc.) omitted....	£2000	
		Eb. Centre band 3½ mm	25	15
813	341	5d. magenta, lt blue, royal blue, olive-brown, green, greenish yellow, red & gold	10	10
		a. Lt blue (sheep, etc.) omitted............	60.00	
		b. Red omitted*	£500	
		c. Gold (Queen's head) omitted	£400	
		d. Green omitted	£200	
		e. Olive-brown, red and gold omitted...		
		Ef. Embossing omitted	20.00	
		Ey. Phosphor omitted.........................	1.00	
814	342	1s. 6d. greenish yellow, brt purple, bluish violet, dp slate, orange, green, new blue & gold....................	30	30
		a. Gold (Queen's head etc.) omitted	80.00	
		b. Dp slate (value) omitted...................	£250	
		c. Greenish yellow omitted.................	£130	
		d. Bluish violet omitted	£300	
		e. New blue omitted	50.00	
		Ef. Embossing omitted	8.00	
		Ey. Phosphor omitted.........................	5.00	
		Eya. Embossing & phosphor omitted	8.00	
		Set of 3..	45	45
		First Day Cover		1.00
		Presentation Pack	2.25	

*The effect of the missing red is shown on the hat, leggings and purse which appear as dull orange.

No. 812 has one centre band 8 mm. wide but this was of no practical use in the automatic facing machines and after about three-quarters of the stamps had been printed the remainder were printed with a 3½mm. band (No. 812Eb).

No. 813e was caused by a paper fold

Used copies of the 5d. have been seen with the olive-brown or greenish yellow omitted.

Special First Day of Issue Postmarks
P.O. Philatelic Bureau, Edinburgh (Type C) 1.25
Bethlehem, Llandeilo, Carms (Type C) 1.50

343 Fife Harling

344 Cotswold Limestone

340 Herald Angel

341 The Three Shepherds

345 Welsh Stucco

346 Ulster Thatch

342 The Three Kings

(Des D. Gentleman (5d., 9d.), Sheila Robinson (1s., 1s. 6d.))

1970 (11 Feb). **British Rural Architecture.** *Chalk-surfaced paper. Two phosphor bands.* P 15 × 14.

815	**343**	5d. grey, grey-black, black, lemon, greenish blue, orange-brown, ultramarine & green	10	10
		a. Lemon omitted	50.00	
		b. Grey (Queen's head & cottage shading) omitted	£4000	
		Ey. Phosphor omitted	1.50	
816	**344**	9d. orange-brown, olive-yellow, brt green, black, grey-black & grey	20	20
		Ey. Phosphor omitted	6.00	
817	**345**	1s. dp blue, reddish lilac, drab & new blue	20	20
		a. New blue omitted	45.00	
		Ey. Phosphor omitted	12.00	
818	**346**	1s. 6d. greenish yellow, black, turquoise-blue & lilac	35	35
		a. Turquoise-blue omitted	£3500	
		Ey. Phosphor omitted	2.25	
		Set of 4	75	75
		First Day Cover		1.25
		Presentation Pack	3.00	

Used examples of the 5d. have been seen with the greenish blue colour omitted.

Special First Day of Issue Postmark
British Philatelic Bureau, Edinburgh (Type C) 2.00

347 Signing the Declaration of Arbroath

348 Florence Nightingale attending Patients

349 Signing of International Co-operative Alliance

350 Pilgrims and *Mayflower*

351 Sir William Herschel, Francis Baily, Sir John Herschel and Telescope

(Des F. Wegner (5d., 9d., and 1s. 6d.), Marjorie Saynor (1s., 1s. 9d.). Queen's head printed in gold and then embossed)

1970 (1 Apr). **Anniversaries.** *Events described on stamps. Chalk-surfaced paper. Two phosphor bands.* P 15 × 14.

819	**347**	5d. black, yellow-olive, blue, emerald, greenish yellow, rose-red, gold & orange-red	10	10
		a. Gold (Queen's head) omitted	£400	
		b. Emerald omitted	50.00	
		Ey. Phosphor omitted	£300	
820	**348**	9d. ochre, dp blue, carmine, black, blue-green, yellow-olive, gold & blue	15	
		a. Ochre omitted	£150	
		Eb. Embossing omitted	10.00	
		Ey. Phosphor omitted	2.25	
821	**349**	1s. green, greenish yellow, brown, black, cerise, gold and lt blue	25	
		a. Gold (Queen's head) omitted	50.00	
		Eb. Green and embossing omitted	75.00	
		c. Green omitted	75.00	
		d. Brown omitted	£100	
		Ee. Embossing omitted	10.00	
		Ey. Phosphor omitted	4.00	
		Eya. Brown and phosphor omitted	£110	
		Eyb. Embossing and phosphor omitted	20.00	
822	**350**	1s. 6d. greenish yellow, carmine, dp yellow-olive, emerald, black, blue, gold & sage-green	30	30
		a. Gold (Queen's head) omitted	75.00	
		b. Emerald omitted	40.00	
		Ec. Embossing omitted	5.00	
		Ey. Phosphor omitted	2.50	
823	**351**	1s. 9d. black, slate, lemon, gold & brt purple	30	30
		Ey. Phosphor omitted	2.50	
		Set of 5	1.00	90
		First Day Cover		1.2
		Presentation Pack	3.00	

The 1s. 9d. with the lemon colour omitted has been seen used on a First Day Cover.

Special First Day of Issue Postmark
British Philatelic Bureau, Edinburgh (Type C) 2.25
First Day of Issue handstamps were provided at Billericay, Essex; Boston, Lincs and Rochdale, Lancs for this issue.

352 "Mr. Pickwick and Sam" (*Pickwick Papers*)

353 "Mr. and Mrs. Micawber" (*David Copperfield*)

354 "David Copperfield and Betsy Trotwood" (*David Copperfield*)

355 "Oliver asking for more" (*Oliver Twist*)

356 "Grasmere" (from engraving by J. Farrington, R.A.)

T **352/5** were issued together se-tenant in blocks of four throughout the sheet.

)es Rosalind Dease. Queen's head printed in gold and then embossed)

970 (3 June). **Literary Anniversaries.** *Death Centenary of Charles Dickens (novelist) (5d. × 4) and Birth Bicentenary of William Wordsworth (poet) (1s. 6d.). Chalk-surfaced paper. Two phosphor bands. P 14 × 15.*

?4	352	5d. black, orange, silver, gold & magenta	10	10
		a. Block of 4. Nos. 824/7	90	90
		ab.* Imperf (block of four)	£600	
?5	353	5d. black, magenta, silver, gold & orange	10	10
?6	354	5d. black, lt greenish blue, silver, gold & yellow-bistre	10	10
		b. Yellow-bistre (value) omitted	£1200	
?7	355	5d. black, yellow-bistre, silver, gold & lt greenish blue	10	10
		b. Yellow-bistre (background) omitted .	£3000	
		c. Lt greenish blue (value) omitted*	£450	
?8	356	1s. 6d. lt yellow-olive, black, silver, gold & bright blue	20	20
		a. Gold (Queen's head) omitted	£225	
		b. Silver ("Grasmere") omitted	60.00	
		Ec. Embossing omitted	5.00	
		Ey. Phosphor omitted	4.00	
		Eya. Embossing & phosphor omitted	20.00	
		Set of 5	1.00	55
		First Day Cover		2.00
		Presentation Pack	3.00	

*No. 827c (unlike No. 826b) comes from a sheet on wnich the colour ~~as~~ only partially omitted so that, although No. 827 was completely ~~i~~thout the light greenish blue colour, it was still partially present on ~~o.~~ 826.

Special First Day of Issue Postmarks

British Philatelic Bureau, Edinburgh (Type C)	2.75
Cockermouth, Cumberland (Type C) (No. 828 only)	1.25
Rochester, Kent (Type C) (Nos. 824/7)	1.25

A First Day of Issue handstamp was provided at Broadstairs, Kent, for this issue.

357 (Value redrawn)

(Des after plaster cast by Arnold Machin. Recess B.W.)

970 (17 June)**–72.** *Decimal Currency. Chalk-surfaced paper or phos-phorised paper* (10p.). *P 12.*

9	357	10p. cerise	1.00	75
0		20p. olive-green	70	15
		Ea. Thinner uncoated paper*		
1		50p. dp ultramarine	1.50	40
		Ea. Thinner uncoated paper*	22.00	
1b		£1 bluish black (6.12.72)	3.50	75
		Set of 4	6.00	1.75
		First Day Cover (829/31)		5.50
		First Day Cover (831b)		7.00
		Presentation Pack (829/31)	7.00	
		Presentation Pack (790 (or 831b), 830/1)	8.00	

*These are not as apparent as uncoated photogravure issues where ~~e~~re is normally a higher degree of chalk-surfacing. The 20p. is known ~~l~~y as a block of four with Plate No. 5. The 50p. comes from Plate No. 9.

The 10p. on phosphorised paper continued the experiments which started with the Machin 1s. 6d. When the experiment had ended a quantity of the 50p. value was printed on the phosphorised paper to use up the stock. These stamps were issued on 1 February 1973, but they cannot be distinguished from No. 831 by the naked eye. (*Price £2*).

A £1 was also issued in 1970, but it is difficult to distinguish it from the earlier No. 790. In common with the other 1970 values it was issued in sheets of 100.

A whiter paper was introduced in 1973. The £1 appeared on 27 Sept. 1973, the 20p. on 30 Nov. 1973 and the 50p. on 20 Feb. 1974.

Special First Day of Issue Postmarks

British Philatelic Bureau, Edinburgh (Type C) (Nos. 829/31)	7.50
Windsor, Berks (Type C) (Nos. 829/31)	15.00
Philatelic Bureau, Edinburgh (Type E) (No. 831b)	10.00
Windsor, Berks (Type E) (No. 831b)	30.00

358 Runners   **359** Swimmers

360 Cyclists

(Des A. Restall. Litho D.L.R.)

1970 (15 July). **Ninth British Commonwealth Games.** *Chalk-surfaced paper. Two phosphor bands. P 13½ × 14.*

832	358	5d. pink, emerald, greenish yellow & dp yellow-green	10	10
		a. Greenish yellow omitted	£3500	
		Ey. Phosphor omitted	£200	
833	359	1s. 6d. lt greenish blue, lilac, bistre-brown & Prussian blue	50	50
		Ey. Phosphor omitted	60.00	
834	360	1s. 9d. yellow-orange, lilac, salmon & dp red-brown	50	50
		Set of 3	1.00	1.00
		First Day Cover		1.25
		Presentation Pack	2.50	

Special First Day of Issue Postmark

British Philatelic Bureau, Edinburgh (Type C) 1.50

Collectors Pack 1970

1970 (14 Sept). *Comprises Nos. 808/28 and 832/4.*

CP834a	Collectors Pack	24.00	

WHEN YOU BUY AN ALBUM LOOK FOR THE NAME "STANLEY GIBBONS"

It means Quality combined with Value for Money.

---

361 1d. Black (1840)

362 1s. Green (1847)

363 4d. Carmine (1855)

(Des D. Gentleman)

1970 (18 Sept). **"Philympia 70" Stamp Exhibition.** *Chalk-surfaced paper. Two phosphor bands.* P 14 × 14½.

835	**361**	5d. grey-black, brownish bistre, black & dull purple	10	10
		Ey. Phosphor omitted	2.75	
836	**362**	9d. lt drab, bluish green, stone, black & dull purple	35	35
		Ey. Phosphor omitted	9.00	
837	**363**	1s. 6d. carmine, lt drab, black & dull purple	40	40
		Ey. Phosphor omitted	3.00	
		Set of 3	75	75
		First Day Cover		1.25
		Presentation Pack	2.50	

Special First Day of Issue Postmark

British Post Office Philatelic Bureau, Edinburgh (Type D).. 1.50

366 The Wise Men bearing gifts

(Des Sally Stiff after De Lisle Psalter. Queen's head printed in gold and then embossed)

1970 (25 Nov). **Christmas.** *Chalk-surfaced paper. One centre phosphor band (4d.) or two phosphor bands (others).* P 14 × 15.

838	**364**	4d. brown-red, turquoise-green, pale chestnut, brown, grey-black, gold & vermilion	10	10
		Ea. Embossing omitted	40.00	
		Ey. Phosphor omitted	55.00	
839	**365**	5d. emerald, gold, blue, brown-red, ochre, grey-black & violet	10	10
		a. Gold (Queen's head) omitted	†	£2500
		b. Emerald omitted	60.00	
		c. Imperf (pair)	£250	
		Ed. Embossing omitted	12.00	
		Ey. Phosphor omitted	2.25	
840	**366**	1s. 6d. gold, grey-black, pale turquoise-green, salmon, ultramarine, ochre & yellow-green	35	35
		a. Salmon omitted	80.00	
		b. Ochre omitted	50.00	
		Ec. Embossing omitted	30.00	
		Ey. Phosphor omitted	3.50	
		Eya. Embossing & phosphor omitted		
		Set of 3	50	50
		First Day Cover		1.00
		Presentation Pack	2.50	

Special First Day of Issue Postmarks

British Post Office Bureau, Edinburgh (Type D)......... 1.25
Bethlehem, Llandeilo, Carms 1.10

364 Shepherds and Apparition of the Angel

365 Mary, Joseph, and Christ in the Manger

(New Currency. 100 new pence=£1)

"X" NUMBERS. The following definitive series has been allocated "X" prefixes to the catalogue numbers to avoid re-numbering all subsequent issues.

NO VALUE INDICATED. Stamps as Types 367/a inscribed "2nd" or "1st" are listed as Nos. 1445/52, 1511/16 and 1663a/6.

ELLIPTICAL PERFORATIONS. These were introduced in 1993 and are listed as Nos. Y1667, etc.

| 367 | 367a |

Printing differences

| Litho | Photo |

(Illustrations enlarged ×6)

Litho. Clear outlines to value and frame of stamp.
Photo. Uneven lines to value and frame formed by edges of screen.

Two types of the 3p, 10p and 26p (Nos. X930/c, X886/b and X971/a)

Figures of face value as I (all ptgs of 3p. brt magenta except the multi-value coil No. 930cl and sheets from 21.1.92 onwards, 10p orange-brown except 1984 "Christmas Heritage" £4 booklet and 26p rosine except 1987 £1.04 barcode booklet.

Figures of face value narrower as II (from coil No. X930cl and in sheets from 21.1.92 (3p.), 1984 "Christian Heritage" £4 booklet (10p.) or 1987 £1.04 barcode booklet (26p.)).

This catalogue includes changes of figure styles on these stamps where there is no other listable difference. Similar changes have also taken place on other values, but only in conjunction with listed colour, paper or perforation changes.

1971 (15 Feb)–93. *Decimal Currency. T 367. Chalk-surfaced paper.*

(a) *Photo Harrison (except for some printings of Nos. X879 and X913 in sheets produced by Enschedé in 1979 (8p.) and 1991 (18p.). With phosphor bands. P 15 × 14.*

X841	½p. turquoise-blue (2 bands)	10	10
	a. Imperf (pair)†	£900	
	l. Booklet pane. No. X841 × 2 se-tenant vert with X849 × 2	5.00	
	lEy. Booklet pane. Phosphor omitted	£150	
	la. Booklet pane. No. X841 × 2 se-tenant horiz with X849 × 2 (14.7.71)	80	
	laEy. Booklet pane. Phosphor omitted	£350	
	m. Booklet pane. No. X841 × 5 plus label	5.00	
	mEy. Booklet pane. Phosphor omitted	90.00	
	n. Coil strip. No. X849Eg, X841Eg × 2 and X844Eg × 2	2.00	
	nEy. Coil strip. Phosphor omitted	30.00	
	nEv. Coil strip. PVA gum. No. X849, X841 × 2 and X844 × 2 (4.74)	35	
	nEvy. Coil strip. Phosphor omitted	9.00	
	o. Booklet pane. No. X841, X851, X852, X852Ea, each × 3 (24.5.72)	12.00	
	oEy. Booklet pane. Phosphor omitted	£1500	
	p. Booklet pane. No. X841 × 3, X842 and X852 × 2 (24.5.72)	70.00	
	pEy. Booklet pane. Phosphor omitted		
	q. Coil strip. No. X870, X849, X844 and X841 × 2 (3.12.75)	80	
	r. Booklet pane. No. X841 × 2, X844 × 3 and X870 (10.3.76)	70	
	s. Booklet pane. No. X841 × 2, X844×2, X873 × 2 and X881 × 4 (8½p. values at right) (26.1.77)	2.50	
	sa. Ditto, but No. X873Ea and 8½p. values at left	2.50	
	t. Booklet pane. No. X841, X844, X894 × 3 and X902 (14p. value at right) (26.1.81)	2.00	
	tEy. Booklet pane. Phosphor omitted	35.00	
	ta. Booklet pane. No. X841, X844, X894Ea × 3 and X902 (14p. value at left)	2.00	
	taEy. Booklet pane. Phosphor omitted	35.00	
	u. Booklet pane. No. X841, X857 × 4 and X899 × 3 (12½p. values at left) (1.2.82)	2.50	
	ua. Ditto, but X899Ea and 12½p. values at right	2.50	
	Eg. Gum arabic (from coil strip, and on 22.9.72 from sheets)	40	
	Egy. Phosphor omitted	50.00	
X842	½p. turquoise-blue (1 side band at left) (24.5.72)	60.00	25.00
X843	½p. turquoise-blue (1 centre band) (14.12.77)	30	20
	l. Coil strip. No. X843 × 2, X875 and X845 × 2 (14.12.77)	55	
	m. Booklet pane. No. X843 × 2, X845 × 2 and X875 plus label (8.2.78)	75	
	mEy. Booklet pane. Phosphor omitted	25.00	
X844	1p. crimson (2 bands)	10	10
	a. Imperf (vert coil)		
	b. Pair, one imperf 3 sides (vert coil)		
	c. Imperf (pair)		
	l. Booklet pane. No. X844 × 2 se-tenant vert with X848 × 2	5.00	
	m. Ditto, but se-tenant horiz (14.7.71)	80	
	mEy. Booklet pane. Phosphor omitted	80.00	
	n. Booklet pane. No. X844 × 2, X876 × 3 and X883 × 3 (9p. values at right) (13.6.77)	4.00	

X844)	na. Ditto, but No. X876Ea and 9p. values at left	2.50		
	Eg. Gum arabic (from coil strip)	40		
	Egy. Phosphor omitted	45.00		
X845	1p. crimson (1 centre band) (14.12.77)	20	20	
	l. Booklet pane. No. X879 and X845 × 2 plus label (17.10.79)	50		
	m. Coil strip. No. X879 and X845 × 2 plus 2 labels (16.1.80)	45		
	n. Booklet pane. No. X845 × 2, X860 and X898 each × 3 (5.4.83)	5.00		
	nEy. Booklet pane. Phosphor omitted	16.00		
	p. Booklet pane. No. X845 × 3, X863 × 2 and X900 × 3 (3.9.84)	3.50		
	pEy. Booklet pane. Phosphor omitted	£180		
	q. Booklet pane. No. X845 × 2 and X896 × 4 (29.7.86)	8.00		
	s. Booklet pane. No. X845, X867 × 2 and X900 × 3 (20.10.86)	3.00		
	sEy. Booklet pane. Phosphor omitted	90.00		
	sa. Ditto, but with vertical edges of pane imperf (29.9.87)	3.00		
X846	1p. crimson ("all-over") (10.10.79)	20	20	
X847	1p. crimson (1 side band at left) (20.10.86)	1.50	1.00	
	Ea. Band at right (3.3.87)	2.75	2.75	
	l. Booklet pane. No. X847, X901 and X912 × 2 (20.10.86)	3.00		
	lEy. Booklet pane. Phosphor omitted	90.00		
	m. Booklet pane. No. X847Ea, X901 × 2, X912 × 5 and X918 with margins all round (3.3.87)	11.50		
X848	1½p. black (2 bands)	20	15	
	a. Uncoated paper*	£110		
	b. Imperf (pair)			
	c. Imperf 3 sides (horiz pair)			
	Ey. Phosphor omitted	10.00		
X849	2p. myrtle-green (2 bands)	20	10	
	a. Imperf (horiz pair)			
	l. Booklet pane. No. X849 × 2, X880 × 2 and X886 × 3 plus label (10p. values at right) (28.8.79)	2.50		
	la. Ditto, but No. X880Ea and 10p. values at left	2.00		
	m. Booklet pane. No. X849 × 3, X889 × 2 and X895 × 2 plus label (12p. values at left) (4.2.80)	2.00		
	mEy. Booklet pane. Phosphor omitted	30.00		
	ma. Booklet pane. No. X849 × 3, X889Ea × 2 and X895 × 2 plus label (12p. values at left)	2.00		
	maEy. Booklet pane. Phosphor omitted	30.00		
	n. Booklet pane. No. X849, X888 × 3, X889Ea and X895 × 4 with margins all round (16.4.80)	3.75		
	nEy. Booklet pane. Phosphor omitted	50.00		
	o. Booklet pane. No. X849 × 6 with margins all round (16.4.80)	80		
	oEy. Booklet pane. Phosphor omitted	50.00		
	p. Booklet pane. No. X849, X857, X898, X899 × 3 and X899Ea × 3 with margins all round (19.5.82)	6.00		
	pEy. Booklet pane. Phosphor omitted	£100		
	Eg. Gum arabic (from coil strip)	2.25		
	Egy. Phosphor omitted	£175		
X850	2p. myrtle-green ("all-over") (10.10.79)	20	15	
X851	2½p. magenta (1 centre band)	15	10	
	a. Imperf (pair)†	£225		
	Ey. Phosphor omitted	6.50		
	l. Booklet pane. No. X851 × 5 plus label	3.00		
	lEy. Booklet pane. Phosphor omitted	35.00		

(X851)	m. Booklet pane. No. X851 × 4 plus two labels	4.00		
	mEy. Booklet pane. Phosphor omitted	75.00		
	n. Booklet pane. No. X851 × 3, X852Ea × 3 and X855 × 6 (24.5.72)	7.00		
	nEy. Booklet pane. Phosphor omitted			
	Eg. Gum arabic (13.9.72)	15		
X852	2½p. magenta (1 band at left)	1.25	1.75	
	l. Booklet pane. No. X852 × 2 and X855 × 4	5.00		
	lEy. Booklet pane. Phosphor omitted	90.00		
	Ea. Band at right (24.5.72)	1.75	2.25	
X853	2½p. magenta (2 bands) (21.5.75)	30	75	
X854	2½p. rose-red (2 bands) (26.8.81)	50	60	
	l. Booklet pane. No. X854 × 3, X862 × 2 and X894 × 3, (11½p. values at left)	5.00		
	la. Ditto, but No. X894Ea and 11½p. values at right	6.50		
X855	3p. ultramarine (2 bands)	20	10	
	a. Imperf (coil strip of 5)	£1000		
	b. Imperf (pair)†	£225		
	c. Uncoated paper*	40.00		
	Ey. Phosphor omitted	2.00		
	l. Booklet pane. No. X855 × 5 plus label	2.00		
	lEy. Booklet pane. Phosphor omitted	£250		
	Eg. Gum arabic (23.8.72)	75		
	Egy. Phosphor omitted	7.00		
X856	3p. ultramarine (1 centre band) (10.9.73)	20	25	
	a. Imperf (pair)†	£250		
	b. Imperf between (vert pair)†	£375		
	c. Imperf horiz (vert pair)†	£150		
	Eg. Gum arabic	30		
	Egy. Phosphor omitted	75.00		
X857	3p. brt magenta (Type I) (2 bands) (1.2.82)	30	25	
X858	3½p. olive-grey (2 bands) (shades)	30	30	
	a. Imperf (pair)	£350		
	Ey. Phosphor omitted	3.50		
	Eb. Bronze-green (18.7.73)	60	50	
	Eby. Phosphor omitted	8.00		
X859	3½p. olive-grey (1 centre band) (24.6.74)	30	15	
X860	3½p. purple-brown (1 centre band) (5.4.83)	1.25	1.25	
X861	4p. ochre-brown (2 bands)	20	20	
	a. Imperf (pair)†	£450		
	Ey. Phosphor omitted	30.00		
	Eg. Gum arabic (1.11.72)	20		
X862	4p. greenish blue (2 bands) (26.8.81)	1.50	1.50	
X863	4p. greenish blue (1 centre band) (3.9.84)	1.00	1.00	
X864	4p. greenish blue (1 band at right) (8.1.85)	2.00	2.00	
	Ea. Band at left	2.00	2.00	
	l. Booklet pane. No. X864, X864Ea, X901 × 2, X901Ea × 2, X909 × 2 and X920 with margins all round (8.1.85)	11.50		
	lEy. Booklet pane. Phosphor omitted	£1000		
X865	4½p. grey-blue (2 bands) (24.10.73)	20	25	
	a. Imperf (pair)	£250		
	Ey. Phosphor omitted	3.50		
X866	5p. pale violet (2 bands)	20	10	
X867	5p. claret (1 centre band) (20.10.86)	1.50	1.50	
	Ey. Phosphor omitted	60.00		
X868	5½p. violet (2 bands) (24.10.73)	25	25	
X869	5½p. violet (1 centre band) (17.3.75)	20	20	
	a. Uncoated paper*	£350		
	Ey. Phosphor omitted	10.00		
X870	6p. lt emerald (2 bands)	30	15	
	a. Uncoated paper*	15.00		
	Ey. Phosphor omitted	65.00		
	Eg. Gum arabic (6.6.73)	1.50		
X871	6½p. greenish blue (2 bands) (4.9.74)	45	45	

X872	6½p. greenish blue (1 centre band) (24.9.75)............................	30	15
	a. Imperf (vert pair)	£300	
	b. Uncoated paper*	£160	
	Ey. Phosphor omitted........................	11.00	
X873	6½p. greenish blue (1 band at right) (26.1.77)............................	60	55
	Ea. Band at left................................	60	75
X874	7p. purple-brown (2 bands) (15.1.75)......	35	25
	a. Imperf (pair)	£250	
	Ey. Phosphor omitted........................	1.25	
X875	7p. purple-brown (1 centre band) (13.6.77)...................................	35	20
	a. Imperf (pair)	£100	
	l. Booklet pane. No. X875 and X883, each × 10 (15.11.78)....................	4.50	
X876	7p. purple-brown (1 band at right) (13.6.77)...................................	60	75
	Ea. Band at left................................	60	75
X877	7½p. pale chestnut (2 bands)	30	25
	Ey. Phosphor omitted........................	15.00	
X878	8p. rosine (2 bands) (24.10.73)	25	20
	a. Uncoated paper*	10.00	
X879	8p. rosine (1 centre band) (20.8.79)	25	15
	a. Uncoated paper*	£550	
	b. Imperf (pair)	£550	
	Ey. Phosphor omitted........................	£110	
	l. Booklet pane. No. X879 and X886, each × 10 (14.11.79)....................	5.00	
X880	8p. rosine (1 band at right) (28.8.79)	60	60
	Ea. Band at left................................	60	60
X881	8½p. lt yellowish green (2 bands) (shades) (24.9.75)...................................	35	20
	a. Imperf (pair)	£750	
	Eb. Yellowish green (24.3.76)................	30	35
X882	9p. yellow-orange and black (2 bands)	60	30
	Ey. Phosphor omitted........................	65.00	
X883	9p. dp violet (2 bands) (25.2.76)	45	25
	a. Imperf (pair)	£180	
	Ey. Phosphor omitted........................	1.50	
X884	9½p. purple (2 bands) (25.2.76)	45	30
	Ey. Phosphor omitted........................	15.00	
X885	10p. orange-brown & chestnut (2 bands) (11.8.71)...................................	40	30
	a. Orange-brown omitted	£150	
	b. Imperf (horiz pair)	£2000	
	Ey. Phosphor omitted........................	7.50	
X886	10p. orange-brown (Type I) (2 bands) (25.2.76)...................................	40	20
	a. Imperf (pair)	£250	
	b. Type II (4.9.84)	7.00	7.00
	bl. Booklet pane. No. X886b, X901Ea and X909 × 7 with margins all round	9.50	
	blEy. Booklet pane. Phosphor omitted		
X887	10p. orange-brown (Type I) ("all-over") (3.10.79)...................................	30	45
X888	10p. orange-brown (Type I) (1 centre band) (4.2.80)	30	20
	a. Imperf (pair)	£225	
	l. Booklet pane. No. X888 × 9 with margins all round...............	2.75	
	lEy. Booklet pane. Phosphor omitted	40.00	
	m. Booklet pane. No. X888 and X895, each × 10 (12.11.80)....................	6.00	
X889	10p. orange-brown (Type I) (1 band at right) (4.2.80)............................	60	60
	Ea. Band at left................................	60	60
X890	10½p. yellow (2 bands) (25.2.76)	40	30
X891	10½p. dp dull blue (2 bands) (26.4.78)........	60	45
X892	11p. brown-red (2 bands) (25.2.76)..........	60	25
	a. Imperf (pair)	£1500	

X893	11½p. drab (1 centre band) (14.1.81).........	45	30
	a. Imperf (pair)	£180	
	Ey. Phosphor omitted........................	5.50	
	l. Booklet pane. No. X893 and X902, each × 10 (11.11.81)....................	7.00	
X894	11½p. drab (1 band at right) (26.1.81)	60	60
	Ea. Band at left................................	60	60
	l. Booklet pane. No. X894/Ea, each × 2 & X902 × 6 (6.5.81)................	4.00	
X895	12p. yellowish green (2 bands) (4.2.80)	60	40
	l. Booklet pane. No. X895 × 9 with margins all round..............	3.00	
	lEy. Booklet pane. Phosphor omitted	40.00	
X896	12p. brt emerald (1 centre band) (29.10.85)	60	40
	Eu. Underprint Type 4 (29.10.85)	60	
	Ey. Phosphor omitted........................	8.00	
	l. Booklet pane. No. X896 × 9 with margins all round (18.3.86).............	3.00	
	lEy. Booklet pane. Phosphor omitted	£160	
X897	12p. brt emerald (1 band at right) (14.1.86)	75	75
	Ea. Band at left................................	75	75
	l. Booklet pane. No. X897/Ea, each × 2 and X909 × 6 (12p. values at left) (14.1.86)...................................	6.00	
	la. Ditto, but 12p. values at right	6.00	
	m. Booklet pane. No. X897/Ea, each × 3, X909 × 2 and X919 with margins all round (18.3.86)...................	9.00	
	mEy. Booklet pane. Phosphor omitted	£1000	
X898	12½p. lt emerald (1 centre band) (27.1.82)	45	25
	a. Imperf (pair)	£100	
	Eu. Underprint Type 1 (10.11.82)	45	
	Eua. Underprint Type 2 (9.11.83)	45	
	Ey. Phosphor omitted........................	5.50	
	l. Booklet pane. No. X898Eu and X907Eu, each × 10 (10.11.82)........	9.00	
X899	12½p. lt emerald (1 band at right) (1.2.82)	60	60
	Ea. Band at left................................	60	60
	l. Booklet pane. No. X899/Ea, each × 2 and X907 × 6 (1.2.82)††...............	5.00	
	m. Booklet pane. No. X899/Ea, each × 3 with margins all round (19.5.82)........	2.50	
	mEy. Booklet pane. Phosphor omitted	25.00	
	n. Booklet pane. No. X899/Ea, each × 2, and X908 × 6 (12½p. values at left) (5.4.83)...................................	8.00	
	na. Ditto, but 12½p. values at right	8.00	
X900	13p. pale chestnut (1 centre band) (28.8.84)...................................	45	35
	a. Imperf (pair)	£400	
	Eu. Underprint Type 2 (2.12.86)	45	
	Ey. Phosphor omitted........................	5.50	
	l. Booklet pane. No. X900 × 9 with margins all round (8.1.85)...............	3.25	
	lEy. Booklet pane. Phosphor omitted	£350	
	m. Booklet pane. No. X900 × 6 with margins all round (3.3.87)...............	2.50	
	n. Booklet pane. No. X900 × 4 with margins all round (4.8.87)...............	2.50	
	o. Booklet pane. No. X900 × 10 with margins all round (4.8.87).............	4.50	
X901	13p. pale chestnut (1 band at right) (3.9.84)...................................	60	60
	Ea. Band at left................................	60	60
	l. Booklet pane. No. X901/Ea, each × 2, and X909 × 6 (13p. values at left)††	7.00	
	la. Ditto, but 13p. values at right	7.00	
	m. Booklet pane. No. X901/Ea, each × 3 with margins all round (4.9.84)	2.50	
	mEy. Booklet pane. Phosphor omitted	£225	
	n. Booklet pane. No. X901Ea and X912 × 5 (20.10.86)	5.00	

	na. Ditto, but with vertical edges of pane		
	imperf (29.9.87)	5.00	
X902	14p. grey-blue (2 bands) (26.1.81)	50	45
X903	14p. dp blue (1 centre band) (23.8.88)	60	40
	a. Imperf (pair)		
	Ey. Phosphor omitted	7.00	
	l. Booklet pane. No. X903 × 4 with margins all round	5.00	
	lEy. Booklet pane. Phosphor omitted		
	m. Booklet pane. No. X903 × 10 with margins all round	7.00	
	n. Booklet pane. No. X903 × 4 with horizontal edges of pane imperf (11.10.88)	5.00	
	p. Booklet pane. No. X903 × 10 with horizontal edges of pane imperf (11.10.88)	7.00	
	pEy. Booklet pane. Phosphor omitted	£100	
	q. Booklet pane. No. X903 × 4 with three edges of pane imperf (24.1.89)	16.00	
	qEy. Booklet pane. Phosphor omitted	16.00	
X904	14p. dp blue (1 band at right) (5.9.88)	2.50	1.75
	l. Booklet pane. No. X904 and X914 × 2 plus label	3.00	
	lEy. Booklet pane. Phosphor omitted	10.00	
	m. Booklet pane. No. X904 × 2 and X914 × 4 with vertical edges of pane imperf	6.00	
X905	15p. brt blue (1 centre band) (26.9.89)	25	20
	a. Imperf (pair)	£250	
	Ey. Phosphor omitted		
X906	15p. brt blue (1 band at left) (10.1.89)	2.00	1.75
	Ea. Band at right (20.3.90)	2.00	1.75
	l. Booklet pane. No. X906 × 2 and X916 plus label	5.00	
	lEy. Booklet pane. Phosphor omitted		
	m. Booklet pane. No. X906Ea, X916, X922, 1446, 1448, 1468Ea, 1470 and 147? plus label with margins all round (20.3.90)	14.00	
X907	15½p. pale violet (2 bands) (1.2.81)	45	45
	Eu. Underprint Type 1 (10.11.82)	45	
	l. Booklet pane. No. X907 × 6 with margins all round (19.5.82)	3.00	
	lEy. Booklet pane. Phosphor omitted	75.00	
	m. Booklet pane. No. X907 × 9 with margins all round (19.5.82)	4.00	
	mEy. Booklet pane. Phosphor omitted	30.00	
X908	16p. olive-drab (2 bands) (5.4.83)	1.00	1.25
X909	17p. grey-blue (2 bands) (3.9.84)	75	75
	Eu. Underprint Type 4 (4.11.85)	70	
	l. Booklet pane. No. X909Eu × 3 plus label (4.11.85)	3.00	
	Ela. Booklet pane. No. X909 × 3 plus label (12.8.86)	3.75	
	lEy. Booklet pane. Phosphor omitted	50.00	
X910	17p. dp blue (1 centre band) (4.9.90)	50	50
	a. Imperf (pair)		
	Ey. Phosphor omitted	6.00	
X911	17p. dp blue (1 band at right) (4.9.90)	1.00	1.00
	Ea. Band at left	50	50
	l. Booklet pane. No. X911 and X911Ea × 2 plus label	3.00	
	lEy. Booklet pane. Phosphor omitted	30.00	
	m. Booklet pane. No. X911 × 2 and X917 × 3 plus three labels with vertical edges of pane imperf	4.00	
X912	18p. dp olive-grey (2 bands) (20.10.86)	75	75
X913	18p. brt green (1 centre band) (10.9.91)	30	35
	a. Imperf (pair)		
X914	19p. brt orange-red (2 bands) (5.9.88)	1.10	1.10
X915	20p. dull purple (2 bands) (25.2.76)	90	40

X916	20p. brownish black (2 bands) (2.10.89)	1.00	1.00
X917	22p. brt orange-red (2 bands) (4.9.90)	1.00	1.00
X918	26p. rosine (Type I) (2 bands) (3.3.87)	6.00	6.00
X919	31p. purple (2 bands) (18.3.86)	8.00	8.00
X920	34p. ochre-brown (2 bands) (8.1.85)	6.00	6.00
X921	50p. ochre-brown (2 bands) (2.2.77)	1.75	40
X922	50p. ochre (2 bands) (20.3.90)	4.50	4.50
	(b) Photo Harrison. On phosphorised paper. P 15×14		
X924	½p. turquoise-blue (10.12.80)	10	10
	a. Imperf (pair)	£130	
	l. Coil strip. No. X924 and X932 × 3 (30.12.81)	45	
X925	1p. crimson (12.12.79)	10	10
	a. Imperf (pair)		
	l. Coil strip. No. X925 and X932Ea × 3 (14.8.84)	60	
	m. Booklet pane. No. X925 and X969, each × 2 (10.9.91)	75	
X926	2p. myrtle-green (face value as T **367**) (12.12.79)	10	10
X927	2p. dp green (face value as T **367**a) (26.7.88)	10	10
	a. Imperf (pair)		
	l. Booklet pane. No. X927 × 2 and X969 × 4 plus 2 labels with vert edges of pane imperf (10.9.91)	1.50	
X928	2p. myrtle-green (face value as T **367**a) (5.9.88)	1.00	75
	l. Coil strip. No. X928 and X932Ea × 3..	1.00	
X929	2½p. rose-red (14.1.81)	20	20
	l. Coil strip. No. X929 and X930 × 3 (6.81)	75	
X930	3p. brt magenta (Type I) (22.10.80)	20	20
	a. Imperf (horiz pair)		
	b. Booklet pane. No. X930, X931 × 2 and X949 × 6 with margins all round (14.9.83)	6.00	
	c. Type II (10.10.89)	10	10
	cl. Coil strip. No. X930c and X933 × 3	1.25	
X931	3½p. purple-brown (30.3.83)	45	45
X932	4p. greenish blue (30.12.81)	25	20
	Ea. Pale greenish blue (14.8.84)	25	25
X933	4p. new blue (26.7.88)	10	10
	l. Coil strip. No. X933 × 3 and X935 (27.11.90)	1.00	
	m. Coil strip. No. X933 and X935, each × 2 (1.10.91)	30	
X934	5p. pale violet (10.10.79)	30	25
X935	5p. dull red-brown (26.7.88)	10	10
	a. Imperf (pair)		
X936	6p. olive-yellow (10.9.91)	10	15
X937	7p. brownish red (29.10.85)	1.50	2.00
X938	8½p. yellowish green (24.3.76)	30	55
X939	10p. orange-brown (Type I) (11.79)	30	20
X940	10p. dull orange (Type II) (4.9.90)	15	15
X941	11p. brown-red (27.8.80)	75	75
X942	11½p. ochre-brown (15.8.79)	50	45
X943	12p. yellowish green (30.1.80)	45	40
X944	13p. olive-grey (15.8.79)	60	45
X945	13½p. purple-brown (30.1.80)	65	60
X946	14p. grey-blue (14.1.81)	50	40
X947	15p. ultramarine (15.8.79)	50	40
X948	15½p. pale violet (14.1.81)	50	40
	a. Imperf (pair)	£200	
X949	16p. olive-drab (30.3.83)	60	30
	a. Imperf (pair)	£160	
	Eu. Underprint Type 3 (10.8.83)	75	
	l. Booklet pane. No. X949 × 9 with margins all round (14.9.83)	3.75	
X950	16½p. pale chestnut (27.1.82)	85	75

X951	17p. lt emerald (30.1.80).........................	70	40
X952	17p. grey-blue (30.3.83).........................	50	40
	a. Imperf (pair)	£225	
	Eu. Underprint Type 3 (5.3.85).............	80	
	l. Booklet pane. No. X952 × 6 with		
	margins all round (4.9.84)	3.00	
	m. Booklet pane. No. X952 × 9 with		
	margins all round (8.1.85)	4.50	
X953	17½p. pale chestnut (30.1.80)...................	80	80
X954	18p. dp violet (14.1.81)	70	75
X955	18p. dp olive-grey (28.8.84)	70	60
	a. Imperf (pair)	£160	
	l. Booklet pane. No. X955 × 9 with		
	margins all round (3.3.87)	4.50	
	m. Booklet pane. No. X955 × 4 with		
	margins all round (4.8.87)	3.00	
	n. Booklet pane. No. X955 × 10 with		
	margins all round (4.8.87)	5.50	
X956	19p. brt orange-red (23.8.88).................	60	40
	a. Imperf (pair)	£225	
	l. Booklet pane. No. X956 × 4 with		
	margins all round	6.00	
	m. Booklet pane. No. X956 × 10 with		
	margins all round	9.00	
	n. Booklet pane. No. X956 × 4 with		
	horizontal edges of pane imperf		
	(11.10.88)	6.00	
	o. Booklet pane. No. X956 × 10 with		
	horizontal edges of pane imperf		
	(11.10.88)	19.00	
	q. Booklet pane. No. X956 × 4 with		
	three edges of pane imperf (24.1.89)	16.00	
X957	19½p. olive-grey (27.1.82)........................	1.75	1.50
X958	20p. dull purple (10.10.79)	80	20
X959	20p. turquoise-green (23.8.88).................	30	35
X960	20p. brownish black (26.9.89)	30	30
	a. Imperf (pair)		
	l. Booklet pane. No. X960 × 5 plus		
	label with vertical edges of pane		
	imperf (2.10.89)	7.00	
X961	20½p. ultramarine (30.3.83).....................	1.00	85
	a. Imperf (pair)	£750	
X962	22p. blue (22.10.80).............................	80	45
	a. Imperf (pair)	£150	
X963	22p. yellow-green (28.8.84)...................	60	55
	a. Imperf (horiz pair)	£950	
X964	22p. brt orange-red (4.9.90)....................	60	50
X965	23p. brown-red (30.3.83)	1.10	60
	a. Imperf (horiz pair)	£750	
X966	23p. brt green (23.8.88).........................	70	40
X967	24p. violet (28.8.84)	1.75	85
X968	24p. Indian red (26.9.89)	60	60
	a. Imperf (horiz pair)		
X969	24p. chestnut (10.9.91).........................	35	40
	a. Imperf (pair)		
X970	25p. purple (14.1.81).............................	90	90
X971	26p. rosine (Type I) (27.1.82).................	90	30
	a. Type II (4.8.87).............................	4.00	3.75
	al. Booklet pane. No. X971a × 4 with		
	margins all round	15.00	
X972	26p. drab (Type II) (4.9.90)....................	70	70
	a. Imperf (horiz pair)		
X973	27p. chestnut (23.8.88)..........................	1.00	85
	l. Booklet pane. No. X973 × 4 with		
	margins all round	7.00	
	m. Booklet pane. No. X973 × 4 with		
	horizontal edges of pane imperf		
	(11.10.88)	22.00	
X974	27p. violet (4.9.90)	75	75
X975	28p. dp violet (30.3.83)	90	90
	a. Imperf (pair)	£1000	
X976	28p. ochre (23.8.88)	75	75

X977	28p. dp bluish grey (10.9.91)..................	45	50
	a. Imperf (pair)		
X978	29p. ochre-brown (27.1.82)...................	2.00	1.25
X979	29p. dp mauve (26.9.89).......................	1.25	60
X980	30p. dp olive-grey (26.9.89)	45	50
X981	31p. purple (30.3.83)	1.25	1.25
	a. Imperf (pair)	£1000	
X982	31p. ultramarine (4.9.90)	90	90
X983	32p. greenish blue (23.8.88)	1.00	1.00
	a. Imperf (pair)		
X984	33p. lt emerald (4.9.90)	70	70
X985	34p. ochre-brown (28.8.84)....................	1.10	80
X986	34p. dp bluish grey (26.9.89)	1.00	80
X987	34p. dp mauve (10.9.91)........................	55	60
X988	35p. sepia (23.8.88)	1.25	75
	a. Imperf (pair)		
X989	35p. yellow (10.9.91).............................	55	60
X990	37p. rosine (26.9.89)	85	85
X991	39p. brt mauve (10.9.91)........................	60	65

(c) Photo Harrison. On ordinary paper. P 15 × 14

X992	50p. ochre-brown (21.5.80)...................	1.50	45
	a. Imperf (pair)	£400	
X993	75p. grey-black (face value as T **367***a*)		
	(26.7.88)......................................	1.10	1.25

(d) Photo Harrison. On ordinary or phosphorised paper. P 15 × 14

X994	50p. ochre (13.3.90)	75	45
	a. Imperf (pair)	£850	

(e) Litho J.W. P 14

X996	4p. greenish blue (2 bands) (30.1.80)	20	25
X997	4p. greenish blue (phosphorised paper)		
	(11.81)...	35	20
X998	20p. dull purple (2 bands) (21.5.80).........	1.00	40
X999	20p. dull purple (phosphorised paper)		
	(11.81)...	1.25	40

(f) Litho Questa. P 14 *(Nos. X1000, X1003/4 and X1023) or* 15 × 14 *(others)*

X1000	2p. emerald-green (face value as T **367**)		
	(phosphorised paper) (21.5.80)	20	20
	a. Perf 15 × 14 (10.7.84)	30	20
X1001	2p. brt green and dp green (face value as		
	T **367***a*) (phosphorised paper)		
	(23.2.88)..	35	35
X1002	4p. greenish blue (phosphorised paper)		
	(13.5.86)...	50	50
X1003	5p. lt violet (phosphorised paper)		
	(21.5.80)...	40	20
X1004	5p. claret (phosphorised paper) (27.1.82)	50	20
	a. Perf 15 × 14 (21.2.84).....................	50	25
X1005	13p. pale chestnut (1 centre band) (9.2.88)	70	70
	l. Booklet pane. No. X1005 × 6 with		
	margins all round	3.00	
X1006	13p. pale chestnut (1 side band at right)		
	(9.2.88)...	60	60
	Ea. Band at left	60	60
	l. Booklet pane. No. X1006/Ea × 3,		
	X1010, X1015 and X1021 with margins		
	all round	14.00	
	lEa. Grey-green (on 18p) ptg double........		
X1007	14p. dp blue (1 centre band) (11.10.88)	1.25	50
X1008	17p. dp blue (1 centre band) (19.3.91)......	1.00	1.00
	Ey. Phosphor omitted		
	l. Booklet pane. No. X1008 × 6 with		
	margins all round	3.50	
	lEy. Booklet pane. Phosphor omitted		
X1009	18p. dp olive-grey (phosphorised paper)		
	(9.2.88)...	1.00	1.00
	l. Booklet pane. No. X1009 × 9 with		
	margins all round	4.50	
	m. Booklet pane. No. X1009 × 6 with		
	margins all round	3.00	

X1010	18p. dp olive-grey (2 bands) (9.2.88)	4.00	4.00
X1011	18p. brt green (1 centre band) (27.10.92)	75	75
	l. Booklet pane. No. X1011 × 6 with margins all round	1.60	
X1012	18p. brt green (1 side band at right) (27.10.92)	1.50	1.50
	Ea. Band at left (10.8.93)	1.50	1.50
	l. Booklet pane. No. X1012 × 2, X1018 × 2, X1022 × 2, 1451a, 1514a and centre label with margins all round (10.8.93)	9.00	
	m. Booklet pane No. X1012Ea, X1020, X1022 and 1451aEb, each × 2, with centre label and margins all round (10.8.93)	9.50	
X1013	19p. brt orange-red (phosphorised paper) (11.10.88)	1.50	1.50
X1014	20p. dull purple (phosphorised paper) (13.5.86)	1.25	1.25
X1015	22p. yellow-green (2 bands) (9.2.88)	5.00	5.00
X1016	22p. brt orange-red (phosphorised paper) (19.3.91)	1.00	1.00
	l. Booklet pane. No. X1016 × 9 with margins all round	5.50	
	m. Booklet pane. No. X1016 × 6, X1019 × 2 and centre label with margins all round	7.00	
X1017	24p. chestnut (phosphorised paper) (27.10.92)	60	60
	l. Booklet pane. No. X1017 × 6 with margins all round	2.10	
X1018	24p. chestnut (2 bands) (27.10.92)	1.50	1.50
X1019	33p. lt emerald (phosphorised paper) (19.3.91)	2.00	2.00
X1020	33p. lt emerald (2 bands) (25.2.92)	1.25	1.25
X1021	34p. ochre-brown (2 bands) (9.2.88)	5.00	5.00
X1022	39p. brt mauve (2 bands) (27.10.92)	2.50	2.50
X1023	75p. black (face value as T **367**) (ordinary paper) (30.1.80)	3.00	1.50
	a. Perf 15 × 14 (21.2.84)	3.00	3.00
X1024	75p. brownish grey and black (face value as T **367**a) (ordinary paper) (23.2.88)	7.50	5.00

(g) Litho Walsall. P 14

X1050	2p. dp green (phosphorised paper) (9.2.93)	10	10
	l. Booklet pane. No. X1050 × 2 and X1053 × 4	1.50	
X1051	14p. dp blue (1 side band at right) (25.4.89)	3.00	3.00
	Ey. Phosphor omitted	£200	
	l. Booklet pane. No. X1051 × 2 and X1052 × 4 with vertical edges of pane imperf	6.00	
	lEy. Booklet pane. Phosphor omitted	£950	
X1052	19p. brt orange-red (2 bands) (25.4.89)	1.00	1.00
	Ey. Phosphor omitted	£150	
X1053	24p. chestnut (phosphorised paper) (9.2.93)	35	40
X1054	29p. dp mauve (2 bands) (2.10.89)	3.50	3.00
	l. Booklet pane. No. X1054 × 4 with three edges of pane imperf	14.00	
X1055	29p. dp mauve (phosphorised paper) (17.4.90)	3.50	3.50
	l. Booklet pane. No. X1055 × 4 with three edges of pane imperf	14.00	
X1056	31p. ultramarine (phosphorised paper) (17.9.90)	1.25	1.25
	l. Booklet pane. No. X1056 × 4 with horizontal edges of pane imperf	4.50	
X1057	33p. lt emerald (phosphorised paper) (16.9.91)	50	55
	l. Booklet pane. No. X1057 × 4 with horiz edges of pane imperf	2.00	

X1058	39p. brt mauve (phosphorised paper) (16.9.91)	60	65
	l. Booklet pane. No. X1058 × 4 with horiz edges of pane imperf	2.40	

*See footnote after No. 744.

†These come from sheets with gum arabic.

††Examples of Booklet panes Nos. X899l, X901l and X901la are known on which the phosphor bands were printed on the wrong values in error with the result that the side bands appear on the 15½p. or 17p. and the two bands on the 12½p. or 13p. Similarly examples of the 1p. with phosphor band at right, instead of left, exist from 50p. booklet pane No. X847l.

Nos. X844a/b come from a strip of eight of the vertical coil. It comprises two normals, one imperforate at sides and bottom, one completely imperforate, one imperforate at top, left and bottom and partly perforated at right due to the bottom three stamps being perforated twice. No. X844b is also known from another strip having one stamp imperforate at sides and bottom.

Nos. X848b/c come from the same sheet, the latter having perforations at the foot of the stamps only.

Multi-value coil strips Nos. X924l, X925l, X928l, X929l, X930cl and X933l/m were produced by the Post Office for use by a large direct mail marketing firm. From 2 September 1981 No. X929l was available from the Philatelic Bureau, Edinburgh, and, subsequently from a number of other Post Office counters. Later multi-value coil strips were sold at the Philatelic Bureau and Post Office philatelic counters.

No. X1020 comes from the *se-tenant* pane in the Wales £6 booklet. This pane is listed under No. W49a in the Wales Regional section.

PANES OF SIX FROM STITCHED BOOKLETS. Nos. X841m, X851l/m and X855l include one or two printed labels showing commercial advertisements. These were originally perforated on all four sides, but from the August 1971 editions of the 25p. and 30p. booklets (Nos. DH42, DQ59) and December 1971 edition of the 50p. (No. DT4) the line of perforation between the label and the binding margin was omitted. Similar panes, with the line of perforation omitted, exist for the 3p., 3½p. and 4½p. values (Nos. X856, X858 and X865), but these are outside the scope of this listing as the labels are blank.

PART-PERFORATED SHEETS. Since the introduction of the "Jumelle" press in 1972 a number of part-perforated sheets, both definitives and commemoratives, have been discovered. It is believed that these occur when the operation of the press is interrupted. Such sheets invariably show a number of "blind" perforations, where the pins have failed to cut the paper. Our listings of imperforate errors from these sheets are for pairs showing no traces whatsoever of the perforations. Examples showing "blind" perforations are outside the scope of this catalogue.

In cases where perforation varieties affect *se-tenant* stamps, fuller descriptions will be found in Vols. 4 and 5 of the *G.B. Specialised Catalogue*.

WHITE PAPER. From 1972 printings appeared on fluorescent white paper giving a stronger chalk reaction than the original ordinary cream paper.

PHOSPHOR OMITTED ERRORS. These are listed for those stamps or booklet panes which were not subsequently issued on phosphorised paper. The following phosphor omitted errors also exist, but can only be identified by the use of an ultra-violet lamp. Prices quoted are for mint examples:

½p. X841 (£1)	8½p. X881 (£1.75)	17p. X909 (£125)
1p. X844 (£2)	10p. X886 (£1)	18p. X912 (£27)
2p. X849 (£5)	11p. X892 (£2.25)	19p. X914 (£2.25)
3p. X857 (£60)	12p. X895 (£5)	20p. X916
3½p. X860 (£5.50)	14p. X902 (£28)	31p. X919 (£650)
4p. X863 (£85)	15½p. X907 (£4)	33p. X1020
5p. X866 (£200)	16p. X908 (£100)	34p. X920 (£750)

No. X909Eu with underprint Type 4 also exists missing phosphor (*price* £11).

"ALL-OVER" PHOSPHOR. To improve mechanised handling most commemoratives from the 1972 Royal Silver Wedding 3p. value to the 1979 Rowland Hill Death Centenary set had the phosphor applied by printing cylinder across the entire surface of the stamp, giving a matt effect. Printings of the 1, 2 and 10p. definitives, released in October 1979, also had "all-over" phosphor, but these were purely a temporary expedient pending the adoption of phosphorised paper. Nos. X883, X890 and X921 have been discovered with "all-over" phosphor in addition to the normal phosphor bands. These errors are outside the scope of this catalogue.

PHOSPHORISED PAPER. Following the experiments on Nos. 743c and 829 a printing of the 4½p. definitive was issued on 13 November 1974, which had, in addition to the normal phosphor bands, phosphor included in the paper coating. Because of difficulties in identifying this phosphorised paper with the naked eye this printing is not listed separately in this catalogue.

No. X938 was the first value printed on phosphorised paper without phosphor bands and was a further experimental issue to test the efficacy of this system. From 15 August 1979 phosphorised paper was accepted for use generally, this paper replacing phosphor bands on values other than those required for the second-class rate.

Stamps on phosphorised paper show a shiny surface instead of the matt areas of those printed with phosphor bands.

DEXTRIN GUM. From 1973 printings in photogravure appeared with PVA gum to which dextrin had been added. Because this is virtually colourless a bluish green colouring matter was added to distinguish it from the earlier pure PVA.

The 4p., 5p. (light violet), 20p. and 75p. printed in lithography exist with PVA and PVAD gum. From 1988 Questa printings were with PVAD gum, but did not show the bluish green additive.

VARNISH COATING. Nos. X841 and X883 exist with and without a varnish coating. This cannot easily be detected without the use of an ultra-violet lamp as it merely reduces the fluorescent paper reaction.

POSTAL FORGERIES. In 1993 a number of postal forgeries of the 24p. chestnut were detected in the London area. These forgeries, produced by lithography, can be identified by the lack of phosphor in the paper, screening dots across the face values and the perforations which were applied by a line machine gauging 11.

First Day Covers

15.2.71	½p., 1p., 1½p., 2p., 2½p., 3p., 3½p., 4p., 5p., 6p., 7½p., 9p., (X841, X844, X848/9, X851, X855, X858, X861, X866, X870, X877, X882) (Covers carry "POSTING DELAYED BY THE POST OFFICE STRIKE 1971" cachet)..	2.25
11.8.71	10p. (X885)	1.00
24.5.72	Wedgwood se-tenant pane ½p., 2½p. (X841p)	25.00
24.10.73	4½p., 5½p., 8p. (X865, X868, X878)	1.00
4.9.74	6½p. (X871)	1.10
15.1.75	7p. (X874)	75
24.9.75	8½p. (X881)	1.25
25.2.76	9p., 9½p., 10p., 10½p., 11p., 20p. (X883/4, X886, X890, X892, X915)	2.75
2.2.77	50p. (X921)	2.25
26.4.78	10½p. (X891)	1.00
15.8.79	11½p., 13p., 15p. (X942, X944, X947)	2.00
30.1.80	4p., 12p., 13½p., 17p., 17½p., 75p. (X996, X943, X945, X951, X953, X1023)	4.50
16.4.80	Wedgwood se-tenant pane 2p., 10p., 12p. (X849n)	4.00
22.10.80	3p., 22p. (X930, X962)	1.00
14.1.81	2½p., 11½p., 14p., 15½p., 18p., 25p. (X929, X893, X946, X948, X954, X973)	2.25
27.1.82	5p., 12½p., 16½p., 19½p., 26p., 29p. (X1004, X898, X950, X957, X971, X978)	3.25

19.5.82	Stanley Gibbons se-tenant pane 2p., 3p., 12½p. (X849z)	3.50
30.3.83	3½p., 16p., 17p., 20½p., 23p., 28p., 31p. (X931, X949, X952, X961, X965, X975, X981)	4.50
14.9.83	Royal Mint se-tenant pane 3p., 3½p., 16p. (X930b)	5.00
28.8.84	13p., 18p., 22p., 24p., 34p. (X900, X955, X963, X967, X985)	5.00
4.9.84	Christian Heritage se-tenant pane 10p., 13p., 17p. (X886bl)	6.00
8.1.85	The Times se-tenant pane 4p., 13p., 17p., 34p. (X864l)	8.50
29.10.85	7p., 12p. (X937, X896)	2.50
18.3.86	British Rail se-tenant pane 12p., 17p., 31p. (X897m)	9.00
3.3.87	P & O se-tenant pane 1p., 13p., 18p., 26p. (X847m)	6.50
9.2.88	Financial Times se-tenant pane 13p., 18p., 22p., 34p. (X1006l)	7.00
23.8.88	14p., 19p., 20p., 23p., 27p., 28p., 32p., 35p. (X903, X956, X959, X966, X973, X976, X983, X988)	5.50
26.9.89	15p., 20p., 24p., 29p., 30p., 34p., 37p. (X905, X960, X968, X979/80, X986, X990)..	4.00
20.3.90	London Life se-tenant pane 15p., (2nd), 20p., (1st), 15p., 20p., 29p. (X906m)	6.50
4.9.90	10p., 17p., 22p., 26p., 27p., 31p., 33p. (X910, X940, X964, X972, X974, X982, X984)	3.50
19.3.91	Alias Agatha Christie se-tenant pane 22p., 33p. (X1016m)	8.00
10.9.91	6p., 18p., 24p., 28p., 34p., 35p., 39p. (X936, X913, X969, X977, X987, X989, X991)	4.50
27.10.92	Tolkien se-tenant pane 18p., (2nd), 24p., (1st), 39p. (X1012l)	4.25
10.8.93	Beatrix Potter se-tenant pane 18p., (2nd), 33p., 39p. (X1012m)	8.50

Post Office Presentation Packs

15.2.71	P.O. Pack No. 26. ½p. (2 bands), 1p. (2 bands), 1½p. (2 bands), 2p. (2 bands), 2½p. magenta (1 centre band), 3p. ultramarine (2 bands), 3½p. olive-grey (2 bands), 4p. ochre-brown (2 bands), 5p. pale violet (2 bands), 6p. (2 bands), 7½p. (2 bands), 9p. yellow-orange and black (2 bands). (Nos. X841, X844, X848/9, X851, X855, X858, X861, X866, X870, X877, X882)	4.00
15.4.71**	"Scandinavia 71". Contents as above	32.00
25.11.71	P.O. Pack No. 37. ½p. (2 bands), 1p. (2 bands), 1½p. (2 bands), 2p. (2 bands), 2½p. magenta (1 centre band), 3p. ultramarine (2 bands) or (1 centre band), 3½p. olive-grey (2 bands) or (1 centre band), 4p. ochre-brown (2 bands), 4½p. (2 bands), 5p. pale violet (2 bands), 5½p. (2 bands) or (1 centre band), 6p. (2 bands), 6½p. (2 bands) or (1 centre band), 7p. (2 bands), 7½p. (2 bands), 8p. (2 bands), 9p. yellow-orange and black (2 bands), 10p. orange-brown and chestnut (2 bands). (Nos. X841, X844, X848/9, X851, X855 or X856, X858 or X859, X861, X865/6, X868 or X869, X870, X871 or X872, X874, X877/8, X882, X885)	4.00

.2.77. P.O. Pack No. 90. ½p. (2 bands), 1p. (2 bands), 1½p. (2 bands), 2p. (2 bands), 2½p. magenta (1 centre band), 3p ultramarine (1 centre band), 5p. pale violet (2 bands), 6½p. (1 centre band), 7p. (2 bands) or (1 centre band), 7½p. (2 bands), 8p. (2 bands), 8½p. (2 bands), 9p. deep violet (2 bands), 9½p. (2 bands), 10p. orange-brown (2 bands), 10½p. yellow (2 bands), 11p. (2 bands), 20p. dull purple (2 bands), 50p. ochre-brown (2 bands). (*Nos.* X841, X844, X848/9, X851, X856, X866, X872, X874
or X875, X877/8, X881, X883/4, X886, X890, X892, X915, X921) 5.00

8.10.81 P.O. Pack No. 129a. 10½p. deep dull blue (2 bands), 11½p. (1 centre band), 2½p. (phos paper), 3p. (phos paper), 11½p. (phos paper), 12p. (phos paper), 13p. (phos paper), 13½p. (phos paper), 14p. (phos paper), 15p. (phos paper), 15½p. (phos paper), 17p. light emerald (phos paper), 17½p. (phos paper), 18p. deep violet (phos paper), 22p. blue (phos paper), 25p. (phos paper), 4p. greenish blue (litho, 2 bands), 75p. (litho). (*Nos.* X891, X893, X929/30, X942/8, X951, X953/4,
X970, X996, X1023) 16.00

.8.83 P.O. Pack No. 1. 10p. orange-brown (1 centre band), 12½p. (1 centre band), ½p. (phos paper), 1p. (phos paper), 3p. (phos paper), 3½p. (phos paper), 16p. (phos paper), 16½p. (phos paper), 17p. grey-blue (phos paper), 20½p. (phos paper), 23p. brown-red (phos paper), 26p. rosine (phos paper), 28p. deep violet (phos paper), 31p. purple (phos paper), 50p. (ord paper), 2p. (litho phos paper), 4p. (litho phos paper), 5p. claret (litho phos paper), 20p. (litho phos paper), 75p. (litho). (*Nos.* X888, X898, X924/5, X930/1, X949/50, X952, X961, X965, X971, X975, X981, X992, X997, X999, X1000, X1004, X1023) 22.00

23.10.84 P.O. Pack No. 5. 13p. (1 centre band), ½p. (phos paper), 1p. (phos paper), 3p. (phos paper), 10p. orange-brown (phos paper), 16p. (phos paper), 17p. grey-blue (phos paper), 18p. dp olive-grey (phos paper), 22p. bright green (phos paper), 24p. violet (phos paper), 26p. rosine (phos paper), 28p. deep violet (phos paper), 31p. purple (phos paper), 34p. ochre-brown (phos paper), 50p. (ord paper), 2p. (litho phos paper), 4p. (litho phos paper), 5p. claret (litho phos paper), 20p. (litho phos paper), 75p. (litho). (*Nos.* X900, X924/5, X930, X939, X949, X952, X955, X963, X967, X971, X975, X981, X985, X992, X1000a, X997, X999, X1004a, X1023a) 20.00

3.3.87 P.O. Pack No. 9. 12p. (1 centre band), 13p. (1 centre band), 1p. (phos paper), 3p. (phos paper), 7p. (phos paper), 10p. orange-brown (phos paper), 17p. grey-blue (phos paper), 18p. dp olive-grey

(phos paper), 22p. bright green (phos paper), 24p. violet (phos paper), 26p. rosine (phos paper), 28p. deep violet (phos paper), 31p. purple (phos paper), 34p. ochre-brown (phos paper), 50p. (ord paper), 2p. (litho phos paper), 4p. (litho phos paper), 5p. claret (litho phos paper), 20p. (litho phos paper). (*Nos.* X896, X900, X925, X930, X937, X939, X952, X955, X963, X967, X971, X975, X981, X985, X992, X997, X999, X1004a, X1004a, X1023a) 16.00

23.8.88 P.O. Pack No. 15. 14p. (1 centre band), 19p. (phos paper), 20p. turquoise-green (phos paper), 23p. bright green (phos paper), 27p. chestnut (phos paper), 28p. ochre (phos paper), 32p. (phos paper), 35p. sepia (phos paper). (Nos. X903, X956, X959, X966, X973, X976, X983, X988) 9.00

26.9.89 P.O. Pack No. 19. 15p. (centre band), 20p. brownish black (phos paper), 24p. Indian red (phos paper), 29p. deep mauve (phos paper), 30p. (phos paper), 34p. deep bluish grey (phos paper), 37p. (phos paper). (Nos. X905, X960, X968, X979/80, X986, X990) 7.00

4.9.90 P.O. Pack No. 22. 10p. dull orange (phos paper), 17p. (centre band), 22p. bright orange-red (phos paper), 26p. drab (phos paper), 27p. violet (phos paper), 31p. ultramarine (phos paper), 33p. (phos paper). (Nos. X910, X940, X964, X972, X974, X982, X984) 6.00

14.5.91 P.O. Pack No. 24. 1p. (phos paper), 2p. (phos paper), 3p. (phos paper), 4p. new blue (phos paper), 5p. dull red-brown (phos paper), 10p. dull orange (phos paper), 17p. (centre band), 20p. turquoise-green (phos paper), 22p. bright orange-red (phos paper), 26p. drab (phos paper), 27p. violet (phos paper), 30p. (phos paper), 31p. ultramarine (phos paper), 32p. (phos paper), 33p. (phos paper), 37p. (phos paper), 50p. (ord paper), 75p. (ord paper). (Nos. X910, X925, X927, X930, X933, X935, X940, X959, X964, X972, X974, X980, X982, X983/4, X990, X993/4) 7.00

10.9.91 P.O. Pack No. 25. 6p. (phos paper), 18p. (centre band), 24p. chestnut (phos paper), 28p. deep bluish grey (phos paper), 34p. deep mauve (phos paper), 35p. yellow (phos paper), 39p. (phos paper). (Nos. X913, X936, X969, X977, X987, X989, X991) 3.25

**The "Scandinavia 71" was a special pack produced for sale during a visit to six cities in Denmark, Sweden and Norway by a mobile display unit between 15 April and 20 May 1971. The pack gives details of this tour and also lists the other stamps which were due to be issued in 1971, the text being in English. A separate insert gives translations in Danish, Swedish and Norwegian. The pack was also available at the Philatelic Bureau, Edinburgh.

DECIMAL MACHIN INDEX

Those booklet stamps shown below with an * after the catalogue number do not exist with perforations on all four sides, but show one or tw
sides imperforate.

Val. Process	Colour	Phosphor	Cat. No.	Source
½p. photo	turquoise-blue	2 bands	X841/Eg	(a) with P.V.A. gum—sheets, 5p. m/v coil (X841nEv), 10p. m/v coil (X841q), 10p booklets (DN46/75, FA1/3), 25p. booklets (DH39/52), 50p. booklets (DT1/12 FB1, FB14/16, FB19/23), £1 Wedgwood booklet (DX1) (b) with gum arabic—sheets, 5p. m/v coil (X841n)
½p. photo	turquoise-blue	1 band at left	X842	£1 Wedgwood booklet (DX1)
½p. photo	turquoise-blue	1 centre band	X843	10p. m/v coil (X843l), 10p. booklets (FA4/9)
½p. photo	turquoise-blue	phos paper	X924	sheets, 12½p. m/v coil (X924l)
1p. photo	crimson	2 bands	X844/Eg	(a) with P.V.A. gum—sheets, coils, 5p. m/v coil (X841nEv), 10p. m/v coil (X841q 10p. booklets (DN46/75, FA1/3), 50p. booklets (FB1/8, FB14/16) (b) with gum arabic—coils, 5p. m/v coil (X841n)
1p. photo	crimson	1 centre band	X845	10p. m/v coils (X843l, X845m), 10p. booklets (FA4/11), 50p. booklets (FB24/30 34/36, 43/6, 48, 50)
1p. photo	crimson	"all-over"	X846	sheets
1p. photo	crimson	phos paper	X925	sheets, coils, 13p. m/v coil (X925l), 50p. booklets (FB59/66)
1p. photo	crimson	1 band at left	X847	50p. booklets (FB37/42, 47, 49)
1p. photo	crimson	1 band at right	X847Ea	£5 P. & O. booklet (DX8)
1½p. photo	black	2 bands	X848	sheets, 10p. booklets (DN46/75)
2p. photo	myrtle-green	2 bands	X849/Eg	(a) with P.V.A. gum—sheets, 5p. m/v coil (X841nEv), 10p. m/v coil (X841q), 10p booklets (DN46/75), 50p. booklets (FB9/13), £3 Wedgwood booklet (DX2), £4 SC booklet (DX3) (b) with gum arabic—5p. m/v coil (X841n)
2p. photo	myrtle-green	"all-over"	X850	sheets
2p. photo	myrtle-green	phos paper	X926	sheets
2p. photo	myrtle-green	phos paper	X928	14p. m/v coil (X928l)
2p. litho	emerald-green	phos paper	X1000/a	sheets
2p. litho	brt grn & dp grn	phos paper	X1001	sheets
2p. photo	dp green	phos paper	X927	sheets, £1 booklets (FH23/7)
2p. litho	dp green	phos paper	X1050*	£1 booklets (FH28/30)
2½p. photo	magenta	1 centre band	X851/Eg	(a) with P.V.A. gum—sheets, coils, 25p. booklets (DH39/52), 50p. booklet (DT1/12), £1 Wedgwood booklet (DX1) (b) with gum arabic— sheets, coils
2½p. photo	magenta	1 side band	X852/Ea	(a) band at left—50p. booklets (DT1/12), £1 Wedgwood booklet (DX1) (b) band at right—£1 Wedgwood booklet (DX1)
2½p. photo	magenta	2 bands	X853	sheets
2½p. photo	rose-red	phos paper	X929	sheets, 11½p. m/v coil (X929l)
2½p. photo	rose-red	2 bands	X854	50p. booklets (FB17/18)
3p. photo	ultramarine	2 bands	X855/Eg	(a) with P.V.A. gum—sheets, coils, 30p. booklets (DQ56/72), 50p. booklet (DT1/12), £1 Wedgwood booklet (DX1) (b) with gum arabic—sheets, coils
3p. photo	ultramarine	1 centre band	X856/Eg	(a) with P.V.A. gum—sheets, coils, 30p. booklets (DQ73/4), 50p. booklet (DT13/14) (b) with gum arabic—sheets
3p. photo	brt magenta	phos paper	X930	Type I. sheets, 11½p. m/v coil (X929l), £4 Royal Mint booklet (DX4)
3p. photo	brt magenta	phos paper	X930c	Type II. sheets (from 21.1.92), 15p. m/v coil (X930cl)
3p. photo	brt magenta	2 bands	X857	Type I. 50p. booklets (FB19/23), £4 SG booklet (DX3)
3½p. photo	olive-grey	2 bands	X858/Eb	sheets, coils, 35p. booklets (DP1/3), 50p. booklets (DT13/14)
3½p. photo	olive-grey	1 centre band	X859	sheets, coils, 35p. booklet (DP4), 85p. booklet (DW1)
3½p. photo	purple-brown	phos paper	X931	sheets, £4 Royal Mint booklet (DX4)
3½p. photo	purple-brown	1 centre band	X860	50p. booklets (FB24/6)
4p. photo	ochre-brown	2 bands	X861/Eg	(a) with P.V.A. gum—sheets. (b) with gum arabic— sheets

Val. Process	Colour	Phosphor	Cat. No.	Source
4p. litho	greenish blue	2 bands	X996	sheets
4p. photo	greenish blue	2 bands	X862	50p. booklets (FB17/18)
4p. litho	greenish blue	phos paper	X997 X1002	sheets J.W. ptg. sheets Questa ptg.
4p. photo	greenish blue	phos paper	X932 X932Ea	12½p. m/v coil (X924l) 13p. m/v coil (X925l), 14p. m/v coil (X928l)
4p. photo	greenish blue	1 centre band	X863	50p. booklets (FB27/30)
4p. photo	greenish blue	1 side band	X864/Ea	(a) band at right—£5 Times booklet (DX6) (b) band at left—£5 Times booklet (DX6)
4p. photo	new blue	phos paper	X933	sheets, 15p. m/v coil (X930cl), 17p. m/v coil (X933l), 18p. m/v coil (X933m)
4½p. photo	grey-blue	2 bands	X865	sheets, coils, 45p. booklets (DS1/2), 85p. booklet (DW1)
5p. photo	pale violet	2 bands	X866	sheets
5p. photo	pale violet	phos paper	X934	sheets
5p. litho	lt violet	phos paper	X1003	sheets
5p. litho	claret	phos paper	X1004/a	sheets
5p. photo	claret	1 centre band	X867	50p. booklets (FB35/36, 43/6, 48, 50)
5p. photo	dull red-brown	phos paper	X935	sheets, 17p. m/v coil (X933l), 18p. m/v coil (X933m)
5½p. photo	violet	2 bands	X868	sheets
5½p. photo	violet	1 centre band	X869	sheets
6p. photo	lt emerald	2 bands	X870/Eg	(a) with P.V.A. gum—sheets, 10p. m/v coil (X841q), 10p. booklets (FA1/3) (b) with gum arabic—sheets
6p. photo	olive-yellow	phos paper	X936	sheets
6½p. photo	greenish blue	2 bands	X871	sheets
6½p. photo	greenish blue	1 centre band	X872	sheets, coils, 65p. booklet (FC1)
6½p. photo	greenish blue	1 side band	X873/Ea	(a) band at right—50p. booklet (FB1A). (b) band at left—50p. booklet (FB1B)
7p. photo	purple-brown	2 bands	X874	sheets
7p. photo	purple-brown	1 centre band	X875	sheets, coils, 10p. m/v coil (X843l), 10p. booklets (FA4/9), 70p. booklets (FD1/7), £1.60 Christmas booklet (FX1)
7p. photo	purple-brown	1 side band	X876/Ea	(a) band at right—50p. booklets (FB2A/8A) (b) band at left—50p. booklets (FB2B/8B)
7p. photo	brownish red	phos paper	X937	sheets
7½p. photo	pale chestnut	2 bands	X877	sheets
8p. photo	rosine	2 bands	X878	sheets
8p. photo	rosine	1 centre band	X879	sheets, coils, 10p. m/v coil (X845m), 10p. booklets (FA10/11), 80p. booklet (FE1), £1.80 Christmas booklet (FX2)
8p. photo	rosine	1 side band	X880/Ea	(a) band at right—50p. booklets (FB9A/10A) (b) band at left—50p. booklets (FB9B/10B)
8½p. photo	lt yellowish green	2 bands	X881	sheets, coils, 50p. booklet (FB1), 85p. booklet (FF1)
8½p. photo	yellowish green	phos paper	X938	sheets
9p. photo	yellow-orange & black	2 bands	X882	sheets
9p. photo	dp violet	2 bands	X883	sheets, coils, 50p. booklets (FB2/8), 90p. booklets (FG1/8), £1.60 Christmas booklet (FX1)
9½p. photo	purple	2 bands	X884	sheets
10p. recess	cerise	phos paper	829	sheets
10p. photo	orange-brown & chestnut	2 bands	X885	sheets
10p. photo	orange-brown	2 bands	X886	Type I. sheets, 50p. booklets (FB9/10), £1.80 Christmas booklet (FX2)
10p. photo	orange-brown	2 bands	X886b	Type II. £4 Christian Heritage booklet (DX5)
10p. photo	orange-brown	"all-over"	X887	Type I. sheets, coils, £1 booklet (FH1)
10p. photo	orange-brown	phos paper	X939	Type I. sheets
10p. photo	orange-brown	1 centre band	X888	Type I. sheets, coils, £1 booklets (FH2/4), £2.20 Christmas booklet (FX3), £3 Wedgwood booklet (DX2)

Val. Process	Colour	Phosphor	Cat. No.	Source
10p. photo	orange-brown	1 side band	X889/Ea	Type I. (a) band at right—50p. booklets (FB11A/13A) (b) band at left—50p. booklets (FB11B/13B), £3 Wedgwood booklet (DX2)
10p. photo	dull orange	phos paper	X940	sheets
10½p. photo	yellow	2 bands	X890	sheets
10½p. photo	dp dull blue	2 bands	X891	sheets
11p. photo	brown-red	2 bands	X892	sheets
11p. photo	brown-red	phos paper	X941	sheets
11½p. photo	ochre-brown	phos paper	X942	sheets
11½p. photo	drab	1 centre band	X893	sheets, coils, £1.15 booklets (FI1/4), £2.55 Christmas booklet (FX4)
11½p. photo	drab	1 side band	X894/Ea	(a) band at right—50p. booklets (FB14A/18A), £1.30 booklets (FL1/2) (b) band at left—50p. booklets (FB14B/18B), £1.30 booklets (FL1/2)
12p. photo	yellowish green	phos paper	X943	sheets, coils, £1.20 booklets (FJ1/3)
12p. photo	yellowish green	2 bands	X895	50p. booklets (FB11/13), £2.20 Christmas booklet (FX3), £3 Wedgwood booklet (DX2)
12p. photo	brt emerald	1 centre band	X896	sheets, coils, 50p. booklet (FB34), £1.20 booklets (FJ4/6), £5 British Rail booklet (DX7)
12p. photo	brt emerald	1 side band	X897/Ea	(a) band at right—£1.50 booklets (FP1/2), £5 British Rail booklet (DX7) (b) band at left—£1.50 booklets (FP1/2), £5 British Rail booklet (DX7)
12p. photo	brt emerald	1 centre band Underprint T.4	X896Eu	sheets
12½p. photo	lt emerald	1 centre band	X898	sheets, coils, 50p. booklets (FB24/6), £1.25 booklets (FK1/8), £4 SG booklet (DX3)
12½p. photo	lt emerald	1 centre band Underprint T.1	X898Eu	£2.80 Christmas booklet (FX5)
12½p. photo	lt emerald	1 centre band Underprint T.2	X898Eua	£2.50 Christmas booklet (FX6)
12½p. photo	lt emerald	1 side band	X899/Ea	(a) band at right—50p. booklets (FB19A/23A), £1.43 booklets (FN1/6), £1.46 booklets (FO1/3), £4 SG booklet (DX3), £4 Royal Mint booklet (DX4) (b) band at left—50p. booklets (FB19B/23B), £1.43 booklets (FN1/6), £1.46 booklets (FO1/3), £4 SG booklet (DX3), £4 Royal Mint booklet (DX4)
13p. photo	olive-grey	phos paper	X944	sheets
13p. photo	pale chestnut	1 centre band	X900	sheets, coils, 50p. booklets (FB27/30, 35/6, 43/6, 48, 50), 52p. booklet (GA1), £1.30 booklets (FL3/14, GI1), £5 Times booklet (DX6), £5 P & O booklet (DX8)
13p. photo	pale chestnut	1 centre band Underprint T.2	X900Eu	£1.30 Christmas booklet (FX9)
13p. photo	pale chestnut	1 side band	X901/Ea	(a) band at right—50p. booklets (FB37/42, 47, 49), £1.54 booklets (FQ1/4), £4 Christian Heritage booklet (DX5), £5 Times booklet (DX6), £5 P & O booklet (DX8) (b) band at left—£1 booklets (FH6/13), £1.54 booklets (FQ1/4), £4 Christian Heritage booklet (DX5), £5 Times booklet (DX6)
13p. litho	pale chestnut	1 centre band	X1005	£5 Financial Times booklet (DX9)
13p. litho	pale chestnut	1 side band	X1006/Ea	£5 Financial Times booklet (DX9)
13½p. photo	purple-brown	phos paper	X945	sheets
14p. photo	grey-blue	phos paper	X946	sheets, coils, £1.40 booklets (FM1/4)
14p. photo	grey-blue	2 bands	X902	50p. booklets (FB14/16), £1.30 booklets (FL1/2), £2.55 Christmas booklet (FX4)
14p. photo	dp blue	1 centre band	X903	sheets, coils, 56p. booklets (GB1/4), £1.40 booklets (FM5/6, GK1, 3)
14p. photo	dp blue	1 band at right	X904	50p. booklets (FB51/4), £1 booklets (FH14/15)
14p. litho	dp blue	1 centre band	X1007	£1.40 booklets (GK2, 4)
14p. litho	dp blue	1 band at right	X1051*	£1 booklet (FH16)
15p. photo	ultramarine	phos paper	X947	sheets
15p. photo	brt blue	1 centre band	X905	sheets, coils
15p. photo	brt blue	1 side band	X906/Ea	(a) band at left—50p. booklet (FB55) (b) band at right—£5 London Life booklet (DX11)
15½p. photo	pale violet	phos paper	X948	sheets, coils, £1.55 booklets (FR1/6)

Val. Process	Colour	Phosphor	Cat. No.	Source
5½p. photo	pale violet	2 bands	X907	£1.43 booklets (FN1/6), £4 SG booklet (DX3)
5½p. photo	pale violet	2 bands Underprint T.1	X907Eu	£2.80 Christmas booklet (FX5)
16p. photo	olive-drab	phos paper	X949	sheets, coils, £1.60 booklets (FS1, 3/4), £4 Royal Mint booklet (DX4)
16p. photo	olive-drab	phos paper Underprint T.3	X949Eu	£1.60 booklet (FS2)
16p. photo	olive-drab	2 bands	X908	£1.46 booklets (FO1/3)
6½p. photo	pale chestnut	phos paper	X950	sheets
17p. photo	lt emerald	phos paper	X951	sheets
17p. photo	grey-blue	phos paper	X952	sheets, coils, £1 booklet (FH5), £1.70 booklets (FT1, 3 & 5/7), £4 Christian Heritage booklet (DX5), £5 Times booklet (DX6), £5 British Rail booklet (DX7)
17p. photo	grey-blue	phos paper Underprint T.3	X952Eu	£1.70 booklet (FT2)
17p. photo	grey-blue	2 bands	X909	50p. booklet (FB33), £1.50 booklets (FP1/3), £1.54 booklets (FQ1/4), £4 Christian Heritage booklet (DX5), £5 Times booklet (DX6), £5 British Rail booklet (DX7)
17p. photo	grey-blue	2 bands Underprint T.4	X909Eu	50p. booklets (FB31/33)
17p. photo	dp blue	1 centre band	X910	sheets, coils
17p. photo	dp blue	1 side band	X911/Ea	(a) band at right— 50p. booklet (FB57/8), £1 booklet (FH21/2) (b) band at left—50p. booklet (FB57/8)
17p. litho	dp blue	1 centre band	X1008	£6 Alias Agatha Christie booklet (DX12)
7½p. photo	pale chestnut	phos paper	X953	sheets
18p. photo	dp violet	phos paper	X954	sheets
18p. photo	dp olive-grey	phos paper	X955	sheets, coils, 72p. booklet (GC1), £1.80 booklets (FU1/8, GM1), £5 P & O booklet (DX8)
18p. photo	dp olive-grey	2 bands	X912	50p. booklets (FB37/42, 47, 49), £1 booklet (FH6/13), £5 P & O booklet (DX8)
18p. litho	dp olive-grey	phos paper	X1009	£5 Financial Times booklet (DX9)
18p. litho	dp olive-grey	2 bands	X1010	£5 Financial Times booklet (DX9)
18p. photo	brt green	1 centre band	X913	sheets, coils
18p. litho	brt green	1 centre band	X1011	£6 Tolkien booklet (DX14)
18p. litho	brt green	1 side band	X1012	(a) band at right—£6 Tolkien booklet (DX14) (b) band at left—£6 (£5.64) Beatrix Potter booklet (DX15)
19p. photo	brt orange-red	2 bands	X914	50p. booklets (FB51/4), £1 booklets (FH14/15, 17)
19p. photo	brt orange-red	phos paper	X956	sheets, coils, 76p. booklets (GD1/4), £1.90 booklets (FV1/2, GN1, 3)
19p. litho	brt orange-red	phos paper	X1013	£1.90 booklets (GN2, 4)
19p. litho	brt orange-red	2 bands	X1052*	£1 booklet (FH16)
9½p. photo	olive-grey	phos paper	X957	sheets
20p. recess	olive-green	none	830	sheets
20p. photo	dull purple	2 bands	X915	sheets
20p. photo	dull purple	phos paper	X958	sheets
20p. litho	dull purple	2 bands	X998	sheets
20p. litho	dull purple	phos paper	X999 X1014	sheets J.W. ptg. sheets Questa ptg.
20p. photo	turquoise-green	phos paper	X959	sheets
20p. photo	brownish black	2 bands	X916	50p. booklet (FB55), £5 London Life booklet (DX11)
20p. photo	brownish black	phos paper	X960	sheets, coils, £1 booklet (FH18)
20½p. photo	ultramarine	phos paper	X961	sheets
22p. photo	blue	phos paper	X962	sheets
22p. photo	yellow-green	phos paper	X963	sheets
22p. litho	yellow-green	2 bands	X1015	£5 Financial Times booklet (DX9)
22p. photo	brt orange-red	2 bands	X917*	£1 booklet (FH21/2)
22p. photo	brt orange-red	phos paper	X964	sheets, coils

Decimal Machin Index (continued)

Val. Process	Colour	Phosphor	Cat. No.	Source
22p. litho	brt orange-red	phos paper	X1016	£6 Alias Agatha Christie booklet (DX12)
23p. photo	brown-red	phos paper	X965	sheets
23p. photo	brt green	phos paper	X966	sheets
24p. photo	violet	phos paper	X967	sheets
24p. photo	Indian red	phos paper	X968	sheets
24p. photo	chestnut	phos paper	X969	sheets, coils, 50p. booklets (FB59/66), £1 booklets (FH23/7)
24p. litho	chestnut	phos paper	X1017 X1053*	£6 Tolkien booklet (DX14) (Questa ptg) £1 booklets (FH28/30) (Walsall ptg)
24p. litho	chestnut	2 bands	X1018	£6 Tolkien booklet (DX14)
25p. photo	purple	phos paper	X970	sheets
26p. photo	rosine	2 bands	X918	Type I. £5 P & O booklet (DX8)
26p. photo	rosine	phos paper	X971	Type I. sheets
26p. photo	rosine	phos paper	X971a	Type II. £1.04 booklet (GE1)
26p. photo	drab	phos paper	X972	sheets
27p. photo	chestnut	phos paper	X973	sheets, £1.08 booklets (GF1/2)
27p. photo	violet	phos paper	X974	sheets
28p. photo	dp violet	phos paper	X975	sheets
28p. photo	ochre	phos paper	X976	sheets
28p. photo	dp bluish grey	phos paper	X977	sheets
29p. photo	ochre-brown	phos paper	X978	sheets
29p. photo	dp mauve	phos paper	X979	sheets
29p. litho	dp mauve	2 bands	X1054*	£1.16 booklet (GG1)
29p. litho	dp mauve	phos paper	X1055*	£1.16 booklet (GG2)
30p. photo	dp olive-grey	phos paper	X980	sheets
31p. photo	purple	2 bands	X919	£5 British Rail booklet (DX7)
31p. photo	purple	phos paper	X981	sheets
31p. photo	ultramarine	phos paper	X982	sheets
31p. litho	ultramarine	phos paper	X1056*	£1.24 booklet (GH1)
32p. photo	greenish blue	phos paper	X983	sheets
33p. photo	lt emerald	phos paper	X984	sheets, coils
33p. litho	lt emerald	phos paper	X1019	£6 Alias Agatha Christie booklet (DX12)
33p. litho	lt emerald	phos paper	X1057*	£1.32 booklet (GJ1)
33p. litho	lt emerald	2 bands	X1020	£6 Wales booklet (DX13), £6 (£5.64) Beatrix Potter booklet (DX15)
34p. photo	ochre-brown	2 bands	X920	£5 Times booklet (DX6)
34p. photo	ochre-brown	phos paper	X985	sheets
34p. litho	ochre-brown	2 bands	X1021	£5 Financial Times booklet (DX9)
34p. photo	dp bluish grey	phos paper	X986	sheets
34p. photo	dp mauve	phos paper	X987	sheets
35p. photo	sepia	phos paper	X988	sheets
35p. photo	yellow	phos paper	X989	sheets
37p. photo	rosine	phos paper	X990	sheets
39p. photo	brt mauve	phos paper	X991	sheets, coils
39p. litho	brt mauve	phos paper	X1058*	78p. booklet (GD4a), £1.56 booklet (GL1)
39p. litho	brt mauve	2 bands	X1022	£6 Tolkien booklet (DX14), £6 (£5.64) Beatrix Potter booklet (DX15)
50p. recess	dp ultramarine	none or phos paper	831/Ea	sheets
50p. photo	ochre-brown	2 bands	X921	sheets
50p. photo	ochre-brown	none	X992	sheets
50p. photo	ochre	2 bands	X922	£5 London Life booklet (DX11)

Val. Process	Colour	Phosphor	Cat. No.	Source
50p. photo	ochre	none or phos paper	X994	sheets
75p. litho	black	none	X1023/a	sheets
75p. litho	brownish grey & black	none	X1024	sheets
75p. photo	grey-black	none	X993	sheets
£1 recess	bluish black	none	831b	sheets
£1 photo	brt yellow-green & blackish olive	none	1026	sheets
£1.30 photo	drab & dp greenish blue	none	1026b	sheets
£1.33 photo	pale mauve & grey-black	none	1026c	sheets
£1.41 photo	drab & dp greenish blue	none	1026d	sheets
£1.50 photo	pale mauve & grey-black	none	1026e	sheets
£1.60 photo	pale drab & dp greenish blue	none	1026f	sheets
£2 photo	lt emerald & purple-brown	none	1027	sheets
£5 photo	salmon & chalky blue	none	1028	sheets

For 1st and 2nd class no value indicated (NVI) stamps, see Nos. 1445/52 and 1511/16.
For table covering Machin stamps with elliptical perforations see after Nos. Y1667, etc, in 1993.

Decimal Machin Booklet Pane Guide

Abbreviations used in the diagrams: 2B = 2 bands, CB = centre band, LB = left band and RB = right band. The shaded squares represent printed labels. Panes completed by unprinted white labels are outside the scope of this catalogue.

Unless otherwise stated the panes were printed in photogravure. Some panes exist in photogravure and lithography and these are separately identified and listed. **Imperforate or straight edges.** These are described under the appropriate illustration and listed as complete panes.

X841l (2 bands)   X841la (2 bands)   X841m (2 bands)   X841o £1 Wedgwood   X841p £1 Wedgwood

X841r (2 bands)   X841s   X841sa   X841t   X841ta   X841u   X841ua   X843m (centre band)

X844l (2 bands)   X844m (2 bands)   X844n   X844na   X845l (centre band)   X845n (centre band)   X845p (centre band)   X845q (centre band)

X845s/sa (centre band) X845sa imperf at left and right   X847l

X847m £5 P & O

X849l

X849la

X849m

X849ma

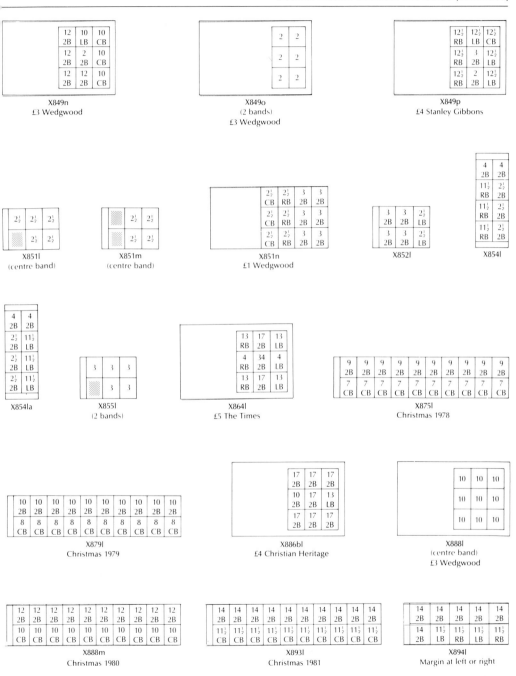

X849n
£3 Wedgwood

X849o
(2 bands)
£3 Wedgwood

X849p
£4 Stanley Gibbons

X851l
(centre band)

X851m
(centre band)

X851n
£1 Wedgwood

X852l

X854l

X854la

X855l
(2 bands)

X864l
£5 The Times

X875l
Christmas 1978

X879l
Christmas 1979

X886bl
£4 Christian Heritage

X888l
(centre band)
£3 Wedgwood

X888m
Christmas 1980

X893l
Christmas 1981

X894l
Margin at left or right

X895l
(2 bands)
£3 Wedgwood

X896l
(centre band)
£5 British Rail

X897l

X897la

X897m
£5 British Rail

X898l
Christmas 1982

X899l
Margin at left or right

X899m
£4 Stanley Gibbons
£4 Royal Mint

X899n

X899na

X900l
(centre band)
£5 The Times
£5 P & O

X900m (photo), X1005l (litho)
(centre band)
£5 P & O (X900m)
£5 Financial Times (X1005l)

X900n
(centre band)
52p. Barcode Booklet

X900o
(centre band)
£1.30 Barcode Booklet

X901l

X901la

X901m
£4 Christian Heritage

X901n/na
X901na imperf at left
and right

X903l
(centre band)
56p. Barcode Bookle

X903m
(centre band)
£1.40 Barcode Booklet

X903n, X903q
(centre band)
56p. Barcode Booklet
X903n imperf at top
and bottom
X903q imperf 3 sides

X903p
(centre band)
£1.40 Barcode Booklet
Imperf at top and bottom

X904l

X904m (photo),
X1051l (litho)
Imperf at left
and right

X906l

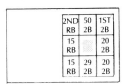

X906m
£5 London Life
The stamps in the bottom row
are Penny Black Anniversary
definitives (Nos. 1468Ea, 1470 and 1472)

X907l
(2 bands)
£4 Stanley Gibbons

X907m
(2 bands)
£4 Stanley Gibbons

X909l
(2 band)
and underprint
X909 Ela (as X909l
but without
underprint)

X911l

X911m
Imperf at left
and right

X925m
(phosphorised paper)

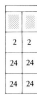

X927l (photo)
X1050l (litho)
(phosphorised paper)
Imperf at left and
right

X930b
(phosphorised paper)
£4 Royal Mint

X949l
(phosphorised paper)
£4 Royal Mint

X952l
(phosphorised paper)
£4 Christian Heritage
£5 The Times
£5 British Rail
X1008l
(centre band)
£6 Agatha Christie

X952m
(phosphorised paper)
£5 The Times
£5 British Rail

X955l (photo), X1009l (litho)
(phosphorised paper)
£5 P & O (X955l)
£5 Financial Times (X1009l)

Decimal Machin Booklet Pane Guide (continued)

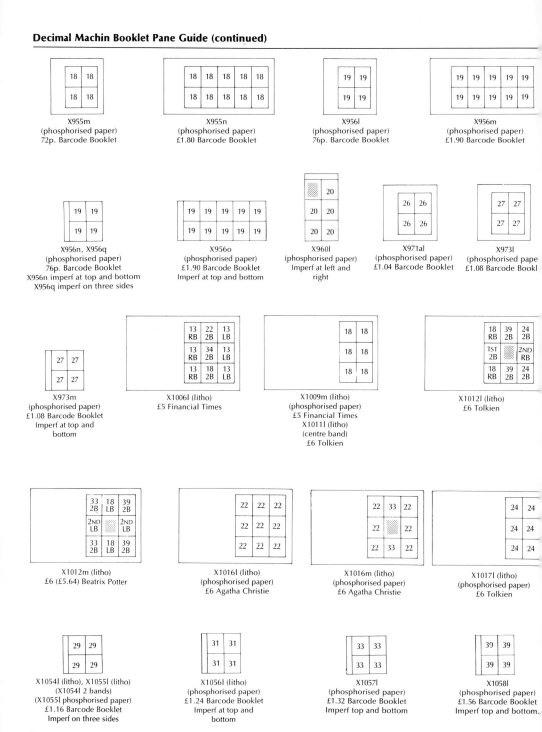

X955m
(phosphorised paper)
72p. Barcode Booklet

X955n
(phosphorised paper)
£1.80 Barcode Booklet

X956l
(phosphorised paper)
76p. Barcode Booklet

X956m
(phosphorised paper)
£1.90 Barcode Booklet

X956n, X956q
(phosphorised paper)
76p. Barcode Booklet
X956n imperf at top and bottom
X956q imperf on three sides

X956o
(phosphorised paper)
£1.90 Barcode Booklet
Imperf at top and bottom

X960l
(phosphorised paper)
Imperf at left and right

X971al
(phosphorised paper)
£1.04 Barcode Booklet

X973l
(phosphorised pape
£1.08 Barcode Bookl

X973m
(phosphorised paper)
£1.08 Barcode Booklet
Imperf at top and bottom

X1006l (litho)
£5 Financial Times

X1009m (litho)
(phosphorised paper)
£5 Financial Times
X1011l (litho)
(centre band)
£6 Tolkien

X1012l (litho)
£6 Tolkien

X1012m (litho)
£6 (£5.64) Beatrix Potter

X1016l (litho)
(phosphorised paper)
£6 Agatha Christie

X1016m (litho)
(phosphorised paper)
£6 Agatha Christie

X1017l (litho)
(phosphorised paper)
£6 Tolkien

X1054l (litho), X1055l (litho)
(X1054l 2 bands)
(X1055l phosphorised paper)
£1.16 Barcode Booklet
Imperf on three sides

X1056l (litho)
(phosphorised paper)
£1.24 Barcode Booklet
Imperf at top and bottom

X1057l
(phosphorised paper)
£1.32 Barcode Booklet
Imperf top and bottom

X1058l
(phosphorised paper)
£1.56 Barcode Booklet
Imperf top and bottom.

368 "A Mountain Road"
(T. P. Flanagan)

369 "Deer's Meadow"
(Tom Carr)

371 John Keats
(150th Death Anniv)

372 Thomas Gray
(Death Bicentenary)

370 "Slieve na brock"
(Colin Middleton)

373 Sir Walter Scott (Birth Bicentenary)

(Des Rosalind Dease. Queen's head printed in gold and then embossed)

1971 (16 June). **"Ulster 1971" Paintings.** *Chalk-surfaced paper. Two phosphor bands. P* 15 × 14.

881	368	3p. yellow-buff, pale yellow, Venetian red, black, blue and drab...............	10	10
		Ey. Phosphor omitted...........................	2.00	
882	369	7½p. olive-brown, brownish grey, pale olive-grey, dp blue, cobalt & grey-blue	50	50
		a. Pale olive-grey omitted*	60.00	
		Ey. Phosphor omitted...........................	12.00	
883	370	9p. greenish yellow, orange, grey, lavender-grey, bistre, black, pale ochre-brown, and ochre-brown.......	50	50
		a. Orange omitted	£500	
		Ey. Phosphor omitted...........................	13.00	
		Set of 3	1.00	1.00
		First Day Cover		1.75
		Presentation Pack...........................	5.00	

A used example of the 3p. has been seen with the Venetian red omitted.

*This only affects the boulder in the foreground, which appears whitish and it only applied to some stamps in the sheet.

1971 (28 July). **Literary Anniversaries.** *Chalk-surfaced paper. Two phosphor bands. P* 15 × 14.

884	371	3p. black, gold & greyish blue..............	10	10
		a. Gold (Queen's head) omitted	75.00	
		Ey. Phosphor omitted...........................	2.00	
885	372	5p. black, gold & yellow-olive	50	50
		a. Gold (Queen's head) omitted	£160	
		Ey. Phosphor omitted...........................	20.00	
886	373	7½p. black, gold & yellow-brown............	50	50
		Eb. Embossing omitted	25.00	
		Ey. Phosphor omitted...........................	13.00	
		Set of 3	1.00	1.00
		First Day Cover		1.50
		Presentation Pack........................	5.00	

Special First Day of Issue Postmarks

Special First Day of Issue Postmarks

British Post Office Philatelic Bureau, Edinburgh (Type
  D, see Introduction) 2.75
London EC 3.25

**FIRST DAY OF ISSUE
16 JUNE 1971
BELFAST**

British Post Office Philatelic Bureau, Edinburgh (Type
  D, see Introduction) 2.50
Belfast.. 4.25
First Day of Issue handstamps, in the same design as that for Belfast, were provided at Armagh, Ballymena, Coleraine, Cookstown, Enniskillen, Londonderry, Newry, Omagh and Portadown for this issue.

374 Servicemen and Nurse of 1921

375 Roman Centurion

376 Rugby Football, 1871

(Des F. Wegner)

1971 (25 Aug). **British Anniversaries.** *Events described on stamps. Chalk-surfaced paper. Two phosphor bands.* P 15 × 14.

887	**374**	3p. red-orange, grey, dp blue, olive-green, olive-brown, black, rosine & violet-blue	10	10
		a. Dp blue omitted*	£600	
		b. Red-orange (nurse's cloak) omitted	£275	
		c. Olive-brown (faces, etc.) omitted	£160	
		d. Black omitted	£10000	
		Ey. Phosphor omitted	1.25	
888	**375**	7½p. grey, yellow-brown, vermilion, mauve, grey-black, black, silver, gold & ochre	50	50
		a. Grey omitted	75.00	
		Ey. Phosphor omitted	6.00	
889	**376**	9p. new blue, myrtle-green, grey-black, lemon, olive-brown, magenta & yellow-olive	50	50
		a. Olive-brown omitted	£110	
		b. New blue omitted	£1750	
		c. Myrtle-green omitted	£2000	
		Ey. Phosphor omitted	£400	
		Set of 3	1.00	1.00
		First Day Cover		1.50
		Presentation Pack	5.00	

*The effect of the missing deep blue is shown on the sailor's uniform, which appears as grey.

A used example has been seen of the 3p. with grey omitted.

Special First Day of Issue Postmarks

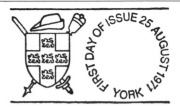

British Post Office Philatelic Bureau, Edinburgh (Type D, see Introduction) 3.00
Maidstone 13.00
Twickenham.. 13.50
York.. 14.00

377 Physical Sciences Building University College of Wales, Aberystwyth

378 Faraday Building, Southampton University

379 Engineering Department Leicester University

380 Hexagon Restaurant, Essex University

(Des N. Jenkins)

1971 (22 Sept). **British Architecture.** *Modern University Buildings. Chalk-surfaced paper. Two phosphor bands.* P 15 × 14.

890	**377**	3p. olive-brown, ochre, lemon, black & yellow-olive	10	10
		a. Lemon omitted		
		b. Black (windows) omitted	£5500	
		Ey. Phosphor omitted	3.75	
891	**378**	5p. rose, black, chestnut & lilac	20	20
		Ey. Phosphor omitted	50.00	
892	**379**	7½p. ochre, black & purple-brown	50	50
		Ey. Phosphor omitted	7.00	
893	**380**	9p. pale lilac, black, sepia-brown & dp blue	90	90
		Ey. Phosphor omitted	10.00	
		Set of 4	1.50	1.50
		First Day Cover		1.50
		Presentation Pack	5.00	

Mint examples of Type **378** exist with a larger "p" following the face value.

Special First Day of Issue Postmarks

British Post Office Philatelic Bureau, Edinburgh (Type
D, see Introduction) 3.50
Aberystwyth 12.00
Colchester 12.00
Leicester 12.00
Southampton 12.00

Collectors Pack 1971

1971 (29 Sept). *Comprises Nos. 835/40 and 881/93.*
CP893a   Collectors Pack 28.00

381 "Dream of the Wise Men"

382 "Adoration of the Magi"

383 "Ride of the Magi"

(Des Clarke-Clements-Hughes design team, from stained-glass windows, Canterbury Cathedral. Queen's head printed in gold and then
embossed)

1971 (13 Oct). **Christmas**. *Ordinary paper. One centre phosphor band
(2½p). or two phosphor bands (orther). P 15 × 14.*

894	**381**	2½p. new blue, black, lemon, emerald, reddish violet, carmine-red, carmine-rose & gold..........	10	10
		a. Imperf (pair)	£450	
		Eb. Embossing omitted		
895	**382**	3p. black, reddish violet, lemon, new blue, carmine-rose, emerald, ultra-marine & gold..........	10	10
		a. Gold (Queen's head) omitted	£350	
		b. Carmine-rose omitted	£1750	
		c. Lemon omitted	60.00	
		d. New blue omitted	†	—
		Ee. Embossing omitted........................	5.00	
		Ey. Phosphor omitted..........................	1.75	
		Eya. Embossing & phosphor omitted..........	50.00	
896	**383**	7½p. black, lilac, lemon, emerald, new blue, rose, green & gold	90	90
		a. Gold (Queen's head) omitted	90.00	
		b. Lilac omitted................................	£400	
		c. Emerald omitted	£200	
		Ed. Embossing omitted........................	30.00	
		Ee. Embossing double	30.00	
		Ey. Phosphor omitted..........................	6.00	
		Eya. Embossing & phosphor omitted..........	20.00	
		Set of 3	1.00	1.00
		First Day Cover		1.50
		Presentation Pack	4.00	

The 3p. is known with reddish violet and embossing omitted, used
in Llandudno and with lemon and carmine-rose both omitted used in
Falkirk. The 7½p. is known in used condition showing the lemon
omitted.

Special First Day of Issue Postmarks

British Post Office Philatelic Bureau, Edinburgh (Type
D, see Introduction) 3.50
Bethlehem, Llandeilo, Carms 6.00
Canterbury 6.00

WHITE CHALK-SURFACED PAPER. From No. 897 all issues, with the exception of Nos. 904/8, were printed on fluorescent white paper, giving a stronger chalk reaction than the original cream paper.

384 Sir James Clark Ross

385 Sir Martin Frobisher

386 Henry Hudson

387 Capt. Scott

(Des Marjorie Saynor. Queen's head printed in gold and then embossed)

1972 (16 Feb). **British Polar Explorers.** *Two phosphor bands.* P 14 × 15.

897	384	3p. yellow-brown, indigo, slate-black, flesh, lemon, rose, brt blue & gold ...	10	10
		a. Gold (Queen's head) omitted	60.00	
		b. Slate-black (hair, etc.) omitted	£2000	
		c. Lemon omitted		
		Ed. Embossing omitted	25.00	
		Ee. Gold (Queen's head) & embossing omitted	75.00	
		Ey. Phosphor omitted..........................	1.25	
		Eya. Embossing & phosphor omitted	20.00	
898	385	5p. salmon, flesh, purple-brown, ochre, black & gold	20	20
		a. Gold (Queen's head) omitted	90.00	
		Eb. Embossing omitted	12.00	
		Ey. Phosphor omitted..........................	7.00	
		Eya. Gold & phosphor omitted	£110	
		Eyb. Embossing & phosphor omitted		
899	386	7½p. reddish violet, blue, dp slate, yellow-brown, buff, black & gold	50	50
		a. Gold (Queen's head) omitted	£200	
		Ey. Phosphor omitted..........................	14.00	
900	387	9p. dull blue, ultramarine, black, greenish yellow, pale pink, rose-red & gold	90	90
		Ey. Phosphor omitted..........................	£275	
		Set of 4	1.50	1.50
		First Day Cover		2.00
		Presentation Pack..........................	4.50	

An example of the 3p. is known used on piece with the flesh colour omitted.

Special First Day of Issue Postmarks

Philatelic Bureau, Edinburgh 6.00
London WC 7.50

388 Statuette of Tutankhamun

389 19th-century Coastguard

390 Ralph Vaughan Williams and Score

(Des Rosalind Dease (3p.), F. Wegner (7½p.), C. Abbott (9p.). Queen's head printed in gold and then embossed (7½p., 9p.))

1972 (26 Apr). **General Anniversaries.** *Events described on stamps. Two phosphor bands.* P 15 × 14.

901	388	3p. black, grey, gold, dull bistre-brown, blackish brown, pale stone & lt brown	10	10
902	389	7½p. pale yellow, new blue, slate-blue, violet-blue, slate & gold	50	50
		Ea. Embossing omitted...........................		
		Ey. Phosphor omitted...........................	£250	
903	390	9p. bistre-brown, black, sage-green, dp slate, yellow-ochre, brown & gold	50	50
		a. Gold (Queen's head) omitted	£1250	
		b. Brown (facial features) omitted	£750	
		c. Deep slate omitted.........................	£7500	
		Ed. Embossing omitted.........................		
		Ey. Phosphor omitted...........................	22.00	
		Set of 3	1.00	1.00
		First Day Cover		1.50
		Presentation Pack	4.00	

Special First Day of Issue Postmarks

Philatelic Bureau, Edinburgh 3.00
London EC 4.00

391 St. Andrew's,
Greensted-juxta-Ongar, Essex

392 All Saints, Earls Barton,
Northants

393 St. Andrew's,
Letheringsett, Norfolk

394 St. Andrew's,
Helpringham, Lincs

395 St. Mary the Virgin, Huish
Episcopi, Somerset

(Des R. Maddox. Queen's head printed in gold and then embossed)

1972 (21 June). **British Architecture.** *Village Churches. Ordinary paper. Two phosphor bands.* P 14 × 15.

904	**391**	3p. violet-blue, black, lt yellow-olive, emerald-green, orange-vermilion & gold	10	10
		a. Gold (Queen's head) omitted	75.00	
		Eb. Embossing omitted	20.00	
		Ey. Phosphor omitted..........................	2.00	
		Eya. Gold (Queen's head) & phosphor omitted	£110	
		Eyb. Embossing & phosphor omitted	10.00	
905	**392**	4p. dp yellow-olive, black, emerald, violet-blue, orange-vermilion & gold	20	20
		a. Gold (Queen's head) omitted	£2000	
		b. Violet-blue omitted........................	£110	
		Ec. Embossing omitted	6.00	
		Ey. Phosphor omitted..........................	10.00	
906	**393**	5p. dp emerald, black, royal blue, lt yellow-olive, orange-vermilion & gold ..	20	25
		a. Gold (Queen's head) omitted	£150	
		Eb. Embossing omitted	25.00	
		Ey. Phosphor omitted..........................	15.00	
907	**394**	7½p. orange-red, black, dp yellow-olive, royal blue, lt emerald & gold	70	80
		Ey. Phosphor omitted..........................	8.00	
908	**395**	9p. new blue, black, emerald-green, dp yellow-olive, orange-vermilion & gold	75	90
		Ea. Embossing omitted	12.00	
		Ey. Phosphor omitted.........................	14.00	
		Set of 5	1.75	2.00
		First Day Cover		3.00
		Presentation Pack	5.00	

Nos. 905a and 906a only exist with the phosphor omitted.

Special First Day of Issue Postmarks

Philatelic Bureau, Edinburgh	5.00	
Canterbury..	6.00	

"Belgica '72" Souvenir Pack

1972 (24 June). *Comprises Nos. 894/6 and 904/8.*
CP908*b* Souvenir Pack 9.50
This pack was specially produced for sale at the "Belgica '72" Stamp Exhibition, held in Brussels between 24 June and 9 July. It contains information on British stamps with a religious theme with text in English, French and Flemish, and was put on sale at Philatelic Bureaux in Britain on 26 June.

396 Microphones, 1924–69

397 Horn Loudspeaker

398 T.V. Camera, 1972

399 Oscillator and Spark
Transmitter, 1897

(Des D. Gentleman)

1972 (13 Sept). **Broadcasting Anniversaries.** *75th Anniv of Marconi and Kemp's Radio Experiments (9p.), and 50th Anniv of Daily Broadcasting by the B.B.C. (others). Two phosphor bands.* P 15 × 14.

909	**396**	3p. pale brown, black, grey, greenish yellow & brownish slate.......................	10	10
		a. Greenish yellow (terminals) omitted .	£1500	

910	**397**	5p. brownish slate, lake-brown, salmon, lt brown, black & red-brown	15	20
		Ey. Phosphor omitted...........................	2.75	
		Eya. Phosphor on back but omitted on front	30.00	
911	**398**	7½p. lt grey, slate, brownish slate, magenta & black	60	60
		a. Brownish slate (Queen's head) omitted	†	—
		Ey. Phosphor omitted...........................	5.00	
912	**399**	9p. lemon, brown, brownish slate, dp brownish slate, bluish slate & black ..	60	60
		a. Brownish slate (Queen's head) omitted	£1300	
		Ey. Phosphor omitted...........................	10.00	
		Set of 4	1.25	1.25
		First Day Cover		2.00
		Presentation Pack	3.50	

In addition to the generally issued Presentation Pack a further pack exists inscribed "1922–1972". This pack of stamps commemorating the 50th Anniversary of the B.B.C. was specially produced as a memento of the occasion for the B.B.C. staff. It was sent with the good wishes of the Chairman and Board of Governors, the Director-General and Board of Management. The pack contains Nos. 909/11 only. (*Price* £35.)

No. 911a is only found on first day covers posted from the Philatelic Bureau in Edinburgh.

Special First Day of Issue Postmarks

Philatelic Bureau, Edinburgh	3.50	
London W1...	7.50	

400 Angel holding Trumpet

401 Angel playing Lute

402 Angel playing Harp

(Des Sally Stiff. Photo and embossing)

1972 (18 Oct). **Christmas.** *One centre phosphor band (2½p.) or two phosphor bands (others).* P 14 × 15.

913	**400**	2½p. cerise, pale reddish brown, yellow-orange, orange-vermilion, lilac, gold, red-brown and dp grey..................	10	15
		a. Gold omitted	£250	
		Eb. Embossing omitted	7.00	
		c. Dp grey omitted		
		Ey. Phosphor omitted...........................	5.00	
914	**401**	3p. ultramarine, lavender, lt turquoise-blue, brt green, gold, red-brown & bluish violet.................................	10	15
		a. Red-brown omitted........................	£500	
		b. Brt green omitted	70.00	
		c. Bluish violet omitted	75.00	
		Ed. Embossing omitted	3.50	
		Ey. Phosphor omitted...........................	2.50	
		Eya. Embossing & phosphor omitted.......	6.00	
915	**402**	7½p. dp brown, pale lilac, lt cinnamon, ochre, gold, red-brown & blackish violet...	90	80
		a. Ochre omitted	55.00	
		Eb. Embossing omitted	7.50	
		Ey. Phosphor omitted...........................	5.00	
		Eya. Embossing & phosphor omitted.......	16.00	
		Set of 3	1.00	1.00
		First Day Cover		1.25
		Presentation Pack	2.75	

The gold printing on the 3p. is from two cylinders: 1E and 1F. Examples have been seen with the gold of the 1F cylinder omitted, but these are difficult to detect on single stamps.

Special First Day of Issue Postmarks

Philatelic Bureau, Edinburgh	2.75	
Bethlehem, Llandeilo, Carms	4.25	

403 Queen Elizabeth and Duke of Edinburgh

404 "Europe"

(Des J. Matthews from photo by N. Parkinson)

1972 (20 Nov). **Royal Silver Wedding.** *"All-over" phosphor (3p.) or without phosphor (20p.). P* 14 × 15.

I. "REMBRANDT" Machine

916	**403**	3p. brownish black, dp blue & silver	20	20
		a. Silver omitted	£300	
917		20p. brownish black, reddish purple & silver	80	80

II. "JUMELLE" Machine

918	**403**	3p. brownish black, dp blue & silver	20	25
		Set of 2	1.00	1.00
		Gutter Pair (No. 918)	1.00	
		Traffic Light Gutter Pair..................	22.00	
		First Day Cover		1.25
		Presentation Pack..........................	2.25	
		Presentation Pack (Japanese)...........	3.50	
		Souvenir Book	3.00	

The souvenir book is a twelve-page booklet containing photographs of the Royal Wedding and other historic events of the royal family and accompanying information.

The 3p. "JUMELLE" has a lighter shade of the brownish black than the 3p. "Rembrandt". It also has the brown cylinders less deeply etched, which can be distinguished in the Duke's face which is slightly lighter, and in the Queen's hair where the highlights are sharper.

3p. "REMBRANDT". Cyls. 3A–1B–11C no dot. Sheets of 100 (10 × 10).
3p. "JUMELLE". Cyls. 1A–1B–3C dot and no dot. Sheets of 100 (two panes 5 × 10, separated by gutter margin).

Special First Day of Issue Postmarks

Philatelic Bureau, Edinburgh	2.00
Windsor, Berks	5.00

Collectors Pack 1972

1972 (20 Nov). *Comprises Nos. 897/917.*
CP918a   Collectors pack 28.00

(Des P. Murdoch)

1973 (3 Jan). *Britain's Entry into European Communities. Two phosphor bands. P* 14 × 15.

919	**404**	3p. dull orange, brt rose-red, ultramarine, lt lilac & black	10	10
920		5p. new blue, brt rose-red, ultramarine, cobalt-blue & black......................	25	35
		a. Pair. Nos. 920/1 ....,................	1.10	1.25
921		5p. lt emerald-green bright rose-red, ultramarine, cobalt-blue and black ...	25	35
		Set of 3	1.10	70
		First Day Cover		1.50
		Presentation Pack..........................	2.25	

Nos. 920/1 were printed horizontally *se-tenant* throughout the sheet.

Philatelic Bureau, Edinburgh 3.25

405 Oak Tree

(Des D. Gentleman)

1973 (28 Feb). **Tree Planting Year. British Trees (1st issue).** *Two phosphor bands. P* 15 × 14.

922	**405**	9p. brownish black, apple-green, dp olive, sepia, blackish green & brownish grey	50	50
		a. Brownish black (value & inscr) omitted	£400	
		b. Brownish grey (Queen's head) omitted	£250	
		Ey. Phosphor omitted.........................	80.00	
		First Day Cover		1.00
		Presentation Pack..........................	2.25	

See also No. 949.

Special First Day of Issue Postmark

Philatelic Bureau, Edinburgh 2.25

CHALK-SURFACED PAPER. The following issues are printed on chalk-surfaced paper but where "all-over" phosphor has been applied there is no chalk reaction except in the sheet margins outside the phosphor area.

406 David Livingstone

407 H. M. Stanley

T **406**/7 were printed together, horizontally *se-tenant* within the sheet

408 Sir Francis Drake

409 Walter Raleigh

410 Charles Sturt

(Des Marjorie Saynor. Queen's head printed in gold and then embossed)

1973 (18 Apr). **British Explorers.** *"All-over"* phosphor. P 14 × 15.

923	**406**	3p. orange-yellow, lt orange-brown, grey-black, lt turquoise-blue, turquoise-blue & gold	25	20
		a. Pair. Nos. 923/4	1.00	1.75
		b. Gold (Queen's head) omitted	32.00	
		c. Turquoise-blue (background & inscr) omitted	£350	
		d. Lt orange-brown omitted	£300	
		Ee. Embossing omitted	20.00	
924	**407**	3p. orange-yellow, lt orange-brown, grey-black, lt turquoise-blue, turquoise-blue & gold	25	20
		b. Gold (Queen's head) omitted	32.00	
		c. Turquoise-blue (background & inscr) omitted	£350	
		d. Lt orange-brown omitted	£300	
		Ee. Embossing omitted	20.00	

925	**408**	5p. lt flesh, chrome-yellow, orange-yellow, sepia, brownish grey, grey-black, violet-blue & gold	20	30
		a. Gold (Queen's head) omitted	90.00	
		b. Grey-black omitted	£500	
		c. Sepia omitted	£350	
		Ed. Embossing omitted	6.50	
926	**409**	7½p. lt flesh, reddish brown, sepia, ultramarine, grey-black, brt lilac & gold	20	30
		a. Gold (Queen's head) omitted	£1750	
		b. Ultramarine (eyes) omitted	£1300	
927	**410**	9p. flesh, pale stone, grey-blue, grey-black, brown-grey, Venetian red, brown-red & gold	25	40
		a. Gold (Queen's head) omitted	90.00	
		b. Brown-grey printing double .... *from*	£800	
		c. Grey-black omitted	£1000	
		Ed. Embossing omitted	22.00	
		Set of 5	1.50	1.25
		First Day Cover		2.00
		Presentation Pack	3.50	

Caution is needed when buying missing gold heads in this issue as they can be removed by using a hard eraser, etc., but this invariably affects the "all-over" phosphor. Genuine examples have the phosphor intact. Used examples off cover cannot be distinguished as much of the phosphor is lost in the course of floating.

In the 5p. value the missing grey-black affects the doublet, which appears as brownish grey, and the lace ruff, which is entirely missing. The missing sepia affects only Drake's hair, which appears much lighter.

The double printing of the brown-grey (cylinder 1F) on the 9p. is a most unusual type of error to occur in a multicoloured photogravure issue. Two sheets are known and it is believed that they stuck to the cylinder and went through a second time. This would result in the following two sheets missing the colour but at the time of going to press this error has not been reported. The second print is slightly askew and more prominent in the top half of the sheets. Examples from the upper part of the sheet showing a clear double impression of the facial features are worth a substantial premium over the price quoted.

Special First Day of Issue Postmark

Philatelic Bureau, Edinburgh 4.50
First Day of Issue handstamps were provided at Blantyre, Glasgow, and Denbigh for this issue.

411

412

413

(T **411/13** show sketches of W. G. Grace by Harry Furniss)

(Des E. Ripley. Queen's head printed in gold and then embossed)

1973 (16 May). **County Cricket 1873–1973.** "All-over" phosphor. P 14 × 15.

928	**411**	3p. black, ochre & gold..........................	10	10
		a. Gold (Queen's head) omitted..........	£1750	
		Eb. Embossing omitted	7.00	
929	**412**	7½p. black, light sage-green & gold	70	70
		Eb. Embossing omitted	16.00	
'930	**413**	9p. black, cobalt & gold	90	90
		Eb. Embossing omitted	50.00	
		Set of 3	1.50	1.50
		First Day Cover		2.00
		Presentation Pack...........................	3.50	
		Souvenir Book	6.25	
		P.H.Q. Card (No. 928)	50.00	£140

The souvenir book is a 24-page illustrated booklet containing a history of County Cricket with text by John Arlott.

Special First Day of Issue Postmarks

Philatelic Bureau, Edinburgh	3.50
Lords, London NW	6.00

414 "Self-portrait"
(Reynolds)

415 "Self-portrait"
(Raeburn)

416 "Nelly O'Brien"
(Reynolds)

417 "Rev. R. Walker
(The Skater)" (Raeburn)

(Des S. Rose. Queen's head printed in gold and then embossed)

1973 (4 July). **British Paintings.** 250th Birth Anniv of Sir Joshua Reynolds and 150th Death Anniv of Sir Henry Raeburn. "All-over" phosphor. P 14 × 15.

931	**414**	3p. rose, new blue, jet-black, magenta, greenish yellow, black, ochre & gold	10	10
		a. Gold (Queen's head) omitted..........	60.00	
		Ec. Gold (Queen's head) & embossing omitted	65.00	
932	**415**	5p. cinnamon, greenish yellow, new blue, lt magenta, black, yellow-olive & gold	20	25
		a. Gold (Queen's head) omitted..........	75.00	
		b. Greenish yellow omitted	£350	
		Ec. Embossing omitted	15.00	
933	**416**	7½p. greenish yellow, new blue, lt magenta, black, cinnamon & gold	45	40
		a. Gold (Queen's head) omitted..........	75.00	
		b. Cinnamon omitted	£3500	
		Ec. Embossing omitted	12.00	
934	**417**	9p. brownish rose, black, dull rose, pale yellow, brownish grey, pale blue & gold	50	50
		b. Brownish rose omitted	30.00	
		Ec. Embossing omitted	£100	
		Set of 4	1.10	1.10
		First Day Cover		1.75
		Presentation Pack..........................	2.75	

Secial First Day of Issue Postmark

Philatelic Bureau, Edinburgh 3.00

418 Court Masque Costumes   **419** St. Paul's Church, Covent Garden

420 Prince's Lodging, Newmarket

421 Court Masque Stage Scene

T **418/19** and T **420/1** were printed horizontally se-tenant within the sheet.

(Des Rosalind Dease. Litho and typo B.W.)

1973 (15 Aug). **400th Birth Anniv of Inigo Jones (architect and designer).** "All-over" phosphor. P 15 × 14.

935	**418**	3p. dp mauve, black & gold	10	15
		a. Pair. Nos. 935/6	35	40
		Eb. 9 mm. phosphor band*	12.00	
936	**419**	3p. dp brown, black & gold	10	15
937	**420**	5p. blue, black & gold	40	45
		a. Pair. Nos. 937/8	1.50	1.50
		Eb. 9 mm. phosphor band*	15.00	
938	**421**	5p. grey-olive, black & gold	40	45
		Set of 4	1.60	1.10
		First Day Cover		2.00
		Presentation Pack	3.50	
		P.H.Q. Card (No. 936)	£125	70.00

*On part of the printings for both values the "all-over" phosphor band missed the first vertical row and a 9 mm. phosphor band was applied to correct this.

Special First Day of Issue Postmark

Philatelic Bureau, Edinburgh 3.00

422 Palace of Westminster seen from Whitehall

423 Palace of Westminster seen from Millbank

(Des R. Downer. Recess and typo B.W.)

1973 (12 Sept). **19th Commonwealth Parliamentary Conference.** "All-over" phosphor. P 15 × 14.

939	**422**	8p. black, brownish grey & stone	50	60
940	**423**	10p. gold & black	50	40
		Set of 2	1.00	1.00
		First Day Cover		1.25
		Presentation Pack	2.00	
		Souvenir Book	5.00	
		P.H.Q. Card (No. 939)	35.00	90.00

The souvenir book is a twelve-page booklet containing a history of the Palace of Westminster.

Special First Day of Issue Postmark

Philatelic Bureau, Edinburgh 2.50

424 Princess Anne and Capt. Mark Phillips

(Des C. Clements and E. Hughes from photo by Lord Litchfield)

1973 (14 Nov). **Royal Wedding.** "All-over" phosphor. P 15 × 14.

941	**424**	3½p. dull violet & silver	10	10
		a. Imperf (horiz pair)	£900	
942		20p. dp brown & silver	90	90
		a. Silver omitted	£900	
		Set of 2	1.00	1.00
		Set of 2 Gutter Pairs	6.00	
		Set of 2 Traffic Light Gutter Pairs	£100	
		First Day Cover		1.25
		Presentation Pack	2.00	
		P.H.Q. Card (No. 941)	8.00	22.00

Special First Day of Issue Postmarks

Philatelic Bureau, Edinburgh 2.00
Westminster Abbey, London SW1 .... 4.50
Windsor, Berks 5.00

425   426

427   428

429

T **425/9** depict the carol "Good King Wenceslas" and were printed horizontally *se-tenant* within the sheet.

430 "Good King Wenceslas, the Page and Peasant"

(Des D. Gentleman)

1973 (28 Nov). **Christmas.** *One centre phosphor band (3p.) or "all-over" phosphor (3½p.). P 15 × 14.*

943	**425**	3p. grey-black, blue, brownish grey, lt brown, brt rose-red, turquoise-green, salmon-pink & gold	15	15
		a. Strip of 5. Nos. 943/7	2.75	2.50
		b. Imperf (horiz strip of 5)	£1000	
		Eg. Gum arabic	20	
		Ega. Strip of 5. Nos. 943Eg/47Eg	2.75	
		Egb. Imperf (strip of 5. Nos. 943Eg/7Eg)		
944	**426**	3p. grey-black, violet-blue, slate, brown, rose-red, rosy mauve, turquoise-green, salmon-pink & gold	15	15
		a. Rosy mauve omitted	£625	
		Eg. Gum arabic	20	
945	**427**	3p. grey-black, violet-blue, slate, brown, rose-red, rosy mauve, turquoise-green, salmon-pink & gold	15	15
		a. Rosy mauve omitted	£625	
		Eg. Gum arabic	20	

946	**428**	3p. grey-black, violet-blue, slate, brown, rose-red, rosy mauve, turquoise-green, salmon-pink & gold	15	15
		a. Rosy mauve omitted	£625	
		Eg. Gum arabic	20	
947	**429**	3p. grey-black, violet-blue, slate, brown, rose-red, rosy mauve, turquoise-green, salmon-pink & gold	15	15
		a. Rosy mauve omitted	£625	
		Eg. Gum arabic	20	
948	**430**	3½p. salmon-pink, grey-black, red-brown, blue, turquoise-green, brt rose-red, rosy mauve, lavender-grey & gold	15	15
		a. Imperf (pair)	£450	
		b. Grey-black (value & inscr, etc.) omitted	75.00	
		c. Salmon-pink omitted	70.00	
		d. Blue (leg, robes) omitted	£130	
		e. Rosy mauve (robe at right) omitted	80.00	
		f. Blue & rosy mauve omitted	£250	
		g. Brt rose-red (King's robe) omitted	75.00	
		h. Red-brown (logs, basket, etc.) omitted		
		i. Turquoise-green (leg, robe, etc.) omitted	£2000	
		Set of 6	2.75	80
		First Day Cover		2.00
		Presentation Pack	3.25	

Examples of the 3½p. with the gold background colour omitted are known used on covers from Gloucester: The same value has been seen with the lavender-grey omitted used on piece.

The 3p. and 3½p. are normally with PVA gum with added dextrin, but the 3½p. exists with normal PVA gum.

Special First Day of Issue Postmarks

Philatelic Bureau, Edinburgh	2.50
Bethlehem, Llandeilo, Carms	4.50

Collectors Pack 1973

1973 (28 Nov). *Comprises Nos. 919/48.*
CP948*j*   Collectors Pack 26.00

431 Horse Chestnut

(Des D. Gentleman)

1974 (27 Feb). **British Trees (2nd issue).** *"All-over" phosphor.*
P 15 × 14.
949 **431** 10p. lt emerald, brt green, greenish yel-
low, brown-olive, black & brownish
grey 50 50
Gutter Pair 3.00
Traffic Light Gutter Pair................... 70.00
First Day Cover 1.00
Presentation Pack......................... 2.25
P.H.Q. Card £100 60.00

Special First Day of Issue Postmark

Philatelic Bureau, Edinburgh 2.50

432 First Motor Fire-engine, 1904 **433** Prize-winning Fire-engine, 1863

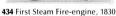

434 First Steam Fire-engine, 1830   **435** Fire-engine, 1766

(Des D. Gentleman)

1974 (24 Apr). **Bicentenary of the Fire Prevention (Metropolis) Act.**
"All-over" phosphor. P 15 × 14.
950 **432** 3½p. grey-black, orange-yellow, greenish
yellow, dull rose, ochre & grey 10 10
a. Imperf (pair) £850
951 **433** 5½p. greenish yellow, dp rosy magenta,
orange-yellow, lt emerald, grey-black
& grey.. 25 25
952 **434** 8p. greenish yellow, lt blue-green, lt
greenish blue, lt chestnut, grey-black
& grey.. 35 35

953 **435** 10p. grey-black, pale reddish brown, lt
brown, orange-yellow & grey 40 40
Set of 4 .... 1.00 1.00
Set of 4 Gutter Pairs 4.00
Set of 4 Traffic Light Gutter Pairs 70.00
First Day Cover 3.00
Presentation Pack......................... 2.50
P.H.Q. Card (No. 950) £100 50.00
The 3½p. exists with ordinary PVA gum.

Special First Day of Issue Postmark

Philatelic Bureau, Edinburgh 3.75

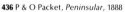

436 P & O Packet, *Peninsular*, 1888   **437** Farman Biplane, 1911

438 Airmail-blue Van and   **439** Imperial Airways "C" Class
Postbox, 1930   Flying-boat, 1937

(Des Rosalind Dease)

1974 (12 June). **Centenary of Universal Postal Union.** *"All-over" phos-*
phor. P 15 × 14.
954 **436** 3½p. dp brownish grey, brt mauve, grey-
black & gold 10 10
955 **437** 5½p. pale orange, lt emerald, grey-black &
gold 20 25
956 **438** 8p. cobalt, brown, grey-black & gold 30 35
957 **439** 10p. dp brownish grey, orange, grey-black
& gold 50 40
Set of 4 .... 1.00 1.00
Set of 4 Gutter Pairs 4.00
Set of 4 Traffic Light Gutter Pairs 50.00
First Day Cover 1.25
Presentation Pack......................... 2.00

Special First Day of Issue Postmark

Philatelic Bureau, Edinburgh 3.25

440 Robert the Bruce

441 Owain Glyndŵr

442 Henry the Fifth

443 The Black Prince

(Des F. Wegner)

1974 (10 July). **Medieval Warriors.** *"All-over" phosphor.* P 15 × 14.

958	**440**	4½p.	greenish yellow, vermilion, slate-blue, red-brown, reddish brown, lilac-grey & gold	10	10
959	**441**	5½p.	lemon, vermilion, slate-blue, red-brown, reddish brown, olive-drab & gold	20	20
960	**442**	8p.	dp grey, vermilion, greenish yellow, new blue, red-brown, dp cinnamon & gold	40	40
961	**443**	10p.	vermilion, greenish yellow, new blue, red-brown, reddish brown, lt blue & gold	40	40
			Set of 4	1.00	1.00
			Set of 4 Gutter Pairs	6.00	
			Set of 4 Traffic Light Gutter Pairs	75.00	
			First Day Cover		2.50
			Presentation Pack	3.50	
			P.H.Q. Cards (set of 4)	30.00	24.00

Special First Day of Issue Postmark

Philatelic Bureau, Edinburgh 3.50

444 Churchill in Royal Yacht Squadron Uniform

445 Prime Minister, 1940

446 Secretary for War and Air, 1919

447 War Correspondent, South Africa, 1899

(Des C. Clements and E. Hughes)

1974 (9 Oct). **Birth Centenary of Sir Winston Churchill.** *"All-over" phosphor.* P 14 × 15.

962	**444**	4½p.	Prussian blue, pale turquoise-green & silver	15	15
963	**445**	5½p.	sepia, brownish grey & silver	20	25
964	**446**	8p.	crimson, lt claret & silver	50	50
965	**447**	10p.	lt brown, stone & silver	55	50
			Set of 4	1.25	1.25
			Set of 4 Gutter Pairs	4.00	
			Set of 4 Traffic Light Gutter Pairs	50.00	
			First Day Cover		1.60
			Presentation Pack	1.75	
			Souvenir Book	2.50	
			P.H.Q. Card (No. 963)	7.00	12.00

The souvenir book consists of an illustrated folder containing a biography of Sir Winston.

Nos. 962/5 come with PVA gum containing added dextrin, but the 8p. also exists with normal PVA.

Special First Day of Issue Postmarks

Philatelic Bureau, Edinburgh 3.50
Blenheim, Woodstock, Oxford 4.50
House of Commons, London SW 4.50

Special First Day of Issue Postmarks

Philatelic Bureau, Edinburgh 2.75
Bethlehem, Llandeilo, Carms 4.75

Collectors Pack 1974

1974 (27 Nov). *Comprises Nos. 949/69.*
CP969*a* Collectors Pack 8.50

452 Invalid in Wheelchair

(Des P. Sharland)

1975 (22 Jan). **Health and Handicap Funds.** *"All-over" phosphor.*
P 15 × 14.
970 **452** 4½p. + 1½p. azure & grey-blue 25   25
                  Gutter Pair 50
                  Traffic Light Gutter Pair 1.00
                  First Day Cover 1.00

Special First Day of Issue Postmark

Philatelic Bureau, Edinburgh 2.25

448 "Adoration of the Magi" (York Minster, *circa* 1355)

449 "The Nativity" (St. Helen's Church, Norwich, *circa* 1480)

450 "Virgin and Child" (Ottery St. Mary Church, *circa* 1350)

451 "Virgin and Child" (Worcester Cathedral, *circa* 1224)

(Des Peter Hatch Partnership)

1974 (27 Nov). **Christmas.** *Church Roof Bosses. One phosphor band (3½p.) or "all-over" phosphor (others). P* 15 × 14.
966 **448** 3½p. gold, lt new blue, lt brown, grey-
                  black & lt stone 10   10
            a. Lt stone (background shading) omit-
                  ted £8000
            Ey. Phosphor omitted 7.00
967 **449** 4½p. gold, yellow-orange, rose-red, lt
                  brown, grey-black, & lt new blue 10   10
968 **450** 8p. blue, gold, lt brown, rose-red, dull
                  green & grey-black 45   45
969 **451** 10p. gold, dull rose, grey-black, lt new
                  blue, pale cinnamon & lt brown 50   50
                  Set of 4 .... 1.00   1.00
                  Set of 4 Gutter Pairs 4.00
                  Set of 4 Traffic Light Gutter Pairs 50.00
                  First Day Cover 1.25
                  Presentation Pack 1.75

The phosphor band on the 3½p. was first applied down the centre of the stamp but during the printing this was deliberately placed to the right between the roof boss and the value; however, intermediate positions, due to shifts, are known.

Two used examples of the 3½p. have been reported with the light brown colour omitted.

453 "Peace—Burial at Sea"

454 "Snowstorm—Steamer off a Harbour's Mouth"

455 "The Arsenal. Venice"   **456** "St. Laurent"

461 National Theatre, London

(Des S. Rose)

(Des P. Gauld)

1975 (19 Feb). **Birth Bicentenary of J. M. W. Turner (painter).** *"All-over" phosphor.* P 15 × 14.

971	**453**	4½p. grey-black, salmon, stone, blue & grey	10	10
972	**454**	5½p. cobalt, greenish yellow, lt yellow-brown, grey-black & rose	15	15
973	**455**	8p. pale yellow-orange, greenish yellow, rose, cobalt & grey-black	40	40
974	**456**	10p. dp blue, lt yellow-ochre, lt brown, dp cobalt & grey-black	45	45
		Set of 4	1.00	1.00
		Set of 4 Gutter Pairs	2.50	
		Set of 4 Traffic Light Gutter Pairs	7.00	
		First Day Cover		1.50
		Presentation Pack	2.50	
		P.H.Q. Card (No. 972)	30.00	11.00

Special First Day of Issue Postmarks

Philatelic Bureau, Edinburgh	2.75
London WC	3.00

457 Charlotte Square, Edinburgh   **458** The Rows, Chester

T **457/8** were printed horizontally *se-tenant* within the sheet.

459 Royal Observatory, Greenwich   **460** St. George's Chapel, Windsor

1975 (23 Apr). **European Architectural Heritage Year.** *"All-over" phosphor.* P 15 × 14.

975	**457**	7p. greenish yellow, brt orange, grey-black, red-brown, new blue, lavender & gold	30	30
		a. Pair. Nos. 975/6	80	90
976	**458**	7p. grey-black, greenish yellow, new blue, brt orange, red-brown & gold	30	30
977	**459**	8p. magenta, dp slate, pale magenta, lt yellow-olive, grey-black & gold	20	25
978	**460**	10p. bistre-brown, greenish yellow, dp slate, emerald-green, grey-black & gold	20	25
979	**461**	12p. grey-black, new blue, pale magenta & gold	20	35
		Set of 5	1.25	1.25
		Set of 5 Gutter Pairs	4.00	
		Set of 5 Traffic Light Gutter Pairs	20.00	
		First Day Cover		2.00
		Presentation Pack	3.00	
		P.H.Q. Cards (Nos. 975/7)	8.00	10.00

Special First Day of Issue Postmark

Philatelic Bureau, Edinburgh	3.00

462 Sailing Dinghies   **463** Racing Keel Yachts

464 Cruising Yachts   **465** Multihulls

99

(Des A. Restall. Recess and photo)

1975 (11 June). **Sailing.** *"All-over"* phosphor. P 15 × 14.

980	**462**	7p. black, bluish violet, scarlet, orange-vermilion, orange & gold	20	20
981	**463**	8p. black, orange-vermilion, orange, lavender, brt mauve, brt blue, dp ultramarine & gold	30	30
		a. Black omitted	55.00	
982	**464**	10p. black, orange, bluish emerald, lt olive-drab, chocolate & gold	30	30
983	**465**	12p. black, ultramarine, turquoise-blue, rose, grey, steel-blue & gold	35	35
		Set of 4	1.00	1.00
		Set of 4 Gutter Pairs	2.50	
		Set of 4 Traffic Light Gutter Pairs	25.00	
		First Day Cover		1.50
		Presentation Pack	1.50	
		P.H.Q. Card (No. 981)	4.50	10.00

On No. 981a the recess-printed black colour is completely omitted.

Special First Day of Issue Postmark

Philatelic Bureau, Edinburgh 2.25
A First Day of Issue handstamp was provided at Weymouth for this issue.

466 Stephenson's *Locomotion*, 1825

467 *Abbotsford*, 1876

468 *Caerphilly Castle*, 1923

469 High Speed Train, 1975

(Des B. Craker)

1975 (13 Aug). **150th Anniv of Public Railways.** *"All-over"* phosphor. P 15 × 14.

984	**466**	7p. red-brown, grey-black, greenish yellow, grey & silver	20	20
985	**467**	8p. brown, orange-yellow, vermilion, grey-black, grey & silver	25	2
986	**468**	10p. emerald-green, grey-black, yellow-orange, vermilion, grey & silver	30	3
987	**469**	12p. grey-black, pale lemon, vermilion, blue, grey & silver	35	3
		Set of 4	1.00	1.0
		Set of 4 Gutter Pairs	3.00	
		Set of 4 Traffic Light Gutter Pairs	12.00	
		First Day Cover		2.50
		Presentation Pack	2.25	
		Souvenir Book	3.00	
		P.H.Q. Cards (set of 4)	55.00	25.0

The souvenir book is an eight-page booklet containing a history of the railways.

Special First Day of Issue Postmarks

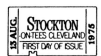

Philatelic Bureau, Edinburgh 3.50
Darlington, Co. Durham 4.50
Shildon, Co. Durham 4.75
Stockton-on-Tees, Cleveland 4.50

470 Palace of Westminster

(Des R. Downer)

1975 (3 Sept). **62nd Inter-Parliamentary Union Conference.** *"All-over"* phosphor. P 15 × 14.

988	**470**	12p. lt new blue, black, brownish grey & gold	50	50
		Gutter Pair	1.00	
		Traffic Light Gutter Pair	3.00	
		First Day Cover		1.00
		Presentation Pack	1.25	

Special First Day of Issue Postmark

Philatelic Bureau, Edinburgh 1.75

Special First Day of Issue Postmark

Philatelic Bureau, Edinburgh 2.50
Steventon, Basingstoke, Hants 3.50

471 Emma and Mr. Woodhouse (*Emma*)

472 Catherine Morland (*Northanger Abbey*)

473 Mr. Darcy (*Pride and Prejudice*)

474 Mary and Henry Crawford (*Mansfield Park*)

(Des Barbara Brown)

1975 (22 Oct). **Birth Bicentenary of Jane Austen (novelist).** "*All-over*" phosphor. P 14 × 15.

989	471	8½p. blue, slate, rose-red, lt yellow, dull green, grey-black & gold.................	20	20
990	472	10p. slate, brt magenta, grey, lt yellow, grey-black & gold	25	25
991	473	11p. dull blue, pink, olive-sepia, slate, pale greenish yellow, grey-black & gold	30	30
992	474	13p. brt magenta; lt new blue, slate, buff, dull blue-green, grey-black & gold ...	35	35
		Set of 4	1.00	1.00
		Set of 4 Gutter Pairs	2.50	
		Set of 4 Traffic Light Gutter Pairs	8.00	
		First Day Cover		1.25
		Presentation Pack..........................	2.00	
		P.H.Q. Cards (set of 4)	16.00	15.00

475 Angels with Harp and Lute

476 Angel with Mandolin

477 Angel with Horn

478 Angel with Trumpet

(Des R. Downer)

1975 (26 Nov). **Christmas.** *One phosphor band* (6½p.), *phosphor-inked background* (8½p.), "*all-over*" *phosphor* (others). P 15 × 14.

993	475	6½p. bluish violet, brt reddish violet, light lavender & gold.............................	20	15
994	476	8½p. turquoise-green, brt emerald-green, slate, lt turquoise-green & gold........	20	20
995	477	11p. vermilion, cerise, pink & gold..........	30	35
996	478	13p. drab, brown, brt orange, buff & gold	40	40
		Set of 4	1.00	1.00
		Set of 4 Gutter Pairs	2.50	
		Set of 4 Traffic Light Gutter Pairs	8.00	
		First Day Cover		1.25
		Presentation Pack..........................	2.00	

The 6½p. exists with both ordinary PVA gum and PVA containing added dextrin.

Special First Day of Issue Postmarks

Philatelic Bureau, Edinburgh 2.25
Bethlehem, Llandeilo, Dyfed 3.25

Collectors Pack 1975

1975 (26 Nov). *Comprises Nos. 970/96.*
CP996a Collectors Pack 7.50

479 Housewife

480 Policeman

481 District Nurse

482 Industrialist

(Des P. Sharland)

1976 (10 Mar). **Telephone Centenary.** *"All-over" phosphor.*
P 15 × 14.
997	**479**	8½p. greenish blue, dp rose, black & blue	20	20
		a. Dp rose (vase and picture frame) omitted	£1750	
998	**480**	10p. greenish blue, black & yellow-olive	25	25
999	**481**	11p. greenish blue, dp rose, black & brt mauve...	30	30
1000	**482**	13p. olive-brown, dp rose, black & orange-red	35	35
		Set of 4	1.00	1.00
		Set of 4 Gutter Pairs	2.50	
		Set of 4 Traffic Light Gutter Pairs	8.00	
		First Day Cover		1.25
		Presentation Pack	2.00	

Special First Day of Issue Postmark

Philatelic Bureau, Edinburgh 2.50

483 Hewing Coal
(Thomas Hepburn)

484 Machinery (Robert Owen)

485 Chimney Cleaning
(Lord Shaftesbury)

486 Hands clutching Prison Bars
(Elizabeth Fry)

(Des D. Gentleman)

1976 (28 Apr). **Social Reformers.** *"All-over" phosphor.* P 15 × 14.
1001	**483**	8½p. lavender-grey, grey-black, black & slate-grey	20	20
1002	**484**	10p. lavender-grey, grey-black, grey & slate-violet	25	25
1003	**485**	11p. black, slate-grey & drab	30	30
1004	**486**	13p. slate-grey, black & dp dull green	35	35
		Set of 4	1.00	1.00
		Set of 4 Gutter Pairs	2.50	
		Set of 4 Traffic Light Gutter Pairs	8.00	
		First Day Cover		1.25
		Presentation Pack	2.00	
		P.H.Q. Card (No. 1001)	5.00	7.50

Special First Day of Issue Postmark

Philatelic Bureau, Edinburgh 2.50

487 Benjamin Franklin (bust by Jean-Jacques Caffieri)

(Des P. Sharland)

1976 (2 June). **Bicentenary of American Revolution.** *"All-over" phosphor.* P 14 × 15.
1005	**487**	11p. pale bistre, slate-violet, pale blue-green, black & gold.......................	50	50
		Gutter Pair	1.00	
		Traffic Light Gutter Pair...................	3.00	
		First Day Cover		1.00
		Presentation Pack..........................	1.25	
		P.H.Q. Card	2.50	8.50

Special First Day of Issue Postmark

Special First Day of Issue Postmark

Philatelic Bureau, Edinburgh 2.00

Philatelic Bureau, Edinburgh 2.25

488 "Elizabeth of Glamis"

489 "Grandpa Dickson"

492 Archdruid

493 Morris Dancing

490 "Rosa Mundi"

491 "Sweet Briar"

(Des Kristin Rosenberg)

494 Scots Piper

495 Welsh Harpist

1976 (30 June). **Centenary of Royal National Rose Society.** *"All-over"* *phosphor.* P 14 × 15.

1006	488	8½p. bright rose-red, greenish yellow, emerald, grey-black & gold..................	20	20
1007	489	10p. greenish yellow, brt green, reddish brown, grey-black & gold..............	30	30
1008	490	11p. brt magenta, greenish yellow, emerald, grey-blue, grey-black & gold	45	50
1009	491	13p. rose-pink, lake-brown, yellow-green, pale greenish yellow, grey-black & gold	45	40
		a. Value omitted*.............................	£20000	
		Set of 4	1.25	1.25
		Set of 4 Gutter Pairs	2.50	
		Set of 4 Traffic Light Gutter Pairs	10.00	
		First Day Cover		1.75
		Presentation Pack.......................	2.25	
		P.H.Q. Cards (set of 4)	30.00	14.00

*During repairs to the cylinder the face value on R.1/9 was temporarily covered with copper. This covering was inadvertently left in place during printing, but the error was discovered before issue and most examples were removed from the sheets. Two mint and one used examples have so far been reported with only one of the mint remaining in private hands.

(Des Marjorie Saynor)

1976 (4 Aug). **British Cultural Traditions.** *"All-over"* *phosphor.* P 14 × 15.

1010	492	8½p. yellow, sepia, brt rose, dull ultramarine, black & gold	20	20
1011	493	10p. dull ultramarine, brt rose-red, sepia, greenish yellow, black & gold.........	25	25
1012	494	11p. bluish green, yellow-brown, yellow-orange, black, brt rose-red & gold....	30	30
1013	495	13p. dull violet-blue, yellow-orange, yellow, black, bluish green & gold	35	35
		Set of 4	1.00	1.00
		Set of 4 Gutter Pairs	2.50	
		Set of 4 Traffic Light Gutter Pairs	10.00	
		First Day Cover		1.25
		Presentation Pack.........................	2.00	
		P.H.Q. Cards (set of 4)	18.00	10.00

The 8½p. and 13p. commemorate the 800th Anniv of the Royal National Eisteddfod.

Special First Day of Issue Postmarks

Special First Day of Issue Postmarks

Philatelic Bureau, Edinburgh 2.25
Cardigan, Dyfed 3.50

Philatelic Bureau, Edinburgh 2.50
London SW1 .... 3.00

 William Caxton 1476 8½ᴾ   William Caxton 1476 10ᴾ

496 Woodcut from
The Canterbury Tales

497 Extract from
The Tretyse of Love

 500 Virgin and Child

 501 Angel with Crown

 William Caxton 1476 11ᴾ

 William Caxton 1476 13ᴾ

498 Woodcut from
The Game and Playe of Chesse

499 Early Printing Press

 502 Angel appearing to Shepherds

 503 The Three Kings

(Des Enid Marx)

1976 (24 Nov). **Christmas.** *English Medieval Embroidery.* One phosphor band (6½p.), "all-over" phosphor (others). P 15 × 14.

1018	**500**	6½p. blue, bistre-yellow, brown & orange.		15	15
		a. Imperf (pair)		£450	
1019	**501**	8½p. sage-green, yellow, brown-ochre, chestnut & olive-black		20	20
1020	**502**	11p. dp magenta, brown-orange, new blue, black & cinnamon		35	35
		a. Uncoated paper*		60.00	30.00
1021	**503**	13p. bright purple, new blue, cinnamon, bronze-green & olive-grey		40	40

Set of 4 .... 1.00 1.00
Set of 4 Gutter Pairs 2.50
Set of 4 Traffic Light Gutter Pairs 8.00
First Day Cover 1.25
Presentation Pack 2.00
P.H.Q. Cards (set of 4) 4.00 8.00

*See footnote after No. 744.

(Des R. Gay. Queen's head printed in gold and then embossed)

1976 (29 Sept). **500th Anniv of British Printing.** *"All-over"* phosphor. P 14 × 15.

1014	**496**	8½p. black, lt new blue & gold	20	20
1015	**497**	10p. black, olive-green & gold	25	25
1016	**498**	11p. black, brownish grey & gold	30	30
1017	**499**	13p. chocolate, pale ochre & gold	35	35

Set of 4 .... 1.00 1.00
Set of 4 Gutter Pairs 2.50
Set of 4 Traffic Light Gutter Pairs 8.00
First Day Cover 1.25
Presentation Pack 2.50
P.H.Q. Cards (set of 4) 14.00 10.00

Special First Day of Issue Postmarks

Philatelic Bureau, Edinburgh	2.50
Bethlehem, Llandeilo, Dyfed	2.75

ollectors Pack 1976

976 (24 Nov). *Comprises Nos. 997/1021.*

P1021a	Collectors Pack	10.00

504 Lawn Tennis

505 Table Tennis

506 Squash

507 Badminton

(Des A. Restall)

977 (12 Jan). **Racket Sports.** *Phosphorised paper. P* 15 × 14.

022	504	8½p. emerald-green, black, grey & bluish green	20	20
		a. Imperf (horiz pair)	£850	
023	505	10p. myrtle-green, black, grey-black & dp blue-green	25	25
024	506	11p. orange, pale yellow, black, slate-black & grey	30	30
025	507	13p. brown, grey-black, grey & brt reddish violet	35	35
		Set of 4	1.00	1.00
		Set of 4 Gutter Pairs	2.50	
		Set of 4 Traffic Light Gutter Pairs	8.00	
		First Day Cover		1.50
		Presentation Pack	2.00	
		P.H.Q. Cards (set of 4)	6.00	9.50

Special First Day of Issue Postmark

Philatelic Bureau, Edinburgh	2.50

508

1977 (2 Feb)–**87**. *T* **508**. *P* 14×15.

1026	£1	brt yellow-green & blackish olive	3.00	20
	a.	Imperf (pair)	£650	
1026b	£1.30	pale drab & dp greenish blue (3.8.83)	6.50	6.00
1026c	£1.33	pale mauve & grey-black (28.8.84)	6.50	6.00
1026d	£1.41	pale drab & dp greenish blue (17.9.85)	7.00	6.00
1026e	£1.50	pale mauve & grey-black (2.9.86)	6.00	4.00
1026f	£1.60	pale drab & dp greenish blue (15.9.87)	6.00	6.00
1027	£2	light emerald & purple-brown	5.50	75
1028	£5	salmon & chalky blue	13.00	2.00
	a.	Imperf (vert pair)		
		Set of 8	48.00	27.00
		Set of 8 Gutter Pairs	£100	
		Set of 8 Traffic Light Gutter Pairs	£130	
		First Day Cover (1026, 1027/8)		8.00
		First Day Cover (1026b)		6.00
		First Day Cover (1026c)		6.00
		First Day Cover (1026d)		6.00
		First Day Cover (1026e)		4.00
		First Day Cover (1026f)		6.00
		Presentation Pack (1026, 1027/8)	22.00	
		Presentation Pack (1026f)	12.00	

Special First Day of Issue Postmarks
(for illustrations see Introduction)

Philatelic Bureau, Edinburgh (Type F) (£1, £2, £5)	9.00
Windsor, Berks (Type F) (£1, £2, £5)	18.00
Philatelic Bureau, Edinburgh (Type F) (£1.30)	7.00
Windsor, Berks (Type F) (£1.30)	10.00
British Philatelic Bureau, Edinburgh (Type F) (£1.33)	6.50
Windsor, Berks (Type F) (£1.33)	10.00
British Philatelic Bureau, Edinburgh (Type G) (£1.41)	6.50
Windsor, Berks (Type G) (£1.41)	10.00
British Philatelic Bureau, Edinburgh (Type G) (£1.50)	5.00
Windsor, Berks (Type G) (£1.50)	8.50
British Philatelic Bureau, Edinburgh (Type G) (£1.60)	6.50
Windsor, Berks (Type G) (£1.60)	8.50

509 Steroids—Conformational Analysis

510 Vitamin C—Synthesis

511 Starch—Chromatography

512 Salt—Crystallography

(Des J. Karo)

1977 (2 Mar). **Royal Institute of Chemistry Centenary.** *"All-over"* *phosphor.* P 15 × 14.

1029 **509**	8½p. rosine, new blue, olive-yellow, brt mauve, yellow-brown, black & gold..	20	20
	a. Imperf (horiz pair)	£850	
1030 **510**	10p. brt orange, rosine, new blue, brt blue, black & gold	30	30
1031 **511**	11p. rosine, greenish-yellow, new blue, dp violet, black & gold	30	30
1032 **512**	13p. new blue, brt green, black & gold	30	30
	Set of 4	1.00	1.00
	Set of 4 Gutter Pairs	2.50	
	Set of 4 Traffic Light Gutter Pairs	8.00	
	First Day Cover		1.40
	Presentation Pack	2.40	
	P.H.Q. Cards (set of 4)	7.00	10.00

Special First Day of Issue Postmark

Philatelic Bureau, Edinburgh 3.00

513

514

515

516

T 513/16 differ in the decorations of "ER".

(Des R. Guyatt)

1977 (11 May–15 June). **Silver Jubilee.** *"All-over"* *phosphor.* P 15 × 14.

1033 **513**	8½p. blackish green, black, silver, olive-grey & pale turquoise-green	20	20
	a. Imperf (pair)	£750	
1034 **513**	9p. maroon, black, silver, olive-grey & lavender (15 June)	25	2
1035 **514**	10p. blackish blue, black, silver, olive-grey & ochre	25	2
	a. Imperf (horiz pair)		
1036 **515**	11p. brown-purple, black, silver, olive-grey & rose-pink	30	3
	a. Imperf (horiz pair)	£1300	
1037 **516**	13p. sepia, black, silver, olive-grey & bistre-yellow	40	4
	a. Imperf (pair)	£1300	
	Set of 5	1.25	1.
	Set of 5 Gutter Pairs	2.75	
	Set of 5 Traffic Light Gutter Pairs	4.50	
	First Day Covers (2)		1.
	Presentation Pack (Nos. 1033, 1035/7)	2.00	
	Souvenir Book	4.00	
	P.H.Q. Cards (set of 5)	12.00	8.

The souvenir book is a 16-page booklet containing a history of the Queen's reign.

Special First Day of Issue Postmarks

Philatelic Bureau, Edinburgh (1033, 1035/7) (11 May)	2.00
Philatelic Bureau, Edinburgh (1034) (15 June)	1.00
Windsor, Berks (1033, 1035/7) (11 May)	3.00
Windsor, Berks (1034) (15 June)	1.00

517 "Gathering of Nations"

(Des P. Murdoch. Recess and photo)

1977 (8 June). **Commonwealth Heads of Government Meeting London.** *"All-over"* *phosphor.* P 14 × 15.

1038 **517**	13p. black, blackish green, rose-carmine & silver	50	
	Gutter Pair	1.00	
	Traffic Light Gutter Pair	1.25	
	First Day Cover		1.
	Presentation Pack	1.00	
	P.H.Q. Card	2.25	3.

106

Special First Day of Issue Postmarks

Philatelic Bureau, Edinburgh 1.25
London SW... 1.50

518 Hedgehog

519 Brown Hare

520 Red Squirrel

521 Otter

522 Badger

T **518/22** were printed horizontally *se-tenant* within the sheet.

(Des P. Oxenham)

1977 (5 Oct). **British Wildlife.** *"All-over"* phosphor. P 14 × 15.
1039 **518**   9p. reddish brown, grey-black, pale le-
mon, brt turquoise-blue, brt magenta
& gold 25   20
   a. Horiz. strip of 5. Nos. 1039/43 .... 1.50   1.50
   b. Imperf (vert pair) ....
   c. Imperf (horiz pair. Nos. 1039/40) ......

1040	**519**	9p. reddish brown, grey-black, pale le-mon, brt turquoise-blue, brt magenta & gold	25	20
1041	**520**	9p. reddish brown, grey-black, pale le-mon, brt turquoise-blue, brt magenta & gold	25	20
1042	**521**	9p. reddish brown, grey-black, pale le-mon, brt turquoise-blue, brt magenta & gold	25	20
1043	**522**	9p. grey-black, reddish brown, pale le-mon, brt turquoise-blue, brt magenta & gold	25	20
		Set of 5	1.50	90
		Gutter Strip of 10	3.75	
		Traffic Light Gutter Strip of 10	4.00	
		First Day Cover		2.25
		Presentation Pack	2.25	
		P.H.Q. Cards (set of 5)	4.00	5.00

Special First Day of Issue Postmark

Philatelic Bureau, Edinburgh 2.75

523 "Three French Hens,
Two Turtle Doves and a
Partridge in a Pear Tree"

524 "Six Geese-a-laying, Five
Gold Rings, Four Colly Birds"

525 "Eight Maids a-milking,
Seven Swans a-swimming"

526 "Ten Pipers piping,
Nine Drummers drumming"

527 "Twelve Lords a-leaping, Eleven Ladies dancing"

T **523/7** depict the carol "The Twelve Days of Christmas" and were
printed horizontally *se-tenant* within the sheet.

528 "A Partridge in a Pear Tree"

(Des D. Gentleman)

1977 (23 Nov). **Christmas.** *One centre phosphor band (7p.) or "all-over" phosphor (9p.). P* 15 × 14.

1044	**523**	7p. slate, grey, brt yellow-green, new blue, rose-red & gold	15	15
		a. Horiz. strip of 5. Nos. 1044/8	90	1.00
		ab. Imperf (strip of 5. Nos. 1044/8)	£1100	
1045	**524**	7p. slate, brt yellow-green, new blue & gold	15	15
1046	**525**	7p. slate, grey, brt yellow-green, new blue, rose-red & gold	15	15
1047	**526**	7p. slate, grey, brt yellow-green, new blue, rose-red & gold	15	15
1048	**527**	7p. slate, grey, bright yellow-green, new blue, rose-red & gold	15	15
1049	**528**	9p. pale brown, pale orange, brt emerald, pale greenish yellow, slate-black & gold	20	20
		a. Imperf (pair)	£850	
		Set of 6	1.00	85
		Set of 6 Gutter Pairs	2.50	
		Traffic Light Gutter Pairs	4.50	
		First Day Cover		1.40
		Presentation Pack	2.00	
		P.H.Q. Cards (set of 6)	3.25	4.00

Special First Day of Issue Postmarks

 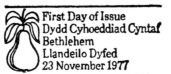

Philatelic Bureau, Edinburgh	1.75	
Bethlehem, Llandeilo, Dyfed	2.75	

Collectors Pack 1977

1977 (23 Nov). *Comprises Nos. 1022/5 and 1029/49.*
CP1049*b* Collectors Pack 7.00

529 Oil—North Sea Production Platform   **530** Coal—Modern Pithead

531 Natural Gas—Flame Rising from Sea   **532** Electricity—Nuclear Power Station and Uranium Atom

(Des P. Murdoch)

1978 (25 Jan). **Energy Resources.** *"All-over" phosphor. P* 14 × 15.

1050	**529**	9p. dp brown, orange-vermilion, grey-black, greenish yellow, rose-pink, new blue & silver	25	20
1051	**530**	10½p. lt emerald-green, grey-black, red-brown, slate-grey, pale apple-green & silver	25	30
1052	**531**	11p. greenish blue, brt violet, violet-blue, blackish brown, grey-black & silver	30	30
1053	**532**	13p. orange-vermilion, grey-black, dp brown, greenish yellow, lt brown, lt blue & silver	30	30
		Set of 4	1.00	1.00
		Set of 4 Gutter Pairs	2.50	
		Set of 4 Traffic Light Gutter Pairs	4.00	
		First Day Cover		1.25
		Presentation Pack	2.00	
		P.H.Q. Cards (set of 4)	4.00	4.00

Special First Day of Issue Postmark

Philatelic Bureau, Edinburgh 2.75

533 The Tower of London   **534** Holyroodhouse

535 Caernarvon Castle   **536** Hampton Court Palace

(Des R. Maddox (stamps), J. Matthews (miniature sheet))

▮78 (1 Mar). **British Architecture.** *Historic Buildings. "All-over" phosphor. P* 15 × 14.

▮54	533	9p.	black, olive-brown, new blue, brt green, lt yellow-olive & rose-red	25	20
▮55	534	10½p.	black, brown-olive, orange-yellow, brt green, lt yellow-olive & violet-blue	25	30
▮56	535	11p.	black, brown-olive, violet-blue, brt green, lt yellow-olive & dull blue	30	30
▮57	536	13p.	black, orange-yellow, lake-brown, brt green & lt yellow-olive..............	30	30
			Set of 4	1.00	1.00
			Set of 4 Gutter Pairs	2.50	
			Set of 4 Traffic Light Gutter Pairs	4.00	
			First Day Cover		1.25
			Presentation Pack..........................	2.00	
			P.H.Q. Cards (set of 4)	4.00	5.00
▮S1058		121 ×	89 mm. Nos. 1054/7 *(sold at 53½p.)*	1.25	1.50
		a.	Imperforate	£4000	
		b.	Lt yellow-olive (Queen's head) omitted	£3000	
		c.	Rose-red (Union Jack on 9p.) omitted	£1750	
		d.	Orange-yellow omitted	£1750	
			First Day Cover		2.00

The premium on No. MS1058 was used to support the London 1980 International Stamp Exhibition.

No. MS1058d is most noticeable on the 10½p. (spheres absent on towers) and around the roadway and arch on the 13p.

Special First Day of Issue Postmarks

Philatelic Bureau, Edinburgh (stamps)	2.00
Philatelic Bureau, Edinburgh (miniature sheet)	2.50
London EC (stamps)	2.00
London EC (miniature sheet)	3.00

539 The Sovereign's Orb   **540** Imperial State Crown

(Des J. Matthews)

1978 (31 May). **25th Anniv of Coronation.** *"All-over" phosphor. P* 14 × 15.

1059	537	9p.	gold & royal blue	20	20
1060	538	10½p.	gold & brown-lake	25	30
1061	539	11p.	gold & dp dull green	30	30
1062	540	13p.	gold & reddish violet.....................	35	30
			Set of 4	1.00	1.00
			Set of 4 Gutter Pairs	2.50	
			Set of 4 Traffic Light Gutter Pairs	4.00	
			First Day Cover		1.25
			Presentation Pack..........................	2.00	
			Souvenir Book	4.00	
			P.H.Q. Cards (set of 4)	2.50	4.00

The souvenir book is a 16-page booklet illustrated with scenes from the Coronation.

Special First Day of Issue Postmarks

Philatelic Bureau, Edinburgh	2.00
London SW1	1.75

541 Shire Horse   **542** Shetland Pony

543 Welsh Pony   **544** Thoroughbred

537 State Coach   **538** St. Edward's Crown

(Des P. Oxenham)

1978 (5 July). **Horses.** *"All-over" phosphor.* P 15 × 14.

1063 **541**	9p.	black, pale reddish brown, grey-black, greenish yellow, lt blue, vermilion & gold	20	20
1064 **542**	10½p.	pale chestnut, magenta, brownish grey, greenish yellow, greenish blue, grey-black & gold	25	25
1065 **543**	11p.	reddish brown, black, lt green, greenish yellow, bistre, grey-black & gold	30	30
1066 **544**	13p.	reddish brown, pale reddish brown, emerald, greenish yellow, grey-black & gold	35	35
		Set of 4	1.00	1.00
		Set of 4 Gutter Pairs	2.50	
		Set of 4 Traffic Light Gutter Pairs	4.00	
		First Day Cover		1.50
		Presentation Pack	2.00	
		P.H.Q. Cards (set of 4)	2.50	6.00

Special First Day of Issue Postmarks

Philatelic Bureau, Edinburgh 2.25
Peterborough 2.75

545 "Penny-farthing" and 1884 Safety Bicycle

546 1920 Touring Bicycles

547 Modern Small-wheel Bicycles

548 1978 Road-racers

(Des F. Wegner)

1978 (2 Aug). **Centenaries of Cyclists Touring Club and British Cycling Federation.** *"All-over" phosphor.* P 15 × 14.

1067 **545**	9p.	brown, dp dull blue, rose-pink, pale olive, grey-black & gold	20	20
		a. Imperf (pair)	£350	

1068 **546**	10½p.	olive, pale yellow-orange, orange-vermilion, rose-red, lt brown, grey-black & gold	25	2
1069 **547**	11p.	orange-vermilion, greenish blue, lt brown, pale greenish yellow, dp grey, grey-black & gold	30	3
1070 **548**	13p.	new blue, orange-vermilion, lt brown, olive-grey, grey-black & gold	35	3
		a. Imperf (pair)	£750	
		Set of 4	1.00	1.0
		Set of 4 Gutter Pairs	2.50	
		Set of 4 Traffic Light Gutter Pairs	4.00	
		First Day Cover		1.2
		Presentation Pack	2.00	
		P.H.Q. Cards (set of 4)	1.50	3.2

Special First Day of Issue Postmarks

Philatelic Bureau, Edinburgh 2.00
Harrogate, North Yorkshire 2.25

549 Singing Carols round the Christmas Tree

550 The Waits

551 18th-century Carol Singers

552 "The Boar's Head Carol"

(Des Faith Jaques)

1978 (22 Nov). **Christmas.** *One centre phosphor band (7p.) or "all over" phosphor (others).* P 15 × 14.

1071 **549**	7p.	brt green, greenish yellow, magenta, new blue, black & gold	20	2
		a. Imperf (vert pair)	£350	
1072 **550**	9p.	magenta, greenish yellow, new blue, sage-green, black & gold	25	2
		a. Imperf (horiz pair)		
1073 **551**	11p.	magenta, new blue, greenish yellow, yellow-brown, black & gold	30	3
		a. Imperf (horiz pair)		

074 **552**	13p.	salmon-pink, new blue, greenish yellow, magenta, black & gold.............	35	35
		Set of 4	1.00	1.00
		Set of 4 Gutter Pairs	2.50	
		Set of 4 Traffic Light Gutter Pairs	3.00	
		First Day Cover		1.25
		Presentation Pack.........................	1.75	
		P.H.Q. Cards (set of 4)	1.50	4.00

Special First Day of Issue Postmarks

Philatelic Bureau, Edinburgh 1.75
Bethlehem, Llandeilo, Dyfed 1.50

Collectors Pack 1978
1978 (22 Nov). Comprises Nos. 1050/7 and 1059/74.
CP1074a Collectors Pack 7.00

553 Old English Sheepdog   **554** Welsh Springer Spaniel

555 West Highland Terrier   **556** Irish Setter

(Des P. Barrett)

1979 (7 Feb). **Dogs.** "All-over" phosphor. P 15 × 14.

1075 **553**	9p.	grey-black, sepia, turquoise-green, pale greenish yellow, pale greenish blue & grey...................................	20	20
1076 **554**	10½p.	grey-black, lake-brown, apple-green, pale greenish yellow, pale greenish blue & grey...................................	30	30
1077 **555**	11p.	grey-black, claret, yellowish green, pale greenish yellow, cobalt & grey ..	30	30
		a. Imperf (horiz pair)	£850	
1078 **556**	13p.	grey-black, lake-brown, green, pale greenish yellow & dp turquoise-blue	30	30
		Set of 4	1.00	1.00
		Set of 4 Gutter Pairs	2.50	
		Set of 4 Traffic Light Gutter Pairs	3.75	
		First Day Cover		1.50
		Presentation Pack.........................	2.00	
		P.H.Q. Cards (set of 4)	3.00	5.00

Special First Day of Issue Postmarks

Philatelic Bureau, Edinburgh 2.00
London SW... 2.00

557 Primrose   **558** Daffodil

559 Bluebell   **560** Snowdrop

(Des P. Newcombe)

1979 (21 Mar). **Spring Wild Flowers.** "All-over" phosphor. P 14 × 15.

1079 **557**	9p.	slate-black, dp brown, pale greenish yellow, dp olive, pale new blue & silver	20	20
		a. Imperf (pair)	£400	
1080 **558**	10½p.	greenish yellow, grey-green, steel-blue, slate-black, new blue & silver ..	30	30
		a. Imperf (vert pair)	£1500	
1081 **559**	11p.	slate-black, dp brown, ultramarine, lt greenish blue, pale greenish yellow & silver	30	30
		a. Imperf (horiz pair)	£1200	
1082 **560**	13p.	slate-black, indigo, grey-green, sepia, ochre & silver..........................	30	30
		a. Imperf (horiz pair)	£750	
		Set of 4	1.00	1.00
		Set of 4 Gutter Pairs	2.50	
		Set of 4 Traffic Light Gutter Pairs	3.75	
		First Day Cover		1.50
		Presentation Pack.........................	2.00	
		P.H.Q. Cards (set of 4)	2.00	4.00

Special First Day of Issue Postmark

Philatelic Bureau, Edinburgh 2.00

Special First Day of Issue Postmarks

Philatelic Bureau, Edinburgh 1.75
London SW 1.75

561   **562**

563   **564**

T **561/4** show Hands placing National Flags in Ballot Boxes.

(Des S. Cliff)

1979 (9 May). **First Direct Elections to European Assembly.** *Phosphorised paper.* P 15 × 14.

1083	**561**	9p.	grey-black, vermilion, cinnamon, pale greenish yellow, pale turquoise-green & dull ultramarine................	20	20
1084	**562**	10½p.	grey-black, vermilion, cinnamon, pale greenish yellow, dull ultramarine, pale turquoise-green & chestnut	30	30
1085	**563**	11p.	grey-black, vermilion, cinnamon, pale greenish yellow, dull ultramarine, pale turquoise-green & grey-green	30	30
1086	**564**	13p.	grey-black, vermilion, cinnamon, pale greenish yellow, dull ultramarine, pale turquoise-green & brown...	30	30
			Set of 4	1.00	1.00
			Set of 4 Gutter Pairs	2.50	
			Set of 4 Traffic Light Gutter Pairs	3.75	
			First Day Cover		1.25
			Presentation Pack..........................	2.00	
			P.H.Q. Cards (set of 4)	1.50	3.50

565 "Saddling 'Mahmoud' for the Derby, 1936" (Sir Alfred Munnings)

566 "The Liverpool Great National Steeple Chase, 1839" (aquatint by F. C. Turner)

567 "The First Spring Meeting, Newmarket, 1793" (J. N. Sartorius)

568 "Racing at Dorsett Ferry, Windsor, 1684" (Francis Barlow)

(Des S. Rose)

1979 (6 June). **Horseracing Paintings.** *Bicentenary of the Derby (9p.).* "All-over" phosphor. P 15 × 14.

1087	**565**	9p.	lt blue, red-brown, rose-pink, pale greenish yellow, grey-black & gold...	25	25
1088	**566**	10½p.	bistre-yellow, slate-blue, salmon-pink, lt blue, grey-black & gold........	30	30
1089	**567**	11p.	rose, vermilion, pale greenish yellow, new blue, grey-black & gold............	30	30
1090	**568**	13p.	bistre-yellow, rose, turquoise, grey-black & gold	30	30
			Set of 4	1.10	1.10
			Set of 4 Gutter Pairs	2.50	
			Set of 4 Traffic Light Gutter Pairs	3.75	
			First Day Cover		1.50
			Presentation Pack..........................	2.00	
			P.H.Q. Cards (set of 4)	1.50	3.00

Special First Day of Issue Postmarks

Special First Day of Issue Postmark

Philatelic Bureau, Edinburgh	2.00
Epsom, Surrey	2.00

Philatelic Bureau, Edinburgh 2.00
First Day of Issue handstamps were provided at Hartfield,
East Sussex and Stourbridge, West Midlands for this issue.

569 *The Tale of Peter Rabbit*
(Beatrix Potter)

570 *The Wind in the Willows*
(Kenneth Grahame)

573 Sir Rowland Hill

574 Postman, *circa* 1839

571 *Winnie-the-Pooh*
(A. A. Milne)

572 *Alice's Adventures in
Wonderland*
(Lewis Carroll)

575 London Postman,
circa 1839

576 Woman and Young Girl
with Letters, 1840

(Des E. Hughes)

1979 (11 July). **International Year of the Child.** *Children's Book Illustrations.* "All-over" phosphor. P 14 × 15.

1091	569	9p. dp bluish green, grey-black, bistre-brown, brt rose, greenish yellow & silver	35	20
1092	570	10½p. dull ultramarine, grey-black, olive-brown, brt rose, yellow-orange, pale greenish yellow & silver	40	35
1093	571	11p. drab, grey-black, greenish yellow, new blue, yellow-orange, agate & silver	45	40
1094	572	13p. pale greenish yellow, grey-black, brt rose, dp bluish green, olive-brown, new blue & silver	50	55
		Set of 4	1.50	1.40
		Set of 4 Gutter Pairs	4.00	
		Set of 4 Traffic Light Gutter Pairs	4.75	
		First Day Cover		2.00
		Presentation Pack	2.25	
		P.H.Q. Cards (set of 4)	2.50	3.00

(Des E. Stemp)

1979 (22 Aug–24 Oct). **Death Centenary of Sir Rowland Hill.** "All-over" phosphor. P 14 × 15.

1095	573	10p. grey-black, brown-ochre, myrtle-green, pale greenish yellow, rosine, brt blue & gold	25	25
1096	574	11½p. grey-black, brown-ochre, brt blue, rosine, bistre-brown, pale greenish yellow & gold	30	35
1097	575	13p. grey-black, brown-ochre, bright blue, rosine, bistre-brown, pale greenish yellow & gold	35	40
1098	576	15p. grey-black, brown-ochre, myrtle-green, bistre-brown, rosine, pale greenish yellow & gold	50	40
		Set of 4	1.25	1.25
		Set of 4 Gutter Pairs	2.50	
		Set of 4 Traffic Light Gutter Pairs	3.75	
		First Day Cover		1.25
		Presentation Pack	2.00	
		P.H.Q. Cards (set of 4)	1.50	3.00

MS1099   89 × 121 mm. Nos. 1095/8 (*sold at 59½p.*)

(24 Oct)	1.25	1.25
a. Imperforate	£1100	
b. Brown-ochre (15p. background, etc.) omitted	£750	
c. Gold (Queen's head) omitted	£150	
d. Brown-ochre, myrtle-green & gold omitted	£3000	
e. Brt blue (13p. background, etc.) omitted	£950	
f. Myrtle-green (10p. background), 15p.) omitted	£1300	
g. Pale greenish yellow omitted	£160	
h. Rosine omitted	£600	
i. Bistre-brown omitted	£750	
First Day Cover		1.25

The premium on No. **MS**1099 was used to support the London 1980 International Stamp Exhibition.

Special First Day of Issue Postmarks

Philatelic Bureau, Edinburgh (stamps) (22 Aug.)	1.60
Philatelic Bureau, Edinburgh (miniature sheet) (24 Oct.)	1.60
London EC (stamps) (22 Aug.)	1.50
London EC (miniature sheet) (24 Oct.)	1.50

First Day of Issue handstamps were provided at Kidderminster, Worcs on 22 August (pictorial) and 24 October (Type C) and at Sanquhar, Dumfries on 22 August (Type C).

577 Policeman on the Beat

579 Mounted Policewoman

578 Policeman directing Traffic

580 River Patrol Boat

(Des B. Sanders)

1979 (26 Sept). **150th Anniv of Metropolitan Police.** *Phosphorised paper.* P 15 × 14.

1100 **577**	10p.	grey-black, red-brown, emerald, greenish yellow, brt blue & magenta	25 25

1101 **578**	11½p.	grey-black, brt orange, purple-brown, ultramarine, greenish yellow & dp bluish green	30	35
1102 **579**	13p.	grey-black, red-brown, magenta, olive-green, greenish yellow & dp dull blue	35	40
1103 **580**	15p.	grey-black, magenta, brown, slate-blue, dp brown & greenish black	50	40
		Set of 4	1.25	1.25
		Set of 4 Gutter Pairs	2.50	
		Set of 4 Traffic Light Gutter Pairs	3.75	
		First Day Cover		1.25
		Presentation Pack	2.00	
		P.H.Q. Cards (set of 4)	1.50	3.00

Special First Day of Issue Postmarks

Philatelic Bureau, Edinburgh	1.75
London SW	1.75

581 The Three Kings

582 Angel appearing to the Shepherds

583 The Nativity

584 Mary and Joseph travelling to Bethlehem

585 The Annunciation

(Des F. Wegner)

1979 (21 Nov). **Christmas.** *One centre phosphor band (8p.) or phosphorised paper (others).* P 15 × 14.

1104 **581**	8p.	blue, grey-black, ochre, slate-violet & gold	20	20
		a. Imperf (pair)	£550	

105	582	10p.	brt rose-red, grey-black, chestnut, chrome-yellow, dp violet & gold	25	25
		a.	Imperf between (vert pair)	£450	
		b.	Imperf (pair)	£600	
106	583	11½p.	orange-vermilion, steel-blue, drab, grey-black, dp blue-green & gold	30	35
107	584	13p.	brt blue, orange-vermilion, bistre, grey-black & gold	40	40
108	585	15p.	orange-vermilion, blue, bistre, grey-black, green & gold.......................	50	45

Set of 5 .... 1.50 1.50
Set of 5 Gutter Pairs 3.00
Set of 5 Traffic Light Gutter Pairs 3.75
First Day Cover 1.50
Presentation Pack.......................... 2.25
P.H.Q. Cards (set of 5) 1.50 3.50

Special First Day of Issue Postmarks

Philatelic Bureau, Edinburgh 2.00
Bethlehem, Llandeilo, Dyfed 1.75

Collectors Pack 1979

1979 (21 Nov).   *Comprises Nos. 1075/98 and 1100/8.*
CP1108a Collectors Pack 9.00

586 Common Kingfisher   **587** Dipper

588 Moorhen   **589** Yellow Wagtails

(Des M. Warren)

1980 (16 Jan).   **Centenary of Wild Bird Protection Act.** *Phosphorised paper. P* 14 × 15.

1109	586	10p.	brt blue, brt yellow-green, vermilion, pale greenish yellow, grey-black & gold	25	25
1110	587	11½p.	sepia, grey-black, dull ultramarine, vermilion, grey-green, pale greenish yellow & gold................................	30	35
1111	588	13p.	emerald-green, grey-black, brt blue, vermilion, pale greenish yellow & gold	40	40
1112	589	15p.	greenish yellow, brown, lt green, slate-blue, grey-black & gold	45	45

Set of 4 .... 1.25 1.25
Set of 4 Gutter Pairs 2.50
First Day Cover 1.40
Presentation Pack.......................... 2.00
P.H.Q. Cards (set of 4) 1.50 3.00

Special First Day of Issue Postmarks

Philatelic Bureau, Edinburgh 2.00
Sandy, Beds.. 2.00

590 *Rocket* approaching Moorish Arch, Liverpool

591 First and Second Class Carriages passing through Olive Mount cutting

592 Third Class Carriage and Cattle Truck crossing Chat Moss

593 Horsebox and Carriage Truck near Bridgewater Canal

594 Goods Truck and Mail-Coach at Manchester

T **590/4** were printed together, *se-tenant*, in horizontal strips of 5 throughout the sheet.

(Des D. Gentleman)

1980 (12 Mar). **150th Anniv of Liverpool and Manchester Railway.** *Phosphorised paper. P* 15 × 14.

1113 **590**	12p.	lemon, lt brown, rose-red, pale blue & grey-black	25	25
	a.	Strip of 5. Nos. 1113/17	1.50	1.60
	ab.	Imperf (horiz strip of 5. Nos. 1113/17)	£1200	
	ac.	Lemon omitted (horiz strip of 5.Nos. 1113/17)		
1114 **591**	12p.	rose-red, lt brown, lemon, pale blue & grey-black	25	25
1115 **592**	12p.	pale blue, rose-red, lemon, lt brown & grey-black	25	25
1116 **593**	12p.	lt brown, lemon, rose-red, pale blue & grey-black	25	25
1117 **594**	12p.	lt brown, rose-red, pale blue, lemon & grey-black	25	25
		Set of 5	1.50	1.10
		Gutter Strip of 10	3.25	
		First Day Cover		1.60
		Presentation Pack	2.50	
		P.H.Q. Cards (set of 5)	1.50	3.75

Special First Day of Issue Postmarks

Philatelic Bureau, Edinburgh	2.00
Liverpool	2.00
Manchester	2.00

INTERNATIONAL STAMP EXHIBITION

595 Montage of London Buildings

During the printing of No. 1118 the die was re-cut resulting in the following two types:

Type I (original). Top and bottom lines of shading in portrait oval broken. Hatched shading below left arm of Tower Bridge and hull of ship below right arm. Other points: Hatched shading on flag on Westminster Abbey, bottom right of Post Office Tower and archway of entrance to Westminster Abbey.

Type II (re-engraved). Lines in oval unbroken. Solid shading on bridge and ship. Also solid shading on flag, Post Office Tower and archway.

(Des J. Matthews. Recess)

1980 (9 Apr–7 May). **"London 1980" International Stamp Exhibition.**
Phosphorised paper. P 14½ × 14.

1118 **595**	50p. agate (I)		1.50	1.50
	Ea.	Type II	1.50	1.50
		Gutter Pair	3.00	
		First Day Cover		1.50
		Presentation Pack........................	2.00	
		P.H.Q. Card	50	1.75
MS1119	90 × 123 mm. No. 1118 (*sold at* 75p.)			
		(7 May)	1.50	1.50
	a.	Error. Imperf...............................	£700	
		First Day Cover		1.50

Examples of No. 1118 are known in various shades of green. Such shades result from problems with the drying of the printed sheets on the press, but are not listed as similar colours can be easily faked.

Special First Day of Issue Postmarks

Philatelic Bureau, Edinburgh (stamp) (9 Apr.)	1.75
Philatelic Bureau, Edinburgh (miniature sheet) (7 May)	2.00
London SW (stamp) (9 Apr.)	1.75
London SW (miniature sheet) (7 May)	1.75

596 Buckingham Palace

597 The Albert Memorial

598 Royal Opera House

599 Hampton Court

600 Kensington Palace

(Des Sir Hugh Casson)

1980 (7 May). **London Landmarks.** *Phosphorised paper.* P 14 × 15.

1120 **596**	10½p. grey, pale blue, rosine, pale greenish yellow, yellowish green & silver.......		25	25
1121 **597**	12p. grey-black, bistre, rosine, yellowish green, pale greenish yellow & silver .		30	30
	a. Imperf (vert pair)		£550	
1122 **598**	13½p. grey-black, pale salmon, pale olive-green, slate-blue & silver		35	35
	a. Imperf (pair)		£550	
1123 **599**	15p. grey-black, pale salmon, slate-blue, dull yellowish green, olive-yellow & silver		40	40
1124 **600**	17½p. grey, slate-blue, red-brown, sepia, yellowish green, pale greenish yellow & silver		40	40
	a. Silver (Queen's head) omitted		£175	
	Set of 5		1.50	1.50
	Set of 5 Gutter Pairs		3.00	
	First Day Cover			1.75
	Presentation Pack........................		2.50	
	P.H.Q. Cards (set of 5)		1.50	3.00

No. 1124a shows the Queen's head in pale greenish yellow, this colour being printed beneath the silver for technical reasons.

Special First Day of Issue Postmarks

Philatelic Bureau, Edinburgh	2.25
Kingston-upon-Thames	2.00

601 Charlotte Brontë
(*Jane Eyre*)

602 George Eliot
(*The Mill on the Floss*)

603 Emily Brontë
(*Wuthering Heights*)

604 Mrs. Gaskell
(*North and South*)

T **601/4** show authoresses and scenes from their novels. T **601/2** also include the "Europa" C.E.P.T. emblem.

(Des Barbara Brown)

1980 (9 July). **Famous Authoresses.** *Phosphorised paper.* P 15 × 14.
1125	**601**	12p. red-brown, brt rose, brt blue, greenish yellow, grey & gold	30	30
		Ea. Missing "p" in value (R.4/6)	25.00	
1126	**602**	13½p. red-brown, dull vermilion, pale blue, pale greenish yellow, grey & gold	35	35
		a. Pale blue omitted	£1500	
1127	**603**	15p. red-brown, vermilion, blue, lemon, grey & gold	40	45
1128	**604**	17½p. dull vermilion, slate-blue, ultramarine, pale greenish yellow, grey & gold	60	60
		a. Imperf & slate-blue omitted (pair)	£700	
		Set of 4	1.50	1.50
		Set of 4 Gutter Pairs	3.00	
		First Day Cover		1.50
		Presentation Pack	2.50	
		P.H.Q. Cards (set of 4)	1.50	3.00

Special First Day of Issue Postmarks

Philatelic Bureau, Edinburgh		1.60
Haworth, Keighley, W. Yorks		1.60

605 Queen Elizabeth the Queen Mother

(Des J. Matthews from photograph by N. Parkinson)

1980 (4 Aug). **80th Birthday of Queen Elizabeth the Queen Mother.** *Phosphorised paper.* P 14 × 15.
1129	**605**	12p. brt rose, greenish yellow, new blue, grey & silver	50	50
		a. Imperf (horiz pair)	£1200	
		Gutter Pair	1.00	
		First Day Cover		60
		P.H.Q. Card	50	1.25

Special First Day of Issue Postmarks

Philatelic Bureau, Edinburgh	1.10
Glamis Castle, Forfar	1.10

606 Sir Henry Wood

607 Sir Thomas Beecham

608 Sir Malcolm Sargent

609 Sir John Barbirolli

(Des P. Gauld)

1980 (10 Sept). **British Conductors.** *Phosphorised paper.* P 14 × 15.
1130	**606**	12p. slate, rose-red, greenish yellow, bistre & gold	30	30
1131	**607**	13½p. grey-black, vermilion, greenish yellow, pale carmine-rose & gold	35	40
1132	**608**	15p. grey-black, bright rose-red, greenish yellow, turquoise-green & gold	45	45
1133	**609**	17½p. black, bright rose-red, greenish yellow, dull violet-blue & gold	55	50
		Set of 4	1.50	1.50
		Set of 4 Gutter Pairs	3.00	
		First Day Cover		1.50
		Presentation Pack	2.00	
		P.H.Q. Cards (set of 4)	1.50	2.50

Special First Day of Issue Postmarks

Special First Day of Issue Postmarks

Philatelic Bureau, Edinburgh	2.00
London SW.	2.00

Philatelic Bureau, Edinburgh	2.00
Cardiff	1.75

610 Running

611 Rugby

614 Christmas Tree

615 Candles

612 Boxing

613 Cricket

616 Apples and Mistletoe

617 Crown, Chains and Bell

(Des R. Goldsmith. Litho Questa)

1980 (10 Oct). **Sport Centenaries.** *Phosphorised paper.* P 14 × 14½.

1134	**610**	12p. pale new blue, greenish yellow, magenta, lt brown, reddish purple & gold	30	30
		a. Gold (Queen's head) omitted	£9000	
1135	**611**	13½p. pale new blue, olive-yellow, brt purple, orange-vermilion, blackish lilac & gold	35	40
1136	**612**	15p. pale new blue, greenish yellow, brt purple, chalky blue & gold	40	40
		a. Gold (Queen's head) omitted		
1137	**613**	17½p. pale new blue, greenish yellow, magenta, dp olive, grey-brown & gold	60	55
		Set of 4	1.50	1.50
		Set of 4 Gutter Pairs	3.00	
		First Day Cover		1.50
		Presentation Pack	2.00	
		P.H.Q. Cards (set of 4)	1.50	2.50

Centenaries:—12p. Amateur Athletics Association; 13½p. Welsh Rugby Union; 15p. Amateur Boxing Association; 17½p. First England–Australia Test Match.

No. 1134a was caused by a paper fold.

618 Holly

(Des J. Matthews)

1980 (19 Nov). **Christmas.** *One centre phosphor band* (10p.) *or phosphorised paper* (others). P 15 × 14.

1138	**614**	10p. black, turquoise-green, greenish yellow, vermilion & blue	25	25
		a. Imperf (horiz pair)		
1139	**615**	12p. grey, magenta, rose-red, greenish grey & pale orange	30	35
1140	**616**	13½p. grey-black, dull yellow-green, brown, greenish yellow & pale olive-bistre	35	40
1141	**617**	15p. grey-black, bistre-yellow, brt orange, magenta & new blue	40	40

119

1142 **618** 17½p. black, vermilion, dull yellowish green
& greenish yellow 40 40
Set of 5 .... 1.50 1.60
Set of 5 Gutter Pairs 3.00
First Day Cover 1.60
Presentation Pack 2.25
P.H.Q. Cards (set of 5) 1.50 2.50

Special First Day of Issue Postmarks

Philatelic Bureau, Edinburgh 2.00
Bethlehem, Llandeilo, Dyfed 2.00

Collectors Pack 1980

1980 (19 Nov). *Comprises Nos. 1109/18 and 1120/42.*
CP1142*a* Collectors Pack 12.00

619 St. Valentine's Day

620 Morris Dancers

621 Lammastide

622 Medieval Mummers

T **619**/20 also include the "Europa" C.E.P.T. emblem.

(Des F. Wegner)

1981 (6 Feb). **Folklore.** *Phosphorised paper. P 15 × 14.*
1143 **619** 14p. cerise, green, yellow-orange, sal-
mon-pink, black & gold 35 35
1144 **620** 18p. dull ultramarine, lemon, lake-brown,
brt green, black & gold.................. 45 50
1145 **621** 22p. chrome-yellow, rosine, brown, new
blue, black & gold 60 60

1146 **622** 25p. brt blue, red-brown, brt rose-red,
greenish yellow, black & gold 75 70
Set of 4 .... 2.00 2.00
Set of 4 Gutter Pairs 4.00
First Day Cover 2.00
Presentation Pack 2.50
P.H.Q. Cards (set of 4) 1.50 2.50

Special First Day of Issue Postmarks

Philatelic Bureau, Edinburgh 2.50
London WC 2.25

623 Blind Man with Guide Dog

624 Hands spelling "Deaf" in Sign Language

625 Disabled Man in Wheelchair

626 Disabled Artist painting with Foot

(Des J. Gibbs)

1981 (25 Mar). **International Year of the Disabled.** *Phosphorised paper. P 15 × 14.*
1147 **623** 14p. drab, greenish yellow, brt rose-red,
dull purple & silver 35 35
a. Imperf (pair) £750
1148 **624** 18p. dp blue-green, brt orange, dull vermilion, grey-black & silver............... 45 50
1149 **625** 22p. brown-ochre, rosine, purple-brown,
greenish blue, black & silver 60 60
1150 **626** 25p. vermilion, lemon, pale salmon, olive-
brown, new blue, black & silver....... 75 70
Set of 4 .... 2.00 2.00
Set of 4 Gutter Pairs 4.00
First Day Cover 2.00
Presentation Pack 2.50
P.H.Q. Cards (set of 4) 1.50 2.75

All known examples of No. 1147*a* are creased.

Edinburgh Philatelic Bureau 2.50
Windsor 2.50

Philatelic Bureau, Edinburgh 2.50
London SW 2.25

631 Glenfinnan, Scotland   **632** Derwentwater, England

627 *Aglais urticae*   **628** *Maculinea arion*

633 Stackpole Head, Wales   **634** Giant's Causeway,
Northern Ireland

629 *Inachis io*   **630** *Carterocephalus palaemon*

(Des G. Beningfield)

635 St. Kilda, Scotland

(Des M. Fairclough)

1981 (13 May). **Butterflies.** *Phosphorised paper.* P 14 × 15.

1151	**627**	14p. greenish yellow, yellow-green, brt rose, brt blue, emerald & gold	35	35
		a. Imperf (pair)	£950	
1152	**628**	18p. black, greenish yellow, dull yellowish green, brt mauve, brt blue, brt green & gold	50	50
1153	**629**	22p. black, greenish yellow, bronze-green, rosine, ultramarine, lt green & gold	60	65
1154	**630**	25p. black, greenish yellow, bronze-green, brt rose-red, ultramarine, brt emerald & gold	70	75
		Set of 4	2.00	2.00
		Set of 4 Gutter Pairs	4.00	
		First Day Cover		2.00
		Presentation Pack	2.50	
		P.H.Q. Cards (set of 4)	2.00	3.00

1981 (24 June). **50th Anniv of National Trust for Scotland.** *British Landscapes. Phosphorised paper.* P 15 × 14.

1155	**631**	14p. lilac, dull blue, reddish brown, bistre-yellow, black & gold	30	30
1156	**632**	18p. bottle green, brt blue, brown, bistre-yellow, black & gold	40	40
1157	**633**	20p. dp turquoise-blue, dull blue, greenish yellow, reddish brown, black & gold	50	50
1158	**634**	22p. chrome-yellow, reddish brown, new blue, yellow-brown, black & gold	60	60
1159	**635**	25p. ultramarine, new blue, olive-green, olive-grey & gold	70	70
		Set of 5	2.25	2.25
		Set of 5 Gutter Pairs	4.50	
		First Day Cover		2.25
		Presentation Pack	2.75	
		P.H.Q. Cards (set of 5)	2.00	2.75

Special First Day of Issue Postmarks

Philatelic Bureau, Edinburgh 2.75
Glenfinnan 3.25
Keswick 3.25

Special First Day of Issue Postmarks

Philatelic Bureau, Edinburgh 2.25
Caernarfon, Gwynedd....................................... 2.50
London EC 2.50

637 "Expeditions" **638** "Skills"

639 "Service" **640** "Recreation"

(Des P. Sharland. Litho J.W.)

636 Prince Charles and Lady Diana Spencer

(Des J. Matthews from photograph by Lord Snowdon)

1981 (22 July). **Royal Wedding.** *Phosphorised paper.* P 14 × 15.

1160	**636**	14p. grey-black, greenish yellow, brt rose-red, ultramarine, pale blue, blue & silver	25	25
1161		25p. drab, greenish yellow, brt rose-red, ultramarine, grey-brown, grey-black & silver	75	75
		Set of 2	1.00	1.00
		Set of 2 Gutter Pairs	2.00	
		First Day Cover		2.00
		Presentation Pack..........................	2.00	
		Souvenir Book	4.00	
		P.H.Q. Cards (set of 2)	1.00	2.75

The souvenir book is a 12-page illustrated booklet with a set of mint stamps in a sachet attached to the front cover.

1981 (12 Aug). **25th Anniv of Duke of Edinburgh Award Scheme.** *Phosphorised paper.* P 14.

1162	**637**	14p. greenish yellow, magenta, pale new blue, black, emerald & silver	35	35
1163	**638**	18p. greenish yellow, magenta, pale new blue, black, cobalt & gold	50	50
1164	**639**	22p. greenish yellow, magenta, pale new blue, black, red-orange & gold	60	60
1165	**640**	25p. brt orange, mauve, pale new blue, black, flesh & bronze	70	70
		Set of 4	2.00	2.00
		Set of 4 Gutter Pairs	4.00	
		First Day Cover		2.00
		Presentation Pack..........................	2.50	
		P.H.Q. Cards (set of 4)	1.60	2.25

Philatelic Bureau, Edinburgh 2.50
Hull 2.25

Philatelic Bureau, Edinburgh 2.50
London W2 .... 2.25

645 Father Christmas   646 Jesus Christ

641 Cockle-dredging from
Linsey II

642 Hauling in Trawl Net

647 Flying Angel   648 Joseph and Mary arriving
at Bethlehem

643 Lobster Potting   644 Hoisting Seine Net

649 Three Kings approaching
Bethlehem

(Des B. Sanders)

1981 (23 Sept). **Fishing Industry.** *Phosphorised paper. P* 15 × 14.

166	**641**	14p. slate, greenish yellow, magenta, new blue, orange-brown, olive-grey & bronze-green	35	35
167	**642**	18p. slate, greenish yellow, brt crimson, ultramarine, black & greenish slate...	50	50
168	**643**	22p. grey, greenish yellow, brt rose, dull ultramarine, reddish lilac & black	60	60
169	**644**	25p. grey, greenish yellow, brt rose, cobalt & black	70	65
		Set of 4	2.00	2.00
		Set of 4 Gutter Pairs	4.00	
		First Day Cover		2.00
		Presentation Pack	2.50	
		P.H.Q. Cards (set of 4)	2.00	2.50

Nos. 1166/9 were issued on the occasion of the centenary of the Royal National Mission to Deep Sea Fishermen.

(Des Samantha Brown (11½p.), Tracy Jenkins (14p.), Lucinda Blackmore (18p.), Stephen Moore (22p.), Sophie Sharp (25p.))

1981 (18 Nov). **Christmas.** *Children's Pictures. One phosphor band (11½p.) or phosphorised paper (others). P* 15 × 14.

1170	**645**	11½p. ultramarine, black, red, olive-bistre, brt green & gold	30	30
1171	**646**	14p. bistre-yellow, brt magenta, blue, greenish blue, brt green, black & gold	40	40
1172	**647**	18p. pale blue-green, bistre-yellow, brt magenta, ultramarine, black & gold ..	50	50
1173	**648**	22p. dp turquoise-blue, lemon, magenta, black & gold	60	60

1174	649	25p.	royal blue, lemon, brt magenta, black & gold	70	70
			Set of 5	2.25	2.25
			Set of 5 Gutter Pairs	4.50	
			First Day Cover		2.25
			Presentation Pack	2.75	
			P.H.Q. Cards (set of 5)	2.00	3.50

Special First Day of Issue Postmarks

Philatelic Bureau, Edinburgh	2.50
Bethlehem, Llandeilo, Dyfed	2.50

Collectors Pack 1981

1981 (18 Nov). *Comprises Nos. 1143/74.*
CP1174a Collectors Pack 18.00

650 Charles Darwin and Giant Tortoises   **651** Darwin and Marine Iguanas

652 Darwin, Cactus Ground Finch and Large Ground Finch   **653** Darwin and Prehistoric Skulls

(Des D. Gentleman)

1982 (10 Feb). **Death Centenary of Charles Darwin.** *Phosphorised paper.* P 15 × 14.

1175	650	15½p.	dull purple, drab, bistre, black & grey-black	35	35
1176	651	19½p.	violet-grey, bistre-yellow, slate-black, red-brown, grey-black & black	60	60
1177	652	26p.	sage green, bistre-yellow, orange, chalky blue, grey-black, red-brown & black	70	70

1178	653	29p.	grey-brown, yellow-brown, brown-ochre, black & grey-black	75	75
			Set of 4	2.25	2.25
			Set of 4 Gutter Pairs	4.50	
			First Day Cover		2.25
			Presentation Pack	3.00	
			P.H.Q. Cards (set of 4)	2.50	6.50

Special First Day of Issue Postmarks

Philatelic Bureau, Edinburgh	2.75
Shrewsbury	2.75

654 Boys' Brigade   **655** Girls' Brigade

656 Boy Scout Movement   **657** Girl Guide Movement

(Des B. Sanders)

1982 (24 Mar). **Youth Organizations.** *Phosphorised paper.* P 15 × 14.

1179	654	15½p.	gold, greenish yellow, pale orange, mauve, dull blue & grey-black	35	35
1180	655	19½p.	gold, greenish yellow, pale orange, brt rose, dp ultramarine, olive-bistre & grey-black	50	50
1181	656	26p.	gold, greenish yellow, olive-sepia, rosine, dp blue, dp dull green & grey black	75	75

1182 **657**	29p.	gold, yellow, dull orange, cerise, dull ultramarine, chestnut & grey-black...	90	90
		Set of 4	2.25	2.25
		Set of 4 Gutter Pairs	4.50	
		First Day Cover		2.25
		Presentation Pack	3.50	
		P.H.Q. Cards (set of 4)	2.50	6.50

Nos. 1179/82 were issued on the occasion of the 75th anniversary of the Boy Scout Movement; the 125th birth anniversary of Lord Baden-Powell and the centenary of the Boys' Brigade (1983).

Special First Day of Issue Postmarks

Edinburgh Philatelic Bureau	2.50
Glasgow	3.00
London SW	2.50

(Des A. George)

1982 (28 Apr). **Europa.** *British Theatre. Phosphorised paper.* P 15 × 14.

1183 **658**	15½p.	carmine-lake, greenish blue, greenish yellow, grey-black, bottle green & silver	35	35
1184 **659**	19½p.	rosine, new blue, greenish yellow, black, ultramarine & silver	50	50
1185 **660**	26p.	carmine-red, brt rose-red, greenish yellow, black, dull ultramarine, lake-brown & silver	75	75
1186 **661**	29p.	rose-red, greenish yellow, brt blue, grey-black & silver	90	90
		Set of 4	2.25	2.25
		Set of 4 Gutter Pairs	4.50	
		First Day Cover		2.25
		Presentation Pack	3.25	
		P.H.Q. Cards (set of 4)	2.50	6.50

Special First Day of Issue Postmarks

Philatelic Bureau, Edinburgh	2.50
Stratford-upon-Avon	2.75

658 Ballerina

659 Harlequin

660 Hamlet

661 Opera Singer

662 Henry VIII and *Mary Rose*

663 Admiral Blake and *Triumph*

664 Lord Nelson and H.M.S. *Victory*

665 Lord Fisher and H.M.S. *Dreadnought*

666 Viscount Cunningham and H.M.S. *Warspite*

(Des Marjorie Saynor. Eng C. Slania. Recess and photo)

1982 (16 June). **Maritime Heritage.** *Phosphorised paper.* P 15 × 14.

1187	662	15½p. black, lemon, bright rose, pale orange, ultramarine & grey	35	35
		a. Imperf (pair)	£750	
1188	663	19½p. black, greenish yellow, brt rose-red, pale orange, ultramarine & grey	60	60
1189	664	24p. black, orange-yellow, brt rose-red, lake-brown, dp ultramarine & grey	70	70
1190	665	26p. black, orange-yellow, brt rose, lemon, ultramarine & grey	80	80
		a. Imperf (pair)		
1191	666	29p. black, olive-yellow, brt rose, orange-yellow, ultramarine & grey	90	90
		Set of 5	3.00	3.00
		Set of 5 Gutter Pairs	6.00	
		First Day Cover		3.00
		Presentation Pack	3.50	
		P.H.Q. Cards (set of 5)	3.00	6.50

Nos. 1187/91 were issued on the occasion of Maritime England Year, the Bicentenary of the Livery Grant by City of London to Worshipful Company of Shipwrights and the raising of *Mary Rose* from Portsmouth Harbour.

Several used examples of the 15½p. have been seen with the black recess (ship and waves) omitted.

Special First Day of Issue Postmarks

Philatelic Bureau, Edinburgh		3.50
Portsmouth		3.25

667 "Strawberry Thief" (William Morris)

668 Untitled (Steiner and Co)

669 "Cherry Orchard" (Paul Nash)

670 "Chevron" (Andrew Foster)

(Des Peter Hatch Partnership)

1982 (23 July). **British Textiles.** *Phosphorised paper.* P 14 × 15.

1192	667	15½p. blue, olive-yellow, rosine, dp blue-green, bistre & Prussian blue	15	15
		a. Imperf (horiz pair)	£950	
1193	668	19½p. olive-grey, greenish yellow, brt magenta, dull green, yellow-brown & black	55	55
		a. Imperf (vert pair)	£1500	
1194	669	26p. brt scarlet, dull mauve, dull ultramarine & brt carmine	70	70
1195	670	29p. bronze-green, orange-yellow, turquoise-green, stone, chestnut & sage-green	90	90
		Set of 4	2.25	2.25
		Set of 4 Gutter Pairs	4.50	
		First Day Cover		2.50
		Presentation Pack	3.25	
		P.H.Q. Cards (set of 4)	3.00	6.50

Nos. 1192/5 were issued on the occasion of the 250th birth anniversary of Sir Richard Arkwright (inventor of spinning machine).

Special First Day of Issue Postmarks

Philatelic Bureau, Edinburgh		3.00
Rochdale		3.00

671 Development of Communications

672 Modern Technological Aids

(Des Delaney and Ireland)

1982 (8 Sept). **Information Technology.** *Phosphorised paper.* P 14 × 15.

1196	671	15½p. black, greenish yellow, brt rose-red, bistre-brown, new blue & lt ochre	45	50
		a. Imperf (pair)	£250	
1197	672	26p. black, greenish yellow, brt rose-red, olive-bistre, new blue & lt olive-grey	80	85
		a. Imperf (pair)	£1300	
		Set of 2	1.25	1.25
		Set of 2 Gutter Pairs	2.50	
		First Day Cover		1.50
		Presentation Pack	2.00	
		P.H.Q. Cards (set of 2)	1.50	4.50

Special First Day of Issue Postmarks

Philatelic Bureau, Edinburgh 2.00
London WC 2.00

Philatelic Bureau, Edinburgh 3.50
Birmingham 3.50
Crewe 3.50

673 Austin "Seven" and "Metro"   **674** Ford "Model T" and "Escort"

677 "While Shepherds Watched"   **678** "The Holly and the Ivy"

675 Jaguar "SS 1" and "XJ6"   **676** Rolls-Royce "Silver Ghost" and "Silver Spirit"

679 "I Saw Three Ships"   **680** "We Three Kings"

(Des S. Paine. Litho Questa)

1982 (13 Oct). **British Motor Cars.** *Phosphorised paper.* P 14½ × 14.
1198 **673** 15½p. slate, orange-vermilion, brt orange, drab, yellow-green, olive-yellow, bluish grey & black...................... 50 50
1199 **674** 19½p. slate, brt orange, olive-grey, rose-red, dull vermilion, grey & black 70 70
    Ea. Rose-red and black ptgs double........
1200 **675** 26p. slate, red-brown, brt orange, turquoise-green, myrtle-green, dull blue-green, grey & olve 85 90
1201 **676** 29p. slate, brt orange, carmine-red, reddish purple, grey & black........... 1.00 1.25
    Ea. Black ptg quadruple £350
    Eb. Brt orange, carmine-red, grey and black ptgs double ....
    Set of 4.. 2.75 3.00
    Set of 4 Gutter Pairs 5.50
    First Day Cover 3.00
    Presentation Pack......................... 3.75
    P.H.Q. Cards (set of 4) 3.00 7.00

681 "Good King Wenceslas"

(Des Barbara Brown)

1982 (17 Nov). **Christmas.** *Carols. One phosphor band (12½p.) or phosphorised paper (others).* P 15 × 14.
1202 **677** 12½p. black, greenish, yellow, brt scarlet, steel blue, red-brown & gold.......... 30 30
1203 **678** 15½p. black, bistre-yellow, brt rose-red, brt blue, brt green & gold 40 40
    a. Imperf. (pair) ....
1204 **679** 19½p. black, bistre-yellow, brt rose-red, dull blue, dp brown & gold 50 60
    a. Imperf (pair) £1300
1205 **680** 26p. black, bistre-yellow, brt magenta, brt blue, chocolate, gold & orange-red .. 60 70
1206 **681** 29p. black, bistre-yellow, magenta, brt blue, chestnut, gold & brt magenta .. 70 80
    Set of 5 .... 2.25 2.50
    Set of 5 Gutter Pairs 4.50
    First Day Cover 2.50
    Presentation Pack......................... 3.00
    P.H.Q. Cards (set of 5) 3.00 7.00

Special First Day of Issue Postmarks

Special First Day of Issue Postmarks

Special First Day of Issue Postmarks

Philatelic Bureau, Edinburgh	2.50
Bethlehem, Llandeilo, Dyfed	3.25

Philatelic Bureau, Edinburgh	2.75
Peterborough	3.00

Collectors Pack 1982

1982 (17 Nov). *Comprises Nos. 1175/1206.*
CP1206a Collectors Pack 24.00

682 Salmon

683 Pike

684 Trout

685 Perch

(Des A. Jardine)

686 Tropical Island

687 Desert

688 Temperate Farmland

689 Mountain Range

(Des D. Fraser)

1983 (26 Jan).   **British River Fishes.** *Phosphorised paper.* P 15 × 14.

1207	**682**	15½p. grey-black, bistre-yellow, brt purple, new blue & silver	35	35
		a. Imperf (pair)	£1300	
1208	**683**	19½p. black, bistre-yellow, olive-bistre, dp claret, silver & dp bluish green	55	55
1209	**684**	26p. grey-black, bistre-yellow, chrome-yellow, magenta, silver & pale blue	70	70
		a. Imperf (pair)	£850	
1210	**685**	29p. black, greenish yellow, brt carmine, new blue & silver	90	90
		Set of 4	2.25	2.25
		Set of 4 Gutter Pairs	4.50	
		First Day Cover		2.50
		Presentation Pack	3.00	
		P.H.Q. Cards (set of 4)	3.00	6.50

All known examples of No. 1209a are creased.

1983 (9 Mar).   **Commonwealth Day.** *Geographical Regions. Phosphorised paper.* P 14 × 15.

1211	**686**	15½p. greenish blue, greenish yellow, brt rose, lt brown, grey-black, dp claret & silver	35	35
1212	**687**	19½p. brt lilac, greenish yellow, magenta, dull blue, grey-black, dp dull blue & silver	55	55
1213	**688**	26p. lt blue, greenish yellow, brt magenta, new blue, grey-black, violet & silver	70	70
1214	**689**	29p. dull violet-blue, reddish violet, slate-lilac, new blue, myrtle-green, black & silver	90	90
		Set of 4	2.25	2.25
		Set of 4 Gutter Pairs	4.50	
		First Day Cover		2.50
		Presentation Pack	3.25	
		P.H.Q. Cards (set of 4)	3.00	6.50

Philatelic Bureau, Edinburgh	3.00
London SW	3.00

690 Humber Bridge

691 Thames Flood Barrier

692 *Iolair* (oilfield emergency support vessel)

(Des M. Taylor)

1983 (25 May). **Europa.** *Engineering Achievements. Phosphorised paper.* P 15 × 14.

1215	**690**	16p. silver, orange-yellow, ultramarine, black & grey	45	45
1216	**691**	20½p. silver, greenish yellow, brt purple, blue, grey-black & grey	95	1.10
1217	**692**	28p. silver, lemon, brt rose-red, chestnut, dull ultramarine, black & grey	1.10	1.25
		Set of 3	2.25	2.50
		Set of 3 Gutter Pairs	4.50	
		First Day Cover		2.75
		Presentation Pack	3.50	
		P.H.Q. Cards (set of 3)	2.50	6.00

Philatelic Bureau, Edinburgh	3.00
Hull	3.00

693 Musketeer and Pikeman, The Royal Scots (1633)

694 Fusilier and Ensign, The Royal Welch Fusiliers (mid-18th century)

695 Riflemen, 95th Rifles (The Royal Green Jackets) (1805)

696 Sergeant (khaki service) and Guardsman (full dress), The Irish Guards (1900)

697 Paratroopers, The Parachute Regiment (1983)

(Des E. Stemp)

1983 (6 July). **British Army Uniforms.** *Phosphorised paper.* P 14 × 15.

1218	**693**	16p. black, buff, dp brown, slate-black, rose-red, gold & new blue	40	40
1219	**694**	20½p. black, buff, greenish yellow, slate-black, brown-rose, gold & brt blue	60	60
1220	**695**	26p. black, buff, slate-purple, green, bistre & gold	70	70
		a. Imperf (pair)	£1300	
1221	**696**	28p. black, buff, lt brown, grey, dull rose, gold & new blue	70	70
1222	**697**	31p. black, buff, olive-yellow, grey, dp magenta, gold & new blue	90	90
		Set of 5	3.00	3.00
		Set of 5 Gutter Pairs	6.00	
		First Day Cover		3.25
		Presentation Pack	4.25	
		P.H.Q. Cards (set of 5)	3.00	6.00

Nos. 1218/22 were issued on the occasion of the 350th anniversary of the Royal Scots, the senior line regiment of the British Army.

Special First Day of Issue Postmarks

Philatelic Bureau, Edinburgh	3.50
Aldershot	4.00

698 20th-century Garden, Sissinghurst

699 19th-century Garden, Biddulph Grange

700 18th-century Garden, Blenheim

701 17th-century Garden, Pitmedden

(Des Liz Butler, Litho J.W.)

1983 (24 Aug). **British Gardens.** *Phosphorised paper.* P 14.

1223	**698**	16p.	greenish yellow, brt purple, new blue, black, brt green & silver	40	40
1224	**699**	20½p.	greenish yellow, brt purple, new blue, black, brt green & silver	50	50
1225	**700**	28p.	greenish yellow, brt purple, new blue, black, brt green & silver	70	90
1226	**701**	31p.	greenish yellow, brt purple, new blue, black, brt green & silver	90	1.00
			Set of 4	2.25	2.50
			Set of 4 Gutter Pairs	4.50	
			First Day Cover		2.75
			Presentation Pack	3.50	
			P.H.Q. Cards (set of 4)	3.00	6.00

Nos. 1223/6 were issued on the occasion of the death bicentenary of "Capability" Brown (landscape gardener)

Special First Day of Issue Postmarks

Philatelic Bureau, Edinburgh	3.50
Oxford	3.50

702 Merry-go-round

703 Big Wheel, Helter-skelter and Performing Animals

704 Side Shows

705 Early Produce Fair

(Des A. Restall)

1983 (5 Oct). **British Fairs.** *Phosphorised paper.* P 15 × 14.

1227	**702**	16p.	grey-black, greenish yellow, orange-red, ochre & turquoise-blue	40	40
1228	**703**	20½p.	grey-black, yellow-ochre, yellow-orange, brt magenta, violet & black	50	65
1229	**704**	28p.	grey-black, bistre-yellow, orange-red, violet & yellow-brown	75	85
1230	**705**	31p.	grey-black, greenish yellow, red, dp turquoise-green, slate-violet & brown	90	90
			Set of 4	2.25	2.50
			Set of 4 Gutter Pairs	4.50	
			First Day Cover		2.75
			Presentation Pack	3.50	
			P.H.Q. Cards (set of 4)	3.00	6.00

Special First Day of Issue Postmarks

Philatelic Bureau, Edinburgh	3.50
Nottingham	3.50

706 "Christmas Post"
(pillar-box)

707 "The Three Kings"
(chimney-pots)

708 "World at Peace"
(Dove and Blackbird)

709 "Light of Christmas"
(street lamp)

710 "Christmas Dove"
(hedge sculpture)
(Des T. Meeuwissen)

1983 (16 Nov). **Christmas.** *One phosphor band (12½p.) or phosphorised paper (others). P 15 × 14.*

1231	**706**	12½p. black, greenish yellow, brt rose-red, brt blue, gold & grey-black..............	30	30
		a. Imperf (horiz pair)	£750	
1232	**707**	16p. black, greenish yellow, brt rose, pale new blue, gold & brown-purple	35	35
		a. Imperf (pair)................................	£850	
1233	**708**	20½p. black, greenish yellow, brt rose, new blue, gold & blue............................	60	60
1234	**709**	28p. black, lemon, brt carmine, bluish violet, gold, dp turquoise-green & purple	70	80
1235	**710**	31p. black, greenish yellow, brt rose, new blue, gold, green & brown-olive	85	1.00
		Set of 5	2.50	2.75
		Set of 5 Gutter Pairs	5.00	
		First Day Cover		2.75
		Presentation Pack	3.50	
		P.H.Q. Cards (set of 5)	3.00	6.00

Special First Day of Issue Postmarks

Philatelic Bureau, Edinburgh	3.00
Bethlehem, Llandeilo, Dyfed................................	3.00

Collectors Pack 1983

1983 (16 Nov). *Comprises Nos. 1207/35.*
CP1235*a* Collectors Pack 40.00

711 Arms of the College
of Arms

712 Arms of King Richard III
(founder)

713 Arms of the Earl Marshal
of England

714 Arms of the City of London

(Des J. Matthews)

1984 (17 Jan). **500th Anniv of College of Arms.** *Phosphorised paper. P 14½.*

1236	**711**	16p. black, chrome-yellow, reddish brown, scarlet-vermilion, brt blue & grey-black	40	40
1237	**712**	20½p. black, chrome-yellow, rosine, brt blue & grey-black	60	60
1238	**713**	28p. black, chrome-yellow, rosine, brt blue, dull green & grey-black..........	85	85
1239	**714**	31p. black, chrome-yellow, rosine, brt blue & grey-black	95	95
		a. Imperf (horiz pair)......................	£1800	
		Set of 4	2.50	2.50
		Set of 4 Gutter Pairs	6.00	
		First Day Cover		2.50
		Presentation Pack...	3.50	
		P.H.Q. Cards (set of 4)	3.00	6.00

Special First Day of Issue Postmarks

Philatelic Bureau, Edinburgh	3.00
London EC	3.50

715 Highland Cow

716 Chillingham Wild Bull

717 Hereford Bull

718 Welsh Black Bull

719 Irish Moiled Cow

(Des B. Driscoll)

1984 (6 Mar). **British Cattle.** *Phosphorised paper. P* 15 × 14.

1240	**715**	16p.	grey-black, bistre-yellow, rosine, yellow-orange, new blue & pale drab....	40	40
1241	**716**	20½p.	grey-black, greenish yellow, magenta, bistre, dull blue-green, pale drab & lt green	65	65
1242	**717**	26p.	black, chrome-yellow, rosine, reddish brown, new blue & pale drab	70	70
1243	**718**	28p.	black, greenish yellow, brt carmine, orange-brown, dp dull blue & pale drab	70	70
1244	**719**	31p.	grey-black, bistre-yellow, rosine, red-brown, lt blue & pale drab	90	90
			Set of 5	3.00	3.00
			Set of 5 Gutter Pairs	6.00	
			First Day Cover		3.00
			Presentation Pack	4.25	
			P.H.Q. Cards (set of 5)	3.00	6.00

Nos. 1240/4 were issued on the occasion of the centenary of the Highland Cattle Society and the bicentenary of the Royal Highland and Agricultural Society of Scotland.

Special First Day of Issue Postmarks

Philatelic Bureau, Edinburgh	3.50
Oban, Argyll	3.25

720 Garden Festival Hall, Liverpool

721 Milburngate Centre, Durham

722 Bush House, Bristol

723 Commercial Street Development, Perth

(Des R. Maddox and Trickett and Webb Ltd)

1984 (10 Apr). **Urban Renewal.** *Phosphorised paper. P* 15 × 14.

1245	**720**	16p.	brt emerald, greenish yellow, cerise, steel-blue, black, silver & flesh	40	40
1246	**721**	20½p.	brt orange, greenish yellow, dp dull blue, yellowish green, azure, black & silver	60	60
		a.	Imperf (horiz pair)	£1000	
1247	**722**	28p.	rosine, greenish yellow, Prussian blue, pale blue-green, black & silver.	75	90
1248	**723**	31p.	blue, greenish yellow, cerise, grey-blue, brt green, black & silver	75	90
		a.	Imperf (pair)	£1000	
			Set of 4	2.25	2.50
			Set of 4 Gutter Pairs	4.50	
			First Day Cover		3.00
			Presentation Pack	3.50	
			P.H.Q. Cards (set of 4)	3.00	6.00

Nos. 1245/8 were issued on the occasion of the 150th anniversaries of the Royal Institute of British Architects and the Chartered Institute of Building, and to commemorate the first International Gardens Festival, Liverpool.

Special First Day of Issue Postmarks

Philatelic Bureau, Edinburgh	3.50
Liverpool	3.75

24 C.E.P.T. 25th Anniversary Logo   **725** Abduction of Europa

726 Lancaster House

(Des J. Larrivière (*T* 724), F. Wegner (*T* 725))

(Des P. Hogarth)

984 (15 May).   **25th Anniv of C.E.P.T. ("Europa")** (*T* 724) **and Second Elections to European Parliament** (*T* 725). *Phosphorised paper.* P 15 × 14.

249	724	16p. greenish slate, dp blue & gold	70	70
		a. Horiz pair. Nos, 1249/50	1.40	1.40
		ab. Imperf (horiz pair).........................	£1300	
250	725	16p. greenish slate, dp blue, black & gold	70	70
251	724	20½p. Venetian red, dp magenta & gold	1.25	1.25
		a. Horiz pair. Nos. 1251/2	2.50	2.50
		ab. Imperf (horiz pair)........................		
252	725	20½p. Venetian red, dp magenta, black & gold	1.25	1.25
		Set of 4	3.50	3.50
		Set of 4 Gutter Pairs	7.00	
		First Day Cover		3.50
		Presentation Pack..........................	5.00	
		P.H.Q. Cards (set of 4)	3.00	6.00

Nos. 1249/50 and 1251/2 were each printed together, *se-tenant,* in horizontal pairs throughout the sheets.

1984 (5 June).   **London Economic Summit Conference.** *Phosphorised paper.* P 14 × 15.

1253	726	31p. silver, bistre-yellow, brown-ochre, black, rosine, brt blue & reddish lilac	1.00	1.00
		Gutter Pair	2.00	
		First Day Cover		2.00
		P.H.Q. Card	1.00	2.75

Special First Day of Issue Postmarks

Philatelic Bureau, Edinburgh 2.50
London SW.. 2.50

Special First Day of Issue Postmarks

Philatelic Bureau, Edinburgh 4.00
London SW.. 4.00

727 View of Earth from "Apollo 11"

728 Navigational Chart of English Channel

729 Greenwich Observatory

730 Sir George Airy's Transit Telescope

STAMP MONTHLY

Finest and most informative magazine for all collectors. Obtainable from your newsagent or by postal subscription – details on request

(Des H. Waller. Litho Questa)

1984 (26 June). **Centenary of the Greenwich Meridian.** *Phosphorised paper.* P 14 × 14½.

1254 **727**	16p.	new blue, greenish yellow, magenta, black, scarlet and blue-black	40	40
1255 **728**	20½p.	olive-sepia, lt brown, pale buff, black & scarlet................................	65	65
1256 **729**	28p.	new blue, greenish yellow, scarlet, black & brt purple.........................	85	90
1257 **730**	31p.	dp blue, cobalt, scarlet & black	90	1.10
		Set of 4	2.50	2.75
		Set of 4 Gutter Pairs	5.00	
		First Day Cover		2.75
		Presentation Pack	3.75	
		P.H.Q. Cards (set of 4)	3.00	6.00

On Nos. 1254/7 the Meridian is represented by a scarlet line.

Special First Day of Issue Postmarks

Philatelic Bureau, Edinburgh 3.50
London SE10 .... 3.50

731 Bath Mail Coach, 1784

732 Attack on Exeter Mail, 1816

733 Norwich Mail in Thunderstorm, 1827

734 Holyhead and Liverpool Mails leaving London, 1828

735 Edinburgh Mail Snowbound, 1831

(Des K. Bassford and S. Paine. Eng C. Slania. Recess and photo)

1984 (31 July). **Bicentenary of First Mail Coach Run, Bath and Bristol to London.** *Phosphorised paper.* P 15 × 14.

1258 **731**	16p.	pale stone, black, grey-black & brt scarlet	60	60
		a. Horiz strip of 5. Nos. 1258/62	2.75	2.75
1259 **732**	16p.	pale stone, black, grey-black & brt scarlet	60	60
1260 **733**	16p.	pale stone, black, grey-black & brt scarlet	60	60
1261 **734**	16p.	pale stone, black, grey-black & brt scarlet	60	60
1262 **735**	16p.	pale stone, black, grey-black & brt scarlet	60	60
		Set of 5	2.75	2.75
		Gutter Strip of 10	5.50	
		First Day Cover		2.75
		Presentation Pack	3.75	
		Souvenir Book	6.00	
		P.H.Q. Cards (set of 5)	3.00	6.50

Nos. 1258/62 were printed together, se-*tenant*, in horizontal strips of 5 throughout the sheet.

The souvenir book is a 24-page illustrated booklet with a set of mint stamps in a sachet attached to the front cover.

Special First Day of Issue Postmarks

Philatelic Bureau, Edinburgh 3.25
Bristol 3.50

736 Nigerian Clinic

737 Violinist and Acropolis, Athens

738 Building Project, Sri Lanka

739 British Council Library, Middle East

(Des F. Newell and J. Sorrell)

1984 (25 Sept). **50th Anniv of the British Council.** *Phosphorised paper.* P 15 × 14.

1263 **736**	17p.	grey-green, greenish yellow, brt purple, dull blue, black, pale green & yellow-green	50	50
1264 **737**	22p.	crimson, greenish yellow, brt rose-red, dull green, black, pale drab & slate-purple	65	65
1265 **738**	31p.	sepia, olive-bistre, red, black, pale stone & olive-brown	90	90
1266 **739**	34p.	steel blue, yellow, rose-red, new blue, black, azure & pale blue	1.00	1.00
		Set of 4	2.75	2.75
		Set of 4 Gutter Pairs	5.50	
		First Day Cover		2.75
		Presentation Pack	3.50	
		P.H.Q. Cards (set of 4)	3.00	6.00

Special First Day of Issue Postmarks

Philatelic Bureau, Edinburgh	3.25
London SW	3.50

1984 (20 Nov). **Christmas.** *One phosphor band (13p.) or phosphorised paper (others).* P 15 × 14.

1267 **740**	13p.	pale cream, grey-black, bistre-yellow, magenta, red-brown & lake-brown	30	30
	Eu.	Underprint Type 4	45	
1268 **741**	17p.	pale cream, grey-black, yellow, magenta, dull blue & dp dull blue	50	50
1269 **742**	22p.	pale cream, grey-black, olive-yellow, brt magenta, brt blue & brownish grey	60	60
1270 **743**	31p.	pale cream, grey-black, bistre-yellow, magenta, dull blue & lt brown	95	95
1271 **744**	34p.	pale cream, olive-grey, bistre-yellow, magenta, turquoise-green & brown-olive	1.00	1.00
		Set of 5	3.00	3.00
		Set of 5 Gutter Pairs	6.00	
		First Day Cover		3.00
		Presentation Pack	3.75	
		P.H.Q. Cards (set of 5)	3.00	6.00

Examples of No. 1267Eu from the 1984 Christmas booklet (No. FX7) show a random pattern of blue double-lined stars printed on the reverse over the gum.

Special First Day of Issue Postmarks

Philatelic Bureau, Edinburgh	3.75
Bethlehem, Llandeilo, Dyfed	3.75

Collectors Pack 1984

1984 (20 Nov). *Comprises Nos. 1236/71.*
CP1271a Collectors Pack 40.00

Post Office Yearbook

1984. *Comprises Nos. 1236/71 in 24-page hardbound book with slip case, illustrated in colour.* 70.00

740 The Holy Family

741 Arrival in Bethlehem

742 Shepherd and Lamb

743 Virgin and Child

744 Offering of Frankincense

745 "The Flying Scotsman"

746 "The Golden Arrow"

747 "The Cheltenham Flyer"

748 "The Royal Scot"

749 "The Cornish Riviera"

(Des T. Cuneo)

1985 (22 Jan). **Famous Trains.** *Phosphorised paper. P* 15 × 14.

1272	**745**	17p.	black, lemon, magenta, dull blue, grey-black & gold	50	50
		a.	Imperf (pair)	£1800	
1273	**746**	22p.	black, greenish yellow, brt rose, dp dull blue, grey-black & gold	70	70
1274	**747**	29p.	black, greenish yellow, magenta, blue, grey-black & gold	90	90
1275	**748**	31p.	black, bistre-yellow, brt magenta, new blue, slate-black & gold	1.00	1.00
1276	**749**	34p.	black, greenish yellow, brt rose, blue, slate-black & gold	1.10	1.10
			Set of 5	4.00	4.00
			Set of 5 Gutter Pairs	8.00	
			First Day Cover		5.00
			Presentation Pack	5.00	
			P.H.Q. Cards (set of 5)	4.00	11.00

Nos. 1272/6 were issued on the occasion of the 150th anniversary of the Great Western Railway Company.

Special First Day of Issue Postmarks

Philatelic Bureau, Edinburgh	7.00
Bristol	7.50

750 *Bombus terrestris* (bee)

751 *Coccinella septempunctata* (ladybird)

752 *Decticus verrucivorus* (bush-cricket)

753 *Lucanus cervus* (stag beetle)

754 *Anax imperator* (dragonfly)

(Des G. Beningtield)

1985 (12 Mar). **Insects.** *Phosphorised paper. P* 14 × 15.

1277	**750**	17p.	black, greenish yellow, magenta, blue, azure, gold & slate-black	40	40
1278	**751**	22p.	black, greenish yellow, brt rose-red, dull blue-green, slate-black & gold	60	60
1279	**752**	29p.	black, greenish yellow, brt rose, greenish blue, grey-black, gold & bistre-yellow	80	80
1280	**753**	31p.	black, greenish yellow, rose, pale new blue & gold	90	90
1281	**754**	34p.	black, greenish yellow, magenta, greenish blue, grey-black & gold	90	90
			Set of 5	3.25	3.25
			Set of 5 Gutter Pairs	6.50	
			First Day Cover		3.50
			Presentation Pack	4.00	
			P.H.Q. Cards (set of 5)	3.00	6.50

Nos. 1277/81 were issued on the occasion of the centenaries of the Royal Entomological Society of London's Royal Charter, and of the Selborne Society.

Special First Day of Issue Postmarks

Philatelic Bureau, Edinburgh	5.00
London SW	5.25

WATER MUSIC
George Frideric Handel

755 "Water Music" (George Frideric Handel)

THE PLANETS SUITE
Gustav Holst

756 "The Planets' Suite" (Gustav Holst)

759 R.N.L.I. Lifeboat and Signal Flags

760 Beachy Head Lighthouse and Chart

THE·FIRST·CUCKOO
Frederick Delius

757 "The First Cuckoo" (Frederick Delius)

SEA·PICTURES
Edward Elgar

758 "Sea Pictures" (Edward Elgar)

761 "Marecs A" Communications Satellite and Dish Aerials

762 Buoys

(Des F. Newell and J. Sorrell. Litho J.W.)

1985 (18 June). **Safety at Sea.** *Phosphorised paper. P* 14.

1286	759	17p. black, azure, emerald, ultramarine, orange-yellow, vermilion, brt blue & chrome-yellow	50	50
1287	760	22p. black, azure, emerald, ultramarine, orange-yellow, vermilion, brt blue & chrome-yellow	65	65
1288	761	31p. black, azure, emerald, ultramarine, orange-yellow, vermilion & brt blue	1.10	1.10
1289	762	34p. black, azure, emerald, ultramarine, orange-yellow, vermilion, brt blue & chrome-yellow	1.10	1.10
		Set of 4	3.00	3.00
		Set of 4 Gutter Pairs	6.00	
		First Day Cover		3.75
		Presentation Pack	4.25	
		P.H.Q. Cards (set of 4)	3.00	6.00

Nos. 1286/9 were issued on the occasion of the bicentenary of the unimmersible lifeboat and the 50th anniversary of radar.

(Des W. McLean)

1985 (14 May). **Europa.** *European Music Year. British Composers. Phosphorised paper.* P 14 × 14½.

282	755	17p. black, brt yellow-green, dp magenta, new blue, grey & gold	65	65
		a. Imperf (vert pair)		
283	756	22p. black, greenish yellow, brt magenta, new blue, grey-black & gold	90	90
		a. Imperf (pair)	£1300	
284	757	31p. black, greenish yellow, magenta, greenish blue, grey-black & gold	1.25	1.25
285	758	34p. black, olive-yellow, bistre, turquoise-blue, slate & gold	1.40	1.40
		Set of 4	3.75	3.75
		Set of 4 Gutter Pairs	7.50	
		First Day Cover		3.75
		Presentation Pack	4.50	
		P.H.Q. Cards (set of 4)	3.00	6.00

Nos. 1282/5 were issued on the occasion of the 300th birth anniversary of Handel.

Special First Day of Issue Postmarks

Philatelic Bureau, Edinburgh	4.50
Worcester	4.50

Special First Day of Issue Postmarks

Philatelic Bureau, Edinburgh	4.50
Eastbourne	4.50

763 Datapost Motorcyclist, City of London

764 Rural Postbus

765 Parcel Delivery in Winter

766 Town Letter Delivery

(Des P. Hogarth)

1985 (30 July). **350 Years of Royal Mail Public Postal Service.** *Phosphorised paper. P* 14 × 15.

1290	763	17p. black, greenish yellow, brt carmine, greenish blue, yellow-brown, grey-black & silver	50	50
		a. Imperf on 3 sides (vert pair)	£1300	
		Eu. Underprint Type 5	70	
1291	764	22p. black, greenish yellow, cerise, steel-blue, lt green, grey-black & silver	65	65
1292	765	31p. black, greenish yellow, brt carmine, dull blue, drab, grey-black & silver	1.10	1.10
		a. Imperf (vert pair)	£1300	
1293	766	34p. black, greenish yellow, cerise, ultra-marine, lt brown, grey-black & silver	1.10	1.10
		Set of 4	3.00	3.00
		Set of 4 Gutter Pairs	6.00	
		First Day Cover		4.00
		Presentation Pack	4.25	
		P.H.Q. Cards (set of 4)	3.00	6.00

No. 1290a shows perforation indentations at right, but is imperforate at top, bottom and on the left-hand side.

Examples of No. 1290Eu from the 1985 £1.70 booklet (sold at £1.53) (No. FT4) show a blue double-lined D in a random pattern, on the reverse over the gum.

Special First Day of Issue Postmarks

Philatelic Bureau, Edinburgh	4.50
Bagshot, Surrey	4.50

767 King Arthur and Merlin

768 Lady of the Lake

769 Queen Guinevere and Sir Lancelot

770 Sir Galahad

(Des Yvonne Gilbert)

1985 (3 Sept). **Arthurian Legends.** *Phosphorised paper. P* 15 × 14.

1294	767	17p. grey-black, lemon, brown-lilac, ultra-marine, grey-black & silver	50	5
		a. Imperf (pair)	£1800	
1295	768	22p. black, lemon, brown-lilac, pale blue, grey-black, silver & grey-black	65	7
1296	769	31p. black, lemon, magenta, turquoise-blue, grey-black, silver & grey-black	1.10	1.1
1297	770	34p. grey, lemon, magenta, new blue, grey-black, silver & grey-black	1.10	1.2
		Set of 4	3.00	3.2
		Set of 4 Gutter Pairs	6.00	
		First Day Cover		4.00
		Presentation Pack	4.75	
		P.H.Q. Cards (set of 4)	3.00	6.00

Nos. 1294/7 were issued on the occasion of the 500th anniversary of the printing of Sir Thomas Malory's *Morte d'Arthur.*

Special First Day of Issue Postmarks

Philatelic Bureau, Edinburgh	4.50
Tintagel, Cornwall	4.50

HAVE YOU READ THE NOTES AT THE BEGINNING OF THIS CATALOGUE?

These often provide answers to the enquiries we receive.

771 Peter Sellers
(from photo by Bill Brandt)

772 David Niven
(from photo by Cornell Lucas)

776 Principal Boy

777 Genie

773 Charlie Chaplin
(from photo by Lord Snowdon)

774 Vivien Leigh
(from photo by Angus McBean)

778 Dame

779 Good Fairy

775 Alfred Hitchcock
(from photo by Howard Coster)

(Des K. Bassford)

780 Pantomime Cat

(Des A. George)

1985 (8 Oct). **British Film Year.** *Phosphorised paper.* P 14½.

1298	771	17p. grey-black, olive-grey, gold & silver..	50	50
1299	772	22p. black, brown, gold & silver	85	85
1300	773	29p. black, lavender, gold & silver	1.00	1.00
1301	774	31p. black, pink, gold & silver	1.25	1.10
1302	775	34p. black, greenish blue, gold & silver ...	1.40	1.25
		Set of 5	4.50	4.25
		Set of 5 Gutter Pairs	9.00	
		First Day Cover		4.50
		Presentation Pack	6.00	
		Souvenir Book	7.00	
		P.H.Q. Cards (set of 5)	3.00	6.00

The souvenir book is a 24-page illustrated booklet with a set of mint stamps in a sachet attached to the front cover.

1985 (19 Nov). **Christmas.** *Pantomime Characters. One phosphor band (12p) or phosphorised paper (others).* P 15 × 14.

1303	776	12p. new blue, greenish yellow, brt rose, gold, grey-black & silver	35	30
		a. Impert (pair)	£1300	
		Eu. Underprint Type 4	40	
1304	777	17p. emerald, greenish yellow, brt rose, new blue, black, gold & silver..........	45	40
		a. Impert (pair)	£1800	
1305	778	22p. brt carmine, greenish yellow, pale new blue, grey, gold & silver	70	80
1306	779	31p. brt orange, lemon, rose, slate-purple, silver & gold	95	1.00
1307	780	34p. brt reddish violet, brt blue, brt rose, black, grey-brown, gold & silver	1.00	1.10
		Set of 5	3.00	3.25
		Set of 5 Gutter Pairs	6.00	
		First Day Cover		3.75
		Presentation Pack.........................	4.50	
		P.H.Q. Cards (set of 5)	3.00	6.00
		Christmas Folder (contains No. 1303 × 50)	20.00	

Examples of No. 1303Eu from the 1985 Christmas booklet (No. FX8) show a random pattern of blue double-lined stars printed on the reverse over the gum.

Special First Day of Issue Postmarks

Philatelic Bureau, Edinburgh	5.00
London WC	5.00

Special First Day of Issue Postmarks

Philatelic Bureau, Edinburgh 4.50
Bethlehem, Llandeilo, Dyfed 4.50

Special First Day of Issue Postmarks

Philatelic Bureau, Edinburgh 5.25
Birmingham 5.25

Collectors Pack 1985

1985 (19 Nov). *Comprises Nos. 1272/1307*
CP1307a Collectors Pack 40.00

Post Office Yearbook

1985. *Comprises Nos. 1272/1307 in 32-page hardbound book with slip
case, illustrated in colour* 75.00

781 Light Bulb and North Sea
Oil Drilling Rig (Energy)

782 Thermometer and Pharm-
aceutical Laboratory (Health)

785 Dr. Edmond Halley
as Comet

786 *Giotto* Spacecraft
approaching Comet

783 Garden Hoe and
Steelworks (Steel)

784 Loaf of Bread and
Cornfield (Agriculture)

787 "Maybe Twice in a Lifetime"

788 Comet orbiting Sun
and Planets

(Des K. Bassford. Litho Questa)

(Des R. Steadman)

1986 (14 Jan). **Industry Year.** *Phosphorised paper.* P 14½ × 14.

1308 **781**	17p. gold, black, magenta, greenish yel- low & new blue	45	45
1309 **782**	22p. gold, pale turquoise-green, black, magenta, greenish yellow & blue	60	60
1310 **783**	31p. gold, black, magenta, greenish yel- low & new blue	90	90
1311 **784**	34p. gold, black, magenta, greenish yel- low & new blue	1.10	1.10
	Set of 4	2.75	2.75
	Set of 4 *Gutter Pairs*	5.50	
	First Day Cover		4.50
	Presentation Pack	4.00	
	P.H.Q. Cards (set of 4)	3.00	6.00

1986 (18 Feb). **Appearance of Halley's Comet.** *Phosphorised paper.*
P 15 × 14.

1312 **785**	17p. black, bistre, rosine, blue, grey- black, gold & dp brown	45	45
1313 **786**	22p. orange-vermilion, greenish yellow, brt purple, new blue, black & gold ...	70	70
1314 **787**	31p. black, greenish yellow, brt purple, dp turquoise-blue, grey-black & gold	1.10	1.10
1315 **788**	34p. blue, greenish yellow, magenta, dp turquoise-blue, black & gold	1.10	1.10
	Set of 4	3.00	3.00
	Set of 4 *Gutter Pairs*	6.00	
	First Day Cover		4.50
	Presentation Pack	4.50	
	P.H.Q. Cards (set of 4)	4.00	6.00

Special First Day of Issue Postmarks

Philatelic Bureau, Edinburgh 5.00
London SE10 .... 5.00

789 Queen Elizabeth in
1928, 1942 and 1952

790 Queen Elizabeth in
1958, 1973 and 1982

T789/90 were printed horizontally *se-tenant* within the sheet

(Des J. Matthews)

1986 (21 Apr). **60th Birthday of Queen Elizabeth II.** *Phosphorised paper.* P 15 × 14.

1316	**789**	17p. grey-black, turquoise-green, brt green, green and dull blue..............	70	70
		a. Pair. Nos. 1316/17	1.40	1.40
1317	**790**	17p. grey-black, dull blue, greenish blue and indigo......................................	70	70
1318	**789**	34p. grey-black, dp dull purple, yellow-orange and red	1.25	1.25
		a. Pair. Nos. 1318/19	2.50	2.50
1319	**790**	34p. grey-black, olive-brown, yellow-brown, olive-brown and red...........	1.25	1.25
		Set of 4	3.50	3.50
		Set of 4 Gutter Pairs	7.00	
		First Day Cover		4.50
		Presentation Pack.........................	5.00	
		Souvenir Book	7.00	
		P.H.Q. Cards (set of 4)	3.00	6.00

The souvenir book is a special booklet, fully illustrated and containing a mint set of stamps.

Special First Day of Issue Postmarks

Philatelic Bureau, Edinburgh 5.25
Windsor.. 5.00

791 Barn Owl

792 Pine Marten

793 Wild Cat

794 Natterjack Toad

(Des K. Lilly)

1986 (20 May). **Europa.** *Nature Conservation – Endangered Species. Phosphorised paper. P* 14½ × 14.

1320	**791**	17p. gold, greenish yellow, rose, yellow-brown, olive-grey, new blue and black	50	50
1321	**792**	22p. gold, greenish yellow, reddish brown, olive-yellow, turquoise-blue, grey-black and black	65	65
1322	**793**	31p. gold, brt yellow-green, magenta, lt brown, ultramarine, olive-brown and black	1.10	1.10
1323	**794**	34p. gold, greenish yellow, brt rose-red, brt green, grey-black and black........	1.10	1.10
		Set of 4	3.00	3.00
		Set of 4 Gutter Pairs	6.00	
		First Day Cover		4.50
		Presentation Pack.........................	4.50	
		PHQ Cards (set of 4)	3.00	6.00

Special First Day of Issue Postmarks

Philatelic Bureau, Edinburgh 5.25
Lincoln.. 5.25

795 Peasants working in Fields

796 Freemen working at Town Trades

801 Weightlifting

802 Rifle Shooting

797 Knight and Retainers

798 Lord at Banquet

(Des Tayburn Design Consultancy)

803 Hockey

(Des N. Cudworth)

1986 (17 Jun). **900th Anniv of Domesday Book.** *Phosphorised paper.*
P 15 × 14.

1324	795	17p. yellow-brown, vermilion, lemon, bright emerald, orange-brown, grey & brownish grey	50	50
1325	796	22p. yellow-ochre, red, greenish blue, chestnut, grey-black & brownish grey	75	75
1326	797	31p. yellow-brown, vermilion, green, Indian red, grey-black & brownish grey	1.10	1.10
1327	798	34p. yellow-ochre, bright scarlet, grey-brown, new blue, lake-brown, grey-black & grey	1.25	1.25
		Set of 4	3.25	3.25
		Set of 4 Gutter Pairs	6.50	
		First Day Cover		4.25
		Presentation Pack	4.50	
		P.H.Q. Cards (set of 4)	3.00	6.00

Special First Day of Issue Postmarks

Philatelic Bureau, Edinburgh 4.50
Gloucester 4.75

799 Athletics

800 Rowing

1986 (15 July). **Thirteenth Commonwealth Games, Edinburgh and World Hockey Cup for Men, London** (34p.). *Phosphorised paper.*
P 15 × 14.

1328	799	17p. black, greenish yellow, orange-vermilion, ultramarine, chestnut & emerald	50	50
1329	800	22p. black, lemon, scarlet, new blue, royal blue, chestnut & dp ultramarine	70	70
1330	801	29p. grey-black, greenish yellow, scarlet, new blue, brown-ochre, brown-rose & pale chestnut	90	90
1331	802	31p. black, greenish yellow, rose, blue, dull yellow-green, chestnut & yellow-green	1.10	1.10
1332	803	34p. black, lemon, scarlet, bright blue, bright emerald, red-brown & vermilion	1.25	1.25
		a. Imperf (pair)	£1300	
		Set of 5	4.00	4.00
		Set of 5 Gutter Pairs	8.00	
		First Day Cover		5.75
		Presentation Pack	5.25	
		P.H.Q. Cards (set of 5)	4.00	6.00

No. 1332 also commemorates the Centenary of the Hockey Association.

Special First Day of Issue Postmarks

Philatelic Bureau, Edinburgh 6.00
Head Post Office, Edinburgh 6.00

STAMP MONTHLY

Finest and most informative magazine for all collectors
Obtainable from your newsagent or by postal subscription
details on request

804   **805**

Prince Andrew and Miss Sarah Ferguson (from photo by Gene Nocon)

(Des J. Matthews)

986 (22 July). **Royal Wedding.** *One phosphor band (12p.) or phosphorised paper (17p.). P 14 × 15.*

333	**804**	12p. lake, greenish yellow, cerise, ultramarine, black & silver	60	60
334	**805**	17p. steel blue, greenish yellow, cerise, ultramarine, black & gold	90	90
		a. Imperf (pair)	£850	
		Set of 2	1.25	1.25
		Set of 2 Gutter Pairs	2.50	
		First Day Cover		2.50
		Presentation Pack.........................	2.00	
		P.H.Q. Cards (set of 2)..................	1.50	5.00

Special First Day of Issue Postmarks

Philatelic Bureau, Edinburgh	3.25
London, SW1	3.25

806 Stylised Cross on Ballot Paper

(Des J. Gibbs. Litho Questa)

1986 (19 Aug). **32nd Commonwealth Parliamentary Association Conference.** *Phosphorised paper. P 14 × 14½.*

335	**806**	34p. pale grey-lilac, black, vermilion, yellow & ultramarine	1.25	1.25
		Gutter Pair	2.50	
		First Day Cover		2.00
		P.H.Q. Card	1.00	2.50

Special First Day of Issue Postmarks

Philatelic Bureau, Edinburgh	2.25
London, SW1	2.25

LORD DOWDING/HURRICANE   LORD TEDDER/TYPHOON

807 Lord Dowding and Hawker "Hurricane"   **808** Lord Tedder and Hawker "Typhoon"

LORD TRENCHARD/DH9A   SIR ARTHUR HARRIS/LANCASTER

809 Lord Trenchard and De Havilland "DH9A"   **810** Sir Arthur Harris and Avro "Lancaster"

LORD PORTAL/MOSQUITO

811 Lord Portal and De Havilland "Mosquito"

(Des B. Sanders)

1986 (16 Sept). **History of the Royal Air Force.** *Phosphorised paper. P 14½.*

336	**807**	17p. pale blue, greenish yellow, brt rose, blue, black & grey-black.................	50	40
		a. Imperf. (pair)..............................	£950	
337	**808**	22p. pale turquoise-green, greenish yellow, magenta, new blue, black & grey-black	70	85
		a. Face value omitted*	£400	
		b. Queen's head omitted*	£400	

143

1338 **809**	29p.	pale drab, olive-yellow, magenta, blue, grey-black & black	90	1.00
1339 **810**	31p.	pale flesh, greenish yellow, magenta, ultramarine, black & grey-black	1.10	1.10
1340 **811**	34p.	buff, greenish yellow, magenta, blue, grey-black & black	1.25	1.25
		Set of 5	4.00	4.25
		Set of 5 Gutter Pairs	8.00	
		First Day Cover		5.00
		Presentation Pack	6.00	
		P.H.Q. Cards (set of 5)	4.00	6.50

Nos. 1336/40 were issued to celebrate the 50th anniversary of the first R.A.F. Commands.

*Nos. 1337a/b come from three consecutive sheets on which the stamps in the first vertical row are without the face value and those in the second vertical row the Queen's head.

Special First Day of Issue Postmarks

Philatelic Bureau, Edinburgh		5.25
Farnborough		5.25

812 The Glastonbury Thorn

813 The Tanad Valley Plygain

814 The Hebrides Tribute

815 The Dewsbury Church Knell

816 The Hereford Boy Bishop

(Des Lynda Gray)

1986 (18 Nov–2 Dec). **Christmas. Folk Customs.** *One phosphor band (12p., 13p.) or phosphorised paper (others).* P 15 × 14.

1341 **812**	12p.	gold, greenish yellow, vermilion, dp brown, emerald & dp blue (2.12)	50	5
	a.	Imperf (pair)		
1342	13p.	dp blue, greenish yellow, vermilion, dp brown, emerald & gold	30	3
	Eu.	Underprint Type 4 (2.12)	50	
1343 **813**	18p.	myrtle-green, yellow, vermilion, dp blue, black, reddish brown & gold	45	45
1344 **814**	22p.	vermilion, olive-bistre, dull blue, dp brown, dp green & gold	65	65
1345 **815**	31p.	dp brown, yellow, vermilion, violet, dp dull green, black & gold	80	80
1346 **816**	34p.	violet, lemon, vermilion, dp dull blue, reddish brown & gold	90	90
		Set of 6	3.25	3.25
		Set of 6 Gutter Pairs	6.50	
		First Day Covers (2)		5.25
		Presentation Pack (Nos. 1342/6)	5.00	
		P.H.Q. Cards (Nos. 1342/6) (Set of 5)	3.00	6.00
		Christmas Folder (contains No. 1342Eu × 36)	17.00	

No. 1341 represented a discount of 1p., available between 2 and 24 December 1986, on the current second class postage rate.

Special First Day of Issue Postmarks

Philatelic Bureau, Edinburgh (Nos. 1342/6) (18 Nov)	4.50
Bethlehem, Llandeilo, Dyfed (Nos. 1342/6) (18 Nov)	4.50
Philatelic Bureau, Edinburgh (No. 1341) (2 Dec)	1.50

Collectors Pack 1986

1986 (18 Nov). *Comprises Nos. 1308/40 and 1342/46.*
CP1346a   Collectors Pack 40.00

Post Office Yearbook

1986 (18 Nov). *Comprises Nos. 1308/46 in 32-page hardbound book with slip case, illustrated in colour* 70.00

HAVE YOU READ THE NOTES AT THE BEGINNING OF THIS CATALOGUE?

These often provide answers to the enquiries we receive.

817 North American
Blanket Flower

818 Globe Thistle

821 *The Principia*
Mathematica

822 *Motion of Bodies*
in Ellipses

819 *Echeveria*

820 Autumn Crocus

(Adapted J. Matthews)

823 *Optick Treatise*

824 *The System of the World*

(Des Sarah Godwin)

987 (20 Jan).   **Flower Photographs by Alfred Lammer.** *Phosphorised*
paper. P 14½ × 14.

347	**817**	18p. silver, greenish yellow, rosine, dp green & black	50	50
348	**818**	22p. silver, greenish yellow, new blue, greenish blue & black	65	65
349	**819**	31p. silver, greenish yellow, scarlet, blue-green, dp green & black	1.10	1.10
		a. Imperf (pair)	£1600	
350	**820**	34p. silver, greenish yellow, magenta, dull blue, dp green & black	1.10	1.10
		Set of 4	3.00	3.00
		Set of 4 Gutter Pairs	6.00	
		First Day Cover		4.25
		Presentation Pack	4.50	
		P.H.Q. Cards (set of 4)	3.00	6.00

1987 (24 Mar).   **300th Anniv of** *The Principia Mathematica* **by Sir Isaac**
Newton. *Phosphorised paper.* P 14 × 15.

1351	**821**	18p. black, greenish yellow, cerise, blue-green, grey-black and silver	50	50
1352	**822**	22p. black, greenish yellow, bright orange, blue, bright emerald, silver & bluish violet	65	65
1353	**823**	31p. black, greenish yellow, scarlet, new blue, bronze-green, silver & slate-green	1.10	1.10
1354	**824**	34p. black, greenish yellow, red, bright blue, grey-black & silver	1.10	1.10
		Set of 4	3.00	3.00
		Set of 4 Gutter Pairs	6.00	
		First Day Cover		4.25
		Presentation Pack	4.50	
		P.H.Q. Cards (set of 4)	3.00	6.00

Special First Day of Issue Postmarks

Special First Day of Issue Postmarks

Philatelic Bureau, Edinburgh	4.75
Richmond, Surrey	4.75

Philatelic Bureau, Edinburgh	4.75
Woolsthorpe, Lincs	4.75

825 Willis Faber and Dumas Building, Ipswich

826 Pompidou Centre, Paris

829 Brigade Members with Ashford Litter, 1887

830 Bandaging Blitz Victim, 1940

827 Staatsgalerie, Stuttgart

828 European Investment Bank, Luxembourg

831 Volunteer with fainting Girl, 1965

832 Transport of Transplant Organ by Air Wing, 1987

(Des B. Tattersfield)

1987 (12 May). **Europa. British Architects in Europe.** *Phosphorised paper.* P 15 × 14.

1355	**825**	18p. black, bistre-yellow, cerise, brt blue, dp grey & grey-black......................	50	50
1356	**826**	22p. black, greenish yellow, carmine, brt blue, dp grey & grey-black	65	65
1357	**827**	31p. grey-black, bistre-yellow, cerise, brt blue, brt green, black & dull violet ..	1.10	1.10
		a. Imperf (horiz pair)........................	£1000	
1358	**828**	34p. black, greenish yellow, cerise, brt blue, grey-black & dp grey	1.10	1.10
		Set of 4	3.00	3.00
		Set of 4 Gutter Pairs	6.00	
		First Day Cover		4.25
		Presentation Pack.........................	4.50	
		P.H.Q. Cards (set of 4)..................	3.00	6.00

Special First Day of Issue Postmarks

(Des Debbie Cook. Litho Questa)

1987 (16 Jun). **Centenary of St. John Ambulance Brigade.** *Phosphorised paper.* P 14 × 14½.

1359	**829**	18p. new blue, greenish yellow, magenta, black, silver & pink......................	50	50
		Ea. Black ptg triple	†	—
1360	**830**	22p. new blue, greenish yellow, magenta, black, silver & cobalt	65	65
1361	**831**	31p. new blue, greenish yellow, magenta, black, silver & bistre-brown	1.10	1.10
1362	**832**	34p. new blue, greenish yellow, magenta, black, silver & greenish grey...........	1.10	1.10
		Set of 4	3.00	3.00
		Set of 4 Gutter Pairs	6.00	
		First Day Cover		4.25
		Presentation Pack.........................	4.50	
		P.H.Q. Cards (set of 4)..................	3.00	6.00

Special First Day of Issue Postmarks

Philatelic Bureau, Edinburgh	4.75
Ipswich	4.75

Philatelic Bureau, Edinburgh	4.75
London, EC1	4.75

833 Arms of the Lord Lyon King of Arms

834 Scottish Heraldic Banner of Prince Charles

837 Crystal Palace, "Monarch of the Glen" (Landseer) and Grace Darling

838 *Great Eastern, Beeton's Book of Household Management* and Prince Albert

835 Arms of Royal Scottish Academy of Painting, Sculpture and Architecture

836 Arms of Royal Society of Edinburgh

839 Albert Memorial, Ballot Box and Disraeli

840 Diamond Jubilee Emblem, Newspaper Placard for Relief of Mafeking and Morse Key

(Des J. Matthews)

1987 (21 July). **300th Anniv of Revival of Order of the Thistle.** *Phosphorised paper. P 14½.*

1363	**833**	18p. black, lemon, scarlet, blue, dp green, slate & brown	50	50
1364	**834**	22p. black, greenish yellow, carmine, new blue, dp green, grey & lake-brown ..	65	65
1365	**835**	31p. black, greenish yellow, scarlet, new blue, dull green, grey & grey-black..	1.10	1.10
1366	**836**	34p. black, greenish yellow, scarlet, dp ultramarine, dull green, grey and yellow-brown	1.10	1.10
		Set of 4	3.00	3.00
		Set of 4 *Gutter Pairs*	6.00	
		First Day Cover		4.25
		Presentation Pack.......................	4.50	
		P.H.Q. Cards (set of 4)..................	3.00	6.00

(Des M. Dempsey. Eng C. Slania. Recess and photo)

1987 (8 Sept). **150th Anniv of Queen Victoria's Accession.** *Phosphorised paper. P 15 × 14.*

1367	**837**	18p. pale stone, dp blue, lemon, rose, greenish blue, brown-ochre & grey-black	50	50
1368	**838**	22p. pale stone, dp brown, lemon, rose, grey-black & brown-ochre	65	65
1369	**839**	31p. pale stone, dp lilac, lemon, cerise, brown-ochre, greenish blue & grey-black	1.10	1.10
1370	**840**	34p. pale stone, myrtle-green, yellow-ochre, reddish brown & brown-ochre	1.10	1.10
		Set of 4	3.00	3.00
		Set of 4 *Gutter Pairs*	6.00	
		First Day Cover		4.25
		Presentation Pack.......................	4.50	
		P.H.Q. Cards (set of 4)..................	3.00	6.00

Special First Day of Issue Postmarks

Special First Day of Issue Postmarks

Philatelic Bureau, Edinburgh	4.75
Rothesay, Isle of Bute	4.75

Philatelic Bureau, Edinburgh	4.75
Newport, Isle of Wight	4.75

841 Pot by Bernard Leach

842 Pot by Elizabeth Fritsch

843 Pot by Lucie Rie

844 Pot by Hans Coper

(Des T. Evans)

1987 (13 Oct). **Studio Pottery.** *Phosphorised paper. P* 14½ × 14.

1371	**841**	18p. gold, lemon, lt red-brown, chestnut, lt grey & black	50	50
1372	**842**	26p. blue over silver, yellow-orange, brt purple, lavender, bluish violet, grey-brown & black	65	65
1373	**843**	31p. rose-lilac over silver, greenish yellow, cerise, new blue, grey-lilac & black	1.10	1.10
1374	**844**	34p. copper, yellow-brown, reddish brown, grey-lilac & black	1.10	1.10
		Set of 4	3.00	3.00
		Set of 4 Gutter Pairs	6.00	
		First Day Cover		4.25
		Presentation Pack	4.50	
		P.H.Q. Cards (set of 4)	3.00	6.00

Special First Day of Issue Postmarks

Philatelic Bureau, Edinburgh 4.75
St. Ives, Cornwall 4.75

845 Decorating the Christmas Tree

846 Waiting for Father Christmas

847 Sleeping Child and Father Christmas in Sleigh

848 Child reading

849 Child playing Recorder and Snowman

(Des M. Foreman)

1987 (17 Nov). **Christmas.** *One phosphor band (13p.) or phosphorised paper (others). P* 15 × 14.

1375	**845**	13p. gold, greenish yellow, rose, greenish blue & black	30	30
		Eu. Underprint Type 4	50	
1376	**846**	18p. gold, greenish yellow, brt purple, greenish blue, brt blue & black	50	50
1377	**847**	26p. gold, greenish yellow, brt purple, new blue, brt blue & black	75	75
1378	**848**	31p. gold, greenish yellow, scarlet, brt magenta, dull rose, greenish blue & black	95	1.10
1379	**849**	34p. gold, greenish yellow, dull rose, greenish blue, brt blue & black	1.10	1.25
		Set of 5	3.25	3.50
		Set of 5 Gutter Pairs	6.50	
		First Day Cover		4.25
		Presentation Pack	4.50	
		P.H.Q. Cards (set of 5)	3.00	6.00
		Christmas Folder (contains No. 1375Eu × 36)	15.00	

Special First Day of Issue Postmarks

Philatelic Bureau, Edinburgh 4.75
Bethlehem, Llandeilo, Dyfed 4.75

Collectors Pack 1987

1987 (17 Nov). *Comprises Nos. 1347/79.*
CP1379a Collectors Pack 32.00

Post Office Yearbook

1987 (17 Nov). *Comprises Nos. 1347/79 in 32-page hardbound book with slip case, illustrated in colour* 45.00

850 Bull-rout (Jonathan Couch)

851 Yellow Waterlily (Major Joshua Swatkin)

852 Whistling ("Bewick's") Swan (Edward Lear)

853 *Morchella esculenta* (James Sowerby)

854 Revd William Morgan (Bible translator, 1588)

855 William Salesbury (New Testament translator, 1567)

856 Bishop Richard Davies (New Testament translator, 1567)

857 Bishop Richard Parry (editor of Revised Welsh Bible, 1620)

(Des E. Hughes)

(Des K. Bowen)

1988 (19 Jan). **Bicentenary of Linnean Society.** *Archive Illustrations. Phosphorised paper.* P 15 × 14.

1380	**850**	18p. grey-black, stone, orange-yellow, brt purple, olive-bistre & gold..............	45	45
1381	**851**	26p. black, stone, bistre-yellow, dull orange, greenish blue, gold & pale bistre	70	70
1382	**852**	31p. black, stone, greenish yellow, rose-red, dp blue, gold & olive-bistre	1.10	1.10
		a. Imperf (horiz pair).......................	£1300	
1383	**853**	34p. black, stone, yellow, pale bistre, olive-grey, gold & olive-bistre	1.10	1.10
		Set of 4	3.00	3.00
		Set of 4 Gutter Pairs	6.00	
		First Day Cover		4.00
		Presentation Pack..........................	4.50	
		P.H.Q. Cards (set of 4)...................	3.00	6.00

Special First Day of Issue Postmarks

1988 (1 Mar). **400th Anniv of Welsh Bible.** *Phosphorised paper.* P 14½ × 14.

1384	**854**	18p. grey-black, greenish yellow, cerise, blue, black & emerald...................	45	45
		a. Imperf (pair)...............................	£1300	
1385	**855**	26p. grey-black, yellow, brt rose-red, turquoise-blue, black & orange	70	70
1386	**856**	31p. black, chrome-yellow, carmine, new blue, grey-black & blue.................	1.10	1.10
1387	**857**	34p. grey-black, greenish yellow, cerise, turquoise-green, black & brt violet ..	1.10	1.10
		Set of 4	3.00	3.00
		Set of 4 Gutter Pairs	6.00	
		First Day Cover		4.00
		Presentation Pack..........................	4.50	
		P.H.Q. Cards (set of 4)...................	3.00	6.00

Special First Day of Issue Postmarks

Philatelic Bureau, Edinburgh	4.75
London, W1	4.75

Philatelic Bureau, Edinburgh	4.75
Ty Mawr, Wybrnant, Gwynedd	4.75

858 Gymnastics (Centenary of British Amateur Gymnastics Association)

859 Downhill Ski-ing (Ski Club of Great Britain)

860 Tennis (Centenary of Lawn Tennis Association)

861 Football (Centenary of Football League)

862 *Mallard* and Mailbags on Pick-up Arms

863 Loading Transatlantic Mail on Liner *Queen Elizabeth*

864 Glasgow Tram No. 1173 and Pillar Box

865 Imperial Airways Handley Page "HP 42" and Airmail Van

(Des J. Sutton)

(Des M. Dempsey)

1988 (22 Mar). **Sports Organizations.** *Phosphor paper. P* 14½.

1388	**858**	18p. violet-blue, greenish yellow, rosine, brt rose, new blue & silver	45	45
1389	**859**	26p. violet-blue, greenish yellow, vermilion, carmine, yellow-orange & silver	70	70
1390	**860**	31p. violet-blue, greenish yellow, rose, blue, pale greenish blue, silver & brt orange	1.10	1.10
1391	**861**	34p. violet-blue greenish yellow, vermilion, blue, brt emerald, silver & pink	1.10	1.10
		Set of 4	3.00	3.00
		Set of 4 Gutter Pairs	6.00	
		First Day Cover		4.00
		Presentation Pack.........................	4.50	
		P.H.Q. Cards (set of 4)..................	2.25	5.00

1988 (10 May). **Europa. Transport and Mail Services in 1930s.** *Phosphorised paper. P* 15 × 14.

1392	**862**	18p. brown, yellow, rose-red, dull blue, dp brown, reddish violet & black	50	50
1393	**863**	26p. brown, yellow, orange-vermilion, dull blue, violet-blue, brt emerald & black	80	80
1394	**864**	31p. brown, yellow-orange, carmine, dull purple, violet-blue, brt green & black	1.10	1.10
1395	**865**	34p. brown, orange-yellow, carmine-rose, bluish violet, brt blue, sepia & black	1.25	1.25
		Set of 4	3.25	3.25
		Set of 4 Gutter Pairs	6.50	
		First Day Cover		4.25
		Presentation Pack.........................	4.50	
		P.H.Q. Cards (set of 4)..................	2.00	5.00

Special First Day of Issue Postmarks

Philatelic Bureau, Edinburgh	5.00
Wembley	5.00

Special First Day of Issue Postmarks

Philatelic Bureau, Edinburgh	4.75
Glasgow	4.75

866 Early Settler and Sailing Clipper

867 Queen Elizabeth II with British and Australian Parliament Buildings

870 Spanish Galeasse off The Lizard

871 English Fleet leaving Plymouth

868 W.G. Grace (cricketer) and Tennis Racquet

869 Shakespeare, John Lennon (entertainer) and Sydney Opera House

872 Engagement off Isle of Wight

873 Attack of English Fire-ships, Calais

(Des G. Emery. Litho Questa)

1988 (21 June). **Bicentenary of Australian Settlement.** *Phosphorised paper.* P 14½.

1396	**866**	18p. dp ultramarine, orange-yellow, scarlet, black, bluish grey & emerald.....	60	60
		a. Horiz pair. Nos. 1396/7..................	1.25	1.25
1397	**867**	18p. dp ultramarine, orange-yellow, black, bluish grey & emerald	60	60
1398	**868**	34p. dp ultramarine, orange-yellow, scarlet, black, bluish grey & emerald.....	1.10	1.10
		a. Horiz pair. Nos. 1398/9..................	2.40	2.40
1399	**869**	34p. dp ultramarine, orange-yellow, black, bluish grey & emerald	1.10	1.10
		Set of 4	3.25	3.25
		Set of 4 Gutter Pairs	6.50	
		First Day Cover		4.25
		Presentation Pack.........................	4.50	
		Souvenir Book	6.00	
		P.H.Q. Cards (set of 4)..................	2.00	5.00

Nos. 1396/7 and 1398/9 were each printed together, *se-tenant,* in horizontal pairs throughout the sheets, each pair showing a background design of the Australian flag.

The 40 page souvenir book contains the British and Australian sets which were issued on the same day in similar designs.

Special First Day Issue Postmarks

Philatelic Bureau, Edinburgh 4.75
Portsmouth 4.75

874 Armada in Storm, North Sea

(Des G. Everndon)

1988 (19 July). **400th Anniv of Spanish Armada.** *Phosphorised paper.* P 15 × 14.

1400	**870**	18p. slate-black, yellow-orange, brt carmine, brt blue, turquoise-blue, yellow-green & gold	65	65
		a. Horiz strip of 5. Nos. 1400/4...........	2.75	2.75
1401	**871**	18p. slate-black, yellow-orange, brt carmine, brt blue, turquoise-blue, yellow-green & gold	65	65
1402	**872**	18p. slate-black, yellow-orange, brt carmine, brt blue, turquoise-blue, yellow-green & gold	65	65
1403	**873**	18p. slate-black, yellow-orange, brt carmine, brt blue, turquoise-blue, yellow-green & gold	65	65
1404	**874**	18p. slate-black, yellow-orange, brt carmine, brt blue, turquoise-blue, yellow-green & gold	65	65
		Set of 5	2.75	2.75
		Gutter strip of 10..........................	5.50	
		First Day Cover		3.75
		Presentation Pack.........................	4.00	
		P.H.Q. Cards (set of 5)....................	2.50	5.50

Nos. 1400/4 were printed together, *se-tenant,* in horizontal strips of 5 throughout the sheet, forming a composite design.

Special First Day of Issue Postmarks

Special First Day of Issue Postmarks

Philatelic Bureau, Edinburgh 4.00
Plymouth 4.00

Philatelic Bureau, Edinburgh (stamps) (6 Sept) 4.50
Philatelic Bureau, Edinburgh (miniature sheet)
(27 Sept.) 9.50
London N7 (stamps) (6 Sept) 4.50
London N22 (miniature sheet) (27 Sept.) 9.50

875 "The Owl and the Pussy-cat"

876 "Edward Lear as a Bird"
(self-portrait)

877 "Cat" (from alphabet
book)

878 "There was a Young Lady
whose Bonnet . . ." (limerick)

(Des M. Swatridge and S. Dew)

1988 (6–27 Sept). **Death Centenary of Edward Lear (artist and author).**
Phosphorised paper. P 15 × 14.

1405	**875**	19p. black, pale cream & carmine..........	50	50
1406	**876**	27p. black, pale cream & yellow.............	65	80
1407	**877**	32p. black, pale cream & emerald..........	1.10	1.10
1408	**878**	35p. black, pale cream & blue...............	1.10	1.25
		Set of 4..	3.00	3.25
		Set of 4 Gutter Pairs	6.00	
		First Day Cover		4.00
		Presentation Pack..........................	4.50	
		P.H.Q. Cards (set of 4)..................	2.00	5.00
MS1409		122 × 90mm. Nos. 1405/8 (*sold at £1.35*)		
		(27 Sept)	8.00	8.50
		First Day Cover		8.50

The premium on No. MS1409 was used to support the "Stamp
World London 90" International Stamp Exhibition.

879 Carrickfergus Castle

880 Caernarfon Castle

881 Edinburgh Castle

882 Windsor Castle

(Des from photos by Prince Andrew, Duke of York. Eng C. Matthews.
Recess Harrison)

1988 (18 Oct).   *Ordinary paper.* P 15 × 14.

1410	**879**	£1 dp green	2.25	50
1411	**880**	£1.50, maroon	3.25	1.00
1412	**881**	£2 indigo	4.50	1.50
1413	**882**	£5 dp brown	11.00	3.00
		Set of 4..	19.00	5.50
		Set of 4 Gutter Pairs	38.00	
		First Day Cover		45.00
		Presentation Pack	22.00	

For similar designs, but with silhouette Queen's head see Nos.
1611/14.

Special First Day of Issue Postmarks
(for illustrations see Introduction)

Philatelic Bureau, Edinburgh (Type H) 50.00
Windsor, Berks (Type I) 50.00

883 Journey to Bethlehem

884 Shepherds and Star

885 Three Wise Men

886 Nativity

887 The Annunciation

(Des L. Trickett)

1988 (15 Nov). **Christmas.** *Christmas Cards. One phosphor band (14p.) or phosphorised paper (others). P 15 × 14.*

1414	**883**	14p. gold, orange-yellow, brt mauve, bluish violet, brt blue & grey-black ..	35	35
		a. Error. "13p." instead of "14p."	£5000	
		b. Imperf (pair)	£600	
1415	**884**	19p. gold, yell-orge, brt violet, ultramarine, rose-red, grey-blk & brt blue	40	45
		a. Imperf (pair)	£600	
1416	**885**	27p. gold, red, dp lavender, dp lilac, emerald, grey-black & brt blue	70	70
1417	**886**	32p. gold, orange-yellow, brt rose, dp mauve, violet, grey-black & brt blue	90	1.00
1418	**887**	35p. gold, green, reddish violet, brt blue, brt purple & grey-black	1.00	1.10
		Set of 5	3.00	3.25
		Set of 5 Gutter Pairs	6.00	
		First Day Cover		4.25
		Presentation Pack	4.25	
		P.H.Q. Cards (set of 5)	2.50	5.25

Examples of No. 1414a were found in some 1988 Post Office Yearbooks.

Special First Day of Issue Postmarks

Philatelic Bureau, Edinburgh 4.50
Bethlehem, Llandeilo, Dyfed 4.50

Collectors Pack 1988

1988 (15 Nov). *Comprises Nos. 1380/1408, 1414/18.*
CP1418a Collectors Pack 32.00

Post Office Yearbook

1988 (15 Nov). *Comprises Nos. 1380/1404,* **MS**1409, *1414/18 in 32-page hardbound book with slip case, illustrated in colour ..* 40.00

888 Atlantic Puffin

889 Avocet

890 Oystercatcher

891 Northern Gannet

(Des D. Cordery)

1989 (17 Jan). **Centenary of Royal Society for the Protection of Birds.** *Phosphorised paper. P 14 × 15.*

1419	**888**	19p. grey, orange-yellow, orange-red, dull ultramarine, grey-black & silver.	45	45
1420	**889**	27p. grey, bistre, rose, steel-blue, lavender, silver & grey-black	1.10	1.10

1421 **890**	32p. grey, bistre, scarlet, orange-red, lavender, silver & black	1.10	1.10
1422 **891**	35p. grey, lemon, rose-carmine, green, new blue, silver & black	1.25	1.25
	Set of 4	3.50	3.50
	Set of 4 Gutter Pairs	7.00	
	First Day Cover		4.50
	Presentation Pack	4.50	
	P.H.Q. Cards (set of 4)	2.50	5.00

Special First Day of Issue Postmarks

Philatelic Bureau, Edinburgh 4.75
Sandy, Bedfordshire 4.75

1424 **893**	19p. black, greenish yellow, brt rose, red, new blue, lt green & gold	2.75	2.25
1425 **894**	19p. black, greenish yellow, brt rose, red, new blue, lt green & gold	2.75	2.25
1426 **895**	19p. black, greenish yellow, brt rose, red, new blue, lt green & gold	2.75	2.25
1427 **896**	19p. black, greenish yellow, brt rose, red, new blue, lt green & gold	2.75	2.25
	Set of 5	12.00	10.00
	First Day Cover		10.00

Nos. 1423/7 were only issued in £1.90 booklets.

Special First Day of Issue Postmarks

Philatelic Bureau, Edinburgh 12.00
Lover, Salisbury, Wilts 12.00

892 Rose

893 Cupid

894 Yachts

895 Fruit

896 Teddy Bear

(Des P. Sutton)

1989 (31 Jan). **Greetings Stamps.** *Phosphorised paper.* P 15 × 14.

1423 **892**	19p. black, greenish yellow, brt rose, red, new blue, lt green & gold	2.75	2.25
	a. Booklet pane. Nos. 1423/7 × 2 plus 12 half stamp-size labels	24.00	

897 Fruit and Vegetables

898 Meat Products

899 Dairy Products

900 Cereal Products

(Des Sedley Place Ltd)

1989 (7 Mar). **Food and Farming Year.** *Phosphorised paper.* P 14 × 14½.

1428 **897**	19p. brownish grey, greenish yellow, rose, new blue, black, pale grey & emerald	50	50
1429 **898**	27p. brownish grey, greenish yellow, brt carmine, new blue, black, pale grey & brt orange	80	80

30 **899**	32p. brownish grey, greenish yellow, rose-red, new blue, black, pale grey & bistre-yellow	1.10	1.10
31 **900**	35p. brownish grey, greenish yellow, brt carmine, new blue, black, pale grey & brown-red	1.25	1.25
	Set of 4	3.25	3.25
	Set of 4 Gutter Pairs	6.50	
	First Day Cover		4.25
	Presentation Pack	4.50	
	P.H.Q. Cards (set of 4)	2.00	5.00

Special First Day of Issue Postmarks

Philatelic Bureau, Edinburgh	4.50
Stoneleigh, Kenilworth, Warwicks	4.50

901 Mortar Board (150th Anniv of Public Education in England)

902 Cross on Ballot Paper (3rd Direct Elections to European Parliament)

903 Posthorn (26th Postal, Telegraph and Telephone International Congress, Brighton)

904 Globe (Inter-Parliamentary Union Centenary Conference London)

(Des Lewis Moberly from firework set-pieces. Litho Questa)

1989 (11 Apr). **Anniversaries.** *Phosphorised paper. P* 14 × 14½.

1432 **901**	19p. new blue, greenish yellow, magenta and black	70	70
	a. Horiz pair. Nos. 1432/3	2.25	2.25
1433 **902**	19p. new blue, greenish yellow, magenta and black	70	70

1434 **903**	35p. new blue, greenish yellow, magenta and black	1.25	1.25
	a. Horiz pair. Nos. 1434/5	3.00	3.00
1435 **904**	35p. new blue, greenish yellow, magenta and black	1.25	1.25
	Set of 4	4.75	3.50
	Set of 2 Gutter Pairs	5.00	
	First Day Cover		4.50
	Presentation Pack	5.25	
	P.H.Q. Cards (set of 4)	2.00	5.00

Nos. 1432/3 and 1434/5 were each printed together, *se-tenant*, in horizontal pairs throughout the sheets.

Special First Day of Issue Postmarks

Philatelic Bureau, Edinburgh	5.00
London SW	5.00

905 Toy Train and Airplane

906 Building Bricks

907 Dice and Board Games

908 Toy Robot, Boat and Doll's House

(Des D. Fern)

1989 (16 May). **Europa. Games and Toys.** *Phosphorised paper. P* 14 × 15.

1436 **905**	19p. black, greenish yellow, vermilion, blue-green, blue, gold and pale ochre	50	50
1437 **906**	27p. black, greenish yellow, reddish orange, blue-green, blue and gold	90	90
1438 **907**	32p. black, greenish yellow, orange-red, blue-green, blue, gold and pale ochre	1.25	1.25

1439 **908** 35p. black, greenish yellow, reddish orange, blue-green, blue, gold and
stone 1.40 1.40
Set of 4 .... 3.50 3.50
Set of 4 Gutter Pairs 7.00
First Day Cover 4.25
Presentation Pack......................... 4.50
P.H.Q. Cards (set of 4).................. 2.00 5.00

Special First Day of Issue Postmarks

Philatelic Bureau, Edinburgh 4.50
Leeds 4.50

909 Ironbridge,
Shropshire

910 Tin Mine, St. Agnes
Head, Cornwall

911 Cotton Mills,
New Lanark, Strathclyde

912 Pontcysyllte
Aqueduct, Clwyd

912a Horizontal versions of T **909/12**

(Des R. Maddox)

1989 (4–25 July). **Industrial Archaeology.** *Phosphorised paper.*
P 14 × 15.
1440 **909** 19p. black, bistre-yellow, rose-red, apple-green, light blue, grey-black and emerald 50 50
1441 **910** 27p. black, bistre-yellow, rose-red, apple-green, light blue, grey-black and dull blue 80 80
1442 **911** 32p. black, yellow-green, apple-green, yellow, dull blue, grey-black and deep reddish violet 1.00 1.00
1443 **912** 35p. black, yellow, bright rose, apple-green, dull blue, grey-black and vermilion 1.10 1.10
Set of 4 .... 3.00 3.00
Set of 4 Gutter Pairs 6.50
First Day Cover 4.25
Presentation Pack......................... 4.50
P.H.Q. Cards (set of 4).................. 2.00 5.00
MS1444 **912a** 122 × 90mm. As Nos. 1440/3, but horizontal. Each black, olive-yellow, bright rose-red, dull blue, apple-green, grey-black and vermilion (*sold at £1.40*) (25 July) 6.00 6.00
First Day Cover 6.00

The premium on No. **MS**1444 was used to support the "Stamp World London 90" International Stamp Exhibition.

Special First Day of Issue Postmarks

Philatelic Bureau, Edinburgh (stamps) (4 July) 4.50
Philatelic Bureau, Edinburgh (miniature sheet) (25 July) 6.50
Telford (stamps) (4 July) 4.50
New Lanark (miniature sheet) (25 July) 6.50

913

914

1989 (22 Aug)–**93.** *Booklet Stamps.*

(a) Photo Harrison. P 15 × 14

1445	**913**	(2nd)	brt blue (1 centre band)	30	35
		a.	Booklet pane. No. 1445 × 10 with horizontal edges of pane imperf	3.00	
		b.	Booklet pane. No. 1445 × 4 with three edges of pane imperf (28.11.89)	3.00	
1446		(2nd)	brt blue (1 band at right) (20.3.90)....	2.25	2.25
1447	**914**	(1st)	brownish black (phosphorised paper)	1.00	50
		a.	Booklet pane. No. 1447 × 10 with horizontal edges of pane imperf	8.00	
		b.	Booklet pane. No. 1447 × 4 with three edges of pane imperf (5.12.89)	4.00	
1448		(1st)	brownish black (2 phosphor bands) (20.3.90)	2.25	2.25
			First Day Cover (Nos. 1445, 1447).....		3.50

(b) Litho Walsall. P 14

1449	**913**	(2nd)	brt blue (1 centre band)	30	35
		a.	Imperf between (vert pair)...............		
		b.	Booklet pane. No. 1449 × 4 with three edges of pane imperf	3.00	
		c.	Booklet pane. No. 1449 × 4 with horiz edges of pane imperf (6.8.91) ...	1.25	
		d.	Booklet pane. No. 1449 × 10 with horiz edges of pane imperf (6.8.91) ...	3.00	
1450	**914**	(1st)	blackish brown (2 phosphor bands) ..	2.00	1.75
		a.	Booklet pane. No. 1450 × 4 with three edges of pane imperf..............	7.50	
		Ey.	Phosphor omitted..........................		

(c) Litho Questa. P 15 × 14

1451	**913**	(2nd)	brt blue (1 centre band) (19.9.89)	30	35
1451*a*		(2nd)	brt blue (1 band at right) (25.2.92)....	1.00	1.00
		a*Eb.*	Band at left (10.8.93)	1.00	1.00
		a*Ey.*	Phosphor omitted..........................		
		a*l.*	Booklet pane. Nos 1451a*Eb* and 1514*a*, each × 3, with margins all round (10.8.93)	8.00	
1452	**914**	(1st)	brownish black (phosphorised paper) (19.9.89)	1.10	1.10

Nos. 1445, 1447 and 1449/52 were initially sold at 14p. (2nd) and 19p. (1st), but these prices were later increased to reflect new postage rates.

Nos. 1446 and 1448 come from the *se-tenant* pane in the London Life £5 Booklet. This pane is listed under No. X906m in the Decimal Machin section.

No. 1451*a* comes from the *se-tenant* panes in the Wales and Tolkien £6 booklets. These panes are listed under Nos. X1012l and W49a (Wales Regionals). No. 1451a*Eb* comes from the £6 (£5.64) Beatrix Potter booklet.

Nos. 1445, 1447 and 1449/50 do not exist perforated on all four sides, but come with either one or two adjacent sides imperforate.

No. 1450*Ey* comes from a pane in which one stamp was without phosphor bands due to a dry print.

For illustrations showing the differences between photogravure and lithography see above Type **367**.

For similar design, but changed colours, see Nos. 1511/16 and for those with elliptical perforations Nos. 1663a/6.

Special First Day of Issue Postmarks
(for illustrations see Introduction)

Philatelic Bureau, Edinburgh (Type G)......................	3.75
Windsor, Berks (Type G).......................................	3.75

HAVE YOU READ THE NOTES AT THE BEGINNING OF THIS CATALOGUE?

These often provide answers to the enquiries we receive.

915 Snowflake (× 10)

916 *Calliphora erythrocephala* (fly)

917 Blood Cells (× 500)

918 Microchip (× 600)

(Des K. Bassford. Litho Questa)

1989 (5 Sept). **150th Anniv of Royal Microscopical Society.** *Phosphorised paper.* P 14½ × 14.

1453	**915**	19p.	gold, lemon, pale blue, grey, black and grey-black	50	50
1454	**916**	27p.	gold, lemon, drab, black and grey-black	85	85
1455	**917**	32p.	gold, lemon, orange-vermilion, flesh, black and grey-black	1.25	1.25
1456	**918**	35p.	gold, lemon, black, bright green and grey-black	1.40	1.40
			Set of 4	3.50	3.50
			Set of 4 Gutter Pairs	7.00	
			First Day Cover		5.00
			Presentation Pack	4.00	
			P.H.Q. Cards (set of 4)..................	2.00	5.00

Special First Day of Issue Postmarks

Philatelic Bureau, Edinburgh	4.50
Oxford	4.50

919 Royal Mail Coach

920 Escort of Blues and Royals

157

921 Lord Mayor's Coach   **922** Passing St. Paul's

924 14th-century Peasants from Stained-glass Window

925 Arches and Roundels, West Front

923 Blues and Royals Drum Horse

926 Octagon Tower

927 Arcade from West Transept

(Des P. Cox)

1989 (17 Oct). **Lord Mayor's Show, London.** *Phosphorised paper.*
P 14 × 15.

1457 **919**	20p.	gold, lemon, rose, orange, pale blue and black	60	60
	a.	Horiz strip of 5. Nos. 1457/61	3.25	3.25
	ab.	Imperforate (horiz strip of 5. Nos. 1457/61)		
	ac.	Imperforate (horiz strip of 4. Nos. 147/60)		
	ad.	Imperforate (horiz strip of 3. Nos. 1457/9)		
1458 **920**	20p.	gold, lemon, rose, orange, pale blue and black	60	60
1459 **921**	20p.	gold, lemon, rose, orange, pale blue and black	60	60
1460 **922**	20p.	gold, lemon, rose, orange, pale blue and black	60	60
1461 **923**	20p.	gold, lemon, rose, orange, pale blue and black	60	60
		Set of 5	3.25	2.75
		Gutter Strip of 10	6.50	
		First Day Cover		3.75
		Presentation Pack	4.50	
		P.H.Q. Cards (set of 5)	2.50	5.00

Nos. 1457/61 wereprinted together, *se-tenant,* in horizontal strips of
5 throughout the sheet. This issue commemorates the 800th anniversary of the installation of the first Lord Mayor of London.
Nos. 1457ab/ad come from a sheet partly imperf at left.

928 Triple Arch from West Front

(Des D. Gentleman)

1989 (14 Nov). **Christmas.** *800th Anniv of Ely Cathedral. One phosphor band (15p., 15p. + 1p.) or phosphorised paper (others).*
P 15 × 14.

1462 **924**	15p.	gold, silver and blue	35	35
1463 **925**	15p. + 1p.	gold, silver and blue	50	40
	a.	Imperf (pair)	£1300	
1464 **926**	20p. + 1p.	gold, silver and rosine	60	50
	a.	Imperf (pair)	£1300	
1465 **927**	34p. + 1p.	gold, silver and emerald	1.25	1.40
1466 **928**	37p. + 1p.	gold, silver and yellow-olive	1.25	1.40
		Set of 5	3.50	3.50
		Set of 5 Gutter Pairs	7.00	
		First Day Cover		4.00
		Presentation Pack	4.50	
		P.H.Q. Cards (set of 5)	2.50	5.00

Special First Day of Issue Postmarks

Special First Day of Issue Postmarks

Philatelic Bureau, Edinburgh 4.00
London, EC4 .... 4.00

Philatelic Bureau, Edinburgh 4.50
Bethlehem, Llandeilo, Dyfed 4.50
Ely, Cambs 4.50

Collectors Pack 1989

1989 (14 Nov). *Comprises Nos. 1419/22, 1428/43 and 1453/66.*
CP1464a Collectors Pack 32.00

Post Office Yearbook

989 (14 Nov). *Comprises Nos. 1419/22, 1428/44 and 1453/66 in hardbound book with slip case, illustrated in colour* 45.00

929 Queen Victoria and Queen Elizabeth II

(Des J. Matthews (after Wyon and Machin)

1990 (10 Jan–12 June). **150th Anniv of the Penny Black.**

(a) Photo Harrison. P 15 × 14

1467 **929**	15p. brt blue (1 centre band)	50	50
	a. Imperf (pair)		
	l. Booklet pane. No. 1467 × 10 with horizontal edges of pane imperf (30.1.90)	5.00	
1468	15p. brt blue (1 side band at left) (30.1.90)	1.50	1.50
	Ea. Band at right (20.3.90)	60	70
	l. Booklet pane. No. 1468 × 2 and 1470 plus label	5.00	
1469	20p. brownish black and cream (phosphorised paper)	75	75
	a. Imperf (pair)		
	l. Booklet pane. No. 1469 × 5 plus label with vertical sides of pane imperf (30.1.90)	7.00	
	m. Booklet pane. No. 1469 × 10 with horizontal edges of pane imperf (30.1.90)	7.00	
	n. Booklet pane. No. 1469 × 6 with margins all round (20.3.90)	2.50	
	r. Booklet pane. No. 1469 × 4 with three edges of pane imperf (17.4.90)	4.50	
1470	20p. brownish black and cream (2 bands) (30.1.90)	1.50	1.50
1471	29p. dp mauve (phosphorised paper)......	1.00	1.00
1472	29p. dp mauve (2 bands) (20.3.90)..........	4.50	4.50
1473	34p. dp bluish grey (phosphorised paper)	1.25	1.25
1474	37p. rosine (phosphorised paper)..........	1.40	1.40

(b) Litho Walsall. P 14 (from booklets)

1475 **929**	15p. brt blue (1 centre band) (30.1.90)	60	60
	l. Booklet pane. No. 1475 × 4 with three edges of pane imperf	3.75	
	m. Booklet pane. No. 1475 × 10 with three edges of pane imperf (12.6.90)	6.00	
1476	20p. brownish black and cream (phosphorised paper) (30.1.90)..............	1.10	80
	l. Booklet pane. No. 1476 × 5 plus label with vertical sides of pane imperf	6.00	
	m. Booklet pane. No. 1476 × 4 with three edges of pane imperf	5.00	
	n. Booklet pane. No. 1476 × 10 with three edges of pane imperf (12.6.90)	8.00	

(c) Litho Questa. P 15 × 14

1477 **929**	15p. brt blue (1 centre band) (17.4.90)	1.00	1.00
1478	20p. brownish black (phosphorised paper) (17.4.90)	1.25	1.25
	Set of 5 (Nos. 1467, 1469, 1471, 1473/4)	4.50	4.50
	First Day Cover (Nos. 1467, 1469, 1471, 1473/4).............................		6.00
	Presentation Pack (Nos. 1467, 1469, 1471, 1473/4).............................	5.75	

Nos. 1468, 1468Ea, 1470, 1472 and 1475/8 come from booklets. Nos. 1468Ea, 1470 and 1472 occur in the *se-tenant* pane from the 1990 London Life £5 booklet. This pane is listed as No. X906m.

Nos. 1475/6 do not exist perforated on all four sides, but come with either one or two adjacent sides imperforate.

For illustrations showing the difference between photogravure and lithography see beneath Type **367**.

For No. 1469 in miniature sheet see No. **MS**1501.

Special First Day of Issue Postmark

Philatelic Bureau, Edinburgh	5.50
Windsor, Berks (Type G, see Introduction)	5.50

930 Kitten

931 Rabbit

932 Duckling

933 Puppy

(Des T. Evans. Litho Questa)

1990 (23 Jan). **150th Anniv of Royal Society for Prevention of Cruelty to Animals.** *Phosphorised paper. P 14 × 14½.*

1479 **930**	20p. new blue, greenish yellow, bright magenta, black and silver	65	50
	a. Silver (Queen's head and face value) omitted	£200	
1480 **931**	29p. new blue, greenish yellow, bright magenta, black and silver	1.00	80
	a. Imperf (horiz pair)........................		
1481 **932**	34p. new blue, greenish yellow, bright magenta, black and silver...............	1.40	1.10
	a. Silver (Queen's head and face value) omitted......................................	£350	
1482 **933**	37p. new blue, greenish yellow, bright magenta, black and silver	1.40	1.10
	Set of 4	4.00	3.25
	Set of 4 Gutter Pairs	6.50	
	First Day Cover		5.25
	Presentation Pack..........................	5.00	
	P.H.Q. Cards (set of 4)....................	2.50	5.50

Special First Day of Issue Postmarks

Philatelic Bureau, Edinburgh 5.50
Horsham 5.50

934 Teddy Bear

935 Dennis the Menace

936 Punch

937 Cheshire Cat

938 The Man in the Moon

939 The Laughing Policeman

940 Clown

941 Mona Lisa

942 Queen of Hearts

943 Stan Laurel (comedian)

(Des Michael Peters and Partners Ltd)

1990 (6 Feb). **Greetings Stamps.** *"Smiles". Two phosphor bands.*
  P 15 × 14.

1483	**934**	20p. gold, greenish yellow, bright rose-red, new blue and grey-black..........	1.25	1.
		a. Booklet pane. Nos. 1483/92 with margins all round	15.00	
1484	**935**	20p. gold, greenish yellow, bright rose-red, new blue, deep blue and grey-black	1.25	1.
1485	**936**	20p. gold, greenish yellow, bright rose-red, new blue, deep blue and grey-black	1.25	1.
1486	**937**	20p. gold, greenish yellow, bright rose-red, new blue and grey-black..........	1.25	1.
1487	**938**	20p. gold, greenish yellow, bright rose-red, new blue and grey-black..........	1.25	1.
1488	**939**	20p. gold, greenish yellow, bright rose-red, new blue and grey-black..........	1.25	1.
1489	**940**	20p. gold, greenish yellow, bright rose-red, new blue and grey-black..........	1.25	1.
1490	**941**	20p. gold, greenish yellow, bright rose-red, new blue and grey-black..........	1.25	1.
1491	**942**	20p. gold, greenish yellow, bright rose-red, new blue and grey-black..........	1.25	1.
1492	**943**	20p. gold and grey-black	1.25	1.
		Set of 10	15.00	11.
		First Day Cover		12.

Nos. 1483/92 were only issued in £2 booklets. The design of Nos.
1483, 1485/7, 1489 and 1492 extend onto the pane margin.
  For Types **934/43** inscribed (1st), see Nos. 1550/59.

Special First Day of Issue Postmarks

Philatelic Bureau, Edinburgh 12.00
Giggleswick, North Yorkshire 12.00

944 Alexandra Palace
("Stamp World London 90"
Exhibition)

945 Glasgow School of
Art

946 British Philatelic Bureau, Edinburgh

947 Templeton Carpet Factory, Glasgow

(Des P. Hogarth)

1990 (6–20 Mar). **Europa** (*Nos. 1493 and 1495*) and **"Glasgow 1990 European City of Culture"** (*Nos. 1494 and 1496*). *Phosphorised paper. P 14 × 15.*

1493	**944**	20p. silver, lemon, flesh, grey-brown, blue, grey-black and black	50	50
		a. Booklet pane. No. 1493 × 4 with margins all round (20 Mar)	2.75	
1494	**945**	20p. silver, greenish yellow, dull orange, blue, grey-black and black	50	50
1495	**946**	29p. silver, stone, orange, olive-sepia, grey-blue, grey-black and black	1.10	1.10
1496	**947**	37p. silver, greenish yellow, bright emerald, salmon, olive-sepia, bright blue and black	1.25	1.25
		Set of 4	3.00	3.00
		Set of 4 Gutter Pairs	6.00	
		First Day Cover		4.25
		Presentation Pack	4.00	
		P.H.Q. Cards (set of 4)	2.50	5.25

Special First Day of Issue Postmarks

Philatelic Bureau, Edinburgh		4.50
Glasgow		4.50

948 Export Achievement Award

949 Technological Achievement Award

(Des S. Broom Litho Questa)

1990 (10 Apr). **25th Anniv of Queen's Awards for Export and Technology.** *Phosphorised paper. P 14 × 14½.*

1497	**948**	20p. new blue, greenish yellow, magenta, black and silver	55	55
		a. Horiz pair. Nos. 1497/8	1.10	1.10
1498	**949**	20p. new blue, greenish yellow, magenta, black and silver	55	55
1499	**948**	37p. new blue, greenish yellow, magenta, black and silver	1.10	1.10
		a. Horiz pair. Nos. 1499/500	2.25	2.25
1500	**949**	37p. new blue, greenish yellow, magenta, black and silver	1.10	1.10
		Set of 4	3.00	3.00
		Set of 2 Gutter Pairs	3.00	
		First Day Cover		4.50
		Presentation Pack	4.00	
		P.H.Q. Cards (set of 4)	2.50	5.25

Nos. 1497/8 and 1499/500 were each printed together, *se-tenant*, in horizontal pairs thoughout the sheets.

Special First Day of Issue Postmarks

Philatelic Bureau, Edinburgh		4.75
London, SW		4.75

949a

(Des Sedley Place Design Ltd. Engraved C. Matthews, Recess and photo Harrison)

1990 (3 May). **"Stamp World 90" International Stamp Exhibition.** *Sheet 122 × 89mm. containing No. 1469. Phosphorised paper. P 15 × 14.*

MS1501	**949a**	20p. brownish black and cream (*sold at £1*)	3.50	4.00
		a. Error. Imperf	£7500	
		b. Black (recess-printing) omitted	£6500	
		c. Black (recess-printing) inverted	£7500	
		First Day Cover		5.50
		Souvenir Book (Nos. 1467, 1469, 1471, 1473/4 and **MS**1501)	12.00	

The premium on No. **MS**1501 was used to support the Stamp World London '90 International Stamp Exhibition. In No. **MS**1501 only the example of the 20p. is perforated.

No. **MS**1501b shows an albino impression on the reverse. The 1d. black and Seahorse background are omitted due to one sheet becoming attached to the underside of another prior to recess-printing.

No. **MS**1501c shows the recess part of the design inverted in relation to the photogravure of Type **929**.

Special First Day of Issue Postmarks

Philatelic Bureau, Edinburgh 5.75
City of London 5.75

950 Cycad and Sir Joseph Banks Building

951 Stone Pine and Princess of Wales Conservatory

952 Willow Tree and Palm House

953 Cedar Tree and Pagoda

(Des P. Leith)

1990 (5 June). **150th Anniv of Kew Gardens.** *Phosphorised paper.* P 14 × 15.

1502	**950**	20p.	black, bright emerald, pale turquoise-green, light brown and lavender	50	50
1503	**951**	29p.	black, bright emerald, turquoise-green, reddish orange and grey-black	80	80
1504	**952**	34p.	Venetian red, bright green, cobalt, dull purple, turquoise-green and yellow-green	1.10	1.25
1505	**953**	37p.	pale violet-blue, bright emerald, red-brown, steel-blue and brown-rose ...	1.25	1.40
			Set of 4	3.25	3.50
			Set of 4 Gutter Pairs	6.50	
			First Day Cover		4.50
			Presentation Pack	4.00	
			P.H.Q. Cards (set of 4)	2.50	5.00

Special First Day of Issue Postmarks

Philatelic Bureau, Edinburgh 4.75
Kew, Richmond 4.75

954 Thomas Hardy and Clyffe Clump, Dorset

(Des J. Gibbs)

1990 (10 July). **150th Birth Anniv of Thomas Hardy (author).** *Phosphorised paper.* P 14 × 15.

1506	**954**	20p.	vermilion, greenish yellow, pale lake-brown, dp brown, lt red-brown & black	60	70
		a.	Imperf (pair)	1.25	
			Gutter Pair	1.25	
			First Day Cover		2.00
			Presentation Pack	1.75	
			P.H.Q. Card	75	2.00

Special First Day of Issue Postmarks

Philatelic Bureau, Edinburgh 2.25
Dorchester 2.25

955 Queen Elizabeth the Queen Mother

956 Queen Elizabeth

957 Elizabeth, Duchess of York   **958** Lady Elizabeth Bowes-Lyon

(Des J. Gorham from photographs by N. Parkinson, (20p.), Dorothy Wilding (29p.), B. Park (34p.), Rita Martin (37p.))

1990 (2 Aug). **90th Birthday of Queen Elizabeth the Queen Mother.** *Phosphorised paper.* P 14 × 15.

1507	**955**	20p. silver, greenish yellow, magenta, turquoise-blue and grey black	50	50
1508	**956**	29p. silver, indigo and grey-blue	80	80
1509	**957**	34p. silver, lemon, red, new blue and grey-black	1.10	1.25
1510	**958**	37p. silver, sepia and stone	1.25	1.40
		Set of 4	3.25	3.50
		Set of 4 Gutter Pairs	6.50	
		First Day Cover		4.75
		Presentation Pack	4.50	
		P.H.Q. Cards (set of 4)	2.50	5.50

Special First Day of Issue Postmarks

Philatelic Bureau, Edinburgh	4.75
Westminster, SW1	4.75

1990 (7 Aug)–**92.** *Booklet Stamps. As T* **913/14**, *but colours changed.*

(a) *Photo Harrison.* P 15 × 14.

1511	**913**	(2nd) deep blue (1 centre band)	50	50
		a. Booklet pane. No. 1511 × 10 with horiz edges of pane imperf	6.00	
1512	**914**	(1st) bright orange-red (phosphorised paper)	40	40
		a. Booklet pane. No. 1512 × 10 with horiz edges of pane imperf	4.00	

(b) *Litho Questa.* P 15 × 14

1513	**913**	(2nd) dp blue (1 centre band)	60	60
1514	**914**	(1st) brt orange-red (phosphorised paper)	40	40
1514a		(1st) brt orange-red (2 bands) (25.2.92)	1.25	1.25

(c) *Litho Walsall.* P 14.

1515	**913**	(2nd) deep blue (1 centre band)	50	50
		a. Booklet pane. No. 1515 × 4 with horiz edges of pane imperf	2.50	
		b. Booklet pane. No. 1515 × 10 with horiz edges of pane imperf	6.00	
1516	**914**	(1st) bright orange-red (phosphorised paper)	40	40
		a. Booklet pane. No. 1516 × 4 with horiz edges of pane imperf	1.60	
		b. Booklet pane. No. 1516 × 10 with edges of pane imperf	4.00	
		c. Perf 13	1.50	1.50
		ca. Booklet pane. No. 1516c × 4 with horiz edges of pane imperf	6.00	
		First Day Cover (Nos. 1515/16)		3.00

Nos. 1511/14 and 1515/16 were initially sold at 15p. (2nd) and 20p. (1st), but these prices were later increased to reflect new postage rates.

Nos. 1511/12 and 1515/16 do not exist with perforations on all four sides, but come with either the top or the bottom edge imperforate.

No. 1514a comes from the *se-tenant* panes in the Wales and Tolkien £6 booklets. These panes are listed under Nos X1012l and W49a (Wales Regionals).

No. 1516c was caused by the use of an incorrect perforation comb.

For similar stamps with elliptical perforations see Nos. 1663a/6.

Special First Day of Issue Postmarks
(for illustration see Introduction)

Philatelic Bureau, Edinburgh (Type G)	3.25
Windsor, Berks (Type G)	3.25

959 Victoria Cross   **960** George Cross

961 Distinguished Service Cross and Distinguished Service Medal

962 Military Cross and Military Medal

963 Distinguished Flying Cross and Distinguished Flying Medal

(Des J. Gibbs and J. Harwood)

1990 (11 Sept). **Gallantry Awards.** *Phosphorised paper. P* 14 × 15 *(vert)* or 15 × 14 *(horiz).*

1517	**959**	20p.	grey-black, pale stone, stone, bistre-brown & brt carmine	65	65
1518	**960**	20p.	grey-black, pale stone, flesh, grey & ultramarine...............................	65	65
1519	**961**	20p.	grey-black, pale stone, flesh, pale blue & ultramarine........................	65	65
			a. Imperf (pair)		
1520	**962**	20p.	grey-black, pale stone, ochre, pale blue, ultramarine, scarlet & violet.....	65	65
1521	**963**	20p.	grey-black, pale stone, yellow-brown, bluish grey & purple	65	65
			Set of 5	3.00	3.00
			Set of 5 Gutter Pairs	6.00	
			First Day Cover		3.75
			Presentation Pack..........................	4.00	
			P.H.Q. Cards (set of 5)...................	3.00	5.50

Special First Day of Issue Postmarks

Philatelic Bureau, Edinburgh 4.25
Westminister, SW1 .... 4.25

(Des. J. Fisher. Litho Questa)

1990 (16 Oct). **Astronomy.** *Phosphorised paper. P* 14 × 14½

1522	**964**	22p.	cream, grey, dull blue-green, slate-blue, blue-green, orange-red, gold & black	50	4•
			a. Gold (Queen's head) omitted		
1523	**965**	26p.	black, yellow, dull purple, pale cream, brown-rose, new blue, greenish yellow, vermilion & gold	80	9•
1524	**966**	31p.	black, cream, pale cream, yellow-orange, salmon, lemon, vermilion & gold	1.00	1.0•
1525	**967**	37p.	black, pale buff, olive-bistre, pale cream, pale flesh, flesh, grey, rose-red & gold	1.10	1.1•
			Set of 4	3.00	3.0•
			Set of 4 Gutter Pairs	6.00	
			First Day Cover		3.7•
			Presentation Pack..........................	4.00	
			P.H.Q. Cards (set of 4)...................	2.50	5.5•

Special First Day of Issue Postmarks

Philatelic Bureau, Edinburgh 3.75
Armagh 3.75

968 Building a Snowman

969 Fetching the Christmas Tree

970 Carol Singing

971 Tobogganing

964 Armagh Observatory, Jodrell Bank Radio Telescope and La Palma Telescope

965 Newton's Moon and Tides Diagram with Early Telescopes

966 Greenwich Old Observatory and Early Astronomical Equipment

967 Stonehenge, Gyroscope and Navigation by Stars

972 Ice-skating

(Des J. Gorham and A. Davidson)

1990 (13 Nov). **Christmas**. *One phosphor band (17p.) or phos-phorised paper (others)*. P 15 × 14.

1526	**968**	17p. gold, greenish yellow, rose, new blue and grey-black	45	35
		a. Booklet pane of 20	9.00	
1527	**969**	22p. gold, greenish yellow, magenta, new blue and black	55	65
		a. Imperf (horiz pair)		
1528	**970**	26p. gold, olive-yellow, pale magenta, agate, new blue, dull violet-blue and black	80	80
1529	**971**	31p. gold, greenish yellow, bright rose-red. dull mauve, new blue, tur-quoise-blue and grey-black	1.00	1.00
1530	**972**	37p. gold, greenish yellow, rose, new blue and slate-green	1.10	1.10
		Set of 5	3.50	3.50
		Set of 5 Gutter Pairs	7.00	
		First Day Cover		4.25
		Presentation Pack	4.25	
		P.H.Q. Cards (set of 5)	3.25	6.00

Booklet pane No. 1526a has the horizontal edges of the pane imperforate.

Special First Day of Issue Postmarks

Philatelic Bureau, Edinburgh	4.50
Bethlehem, Llandeilo, Dyfed	4.50

Collectors Pack 1990

1990 (13 Nov). *Comprises Nos. 1479/82, 1493/1510 and 1517/30.*

CP1530a Collectors Pack	28.00

Post Office Yearbook

1990 (13 Nov). *Comprises Nos. 1479/82, 1493/500, 1502/10 and 1517/30 in hardbound book with slip case, illustrated in colour* | 40.00

973 "King Charles Spaniel"

974 "A Pointer"

975 "Two Hounds in a Landscape"

976 "A Rough Dog"

977 "Fino and Tiny"

(Des Carroll Dempsey and Thirkell Ltd)

1991 (8 Jan). **Dogs**. *Paintings by George Stubbs. Phosphorised paper.* P 14 × 14½.

1531	**973**	22p. gold, greenish yellow, magenta, new blue, black & drab	75	75
		a. Imperf (pair)	£350	
1532	**974**	26p. gold, greenish yellow, magenta, new blue, black & drab	80	80
1533	**975**	31p. gold, greenish yellow, magenta, new blue, black & drab	85	85
		a. Imperf (pair)	£750	
1534	**976**	33p. gold, greenish yellow, magenta, new blue, black & drab	95	95
1535	**977**	37p. gold, greenish yellow, magenta, new blue, black & drab	1.10	1.10
		Set of 5	4.00	4.00
		Set of 5 Gutter Pairs	8.00	
		First Day Cover		5.00
		Presentation Pack	5.00	
		P.H.Q. Cards (set of 5)	3.25	6.00

Special First Day of Issue Postmarks

Philatelic Bureau, Edinburgh	5.25
Birmingham	5.25

HAVE YOU READ THE NOTES AT THE BEGINNING OF THIS CATALOGUE?

These often provide answers to the enquiries we receive.

978 Thrush's Nest

979 Shooting Star and Rainbow

980 Magpies and Charm Bracelet

981 Black Cat

982 Common Kingfisher with Key

983 Mallard and Frog

984 Four-leaf Clover in Boot and Match Box

985 Pot of Gold at End of Rainbow

986 Heart-shaped Butterflies

987 Wishing Well and Sixpence

(Des T. Meeuwissen)

1991 (5 Feb). **Greetings Stamps.** *"Good Luck". Two phosphor bands.*
P 15 × 14.

1536	978	(1st) silver, greenish yellow, magenta, new blue, olive-brown and black......	75	90
		a. Booklet pane. Nos. 1536/45 plus 12 half stamp-size labels with margins on 3 sides	7.50	
1537	979	(1st) silver, greenish yellow, magenta, new blue, olive-brown and black.....	75	9(
1538	980	(1st) silver, greenish yellow, magenta, new blue, olive-brown and black.....	75	9(
1539	981	(1st) silver, greenish yellow, magenta, new blue, olive-brown and black.....	75	9(
1540	982	(1st) silver, greenish yellow, magenta, new blue, olive-brown and black.....	75	9(
1541	983	(1st) silver, greenish yellow, magenta, new blue, olive-brown and black.....	75	9(
1542	984	(1st) silver, greenish yellow, magenta, new blue, olive-brown and black.....	75	90(
1543	985	(1st) silver, greenish yellow, magenta, new blue, olive-brown and black.....	75	90(
1544	986	(1st) silver, greenish yellow, magenta, new blue, olive-brown and black.....	75	90(
1545	987	(1st) silver, greenish yellow, magenta, new blue, olive-brown and black.....	75	9(
		Set of 10	7.50	8.0(
		First Day Cover		8.5(

Nos. 1536/45 were only issued in £2.20 booklets (sold at £2.40 from 16 September 1991). The backgrounds of the stamps form a composite design.

Special First Day of Issue Postmarks

Philatelic Bureau, Edinburgh 8.50
Greetwell, Lincs 8.50

988 Michael Faraday (inventor of electric motor) (Birth Bicentenary)

989 Charles Babbage (computer science pioneer) (Birth Bicentenary)

990 Radar Sweep of East Anglia (50th Anniv of Operational Radar Network)

991 Gloster E28/39 Aircraft over East Anglia (50th Anniv of First Flight of Sir Frank Whittle's Jet Engine)

(Des P. Till (Nos. 1546/7), J. Harwood (Nos. 1548/9))

1991 (5 Mar). **Scientific Achievements.** *Phosphorised paper. P* 14 × 15.

1546	**988**	22p. silver, olive-brown, greenish yellow, magenta, slate-blue, grey & black	65	65
		a. Imperf (pair)	£275	
1547	**989**	22p. silver, chrome-yellow, red, grey-black, brownish grey & sepia	65	65
1548	**990**	31p. silver, dp turquoise-green, violet-blue, steel-blue & dp dull blue	95	95
1549	**991**	37p. silver, olive-bistre, rose-red, turquoise-blue, new blue & grey-black	1.10	1.10
		Set of 4	3.00	3.00
		Set of 4 Gutter Pairs	6.00	
		First Day Cover		4.00
		Presentation Pack	3.75	
		P.H.Q. Cards (set of 4).................	3.00	5.50

Special First Day of Issue Postmarks

Philatelic Bureau, Edinburgh	4.25
South Kensington, London, SW7	4.25

992 Teddy Bear

1991 (26 Mar). **Greeting Stamps.** *As Nos. 1483/92, but inscribed* (1st) *as T* **992.** *Two phosphor bands. P* 15 × 14.

1550	**992**	(1st) gold, greenish yellow, bright rose-red, new blue and grey-black..........	40	45
		a. Booklet pane. Nos. 1550/59 plus 12 half stamp-size labels with margins on 3 sides	3.50	
1551	**935**	(1st) gold, greenish yellow, bright rose-red, new blue, deep blue and grey-black	40	45
1552	**936**	(1st) gold, greenish yellow, bright rose-red, new blue, deep blue and grey-black	40	45
1553	**937**	(1st) gold, greenish yellow, bright rose-red, new blue and grey-black..........	40	45
1554	**938**	(1st) gold, greenish yellow, bright rose-red, new blue and grey-black..........	40	45
1555	**939**	(1st) gold, greenish yellow, bright rose-red, new blue and grey-black..........	40	45
1556	**940**	(1st) gold, greenish yellow, bright rose-red, new blue and grey-black..........	40	45
1557	**941**	(1st) gold, greenish yellow, bright rose-red, new blue and grey-black..........	40	45
1558	**942**	(1st) gold, greenish yellow, bright rose-red, new blue and grey-black..........	40	45
1559	**943**	(1st) gold and grey-black	40	45
		Set of 10	3.50	4.00
		First Day Cover		7.50

Nos. 1550/9 were only issued in £2.20 booklets (sold at £2.40 from 16 September 1991 and at £2.50 from 1 November 1993). The designs of Nos. 1550, 1552/4, 1556 and 1559 extend onto the pane margin.

Special First Day of Issue Postmarks

Philatelic Bureau, Edinburgh	7.75
Laughterton, Lincs...	7.75

993   **994**

Man Looking at Space

995   **996**

Space Looking at Man

(Des J.-M. Folon)

1991 (23 Apr). **Europa. Europe in Space.** *Phosphorised paper. P* 14 × 15.

1560	**993**	22p. silver-mauve, greenish yellow, scarlet, violet-blue, brt blue, brt green & black	55	55
		a. Horiz pair. Nos. 1560/1...................	1.10	1.10
1561	**994**	22p. silver-mauve, greenish yellow, scarlet, violet-blue, brt blue & black	55	55
1562	**995**	37p. silver-mauve, bistre-yellow, dull vermilion, blue & black.................	1.10	1.10
		a. Horiz pair. Nos. 1562/3.................	2.25	2.25
1563	**996**	37p. silver-mauve, bistre-yellow, dull vermilion, blue & black.................	1.10	1.10
		Set of 4	3.00	3.00
		Set of 4 Gutter Pairs	6.00	
		First Day Cover		4.00
		Presentation Pack	4.00	
		PHQ Cards (set of 4)	3.00	5.50

Nos. 1560/1 and 1562/3 were each printed together, *se-tenant*, in horizontal pairs throughout the sheets each pair forming a composite design.

167

Special First Day of Issue Postmarks

Philatelic Bureau, Edinburgh................................. 4.50
Cambridge 4.50

997 Fencing

998 Hurdling

999 Diving

1000 Rugby

(Des Huntley Muir Partners)

1991 (11 June). **World Student Games, Sheffield** (*Nos.* 1564/6) **and World Cup Rugby Championship, London** (*No.* 1567). *Phosphorised paper. P* 14½ × 14.

1564	**997**	22p. black, greenish yellow, vermilion, brt orange, ultramarine & grey	50	50
1565	**998**	26p. pale blue, greenish yellow, red, brt blue & black.................................	80	80
1566	**999**	31p. brt blue, bistre-yellow, rose, vermilion, new blue & black	95	95
1567	**1000**	37p. yellow-orange, greenish yellow, rose, brt blue, emerald & black	1.10	1.10
		Set of 4...................................	3.00	3.00
		Set of 4 Gutter Pairs	6.00	
		First Day Cover		4.00
		Presentation Pack	4.00	
		PHQ Cards (set of 4)	3.00	5.50

Special First Day of Issue Postmarks

Philatelic Bureau, Edinburgh................................. 4.50
Sheffield 4.50

1001 "Silver Jubilee"

1002 "Mme Alfred Carrière"

1003 *Rosa moyesii*

1004 "Harvest Fayre"

1005 "Mutabilis"

(Des Yvonne Skargon. Litho Questa)

1991 (16 July). **9th World Congress of Roses, Belfast**. *Phosphorised paper. P* 14½ × 14.

1568	**1001**	22p. new blue, greenish yellow, magenta, black & silver..................	75	50
		a. Silver (Queen's head) omitted		
		Eb. Black printing double		
1569	**1002**	26p. new blue, greenish yellow, magenta, black & silver..................	80	80
1570	**1003**	31p. new blue, greenish yellow, magenta, black & silver..................	85	85
1571	**1004**	33p. new blue, greenish yellow, magenta, black & silver..................	95	95
1572	**1005**	37p. new blue, greenish yellow, magenta, black & silver..................	1.10	1.10
		Set of 5...................................	4.00	4.00
		Set of 5 Gutter Pairs	8.00	
		First Day Cover		5.50
		Presentation Pack	4.50	
		PHQ Cards (set of 5)	3.25	6.50

Special First Day of Issue Postmarks

Philatelic Bureau, Edinburgh................................. 5.00
Belfast 5.00

1006 Iguanodon

1007 Stegosaurus

1008 Tyrannosaurus

1009 Protoceratops

1010 Triceratops

(Des B. Kneale)

Special First Day of Issue Postmarks

Philatelic Bureau, Edinburgh	6.00
Plymouth	6.00

1011 Map of 1816

1012 Map of 1906

1013 Map of 1959

1014 Map of 1991

(Des H. Brown. Recess and litho Harrison (24p.), Litho Harrison (28p.), Questa (33p., 39p.))

1991 (20 Aug). **150th Anniversary of Dinosaurs' Identification by Owen.** *Phosphorised paper.* P 14½ × 14.

973	1006	22p. grey, pale blue, magenta, brt blue, dull violet & grey-black	75	50
		a. Imperf (pair)	£750	
974	1007	26p. grey, greenish yellow, pale emerald, brt blue-green, pale brt blue, grey-black & black	90	1.00
975	1008	31p. grey, lt blue, magenta, brt blue, pale blue, brown & grey-black	1.00	1.10
976	1009	33p. grey, dull rose, pale brt blue, brt rose-red, yellow-orange, grey-black & black	1.10	1.10
977	1010	37p. grey, greenish yellow, turquoise-blue, dull violet, yellow-brown & black	1.25	1.25
		Set of 5	4.50	4.50
		Set of 5 Gutter Pairs	9.00	
		First Day Cover		5.50
		Presentation Pack	5.00	
		PHQ Cards (set of 5)	3.25	6.00

1991 (17 Sept). **Bicentenary of Ordnance Survey. Maps of Hamstreet, Kent.** *Phosphorised paper.* P 14½ × 14.

1578	1011	24p. black, magenta & cream	50	50
		Ea. Black (litho) printing treble and magenta printing double	£950	
1579	1012	28p. black, brt yellow-green, new blue, reddish orange, magenta, olive-sepia & cream	80	85
1580	1013	33p. dull blue-green, orange-brown, magenta, olive-grey greenish yellow, vermilion, greenish grey, pale blue, blue, dull orange, apple green & black	95	1.00
1581	1014	39p. black, magenta, greenish yellow & new blue	1.10	1.25
		Set of 4	3.00	3.25
		Set of 4 Gutter Pairs	6.00	
		First Day Cover		4.25
		Presentation Pack	4.00	
		PHQ Cards (set of 4)	3.00	6.00

Mint examples of Type **1012** exist with a face value of 26p.

Special First Day of Issue Postmarks

Philatelic Bureau, Edinburgh	4.50
Southampton	4.50

1015 Adoration of the Magi

1016 Mary and Baby Jesus in the Stable

1017 The Holy Family and Angel

1018 The Annunciation

1019 The Flight into Egypt

(Des D. Driver)

1991 (12 Nov). **Christmas. Illuminated Letters from "Acts of Mary and Jesus" Manuscript in Bodleian Library, Oxford.** *One phosphor band* (18p.) *or phosphorised paper* (*others*). P 15 × 14.

1582	**1015**	18p. steel-blue, greenish yellow, rose-red, orange-red, black & gold	70	40
		a. Imperf (pair)	£1500	
		b. Booklet pane of 20	8.25	
1583	**1016**	24p. brt rose-red, greenish yellow, vermilion, slate-blue, yellow-green, grey-black & gold	80	50
1584	**1017**	28p. reddish brown, bistre-yellow, orange-vermilion, orange-red, dp dull blue, grey-black & gold	85	1.00
1585	**1018**	33p. green, greenish yellow, red, orange-red, blue, grey & gold	95	1.10
1586	**1019**	39p. orange-red, greenish yellow, orange-vermilion, dp dull blue, olive-sepia, black & gold	1.10	1.
		Set of 5	4.00	4.
		Set of 5 Gutter Pairs	8.00	
		First Day Cover		4.
		Presentation Pack	4.25	
		PHQ Cards (set of 5)	3.00	6.

Booklet pane No. 1582b has margins at left, top and bottom.

Special First Day of Issue Postmarks

Philatelic Bureau, Edinburgh	5.00
Bethlehem, Landeilo, Dyfed	5.00

Collectors Pack 1991

1991 (12 Nov). *Comprises Nos. 1531/5, 1546/9 and 1560/86.*
CP1586a Collectors Pack 28.00

Post Office Yearbook

1991 (13 Nov). *Comprises Nos. 1531/5, 1546/9 and 1560/86 hardbound book with slip case, illustrated in colour* 50.00

1020 Fallow Deer in Scottish Forest

1021 Hare on North Yorkshire Moors

1022 Fox in the Fens

1023 Redwing and Home Counties Village

1024 Welsh Mountain Sheep in Snowdonia

(Des J. Gorham and K. Bowen)

1992 (14 Jan–25 Feb). **The Four Seasons. Wintertime.** *One phosphor band (18p.) or phosphorised paper (others).* P 15 × 14.

1587	1020	18p.	silver, greenish yellow, grey, dull rose, new blue & black	45	50
1588	1021	24p.	silver, lemon, rose, blue & grey-black	60	65
		a.	Imperf (pair)	£1250	
1589	1022	28p.	silver, greenish yellow, bright rose, steel-blue & grey-black	70	75
1590	1023	33p.	silver, greenish yellow, brt orange, brt purple, greenish blue & grey......	85	90
1591	1024	39p.	silver, yellow, yellow-orange, grey, vermilion, new blue & black	1.00	1.10
		a.	Booklet pane. No. 1591 × 4 with margins all round (25 Feb)	3.25	
			Set of 5...	3.25	3.50
			Set of 5 Gutter Pairs	6.50	
			First Day Cover		4.50
			Presentation Pack	4.25	
			PHQ Cards (set of 5)	3.00	6.50

Special First Day of Issue Postmarks

Philatelic Bureau, Edinburgh 4.75
Brecon 4.75

1025 Flower Spray

1026 Double Locket

1027 Key

1028 Model Car and Cigarette Cards

1029 Compass and Map

1030 Pocket Watch

1031 1854 1d. Red Stamp and Pen

1032 Pearl Necklace

1033 Marbles

1034 Bucket, Spade and Starfish

(Des Trickett and Webb Ltd)

1992 (28 Jan). **Greetings Stamps. "Memories".** *Two phosphor bands.* P 15 × 14.

1592	1025	(1st)	gold, greenish yellow, magenta, ochre, lt blue & grey-black	40	45
		a.	Booklet pane. Nos. 1592/1601 plus 12 half stamp-size labels with margins on 3 sides	3.50	
1593	1026	(1st)	gold, greenish yellow, magenta, ochre, lt blue & grey-black	40	45
1594	1027	(1st)	gold, greenish yellow, magenta, ochre, lt blue & grey-black	40	45
1595	1028	(1st)	gold, greenish yellow, magenta, ochre, lt blue & grey-black	40	45
1596	1029	(1st)	gold, greenish yellow, magenta, ochre, lt blue & grey-black	40	45
1597	1030	(1st)	gold, greenish yellow, magenta, ochre, lt blue & grey-black	40	45
1598	1031	(1st)	gold, greenish yellow, magenta, ochre, lt blue & grey-black	40	45
1599	1032	(1st)	gold, greenish yellow, magenta, ochre, lt blue & grey-black	40	45
1600	1033	(1st)	gold, greenish yellow, magenta, ochre, lt blue & grey-black	40	45
1601	1034	(1st)	gold, greenish yellow, magenta, ochre, lt blue & grey-black	40	45
			Set of 10	3.50	4.00
			First Day Cover		7.50
			Presentation Pack	4.00	

Nos. 1592/1601 were only issued in £2.40 booklets (sold at £2.50 from 1 November 1993). The backgrounds of the stamps form a composite design.

Special First Day of Issue Postmarks

Philatelic Bureau, Edinburgh 8.00
Whimsey, Gloucestershire.................... 8.00

1035 Queen Elizabeth in Coronation Robes and Parliamentary Emblem

1036 Queen Elizabeth in Garter Robes and Archiepiscopal Arms

1037 Queen Elizabeth with Baby Prince Andrew and Royal Arms

1038 Queen Elizabeth at Trooping the Colour and Service Emblems

1039 Queen Elizabeth and Commonwealth Emblem

(Des Why Not Associates. Litho Questa)

1992 (6 Feb). **40th Anniv of Accession.** *Two phosphor bands.* P 14½ × 14.

1602	**1035**	24p. new blue, greenish yellow, magenta, black, silver & gold	60	65
		a. Horiz strip of 5. Nos. 1602/6	4.00	3.50
1603	**1036**	24p. new blue, greenish yellow, magenta, black, silver & gold	60	65
1604	**1037**	24p. new blue, greenish yellow, magenta, black & silver	60	65
1605	**1038**	24p. new blue, greenish yellow, magenta, black, silver & gold	60	65
1606	**1039**	24p. new blue, greenish yellow, magenta, black, silver & gold	60	65
		Set of 5	4.00	3.00
		Gutter strip of 10	8.00	
		First Day Cover		5.00
		Presentation Pack	4.25	
		PHQ Cards (set of 5)	3.00	5.00

Nos. 1602/6 were printed together, *se-tenant*, in horizontal strips of five throughout the sheet.

Special First Day of Issue Postmarks

Philatelic Bureau, Edinburgh	5.25
Buckingham Palace, London SW1	5.25

1040 Tennyson in 1888 and "The Beguiling of Merlin" (Sir Edward Burne-Jones)

1041 Tennyson in 1864 and "I am Sick of the Shadows" (John Waterhouse)

1042 Tennyson in 1856 and "April Love" (Arthur Hughes)

1043 Tennyson as a Young Man and "Mariana" (Dante Gabriel Rossetti)

(Des Irene von Treskow)

1992 (10 Mar). **Death Centenary of Alfred, Lord Tennyson (poet** *Phosphorised paper.* P 14½ × 14.

1607	**1040**	24p. gold, greenish yellow, magenta, new blue & black	50	5
1608	**1041**	28p. gold, greenish yellow, magenta, new blue & black	65	6
1609	**1042**	33p. gold, greenish yellow, magenta, new blue & black	1.10	1.1
1610	**1043**	39p. gold, greenish yellow, magenta, new blue, bistre & black	1.10	1.1
		Set of 4	3.00	3.0
		Set of 4 Gutter Pairs	6.00	
		First Day Cover		4.0
		Presentation Pack	3.75	
		PHQ Cards (set of 4)	2.50	5.0

Special First Day of Issue Postmarks

Philatelic Bureau, Edinburgh	4.50
Isle of Wight	4.50

ALBUM LISTS

Write for our latest list of albums and accessories.
This will be sent on request.

CARRICKFERGUS CASTLE

1044 Carrickfergus Castle

(Des from photos by Prince Andrew, Duke of York. Eng C. Matthews. Recess Harrison)

1992 (24 Mar). *Designs as Nos. 1410/13, but showing Queen's head in silhouette as T 1044. P 15 × 14 (with one elliptical hole on each vertical side).*

1611	1044	£1 bottle green & gold†	1.50	1.50
1612	880	£1.50, maroon & gold†	2.25	2.25
1613	881	£2 indigo & gold†	3.00	3.00
1614	882	£5 dp brown & gold†	7.50	7.50
		a. Gold† (Queen's head) omitted	£250	
		Set of 4	13.00	13.00
		Set of 4 Gutter Pairs	27.00	
		First Day Cover		30.00
		Presentation Pack	14.50	
		PHQ Cards†† (set of 4)	1.40	

†The Queen's head on these stamps is printed in optically variable ink which changes colour from gold to green when viewed from different angles.

††The PHQ cards for this issue did not appear until 16 February 1993. They do not exist used on the first day of issue of Nos. 1611/14.

Special First Day of Issue Postmarks
(for illustrations see Introduction)

Philatelic Bureau, Edinburgh (Type H)	32.00
Windsor, Berkshire (Type I)	32.00

1049 British Pavilion, "EXPO '92", Seville

(Des K. Bassford (Nos. 1615/16, 1619), K. Bassford and S. Paine, Eng. C. Matthews (Nos. 1617/18). Litho Questa (Nos. 1615/16, 1619) or recess and litho Harrison (Nos. 1617/18))

1992 (7 Apr). **Europa. International Events.** *Phosphorised paper. P 14 × 14½.*

1615	1045	24p. new blue, lemon, magenta & black	65	65
		a. Horiz pair. Nos. 1615/16	1.25	1.25
1616	1046	24p. new blue, lemon, magenta & black	65	65
1617	1047	24p. black, grey, carmine, cream & gold	65	65
1618	1048	39p. black, grey, carmine, cream & gold	1.10	1.10
1619	1049	39p. new blue, lemon, magenta & black	1.10	1.10
		Set of 5	3.75	3.75
		Set of 4 Gutter Pairs	7.50	
		First Day Cover		4.50
		Presentation Pack	4.25	
		PHQ Cards (set of 5)	3.00	6.00

Nos. 1615/16 were printed together, *se-tenant*, throughout the sheets.

No. 1617 is know with cream omitted used from Cornwall in September 1992.

Special First Day of Issue Postmarks

Philatelic Bureau, Edinburgh	4.75
Liverpool	4.75

1045 British Olympic Association Logo (Olympic Games, Barcelona)

1046 British Paralympic Association Symbol (Paralympics '92, Barcelona)

1047 *Santa Maria* (500th Anniv of Discovery of America by Columbus)

1048 *Kaisei* (Japanese cadet brigantine) (Grand Regatta Columbus, 1992)

1050 Pikeman

1051 Drummer

THE CIVIL WAR 1642-51
fought between the forces of KING
& PARLIAMENT: *Musketeer*

1052 Musketeer

THE CIVIL WAR 1642-51
fought between the forces of KING
& PARLIAMENT: *Standard Bearer*

1053 Standard Bearer

GILBERT & SULLIVAN
The Mikado

1056 *The Mikado*

GILBERT & SULLIVAN
The Pirates of Penzance

1057 *The Pirates of Penzance*

(Des J. Sancha)

1992 (16 June). **350th Anniv of the Civil War.** *Phosphorised paper.*
P $14\frac{1}{2}$ × 14.

1620	**1050**	24p.	black, stone, bistre, scarlet, indigo, grey-green & yellow-ochre	55	55
1621	**1051**	28p.	black, yellow-ochre, ochre, rose-pink, blue, dull yellow-green & slate-lilac	70	70
1622	**1052**	33p.	black, ochre, pale orange, lemon, reddish orange, new blue & olive-green	1.00	1.00
1623	**1053**	39p.	black, yellow-ochre, yellow, greenish yellow, vermilion, indigo & orange-brown	1.10	1.10
			Set of 4	3.00	3.00
			Set of 4 Gutter Pairs	6.00	
			First Day Cover		4.00
			Presentation Pack	3.75	
			PHQ Cards (set of 4)	2.00	5.00

Special First Day of Issue Postmarks

Philatelic Bureau, Edinburgh	4.25
Banbury, Oxfordshire	4.25

GILBERT & SULLIVAN
Iolanthe

1058 *Iolanthe*

(Des Lynda Gray)

1992 (21 July). **150th Birth Anniv of Sir Arthur Sullivan (composer) Gilbert and Sullivan Operas.** *One phosphor band* (18p.) or *phosphorised paper* (others). P $14\frac{1}{2}$ × 14.

1624	**1054**	18p.	bluish violet, bistre-yellow, scarlet, stone, blue & grey-black	40	45
1625	**1055**	24p.	purple-brown, lemon, scarlet, stone, blue, olive- bistre & black	55	55
			a. Imperf (pair)	£250	
1626	**1056**	28p.	rose-red, lemon, stone, new blue, bluish violet, brt emerald & black	70	70
1627	**1057**	33p.	blue-green, orange-yellow, scarlet, olive-bistre, blue, brown-purple & black	90	90
1628	**1058**	39p.	dp blue, lemon, scarlet, stone, lavender, olive-bistre & lake-brown	1.10	1.10
			Set of 5	3.25	3.25
			Set of 5 Gutter Pairs	6.50	
			First Day Cover		4.75
			Presentation Pack	4.00	
			PHQ Cards (set of 5)	2.25	6.00

GILBERT & SULLIVAN
The Yeomen of the Guard

1054 *The Yeomen of the Guard*

GILBERT & SULLIVAN
The Gondoliers

1055 *The Gondoliers*

Special First Day of Issue Postmarks

Philatelic Bureau, Edinburgh	5.00
Birmingham	5.00

1059 "Acid Rain Kills"

1060 "Ozone Layer"

1061 "Greenhouse Effect"

1062 "Bird of Hope"

(Des Christopher Hall (24p.), Lewis Fowler (28p.), Sarah Warren (33p.), Alice Newton-Mold (39p.). Adapted Trickett and Webb Ltd)

1992 (15 Sept). **Protection of the Environment. Children's Paintings.** *Phosphorised paper.* P 14 × 14½.

1629	**1059**	?4p. emerald, greenish yellow, pale olive-yellow, brt carmine & black.....	60	45
1630	**1060**	28p. vermilion, lemon, brt blue, new blue, brt green, ultramarine & black.	75	80
1631	**1061**	33p. greenish blue, greenish yellow, brt rose-red, brt green, emerald, blue & black	80	90
1632	**1062**	39p. emerald, greenish yellow, brt magenta, brt orange, brt blue & black	90	90
		Set of 4	2.75	2.75
		Set of 4 Gutter Pairs	5.50	
		First Day Cover		3.75
		Presentation Pack	3.50	
		PHQ Cards (set of 4)	2.00	5.50

Special First Day of Issue Postmarks

Philatelic Bureau, Edinburgh	4.00
Torridon	4.00

GIBBONS STAMP MONTHLY

— finest and most informative magazine for all collectors. Obtainable from your newsagent or by postal subscription — details on request.

1063 European Star

(Des D. Hockney)

1992 (13 Oct). **Single European Market.** *Phosphorised paper.* P 15 × 14.

1633	**1063**	24p. gold, greenish yellow, brt magenta, dull ultramarine & black	60	60
		Gutter Pair	1.25	
		First Day Cover		1.50
		Presentation Pack	1.40	
		PHQ Card	60	1.60

Special First Day of Issue Postmarks

Philatelic Bureau, Edinburgh	1.75
Westminster	1.75

1064 "Angel Gabriel", St. James's, Pangbourne

1065 "Madonna and Child", St. Mary's Bilbury

1066 "King with Gold", Our Lady and St. Peter, Leatherhead

1067 "Shepherds", All Saints, Porthcawl

1068 "Kings with Frankincense and Myrrh", Our Lady and St. Peter, Leatherhead

(Des Carroll, Dempsey and Thirkell Ltd from windows by Karl Parsons (18, 24, 33p.) and Paul Woodroffe (28, 39p.))

1992 (10 Nov). **Christmas. Stained Glass Windows.** *One centre band (18p.) or phosphorised paper (others). P 15 × 14.*

1634	**1064**	18p. black, greenish yellow, mauve, ultramarine, brt emerald & gold	40	40
		a. Booklet pane of 20	7.50	
1635	**1065**	24p. black, greenish yellow, brt purple, ultramarine, new blue, brt greenish yellow & gold..............................	65	65
1636	**1066**	28p. black, lemon, rosine, ultramarine, reddish lilac, red-orange & gold	80	80
1637	**1067**	33p. brt ultramarine, greenish yellow, rosine, brown, yellow-orange, black & gold...................................	95	95
1638	**1068**	39p. black, lemon, rosine, brt blue, dp violet, yellow-orange & gold	1.10	1.10
		Set of 5...	3.50	3.50
		Set of 5 Gutter Pairs	7.00	
		First Day Cover		4.25
		Presentation Pack	4.00	
		PHQ Cards (set of 5)	2.25	5.50

Booklet pane No. 1634a comes from a special £3.60 Christmas booklet and has margins at left, top and bottom.

Special First Day of Issue Postmarks

Philatelic Bureau, Edinburgh	4.50
Bethlehem, Llandeilo, Dyfed...................................	4.50
Pangbourne	4.50

Collectors Pack 1992

1992 (10 Nov). *Comprises Nos. 1587/91, 1602/10 and 1615/38.*
CP1638a Collectors Pack 24.00

Post Office Yearbook

1992 (11 Nov). *Comprises Nos. 1587/91, 1602/10 and 1615/38 in hardbound book with slip case, illustrated in colour*... 40.00

1069 Mute Swan Cob and St. Catherine's Chapel, Abbotsbury

1070 Cygnet and Decoy

1071 Swans and Cygnet

1072 Eggs in Nest and Tithe Barn, Abbotsbury

1073 Young Swan and the Fleet

(Des D. Gentleman)

1993 (19 Jan). **600th Anniv of Abbotsbury Swannery.** *One phosph band (18p.) or phosphorised paper (others). P 14 × 15.*

1639	**1069**	18p. gold, greenish yellow, bistre, green, vermilion & black................	40	
1640	**1070**	24p. gold, cream, brt green, grey-brown, dull blue & grey-black..................	55	
1641	**1071**	28p. gold, greenish grey, yellow-brown, myrtle-green, brown, vermilion & black	65	
1642	**1072**	33p. gold, ochre, apple-green, olive-brown, brt orange & grey-black.......	80	
1643	**1073**	39p. gold, cream, brt green, cobalt, lt brown & black..............................	95	
		Set of 5...	3.00	3.
		Set of 5 Gutter Pairs	6.00	
		First Day Cover		4.
		Presentation Pack	4.00	
		PHQ Cards (set of 5)	2.25	5.

Special First Day of Issue Postmarks

Philatelic Bureau, Edinburgh	4.50
Abbotsbury, Dorset..	4.50

1074 Long John Silver and Parrot (*Treasure Island*)

1075 Tweedledum and Tweedledee (*Alice Through the Looking-Glass*)

076 William (*William* books)

1077 Mole and Toad (*The Wind in the Willows*)

1078 Teacher and Wilfrid ("The Bash Street Kids")

1079 Peter Rabbit and Mrs. Rabbit (*The Tale of Peter Rabbit*)

1080 Snowman and Father Christmas (*The Snowman*)

1081 The Big Friendly Giant and Sophie (*The BFG*)

1082 Bill Badger and Rupert Bear

1083 Aladdin and the Genie

(Des Newell and Sorell)

1993 (2 Feb–10 Aug). **Greetings Stamps. "Gift Giving".** *Two phosphor bands. P 15 × 14 (with one elliptical hole in each vertical side).*

1644	1074	(1st) gold, greenish yellow, magenta, pale brown, lt blue & black		40	45
		a. Booklet pane. Nos. 1644/53		3.50	
1645	1075	(1st) gold, cream & black		40	45
1646	1076	(1st) gold, greenish yellow, magenta, cream, new blue & black		40	45
1647	1077	(1st) gold, greenish yellow, magenta, cream, new blue & black		40	45
1648	1078	(1st) gold, greenish yellow, magenta, cream, new blue & black		40	45
1649	1079	(1st) gold, greenish yellow, magenta, cream, new blue & black		40	45
		a. Booklet pane. No. 1649 × 4 with margins all round (10 Aug)		2.50	
1650	1080	(1st) gold, greenish yellow, magenta, cream, new blue & black		40	45
1651	1081	(1st) gold, greenish yellow, magenta, cream, new blue & black		40	45
1652	1082	(1st) gold, greenish yellow, magenta, cream new blue & black		40	45
1653	1083	(1st) gold, greenish yellow, magenta, cream, new blue & black		40	45
		Set of 10		3.50	4.00
		First Day Cover			7.50
		Presentation Pack		4.00	
		PHQ Cards (set of 10)		3.00	7.75

Nos. 1644/53 were issued in £2.40 booklets (sold at £2.50 from 1 November 1993), together with a pane of 20 half stamp-sized labels. The stamps and labels were affixed to the booklet cover by a common gutter margin.

Booklet pane No. 1079a comes from the £6 (£5.64) Beatrix Potter Booklet.

Special First Day of Issue Postmarks

British Philatelic Bureau, Edinburgh (No. 1644a) (2 Feb) 8.00
Greetland (No. 1644a) (2 Feb) 8.00
British Philatelic Bureau, Edinburgh (No. 1649a) (10 Aug) 5.00
Keswick (No. 1649a) (10 Aug) 5.00

1084 Decorated Enamel Dial

1085 Escapement, Remontoire and Fusee

1086 Balance, Spring and Temperature Compensator

1087 Back of Movement

(Des H. Brown and D. Penny. Litho Questa)

1993 (16 Feb). **300th Birth Anniv of John Harrison (inventor of the marine chronometer).** *Details of "H4" Clock. Phosphorised paper.* P 14½ × 14.

1654	**1084**	24p. new blue, greenish yellow, magenta, black, grey-black and pale cream	50	50
1655	**1085**	28p. new blue, greenish yellow, magenta, black, grey-black and pale cream	70	70
1656	**1086**	33p. new blue, greenish yellow, magenta, black, grey-black & pale cream	85	85
1657	**1087**	39p. new blue, greenish yellow, magenta, black, grey-black & pale cream	1.00	1.00
		Set of 4	2.75	2.75
		Set of 4 Gutter Pairs	5.50	
		First Day Cover		3.75
		Presentation Pack	4.00	
		PHQ Cards (set of 4)	2.00	4.50

Special First Day of Issue Postmarks

British Philatelic Bureau, Edinburgh......................... 4.00
Greenwich 4.00

1088 Britannia

(Des B. Craddock, adapted Roundel Design Group. Litho (silver die-stamped, braille symbol for "10" embossed) Questa)

1993 (2 Mar). *Granite paper. P* 14 × 14½ *(with two elliptical holes on each horizontal side).*

1658	**1088**	£10 greenish grey, rosine, yellow, new blue, reddish violet, vermilion, violet, brt green and silver	15.00	16.00
		First Day Cover		22.00
		Presentation Pack	15.00	
		PHQ Card	35	22.00

The paper used for No. 1658 contains fluorescent coloured fibre which together with the ink used on the shield, react under U.V. light.

Special First Day of Issue Postmarks

British Philatelic Bureau, Edinburgh......................... 24.00
Windsor 24.00

1089 *Dendrobium hellwigianum*

1090 *Paphiopedilum* Maudiae "Magnificum"

1091 *Cymbidium lowianum*

1092 *Vanda* Rothschildiana

1093 *Dendrobium vexillarius* var *albiviride*

(Des Pandora Sellars)

993 (16 Mar). **14th World Orchid Conference, Glasgow.** *One phosphor band (18p.) or phosphorised paper (others). P* 15 × 14.

659	1089	18p. green, greenish yellow, magenta, pale blue, apple-green & slate	40	40
		a. Imperf (pair)		
660	1090	24p. green, greenish yellow, brt green & grey-black	50	50
661	1091	28p. green, greenish yellow, red, brt turquoise-blue & drab	75	75
662	1092	33p. green, greenish yellow, pale magenta, brt violet, brt green & grey	85	85
663	1093	39p. green, greenish yellow, red, pale olive-yellow, brt green, violet & grey-black	1.10	1.10
		Set of 5	3.25	3.25
		Set of 5 Gutter Pairs	6.50	
		First Day Cover		4.25
		Presentation Pack	4.00	
		PHQ Cards (set of 5)	2.25	5.00

Special First Day of Issue Postmarks

British Philatelic Bureau, Edinburgh	4.50
Glasgow	4.50

1993 (6 Apr-7 Sept). *Booklet Stamps. As T* **913/14,** *but P* 15 × 14 *(with one elliptical hole on each vertical side).*

(a) Photo Harrison

663a	913	(2nd) brt blue (1 centre band) (7 Sept)	30	35
664	914	(1st) brt orange-red (phosphorised paper)	40	45

(b) Litho Questa or Walsall

665	913	(2nd) brt blue (1 centre band)	30	35
		Ey. Phosphor omitted		
666	914	(1st) brt orange-red (2 phosphor bands)	40	45
		Ey. Phosphor omitted		

Nos. 1663a/6 were issued in booklet panes showing perforations on all four edges.

Nos. 1663a comes from Barcode booklet No. HA7, No. 1664 from Barcode booklets Nos. HB5 and HD9, No. 1665 from Barcode booklets Nos. HA6 (Walsall) and HC11 (Questa) and No. 1666 from Barcode booklets Nos. HB6 (Walsall), HD10 (Walsall), HD11 (Questa) and HD12 (Walsall).

On 6 September 1993 Nos. 1665/6 printed in lithography by Questa were made available in sheets, from post offices in Birmingham, Coventry, Falkirk and Milton Keynes. These sheets stamps became available nationally on 5 October 1993.

1993 (27 Apr-14 Dec). *As Nos. X841, etc, but P* 15 × 14 *(with one elliptical hole on each vertical side).*

(a) Photo Enschedé. Two phosphor bands.

Y1667	369	1p. crimson (8.6.93)	10	10
Y1669		4p. new blue (14.12.93.)	10	10
Y1670		5p. dull red-brown (8.6.93)	10	10
Y1671		6p. yellow-olive	10	15

Y1672		10p. dull orange (8.6.93)	15	20
Y1673		20p. turquoise-green (14.12.93.)	30	35
Y1674		29p. grey (26.10.93)	45	50
Y1675		30p. dp olive-grey (27.7.93)	45	50
Y1676		35p. yellow (17.8.93)	55	60
Y1677		36p. brt ultramarine (26.10.93)	55	60
Y1678		38p. rosine (26.10.93)	60	65
Y1679		41p. grey-brown (26.10.93)	65	70
Y1680		50p. ochre (14.12.93.)	75	80

(b) Photo Harrison.

Y1700	369	19p. bistre (1 centre band) (26.10.93)	30	35
Y1701		25p. rose-red (phosphorised paper) (26.10.93)	40	45
		a. Booklet pane. No. Y1701 × 2 plus 2 labels (1.11.93)	80	
Y1702		35p. yellow (phosphorised paper) (1.11.93)	55	60
Y1703		41p. drab (phosphorised paper) (1.11.93)	65	70

(c) Litho Walsall. Two phosphor bands.

Y1750	369	25p. red (1.11.93)	40	45
Y1751		35p. yellow (1.11.93)	55	65
Y1752		41p. drab (1.11.93)	65	70
		First Day Cover (Nos. Y1674, Y1677/9, Y1700/1)		4.25
		Presentation Pack (Nos. Y1674, Y1677/9, Y1700/1)	3.25	

DECIMAL MACHIN WITH ELLIPTICAL PERFORATIONS INDEX

Val. Process and Printer	Colour	Phosphor	Cat No.	Source
1p. photo Enschedé	crimson	2 bands	Y1667	sheets
4p. photo Enschedé	new blue	2 bands	Y1669	sheets
5p. photo Enschedé	dull red-brown	2 bands	Y1670	sheets
6p. photo Enschedé	yellow-olive	2 bands	Y1671	sheets
10p. photo Enschedé	dull orange	2 bands	Y1672	sheets
19p. photo Harrison	bistre	1 centre band	Y1700	sheets, coils
20p. photo Enschedé	turquoise-green	2 bands	Y1673	sheets
25p. photo Harrison	rose-red	phos paper	Y1701	sheets, coils, 50p. booklet (FB67/8), £2 booklet (FW1)
25p. litho Walsall	red	2 bands	Y1750	£1 booklet (FH31/2)
29p. photo Enschedé	grey	2 bands	Y1674	sheets
30p. photo Enschedé	dp olive-grey	2 bands	Y1675	sheets
35p. photo Enschedé	yellow	2 bands	Y1676	sheets
35p. photo Harrison	yellow	phos paper	Y1702	coils
35p. litho Walsall	yellow	2 bands	Y1751	£1.40 booklet (GK5)
36p. photo Enschedé	brt ultramarine	2 bands	Y1677	sheets
38p. photo Enschedé	rosine	2 bands	Y1678	sheets
41p. photo Enschedé	grey-brown	2 bands	Y1679	sheets
41p. photo Harrison	drab	phos paper	Y1703	coils
41p. litho Walsall	drab	2 bands	Y1752	£1.64 booklet (GM1)
50p. photo Enschedé	ochre	2 bands	Y1680	sheets

1094 "Family Group"
(bronze sculpture)
(Henry Moore)

1095 "Kew Gardens"
(lithograph) (Edward
Bawden)

1096 "St. Francis and the
Birds" (Stanley Spencer)

1097 "Still Life: Odyssey
I" (Ben Nicholson)

(Des A. Dastor)

1993 (11 May). **Europa. Contemporary Art.** *Phosphorised paper.*
P 14 × 14½.

1767	**1094**	24p. brownish grey, lemon, magenta, turquoise-blue, & grey-black	40	45
1768	**1095**	28p. brownish grey, buff, lt green, yellow-brown, brt orange, new blue & grey-black	45	50
1769	**1096**	33p. brownish grey, cream, greenish yellow, magenta, new blue & grey-black	50	55
1770	**1097**	39p. brownish grey, cream, yellow-ochre, rose-lilac, red, lt blue & grey-black	60	65
		Set of 4....................................	1.75	2.00
		Set of 4 Gutter Pairs......................	3.75	
		First Day Cover		3.75
		Presentation Pack	2.40	
		PHQ Cards (set of 4)	2.00	4.00

Special First Day of Issue Postmarks

British Philatelic Bureau, Edinburgh	4.00
London SW	4.00

1098 Emperor Claudius
(from gold coin)

1099 Emperor Hadrian
(bronze head)

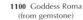

1100 Goddess Roma
(from gemstone)

1101 Christ (Hinton
St. Mary mosaic)

(Des J. Gibbs)

1993 (15 June). **Roman Britain.** *Phosphorised paper with two phosphor bands.* P 14 × 14½.

1771	**1098**	24p. black, pale orange, lt brown & silver	40	45
1772	**1099**	28p. black, greenish yellow, brt rose-red, silver, brt blue & grey-black	45	50
1773	**1100**	33p. black, greenish yellow, brt rose-red, silver & grey	50	55
1774	**1101**	39p. black, greenish yellow, rosine, silver, pale violet & grey...............	60	65
		Set of 4....................................	1.75	2.00
		First Day Cover		3.75
		Presentation Pack	2.40	
		PHQ Cards (set of 4)	1.40	4.00

Special First Day of Issue Postmarks

British Philatelic Bureau, Edinburgh	4.00
Caerllion..	4.00

STAMP MONTHLY

Finest and most informative magazine for all collectors.
Obtainable from your newsagent or by postal subscription –
details on request

1102 *Midland Maid* and other Narrow Boats, Grand Junction Canal

1103 *Yorkshire Lass* and other Humber Keels, Stainforth and Keadby Canal

1104 *Valley Princess* and other Horse-drawn Barges, Brecknock and Abergavenny Canal

1105 Steam Barges, including *Pride of Scotland*, and Fishing Boats, Crinan Canal

(Des T. Lewery. Litho Questa)

1993 (20 July). **Inland Waterways**. *Two phosphor bands. P 14½ × 14.*

1775	**1102**	24p.	new blue, greenish yellow, brt magenta, black, blue, vermilion, brownish grey & sage-green	40	45
1776	**1103**	28p.	new blue, greenish yellow, brt magenta, black, blue, bluish grey, vermilion & sage-green	45	50
1777	**1104**	33p.	new blue, greenish yellow, brt magenta, black, blue, vermilion, greenish grey & sage-green	50	55
1778	**1105**	39p.	new blue, greenish yellow, brt magenta, black, blue, vermilion, sage-green & dull mauve	60	65
			Set of 4	1.75	2.00
			Set of 4 Gutter Pairs	3.75	
			First Day Cover		3.75
			Presentation Pack	2.40	
			PHQ Cards (set of 4)	1.40	4.00

Nos. 1775/8 commemorate the bicentenary of the Acts of Parliament authorising the canals depicted.

1106 Horse Chestnut

1107 Blackberry

1108 Hazel

1109 Rowan

1110 Pear

(Des Charlotte Knox)

1993 (14 Sept). **The Four Seasons. Autumn**. *Fruits and Leaves. One phosphor band (18p.) or phosphorised paper (others). P 15 × 14.*

1779	**1106**	18p.	black, greenish yellow, cerise, brt green, gold & chestnut	30	35
1780	**1107**	24p.	black, lemon, cerise, myrtle-green, gold, brt green & brown	40	45
1781	**1108**	28p.	grey, lemon, emerald, lake-brown & gold	45	50
1782	**1109**	33p.	grey-black, greenish yellow, rosine, lt green, gold & brown	50	55
1783	**1110**	39p.	myrtle-green, greenish yellow, rosine, olive-sepia, gold, apple-green & dp myrtle-green	60	65
			Set of 5	2.00	2.25
			Set of 5 Gutter Pairs	4.25	
			First Day Cover		3.75
			Presentation Pack	2.50	
			PHQ Cards (set of 5)	1.50	4.50

Special First Day of Issue Postmarks

British Philatelic Bureau, Edinburgh	4.00
Gloucester	4.00

Special First Day of Issue Postmarks

British Philatelic Bureau, Edinburgh	4.00
Taunton	4.00

1111 *The Reigate Squire*

1112 *The Hound of the Baskervilles*

1113 *The Six Napoleons*

1114 *The Greek Interpreter*

1115 *The Final Problem*

(Des A. Davidson. Litho Questa)

1993 (12 Oct). **Sherlock Holmes. Centenary of the Publication of "The Final Problem".** *Phosphorised paper.* P 14 × 14½.

1784	**1111**	24p.	new blue, greenish yellow, magenta, black & gold	40	45
			a. Horiz strip. Nos. 1784/8	1.75	2.00
1785	**1112**	24p.	new blue, greenish yellow, magenta, black & gold	40	45
1786	**1113**	24p.	new blue, greenish yellow, magenta, black & gold	40	45
1787	**1114**	24p.	new blue, greenish yellow, magenta, black & gold	40	45

1788	**1115**	24p.	new blue, greenish yellow, magenta, black & gold	40	45
			Set of 5	1.75	2.00
			Gutter strip of 10	3.75	
			First Day Cover		3.75
			Presentation Pack	2.25	
			PHQ Cards (set of 5)	1.50	4.00

Nos. 1785/8 were printed together, *se-tenant*, in horizontal strips of 5 throughout the sheet.

Special First Day of Issue Postmarks

British Philatelic Bureau, Edinburgh	4.00
London NW1	4.00

1116

(Des J. Matthews. Litho Walsall)

1993 (19 Oct). *Self-adhesive Booklet Stamp. Two phosphor bands.* P 14 × 15 *(with one elliptical hole on each vertical side).*

1789	**1116**	(1st)	orange-red	40	45
			a. Booklet pane. No. 1789 × 20	1.25	
			First Day Cover (No. 1789)		1.25
			Presentation Pack (No. 1789a)	7.50	
			PHQ Card	30	1.00

No. 1789 was initially sold at 24p. which was increased to 25p. on 1 November 1993. It was only issued in booklets containing 20 stamps, each surrounded by die-cut perforations.

Special First Day of Issue Postmarks

British Philatelic Bureau, Edinburgh	1.50
Newcastle upon Tyne	1.50

1117 Bob Cratchit and Tiny Tim

1118 Mr. and Mrs. Fezziwig

1119 Scrooge

1120 The Prize Turkey

1121 Mr. Scrooge's Nephew

(Des Q. Blake)

1993 (9 Nov). **Christmas. 150th Anniv of Publication of "A Christmas Carol" by Charles Dickens**. *One phosphor band* (19p.) *or phosphorised paper* (others). P 15 × 14.

1790	**1117**	19p. new blue, yellow, magenta, salmon, brt emerald & grey-black	30	35
		a. Imperf (pair)		
1791	**1118**	25p. yellow-orange, brown- ::, steel-blue, lake-brown, lt green, grey-black & black	40	45
1792	**1119**	30p. cerise, bistre-yellow, dull blue, brown-rose, pale green, grey-black & black	45	50
1793	**1120**	35p. dp turquoise-green, lemon, vermilion, dull ultramarine, Indian red, bluish grey & black	55	60
1794	**1121**	41p. reddish purple, lemon, purple, lt blue, salmon, brt green & black	65	70
		Set of 5	2.10	2.25
		Set of 5 Gutter Pairs	4.50	
		First Day Cover		3.75
		Presentation Pack	2.75	
		PHQ Cards (set of 5)	1.90	5.25

Special First Day of Issue Postmarks

British Phialetelic Bureau, Edinburgh	4.00
Bethlehem, Llandeilo	4.00

1122 Class "5" No. 44957 and Class "B1" No. 61342 on West Highland Line

1123 Class "A1" No. 60149 *Amadis* at Kings Cross

1124 Class "4" No. 43000 on Turntable at Blyth North

1125 Class "4" No. 42455 near Wigan Central

1126 Class "Castle" No. 7002 *Devizes Castle* on Bridge crossing Worcester and Birmingham Canal

(Des B. Delaney)

1994 (18 Jan). **The Age of Steam**. *Railway Photographs by Colin Gifford. One phosphor band* (19p.) *or phosphorised paper with two bands* (others). P 14½.

1795	**1122**	19p. deep blue-green, grey-black and black	30	35
1796	**1123**	25p. slate-lilac, grey-black and black	40	45
1797	**1124**	30p. lake-brown, grey-black and black	45	50
1798	**1125**	35p. deep claret, grey-black and black	55	60
1799	**1126**	41p. indigo, grey-black and black	65	70
		Set of 5	2.10	2.25
		Set of 5 Gutter Pairs	4.50	
		First Day Cover		2.40
		Presentation Pack	2.75	
		PHQ Cards (set of 5)	1.90	4.00

Nos. 1796/9 are on phosphorised paper and also show two phosphor bands.

Special First Day of Issue Postmarks

British Philatelic Bureau, Edinburgh 2.50
York 2.50

1127 Dan Dare and the Mekon

1128 The Three Bears

1129 Rupert the Bear

1130 Alice (*Alice in Wonderland*)

1131 Noggin and the Ice Dragon

1132 Peter Rabbit posting Letter

1133 Red Riding Hood and Wolf

1134 Orlando the Marmalade Cat

1135 Biggles

1136 Paddington Bear on Station

(Des Newell and Sorrell)

1994 (1 Feb). **Greetings Stamps. "Messages".** *Two phosphor bands.* P 15 × 14 (*with one elliptical hole on each vertical side*).

1800	**1127**	(1st)	gold, greenish yellow, bright purple, bistre-yellow, new blue & black	40	45
		a.	Booklet pane. Nos. 1800/9	3.50	
1801	**1128**	(1st)	gold, greenish yellow, bright purple, bistre-yellow, new blue & black	40	45
1802	**1129**	(1st)	gold, greenish yellow, bright purple, bistre-yellow, new blue & black	40	45
1803	**1130**	(1st)	gold, bistre-yellow & black	40	45
1804	**1131**	(1st)	gold, greenish yellow, bright purple, bistre-yellow, new blue & black	40	45
1805	**1132**	(1st)	gold, greenish yellow, bright purple, bistre-yellow, new blue & black	40	45
1806	**1133**	(1st)	gold, greenish yellow, bright purple, bistre-yellow, new blue & black	40	45
1807	**1134**	(1st)	gold, greenish yellow, bright purple, bistre-yellow, new blue & black	40	45
1808	**1135**	(1st)	gold, greenish yellow, bright purple, bistre-yellow, new blue & black	40	45
1809	**1136**	(1st)	gold, greenish yellow, bright purple, bistre-yellow, new blue & black	40	45
			Set of 10	3.50	4.00
			First Day Cover		5.50
			Presentation Pack	4.25	
			PHQ Cards (set of 10)	3.75	7.50

Nos. 1800/9 were only issued in £2.50, stamp booklets, together with a pane of 20 half stamp-sized labels. The stamps and labels were affixed to the booklet cover by a common gutter margin

Special First Day of Issue Postmarks

British Philatelic Bureau, Edinburgh 5.75
Penn, Wolverhampton 5.75

1137 Castell Y Waun (Chirk Castle), Clwyd, Wales

1138 Ben Arkle, Sutherland, Scotland

1139 Mourne Mountains, County Down, Northern Ireland

1140 Dersingham, Norfolk, England

1141 Dolwyddelan, Gwynedd, Wales

1994 (1 Mar). **25th Anniv of Investiture of the Prince of Wales. Paintings by Prince Charles.** *One phosphor band* (19p.) *or phosphorised paper* (*others*). P 15 × 14.

1810	**1137**	19p. grey-black, greenish yellow, magenta, new blue, black & silver....	30	35
1811	**1138**	25p. grey-black, orange-yellow, bright magenta, new blue, silver & black....	40	45
1812	**1139**	30p. grey-black, greenish yellow, magenta, new blue, silver & black....	45	50
1813	**1140**	35p. grey-black, greenish yellow, magenta, new blue, silver & black....	55	60
1814	**1141**	41p. grey-black, lemon, magenta, new blue, silver & black	65	70
		Set of 5	2.10	2.40
		First Day Cover...........................		3.25
		Presentation Pack	3.75	
		PHQ Cards (set of 5)	1.90	4.50

Special First Day of Issue Postmarks

British Philatelic Bureau, Edinburgh 3.50
Caernarfon 3.50

ROYAL MAIL POSTAGE LABELS

These imperforate labels were issued as an experiment by the Post Office. Special microprocessor controlled machines were installed at post offices in Cambridge, London, Shirley (Southampton) and Windsor to provide an after-hours sales service to the public. The machines printed and dispensed the labels according to the coins inserted and the buttons operated by the customer. Values were initially available in ½p. steps to 16p. and in addition, the labels were sold at philatelic counters in two packs containing either 3 values (3½, 12½, 16p.) or 32 values (½p. to 16p.).

From 28 August 1984 the machines were adjusted to provide values up to 17p. After 31 December 1984 labels including ½p. values were withdrawn. The machines were taken out of service on 30 April 1985.

Machine postage-paid impression in red on phosphorised paper with grey-green background design. No watermark. Imperforate.

1984 (1 May–28 Aug).

Set of 32 (½p. to 16p.)	20.00	30.00
Set of 3 (3½p., 12½p., 16p.)	4.00	4.50
Set of 3 on First Day Cover (1.5.84)		6.50
Set of 2 (16½p., 17p.) (28.8.84)	6.00	6.00

REGIONAL ISSUES

I. CHANNEL ISLANDS

C 1 Gathering Vraic

C 2 Islanders gathering Vraic

(Des J. R. R. Stobie (1d.) or from drawing by E. Blampied (2½d.). Photo Harrison)

1948 (10 May). *Third Anniv of Liberation.* W **127** *of Great Britain.* P 15 × 14.

C1	**C 1**	1d. scarlet	20	20
C2	**C 2**	2½d. ultramarine	30	30
		First Day Cover		18.00

PRINTERS (£ s. d. stamps of all regions):—Photo Harrison & Sons. Portrait by Dorothy Wilding Ltd.

DATES OF ISSUE. Conflicting dates of issue have been announced for some of the regional issues, partly explained by the stamps being released on different dates by the Philatelic Bureau in Edinburgh or the Philatelic Counter in London and in the regions. We have adopted the practice of giving the earliest known dates, since once released the stamps could have been used anywhere in the U.K.

II. NORTHERN IRELAND

N 1   N 2   N 3

(Des W. Hollywood (3d., 4d., 5d.), L. Pilton (6d., 9d.), T. Collins (1s. 3d., 1s. 6d.))

1958–67. W 179. P 15 × 14.

N11	N 1	3d. deep lilac (18.8.58)	20	10
		p. One centre phosphor band (9.6.67)	20	15
N12		4d. ultramarine (7.2.66)	20	15
		p. Two phosphor bands (10.67)	20	15
N13	N 2	6d. deep claret (29.9.58)	20	20
N14		9d. bronze-green (2 phosphor bands) (1.3.67)	30	50
N15	N 3	1s. 3d. green (29.9.58)	30	50
N16		1s. 6d. grey-blue (2 phosphor bands) (1.3.67)	30	50
		Ey. Phosphor omitted	£200	

First Day Covers

18.8.58	3d. (*N11*)	20.00
29.9.58	6d., 1s. 3d. (*N13, N15*)	25.00
7.2.66	4d. (*N12*)	4.00
1.3.67	9d., 1s. 6d. (*N14, N16*)	1.50

For Nos. N11, 3 and 5 in Presentation Pack, see below Wales No. W6.

1968–69. *No watermark. Chalk-surfaced paper. One centre phosphor band (Nos. N18/9) or two phosphor bands (others). Gum arabic (No. N17) or PVA gum (others).* P 15 × 14.

NI 7	N 1	4d. dp brt blue (27.6.68)	20	15
		Ev. PVA gum* (23.10.68)	7·00	
NI 8		4d. olive-sepia (4.9.68)	20	15
		Ey. Phosphor omitted	£200	
NI 9		4d. brt vermilion (26.2.69)	20	20
		Ey. Phosphor omitted	4.50	
NI10		5d. royal blue (4.9.68)	20	20
		Ey. Phosphor omitted	25.00	
NI11	N 3	1s. 6d. grey-blue (20.5.69)	2.00	3.00
		Ey. Phosphor omitted		

4.9.68	First Day Cover (*NI8, NI10*)	50
	Presentation Pack (containing Nos. NI1p, NI4/6, NI8/10) (9.12.70)	3.00

*No. NI7Ev was never issued in Northern Ireland. After No. NI7 (gum arabic) had been withdrawn from Northern Ireland but whilst still on sale at the philatelic counters elsewhere, about fifty sheets with PVA gum were sold over the London Philatelic counter on 23 October, 1968, and some were also on sale at the British Philatelic Exhibition Post Office.

For full information on all future British issues, collectors should write to the British Post Office Philatelic Bureau, 20 Brandon Street, Edinburgh EH3 5TT

N 4

I	II

Redrawn design of Type N 4 (litho ptgs.)

Two Types of Crown

Type I:– Crown with all pearls individually drawn.

Type II:–Crown with clear outlines, large pearls and strong white line below them. First 3 pearls at left are joined, except on Nos. NI39 and NI48.

The following stamps printed in lithography show a screened background behind and to the left of the emblem: 11½p., 12½p., 14p. (No. NI38), 15½p., 16p., 18p., (No. NI45), 19½p., 22p., (No. NI53) and 28p. (NI62). The 13p. and 17p. (No. NI43) also showed screened backgrounds in Type I, but changed to solid backgrounds for Type II. The 31p. had a solid background in Type I, but changed to a screened background for Type II. All other values printed in lithography have solid backgrounds.

(Des J. Matthews after plaster cast by Arnold Machin)

1971 (17 July)–**93**. *Decimal Currency. Chalk-surfaced paper. Type N **4**.*

(a) *Photo Harrison. With phosphor bands.* P 15 × 14

NI12	2½p. brt magenta (1 centre band)	75	25
NI13	3p. ultramarine (2 bands)	40	15
	Ey. Phosphor omitted	20.00	
NI14	3p. ultramarine (1 centre band) (23.1.74).	20	15
NI15	3½p. olive-grey (2 bands)(23.1.74)	20	20
NI16	3½p. olive-grey (1 centre band) (6.11.74)...	20	25
NI17	4½p. grey-blue (2 bands) (6.11.74)	25	25
NI18	5p. reddish violet (2 bands)	1.00	1.00
NI19	5½p. violet (2 bands) (23.1.74)	20	20
	Ey. Phosphor omitted	£225	
NI20	5½p. violet (1 centre band) (21.5.75)	20	20
NI21	6½p. greenish blue (1 centre band) (14.1.76)	20	20
NI22	7p. purple-brown (1 centre band) (18.1.78)	35	25
NI23	7½p. chestnut (2 bands)	2.00	2.00
	Ey. Phosphor omitted	55.00	
NI24	8p. rosine (2 bands) (23.1.74)	30	30
	Ey. Phosphor omitted	45.00	
NI25	8½p. yellow-green (2 bands) (14.1.76)	30	30
NI26	9p. dp violet (2 bands) (18.1.78)	30	30
	Ey. Phosphor omitted	25.00	
NI27	10p. orange-brown (2 bands) (20.10.76)....	35	35
NI28	10p. orange-brown (1 centre band) (23.7.80)	35	35
NI29	10½p. steel-blue (2 bands) (18.1.78)	40	40
NI30	11p. scarlet (2 bands) (20.10.76)	40	40
	Ey. Phosphor omitted	4.50	

(b) *Photo Harrison. On phosphorised paper.* P 15 × 14

NI31	12p. yellowish green (23.7.80)	50	45
NI32	13½p. purple-brown (23.7.80)	60	70
NI33	15p. ultramarine (23.7.80)	60	50

(c) *Litho Questa (Type II unless otherwise stated). P 14 (11½p., 12½p., 14p., (No. NI38), 15½p., 16p., 18p. (NI45), 19½p., 20½p., 22p, (NI53), 26p,* (NI60), *28p.* (NI62) *or 15 × 14 (others).*

NI34	11½p. drab (Type I) (1 side band) (8.4.81)	80	60
NI35	12p. brt emerald (1 side band) (7.1.86)	50	50
NI36	12½p. lt emerald (Type I) (1 side band) (24.2.82)	50	40
	a. Perf 15 × 14 (28.2.84)	4.50	4.50
NI37	13p. pale chestnut (Type I) (1 side band) (23.10.84)	70	35
	Ea. Type II (28.11.86)	60	30
	Ey. Phosphor omitted (Type I)		
NI38	14p. grey-blue (Type I) (phosphorised paper) (8.4.81)	70	50
NI39	14p. dp blue (1 centre band) (8.11.88)	55	35
NI40	15p. brt blue (1 centre band) (28.11.89)	60	30
NI41	15½p. pale violet (Type I) (phosphorised paper) (24.2.82)	80	65
NI42	16p. drab (Type I) (phosphorised paper) (27.4.83)	90	1.00
	a. Perf 15 × 14 (28.2.84)	7.50	5.00
NI43	17p. grey-blue (Type I) (phosphorised paper) (23.10.84)	80	40
	Ea. Type II (9.9.86)	35.00	16.00
NI44	17p. dp blue (1 centre band) (4.12.90)	50	40
NI45	18p. dp violet (Type I) (phosphorised paper) (8.4.81)	80	80
NI46	18p. dp olive-grey (phosphorised paper) (6.1.87)	80	70
NI47	18p. brt green (1 centre band) (3.12.91)	30	35
	a. Perf 14 (31.12.92*)	75	75
NI48	18p. brt green (1 side band) (10.8.93)	2.00	2.00
	I. Booklet pane. Nos. NI48, NI59, S61, S71, W49Eb and W60 with margins all round	10.00	
NI49	19p. brt orange-red (phosphorised paper) (8.11.88)	60	60
NI50	19½p. olive-grey (Type I) (phosphorised paper) (24.2.82)	1.75	1.75
NI51	20p. brownish black (phosphorised paper) (28.11.89)	30	30
NI52	20½p. ultramarine (Type I) (phosphorised paper) (27.4.83)	4.00	4.00
NI53	22p. blue (Type I) (phosphorised paper) (8.4.81)	90	1.10
NI54	22p. yellow-green (Type I) (phosphorised paper) (23.10.84)	85	1.10
NI55	22p. brt orange-red (phosphorised paper) (4.12.90)	85	40
NI56	23p. brt green (phosphorised paper) (8.11.88)	80	1.10
NI57	24p. Indian red (phosphorised paper) (28.11.89)	70	1.10
NI58	24p. chestnut (phosphorised paper) (3.12.91)	40	45
NI59	24p. chestnut (2 bands) (10.8.93)	2.00	2.00
NI60	26p. rosine (Type I) (phosphorised paper) (24.2.82)	90	1.25
	a. Perf 15 × 14 (Type II) (27.1.87)	2.00	2.00
NI61	26p. drab (phosphorised paper) (4.12.90)	40	45
NI62	28p. dp violet-blue (Type I) (phosphorised paper) (27.4.83)	1.00	1.00
	a. Perf 15 × 14 (Type II) (27.1.87)	80	80
NI63	28p. dp bluish grey (phosphorised paper) (3.12.91)	45	50

NI64	31p. brt purple (Type I) (phosphorised		
	paper) (23.10.84)	1.25	1.10
	Ea. Type II (14.4.87)	1.40	1.25
NI65	32p. greenish blue (phosphorised paper)		
	(8.11.88)	1.10	1.10
NI66	34p. dp bluish grey (phosphorised paper)		
	(28.11.89)	1.00	1.00
NI67	37p. rosine (phosphorised paper) (4.12.90)	1.00	1.10
NI68	39p. brt mauve (phosphorised paper)		
	(3.12.91)	60	65

*Earliest known date of use.

No. NI47a was caused by the use of a reserve perforating machine for some printings in the second half of 1992.

From 1972 printing were made on the fluorescent white paper and from 1973 most printings had dextrin added to the PVA gum (see notes after 1971 Decimal Machin issue).

First Day Covers

7.7.71	2½p., 3p., 5p., 7½p. (NI12/13, NI18, NI23)	4.50
23.1.74	3p., 3½p., 5½p., 8p. (NI14/15, NI19, NI24)	1.50
6.11.74	4½p. (NI17)	1.00
14.1.76	6½p., 8½p. (NI21, NI25)	60
20.10.76	10p., 11p. (NI27, NI30)	1.00
18.1.78	7p., 9p., 10½p. (NI22, NI26, NI29)	1.00
23.7.80	12p., 13½p., 15p. (NI31/3)	2.00
8.4.81	11½p., 14p., 18p., 22p. (NI34, NI38, NI45, NI53)	2.00
24.2.82	12½p., 15½p., 19½p., 26p. (NI36, NI41, NI50, NI60)	4.25
27.4.83	16p., 20½p., 28p. (NI42, NI52, NI62) ..	6.50
23.10.84	13p., 17p., 22p., 31p. (NI37, NI43, NI54, NI64)	4.50
7.1.86	12p. (NI35)	1.25
6.1.87	18p. (NI46)	2.00
8.11.88	14p., 19p., 23p., 32p. (NI39, NI49, NI56, NI65)	4.50
28.11.89	15p., 20p., 24p., 34p. (NI40, NI51, NI57, NI66)	4.00
4.12.90	17p., 22p., 26p., 37p. (NI44, NI55, NI61, NI67)	4.50
3.12.91	18p., 24p., 28p., 39p. (NI47, NI58, NI63, NI68)	4.00

Presentation Packs

7.7.71	2½p., 3p. (2 bands), 5p., 7½p. (Nos. NI12/13, NI18, NI23)	4.00
29.5.74	3p. (1 centre band), 3½p. (2 bands) or (1 centre band), 5½p. (2 bands) or (1 centre band), 8p. (Nos. NI14, NI15 or NI16, NI19 or NI20, NI24). The 4½p. (No. NI17) was added later	2.25
20.10.76	6½p., 8½p., 10p. (2 bands), 11p. (Nos. NI21, NI25, NI27, NI30)	1.75
28.10.81	7p., 9p., 10½p., 12p. (photo), 13½p., 15p. (photo), 11½p., 14p. grey-blue, 18p. dp violet, 22p, blue (Nos. NI22, NI26, NI29, NI31/4, NI38, NI45, NI53)..	7.00
3.8.83	10p. (1 centre band), 12½p., 16p., 20½p., 26p. rosine, 28p. dp violet-blue (Nos. NI28, NI36, NI42, NI52, NI60, NI62)	7.00
23.10.84	10p. (1 centre band), 13p., 16p., 17p. grey-blue, 22p. yellow-green, 26p. rosine, 28p. dp violet-blue, 31p. (Nos. NI28, NI37, NI42a, NI43, NI54, NI60, NI62)	10.00

3.3.87	12p. (litho), 13p., 17p. grey-blue, 18p. dp olive- grey, 22p. yellow-green, 26p rosine, 28p. dp violet-biue, 31p. (Nos. NI35, NI37, NI43, NI46, NI54, NI60, NI62, NI64)	9.00

Presentation Packs for Northern Ireland, Scotland and Wales.

8.11.88	14p. dp blue, 19p., 23p., 32p. (Nos. NI39, NI48, NI56, NI65), 14p. (1 centre band), 19p. (phosphorised paper), 23p. (phosphorised paper), 32p. (Nos. S54, S62, S67, S77), 14p. dp blue, 19p., 23p., 32p. (Nos. W40, W50, W57, W66)	8.00
28.11.89	15p. (litho), 20p., 24p. Indian red, 34p. (Nos. NI40, NI51, NI57, NI66), 15p. (litho), 20p., 24p. Indian red, 34p. (Nos. S56, S64, S69, S78), 15p. (litho), 20p., 24p. Indian red, 34p. (Nos. W41, W52, W58, W67)	7.50
4.12.90	17p. dp blue, 22p. brt orange-red, 26p. drab, 37p. (Nos. NI44, NI55, NI61, NI67), 17p. dp blue, 22p. brt orange-red, 26p. drab, 37p., (Nos. S58, S66, S73, S79), 17p. dp blue, 22p. brt orange-red, 26p. drab, 37p. (Nos. W45, W56, W62, W68)	8.50
3.12.91	18p. brt green, 24p. chestnut, 28p. dp bluish grey, 39p. (Nos. NI47, NI58, NI63, NI68), 18p. brt green, 24p. chestnut, 28p. dp bluish grey, 39p. (Nos. S60, S70, S75, S80), 18p. brt green, 24p. chestnut, 28p. dp bluish grey, 39p. (W48, W59, W64, W69)	5.50

(Des J. Matthews after plaster cast by Arnold Machin. Litho Questa)

1993 (7 Dec). *Chalk-surfaced paper. One centre phosphor band (19p.) or phosphorised paper (others). P 15 × 14 (with one elliptical hole on each vertical side).*

NI69	N **4**	19p. bistre	30	35
NI70		25p. red	40	45
NI71		30p. deep olive-grey	45	50
NI72		41p. grey-brown	65	70

First Day Cover

7.12.93	19p., 25p., 30p., 41p., (NI69/72)........	2.75

Presentation Packs for Northern Ireland, Scotland and Wales

7.12.93	19p., 25p., 30p., 41p., each × 3 (Nos. NI69/72, S81/4, W70/3)	5.75

III. SCOTLAND

S 1   S 2   S 3

(Des. G. Huntly (3d., 4d., 5d.), J. Fleming (6d., 9d.), A. Imrie (1s. 3d., 1s. 6d.))

1958–67. *W* 179. *P* 15 × 14.

S1	S 1	3d. dp lilac (18.8.58)	20	15
		p. Two phosphor bands (29.1.63)	12.00	1.00
		pa. One side phosphor band (30.4.65)....	20	25
		pb. One centre phosphor band (9.11.67)	20	15
S2		4d. ultramarine (7.2.66)	20	10
		p. Two phosphor bands	20	20
S3	S 2	6d. dp claret (29.9.58)	20	15
		p. Two phosphor bands (29.1.63)	20	25
S4		9d. bronze-green (2 phosphor bands) (1.3.67)	30	30
S5	S 3	1s. 3d. green (29.9.58)	30	30
		p. Two phosphor bands (29.1.63)	30	30
S6		1s. 6d. grey-blue (2 phosphor bands) (1.3.67)	35	30

First Day Covers

18.8.58	3d. (S1)	6.00
29.9.58	6d., 1s. 3d. (S3, S5)	12.00
7.2.66	4d. (S2)	4.00
1.3.67	9d., 1s. 6d. (S4, S6)	1.50

The one phosphor band on No. S1pa was produced by printing broad phosphor bands across alternate vertical perforations. Individual stamps show the band at right or left (same prices either way).

For Nos. S1, 3 and 5 in Presentation Pack, see below Wales No. W6.

1967–70. *No watermark. Chalk-surfaced paper. One centre phosphor band (S7, S9/10) or two phosphor bands (others). Gum arabic (Nos. S7, S8) or PVA gum (others). P* 15 × 14.

S 7	S 1	3d. dp lilac (16.5.68)	10	15
		Ey. Phosphor omitted	5.50	
		Ev. PVA gum	10	
		Eya. Phosphor omitted (No. S7Ev)	2.50	
S 8		4d. dp brt blue (28.11.67)	10	15
		Ey. Phosphor omitted	7.00	
		Ev. PVA gum (25.7.68)	10	
S 9		4d. olive-sepia (4.9.68)	10	10
		Ey. Phosphor omitted	1.75	
S10		4d. brt vermilion (26.2.69)	10	10
		Ey. Phosphor omitted	1.75	
S11		5d. royal blue (4.9.68)	20	10
		Ey. Phosphor omitted	42.00	
S12	S 2	9d. bronze-green (28.9.70)	5.00	5.50
		Ey. Phosphor omitted	£140	
S13	S 3	1s. 6d. grey-blue (12.12.68)	1.40	1.00
		Ey. Phosphor omitted	£110	

4.9.68	First Day Cover (S9, S11)	50
	Presentation Pack (containing Nos. S3, S5p., S7, S9/13) (9.12.70)	13.00

STAMP MONTHLY

Finest and most informative magazine for all collectors. Obtainable from your newsagent or by postal subscription – details on request

S 4

I   II

Redrawn design of Type S 4 (litho ptgs.)

The introduction of the redrawn lion took place in 1983 when Waddington's had the contract and therefore the 13, 17, 22 and 31p. exist in both types and perforated 14. The Questa printings, perforated 15 × 14, are all Type II.

The Types of Lion

Type I:– The eye and jaw appear larger and there is no line across the bridge of the nose.

Type II:– The tongue is thick at the point of entry to the mouth and the eye is linked to the background by a solid line.

The following stamps printed in lithography show a screened background behind and to the left of the emblem: 12½p., 15½p., 16p., 19½p., 28p. (Nos. S50 and S74) and 31p. (Nos. S51 and S76). The 13p. and 17p. (No. S43) also show screened backgrounds for both Type I and II of the John Waddington printings, but changed to solid backgrounds for the Questa Type II. All other values printed in lithography have solid backgrounds.

(Des J. Matthews after plaster cast by Arnold Machin)

1971 (7 July)**–93.** *Decimal Currency. Chalk-surfaced paper. Type S* **4.**

(a) Photo Harrison. With phosphor bands. P 15 x 14

S14	2½p. brt magenta (1 centre band)	25	15
	Ey. Phosphor omitted	3.50	
	Eg. Gum arabic (22.9.72)	20	
S15	3p. ultramarine (2 bands)	30	15
	Ey. Phosphor omitted	5.50	
	Eg. Gum arabic (14.12.72)	30	
	Ega. Imperf (pair)	£400	
S16	3p. ultramarine (1 centre band) (23.1.74)	15	15
S17	3½p. olive-grey (2 bands) (23.1.74)	20	20
	Ey. Phosphor omitted	20.00	
S18	3½p. olive-grey (1 centre band) (6.11.74)	20	20
S19	4½p. grey-blue (6.11.74)	25	20
S20	5p. reddish violet (2 bands)	1.25	1.25
S21	5½p. violet (2 bands) (23.1.74)	20	20
S22	5½p. violet (1 centre band) (21.5.75)	20	20
	a. Imperf (pair)	£350	
S23	6½p. greenish blue (1 centre band) (14.1.76)	20	20
S24	7p. purple-brown (1 centre band) (18.1.78)	25	25
S25	7½p. chestnut (2 bands)	1.50	1.50
	Ey. Phosphor omitted	4.50	
S26	8p. rosine (2 bands) (23.1.74)	30	40
S27	8½p. yellow-green (2 bands) (14.1.76)	30	30
S28	9p. dp violet (2 bands) (18.1.78)	30	30
S29	10p. orange-brown (2 bands) (20.10.76)....	35	30

S30	10p. orange-brown (1 centre band) (23.7.80)	35	35
S31	10½p. steel-blue (2 bands) (18.1.78)	45	35
S32	11p. scarlet (2 bands) (20.10.76)	45	35
	Ey. Phosphor omitted	1.75	

(b) Photo Harrison. On phosphorised paper. P 15 × 14

S33	12p. yellowish green (23.7.80)	50	30
S34	13½p. purple-brown (23.7.80)	60	65
S35	15p. ultramarine (23.7.80)	60	45

(c) Litho J.W. (Type I unless otherwise stated). One side phosphor band (11½p., 12p., 12½p., 13p.) or phosphorised paper (others). P 14

S36	11½p. drab (8.4.81)	85	60
S37	12p. brt emerald (Type II) (7.1.86)	90	70
S38	12½p. lt emerald (24.2.82)	50	40
S39	13p. pale chestnut (Type I) (23.10.84)	80	30
	Ea. Type II (1.85)	2.00	50
S40	14p. grey-blue (8.4.81)	60	50
S41	15½p. pale violet (24.2.82)	70	65
S42	16p. drab (Type II) (27.4.83)	70	45
S43	17p. grey-blue (Type I) (23.10.84)	3.25	2.00
	Ea. Type II (1.85)	1.25	1.00
S44	18p. dp violet (8.4.81)	80	80
S45	19½p. olive-grey (24.2.82)	1.75	1.75
S46	20½p. ultramarine (Type II) (27.4.83)	4.00	4.00
S47	22p. blue (8.4.81)	80	1.10
S48	22p. yellow-green (Type I) (23.10.84)	1.75	1.10
	Ea. Type II (1.86)	3.50	1.25
S49	26p. rosine (24.2.82)	1.00	1.10
S50	28p. dp violet-blue (Type II) (27.4.83)	1.00	80
S51	31p. brt purple (Type I) (23.10.84)	1.75	1.10
	Ea. Type II (4.12.85)	85.00	40.00

(d) Litho Questa (Type II). P 15 × 14

S52	12p. brt emerald (1 side band) (29.4.86)	1.50	1.00
S53	13p. pale chestnut (1 side band) (4.11.86)	70	30
S54	14p. dp blue (1 centre band) (8.11.88)	40	30
	l. Booklet pane. No. S54 × 6 with margins all round (21.3.89)	2.50	
S55	14p. dp blue (1 side band) (21.3.89)	60	1.00
	l. Booklet pane. No. S55 × 5, S63 × 2, S68 and centre label with margins all round	9.00	
	la. Error. Booklet pane imperf		
S56	15p. brt blue (1 centre band) (28.11.89)	50	30
	a. Imperf (three sides) (blk. of four)		
S57	17p. grey-blue (phosphorised paper) (29.4.86)	3.50	2.00
S58	17p. dp blue (1 centre band) (4.12.90)	50	35
S59	18p. dp olive-grey (phosphorised paper) (6.1.87)	80	1.50
S60	18p. brt green (1 centre band) (3.12.91)	30	35
	a. Perf (26.9.92*)	30	35
S61	18p. brt green (2 bands) (10.8.93)	2.00	2.00
S62	19p. brt orange-red (phosphorised paper) (8.11.88)	60	45
	l. Booklet pane. No. S62 × 9 with margins all round (21.3.89)	5.00	
	m. Booklet pane. No. S62 × 6 with margins all round (21.3.89)	3.00	
S63	19p. brt orange-red (2 bands) (21.3.89)	1.40	1.40
S64	20p. brownish black (phosphorised paper) (28.11.89)	60	30
S65	22p. yellow-green (phosphorised paper) (27.1.87)	1.00	1.10
S66	22p. brt orange-red (phosphorised paper) (4.12.90)	90	40
S67	23p. brt green (phosphorised paper) (8.11.88)	90	1.10
S68	23p. brt green (2 bands) (21.3.89)	5.50	5.50

S69	24p. Indian red (phosphorised paper) (28.11.89)	70	70
S70	24p. chestnut (phosphorised paper) (3.12.91)	40	45
	a. Perf 14 (10.92*)	75	75
S71	24p. chestnut (2 bands) (10.8.93)	2.00	2.00
S72	26p. rosine (phosphorised paper) (27.1.87)	1.50	1.50
S73	26p. drab (phosphorised paper) (4.12.90)	70	70
S74	28p. dp violet-blue (phosphorised paper) (27.1.87)	85	75
S75	28p. dp bluish grey (phosphorised paper) (3.12.91)	45	50
	a. Perf 14 (18.2.93*)	1.00	1.00
S76	31p. brt purple (phosphorised paper) (29.4.86)	1.50	1.50
S77	32p. greenish blue (phosphorised paper) (8.11.88)	1.10	1.00
S78	34p. dp bluish grey (phosphorised paper) (28.11.89)	1.00	1.00
S79	37p. rosine (phosphorised paper) (4.12.90)	1.00	1.00
S80	39p. brt mauve (phosphorised paper) (3.12.91)	60	65
	a. Perf 14 (11.92)	1.60	1.00

*Earliest known date of use.

No. S56a occurred in the second vertical row of two sheets. It is best collected as a block of four including the left-hand vertical pair imperforate on three sides.

Nos. S60a, S70a, S75a and S80a were caused by the use of a reserve perforating machine for some printings in the second half of 1992.

From 1972 printings were on fluorescent white paper. From 1973 most printings had dextrin added (see notes after the 1971 Decimal Machin issue).

First Day Covers

7.7.71	2½p., 3p., 5p., 7½p. (S14/15, S20, S25)	2.50
23.1.74	3p., 3½p., 5½p., 8p. (S16/17, S21, S26)	1.50
6.11.74	4½p. (S19)	1.00
14.1.76	6½p., 8½p. (S23, S27)	60
20.10.76	10p., 11p. (S29, S32)	75
18.1.78	7p., 9p., 10½p. (S24, S28, S31)	75
23.7.80	12p., 13½p., 15p. (S33/5)	1.75
8.4.81	11½p., 14p., 18p., 22p. (S36, S40, S44, S47)	1.75
24.2.82	12½p., 15½p., 19½p., 26p. (S38, S41, S45, S49)	3.75
27.4.83	16p., 20½p., 28p. (S42, S46, S50)	6.00
23.10.84	13p., 17p., 22p., 31p. (S39, S43, S48, S51)	4.50
7.1.86	12p. (S37)	1.25
6.1.87	18p. (S59)	2.00
8.11.88	14p., 19p., 23p., 32p. (S54, S62, S67, S77)	4.50
21.3.89	Scots Connection se-tenant pane 14p., 19p., 23p. (S551)	8.00
28.11.89	15p., 20p., 24p., 34p. (S56, S64, S69, S78)	4.00
4.12.90	17p., 22p., 26p., 37p. (S58, S66, S73, S79)	4.50
3.12.91	18p., 24p., 28p., 39p. (S60, S70, S75, S80)	4.00

Presentation Packs

7.7.71	2½p., 3p. (2 bands), 5p., 7½p. (Nos. S14/15, S20, S25)	4.00
29.5.74	3p. (1 centre band), 3½p. (2 bands) or (1 centre band), 5½p. (2 bands) or (1 centre band), 8p. (Nos. S16, S17 or S18, S21 or S22, S26). The 4½p. (No. S19) was added later	2.25
20.10.76	6½p., 8½p., 10p. (2 bands), 11p. (Nos. S23, S27, S29, S32)	1.75

28.10.81	7p., 9p., 10½p., 12p. (photo), 13½p., 15p. (photo), 11½p., 14p grey-blue, 18p. dp violet, 22p. blue (Nos. S24, S28, S31, S33/6, S40, S44, S47)	7.00	
3.8.83	10p. (1 centre band), 12½p., 16p., 20½p., 26p. (J.W.), 28p. (J.W.), (Nos. S30, S38, S42, S46, S49/50)	7.00	
23.10.84	10p. (1 centre band), 13p. (J.W.), 16p., 17p. (J.W.), 22p. yellow-green, 26p. (J.W.), 28p. (J.W.), 31p. (J.W.) (Nos. S30, S39, S42/3, S48/51)	9.50	
3.3.87	12p. (litho), 13p. (Questa), 17p. grey-blue (Questa), 18p. dp olive-grey, 22p. yellow-green, 26p. rosine (Questa), 28p. dp violet-blue (Questa), 31p. (Questa) (Nos. S52/3, S57, S59, S65, S72, S74, S76)	9.00	

Presentation Packs containing stamps of Northern Ireland, Scotland and Wales are listed after those in Northern Ireland.

1977–78. EXPERIMENTAL MACHINE PACKETS. These are small cartons containing loose stamps for sale in vending machines. The experiment was confined to the Scottish Postal Board area, where six vending machines were installed, the first becoming operational in Dundee about February 1977.

The cartons carry labels inscribed "ROYAL MAIL STAMPS", their total face value (30p. or 60p.) and their contents.

At first the 30p. packet contained two 6½p. and two 8½p. Scottish Regional stamps and the 60p. packet had four of each. The stamps could be in pairs or blocks, but also in strips or singles.

With the change in postal rates on 13 June 1977 these packets were withdrawn on 11 June and on the 13 June the contents were changed, giving three 7p. and one 9p. for the 30p. packet and double this for the 60p. packet. However, this time ordinary British Machin stamps were used. Moreover the Edinburgh machine, situated in an automatic sorting area, was supplied with 7p. stamps with two phosphor bands instead of the new centre band 7p. stamps, despite instructions having been given to withdraw the two band stamps. However, the demand for these packets was too great to be filled and by 27 June the machine was closed down. It was brought back into use on 16 August 1977, supplying 7p. stamps with the centre band.

The 6½p. and 8½p. Scottish Regional packets were put on sale at the Edinburgh Philatelic Bureau in June 1977 and withdrawn in April 1978. The packets with the 7p. and 9p. Machin stamps were put on sale at the Bureau in June 1977 and withdrawn in December 1978.

Such machine packets are outside the scope of this catalogue.

(Des J. Matthews after plaster cast by Arnold Machin. Litho Questa)

1993 (7 Dec). *Chalk-surfaced paper. One centre phosphor band (19p.) or phosphorised paper (others). P 15 × 14 (with one elliptical hole on each vertical side).*

S81	S 4	19p. bistre	30	35
S82		25p. red..	40	45
S83		30p. deep olive-grey.............................	45	50
S84		41p. grey-brown	65	70

First Day Cover.

7.12.93	19p., 25p., 30p., 41p., (S81/4)............	2.75

For Presentation Pack containing stamps of Northern Ireland, Scotland and Wales see after No. NI72 of Northern Ireland.

IV. WALES

From the inception of the Regional stamps, the Welsh versions were tendered to members of the public at all Post Offices within the former County of Monmouthshire but the English alternatives were available on request. Offices with a Monmouthshire postal address but situated outside the County, namely Beachley, Brockweir, Redbrook, Sedbury, Tutshill, Welsh Newton and Woodcroft, were not supplied with the Welsh Regional stamps.

With the re-formation of Counties, Monmouthshire became known as Gwent and was also declared to be part of Wales. From 1 July 1974, therefore, except for the offices mentioned above, only Welsh Regional stamps were available at the offices under the jurisdiction of Newport, Gwent.

W 4

| I | II |

Redrawn design of Type W 4 (litho ptgs.)

Two Types of Dragon

Type I: – The eye is complete with white dot in the centre. Wing-tips, tail and tongue are thin.

Type II: – The eye is joined to the nose by a solid line. Tail, wing-tips, claws and tongue are wider than in Type I.

The following stamps printed in lithography show a screened background behind and to the left of the emblem: 11½p., 12½p, 14p. (No. W39), 15½p., 16p., 18p. (No. W46), 19½p., 22p. (No. W54) and 28p. (No. W63). The 13p and 17p. (No. W44) also show screened backgrounds in Type I but changed to solid backgrounds for Type II. All other values printed in lithography have solid backgrounds.

| W 1 | W 2 | W 3 |

(Des R. Stone)

1958–67. W 179. *P* 15 × 14.

W1	W 1	3d. dp lilac (18.8.58)	20	10
		p. One centre phosphor band (16.5.67)	20	15
W2		4d. ultramarine (7.2.66)......................	20	15
		p. Two phosphor bands (10.67)...........	20	15
W3	W 2	6d. dp claret (29.9.58)	40	20
W4		9d. bronze-green (2 phosphor bands)		
		(1.3.67)	30	35
		Ey. Phosphor omitted.........................	£300	
W5	W 3	1s. 3d. green (29.9.58)	30	30
W6		1s. 6d. grey-blue (2 phosphor bands)		
		(1.3.67)	35	30
		Ey. Phosphor omitted.........................	40.00	

First Day Covers

18.8.58	3d. (W1)	6.00
29.9.58	6d., 1s. 3d. (W3, W5)	12.00
7.2.66	4d. (W2)	4.00
1.3.67	9d., 1s. 6d. (W4, W6)	1.50
	Presentation Pack*	90.00

*This was issued in 1960 and comprises Guernsey No. 7, Jersey No. 10, Isle of Man No. 2, Northern Ireland Nos. NI1, 3 and 5, Scotland Nos. S1, 3 and 5 and Wales and Monmouthshire Nos. W1, 3 and 5 together with 6-page printed leaflet describing the stamps. There exist two forms: (a) inscribed "7s.3d." for sale in U.K.; and (b) inscribed "$1.20" for sale in the U.S.A.

1967–69. No wmk. Chalk-surfaced paper. One centre phosphor band (W7, W9/10) or two phosphor bands (others). Gum arabic (3d.) or PVA gum (others). P 15 × 14.

W 7	W 1	3d. dp lilac (6.12.67)	20	10
		Ey. Phosphor omitted.........................	40.00	
W 8		4d. ultramarine (21.6.68)	20	10
W 9		4d. olive-sepia (4.9.68)......................	20	10
W10		4d. brt vermilion (26.2.69)	20	20
		Ey. Phosphor omitted.........................	1.75	
W11		5d. royal blue (4.9.68)	20	10
		Ey. Phosphor omitted.........................	2.25	
W12	W 3	1s. 6d. grey-blue (1.8.69)	3.00	3.00

4.9.68	First Day Cover (W9, W11)	50	
	Presentation Pack (containing Nos. W4, W6/7, W9/11) (9.12.70).............	2.50	

(Des J. Mathews after plaster cast by Arnold Machin)

1971 (7 July)–**93**. Decimal Currency. Chalk-surfaced paper. Type W **4**.

(a) Photo Harrison. With phosphor bands. P 15 × 14

W13	2½p. brt magenta (1 centre band)		20	15
	Ey. Phosphor omitted.........................		5.50	
	Eg. Gum arabic (22.9.72)		20	
	Ega. Imperf (pair).............................		£350	
W14	3p. ultramarine (2 bands)		25	15
	Ey. Phosphor omitted.........................		15.00	
	Eg. Gum arabic (6.6.73).........................		30	
	Eya. Phosphor omitted (No. W14Eg.).......		3.50	
W15	3p. ultramarine (1 centre band) (23.1.74).		20	20
W16	3½p. olive-grey (2 bands) (23.1.74)		20	25
W17	3½p. olive-grey (1 centre band) (6.11.74) ...		20	25
W18	4½p. grey-blue (2 bands) (6.11.74)...........		25	25
W19	5p. reddish violet (2 bands)		1.00	1.00
	Ey. Phosphor omitted.........................		11.00	
W20	5½p. violet (2 bands) (23.1.74)		20	25
	Ey. Phosphor omitted.........................		£160	
W21	5½p. violet (1 centre band) (21.5.75)		20	25
	a. Imperf (pair)		£400	
W22	6½p. greenish blue (1 centre band) (14.1.76)		20	20
W23	7p. purple-brown (1 centre band) (18.1.78)		25	25
W24	7½p. chestnut (2 bands)		1.75	1.90
	Ey. Phosphor omitted.........................		75.00	
W25	8p. rosine (2 bands) (23.1.74)		30	30
	Ey. Phosphor omitted		£450	
W26	8½p. yellow-green (2 bands) (14.1.76)		30	30
W27	**9p.** dp violet (2 bands) (18.1.78)		30	30
W28	10p. orange-brown (2 bands) (20.10.76)....		35	30

W29	10p. orange-brown (1 centre band) (23.7.80)	35	30
W30	10½p. steel-blue (2 bands) (18.1.78)	40	35
W31	11p. scarlet (2 bands) (20.10.76)	40	45

(b) Photo Harrison. On phosphorised paper. P 15 × 14

W32	12p. yellow-green (23.7.80)	50	45
W33	13½p. purple brown (23.7.80)	60	70
W34	15p. ultramarine (23.7.80)	60	50

(c) Litho Questa (Type II unless otherwise stated). P 14 (11½p., 12½p., 14p. (No. W39), 15½p., 16p., 18p. (W46), 19½p., 20½p., 22p. (W54), 26p. (W61), 28p. (W63)) or 15 × 14 (others).

W35	11½p. drab (Type I) (1 side band) (8.4.81)	85	60
W36	12p. brt emerald (1 side band) (7.1.86)	2.00	1.10
W37	12½p. lt emerald (Type I) (1 side band) (24.2.82)	70	60
	a. Perf 15 × 14 (10.1.84)	7.00	6.00
W38	13p. pale chestnut (Type I) (1 side band) (23.10.84)	50	35
	Ea. Type II (1.87)	60	35
W39	14p. grey-blue (Type I) (phosphorised paper) (8.4.81)	65	50
W40	14p. dp blue (1 centre band) (8.11.88)	55	30
W41	15p. brt blue (1 centre band) (28.11.89)	40	30
	Ey. Phosphor omitted		
W42	15½p. pale violet (Type I) (phosphorised paper) (24.2.82)	80	65
W43	16p. drab (Type I) (phosphorised paper) (27.4.83)	1.50	1.25
	a. Perf 15 × 14 (10.1.84)	1.60	1.25
W44	17p. grey-blue (Type I) (phosphorised paper) (23.10.84)	80	55
	Ea. Type II (18.8.86)	11.00	8.00
W45	17p. dp blue (1 centre band) (4.12.90)	50	35
	Ey. Phosphor omitted		
W46	18p. dp violet (Type I) (8.4.81)	80	75
W47	18p. dp olive-grey (phosphorised paper) (6.1.87)	1.00	45
W48	18p. brt green (1 centre band) (3.12.91)	30	35
	Ey. Phosphor omitted		
	a. Booklet pane. No. W48 × 6 with margins all round (25.2.92)	1.90	
	aEy. Phosphor omitted		
	b. Perf 14 (12.1.93*)	1.00	1.00
W49	18p brt green (1 side band at right) (25.2.92)	75	75
	a. Booklet pane No. X1020 × 2, 1451a, 1514a, W49 × 2, W60 × 2 and centre label with margins all round	9.00	
	aEy. Phosphor omitted		
	Eb. Band at left (10.8.93)	2.00	2.00
W50	19p. brt orange-red (phosphorised paper) (8.11.88)	60	45
W51	19½p. olive-grey (Type I) (phosphorised paper) (24.2.82)	1.75	1.75
W52	20p. brownish black (phosphorised paper) (28.11.89)	30	30
W53	20½p. ultramarine (Type I) (phosphorised paper) (27.4.83)	4.00	4.00
W54	22p. blue (Type I) (phosphorised paper) (8.4.81)	1.00	1.00
W55	22p. yellow-green (Type I) (phosphorised paper) (23.10.84)	80	1.10
W56	22p. brt orange-red (phosphorised paper) (4.12.90)	60	50
W57	23p. brt green (phosphorised paper) (8.11.88)	80	1.10
W58	24p. Indian red (phosphorised paper) (28.11.89)	70	1.10

W59	24p. chestnut (phosphorised paper) (3.12.91)	40	45
	a. Booklet pane. No. W59 × 6 with margins all round (25.2.92)	2.50	
	b. Perf 14 (14.9.92*)	1.00	1.00
W60	24p. chestnut (2 bands) (25.2.92)	1.10	85
W61	26p. rosine (Type I) (phosphorised paper) (24.2.82)	90	1.10
	a. Perf 15 × 14 (Type II) (27.1.87)	4.00	4.00
W62	26p. drab (phosphorised paper) (4.12.90)	70	70
W63	28p. dp violet-blue (Type I) (phosphorised paper) (27.4.83)	1.00	1.10
	a. Perf 15 × 14 (Type II) (27.1.87)	80	65
W64	28p. dp bluish grey (phosphorised paper) (3.12.91)	45	50
W65	31p. brt purple (Type I) (phosphorised paper) (23.10.84)	1.10	1.10
W66	32p. greenish blue (phosphorised paper) (8.11.88)	1.10	1.10
W67	34p. dp bluish grey (phosphorised paper) (28.11.89)	1.00	1.00
W68	37p. rosine (phosphorised paper) (4.12.90)	1.00	1.00
W69	39p. brt mauve (phosphorised paper) (3.12.91)	60	65

Nos W48b and W59b were caused by the use of a reserve perforating machine for some printings in the second half of 1992.

From 1972 printings were on fluorescent white paper. From 1973 most printings had dextrin added (see notes after 1971 Decimal Machin issue).

First Day Covers

7.7.71	2½p., 3p., 5p., 7½p., (W13/14, W19, W24)	2.50
23.1.74	3p., 3½p., 5½p., 8p. (W15/16, W20, W25)	1.50
6.11.74	4½p. (W18)	1.00
14.1.76	6½p., 8½p. (W22, W26)	60
20.10.76	10p., 11p. (W28, W31)	75
18.1.78	7p., 9p., 10½p. (W23, W27, W30)	75
23.7.80	12p., 13½p., 15p. (W32/4)	1.75
8.4.81	11½p., 14p., 18p., 22p. (W35, W39, W46, W54)	1.75
24.2.82	12½p., 15½p., 19½p., 26p. (W37, W42, W51, W61)	4.25
27.4.83	16p., 20½p., 28p. (W43, W53, W63)	6.50
23.10.84	13p., 17p., 22p., 31p. (W38, W44, W55, W65)	4.50
7.1.86	12p. (W36)	1.25
6.1.87	18p. (W47)	2.00
8.11.88	14p., 19p., 23p., 32p. (W40, W50, W57, W66)	4.50
28.11.89	15p., 20p., 24p., 34p. (W41, W52, W58, W67)	4.00
4.12.90	17p., 22p., 26p., 37p. (W45, W56, W62, W68)	4.50
3.12.91	18p., 24p., 28p., 39p. (W48, W59, W64, W69)	4.00
25.2.92	Cymru–Wales se-tenant pane 18p., (2nd), 24p., (1st), 33p. (W49a)	9.00

Presentation Packs

7.7.71	2½p., 3p. (2 bands) 5p., 7½p., (Nos. W13/14, W19, W24)	4.00
29.5.74	3p. (1 centre band), 3½p. (2 bands) or (1 centre band), 5½p. (2 bands) or (1 centre band), 8p. (Nos. W15, W16 or W17, W20 or W21, W25). The 4½p. (No. W18) was added later	2.25
20.10.76	6½p., 8½p., 10p. (2 bands), 11p. (Nos. W22, W26, W28, W31)	1.75

28.10.81	7p., 9p., 10½p., 12p. (photo), 13½p., 15p. (photo), 11½p., 14p. grey-blue, 18p. dp violet, 22p. blue (*Nos.* W23, W27, W30, W32/5, W39, W46, W54)	7.00
3.8.83	10p. (1 centre band), 12½p., 16p., 20½p., 26p. rosine, 28p. dp violet-blue (*Nos.* W29, W37, W43, W53, W61, W63)	7.00
23.10.84	10p. (1 centre band), 13p., 16p., 17p. grey-blue, 22p. yellow-green, 26p. rosine, 28p. dp violet-blue, 31p. (*Nos.* W29, W38, W43a, W44, W55, W61, W63, W65)	9.50
3.3.87	12p. (litho), 13p., 17p. grey-blue, 18p. dp olive-grey, 22p. yellow-green, 26p. rosine, 28p. dp violet-blue, 31p. (*Nos.* W36, W38, W44, W47, W55, W61, W63, W65)	9.50

Presentation Packs containing stamps of Northern Ireland, Scotland and Wales are listed after those of Northern Ireland.

(Des J. Matthews after plaster cast by Arnold Machin.
Litho Questa)

1993 (7 Dec). *Chalk-surfaced paper. One centre phosphor band (19p.) or phosphorised paper (others). P 15 × 14 (with one elliptical hole on each vertical side).*

W70	W **4**	19p. bistre..	30	35
W71		25p. red	40	45
W72		30p. deep olive-grey	45	50
W73		41p. grey-brown.................................	65	70

First Day Cover
7.12.93   19p., 25p., 30p., 41p. (*W70/3*) 2.75

For Presentation Pack containing stamps of Northern Ireland, Scotland and Wales see after No. NI72 of Northern Ireland.

V. GUERNSEY

War Occupation Issues

SECTS. On 24 December 1940 authority was given, by Post Office notice, that prepayment of penny postage could be effected by using half a British 2d. stamp, diagonally bisected. Such stamps were first used on 27 December 1940.

The 2d. stamps generally available were those of the Postal Centenary issue, 1940 (S.G. 482) and the first colour of the King George VI issue (S.G. 465). These are listed under Nos. 482a and 465b. A number of the 2d. King George V, 1912–22, and of the King George V photogravure stamp (S.G. 442) which were in the hands of philatelists, were also bisected and used.

1

1a Loops (half actual size)

(Des E. W. Vaudin. Typo Guernsey Press Co Ltd)

41–44. Rouletted. (a) White paper. No wmk.

1	½d. light green (7.4.41)		2.50	2.75
	a. Emerald-green (6.41)		2.50	2.75
	b. Bluish green (11.41)		40.00	28.00
	c. Bright green (2.42)		24.00	12.00
	d. Dull green (9.42)		5.00	3.50
	e. Olive-green (2.43)		28.00	22.00
	f. Pale yellowish green (7.43 and later)			
	(shades)		2.50	2.75
	g. Imperf (pair)		£150	
	h. Imperf between (horiz pair)		£600	
	i. Imperf between (vert pair)		£700	
	1d. scarlet (18.2.41)		2.50	1.25
	a. Pale vermilion (7.43) (etc.)		2.00	2.00
	b. Carmine (1943)		2.50	3.50
	c. Imperf. (pair)		£150	75.00
	d. Imperf between (horiz pair)		£600	
	da. Imperf vert (centre stamp of horiz strip of 3)		£700	
	e. Imperf between (vert pair)		£700	
	f. Printed double (scarlet shade)		75.00	
	2½d. ultramarine (12.4.44)		5.50	5.50
	a. Pale ultramarine (7.44)		5.50	4.50
	b. Imperf (pair)		£350	
	c. Imperf between (horiz pair)		£800	
	Set of 3		9.00	7.50

First Day Covers

7.4.41	½d.	6.00
18.2.41	1d.	6.00
12.4.44	2½d.	7.50

(b) Bluish French bank-note paper. W 1a (sideways)

4	1	½d. bright green (11.3.42)		19.00	20.00
5		1d. scarlet (9.4.42)		8.00	25.00
		Set of 2		27.00	45.00

First Day Covers

11.3.42	½d.	75.00
9.4.42	1d.	40.00

The dates given for the shades of Nos. 1/3 are the months in which they were printed as indicated on the printer's imprints. Others are issue dates.

Regional Issues

2   3

(Des E. A. Piprell. Portrait by Dorothy Wilding Ltd.
Photo Harrison & Sons)

1958 (18 Aug)–**67.** W **179** of Great Britain. P 15 × 14.

6	**2**	2½d. rose-red (8.6.64)		35	40
7	**3**	3d. dp lilac		35	30
		p. One centre phosphor band (24.5.67)		20	20
8		4d. ultramarine (7.2.66)		25	30
		p. Two phosphor bands (24.10.67)		20	20
		Set of 3 (cheapest)		70	75

First Day Covers

18.8.58	3d.	8.00
8.6.64	2½d.	15.00
7.2.66	4d.	7.00

For No. 7 in Presentation Pack, see Regional Issues below Wales No. W6.

1968–69. No wmk. Chalk-surfaced paper. PVA gum*. One centre phosphor band (Nos. 10/11) or two phosphor bands (others). P 15 × 14.

9	**3**	4d. pale ultramarine (16.4.68)		10	25
		Ey. Phosphor omitted		40.00	
10		4d. olive-sepia (4.9.68)		15	20
		Ey. Phosphor omitted		40.00	
11		4d. brt vermilion (26.2.69)		15	30
12		5d. royal blue (4.9.68)		15	30
		Set of 4		40	95

First Day Cover

4.9.68	4d., 5d.	1.00

No. 9 was not issued in Guernsey until 22 April.
*PVA Gum. See note after No. 722 of Great Britain.

VI. ISLE OF MAN

Although specifically issued for use in the Isle of Man, these issues were also valid for use throughout Great Britain.

DATES OF ISSUE. The note at the beginning of Northern Ireland also applies here.

Nos. 8/11 and current stamps of Great Britain were withdrawn from sale on the island from 5 July 1973 when the independent postal administration was established but remained valid for use there for a time. They also remained on sale at the Philatelic Sales counters in the United Kingdom until 4 July 1974.

1　　　　**2**

(Des J. Nicholson. Portrait by Dorothy Wilding Ltd. Photo Harrison)

1958 (18 Aug)–**68.** *W* **179.** *P* 15 × 14.

1	**1**	2½d. carmine-red (8.6.64)		45	80
2	**2**	3d. dp lilac		20	10
		a. Chalk-surfaced paper (17.5.63)		16.00	11.00
		p. One centre phosphor band (27.6.68)		20	30
3		4d. ultramarine (7.2.66)		1.50	1.10
		p. Two phosphor bands (5.7.67)		20	15
		Set of 3 (cheapest)		75	90

First Day Covers

18.8.58	3d.		20.00
8.6.64	2½d.		20.00
7.2.66	4d.		7.00

No. 2a was released in London sometime after 17 May 1963, this being the date of issue in Douglas.

For No. 2 in Presentation Pack, see Regional Issues below Wales No. W6.

1968–69. *No wmk. Chalk-surfaced paper. PVA gum. One centre phosphor band (Nos. 5/6) or two phosphor bands (others). P 15 × 14.*

4	**2**	4d. blue (24.6.68)		20	25
5		4d. olive-sepia (4.9.68)		20	30
		Ey. Phosphor omitted		20.00	
6		4d. brt vermilion (26.2.69)		45	60
7		5d. royal blue (4.9.68)		45	60
		Ey. Phosphor omitted		£150	
		Set of 4		1.00	1.60

First Day Cover

4.9.68	4d., 5d.		1.75

3

(Des J. Matthews. Portrait after plaster cast by Arnold Machin. Photo Harrison)

1971 (7 July). *Decimal Currency. Chalk-surfaced paper. One centre phosphor band (2½p.) or two phosphor bands (others). P 15 × 14.*

8	**3**	2½p. brt magenta		20	15
		Ey. Phosphor omitted		£900	
9		3p. ultramarine		20	15

10	**3**	5p. reddish violet		70	75
		Ey. Phosphor omitted		£200	
11		7½p. chestnut		70	90
		Set of 4		1.50	1.75
		Presentation Pack		2.00	

First Day Cover

7.7.71	2½p., 3p., 5p., 7½p.		3.50

All values exist with PVA gum on ordinary cream paper and the 2½p. and 3p. also on fluorescent white paper.

VII. JERSEY

War Occupation Issues

(Des Major N. V. L. Rybot. Typo *Evening Post*, Jersey)

1941–43. *White paper (thin to thick). No wmk. P 11.*

1	**1**	½d. bright green (29.1.42)		3.75	2.50
		a. Imperf between (vert pair)		£650	
		b. Imperf. between (horiz pair)		£550	
		c. Imperf (pair)		£180	
		d. On greyish paper (1.43)		5.00	6.50
2		1d. scarlet (1.4.41)		4.00	2.75
		a. Imperf between (vert pair)		£650	
		b. Imperf between (horiz pair)		£550	
		c. Imperf (pair)		£200	
		d. On chalk-surfaced paper		40.00	40.00
		e. On greyish paper (1.43)		4.50	6.50

First Day Covers

29.1.42	½d.		4.50
1.4.41	1d.		4.50

2 Old Jersey Farm　　**3** Portelet Bay

4 Corbière Lighthouse　　**5** Elizabeth Castle

6 Mont Orgueil Castle　　**7** Gathering Vraic (seaweed)

(Des E. Blampied. Eng H. Cortot. Typo French Govt Works, Paris)

943–44. No wmk. P 13½.

2	½d. green (1 June)		7.00	5.50
	a. Rough, grey paper (6.10.43)		8.50	9.00
3	1d. scarlet (1 June)		1.50	50
	a. On newsprint (28.2.44)		2.00	2.75
4	1½d. brown (8 June)		2.50	3.00
5	2d. orange-yellow (8 June)		4.00	2.25
6	2½d. blue (29 June)		1.50	1.50
	a. On newsprint (25.2.44)		75	1.50
	ba. Thin paper*		£180	
7	3d. violet (29 June)		1.00	2.75
	Set of 6		15.00	12.50
	First Day Covers (3)			18.00

*On No. 7ba the design shows clearly through the back of the
.amp.

Regional Issues

8   **9**

Des E. Blampied (T **8**), W. Gardner (T **9**). Portrait by Dorothy Wilding
Ltd. Photo Harrison & Sons)

958 (18 Aug)–67. W 179 of Great Britain. P 15 × 14.

9	8	2½d. carmine-red (8.6.64)	35	50
		a. Imperf three sides (pair)	£1800	
10	9	3d. dp lilac	35	30
		p. One centre phosphor band (9.6.67)	20	20
11		4d. ultramarine (7.2.66)	25	30
		p. Two phosphor bands (5.9.67)	20	25
		Set of 3 (cheapest)	60	85

First Day Covers

18.8.58	3d.	8.00
8.6.64	2½d.	15.00
7.2.66	4d.	7.00

For No. 10 in Presentation Pack, see Regional Issues below Wales No.
V6.

968–69. No wmk. Chalk-surfaced paper, PVA gum*. One centre
phosphor band (4d. values) or two phosphor bands (5d.). P 15 × 14.

12	9	4d. olive-sepia (4.9.68)	20	25
		Ey. Phosphor omitted	£750	
13		4d. brt vermilion (26.2.69)	20	30
14		5d. royal blue (4.9.68)	20	40
		Set of 3	50	85

First Day Cover

4.9.68	4d., 5d.	1.25

*PVA Gum. See note after No. 722 of Great Britain.

POSTAGE DUE STAMPS

ERFORATIONS. All postage due stamps are perf 14 × 15.
VATERMARK. The watermark always appears sideways and this is the
normal" listed in this Catalogue for Nos. D1/D68. Varieties occur as
llows. The point of identification is which way the top of the crown
ints, but (where they occur) the disposition of the letters needs to be
ted also.

The meaning of the terms is given below: (1) as described and
illustrated in the Catalogue, i.e. as read through the front of the stamp,
and (2) what is seen during watermark detection when the stamp is face
down and the back is under examination.

(1) As described

Watermark	Crown pointing	Letters reading
Sideways	left	upwards
Sideways-inverted	right	downwards
Sideways and reversed	left	downwards, back to front
Sideways-inverted and reversed	right	upwards, back to front

(2) As detected (stamp face down)

Watermark		
Sideways	right	upwards, back to front
Sideways-inverted	left	downwards, back to front
Sideways and reversed	right	downwards
Sideways-inverted and reversed	left	upwards

D 1   **D 2**

(Typo by Somerset House (early trial printings of ½d., 1d., 2d. and 5d.;
all printings of 1s.) and by Harrison (later printings of all values except
1s.). Not easily distinguishable except by the control)

1914 (20 Apr)–23. W 100 (Simple Cypher) sideways-inverted on 1½d.,
4d. and 1s. and sideways on others.

			Unmtd mint	Mtd mint	Used
D1	D 1	½d. emerald	1.00	50	50
		Wi. Watermark sideways-inverted	1.50	75	75
		Wj. Watermark sideways and reversed	15.00	10.00	12.00
		Wk. Watermark sideways-inverted and reversed			
D2		1d. carmine	1.50	50	50
		a. Pale carmine	1.50	75	75
		Wi. Watermark sideways-inverted	1.50	75	75
		Wj. Watermark sideways-inverted and reversed	12.00	10.00	10.00
D3		1½d. chestnut (1923)	95.00	40.00	15.00
		Wi. Watermark sideways	95.00	40.00	12.00
D4		2d. agate	1.50	50	40
		Wi. Watermark sideways-inverted	2.25	1.50	1.50
		Wj. Watermark sideways-inverted and reversed	8.00	5.00	5.00
D5		3d. violet (1918)	20.00	2.00	1.00
		a. Bluish violet	20.00	3.50	3.50
		Wi. Watermark sideways-inverted	20.00	7.50	2.00
		Wj. Watermark sideways-inverted and reversed			
D6		4d. dull grey-green (12.20)	80.00	25.00	3.00
		Wi. Watermark sideways	80.00	10.00	5.00

Postage Due

D7	D **1**	5d. brownish cinnamon	10.00	5.00	2.00
		Wi. Watermark sideways-inverted	30.00	15.00	15.00
D8		1s. brt blue (1915)	80.00	25.00	2.50
		a. Dp brt blue	80.00	25.00	2.50
		Wi. Watermark sideways	70.00	20.00	20.00
		Wj. Watermark sideways-inverted and reversed			
		Set of 8	£250	90.00	22.00

The 1d. is known bisected and used to make up a 1½d. rate on understamped letters from Ceylon (1921), and to pay ½d. on a returned printed paper matter envelope at Kilburn, London (1923). The 2d. was bisected and used as 1d. at Christchurch, Malvern, Streatham and West Kensington all in 1921.

1924. *As 1914–23, but on thick chalk-surfaced paper.*

D9	D **1**	1d. carmine	6.50	2.25	3.00

(Typo Waterlow and (from 1934) Harrison)

1924–31. W **111** (*Block Cypher*) *sideways.*

D10	D **1**	½d. emerald (6.25)	2.50	50	30
		Wi. Watermark sideways-inverted	5.00	2.50	1.25
D11		1d. carmine (4.25)	2.50	50	30
		Wi. Watermark sideways-inverted	—	—	10.00
D12		1½d. chestnut (10.24)	80.00	35.00	15.00
		Wi. Watermark sideways-inverted	—	—	30.00
D13		2d. agate (7.24)	8.00	1.00	40
		Wi. Watermark sideways-inverted	—	—	10.00
D14		3d. dull violet (10.24)	9.00	1.50	40
		a. Printed on gummed side	£100	60.00	†
		b. Experimental paper W **111**a	50.00	35.00	30.00
		Wi. Watermark sideways-inverted	9.00	4.00	1.50
D15		4d. dull grey-green (10.24)	30.00	10.00	2.00
		Wi. Watermark sideways-inverted	35.00	15.00	10.00
D16		5d. brownish cinnamon (1.31)	60.00	24.00	20.00
D17		1s. dp blue (9.24)	15.00	6.00	75
		Wi. Watermark sideways-inverted			
D18	D **2**	2s. 6d. purple/yellow (10.24)	£160	30.00	1.75
		Wi. Watermark sideways-inverted			
		Set of 9	£325	95.00	40.00

The 2d. is known bisected to make up the 2½d. rate at Perranwell Station, Cornwall, in 1932.

			Unmtd mint	Used
1936–37.	W **125** (E 8 R) *sideways.*			
D19	D **1**	½d. emerald (5.37)	7.50	6.00
D20		1d. carmine (5.37)	1.50	1.60
D21		2d. agate (5.37)	7.00	6.00
D22		3d. dull violet (3.37)	1.50	1.60
D23		4d. dull grey-green (12.36)	23.00	17.00
D24		5d. brownish cinnamon (11.36)	40.00	22.00
		a. Yellow-brown (1937)	15.00	17.00
D25		1s. dp blue (12.36)	11.00	4.75
D26	D **2**	2s. 6d. purple/yellow (5.37)	£250	8.50
		Set of 8	£300	60.00

The 1d. is known bisected (Solihull, 3 July 1937).

1937–38. W **127** (G VI R) *sideways.*

D27	D **1**	½d. emerald (1938)	8.00	3.25
D28		1d. carmine (1938)	2.50	40
		Wi. Watermark sideways-inverted		
D29		2d. agate (1938)	2.50	40
		Wi. Watermark sideways-inverted	10.00	

D30	D **1**	3d. violet (1938)	10.00	
		Wi. Watermark sideways-inverted	25.00	
D31		4d. dull grey-green (1937)	60.00	7.5
		Wi. Watermark sideways-inverted		
D32		5d. yellow-brown (1938)	10.00	1.0
		Wi. Watermark sideways-inverted	35.00	
D33		1s. dp blue (1937)	55.00	1.0
		Wi. Watermark sideways-inverted	55.00	
D34	D **2**	2s. 6d. purple/yellow (1938)	55.00	3.
		Set of 8	£180	15.

The 2d. is known bisected in June 1951 (Harpenden and St. Albans and on 30 October 1954 (Harpenden).

DATES OF ISSUE. The dates for Nos. D35/68 are those on whic stamps were first issued by the Supplies Department to postmasters

1951–52. *Colours changed and new value (1½d.). W* **127** *(G VI R) side ways.*

D35	D **1**	½d. orange (18.9.51)	1.50	2.
D36		1d. violet-blue (6.6.51)	1.00	7
		Wi. Watermark sideways-inverted		
D37		1½d. green (11.2.52)	1.50	1.7
		Wi. Watermark sideways-inverted	8.50	
D38		4d. blue (14.8.51)	26.00	9.
D39		1s. ochre (6.12.51)	23.00	4.
		Wi. Watermark sideways-inverted		
		Set of 5	48.00	16.

The 1d. is known bisected (Dorking, 1952, and Camberley, 6 Ap 1954).

1954–55. W **153** (*Mult Tudor Crown and* E 2 R) *sideways.*

D40	D **1**	½d. orange (8.6.55)	4.00	2.
		Wi. Watermark sideways-inverted	10.00	
D41		2d. agate (28.7.55)	2.00	2.
		Wi. Watermark sideways-inverted		
D42		3d. violet (4.5.55)	42.00	25.
D43		4d. blue (14.7.55)	15.00	16.
		a. Imperf (pair)	£225	
D44		5d. yellow-brown (19.5.55)	20.00	6.
D45	D **2**	2s. 6d. purple/yellow (11.54)	£120	3.
		Wi. Watermark sideways-inverted		
		Set of 6	£180	50.0

1955–57. W **165** (*Mult St. Edward's Crown and* E 2 R) *sideways.*

D46	D **1**	½d. orange (16.7.56)	1.50	2.25
		Wi. Watermark sideways-inverted	10.00	
D47		1d. violet-blue (7.6.56)	4.00	1.25
D48		1½d. green (13.2.56)	3.75	3.75
		Wi. Watermark sideways-inverted	12.00	
D49		2d. agate (22.5.56)	35.00	3.0(
D50		3d. violet (5.3.56)	4.50	1.25
		Wi. Watermark sideways-inverted	25.00	
D51		4d. blue (24.4.56)	18.00	3.0(
		Wi. Watermark sideways-inverted	30.00	
D52		5d. brown-ochre (23.3.56)	27.00	2.0(
D53		1s. ochre (22.11.55)	65.00	1.25
		Wi. Watermark sideways-inverted		
D54	D **2**	2s. 6d. purple/yellow (28.6.57)	£160	7.5(
		Wi. Watermark sideways-inverted		
D55		5s. scarlet/yellow (25.11.55)	90.00	19.0(
		Wi. Watermark sideways-inverted		
		Set of 10	£375	40.0(

The 2d. is known bisected (June 1956), and also the 4d. (Poplar London, April 1959).

1959–63. W **179** (*Mult St. Edward's Crown*) *sideways.*

D56	D **1**	½d. orange (18.10.61)	10	45
		Wi. Watermark sideways-inverted	1.50	
D57		1d. violet-blue (9.5.60)	10	15
		Wi. Watermark sideways-inverted	5.00	
D58		1½d. green (5.10.60)	90	2.00

59	D 1	2d. agate (14.9.59)	1.25	30
		Wi. Watermark sideways-inverted	15.00	
50		3d. violet (24.3.59)	40	15
		Wi. Watermark sideways-inverted	3.50	
51		4d. blue (17.12.59)	40	20
		Wi. Watermark sideways-inverted	10.00	
52		5d. yellow-brown (6.11.61)	45	45
		Wi. Watermark sideways-inverted	5.00	
53		6d. purple (29.3.62)	60	30
		Wi. Watermark sideways-inverted	12.00	
54		1s. ochre (11.4.60)	1.40	25
		Wi. Watermark sideways-inverted	5.00	
55	D 2	2s. 6d. purple/yellow (11.5.61)	4.00	45
		Wi. Watermark sideways-inverted	7.50	
56		5s. scarlet/yellow (8.5.61)	7.50	80
		Wi. Watermark sideways-inverted	12.00	
57		10s. blue/yellow (2.9.63)	9.00	4.00
		Wi. Watermark sideways-inverted	30.00	
58		£1 black/yellow (2.9.63)	45.00	7.00
		Set of 13	60.00	15.00

Whiter paper. The note after No. 586 also applies to Postage Due stamps.

The 1d. is known bisected (Newbury, Dec. 1962).

58–69. *Typo. No wmk. Chalk-surfaced paper.*

59	D 1	2d. agate (11.4.68)	20	40
		Ev. PVA gum (26.11.68)	75	
70		3d. violet (9.9.68)	25	40
71		4d. blue (6.5.68)	25	40
		Ev. PVA gum	75	
72		5d. orange-brown (31.1.69)	4.50	5.25
73		6d. purple (9.9.68)	60	60
74		1s. ochre (19.11.68)	2.00	1.00
		Set of 6	7.00	7.00

The 2d. and 4d. exist with gum arabic and PVA gum; remainder with PVA gum only.

68–69. *Photo. No wmk. Chalk-surfaced paper. PVA gum. P 14 × 15.*

75	D 1	4d. blue (12.6.69)	5.00	5.00
76		8d. red (3.10.68)	75	75

Nos. D75/6 are smaller, 21½ × 17½mm.

| | D 3 | | D 4 | |

(Des J. Matthews. Photo Harrison)

70 (17 June)–**75.** *Decimal Currency. Chalk-surfaced paper. P 14 × 15.*

77	D 3	½p. turquoise-blue (15.2.71)	10	20
78		1p. dp reddish purple (15.2.71)	10	15
79		2p. myrtle-green (15.2.71)	10	15
80		3p. ultramarine (15.2.71)	15	15
81		4p. yellow-brown (15.2.71)	15	15
82		5p. violet (15.2.71)	20	20
83		7p. red-brown (21.8.74)	35	45
84	D 4	10p. carmine	30	20
85		11p. slate-green (18.6.75)	50	60
86		20p. olive-brown	60	50
87		50p. ultramarine	1.50	40
88		£1 black	2.75	60
89		£5 orange-yellow and black (2.4.73)	30.00	2.00
		Set of 13	35.00	5.00
		Presentation Pack (Nos. D77/82, D84, D86/8) (3.11.71)	10.00	
		Presentation Pack (Nos. D77/88) (30.3.77)	6.00	

Later printings were on fluorescent white paper, some with dextrin added to the PVA gum (see notes after X1025).

| | D 5 | | D 6 | |

(Des Sedley Place Design Ltd. Photo Harrison)

1982 (9 June). *Chalk-surfaced paper. P 14 × 15.*

D90	D 5	1p. lake	10	10
D91		2p. bright blue	10	10
D92		3p. dp mauve	10	15
D93		4p. dp blue	10	20
D94		5p. sepia	10	20
D95	D 6	10p. lt brown	15	25
D96		20p. olive-green	30	30
D97		25p. dp greenish blue	40	70
D98		50p. grey-black	75	50
D99		£1 red	1.50	50
D100		£2 turquoise-blue	3.00	50
D101		£5 dull orange	7.50	50
		Set of 12	12.50	3.75
		Set of 12 Gutter Pairs	30.00	
		Presentation Pack	14.00	

D 7

(Des Sedley Place Design Ltd. Litho Questa)

1994 (15 Feb). *P 15 × 14 (with one elliptical hole on each vertical side).*

D102	D 7	1p. red, yellow & black	10	10
D103		2p. magenta, purple & black	10	10
D104		5p. yellow, red-brown & black	10	10
D105		10p. yellow, emerald & black	20	25
D106		20p. blue-green, violet & black	30	35
D107		25p. cerise, rosine & black	40	45
D108		£1 violet, magenta & black	1.50	1.60
D109		£1.20, greenish blue, blue-green & black	1.75	1.90
D110		£5 greenish black, blue-green & black	7.50	8.00
		Set of 9	10.50	11.50
		First Day Cover		12.00
		Presentation Pack	12.00	

Special First Day of Issue Postmark

London EC3 .... 12.50

OFFICIAL STAMPS

In 1840 the 1d. black (Type **1**), with "V R" in the upper corners, was prepared for official use, but never issued for postal purposes. Obliterated specimens are those which were used for experimental trials of obliterating inks, or those that passed through the post by oversight.

V **1**

1840. *Prepared for use but not issued; "V" "R" in upper corners. Imperf.*

			Un	Used	Used on cover
V1	V **1**	1d. black	£6000	£5000	£15000

The following Official stamps would be more correctly termed Departmental stamps as they were exclusively for the use of certain government departments. Until 1882 official mail used ordinary postage stamps purchased at post offices, the cash being refunded once a quarter. Later the government departments obtained Official stamps by requisition.

Official stamps were on sale to the public for a short time at Somerset House but they were not sold from post offices. The system of only supplying the Government departments with stamps was open to abuse so that all official stamps were withdrawn on 14 May 1904.

OVERPRINTS, PERFORATIONS, WATERMARKS. All Official stamps were overprinted by Thomas De La Rue & Co. and are perf 14. Except for the 5s., and 10s. on Anchor, they are on Crown watermarked paper unless otherwise stated.

INLAND REVENUE

These stamps were used by revenue officials in the provinces, mail to and from Head Office passing without a stamp. The London Office used these stamps only for foreign mail.

I.R.   I. R.

OFFICIAL   OFFICIAL

(O **1**)   (O **2**)

*Optd with Types O **1** (½d. to 1s.) or O **2** (others)*

1882–1901. *Stamps of Queen Victoria. (a) Issues of 1880–81.*

			Un	Used	★ Used on cover
O1		½d. green (1.11.82)	12.00	3.00	40.00
O3		1d. lilac (Die II) (1.10.82)	1.50	65	10.00
	a.	Optd in blue-black	60.00	35.00	
	b.	"OFFICIAL" omitted	—	£2250	
	Wi.	Watermark inverted			
O4		6d. grey (Plate 18) (3.11.82)	75.00	20.00	

No. O3 with the lines of the overprint transposed is an essay.

(b) Issues of 1884–88

O5	½d. slate-blue (8.5.85)		25.00	15.00	75.
O6	2½d. lilac (12.3.85)		£110	35.00	£5
O7	1s. green (12.3.85)		£2500	£450	
O8	5s. rose (*blued paper*) (12.3.85)		£2750	£475	
O9	5s. rose (12.3.85)		£1300	£400	
	a. Raised stop after "R"		£1600	£325	
	b. Optd in blue-black		£2000	£450	
O9c	10s. cobalt (*blued paper*) (12.3.85)		£5000	£700	
O9d	10s. ultramarine (*blued paper*) (12.3.85)		£5000	£1400	
O10	10s. ultramarine (3.90)		£2250	£475	
	a. Raised stop after "R"		£3000	£500	
	b. Optd in blue-black		£3500	£700	
O11	£1 brown-lilac (watermark Crowns) (12.3.85)		£18000		
	a. Frame broken		£22000		
O12	£1 brown-lilac (watermark Orbs) (3.90)		£25000		
	a. Frame broken		£27000		

(c) Issues of 1887–92

O13	½d. vermilion (5.88)		1.50	50	20
	a. Without "I.R."		£1500		
	b. Imperf		£850		
	c. Opt double (imperf)		£1000		
O14	2½d. purple/*blue* (2.92)		50.00	4.00	£
O15	1s. green (9.89)		£200	20.00	£1
O16	£1 green (6.92)		£3750	£450	
	a. No stop after "R"		—	£800	
	b. Frame broken		£5500	£900	

Nos. O3, O13, O15 and O16 may be found with two varieties overprint, *thin* letters, and from 1894 printings, *thicker* letters.

(d) Issues of 1887 and 1900

O17	½d. blue-green (4.01)		4.00	3.00	85
O18	6d. purple/*rose-red* (1.7.01)		£100	22.00	
O19	1s. green and carmine (12.01)		£600	£100	
★O1/19	**For well-centred, lightly used**			+35%	

1902–4. *Stamps of King Edward VII. Ordinary paper.*

O20	½d. blue-green (4.2.02)		17.00	1.50	80
O21	1d. scarlet (4.2.02)		10.00	70	40
O22	2½d. ultramarine (19.2.02)		£400	60.00	
O23	6d. dull purple (14.3.04)		£85000	£65000	
O24	1s. green & carmine (29.4.02)		£500	65.00	
O25	5s. carmine (29.4.02)		£4000	£1300	
	a. Raised stop after "R"		£4500	£1500	
O26	10s. ultramarine (29.4.02)		£15000	£9500	
	a. Raised stop after "R"		£17000	£11000	
O27	£1 dull blue-green (29.4.02)		£12000	£6000	

OFFICE OF WORKS

These were issued to Head and Branch (local) offices in London and to Branch (local) offices at Birmingham, Bristol, Edinburgh, Glasgow, Leeds, Liverpool, Manchester and Southampton. The overprinted stamps of value 2d. and upwards were created later in 1902, the 2d. registration fees and the rest for overseas mail.

O. W.

OFFICIAL

(O **3**)

Optd with Type O 3

896 (24 Mar)–**02.** Stamps of Queen Victoria

				★ Used on
		Un	Used	cover
)31	½d. vermilion	90.00	40.00	£180
)32	½d. blue-green (2.02)	£150	75.00	
)33	1d. lilac (Die II)	£150	40.00	£200
)34	5d. dull purple & blue (II) (29.4.02)	£750	£150	
)35	10d. dull purple & carmine (28.5.02)	£1300	£225	

902 (11 Feb)–**03.** Stamps of King Edward VII. Ordinary paper.

)36	½d. blue-green (8.02)	£350	80.00	£850
)37	1d. scarlet	£350	80.00	£150
)38	2d. green & carmine (29.4.02)	£600	75.00	£1100
)39	2½d. ultramarine (29.4.02)	£700	£200	
)40	10d. purple & carmine (28.5.03)	£5000	£1500	
★O31/40	**For well-centred, lightly used**		+25%	

ARMY

Letters to and from the War Office in London passed without postage. The overprinted stamps were distributed to District and tation Paymasters nationwide, including Cox and Co., the Army gents, who were paymasters to the Household Division.

ARMY

ARMY

ARMY

OFFICIAL

OFFICIAL

OFFICIAL

(O **4**)　　　(O **5**)　　　(O **6**)

896 (1 Sept)–**01.** Stamps of Queen Victoria optd with Type O **4** (½d., 1d.) or O **5** (2½d., 6d.)

)41	½d. vermilion	1.50	75	20.00
	a. "OFFICIAI" (R.13/7)	35.00	16.00	
	b. Lines of opt transposed	£1000		
	Wi. Watermark inverted	£170	60.00	
)42	½d. blue-green (6.00)	1.75	4.00	
	Wi. Watermark inverted	£130	40.00	
)43	1d. lilac (Die II)	1.50	75	30.00
	a. "OFFICIAI" (R. 13/7)	35.00	16.00	
)44	2½d. purple/blue	4.00	3.00	£250
)45	6d. purple/rose-red (9.01)	16.00	10.00	£450

Nos. O41a and O43a occur in sheets overprinted by Forme 1.

902–03. Stamps of King Edward VII optd with Type O **4** (Nos. O48/50) or Type O **6** (O52). Ordinary paper.

)48	½d. blue-green (11.2.02)	2.00	65	50.00
)49	1d. scarlet (11.2.02)	1.50	55	50.00
	a. "ARMY" omitted			
)50	6d. dull purple (23.8.02)	60.00	32.00	
)52	6d. dull purple (12.03)	£850	£275	

GOVERNMENT PARCELS

These stamps were issued to all departments, including the Head Office, for use on parcels weighing over 3 lb. Below this weight overnment parcels were sent by letter post to avoid the 55% of the ostage paid from accruing to the railway companies, as laid down by arcel-post regulations. Most government parcels stamps suffered eavy postmarks in use.

GOVT

PARCELS

(O **7**)

Optd as Type O **7**

1883 (1 July)–**86.** Stamps of Queen Victoria

			★
		Un	Used
O61	1½d. lilac (30.4.86)	£100	25.00
	a. No dot under "T"	£130	28.00
	b. Dot to left of "T"	£100	28.00
O62	6d. dull green (30.4.86)	£800	£275
O63	9d. dull green (1.8.83)	£650	£180
O64	1s. orange-brown (watermark Crown, Pl 13)	£425	70.00
	a. No dot under "T"	£475	80.00
	b. Dot to left of "T"	£475	80.00
O64c	1s. orange-brown (Pl 14)	£750	£110
	ca. No dot under "T"	£825	£100
	cb. Dot to left of "T"		

1887–90. Stamps of Queen Victoria

O65	1½d. dull purple & pale green (29.10.87)	14.00	2.00
	a. No dot under "T"	18.00	6.00
	b. Dot to right of "T"	16.00	5.00
	c. Dot to left of "T"	16.00	5.00
O66	6d. purple/rose-red (19.12.87)	28.00	10.00
	a. No dot under "T"	30.00	12.00
	b. Dot to right of "T"	30.00	12.00
	c. Dot to left of "T"	30.00	11.00
O67	9d. dull purple & blue (21.8.88)	55.00	15.00
O68	1s. dull green (25.3.90)	£120	70.00
	a. No dot under "T"	£140	75.00
	b. Dot to right of "T"	£140	75.00
	c. Dot to left of "T"	£160	80.00
	d. Optd in blue-black		

1891–1900. Stamps of Queen Victoria

O69	1d. lilac (Die II) (6.97)	28.00	8.00
	a. No dot under "T"	30.00	20.00
	b. Dot to left of "T"	30.00	20.00
	c. Opt inverted	£800	£600
	d. Ditto. Dot to left of "T"	£900	£500
	Wi. Watermark inverted	—	50.00
O70	2d. grey-green & carmine (24.10.91)	45.00	7.00
	a. No dot under "T"	50.00	8.00
	b. Dot to left of "T"	50.00	9.00
O71	4½d. green & carmine (9.92)	£100	75.00
	b. Dot to right of "T"		
	Wi. Watermark inverted		
O72	1s. green & carmine (11.00)	£160	50.00
		—	£3750
★O61/72	**For well-centred lightly used**		+100%

1902. Stamps of King Edward VII. Ordinary paper.

O74	1d. scarlet (30.10.02)	17.00	6.00
O75	2d. green & carmine (29.4.02)	65.00	18.00
O76	6d. dull purple (19.2.02)	£100	18.00
	a. Overprint double, one albino	£3500	
O77	9d. purple & ultramarine (28.8.02)	£225	50.00
O78	1s. green & carmine (17.12.02)	£350	85.00

The "no dot under T" variety occurred on R.12/3 and 20/2. The "dot to left of T" comes four times in the sheet on R.2/7, 6/7, 7/9 and 12/9. The best example of the "dot to right of T" is on R.20/1. All three varieties were corrected around 1897.

BOARD OF EDUCATION

BOARD

OF

EDUCATION

(O **8**)

Optd with Type O **8**

1902 (19 Feb). *Stamps of Queen Victoria.*

		Un	Used	Used on cover
O81	5d. dull purple & blue (II)	£525	£100	
O82	1s. green & carmine	£950	£375	

1902–4. *Stamps of King Edward VII. Ordinary paper.*

O83	½d. blue-green (19.2.02)	18.00	6.00	£200
O84	1d. scarlet (19.2.02)	18.00	5.00	£125
O85	2½d. ultramarine (19.2.02)	£500	50.00	
O86	5d. purple & blue (6.2.04)	£2000	£950	
O87	1s. green & carmine (23.2.02)	£35000	£25000	

ROYAL HOUSEHOLD

R.H.

OFFICIAL

(O **9**)

1902. *Stamps of King Edward VII optd with Type O* **9.** *Ordinary paper.*

O91	½d. blue-green (29.4.02)	£150	95.00	£500
O92	1d. scarlet (19.2.02)	£130	85.00	£300

ADMIRALTY

ADMIRALTY   ADMIRALTY

OFFICIAL   OFFICIAL

(O **10**)   (O **11**)

1903 (3 Mar). *Stamps of King Edward VII optd with Type O* **10.** *Ordinary paper.*

O101	½d. blue-green	10.00	4.00	£225
O102	1d. scarlet	5.00	2.50	£150
O103	1½d. purple & green	60.00	45.00	
O104	2d. green & carmine	£100	50.00	
O105	2½d. ultramarine	£120	40.00	
O106	3d. purple/*yellow*	£100	38.00	

1903–4. *Stamps of King Edward VII optd with Type O* **11.** *Ordinary paper.*

O107	½d. blue-green (9.03)	7.00	4.00	£250
O108	1d. scarlet (11.03)	6.50	3.50	50.00
O109	1½d. purple & green (2.04)	£180	50.00	
O110	2d. green & carmine (3.04)	£400	£100	
O111	2½d. ultramarine (3.04)	£450	£225	
O112	3d. purple/*yellow* (2.04)	£350	85.00	

Stamps of various issues perforated with a Crown and initials ("H.M.O.W.", "O.W.", "B.T." or "S.O.") or with initials only ("H.M.S.O." or "D.S.I.R.") have also been used for official purposes, but these are outside the scope of the catalogue.

POSTAL FISCAL STAMPS

ICES. Prices in the used column are for stamps with genuine postal cancellations dated from the time when they were authorised for use as postage stamps. Beware of stamps with fiscal cancellations removed d fraudulent postmarks applied.

LIDITY. The 1d. surface-printed stamps were authorised for postal e from 1 June 1881 and at the same time the 1d. postage issue, No. 6, was declared valid for fiscal purposes. The 3d. and 6d. values, gether with the embossed issues, were declared valid for postal rposes by another Act effective from 1 January 1883.

SURFACE-PRINTED ISSUES

(Typo Thomas De La Rue & Co.)

F 1
Rectangular Buckle

F 2

F 3
Octagonal Buckle

F 4

F 5
Double-lined Anchor

F 6
Single-lined Anchor

853–57. *P 15½ × 15. (a) Wmk F 5 (inverted) (1853–55).*

			Un	Used	Used on cover
1	F 1	1d. lt blue (10.10.53)	12.00	16.00	75.00
2	F 2	1d. ochre (10.53)	50.00	35.00	£150
		a. *Tête-bêche* (in block of four)	£8000		
3	F 3	1d. pale turquoise-blue (1854)	15.00	15.00	£130
		Wi. Watermark upright	50.00	35.00	
4		1d. lt blue/*blue* (1854)	30.00	22.00	£150
		Wi. Watermark upright	80.00	80.00	

F5	F 4	1d. reddish lilac/*blue glazed paper* (25.3.55)	45.00	11.00	£100
		Wi. Watermark upright	85.00	25.00	

Only one example is known of No. F2a outside the National Postal Museum and the Royal Collection.

(b) Wmk F 6 (1856–57)

F6	F 4	1d. reddish lilac (*shades*)	5.50	4.00	80.00
F7		1d. reddish lilac/*bluish* (*shades*) (1857)	5.50	4.00	80.00

INLAND REVENUE

(F 7)

1860 (3 Apr). *No. F7 optd with Type F 7, in red.*

F8	F 4	1d. dull reddish lilac/*blue*	£350	£300	£500
		Wj. Wmk reversed			

BLUE PAPER. In the following issues we no longer distinguish between bluish and white paper. There is a range of papers from white or greyish to bluish.

F 8 **F 9**

F 10

1860–67. *Bluish to white paper. P 15½ × 15. (a) Wmk F 6 (1860).*

F9	F 8	1d. reddish lilac (May)	6.00	6.00	80.00
F10	F 9	3d. reddish lilac (June)	£225	80.00	£150
F11	F 10	6d. reddish lilac (Oct)	85.00	60.00	£180
		Wi. Watermark inverted	£130	85.00	
		Wj. Watermark reversed	£120	85.00	

(b) W 40. (Anchor 16mm high) (1864)

F12	F 8	1d. pale reddish lilac (Nov)	4.75	4.75	65.00
F13	F 9	3d. pale reddish lilac	75.00	55.00	
F14	F 10	6d. pale reddish lilac	75.00	55.00	£150
		Wi. Watermark inverted	£150		

(c) W 40 (Anchor 18mm high) (1867)

F15	F 8	1d. reddish lilac	13.00	6.00	£130
F16	F 9	3d. reddish lilac	60.00	60.00	£160
F17	F 10	6d. reddish lilac	70.00	35.00	£150

For stamps perf 14, see Nos. F24/7.

F 11   F 12

Four Dies of Type F 12

Die 1. Corner ornaments small and either joined or broken; heavy
shading under chin

Die 2. Ornaments small and always broken; clear line of shading
under chin

Die 3. Ornaments larger and joined; line of shading under chin
extended half way down neck

Die 4. Ornaments much larger; straight line of shading continued to
bottom of neck

1867–81.   *White to bluish paper. P 14. (a) W **47** (Small Anchor).*

F18	F **11**	1d. purple (1.9.67)	8.00	5.00	60.0
		Wi. Watermark inverted.............			
F19	F **12**	1d. purple (Die I) (6.68)	1.75	1.50	40.0
		Wi. Watermark inverted.............	50.00		
F20		1d. purple (Die 2) (6.76)............	10.00	10.00	£18
F21		1d. purple (Die 3) (3.77)............	4.00	4.00	75.0
F22		1d. purple (Die 4) (7.78)............	3.00	2.50	65.0

*(b) W **48** (Orb)*

F23	F **12**	1d. purple (Die 4) (1.81).............	2.00	1.50	40.0
		Wi. Watermark inverted.............	50.00		

1881.   *White to bluish paper. P 14.*

*(a) W **40** (Anchor 18mm high) (Jan)*

F24	F **9**	3d. reddish lilac	£325	£200	£32
F25	F **10**	6d. reddish lilac	£170	50.00	£1£

*(b) W **40** (Anchor 20 mm high) (May)*

F26	F **9**	3d. reddish lilac	£250	55.00	£15
F27	F **10**	6d. reddish lilac	£110	75.00	£25

ISSUES EMBOSSED IN COLOUR

(Made at Somerset House)

The embossed stamps were struck from dies not appropriated to any
special purpose on paper which had the words "INLAND REVENUE"
previously printed, and thus became available for payment of any
duties for which no special stamps had been provided.

The die letters are included in the embossed designs and holes were
drilled for the insertion of plugs showing figures indicating dates of
striking.

F **13**   F **14**

INLAND
REVENUE
(F **15**)

INLAND
REVENUE
(F **16**)

1860 (3 Apr)–**71.** *Types F **13/14** and similar types embossed on bluish
paper. Underprint Type F **15**. No wmk. Imperf.*

			Un	Use
F28		2d. pink (Die A) (1.1.71)	£120	£12
F29		3d. pink (Die C)................................	90.00	80.0
		a. *Tête-bêche* (vert pair).....................	£1000	
F30		3d. pink (Die D)................................	£325	
F31		6d. pink (Die T)	£650	
F32		6d. pink (Die U)................................	95.00	80.0
		a. *Tête-bêche* (vert pair).....................	£1200	

33	9d. pink (Die C) (1.1.71)	£225		
34	1s. pink (Die E) (28.6.61)	£325	£130	
35	1s. pink (Die F) (28.6.61)	£110	90.00	
	a. *Tête-bêche* (vert pair)	£500		
36	2s. pink (Die K) (6.8.61)	£250	£150	
37	2s. 6d. pink (Die N) (28.6.61)	£750		
38	2s. 6d. pink (Die O) (28.6.61)	75.00	65.00	

361–71. *As last but perf 12½.*

39	2d. pink (Die A) (8.71)	£225	£110
40	3d. pink (Die C)		
41	3d. pink (Die D)		
42	9d. pink (Die C) (8.71)	£250	£120
43	1s. pink (Die E) (8.71)	£190	£110
44	1s. pink (Die F) (8.71)	£170	£110
45	2s. 6d. pink (Die O) (8.71)	£100	50.00

374 (Nov). *Types as before embossed on white paper. Underprint Type F **16**, in green. W **47** (Small Anchor). P 12½.*

46	2d. pink (Die A)	—	£150
47	9d. pink (Die C)		
48	1s. pink (Die F)	£170	90.00
49	2s. 6d. pink (Die O)	—	£130

375 (Nov)**–80.** *As last but colour changed and on white or bluish paper.*

50	2d. vermilion (Die A) (1880)	£250	85.00
51	9d. vermilion (Die C) (1876)	£250	£120
52	1s. vermilion (Die E)	£150	55.00
53	1s. vermilion (Die F)	£150	55.00
54	2s. 6d. vermilion (Die O) (1878)	£190	85.00

382 (Oct). *As last but W **48** (Orbs).*

55	2d. vermilion (Die A)		
56	9d. vermilion (Die C)		
57	1s. vermilion (Die E)		
58	2s. 6d. vermilion (Die O)	£400	£190

The sale of Inland Revenue stamps up to the 2s. value ceased from 30 December 1882 and stocks were called in and destroyed. The 2s. 6d. value remained on sale until 2 July 1883 when it was replaced by the 2s. 6d. "Postage & Revenue" stamp. Inland Revenue stamps still in the hands of the public continued to be accepted for revenue and postal purposes.

POSTMASTER AND U.P.U. SPECIMEN OVERPRINTS

At various times since 1847 the British Post Office, or its printers, has applied "SPECIMEN" or "CANCELLED" overprints to certain stamp issues.

Many of these overprints were purely intended for internal record purposes, but some had a wider use connected to the postal service. Between 1847 and 1873 the G.P.O. circulated examples of new stamps overprinted "SPECIMEN" to its postmasters and from 1879 similar overprints were applied to samples forwarded to the Universal Postal Union for distribution to member administrations. After 1892 such U.P.U. overprints were restricted to stamps with a face value of 1 shilling or above and they were discontinued altogether after March 1948.

In the listings below Types P **1** to P **6** are postmaster specimens and the remainder for the U.P.U.

For a complete listing of all other "SPECIMEN" overprints see the *Great Britain Specialised Catalogue.*

SPECIMEN

SPECIMEN   SPECIMEN

P 1   P 3   P 4

SPECIMEN   SPECIMEN   SPECIMEN

P 5   P 6   P 9

SPECIMEN   *SPECIMEN*   SPECIMEN

P 16   P 23   P 26

SPECIMEN

P 32

1847–54. *Embossed issues.*

No.	Type No.	Specimen	Unused Price
SP1	P **1**	1s. pale green (No. 54) (red opt)	£325
		a. Black opt	£450
SP2		10d. brown (No. 57)	£275
SP3		6d. mauve (No. 58)	£550

Specimen Overprints

1855–57. *Surface-printed issues. No corner letters.*

No.	Type No.	Specimen	Unused Price
SP4	P **3**	4d. carmine/*blued* (No. 62)	£160
SP5	P **4**	4d. rose/*white* (No. 65)	
SP6		6d. dp lilac/*white* (No. 69)	£100
		a. On azure paper	£140
SP7		1s. dp green (No. 71)	£100

1858–70. *Line-engraved issues.*

No.	Type No.	Specimen	Unused Price
SP8	P **9**	½d. rose-red (pl 10) (No. 48)	£100
SP9		1d. rose-red (pl 146) (No. 43)	£100
SP10		1½d. rose-red (pl 3) (No. 51)	£110
SP11		2d. blue (pl 15) (No. 46)	£150

1862–64. *Surface-printed issue. Small uncoloured corner letters.*

SP12	P **5**	3d. dp carmine-rose (No. 75)	80.00
SP13		4d. brt red (No. 79)	60.00
SP14	P **6**	9d. bistre (No. 86)	£100

1867–80. *Large uncoloured corner letters. Wmk Spray of Rose.*

SP15	P **5**	10d. red-brown (No. 1	80.00
SP16		2s. dull blue (pl 1) (No. 118)	70.00
SP17	P **9**	2s. dull blue (pl 1) (No. 118)	70.00
SP18		2s. brown (No. 121)	£500

1867–83. *Wmk Maltese Cross or Anchor (£5).*

SP19	P **6**	5s. rose (pl 1) (No. 126)	£225
SP20	P **9**	5s. pale rose (pl 2) (No. 127)	£250
SP21		10s. greenish grey (No. 128)	£550
SP22		£1 brown-lilac (No. 129)	£900
SP23		£5 orange/*blued* (No. 133)	£700

1872–73. *Uncoloured letters in corner. Wmk Spray of Rose.*

SP24	P **6**	6d. chestnut (pl 11) (No. 123)	60.00
SP25		6d. grey (pl 12) (No. 125)	70.00

1873–80. *Large coloured corner letters.*

SP26	P **9**	2½d. rosy-mauve (pl 6) (No. 141)	50.00
SP27		2½d. blue (pl 17) (No. 142)	45.00
SP28		3d. rose (pl 18) (No. 143)	60.00
SP29		4d. sage-green (pl 15) (No. 153)	70.00
SP30		4d. grey-brown (pl 17) (No. 154)	£120
SP31		6d. grey (pl 16) (No. 147)	60.00
SP32		8d. orange (pl 1) (No. 156)	60.00
SP33		1s. green (pl 12) (No. 150)	60.00
SP34		1s. orange-brown (pl 13) (No. 151)	£100

1880–83. *Wmk Imperial Crown.*

SP35	P **9**	3d. on 3d. lilac (No. 159)	90.00
SP36		6d. on 6d. lilac (No. 162)	90.00

1880–81. *Wmk Imperial Crown.*

SP37	P **9**	½d. dp green (No. 164)	20.00
SP38		1d. Venetian red (No. 166)	20.00
SP39		1½d. Venetian red (No. 167)	20.00
SP40		2d. pale rose (No. 168)	30.00
SP41		5d. indigo (No. 169)	30.00

1881. *Wmk Imperial Crown.*

SP42	P **9**	1d. lilac (14 dots) (No. 170)	25.00
SP43		1d. lilac (16 dots) (No. 172)	20.00

1883–84. *Wmk Anchor or Three Imperial Crowns (£1).*

SP44	P **9**	2s.6d. lilac/*blued* (No. 175)	£175
SP45		5s. crimson (No. 181)	£175
SP46		10s. ultramarine (No. 183)	£175
SP47		£1 brown-lilac (No. 185)	£350

1883–84. *Wmk Imperial Crown.*

SP48	P **9**	½d. slate-blue (No. 187)	20.00
SP49		1½d. lilac (No. 188)	45.00
SP50		2d. lilac (No. 189)	45.00

No.	Type No.	Specimen	Unused Price
SP51	P **9**	2½d. lilac (No. 190)	45.00
SP52		3d. lilac (No. 191)	45.00
SP53		4d. dull green (No. 192)	70.00
SP54		5d. dull green (No. 193)	70.00
SP55		6d. dull green (No. 194)	£13
SP56		9d. dull green (No. 195)	70.00
SP57		1s. dull green (No. 196)	70.00

1887–91. *"Jubilee" issue.*

SP58	P **9**	½d. vermilion (No. 197)	22.0
SP59		1½d. dull purple & pale green (No. 198)	35.0
SP60		2d. green & scarlet (No. 199)	35.0
SP61		2½d. purple/*blue* (No. 201)	40.0
SP62		3d. purple/*yellow* (No. 202)	30.0
SP63		4d. green & purple-brown (No. 205)	30.0
SP64		5d. dull purple & blue (Die I) (No. 207)	30.0
SP65		6d. purple/*rose-red* (No. 208)	20.0
SP66		9d. dull purple & blue (No. 209)	30.0
SP67		10d. dull purple & carmine (No. 210)	55.0
SP68		1s. dull green (No. 211)	30.0

1902–10. *King Edward VII. De La Rue printings.*

SP69	P **16**	2s. 6d. lilac (No. 260)	£12
SP70		5s. brt carmine (No. 263)	£13
SP71		10s. ultramarine (No. 265)	£20
SP72		£1 dull blue-green (No. 266)	£40

1913. *King George V. Wmk Royal Cypher.*

SP73	P **26**	1s. bistre-brown (No. 395)	£12

1913. *"Seahorse" high values. Printed by Waterlow.*

SP74	P **26**	2s. 6d. dp sepia-brown (No. 399)	£20
SP75		5s. rose-carmine (No. 401)	£17
SP76		10s. indigo-blue (No. 402)	£40
SP77		£1 green (No. 403)	£100

1929. *Ninth U.P.U. Congress.*

SP78	P **32**	£1 black (No. 438) (opt in red)	£75

1936. *Photogravure.*

SP79	P **32**	1s. bistre-brown (No. 449)	40.0

1939. *King George VI.*

SP80	P **23**	1s. bistre-brown (No. 475)	28.0
SP81		2s. 6d. brown (No. 476)	£20
SP82		2s. 6d. yellow-green (No. 476a)	£20
SP83		5s. red (No. 477)	£20
SP84		10s. dark blue (No. 478)	£35
SP85		10s. ultramarine (No. 478a)	£30

POSTAGE DUE STAMPS

1915. *Wmk Simple Cypher.*

SP86	P **23**	1s. brt blue (No. D8)	25.0

1924. *Wmk Block Cypher.*

SP87	P **23**	2s.6d. purple/*yellow* (No. D18)	

OFFICIAL STAMPS

1887–91. *Optd "GOVT PARCELS".*

SP88	P **9**	1½d. dull purple & pale green (No. O65)	65.00
SP89		2d. grey-green & carmine (No. O70)	50.00
SP90		6d. purple/*rose-red* (No. O66)	65.00
SP91		9d. dull purple & blue (No. O67)	50.00
SP92		1s. dull green (No. O68)	65.00

POST OFFICE STAMP BOOKLETS

The following listing covers all booklets sold by post offices from 904 until March 1991.

All major variations of contents and cover are included, but minor changes to the covers and differences on the interleaves have been ignored.

From 1913 each booklet carried an edition number, linked to an internal Post Office system of identification which divided the various booklets into series. In 1943 these edition numbers were replaced by edition dates. No attempt has been made to list separately edition numbers for booklets issued prior to 1943, although notes giving their extent are provided for each booklet. Edition dates from August 1943 are listed separately and exist for all £.s.d. and most Decimal Stitched booklets (except for the 1s. booklets, the 2s. booklets (N1/3), the 5s. "Philympia" booklet (No. HP34), the £1 "Stamps for Cooks" booklet (No. ZP1) and the Decimal Sponsored booklets). They are those found printed upon the booklets, either on the outer back cover or on the white leaves.

ERRORS OF MAKE-UP of booklets exist but we do not list them here. More detailed listings can be found in the 2nd, 3rd and 4th volumes of the *Great Britain Specialised Catalogue*.

ILLUSTRATIONS. The illustrations of the covers are $\frac{3}{4}$ size except where otherwise stated.

PRICES quoted are for complete booklets containing stamps with "average" perforations (ie. full perforations on two edges of the pane only). Booklets containing panes with complete perforations are worth more.

KING EDWARD VII

2s. Booklets

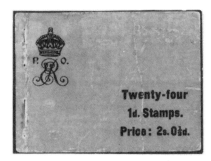

Type BA1

1904 (Mar). *Red cover printed in black as Type BA1. Pages of six stamps: 24 × 1d. Wmk Imperial Crown (No. 219)*
BA1 .... £130

HAVE YOU READ THE NOTES AT THE BEGINNING OF THIS CATALOGUE?

These often provide answers to the enquiries we receive.

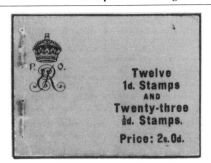

Type BA2

1906 (June). *Red cover printed in black as Type BA2. As before but make-up changed to include 12 × 1d. and 23 × ½d. and label showing one green cross (Nos. 217 and 219).*
BA2 .... £400

1907 (Aug). *Red cover printed in black as Type BA2. Make-up changed to include 18 × 1d. and 11 × ½d. and label showing one green cross (Nos. 217 and 219).*
BA3 .... £400

1911 (June). *Red cover printed in black as Type BA2 but showing a larger Post Office cypher on cover. As before, but containing stamps by Harrison & Sons (Nos. 267 and 272).*
BA6 .... £450

KING GEORGE V

2s. Booklets

1911 (Aug). *Red cover printed in black as Type BA2 showing King George V cypher. Pages of six stamps: 18 × 1d. and 12 × ½d. Wmk Crown (Nos. 325, 329) Die 1B.*
BB1 .... £250

Type BB2

1912 (April). *As before, but red cover printed in black as Type BB2.*
BB2 .... £350

1912 (Sept). *As before, but Wmk Simple Cypher (Nos. 334, 336) Die 1B.*
BB3 .... £400

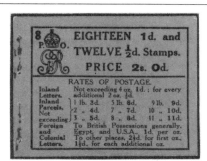

Type BB5

1913 (Jan). *As before, but red cover printed in black as Type BB5.*
BB5   No Edition number or 8 or 9 .... £400

1913 (April). *As before, but 1912–22 Wmk Simple Cypher (Nos. 351, 357).*
BB6   Edition numbers 10 to 45 .... £125

1916 (July). *As before, but orange cover printed in black as Type BB5.*
BB9   Edition numbers 46 to 64 .... £150

Type BB10

1917 (Sept). *As before, but orange cover printed in black as Type BB10.*
BB10   Edition numbers 65 to 81 .... £180

Type BB11

1924 (Feb). *Blue cover printed in black as Type BB11. Pages of six stamps: 10 × 1½d. (first completed by two perforated labels), 6 × 1d. and 6 × ½d. 1912–22 Wmk Simple Cypher (Nos. 351, 357, 362).*
BB11   Edition Nos. 1 or 2 .... £450

1933 (Oct). *As before, but 1924–26 Wmk Block Cypher (Nos. 418/20).*
BB12   Edition numbers 3 to 102 & 108 to 254 ...., £125

Type BB13

1929 (May). *Postal Union Congress issue. Cover of special design as Type BB13 printed in blue on buff as before but containing stamps of the P.U.C. issue (Nos. 434/6).*
BB13   Edition numbers 103 to 107 .... £250

1934 (Feb). *Blue cover printed in black as Type BB11, but containing stamps with Block Cypher wmk printed by Harrison & Sons. (Nos. 418/20).*
BB14   Edition numbers 255 to 287 .... £170

1935 (Jan). *As before, but containing stamps of the photogravure issue with the se-tenant advertisements printed in brown (Nos. 439/41).*
BB15   Edition numbers 288 to 297 .... £350

Type BB16

1935 (May). *Silver Jubilee issue. Larger size cover printed in blue or buff as Type BB16 and containing pages of four stamps with no se tenant advertisements: 12 × 1½d., 4 × 1d. and 4 × ½d. (Nos. 453/5).*
BB16   Edition numbers 298 to 304 .... 40.00

1935 (July). *As No. BB15, but containing stamps of the photogravure issue with se-tenant advertisements printed in black (Nos. 439/41).*
BB17   Edition numbers 305 to 353 .... 75.00

3s. Booklets

Type BB18

918 (Oct). *Orange cover printed in black as Type BB18. Pages of six stamps: 12 × 1½d., 12 × 1d. and 12 × ½d. 1912–22 Wmk Simple Cypher (Nos. 351, 357, 362).*
BB18 Edition numbers 1 to 11 .... £200

919 (July). *As before, but make-up altered to contain 18 × 1½d., 6 × 1d. and 6 × ½d.*
BB19 Edition numbers 12 to 26 .... £200

Type BB20

1921 (April). *Experimental booklet bound in blue covers as Type BB20, containing pages of six stamps: 18 × 2d. (Die I) (No. 368).*
BB20 Edition numbers 35 and part 37 .... £250

1921 (Dec). *As before, but containing 2d. (Die II) (No. 370).*
BB21 Edition numbers 12, 13 and part 37 .... £225

Type BB22

1922 (May). *Scarlet cover printed in black as Type BB22. Pages of six stamps: 18 × 1½d., 6 × 1d. and 6 × ½d. (Nos. 351, 357, 362).*
BB22 Edition numbers 19, 20, 22, 23 and 25 to 54 .... £200

1922 (June). *Experimental booklet as Edition numbers 12 and 13 bound in blue covers as Type BB22, containing pages of six stamps: 24 × 1½d. (No. 362).*
BB23 Edition numbers 21 or 24 .... £250

1924 (Feb). *Scarlet cover printed in black as Type BB22, but containing stamps with Block Cypher wmk, printed by Waterlow & Sons. (Nos. 418/20).*
BB24 Edition numbers 55 to 167 & 173 to 273 .... 65.00

1929 (May). *Postal Union Congress issue. Cover of special design as Type BB13 printed in red on buff as before but containing stamps of the P.U.C. issue. (Nos. 434/6).*
BB25 Edition numbers 168 to 172 .... £200

1934 (March). *Scarlet cover printed in black as Type BB22, but containing stamps with the Block Cypher wmk printed by Harrison & Sons. (Nos. 418/20).*
BB26 Edition numbers 274 to 288 .... £110

1935 (May). *Silver Jubilee issue. Larger size cover printed in red on buff as Type BB16 and containing pages of four stamps: 20 × 1½d., 4 × 1d. and 4 × ½d. (Nos. 453/5).*
BB28 Edition numbers 294 to 297 .... 40.00

1935 (July). *As No. BB26, but containing stamps of the photogravure issue. (Nos. 439/41).*
BB29 Edition numbers 289 to 293 & 298 to 319 .... 90.00

3s. 6d. Booklets

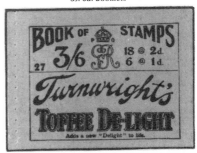

Type BB30

1920 (July). *Orange cover printed in black as Type BB30, containing pages of six stamps: 18 × 2d. and 6 × 1d. (Nos. 357, 368).*
BB30 Edition numbers 27 to 32 .... £250

Type BB31

1921 (Jan). *Orange-red cover printed in black as Type BB31, as before but make-up changed to include stamps of 1912–22 issue with the Simple Cypher wmk: 12 × 2d., 6 × 1½d., 6 × 1d. and 6 × ½d. (Nos. 351, 357, 362, 368 or 370).*

BB31   Edition numbers 1 to 11, 14 to 18, 33, 34, 36 & 38 .... £225

5s. Booklets

Type BB33

1931 (Aug). *Green cover printed in black as Type BB33. Pages of six stamps: 34 × 1½d., 6 × 1d. and 6 × ½d. The first 1½d. pane completed by two se-tenant advertisements. Printed by Waterlow & Son on paper with Block Cypher wmk. (Nos. 418/20).*

BB33   Edition number 1 .... £600

1932 (June). *As before, but buff cover printed in black.*

BB34   Edition numbers 2 to 6 .... £200

1934 (July). *As before, but containing stamps with Block Cypher wmk printed by Harrison & Sons. (Nos. 418/20).*

BB35   Edition numbers 7 or 8 .... £225

1935 (Feb). *As before, but containing stamps of the photogravure issue with se-tenant advertisements printed in brown. (Nos. 439/41).*

BB36   Edition number 9 .... £600

1935 (July). *As before, but containing stamps of the photogravure issue with se-tenant advertisements printed in black. (Nos. 439/41).*

BB37   Edition numbers 10 to 15 .... 75.00

KING EDWARD VIII

6d. Booklet

1936. *Buff unglazed cover without inscription containing 4 × 1½d. stamps, in panes of two (No. 459).*

BC1 .... 30.00

2s. Booklet

1936 (Oct). *As No. BB17, except for the K.E.VIII cypher on the cover and containing Nos. 457/9.*

BC2   Edition numbers 354 to 385 .... 50.00

3s. Booklet

1936 (Nov). *As No. BB29, except for the K.E.VIII cypher on the cover but without "P" and "O" on either side of the crown, and containing Nos. 457/9.*

BC3   Edition numbers 320 to 332 .... 40.00

5s. Booklet

1937 (Mar). *As No. BB37, but with the K.E.VIII cypher on the cover and containing Nos. 457/9.*

BC4   Edition numbers 16 or 17 .... £100

KING GEORGE VI

6d. Booklets

1938 (Jan). *As No. BC1, but containing stamps in the original dark colours. Buff cover without inscription (No. 464).*

BD1 .... 18.00

1938 (Feb). *As before, but pink unprinted cover and make-up changed to contain 2 × 1½d., 2 × 1d. and 2 × ½d. in the original dark colours (Nos. 462/4).*

BD2 .... 90.00

1940 (June). *Pale green unprinted cover and make-up changed to include two panes of four stamps with wmk sideways. Stamps in original dark colours with binding margin either at the top or bottom of the pane: 4 × 1d., 4 × ½d. (Nos. 462a/3a).*

BD3 .... 55.00

1s. Booklets

1947 (Dec.). *Cream cover, unglazed and without inscription containing panes of two stamps in pale shades, all with wmk normal. Panes of two stamps: 4 × ½d., 4 × 1d. and 4 × 1½d. (Nos. 485/7).*

BD4 .... 12.00

1951 (May). *As before, but containing stamps in changed colours (Nos. 503/5).*

BD5 .... 10.00

1948. *Cream cover as before, but make-up changed to contain 4 × 1½d., 4 × 1d. and 4 × ½d. in panes of four of the pale shades with wmk normal (Nos. 485/7).*

BD6 .... £2500

1951 (May). *As before, but stamps in new colours all wmk normal, margin at either top or at the bottom. (Nos. 503/5).*

BD7 .... 10.00

Type BD8

1952 (Dec). *Cream cover printed in black as Type BD8. Make-up as before but with wmk either upright or inverted and margins only at the top. (Nos. 503/5).*

BD8 .... 10.00

Type BD10

1954. As before but cover showing GPO emblem with St. Edward's crown and oval frame as Type BD10 (Nos. 503/5).

BD10 .... 14.00

2s. Booklets

1937 (Aug). Blue cover printed in black as Type BB11, but with K.G.VI cypher on the cover and containing stamps in the original dark colours. Panes of six stamps: 10 × 1½d., 6 × 1d. and 6 × ½d. The first 1½d. pane completed by two se-tenant advertisements. (Nos. 462/4).

BD11 Edition numbers 386 to 412 .... £150

Type BD12

1938 (April). Blue cover printed in black as Type BD12 (Nos. 462/4).

BD12 Edition numbers 413 to 508 .... £150

2s. 6d. Booklets

Type BD13

1940 (June). Scarlet cover printed in black as Type BD13, containing panes of six stamps in original dark colours: 6 × 2½d., 6 × 2d. and 6 × ½d. (Nos. 462, 465/6).

BD13 Edition numbers 1 to 7 .... £350

1940 (Sept). As before, but blue cover printed in black as Type BD13.

BD14 Edition numbers 8 to 13 .... £350

Type BD15

1940 (Oct). As before, but with green cover printed in black as Type BD15 (Nos. 462, 465/6).

BD15 Edition numbers 14 to 94 .... £150

1942 (Mar). As before, but containing stamps in pale shades (Nos. 485, 488/9).

BD16 Edition numbers 95 to 214 .... £200

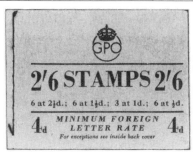

Type A
Circular GPO Cypher

1943 (Aug). *As before, but green cover printed in black as Type A, with different contents details (Nos. 485, 488/9).*
BD18   Edition dates August 1943 to February 1951 .... 20.00

(1) AUG 1943 .... 25.00		(46) MAY 1947 .... 35.00
(2) SEPT 1943 .... 35.00		(47) JUNE 1947 .... 35.00
(3) OCT 1943 .... 35.00		(48) JULY 1947 .... 35.00
(4) NOV 1943 .... 35.00		(49) AUG 1947 .... 35.00
(5) DEC 1943 .... 35.00		(50) SEPT 1947 .... 35.00
(6) JAN 1944 .... 35.00		(51) OCT 1947 .... 35.00
(7) FEB 1944 .... 35.00		(52) NOV 1947 .... 35.00
(8) MAR 1944 .... 35.00		(53) DEC 1947 .... 35.00
(9) APR 1944 .... 35.00		(54) JAN 1948 .... 30.00
(10) MAY 1944 .... 35.00		(55) FEB 1948 .... 30.00
(11) JUNE 1944 .... 35.00		(56) MAR 1948 .... 30.00
(12) JULY 1944 .... 35.00		(57) APR 1948 .... 30.00
(13) AUG 1944 .... 35.00		(58) MAY 1948 .... 30.00
(14) SEPT 1944 .... 35.00		(59) JUNE 1948 .... 30.00
(15) OCT 1944 .... 35.00		(60) JULY 1948 .... 30.00
(16) NOV 1944 .... 35.00		(61) AUG 1948 .... 30.00
(17) DEC 1944 .... 35.00		(62) SEPT 1948 .... 30.00
(18) JAN 1945 .... 35.00		(63) OCT 1948 .... 30.00
(19) FEB 1945 .... 35.00		(64) NOV 1948 .... 30.00
(20) MAR 1945 .... 35.00		(65) DEC 1948 .... 30.00
(21) APR 1945 .... 35.00		(66) JAN 1949 .... 30.00
(22) MAY 1945 .... 35.00		(67) FEB 1949 .... 30.00
(23) JUNE 1945 .... 35.00		(68) MAR 1949 .... 30.00
(24) JULY 1945 .... 35.00		(69) APR 1949 .... 30.00
(25) AUG 1945 .... 35.00		(70) MAY 1949 .... 30.00
(26) SEPT 1945 .... 35.00		(71) JUNE 1949 .... 30.00
(27) OCT 1945 .... 35.00		(72) JULY 1949 .... 30.00
(28) NOV 1945 .... 35.00		(73) AUG 1949 .... 30.00
(29) DEC 1945 .... 35.00		(74) OCT 1949 .... 30.00
(30) JAN 1946 .... 35.00		(75) NOV 1949 .... 30.00
(31) FEB 1946 .... 35.00		(76) DEC 1949 .... 30.00
(32) MAR 1946 .... 35.00		(77) JAN 1950 .... 20.00
(33) APR 1946 .... 35.00		(78) FEB 1950 .... 20.00
(34) MAY 1946 .... 35.00		(79) MAR 1950 .... 20.00
(35) JUNE 1946 .... 35.00		(80) APR 1950 .... 20.00
(36) JULY 1946 .... 35.00		(81) MAY 1950 .... 20.00
(37) AUG 1946 .... 35.00		(82) JUNE 1950 .... 20.00
(38) SEPT 1946 .... 35.00		(83) JULY 1950 .... 20.00
(39) OCT 1946 .... 35.00		(84) AUG 1950 .... 20.00
(40) NOV 1946 .... 35.00		(85) SEPT 1950 .... 20.00
(41) DEC 1946 .... 35.00		(86) OCT 1950 .... 20.00
(42) JAN 1947 .... 35.00		(87) NOV 1950 .... 20.00
(43) FEB 1947 .... 35.00		(88) DEC 1950 .... 20.00
(44) MAR 1947 .... 35.00		(89) JAN 1951 .... 20.00
(45) APR 1947 .... 35.00		(90) FEB 1951 .... 20.00

1951 (May). *As before, but containing stamps in the new colours (Nos. 503, 506/7).*
BD19   Edition dates May 1951 to February 1952 .... 15.00

(1) MAY 1951 .... 15.00	(6) OCT 1951 .... 15.00
(2) JUNE 1951 .... 16.00	(7) NOV 1951 .... 15.00
(3) JULY 1951 .... 15.00	(8) DEC 1951 .... 15.00
(4) AUG 1951 .... 16.00	(9) JAN 1952 .... 15.00
(5) SEPT 1951 .... 15.00	(10) FEB 1952 .... 15.00

1952 (March). *As before, but make-up changed to contain: 6 × 2½d., 6 × 1½d., 3 × 1d. and 6 × ½d. The 1d. pane was completed by three perforated labels in the lower row inscribed "MINIMUM INLAND PRINTED PAPER RATE 1½d." (Nos. 503/5, 507).*
BD20 Edition dates March 1952 to May 1953 ....15.00

(1) MAR 1952 .... 15.00	(9) NOV 1952 .... 15.00
(2) APR 1952 .... 16.00	(10) DEC 1952 .... 15.00
(3) MAY 1952 .... 15.00	(11) JAN 1953 .... 15.00
(4) JUNE 1952 .... 16.00	(12) FEB 1953 .... 15.00
(5) JULY 1952 .... 15.00	(13) MAR 1953 .... 15.00
(6) AUG 1952 .... 15.00	(14) APR 1953 .... 15.00
(7) SEPT 1952 .... 15.00	(15) MAY 1953 .... 16.00
(8) OCT 1952 .... 15.00	

3s. Booklets

1937 (Aug). *Scarlet cover Type BB22 printed in black as No. BC3, except for K.G.VI cypher on the cover and containing stamps in the original dark colours (Nos. 462/4).*
BD21   Edition numbers 333 to 343 .... £25

1938 (April). *As before, but scarlet cover printed in black as Type BD12 (Nos. 462/4).*
BD22   Edition numbers 344 to 377 .... £250

5s. Booklets

1937 (Aug). *Buff cover printed in black as Type BB33, containing stamps of the new reign in the original dark colours. Pages of six stamps: 34 × 1½d., 6 × 1d. and 6 × ½d. The first 1½d. pane completed by two se-tenant advertisements. (Nos. 462/4).*
BD23   Edition numbers 18 to 20 .... £300

Type BD24

1938 (May). *As before, but with redesigned front cover showing GPO emblem as Type BD24 instead of royal cypher.*
BD24   Edition numbers 21 to 29 .... £250

1940 (July). *As before, but make-up changed to contain: 18 × 2½d., 6 × 2d. and 6 × ½d. in the original dark colours (Nos. 462, 465/6).*
BD25 Edition numbers 1 to 16 (part) £250

1942 (Mar). *As before, but containing stamps in pale shades (Nos. 485, 488/9).*
BD26 Edition numbers 16 (part) to 36 .... £250

1943 (Sept). *As before, but buff cover printed in black as Type A (see No. BD18, 2s. 6d.) (Nos. 485, 488/9).*
BD28 Edition dates September 1943 to December 1950 .... 50.00

(1) SEPT 1943 .... 60.00	(26) JUNE 1947 .... 60.00
(2) OCT 1943 .... 60.00	(27) AUG 1947 .... 60.00
(3) NOV 1943 .... 60.00	(28) OCT 1947 .... 60.00
(4) DEC 1943 .... 60.00	(29) DEC 1947 .... 60.00
(5) FEB 1944 .... 60.00	(30) FEB 1948 .... 60.00
(6) MAR 1944 .... 60.00	(31) APR 1948 .... 60.00
(7) AUG 1944 .... 60.00	(32) JUNE 1948 .... 60.00
(8) OCT 1944 .... 60.00	(33) JULY 1948 .... 60.00
(9) NOV 1944 .... 60.00	(34) AUG 1948 .... 60.00
(10) JAN 1945 .... 60.00	(35) OCT 1948 .... 60.00
(11) FEB 1945 .... 60.00	(36) DEC 1948 .... 60.00
(12) APR 1945 .... 60.00	(37) FEB 1949 .... 60.00
(13) JUNE 1945 .... 60.00	(38) APR 1949 .... 60.00
(14) AUG 1945 .... 60.00	(39) JUNE 1949 .... 60.00
(15) OCT 1945 .... 60.00	(40) AUG 1949 .... 60.00
(16) DEC 1945 .... 60.00	(41) SEPT 1949 .... 60.00
(17) JAN 1946 .... 60.00	(42) OCT 1949 .... 60.00
(18) MAR 1946 .... 60.00	(43) DEC 1949 .... 60.00
(19) MAY 1946 .... 60.00	(44) FEB 1950 .... 50.00
(20) JUNE 1946 .... 60.00	(45) APR 1950 .... 50.00
(21) AUG 1946 .... 60.00	(46) JUNE 1950 .... 50.00
(22) OCT 1946 .... 60.00	(47) AUG 1950 .... 50.00
(23) DEC 1946 .... 60.00	(48) OCT 1950 .... 50.00
(24) FEB 1947 .... 60.00	(49) DEC 1950 .... 50.00
(25) APR 1947 .... 60.00	

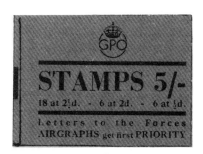

Type BD29

1944 (April). *As before, but buff cover printed in black as Type BD29 (Nos. 485, 488/9).*
BD29 Edition dates April or June 1944 .... £325

(1) APR 1944 .... £325   (2) JUNE 1944 .... £325

1951 (May). *As before, but buff cover changed back to Type A (see No. BD18, 2s. 6d.) and containing stamps in the new colours. (Nos. 503, 506/7).*
BD30 Edition dates May 1951 to January 1952 .... 15.00

(1) MAY 1951 .... 15.00   (4) NOV 1951 .... 15.00
(2) JULY 1951 .... 15.00   (5) JAN 1952 .... 15.00
(3) SEPT 1951 .... 15.00

1952 (Mar). *As before, make-up changed to contain: 18 × 2½d., 6 × 1½d., 3 × 1d. and 6 × ½d. The 1d. pane was completed by three perforated labels in the lower row inscribed "MINIMUM INLAND PRINTED PAPER RATE 1½d." (Nos. 503/5, 507).*
BD31 Edition dates March to November 1952 .... 15.00

(1) MAR 1952 .... 15.00   (4) SEPT 1952 .... 15.00
(2) MAY 1952 .... 15.00   (5) NOV 1952 .... 15.00
(3) JULY 1952 .... 15.00

1953 (Jan). *As before, but make-up changed again to include the 2d. value and containing: 12 × 2½d., 6 × 2d., 6 × 1½d., 6 × 1d. and 6 × ½d. (Nos. 503/7).*
BD32 Edition dates January or March 1953 .... 25.00

(1) JAN 1953 .... 25.00   (2) MAR 1953 .... 25.00

QUEEN ELIZABETH II

l.£.s.d. Booklets, 1953–70.

TYPES OF BOOKLET COVER WITH GPO CYPHER

Type A
Circular GPO Cypher
(See illustration above No. BD18)

Type B
Oval Type GPO Cypher

Type C
New GPO Cypher (small)

Type D
New GPO Cypher (large)

1s. Booklets

1953 (2 Sept)–**59.** *I. White unprinted cover. Pages of two stamps:
4 × 1½d., 4 × 1d., 4 × ½d. For use in experimental "D" machines.*

A. *Wmk Tudor Crown (Nos. 515/17)*
E1 No date... 2.25

B. *Wmk St. Edward's Crown (Nos. 540/2)*
E2 No date (11.57).. 4.50

*II. White printed cover as Type B. Pages of four stamps: 4 × 1½d.,
4 × 1d., 4 × ½d. For use in "E" machines.*

A. *Wmk Tudor Crown (Nos. 515/17)*
K1 No date (22.7.54).. 4.00

B. *Wmk St. Edward's Crown (Nos. 540/2)*
K2 No date (5.7.56).. 2.50

C. *Wmk Crowns (Nos. 570/2)*
K3 No date (13.8.59)... 3.00

2s. Booklets

1959 (22 Apr)–**65.** *Pages of four stamps: 4 × 3d., 4 × 1½d., 4 × 1d.,
4 × ½d.
I. Salmon cover as Type B. Wmk. St. Edward's Crown (Nos. 540/2 and
545).*
N1 No date... 4.00

II. Salmon cover as Type C. Wmk Crowns (Nos. 570/2 and 575).
N2 No date (2.11.60)... 3.75

III. Lemon cover as Type C. Wmk Crowns (Nos. 570/2 and 575).
N3 No date (2.61)... 4.00

*IV. Lemon cover as Type C. Wmk Crowns (sideways) (Nos. 570a, 571a,
572b, 575a) or phosphor (Nos. 610a, 611a, 612a, 615b).*
N 4 APR 1961 .... 15.00
       p. With phosphor bands.................................... 40.00
N 5 SEPT 1961 .... 24.00
N 6 JAN 1962 .... 24.00
N 7 APR 1962 .... 24.00
N 8 JULY 1962 .... 24.00
       p. With phosphor bands.................................... 45.00
N 9 NOV 1962 .... 24.00
       p. With phosphor bands.................................... 40.00
N10 JAN 1963 .... 24.00
       p. With phosphor bands.................................... 50.00
N11 MAR 1963 .... 24.00

N12 JUNE 1963.. 24.00
       p. With phosphor bands.................................... 40.00
N13 AUG 1963 .... 24.00
       p. With phosphor bands.................................... 40.00
N14 OCT 1963 .... 24.00
       p.With phosphor bands..................................... 55.00
N15 FEB 1964... 24.00
       p. With phosphor bands.................................... 38.00
N16 JUNE 1964.. 24.00
       p. With phosphor bands.................................... 55.00
N17 AUG 1964 .... 24.00
       p.With phosphor bands..................................... 55.00
N18 OCT 1964 .... 26.00
       p. With phosphor bands.................................... 40.00
N19 DEC 1964.. 26.00
       p. With phosphor bands.................................... 40.00
N20 APR 1965 .... 22.00
       p. With phosphor bands.................................... 38.00

1965 (16 Aug)–**67.** *New Composition. Pages of four stamps: 4 × 4d.
and pane of 2 × 1d. and 2 × 3d. arranged se-tenant horiz.*

*Orange-yellow cover as Type C printed in black. Wmk Crowns (side-
ways) (Nos. 571a, 575a and 576ab) or phosphor (Nos. 611a, 615d (one
side phosphor band) and 616ab).*
N21 JULY 1965 .... 1.50
       p. With phosphor bands.................................... 14.00
N22 OCT 1965 .... 1.50
       p. With phosphor bands.................................... 8.50
N23 JAN 1966 .... 2.50
       p. With phosphor bands.................................... 12.00
N24 APR 1966 .... 2.50
       p. With phosphor bands.................................... 6.00
N25 JULY 1966 .... 2.50
       p. With phosphor bands.................................... 30.00
N26 OCT 1966 .... 2.10
       p. With phosphor bands.................................... 6.00
N27 JAN 1967 .... 2.25
       p. With phosphor bands.................................... 5.00
N28p APR 1967. With phosphor bands.............................. 5.00
N29p JULY 1967. With phosphor bands 4.00
N30p OCT 1967. With phosphor bands 4.00
    *In the se-tenant pane the 3d. appears at left or right to facilitate the
application of phosphor bands.*
    The following illustration shows how the se-tenant stamps with one
phosphor band on 3d. are printed and the arrows indicate where the
guillotine falls. The result gives 1d. stamps with two bands and the 3d.
stamps with one band either at left or right.

3d.   1d.   1d.   3d.   3d.   1d.   1d.   3d.

1967 (Nov)–**68.** *Composition and cover as Nos. N21/30. Wmk Crowns
(sideways) (Nos. 611a, 615b (two phosphor bands) and 616ab).*
N31p JAN 1968 .... 2.25
N32p MAR 1968 .... 2.25

2s. Booklets with Machin type stamps

1968 (6 Apr–Aug). *Orange-yellow cover as Type C. Pages of four
stamps: 4 × 4d. and pane of 2 × 1d. and 2 × 3d. arranged se-tenant
horiz. PVA gum (Nos. 724, 730, 731Ev).*
NP27 MAY 1968 70
NP28 JULY 1968 70
NP29 AUG 1968 .... 2.00

1968 (16 Sept)–**70.** *Grey cover as Type C. New composition. 4d. stamps only comprising page of 4 × 4d. with two phosphor bands (No. 731Ev) and page of 2 × 4d. with one centre phosphor band (No. 732) se-tenant with two printed labels.*

NP30	SEPT 1968	55
NP31	JAN 1969	£100

Same composition but all six 4d. stamps have one centre phosphor band (No. 732).

NP31a	SEPT 1968	£325
NP32	NOV 1968	55
NP33	JAN 1969	55

Same composition but change to 4d. bright vermilion with one centre phosphor band (No. 733).

NP34	MAR 1969	90
NP35	MAY 1969	1.10
NP36	JULY 1969	1.40
NP37	SEPT 1969	1.25
NP38	NOV 1969	1.25
NP39	JAN 1970	1.25
NP40	MAR 1970	1.25
NP41	MAY 1970	1.25
NP42	JULY 1970	1.25
NP43	AUG 1970	1.25
NP44	OCT 1970	1.25
NP45	DEC 1970	1.25

2s. Booklets for Holiday Resorts

1963 (15 July)–**64.** *I. Lemon cover as Type C and printed in red. New composition. Pages of four stamps: two of 4 × 2½d. and one of 3 × ½d., and 1 × 2½d. arranged se-tenant. Chalky paper. Wmk Crowns (Nos. 570k and 574k).*

NR1	No date, black stitching	2.50
	a. White stitching (3.9.63)	3.00

II. Lemon cover as Type C and printed in red. Composition changed again. Pages of four stamps 2 × ½d. and 2 × 2½d. arranged sideways, vertically se-tenant. Wmk Crowns (sideways) (No. 570m × 4).

NR2	1964 (1.7.64)	1.10

2s. Booklet for Christmas Cards

1965 (6 Dec). *Orange-yellow cover as Type C printed in red. Two panes of 4 × 3d. arranged sideways. Wmk Crowns (sideways) (No. 575a).*

NX1	1965	55

2s. 6d. Booklets

Green cover. Pages of six stamps: 6 × 2½d., 6 × 1½d., 3 × 1d. (page completed by three perforated labels), 6 × ½d.

LABELS. The wording printed on the labels differs as follows:

"PPR" = "MINIMUM INLAND PRINTED PAPER RATE 1½d." Two types exist:
A. Printed in photogravure 17 mm high.
B. Typographed, 15 mm high.
"Shorthand" = "SHORTHAND IN 1 WEEK" (covering all three labels).
"Post Early" = "PLEASE POST EARLY IN THE DAY".
"PAP" = "PACK YOUR PARCELS SECURELY" (1st label) "ADDRESS YOUR LETTERS CORRECTLY" (2nd label), "AND POST EARLY IN THE DAY" (3rd label).

1953–54. *Composite booklets containing stamps of George VI and Queen Elizabeth II.*

A. *K.G.VI ½d. and 1d. (Nos. 503/4) and Q.E.II 1½d. and 2½d. (Nos. 517 and 519b). Cover as Type A. No interleaving pages.*

F 1	MAY 1953 (PPR 17 mm)	11.00
F 2	JUNE 1953 (PPR 17 mm)	12.00
F 3	JULY 1953 (PPR 17 mm)	15.00
F 4	AUG 1953 (PPR 17 mm)	13.00

B. *Same composition but with addition of two interleaving pages, one at each end. Cover as Type A.*

F 5	SEPT 1953 (PPR 17 mm)	65.00
F 6	SEPT 1953 (PPR 15 mm)	14.00

C. *Same composition and with interleaving pages but cover as Type B.*

F 7	OCT 1953 (PPR 17 mm)	15.00
F 8	OCT 1953 (PPR 15 mm)	18.00
F 9	NOV 1953 (PPR 17 mm)	15.00
F10	NOV 1953 (PPR 15 mm)	60.00
F11	DEC 1953 (PPR 17 mm)	15.00
F12	JAN 1954 (Shorthand)	20.00
F13	FEB 1954 (Shorthand)	15.00

D. *New composition: K.G.VI 1d. (No. 504) and Q.E.II ½d., 1½d. and 2½d. (Nos. 515, 517 and 519b).*

F14	MAR 1954 (PPR 17 mm)	£350

1954–57. *Booklets containing only Queen Elizabeth II stamps. All covers as Type B.*

A. *Wmk Tudor Crown (Nos. 515/17 and 519b).*

F15	MAR 1954 (PPR 15 mm)	£150
F16	APR 1954 (Post Early)	15.00
F17	MAY 1954 (Post Early)	15.00
F18	JUNE 1954 (Post Early)	15.00
F19	JULY 1954 (Post Early)	16.00
F20	AUG 1954 (Post Early)	18.00
F21	SEPT 1954 (Post Early)	15.00
F22	OCT 1954 (Post Early)	15.00
F23	NOV 1954 (Post Early)	15.00
F24	DEC 1954 (Post Early)	15.00

B. *Same composition but with interleaving pages between each pane of stamps.*

F25	JAN 1955 (Post Early)	18.00
F26	JAN 1955 (PAP)	35.00
F27	FEB 1955 (PAP)	16.00
F28	MAR 1955 (PAP)	15.00
F29	APR 1955 (PAP)	17.00
F30	MAY 1955 (PAP)	17.00
F31	JUNE 1955 (PAP)	16.00
F32	JULY 1955 (PAP)	17.00
F33	AUG 1955 (PAP)	16.00

C *Mixed watermarks. Wmk Tudor Crown (Nos. 515/17 and 519b) and wmk St. Edward's Crown (Nos. 540/2 and 544b) in various combinations.*

F34	SEPT 1955 (PAP)	*From* 15.00

2s. 6d. booklets dated AUGUST, OCTOBER, NOVEMBER and DECEMBER 1955, JANUARY, MAY and JUNE 1956 exist both as listed and with the two watermarks mixed. There are so many different combinations that we do not list them separately, but when in stock selections can be submitted. The SEPTEMBER 1955 booklet (No. F34) only exists in composite form.

D. *Wmk St. Edward's Crown (Nos. 540/2 and 544b).*

F35	OCT 1955 (PAP)	15.00
F36	NOV 1955 (PAP)	15.00
F37	DEC 1955 (PAP)	15.00

F38	JAN 1956 (PAP)	12.00
F39	FEB 1956 (PAP)	15.00
F40	MAR 1956 (PAP)	15.00
F41	APR 1956 (PAP)	15.00
F42	MAY 1956 (PAP)	15.00
F43	JUNE 1956 (PAP)	15.00
F44	JULY 1956 (PAP)	15.00
F45	AUG 1956 (PAP)	15.00
F46	SEPT 1956 (PAP)	15.00
F47	OCT 1956 (PAP)	15.00
F48	NOV 1956 (PAP)	14.00
F49	DEC 1956 (PAP)	14.00
F50	JAN 1957 (PAP)	16.00
F51	FEB 1957 (PAP)	15.00
F52	MAR 1957 (PAP)	12.00

E. *Same wmk but new composition. Pages of six stamps:* $6 \times 2\frac{1}{2}d.$ *(No. 544b),* $6 \times 2d.$ *(No. 543b) and* $6 \times \frac{1}{2}d.$ *(No. 540).*

F53	APR 1957	13.00
F54	MAY 1957	15.00
F55	JUNE 1957	13.00
F56	JULY 1957	13.00
F57	AUG 1957	11.00
F58	SEPT 1957	12.00
F59	OCT 1957	11.00
F60	NOV 1957	10.00
F61	DEC 1957	13.00

3s. Booklets

1958–65. *Pages of six stamps:* $6 \times 3d., 6 \times 1\frac{1}{2}d., 6 \times 1d., 6 \times \frac{1}{2}d.$

I. Red cover as Type B.
A. *Wmk St. Edward's Crown (Nos. 540/2 and 545).*

M1	JAN 1958	10.00
M2	FEB 1958	10.00
M3	MAR 1958	10.00
M4	APR 1958	10.00
M5	MAY 1958	10.00
M6	JUNE 1958	10.00
M7	JULY 1958	10.00
M8	AUG 1958	10.00
M9	NOV 1958	10.00

The 3s. booklet dated NOVEMBER 1958, DECEMBER 1958 and JANU-ARY 1959 exist both as listed and with mixed St. Edward's Crown and Crowns wmks.

B. *Wmk crowns (Nos. 570/2 and 575) or graphite lines (Nos. 587/9 and 592).*

M10	DEC 1958	14.00
M11	JAN 1959	13.00
M12	FEB 1959	13.00
M13	AUG 1959	13.00
	g. With graphite lines	£120
M14	SEPT 1959	13.00
	g. With graphite lines	£140

II. Brick-red cover as Type C. Wmk Crowns (Nos. 570/2 and 575), graphite lines (Nos. 587/9 and 592) or phosphor (Nos. 610/12 and 615).

M15	OCT 1959	13.00
	g. With graphite lines	£120
M16	NOV 1959	13.00
M17	DEC 1959	13.00
M18	JAN 1960	13.00
M19	FEB 1960	14.00
	g. With graphite lines	£140
M20	MAR 1960	13.00
	g. With graphite lines	£150
M21	APR 1960	14.00
	g. With graphite lines	£140
M22	MAY 1960	14.00

M23	JUNE 1960	14.00
M24	JULY 1960	14.00
M25	AUG 1960	14.00
	p. With phosphor bands	30.00
M26	SEPT 1960	14.00
M27	OCT 1960	14.00
M28	NOV 1960	14.00
	p. With phosphor bands	32.00

III. Brick-red cover as Type D. Wmk Crowns (Nos. 570/2 and 575) or phosphor (Nos. 610/12 and 615).

M29	DEC 1960	14.00
	p. With phosphor bands	35.00
M30	JAN 1961	14.00
M31	FEB 1961	14.00
M32	MAR 1961	14.00
M33	APR 1961	14.00
	p. With phosphor bands	25.00
M34	MAY 1961	14.00
M35	JUNE 1961	14.00
M36	JULY 1961	14.00
	p. With phosphor bands	25.00
M37	AUG 1961	14.00
	p. With phosphor bands	25.00
M38	SEPT 1961	14.00
	p. With phosphor bands	30.00
M39	OCT 1961	14.00
	p. With phosphor bands	25.00
M40	NOV 1961	14.00
M41	DEC 1961	14.00
M42	JAN 1962	14.00
M43	FEB 1962	14.00
	p. With phosphor bands	25.00
M44	MAR 1962	14.00
	p. With phosphor bands	25.00
M45	APR 1962	14.00
	p. With phosphor bands	25.00
M46	MAY 1962	14.00
	p. With phosphor bands	25.00
M47	JUNE 1962	16.00
	p. With phosphor bands	25.00
M48	JULY 1962	14.00
M49	AUG 1962	14.00
	p. With phosphor bands	25.00
M50	SEPT 1962	14.00
	p. With phosphor bands	25.00
M51	OCT 1962	14.00
	p. With phosphor bands	25.00
M52	NOV 1962	14.00
	p. With phosphor bands	25.00
M53	DEC 1962	14.00
	p. With phosphor bands	25.00
M54	JAN 1963	16.00
M55	FEB 1963	14.00
	p. With phosphor bands	25.00
M56	MAR 1963	14.00
	p. With phosphor bands	25.00
M57	APR 1963	14.00
	p. With phosphor bands	25.00
M58	MAY 1963	14.00
	p. With phosphor bands	80.00
M59	JUNE 1963	14.00
	p. With phosphor bands	23.00
M60	JULY 1963	14.00
	p. With phosphor bands	25.00
M61	AUG 1963	14.00
	p. With phosphor bands	25.00
M62	SEPT 1963	14.00
M63	OCT 1963	14.00
M64	NOV 1963	14.00
	p. With phosphor bands	23.00

M65	DEC 1963	14.00
	p. With phosphor bands	30.00
M66	JAN 1964	16.00
	p. With phosphor bands	25.00
M67	MAR 1964	14.00
	p. With phosphor bands	25.00
M68	MAY 1964	14.00
	p. With phosphor bands	35.00
M69	JULY 1964	14.00
	p. With phosphor bands	25.00
M70	SEPT 1964	14.00
	p. With phosphor bands	25.00
M71	NOV 1964	14.00
	p. With phosphor bands	23.00
M72	JAN 1965	14.00
	p. With phosphor bands	23.00
M73	MAR 1965	10.00
	p. With phosphor bands	23.00
M74	MAY 1965	10.00
	p. With phosphor bands	25.00

3s. 9d. Booklets

1953–57. *Red cover as Type B. Pages of six stamps: 18 × 2½d.*
A. *Wmk Tudor Crown (No. 519b).*

G 1	NOV 1953	14.00
G 2	JAN 1954	15.00
G 3	MAR 1954	14.00
G 4	DEC 1954	14.00
G 5	FEB 1955	14.00
G 6	APR 1955	15.00
G 7	JUNE 1955	15.00
G 8	AUG 1955	15.00

3s. 9d. booklets dated OCTOBER and DECEMBER 1955 exist both as listed and with the two wmks mixed.

G 9	OCT 1955	14.00
G10	DEC 1955	16.00

Wmk St. Edward's Crown (No. 544b).
B. *Same composition but with interleaving pages between each pane of stamps.*

G12	FEB 1956	8.00
G13	APR 1956	8.00
G14	JUNE 1956	8.00
G15	AUG 1956	8.00
G16	OCT 1956	8.00
G17	DEC 1956	8.00
G18	FEB 1957	8.00
G19	APR 1957	8.00
G20	JUNE 1957	6.00
G21	AUG 1957	14.00

4s. 6d. Booklets

1957–65. *Pages of six stamps: 18 × 3d.*

I. Purple cover as Type B.
A. *Wmk St. Edward's Crown (No. 545).*

L1	OCT 1957	9.00
L2	DEC 1957	8.00
L3	FEB 1958	10.00
L4	APR 1958	8.00
L5	JUNE 1958	10.00
L6	OCT 1958	10.00
L7	DEC 1958	10.00

B. *Wmk Crowns (No. 575).*

L8	DEC 1958	32.00

II. Purple cover as Type C. Wmk Crowns (No. 575) or graphite lines (No. 592).

L9	FEB 1959	11.00
L10	JUNE 1959	11.00
L11	AUG 1959	11.00
	g. With graphite lines	10.00
L12	OCT 1959	11.00
L13	DEC 1959	11.00

III. Violet cover as Type C. Wmk Crowns (No. 575), graphite lines (No. 592) or phosphor (No. 615).

L14	FEB 1959	12.00
L15	APR 1959	11.00
	g. With graphite lines	10.00
L16	JUNE 1959	11.00
	g. With graphite lines	10.00
L17	DEC 1959	10.00
L18	FEB 1960	12.50
	g. With graphite lines	11.00
L19	APR 1960	12.50
	g. With graphite lines	11.00
L20	JUNE 1960	12.50
L21	AUG 1960	13.00
	p. With phosphor bands	24.00
L22	OCT 1960	14.00

IV. Violet cover as Type D. Wmk Crowns (No. 575) or phosphor (No. 615).

L23	DEC 1960	15.00
L24	FEB 1961	16.00
	p. With phosphor bands	18.00
L25	APR 1961	14.00
	p. With phosphor bands	18.00
L26	JUNE 1961	14.00
L27	AUG 1961	14.00
	p. With phosphor bands	18.00
L28	OCT 1961	14.00
	p. With phosphor bands	18.00
L29	DEC 1961	14.00
L30	FEB 1962	14.00
	p. With phosphor bands	18.00
L31	APR 1962	15.00
	p. With phosphor bands	18.00
L32	JUNE 1962	15.00
	p. With phosphor bands	26.00
L33	AUG 1962	15.00
	p. With phosphor bands	26.00
L34	OCT 1962	15.00
	p. With phosphor bands	90.00
L35	DEC 1962	15.00
	p. With phosphor bands	18.00
L36	FEB 1963	15.00
	p. With phosphor bands	18.00
L37	APR 1963	15.00
	p. With phosphor bands	18.00
L38	JUNE 1963	15.00
	p. With phosphor bands	20.00
L39	AUG 1963	15.00
	p. With phosphor bands	18.00
L40	OCT 1963	15.00
	p. With phosphor bands	18.00
L41	NOV 1963	15.00
	p. With phosphor bands	18.00
L42	DEC 1963	16.00
	p. With phosphor bands	80.00
L43	JAN 1964	15.00
L44	FEB 1964	15.00
	p. With phosphor bands	20.00
L45	MAR 1964	15.00
	p. With phosphor bands	26.00

L46	APR 1964	20.00
	p. With phosphor bands................................	18.00
L47	MAY 1964	15.00
	p. With phosphor bands................................	18.00
L48	JUNE 1964...	15.00
	p. With phosphor bands................................	18.00
L49	JULY 1964...	15.00
	p. With phosphor bands................................	18.00
L50	AUG 1964	20.00
	p. With phosphor bands................................	18.00
L51	SEPT 1964	15.00
	p. With phosphor bands................................	18.00
L52	OCT 1964	15.00
	p. With phosphor bands................................	20.00
L53	NOV 1964	15.00
	p. With phosphor bands................................	18.00
L54	DEC 1964	12.00
	p. With phosphor bands................................	18.00
L55	JAN 1965	12.00
	p. With phosphor bands................................	18.00
L56	FEB 1965	12.00
	p. With phosphor bands................................	18.00
L57	MAR 1965	12.00
	p. With phosphor bands................................	£120
L58	APR 1965	8.00

1965 (26 July)–**67.** *New composition. Pages of six stamps. 12 × 4d.,
6 × 1d. Slate-blue cover as Type D. Wmk Crowns (Nos. 571 and 576a)
or phosphor (Nos. 611 and 616a).*

L59	JULY 1965	8.00
	p. With phosphor bands................................	15.00
L60	SEPT 1965	8.00
	p. With phosphor bands................................	15.00
L61	NOV 1965	7.50
	p. With phosphor bands................................	15.00
L62	JAN 1966	8.00
	p. With phosphor bands................................	15.00
L63	MAR 1966	8.00
	p. With phosphor bands................................	7.00
L64	JAN 1967	7.50
	p. With phosphor bands................................	7.00
L65	MAR 1967	15.00
	p. With phosphor bands................................	8.00
L66p	MAY 1967. With phosphor bands....................	7.00
L67p	JULY 1967. With phosphor bands	7.00
L68p	SEPT 1967. With phosphor bands...................	6.00
L69p	NOV 1967. With phosphor bands....................	5.50
L70p	JAN 1968. With phosphor bands....................	5.50
L71p	MAR 1968. With phosphor bands...................	5.50

4s. 6d. Booklets with Machin type stamps

1968–70. *Slate-blue cover as Type D. Pages of six stamps: 12 × 4d.,
6 × 1d. PVA gum (Nos. 724, 731Ev).*

LP45	MAY 1968	5.00

Type LP46
Ships Series with GPO Cypher

220

(Des S. Rose)

Blue cover as Type LP46. Ships Series. Composition as last.

LP46	JULY 1968 (*Cutty Sark*)	1.25

Same composition but change to one centre phosphor band (No. 732).

LP47	SEPT 1968 (*Golden Hind*)...........................	1.25
LP48	NOV 1968 (*Discovery*)	1.25

*Same composition but change to 4d. bright vermilion with one centre
phosphor band (No. 733).*

LP49	JAN 1969 (*Queen Elizabeth 2*)	1.25
LP50	MAR 1969 (*Sirius*)...................................	1.25
LP51	MAY 1969 (*Sirius*)	1.60
LP52	JULY 1969 (*Dreadnought*)	2.25
LP53	SEPT 1969 (*Dreadnought*)	3.25
LP54	NOV 1969 (*Mauretania*)	2.50
LP55	JAN 1970 (*Mauretania*)	2.50
LP56	MAR 1970 (*Victory*).................................	2.50
LP57	MAY 1970 (*Victory*)..................................	5.00

Type LP58
Ships Series with Post Office
Corporation Crown Symbol

(Des S. Rose)

As last but cover changed to Type LP58.

LP58	AUG 1970 (*Sovereign of the Seas*)...............	3.00
LP59	OCT 1970 (*Sovereign of the Seas*)...............	4.75

5s. Booklets

1953–57. *Buff cover. Pages of six stamps. 12 × 2½d., 6 × 2d., 6 × 1½d.,
6 × 1d., 6 × ½d.*

*I. Composite booklets containing stamps of King George VI and Queen
Elizabeth II.*
A. *K.G.VI.½d., 1d. and 2d. (Nos. 503/4 and 506) and Q.E.II 1½d. and 2½d.
(Nos. 517 and 519b). Cover as Type A. No interleaving pages.*

H1	MAY 1953	17.00
H2	JULY 1953	17.00

B. *Same composition but with addition of two interleaving pages, one
at each end. Cover as Type A.*

H3	SEPT 1953	18.00

C. *Same composition and with interleaving pages but cover as Type B.*

H4	NOV 1953	18.00
H5	JAN 1954	19.00

D. *New composition: K.G.VI 1d. and 2d. (Nos. 504 and 506) and Q.E.II ½d., 1½d. and 2½d. (Nos. 515, 517 and 519b).*

H6	MAR 1954	£140

E. *New composition: K.G.VI 2d. (No. 506) and Q.E.II ½d., 1d., 1½d. and 2½d. (Nos. 515/17 and 519b).*

H7	MAR 1954	65.00

II. Booklets containing only Queen Elizabeth II stamps. Buff cover as Type B. Two interleaving pages as before.
A. *Wmk Tudor Crown (Nos. 515/18 and 519b).*

H8	MAR 1954	55.00
H9	MAY 1954	18.00
H10	JULY 1954	27.00
H11	SEPT 1954	20.00
H12	NOV 1954	20.00

B. *Same composition but with interleaving pages between each pane of stamps.*

H13	JAN 1955	20.00
H14	MAR 1955	20.00
H15	MAY 1955	20.00
H16	JULY 1955	20.00

5s. booklets dated SEPTEMBER and NOVEMBER 1955 and JANUARY 1956 exist both as listed and with the two watermarks mixed. There are so many different combinations that we do not list them separately, but when in stock selections can be submitted.

C. *Wmk St. Edward's Crown (Nos. 540/3 and 544b).*

H17	SEPT 1955	14.00
H18	NOV 1955	17.00
H19	JAN 1956	17.00
H20	MAR 1956	18.00
H21	MAY 1956	17.00
H22	JULY 1956	17.00
H23	SEPT 1956	17.00
H24	NOV 1956	20.00
H25	JAN 1957	22.00

D. *Same watermark. Introduction of 2d. light red-brown (No. 543b) in place of No. 543.*

H26	JAN 1957	18.00
H27	MAR 1957	18.00
H28	MAY 1957	16.00
H29	JULY 1957	16.00
H30	SEPT 1957	16.00
H31	NOV 1957	16.00

1958–65. E. *New composition. Pages of six stamps: 12 × 3d. (No. 545), 6 × 2½d. (No. 544b), 6 × 1d. (No. 541), 6 × ½d. (No. 540). Wmk St. Edward's Crown.*

H32	JAN 1958	16.00
H33	MAR 1958	16.00
H34	MAY 1958	14.00
H35	JULY 1958 (11.58)	12.00
H36	NOV 1958	12.00

5s. booklets dated JULY 1958, NOVEMBER 1958 and JANUARY 1959 exist with mixed watermarks.

F. *Blue cover as Type C. Wmk Crowns (Nos. 570/1, 574/5), graphite lines (Nos. 587/8 and 591/2) or phosphor (Nos. 610/11, 614 and 615).*

H37	JAN 1959	14.00
H38	MAR 1959	16.00

H39	JULY 1959	16.00
	g. With graphite lines	60.00
H40	SEPT 1959	16.00
H41	NOV 1959	16.00
H42	JAN 1960	16.00
H43	MAR 1960	16.00
	g. With graphite lines	70.00
H44	MAY 1960	16.00
H45	JULY 1960	18.00
H46	SEPT 1960	18.00
	g. With graphite lines	70.00
	p. With phosphor bands	38.00
H47	NOV 1960	18.00

G. *As last but blue cover as Type D. Same composition.*
I. *Phosphor has two bands on 2½d.*

H48	JAN 1961	19.00
H49	MAR 1961	19.00
	p. With phosphor bands	45.00
H50	MAY 1961	18.00
H51	JULY 1961	18.00
	p. With phosphor bands	45.00
H52	SEPT 1961	19.00
	p. With phosphor bands	45.00
H53	NOV 1961	18.00
H54	JAN 1962	18.00
	p. With phosphor bands	45.00

II. *As last but phosphor has one band on 2½d.*

H55	MAR 1962	18.00
	p. With phosphor bands	45.00
H56	MAY 1962	18.00
	p. With phosphor bands	45.00
H57	JULY 1962	18.00
	p. With phosphor bands	45.00
H58	SEPT 1962	18.00
	p. With phosphor bands	45.00
H59	NOV 1962	18.00
	p. With phosphor bands	45.00
H60	JAN 1963	18.00
	p. With phosphor bands	£150
H61	MAR 1963	18.00
	p. With phosphor bands	50.00
H62	MAY 1963	18.00
	p. With phosphor bands	45.00
H63	JULY 1963	18.00
	p. With phosphor bands	45.00
H64	SEPT 1963	18.00
	p. With phosphor bands	50.00
H65	NOV 1963	18.00
	p. With phosphor bands	45.00
H66	JAN 1964	18.00
	p. With phosphor bands	45.00
H67	MAR 1964	18.00
	p. With phosphor bands	45.00
H68	MAY 1964	18.00
	p. With phosphor bands	50.00
H69	JULY 1964	18.00
	p. With phosphor bands	45.00
H70	SEPT 1964	18.00
	p. With phosphor bands	45.00
H71	NOV 1964	19.00
	p. With phosphor bands	45.00
H72	JAN 1965	18.00
	p. With phosphor bands	38.00
H73	MAR 1965	18.00
	p. With phosphor bands	45.00
H74	MAY 1965	18.00
	p. With phosphor bands	45.00

5s. Booklets with Machin type stamps

Type HP26
English Homes Series with
GPO Cypher

(Des S. Rose)

1968 (27 Nov)–**70.** *Cinnamon cover as Type HP26 (English Homes Series). Pages of six stamps: 12 × 5d. (No. 735).*
HP26	DEC 1968 (Ightham Mote)	1.10
HP27	FEB 1969 (Little Moreton Hall)	1.10
HP28	APR 1969 (Long Melford Hall)	1.10
HP29	JUNE 1969 (Long Melford Hall)	1.50
HP30	AUG 1969 (Long Melford Hall)	1.50

Type HP31
English Homes Series with Post
Office Corporation Crown Symbol

(Des S. Rose)

As last but cover change to Type HP31.
HP31	OCT 1969 (Mompesson House)	1.50
HP32	DEC 1969 (Mompesson House)	2.40
HP33	FEB 1970 (Cumberland Terrace)	2.00

STAMP MONTHLY

Finest and most informative magazine for all collectors.
Obtainable from your newsagent or by postal subscription –
details on request

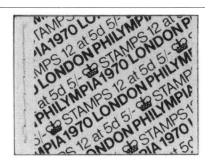

Type HP34

(Des Peter Gauld)

As last but cover change to Type HP34 (special edition to advertise "Philympia" International Philatelic Exhibition, London, September 1970).
HP34	(no date) (3.3.70)	1.00

As last but cover changed to Type HP31.
HP35	JUNE 1970 (The Vineyard, Saffron, Walden)	2.00
HP36	AUG 1970 (The Vineyard, Saffron, Walden)	2.00
HP37	OCT 1970 (Mereworth Castle)	2.25
HP38	DEC 1970 (Mereworth Castle)	2.50

6s. Booklets

1965 (21 June)–**67.** *Claret cover as Type D. Wmk Crowns (No. 576a) or phosphor (No. 616a). Pages of six stamps: 18 × 4d.*
Q 1	JUNE 1965	15.00
	p. With phosphor bands	15.00
Q 2	JULY 1965	15.00
	p. With phosphor bands	15.00
Q 3	AUG 1965	15.00
	p. With phosphor bands	18.00
Q 4	SEPT 1965	15.00
	p. With phosphor bands	18.00
Q 5	OCT 1965	15.00
	p. With phosphor bands	18.00
Q 6	NOV 1965	15.00
	p. With phosphor bands	18.00
Q 7	DEC 1965	15.00
	p. With phosphor bands	18.00
Q 8	JAN 1966	15.00
	p. With phosphor bands	18.00
Q 9	FEB 1966	15.00
	p. With phosphor bands	18.00
Q10	MAR 1966	15.00
	p. With phosphor bands	18.00
Q11	APR 1966	15.00
	p. With phosphor bands	20.00
Q12	MAY 1966	15.00
	p. With phosphor bands	18.00
Q13	JUNE 1966	15.00
	p. With phosphor bands	17.00
Q14	JULY 1966	15.00
	p. With phosphor bands	22.00
Q15	AUG 1966	15.00
	p. With phosphor bands	45.00
Q16	SEPT 1966	15.00
	p. With phosphor bands	15.00
Q17	OCT 1966	15.00
	p. With phosphor bands	22.00

Q18	NOV 1966	15.00
	p. With phosphor bands	15.00
Q19	DEC 1966	15.00
	p. With phosphor bands	15.00
Q20	JAN 1967	18.00
	p. With phosphor bands	18.00
Q21	FEB 1967	18.00
	p. With phosphor bands	15.00
Q22	MAR 1967	15.00
	p. With phosphor bands	15.00
Q23	APR 1967	15.00
	p. With phosphor bands	15.00
Q24p	MAY 1967. With phosphor bands	15.00
Q25p	JUNE 1967. With phosphor bands	15.00
Q26p	JULY 1967. With phosphor bands	15.00
Q27p	AUG 1967. With phosphor bands	18.00

6s. Booklets with Machin type stamps

1967–70. *Claret cover as Type D. Pages of six stamps: 18 × 4d. Two phosphor bands. Gum arabic (No. 731).*

QP28	SEPT 1967	26.00
QP29	OCT 1967	28.00
QP30	NOV 1967	30.00
QP31	DEC 1967	32.00
QP32	JAN 1968	32.00
QP33	FEB 1968 (No. 731Ea)	32.00
QP34	MAR 1968 (No. 731Ea)	26.00
QP35	APR 1968 (No. 731Ea)	24.00
QP36	MAY 1968 (No. 731Ea)	13.00

Change to PVA gum (No. 731Ev).

QP37	MAY 1968	£200

Type QP38
Birds Series with GPO Cypher

(Des S. Rose)

Orange-red cover as Type QP38 (Birds Series). Same composition. Two phosphor bands. PVA gum (No. 731Ev).

QP38	JUNE 1968 (Kingfisher) (4.6.68)	1.25
QP39	JULY 1968 (Kingfisher)	4.50
QP40	AUG 1968 (Peregrine Falcon)	1.25

Change to one centre phosphor band (No. 732).

QP41	SEPT 1968 (Peregrine Falcon) (16.9.68)	1.25
QP42	OCT 1968 (Pied Woodpecker)	1.50
QP43	NOV 1968 (Pied Woodpecker)	1.75
QP44	DEC 1968 (Great Crested Grebe)	1.75
QP45	JAN 1969 (Barn Owl)	1.75

Change to 4d. bright vermilion with one centre phosphor band (No. 733).

QP46	FEB 1969 (Barn Owl) (20.2.69)	1.75

QP47	MAR 1969 (Jay)	1.75
QP48	MAY 1969 (Jay)	2.00
QP49	JULY 1969 (Puffin)	2.00
QP50	SEPT 1969 (Puffin)	2.25

Type QP51
Birds Series with Post Office
Corporation Crown Symbol

(Des S. Rose)

As last but cover change to Type QP51.

QP51	NOV 1969 (Cormorant)	2.25
QP52	JAN 1970 (Cormorant)	2.25
QP53	APR 1970 (Wren)	2.25
QP54	AUG 1970 (Golden Eagle)	2.50
QP55	OCT 1970 (Golden Eagle)	2.50

10s. Booklets

1961 (10 Apr–Oct). *Green cover as Type D. Pages of six stamps: 30 × 3d., 6 × 2d., 6 × 1½d., 6 × 1d., 6 × ½d. Wmk Crowns (Nos. 570/3 and 575).*

X1	No date	45.00
X2	OCT 1961	45.00

1962–64. *New composition. Pages of six stamps: 30 × 3d., 6 × 2½d., 6 × 1½d., 6 × 1d. (Nos. 571/2 and 574/5).*

X3	APR 1962	35.00
X4	AUG 1962	38.00
X5	MAR 1963	35.00
X6	JULY 1963	35.00
X7	DEC 1963	35.00
X8	JULY 1964	30.00
X9	DEC 1964	50.00

1965 (23 Aug)–**66.** *Ochre cover as Type D. Pages of six stamps: 24 × 4d., 6 × 3d., 6 × 1d. Wmk Crowns (Nos. 571, 575, 576a)*

X10	AUG 1965	16.00
X11	DEC 1965	18.00
X12	FEB 1966	18.00
X13	AUG 1966	14.00
X14	NOV 1966	12.00

1967–68. *Ochre cover as Type D. Pages of six phosphor stamps: 24 × 4d., 6 × 3d., 6 × 1d. Wmk Crowns (Nos. 611, 615c (one side phosphor band), 616a).*

X15p	FEB 1967	5.00

Composition as No. X15p. Wmk Crowns (Nos. 611, 615e (one centre phosphor band) 616a).

X16p	AUG 1967	6.00
X17p	FEB 1968	5.00

10s. Booklets with Machin type stamps

Type XP4
Explorers Series with GPO Cypher

(Des S. Rose)

1968 (25 Mar–Aug). *Bright purple cover as Type XP4 (Explorers Series).
Pages of six stamps: 24 × 4d., 6 × 3d., 6 × 1d. PVA gum (Nos. 724,
729Ev, 731Ev).*

XP4	MAY 1968 (Livingstone)	3.50
XP5	AUG 1968 (Livingstone)	3.50

1968 (16 Sept)–**70.** *Yellow-green covers as Type XP4 (Explorers Series).
New composition. Pages of six stamps: 12 × 5d. (with two phosphor
bands), 12 × 4d. (with one centre phosphor band) and pane comprising 4 × 1d. se-tenant with vert pair of 4d. (each with one centre
phosphor band). PVA gum (Nos. 725, 732 and 735).*

XP6	SEPT 1968 (Scott)	3.50

*Change to 4d. bright vermilion (one centre band) but se-tenant pane
comprises 1d. with two phosphor bands and 4d. with one left side
phosphor band (Nos. 724 and 733/4).*

XP 7	FEB 1969 (Mary Kingsley) (6.1.69)	2.25
XP 8	MAY 1969 (Mary Kingsley)	3.00
XP 9	AUG 1969 (Shackleton)	2.25
XP10	NOV 1969 (Shackleton)	5.00

Type XP11
Explorers Series with Post Office
Corporation Crown Symbol

(Des S. Rose)

As last but cover change to Type XP11.

XP11	FEB 1970 (Frobisher)	5.00
XP12	NOV 1970 (Captain Cook)	5.00

£1 Booklet with Machin type stamps

Type ZP1

1969 (1 Dec). *"Stamps for Cooks". Type ZP1 (150 × 72 mm) with full
colour pictorial cover showing "Baked, Stuffed Haddock". Contains
12 recipes on interleaving pages and on se-tenant label attached to
booklet panes. PVA gum. Stapled.*

ZP1	£1 containing panes of fifteen stamps (5 × 3): 15 × 5d. (No. 735), 30 × 4d. (No. 733) and pane comprising 6 × 4d. (three each of Nos. 734 and 734Eb) se-tenant with 6 × 1d. (No. 724) and 3 × 5d. (No. 735)	65.00
ZP1a	As last but booklet is sewn with thread instead of being stapled	10.00

II. Decimal Booklets, 1971 onwards.

A. Stitched Booklets.

The 25p., 30p., 35p., 45p. and 50p. booklets have pictorial covers
(except for the 35p. and 45p.) without the design inscription.

This was no longer necessary as the designs and background information were given on the inside of the front cover. Each series was
numbered.

10p. Booklets

Type DN46
British Pillar Box Series

(Des R. Maddox)

1971 (15 Feb–1 June). *British Pillar Box Series. Orange-yellow cover as
Type DN46. Pages of four stamps: 2 × 2p. se-tenant vertically with
2 × ½p. and 2 × 1p. se-tenant vertically with 2 × 1½p. (Nos. X841l and
X844l).*

DN46	FEB 1971 (No. 1 1855 type)	1.25
DN47	APR 1971 (No. 1 1855 type) (19.3.71)	1.50
DN48	JUNE 1971 (No. 2 1856 type) (1.6.71)	1.25

1971 (14 July)–**74.** *British Pillar Box Series continued. Orange-yellow cover as Type DN46. Contents unchanged, but panes are se-tenant horizontally (Nos. X841la and X844m).*

DN49	AUG 1971 (No. 2 1856 type) (14.7.71)	2.00
DN50	OCT 1971 (No. 3 1857–9 type) (27.8.71)	2.00
DN51	DEC 1971 (No. 3 1857–9 type) (6.10.71)	2.00
DN52	FEB 1972 (No. 4 1866–79 type) (8.12.71)	2.00
DN53	APR 1972 (No. 4 1866–79 type) (24.2.72)	2.00
DN54	JUNE 1972 (No. 5 1899 type) (12.4.72)	2.00
DN55	AUG 1972 (No. 5 1899 type) (8.6.72)	2.00
DN56	OCT 1972 (No. 6 1968 type) (2.8.72)	2.00
DN57	DEC 1972 (No. 6 1968 type) (30.10.72)	2.00
DN58	FEB 1973 (No. 7 1936 type) (5.1.73)	2.00
DN59	APR 1973 (No. 7 1936 type) (2.4.73)	2.00
DN60	JUNE 1973 (No. 8 1952 type) (18.4.73)	2.00
DN61	AUG 1973 (No. 8 1952 type) (4.7.73)	10.00
DN62	OCT 1973 (No. 9 1973 type) (16.8.73)	2.00
DN63	DEC 1973 (No. 9 1973 type) (12.11.73)	2.00
DN64	FEB 1974 (No. 9 1973 type) (17.12.73)	2.00
DN65	APR 1974 (No. 10 1974 type) (22.2.74)	1.50
DN66	JUNE 1974 (No. 10 1974 type) (23.4.74)	1.50

In No. DN47 the pillar box is slightly reduced in size.

Type DN67
Postal Uniforms Series

(Des C. Abbott)

1974 (23 July)–**76.** *Postal Uniforms Series. Orange-yellow cover as Type DN67. Contents unchanged.*

DN67	AUG 1974 (No. 1 1793 type)	1.50
DN68	OCT 1974 (No. 1 1793 type) (27.8.74)	1.50
DN69	DEC 1974 (No. 2 1837 type) (25.10.74)	1.50
DN70	FEB 1975 (No. 2 1837 type) (12.12.74)	1.50
DN71	APR 1975 (No. 3 1855 type) (26.3.75)	1.50
DN72	JUNE 1975 (No. 3 1855 type) (21.5.75)	1.50
DN73	AUG 1975 (No. 3 1855 type) (27.6.75)	1.00
DN74	OCT 1975 (No. 3 1855 type) (3.10.75)	75
DN75	JAN 1976 (No. 3 1855 type) (16.3.76)	75

HAVE YOU READ THE NOTES AT THE BEGINNING OF THIS CATALOGUE?

These often provide answers to the enquiries we receive.

25p. Booklets

Type DH39
Veteran Transport Series

(Des D. Gentleman)

1971 (15 Feb). *Veteran Transport Series. Dull purple cover as Type DH39. Pages of six stamps: $5 \times 2\frac{1}{2}$p. with one printed label, $4 \times 2\frac{1}{2}$p. with two printed labels, $5 \times \frac{1}{2}$p. with one printed label (Nos. X841m and X851l/m).*

DH39	FEB 1971 (No. 1 Knife-board omnibus)	3.00

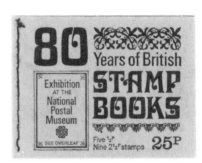

Type DH40

1971 (19 Mar). *Issued to publicise the National Postal Museum Exhibition of 80 Years of British Stamp Booklets. Dull purple cover as Type DH40.*

DH40	APR 1971	5.00

1971 (11 May)–**73.** *Dull purple cover as Type DH39. Veteran Transport Series continued.*

DH41	JUNE 1971 (No. 2 B-type omnibus)	5.00
DH42	AUG 1971 (No. 2 B-type omnibus) (17.9.71)	7.00
DH43	OCT 1971 (No. 3 Showman's Engine) (22.11.71)	7.00
DH44	FEB 1972 (No. 4 Mail Van) (23.12.71)	5.50
DH45	APR 1972 (No. 4 Mail Van) (13.3.72)	7.00
DH46	JUNE 1972 (No. 5 Motor Wagonette) (24.4.72)	6.00
DH47	AUG 1972 (No. 5 Motor Wagonette) (14.6.72)	6.00
DH48	OCT 1972 (No. 6 Taxi Cab) (17.7.72)	6.00
DH49	DEC 1972 (No. 6 Taxi Cab) (19.10.72)	5.50
DH50	DEC 1972 "Issue S" (No. 6 Taxi Cab) (6.11.72)	6.00
DH51	FEB 1973 (No. 7 Electric Tramcar) (26.2.73)	8.00

Nos. DH42/51 contain panes showing the perforations omitted between the label and the binding margin.

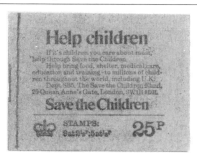

Type DH52

1973 (7 June). *Dull mauve cover as Type DH52.*
DH52   JUNE 1973..   8.00
   No. DH52 contains panes showing the perforations omitted between the label and the binding margin.

30p. Booklets

Type DQ56
British Birds Series

(Des H. Titcomb)

1971 (15 Feb). *British Birds Series. Bright purple cover as Type DQ56. Pages of six stamps: 2 panes of 5 × 3p. with one printed label (No. X855l).*
DQ56   FEB 1971 (No. 1 Curlew) 4.00

1971 (19 Mar). *Bright purple cover as Type DH40.*
DQ57   APR 1971 ....   3.50

1971 (26 May)–**73.** *Bright purple cover as Type DQ56. British Birds Series continued.*
DQ58   JUNE 1971 (No. 2 Lapwing) 3.50
DQ59   AUG 1971 (No. 2 Lapwing) (23.7.71) 4.00
DQ60   OCT 1971 (No. 3 Robin) (1.10.71).............................   4.00
DQ61   DEC 1971 (No. 3 Robin) (10.11.71)............................   4.00
DQ62   FEB 1972 (No. 4 Pied Wagtail) (21.12.71) 4.00
DQ63   APR 1972 (No. 4 Pied Wagtail) (9.2.72).......................   4.00
DQ64   JUNE 1972 (No. 5 Kestrel) (12.4.72)...........................   4.00
DQ65   AUG 1972 (No. 5 Kestrel) (8.6.72)..............................   5.00
DQ66   OCT 1972 (No. 6 Black Grouse) (31.7.72).....................   4.00
DQ67   DEC 1972 (No. 6 Black Grouse) (30.10.72)...................   4.00
DQ68   DEC 1972 "Issue S" (No. 6 Black Grouse) (6.12.72) 4.00
DQ69   FEB 1973 (No. 7 Skylark) (29.1.73).............................   4.00
DQ70   APR 1973 (No. 7 Skylark) (2.4.73) 5.00
DQ71   JUNE 1973 (No. 8 Oyster-catcher) (8.5.73) 4.50
DQ72   AUG 1973 (No. 8 Oyster-catcher) (7.6.73)...................   5.00
DQ72a   As DQ72 but buff cover (10.8.73)* 5.00
   Nos. DQ59/72a contain panes showing the perforations omitted between the label and the binding margin.
   No. DQ72a was printed with a buff cover because of a shortage of the original purple-coloured card.

1974 (30 Jan).   *Red cover similar to Type DH52. Make-up as before but with blank label.*
DQ73   SPRING 1974..   3.75

1974 (21 June).   *Red cover similar to Type DT9. Make-up as before.*
DQ74   JUNE 1974...   3.75

35p. Booklets

Type DP1
British Coins Series

(Des P. Gauld)

1973 (12 Dec)–**74.** *British Coins Series. Blue cover as Type DP1. Pages of six stamps: 2 pages of 5 × 3½p. with one blank label (No. X858Eb).*
DP1   AUTUMN 1973 (No. 1 Cuthred's Penny) 2.50
DP2   APR 1974 (No. 1 Cuthred's Penny) (10.4.74) 4.50
DP3   JUNE 1974 (No. 2 Silver Groat) (4.7.74).......................   2.50

1974 (23 Oct).   *Blue cover as Type DT9. Make-up as before but with No. X859.*
DP4   SEPT 1974 ....   2.50

45p. Booklets

1974 (9 Oct–26 Nov). *British Coins Series continued. Yellow-brown cover as Type DP1. Pages of six stamps: 2 pages of 5 × 4½p. (No. X865) with one blank label.*
DS1   SEPT 1974 (No. 3 Elizabeth Gold Crown) 4.00
DS2   DEC 1974 (No. 3 Elizabeth Gold Crown) (1.11.74) 4.50
DS2a   As DS2 but orange-brown cover (26.11.74)* 6.00
*No. DS2a was printed with an orange-brown cover because of a shortage of the original yellow-brown card.

50p. Booklets

Type DT1

(Des Rosalie Southall)

1971 (15 Feb)–**72**. *British Flowers Series. Turquoise-green cover as Type DT1. Pages of six stamps: 6 × 3p., 4 × 3p. se-tenant horizontally with 2 × 2½p. (side band), 5 × 2½p. (centre band) with one printed label and 5 × ½p. with one printed label (Nos. X841m, X851l, X852l and X855 × 6)*

DT1	FEB 1971 (No. 1 Large Bindweed)	8.00
DT2	MAY 1971 (No. 2 Primrose) (24.3.71)	7.00
DT3	AUG 1971 (No. 3 Honeysuckle) (28.6.71)	7.00
DT4	NOV 1971 (No. 4 Hop) (17.9.71)	8.00
DT5	FEB 1972 (No. 5 Common Violet) (23.12.71)*	8.00
DT6	MAY 1972 (No. 6 Lords-and-Ladies) (13.3.72)	7.00
DT7	AUG 1972 (No. 7 Wood Anemone) (31.5.72)	7.00
DT8	NOV 1972 (No. 8 Deadly Nightshade) (15.9.72)	7.00

Nos. DT4/8 contain panes showing the perforations omitted between the label and the binding margin.

*Although generally released on 24 December, this booklet was put on sale at the London E.C.1 Philatelic Counter and also at one other Philatelic Counter on the 23 December.

Type DT9

1973 (19 Jan–June). *Turquoise-green cover as Type DT9.*

DT9	FEB 1973	7.00
DT10	APR 1973 (26.2.73)	9.00
DT11	MAY 1973 (2.4.73)	9.00
DT12	AUG 1973 (14.6.73)	12.00

1973 (14 Nov)–**74**. *Moss-green cover similar to Type DT9. Pages of six stamps: 2 pages of 5 × 3½p. with one blank label (No. X858Eb) and 1 page of 5 × 3p. (centre band) with one blank label (No. X856).*

DT13	AUTUMN 1973	6.00
DT14	MAR 1974 (18.2.74)	4.00

85p. Booklet

1974 (13 Nov). *Purple cover similar to Type DT9.*

DW1 Containing 3 pages of 5 × 4½p. (No. X865) with one blank label and 1 page of 5 × 3½p. (No. X859) with one blank label 6.00

Sponsored Booklets

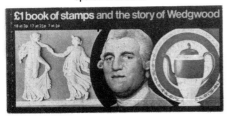

Type DX1

(Des J. Wallis)

1972 (24 May). *"The Story of Wedgwood". Full colour pictorial cover, Type DX1 (150 × 72 mm). Containing information and illustrations on interleaving panes and on se-tenant label attached to booklet panes.*

DX1 £1 containing 12 × 3p. (No. X855) and booklet panes X851n, X841o and X841p....................... 75.00

Price quoted for No. DX1 is for examples showing the ½p. 1 side band, No. X842, (in pane No. X841p) with full perforations. Examples of the booklet with this ½p. value showing trimmed perforations are priced at £25.

Type DX2

(Des J. Wallis)

1980 (16 Apr). *"The Story of Wedgwood". Multicoloured cover, Type DX2 (163 × 97 mm) showing painting "Josiah Wedgwood and his Family" by George Stubbs. Booklet contains text and illustrations on the labels attached to panes and on interleaving pages.*

DX2 £3 containing booklet panes Nos. X849n, X849o, X888l and X895l 7.50

No. DX2 is inscribed "January 1980".

Type DX3

(Des B. Dedman)

1982 (19 May). *"Story of Stanley Gibbons". Multicoloured cover, Type DX3 (163 × 97 mm) showing early envelope design on front and stamp album with text on back. Booklet contains text and illustrations on labels attached to panes and on interleaving pages.*

DX3 £4 containing booklet panes Nos. X849p, X899m and X907l/m 11.00

No. DX3 is inscribed "February 1982".

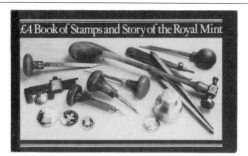

Type DX4

(Des B. West)

1983 (14 Sept). *"Story of the Royal Mint". Multicoloured cover, Type DX4 (163 × 97 mm) showing current coins, die and tools. Booklet contains text and illustrations on labels attached to panes and on interleaving pages.*
DX4   £4 containing booklet panes Nos. X899m × 2, X930b
and X949l 11.00

Type DX5

(Des P. Miles)

1984 (4 Sept). *"The Story of our Christian Heritage". Multicoloured cover, Type DX5 (163 × 97 mm) showing mosaic of Christ from Hinton St. Mary Roman villa. Booklet contains text and illustrations on labels attached to panes and on interleaving pages.*
DX5   £4 containing booklet panes Nos. X886bl, X901m × 2
and X952l 20.00

Type DX6

(Des D. Driver)

1985 (8 Jan). *"Story of the Times" (newspaper). Multicoloured cover, Type DX6 (163 × 95 mm) showing "Waiting for the Times" (painting by Haydon). Booklet contains text and illustrations on labels attached to panes and on interleaving pages.*
DX6   £5 containing booklet panes Nos. X864l, X900l, X952l
and X952m 20.00

Type DX7

(Des Trickett and Webb Ltd)

1986 (18 Mar). *"The Story of British Rail". Multicoloured cover, Type DX7 (162 × 95mm) showing diesel locomotive. Booklet contains text and illustrations on labels attached to panes and on interleaving pages.*
DX7   £5 containing booklet panes Nos. X896l, X897m, X952l
and X952m 20.00

Type DX8

(Des Aitken Blakeley Designers)

1987 (3 Mar). *"The Story of P & O". Multicoloured cover, Type DX8 (162 × 95 mm) showing the "William Fawcett". Booklet contains text and illustrations on labels attached to panes and on interleaving pages.*
DX8   £5 containing booklet panes Nos. X847m, X900l,
X900m and X955l 20.00

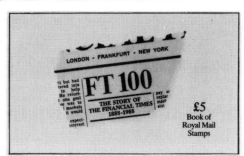

Type DX9

(Des The Partners Limited)

1988 (9 Feb). *"The Story of the Financial Times"* (newspaper). *Multi-coloured cover, Type DX9* (162 × 97 mm). *Booklet contains text and illustrations on labels attached to the panes and on interleaving pages.*
DX9   £5 containing booklet panes Nos. X1005l, X1006l, X1009l and X1009m 23.00

Type DX10

(Des Tayburn)

1989 (21 Mar). *"The Scots Connection". Multicoloured cover, Type DX10* (162 × 97mm). *Booklet contains text and illustrations on labels attached to the panes and on interleaving pages.*
DX10   £5 containing booklet panes Nos. S54l, S55l, S61l, and S61m 16.00

Type DX11

(Des D. Driver)

1990 (20 Mar). *"London Life". Multicoloured cover, Type DX11* (162 × 97mm). *Booklet contains text and illustrations on labels attached to the panes and on interleaving pages.*
DX11   £5 containing booklet panes Nos. X906m, 1469n × 2 and 1493a 20.00

Type DX12

(Des Trickett and Webb Ltd)

1991 (19 Mar). *"Alias Agatha Christie". Multicoloured cover, Type DX12* (162 × 97 mm). *Booklet contains text and illustrations on labels attached to the panes and on interleaving pages.*
DX12   £6 containing booklet panes Nos. X1008l × 2, X1016l and X1016m 19.00

Type DX13

(Des G. Evernden and J. Gibbs)

1992 (25 Feb). *"Cymru-Wales". Multicoloured cover; Type DX13* (162 × 97 mm.). *Booklet contains text and illlustrations on labels attached to the panes and on interleaving pages.*
DX13   £6 containing booklet panes Nos. 1591a, W48a, W49a, and W59a 17.00

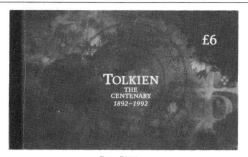

Type DX14

(Des The Partners)

Type DX15

(Des The Partners)

1992 (27 Oct). *Birth Centenary of J. R. R. Tolkien (author).*
Multicoloured cover, Type DX14 (162 × 97 mm). Booklet contains
text and illustrations on labels attached to the panes and on
interleaving pages.
DX14   £6 containing booklet panes Nos. X1011l, X1012l and
    X1017l × 2 .... 14.00

1993 (10 Aug). *"The Story of Beatrix Potter". Multicoloured cover,*
Type DX15 (162 × 197 mm). Booklet contains text and illustrations
on labels attached to the panes and on interleaving pages.
DX15   £5.64, containing booklet panes Nos. X1012m, 1451al,
    1649a and NI48l 18.00
  Although inscribed "£6.00" No. DX15 was sold at the face value of its
contents, £5.64.

3. Folded Booklets.

NOTE. All panes are attached to the covers by the selvedge.

10p. Booklets

Type FA1

(Des Post Office artist)

1976 (10 Mar)–**77.** *Cover as Type FA1 printed in dull rose on very pale lavender. Containing booklet pane X841r.*
FA1   NOV 1975   70
FA2   MAR 1976 (9.6.76)   80
FA3   JUNE 1977 (13.6.77)   70

Type FA4

(Des N. Battershill)

1978 (8 Feb)–**79.** *Farm Buildings Series. Bistre-brown and turquoise-blue covers as Type FA4, containing booklet pane No. X843m.*
FA4   Design No. 1, Oast Houses   75
FA5   Design No. 2, Buildings in Ulster (3.5.78)   75
FA6   Design No. 3, Buildings in Yorkshire (9.8.78)   75
FA7   Design No. 4, Buildings in Wales (25.10.78)   75
FA8   Design No. 5, Buildings in Scotland (10.1.79)   75
FA9   Design No. 6, Buildings in Sussex (4.4.79)   75
Nos. FA4/5 are inscribed "January 1978", FA6 "July 1978", FA7 "October 1978", FA8 "December 1978" and FA9 "March 1979".

Type FA10

(Des Hamper and Purssell)

1979 (17 Oct)–**80.** *"London 1980" International Stamp Exhibition. Red and blue cover as Type FA10 showing Post Office exhibition stand and containing No. X845l.*
FA10   Inscr "August 1979"   50
FA11   Inscr "January 1980" (12.1.80)   60

50p. Booklets

All booklets were sold at the cover price of 50p. although some contain stamps to a greater value.

Type FB1

1977 (26 Jan). *Cover as Type FB1 printed in maroon and pale blue.*
FB1A   Containing booklet pane X841s....................   2.50
FB1B   Containing booklet pane X841sa 2.50

1977 (13 June). *Cover as Type FB1. Printed in chestnut and stone.*
FB2A   Containing booklet pane X844n 4.00
FB2B   Containing booklet pane X844na..................   2.50

Type FB3

(Des J. Ireland)

1978 (8 Feb)–**79.** *Commercial Vehicles Series. Olive-yellow and grey covers as Type FB3. A. Containing booklet pane No. X844n. B. Containing booklet pane No. X844na.*

		A	B
FB3	Design No. 1, Clement Talbot van	4.00	3.00
FB4	Design No. 2, Austin taxi (3.5.78)	4.00	2.50
FB5	Design No. 3, Morris Royal Mail van (9.8.78)......	4.50	2.50
FB6	Design No. 4, Guy Electric dustcart (25.10.78)....	4.00	3.00
FB7	Design No. 5, Albion van (10.1.79)	5.00	2.50
FB8	Design No. 6, Leyland fire engine (4.4.79)	4.00	2.50

Nos. FB3/4 are inscribed "January 1978", FB5 "July 1978", FB6 "October 1978", FB7 "December 1978" and FB8 "March 1979".

1979 (28 Aug). *Contents changed. A. Containing booklet pane No. X849l. B. Containing booklet pane No. X849la.*

		A	B
FB9	Design No. 6 Leyland fire engine....................	2.00	2.00

Type FB10

(Des B. Smith)

1979 (3 Oct)–**81.** *Veteran Cars Series. Orange-red and reddish lilac covers as Type FB10. A. Containing booklet pane No.* X849l. *B. Containing booklet pane No.* X849la.

	A	B
FB10 Design No. 1, 1907 Rolls-Royce Silver Ghost......	2.50	2.50

No. FB10 is inscribed "August 1979".

Contents changed. A. Containing booklet pane No. X849m. *B. Containing booklet pane No.* X849ma.

	A	B
FB11 Design No. 2, 1908 Grand Prix Austin (4.2.80)	2.50	2.00
FB12 Design No. 3, 1903–5 Vauxhall (25.6.80)	2.50	2.00
FB13 Design No. 4, 1897–1900 Daimler (24.9.80)	2.50	2.00

No. FB11 is inscribed "January 1980", No. FB12 "May 1980" and No. FB13 "July 1980".

Contents changed. A. Containing No. X841t. *B. Containing No.* X841ta.

	A	B
FB14 Design No. 5, 1896 Lanchester (26.1.81)	2.25	2.25
FB15 Design No. 6, 1913 Bull-nose Morris (18.3.81)	2.25	2.25

Nos. FB14/15 are inscribed "January 1981".

Type FB16

(Des R. Downer)

1981 (6 May)–**82.** *Follies Series. Brown and orange-brown covers as Type FB16. A. Containing No.* X841t. *B. Containing No.* X841ta.

	A	B
FB16 Design No. 1, Mugdock Castle, Stirlingshire	2.00	2.00

No. FB16 is inscribed "January 1981".

Contents changed. A. Containing No. X854l. *B. Containing No.* X854la.

	A	B
FB17 Design No. 1, Mugdock Castle, Stirlingshire (26.8.81)	5.00	9.00
FB18 Design No. 2, Mow Cop Castle, Cheshire-Staffs border (30.9.81).......................................	4.00	7.00

Nos. FB17/18 are inscribed "January 1981".

Contents changed. A. Containing No. X841u. *B. Containing No.* X841ua.

	A	
FB19 Design No. 3, Paxton's Tower, Llanarthney, Dyfed (1.2.82)	2.50	2.5
FB20 Design No. 4, Temple of the Winds, Mount Stewart, Northern Ireland (6.5.82)................	2.50	2.5
FB21 Design No. 5, Temple of the Sun, Stourhead, Wilts (11.8.82)	2.50	2.5
FB22 Design No. 6, Water Garden Cliveden, Bucks 6.10.82)	2.50	2.5

Nos. FB19/22 are inscribed "February 1982".

Type FB23

(Des H. Titcombe)

1983 (16 Feb–26 Oct). *Rare Farm Animals Series. Bright green and black covers as Type FB23. A. Containing booklet pane No.* X841u *B. Containing booklet pane No.* X841ua.

	A	
FB23 Design No. 1, Bagot Goat..............................	2.50	2.5

Contents changed. Containing No. X845n.

FB24 Design No. 2, Gloucester Old Spot Pig (5.4.83)..........	5.0
b. Corrected rate	10.0
FB25 Design No. 3, Toulouse Goose (27.7.83)	5.0
FB26 Design No. 4, Orkney Sheep (26.10.83)	5.0

No. FB23 is inscribed "February 1982" and Nos. FB24/6 "April 1983" The corrected rate reads, "36p. for 200g" instead of "37p. for 200g".

Type FB27

(Des P. Morter)

1984 (3 Sept)–**85.** *Orchids Series. Yellow-green and lilac covers a Type FB27. Containing booklet pane No.* X845p.

FB27 Design No. 1, *Dendrobium nobile* and *Miltonia hybrid*	3.5
FB28 Design No. 2, *Cypripedium calceolus* and *Ophrys apifera* (15.1.85)	3.5
FB29 Design No. 3, *Bifrenaria* and *Vanda tricolour* (23.4.85) .	3.5
FB30 Design No. 4, *Cymbidium* and *Arpophyllum* (23.7.85)..	3.5

Nos. FB27/30 are inscribed "September 1984".

Type FB31

(Des M. Thierens Design Ltd)

1985 (4 Nov). *Cover as Type FB31 printed in black and bright scarlet. Containing booklet pane No. X909I.*

FB31   Pillar box design 3.00
No. FB31 is inscribed "November 1985".

Type FB32

(Des P. Morter)

1986 (20 May–12 Aug). *Pond Life Series. Dull blue and emerald covers as Type FB32. Containing booklet pane No. X907I.*

FB32   Design No. 1, Emperor Dragonfly, Four-spotted Libel-
         lula and Yellow Flag 2.75
FB33   Design No. 2, Common Frog, Fennel-leaved Pond-
         weed and Long-stalked Pondweed (29.7.86) 3.50
         FB33 was originally issued with double-lined blue stars 2.75
Nos. FB32/33 are inscribed "November 1985".

Type FB34

(Des N. Battershill)

1986 (29 July). *Roman Britain Series. Brown-ochre and Indian red cover as Type FB34. Containing booklet pane No. X845q.*

FB34   Design No. 1, Hadrian's Wall 8.00
No. FB34 is inscribed "November 1985".

1986 (20 Oct)–**87**. *Pond Life Series continued. Dull blue and emerald covers as Type FB32. Containing booklet pane No. X845s.*

FB35   Design No. 3, Moorhen and Little Grebe 4.00
FB36   Design No. 4, Giant Pond and Great Ramshorn Snails
         (27.1.87) 4.00
No. FB36 is inscribed "October 1986"

1986 (20 Oct)–**87**. *Roman Britain Series continued. Brown-ochre and Indian red covers as Type FB34. Containing booklet pane No. X847I.*

FB37   Design No. 2, Roman Theatre of Verulamium, St.
         Albans 3.00
FB38   Design No. 3, Portchester Castle, Hampshire (27.1.87) 3.00
No. FB38 is inscribed "October 1986".

Type FB39

(Des Patricia Howes)

1987 (14 Apr)–**88**. *Bicentenary of Marylebone Cricket Club Series. Brown and dull ultramarine covers as Type FB39. Containing booklet pane No. X847I.*

FB39   Design No. 1, Father Time weathervane 3.00
FB40   Design No. 2, Ashes urn and embroidered velvet
         bag (14.7.87) 3.00
FB41   Design No. 3, Lord's Pavilion and wrought iron
         decoration on roof (29.9.87) 3.00
FB42   Design No. 4, England team badge and new stand at
         Lord's (26.1.88) 3.00
Nos. FB39/42 are inscribed "October 1986".

Type FB43

(Des G. Evernden)

1987 (14 Apr)–**88**. *Botanical Gardens Series. Covers as Type FB43. Containing booklet pane No. X845s (FB43/4) or X845sa (FB45/6).*

FB43   Design No. 1 (cover in ultramarine and rose-red),
         Rhododendron "Elizabeth", Bodnant 3.25
FB44   Design No. 2 (cover in deep ultramarine and cobalt),
         Gentiana sino-ornata, Edinburgh (14.7.87) 3.25
FB45   Design No. 3 (cover in dull ultramarine and orange-
         yellow), Lilium auratum and "Mount Stuart"
         (incorrect inscr) (29.9.87) 3.25
         a. With corrected spelling "Mount Stewart"
         (30.10.87) 3.25
FB46   Design No. 4 (cover in dull ultramarine and yellow-
         orange), Strelitzia reginae, Kew (26.1.88) 3.00
Nos. FB43/6 are inscribed "October 1986".
The panes from Nos. FB45/6 have imperforate vertical sides

Type FB47

1988 (12 Apr–5 July). *London Zoo. Children's Drawings Series. Covers as Type* FB47.

FB47   Pigs design (cover in black and rose) containing
         booklet pane No. X847l 3.00
FB48   Birds design (cover in black and yellow) containing
         booklet pane No. X845sa 3.25
FB49   Elephants design (cover in black and grey) containing
         booklet pane No. X847l (5.7.88) 3.00
   Nos. FB47/9 are inscribed "October 1986". The pane from No. FB48
has imperforate vertical sides.

Type FB50

(Des P. Morter)

1988 (5 July). *Marine Life Series. Blue and orange-brown cover as Type* FB50. *Containing booklet pane No.* X845sa.

FB50   Design No. 1, Parasitic Anemone on Common Whelk
         Shell and Umbrella Jellyfish 3.00
   No. FB50 is inscribed "October 1986" and has the vertical sides of
the pane imperforate.

Type FB51

(Des Lynda Gray)

1988 (5 Sept)–**89**. *Gilbert and Sullivan Operas Series. Black and red covers as Type* FB51. *Containing booklet pane No.* X904l.

FB51   Design No. 1 *The Yeomen of the Guard* 3.00
FB52   Design No. 2 *The Pirates of Penzance* (24.1.89) 3.00
FB53   Design No. 3 *The Mikado* (25.4.89) 3.00

1989 (18 July). *Marine Life Series continued. Blue and orange-brown cover as Type* FB50. *Containing booklet pane No.* X904l.
FB54   Design No. 2, Common Hermit Crab, Bladder Wrack
         and Laver Spire Shell .... 4.
For Design No. 3, see £1 Booklet No. FH17.

Type FB55

(Des P. Hutton)

1989 (2 Oct)–**90**. *Aircraft Series. Turquoise-green and light brown covers as Type* FB55. *Containing booklet pane No.* X906l.
FB55   Design No. 1, "HP42", Armstrong Whitworth "Ata-
         lanta" and De Havilland "Dragon Rapide" 5.0
   No. FB55 was incorrectly inscribed "Atlanta".

As before, but containing Penny Black Anniversary booklet pane No. 1468l.
FB56   Design No. 2, Vickers Viscount 806 and De Havilland
         Comet 4 (30.1.90) .... 5.

1990 (4 Sept)–**91**. *Aircraft Series continued. Turquoise-green and light brown covers as Type* FB55. *Containing booklet pane No.* X911l.
FB57   Design No. 3, BAC "1-11" and "VC10" .... 3.
FB58   Design No. 4, BAe "ATP", BAe "146" and Aerospatiale–
         BAC "Concorde" (25.6.91) .... 3.

Type FB59

(Des A. Drummond)

1991 (10 Sept)–**92**. *Archaeology Series. Covers as Type* FB. *Containing booklet pane No.* X925m.
FB59   Design No. 1 (cover in bright blue and lake-brown),
         Sir Arthur Evans at Knossos, Crete 2
         a. Corrected rate (10.91) 3
FB60   Design No. 2 (cover in bright blue and yellow),
         Howard Carter in the Tomb of Tutankhamen
         (21.1.92) .... 2.
FB61   Design No. 3 (cover in bright blue and yellow), Sir
         Austen Layard at Assyrian site (28.4.92) .... 2.
FB62   Design No.4 (cover in new blue and yellow), Sir
         Flinders Petrie surveying the Pyramids and Temples
         of Giza (28.7.92) .... 2.
   On the inside front cover of No. FB59 the inland letter rates a
shown as: 1st class 24, 35, 43, 51p. and 2nd class 18, 28, 33, 39p. The
were corrected on No. FB59a to read: 1st class 24, 36, 45, 54p. and 2
class 18, 28, 34, 41p.

Type FB63

(Des J. Matthews)

1992 (22 Sept). *1000th Anniv of Appointment of Sheriffs. Dull blue and scarlet cover as Type FB63. Containing booklet pane No. X925m.*
FB63 Design showing Crest, with Helm and Mantling, and Badge of The Shrievalty Association...................... 2.00

Type FB64

(Des M. Newton)

1993 (9 Feb–6 July). *Postal History Series. Covers as Type FB64. Containing booklet pane No. X925m.*
FB64 Design No. 1 (cover in grey-green and grey-black), Airmail postmarks 1.50
FB65 Design No. 2 (cover in dull orange and black), Ship mail postmarks (6.4.93) 1.50
FB66 Design No. 3 (cover in blue and grey-black), Registered mail postmarks (6.7.93)...................... 75

1993 (1 Nov). *Postal History Series continued. Rose-red and grey-black cover as Type FB64 containing booklet pane No. Y1701a.*
FB67 Design No. 4, "Paid" postmarks 75

Type FB68

(Des A. Davidson)

1994 (25 Jan). *Coaching Inns Series. Myrtle-green and pale myrtle-green cover as Type FB68 containing booklet pane No. Y1701a.*
FB68 Design No. 1, "Swan with Two Necks".................... 75

65p. Booklet

1976 (14 July). *Cover as Type FB1, but larger (90 × 49 mm). Printed in turquoise-blue and pale buff. A. Selvedge at left. B. Selvedge at right.*

		A	B
FC1	Containing ten 6½p. (No. X872)	8.00	6.00

70p. Booklets

1977 (13 June). *Cover as Type FB1, but larger (90 × 49 mm). Printed in purple-brown and dull rose. A. Selvedge at left. B. Selvedge at right.*

		A	B
FD1	Containing ten 7p. (No. X875)	5.00	5.00

Type FD2

(Des E. Stemp)

1978 (8 Feb)–79. *Country Crafts Series. Grey-green and red-brown covers as Type FD2 (90 × 49 mm). Containing ten 7p. (No. X875). A. Selvedge at left. B. Selvedge at right.*

		A	B
FD2	Design No. 1, Horse-shoeing	11.00	4.00
FD3	Design No. 2, Thatching (3.5.78)	40.00	4.00
FD4	Design No. 3, Dry-stone-walling (9.8.78)	£120	4.00
FD5	Design No. 4, Wheel-making (25.10.78)	7.00	4.50
FD6	Design No. 5, Wattle fence-making (10.1.79)	14.00	5.00

Nos. FD2/3 are inscribed "January 1978", FD4 "July 1978", FD5 "October 1978" and FD6 "December 1978".

Type FD7

(Des F. Wegner)

1979 (5 Feb). *Official opening of Derby Mechanised Letter Office. Pale yellow-green and lilac cover as Type FD7 (90 × 49 mm). Containing ten 7p. (No. X875). A. Selvedge at left. B. Selvedge at right.*

		A	B
FD7	Kedleston Hall	7.00	7.00

No. FD7 is inscribed "December 1978".

On sale only in the Derby Head Post Office area to promote postcode publicity and also at the Philatelic Bureau and philatelic sales counters.

1979 (4 Apr). *Country Crafts Series continued. Grey-green and red-brown cover as Type FD2 (90 × 49 mm). A. Selvedge at left. B. Selvedge at right.*

		A	B
FD8	Design No. 6, Basket-making	6.00	4.00

No. FD8 is inscribed "March 1979".

80p. Booklet

Type FE1

(Des P. Hutton)

1979 (3 Oct). *Military Aircraft Series. Blue and grey cover as Type FE1 (90 × 49 mm). Containing ten 8p. (No. X879) attached by the selvedge. A. Selvedge at left. B. Selvedge at right.*

		A	B
FE1	Design No. 1, BE2B, 1914, & Vickers Gun Bus, 1915	3.00	3.00

No. FE1 is inscribed "August 1979".

85p. Booklet

1976 (14 July). *Cover as Type FB1 but larger (90 × 49 mm). Printed in light yellow-olive and brownish grey. A. Selvedge at left. B. Selvedge at right.*

		A	B
FF1	Containing ten 8½p. (No. X881)	5.50	5.50

90p. Booklets

1977 (13 June). *Cover as Type FB1, but larger (90 × 49 mm). Printed in deep grey-blue and cobalt. A. Selvedge at left. B. Selvedge at right.*

		A	B
FG1	Containing ten 9p. (No. X883)	4.50	5.00

Type FG2

(Des R. Maddox)

1978 (8 Feb)–79. *British Canals Series. Yellow-olive and new blue cover as Type FG2 (90 × 49 mm). Containing ten 9p. (No. X883) A. Selvedge at left. B. Selvedge at right.*

		A	B
FG2	Design No. 1, Grand Union	18.00	6.00
FG3	Design No. 2, Llangollen (3.5.78)	5.00	£25
FG4	Design No. 3, Kennet & Avon (9.8.78)	12.00	8.00
FG5	Design No. 4, Caledonian (25.10.78)	4.50	6.00
FG6	Design No. 5, Regents (10.1.79)	15.00	7.00

Nos. FG2/3 are inscribed "January 1978", FG4 "July 1978", FG5 "October 1978" and FG6 "December 1978".

(Des F. Wegner)

1979 (5 Feb). *Official Opening of Derby Mechanised Letter Office. Violet-blue and rose cover as Type FD7 (90 × 49 mm). Containing ten 9p. (No. X883). A. Selvedge at left. B. Selvedge at right.*

		A	B
FG7	Tramway Museum, Crich	8.00	8.00

No. FG7 is inscribed "December 1978".

On sale only in the Derby Head Post Office area to promote postcode publicity and also at the Philatelic Bureau and philatelic sales counters.

1979 (4 Apr). *British Canals Series continued. Yellow-olive and new blue cover as Type FG2. A. Selvedge at left. B. Selvedge at right.*

		A	B
FG8	Design No. 6, Leeds & Liverpool	4.00	4.00

No. FG8 is inscribed "March 1979".

£1 Booklets

All booklets were sold at the cover price of £1 although some contain stamps to a greater value.

Type FH1

(Des N. Battershill)

1979 (3 Oct). *Industrial Archaeology Series. Red and green cover as Type FH1 (90 × 49 mm). Containing ten 10p. (No. X887). A. Selvedge at left. B. Selvedge at right.*

		A	B
FH1	Design No. 1, Ironbridge, Telford, Salop	4.00	3.75

No. FH1 is inscribed "August 1979".

1980 (4 Feb–24 Sept). *Military Aircraft Series continued. Blue and grey cover as Type FE1 (90 × 49 mm). Containing ten 10p. (No. X888). A. Selvedge at left. B. Selvedge at right.*

		A	B
FH2	Design No. 2, Sopwith Camel & Vickers Vimy	3.25	3.25
FH3	Design No. 3, Hawker Hart* & Handley Page Heyford (25.6.80)	4.00	4.00
FH4	Design No. 4, Hurricane & Wellington (24.9.80)	4.00	4.00

No. FH2 is inscribed "January 1980", No. FH3 "May 1980" and No. FH4 "July 1980".

*On the booklet cover the aircraft is wrongly identified as a Hawker Fury.

Type FH5

(Des M. Newton and S. Paine)

1986 (29 July)–**87.** *Musical Instruments Series. Scarlet and black covers as Type FH5. Containing six 17p. (X952).*

FH5   Design No. 1, Violin 5.00
    No. FH5 is inscribed "November 1985".

Contents changed. Containing No. X901n.

FH6   Design No. 2, French horn (20.10.86) 5.00
FH7   Design No. 3, Bass clarinet (27.1.87) 5.00
    No. FH7 is inscribed "October 1986".

Type FH8

(Des A. Davidson)

1987 (14 Apr)–**88.** *Sherlock Holmes Series. Bright scarlet and grey-black covers as Type FH8. Containing booklet pane No. X901n (FH8/9) or X901na (FH10/11).*

FH8   Design No. 1, *A Study in Scarlet* 5.00
FH9   Design No. 2, *The Hound of the Baskervilles* (14.7.87).. 5.00
FH10   Design No. 3, *The Adventure of the Speckled Band* (29.9.87)... 5.00
FH11   Design No. 4, *The Final Problem* (26.1.88) 5.00
    Nos. FH8/11 are inscribed "October 1986".
    The panes from Nos. FH10/11 have imperforate vertical sides.

1988 (12 Apr). *London Zoo. Children's Drawings Series. Cover as Type FB47 in black and brown. Containing booklet pane No. X901na.*

FH12   Bears design 5.00
    No. FH12 is inscribed "October 1986" and has the vertical sides of the pane imperforate.

Type FH13

(Des Liz Moyes)

1988 (5 July)–**89.** *Charles Dickens Series. Orange-red and maroon covers as Type FH13.*

FH13   Design No. 1, *Oliver Twist*, containing booklet pane No. X901na... 6.00
FH14   Design No. 2, *Nicholas Nickleby*, containing booklet pane No. X904m (5.9.88) 6.00
FH15   Design No. 3, *David Copperfield*, containing booklet pane No. X904m (24.1.89)................................... 6.00
FH16   Design No. 4, *Great Expectations*, containing booklet pane No. X1051l (25.4.89)................................... 6.00
    No. FH13 is inscribed "October 1986" and No. FH16 "September 1988". Nos. FH13/16 have the vertical sides of the pane imperforate.

1989 (18 July). *Marine Life Series continued. Cover as Type FB50 in turquoise-green and scarlet. Containing booklet pane No. X904m.*

FH17   Design No. 3, Edible Sea Urchin, Common Starfish and Common Shore Crab 6.00
    No. FH17 has the vertical edges of the pane imperforate.

Type FH18

(Des J. Sancha)

1989 (2 Oct)–**90.** *Mills Series. Grey-black and grey-green matt card cover as Type FH18.*

FH18   Design No. 1, Wicken Fen, Ely containing booklet pane No. X960l... 7.00

As Type FH18 but glossy card cover containing Penny Black Anniversary booklet pane No. 1476l printed in litho by Walsall.

FH19   Design No. 1 (cover in bottle-green and pale green), Wicken Fen, Fly (30.1.90) 7.00
    No. FH19 was an experimental printing to test a new cover material. This appears glossy when compared with Nos. FH18 and FH20.

As Type FH18 but changed to matt card cover containing Penny Black Anniversary booklet pane No. 1469l printed in photo by Harrison.

FH20   Design No. 2 (cover in grey-black and bright green), Click Mill, Dounby, Orkney (30.1.90) 7.00

1990 (4 Sept)–**91.** *Mills Series continued. Covers as Type FH18. Containing booklet pane No. X911m.*

FH21   Design No. 3, (cover printed in light blue and buff) Jack and Jill Mills, Clayton, Sussex........................ 4.00

FH22 Design No. 4, (cover printed in dull blue and bright
yellow-green) Howell Mill, Llanddeusant, Anglesey
(25.6.91)... 4.00
Nos. FH18/22 have the vertical edges of the pane imperforate.

Type FH23

(Des J. Gibbs)

1991 (10 Sept)–**92.** *150th Anniv of Punch magazine. Magenta and
grey-black covers as Type* FH23 *containing booklet pane No.* X927I.
FH23 Design No. 1, Illustrations by Richard Doyle and
Hoffnung.. 4.00
a. Corrected rate (10.91) 5.00
FH24 Design No. 2, Illustrations by Sir John Tenniel and Eric
Burgin (21.1.92)... 4.00
FH25 Design No. 3, Illustrations by Sir John Tenniel and
Anton (28.4.92) 4.00
FH26 Design No. 4, Illustrations by Sir John Tenniel and
Hewison (28.7.92).. 3.75
Nos. FH23/6 have the vertical edges of the pane imperforate.
No. FH23a has corrected letter rates as No. FB59a.

(Des J. Matthews)

1992 (22 Sept). *1000th Anniv of Appointment of Sheriffs. Scarlet and
dull blue cover as Type* FB63 *containing booklet pane No.* X927I.
FH27 Design as Type FB63 but elements in reverse order 3.75

Type FH28

(Des J. Lawrence)

1993 (9 Feb–6 July). *Educational Institutions Series. Covers as Type*
FH28 *containing booklet pane No.* X1050I *printed in litho by Walsall.*
FH28 Design No. 1 (cover in lake-brown and light blue),
University of Wales 2.50
FH29 Design No. 2 (cover in deep dull green and lemon), St.
Hilda's College, Oxford (6.4.93) 2.50
FH30 Design No. 3 (cover in purple-brown and flesh),
Marlborough College, Wiltshire (6.7.93) 1.50

1993 (1 Nov). *Educational Institutions Series continued. Deep bluish
green and lilac cover as Type* FH28 *containing four 25p.* (No. Y1750)
printed in litho by Walsall.
FH31 Design No. 4, Free Church of Scotland College,
Edinburgh.. 1.50

Type FH32

(Des H. Brockway)

1994 (25 Jan). *20th-century Prime Ministers Series. Brown and pale
brown cover as Type* FH32 *containing four 25p.* (No. Y1750) *printed
in litho by Walsall.*
FH32 Design No. 1, Herbert Asquith 1.5

£1.15 Booklets

981 (26 Jan–18 Mar). *Military Aircraft Series continued. Blue and grey cover as Type FE1 (90 × 49 mm). Containing ten 11½p. (No. X893).*
A. *Selvedge at left.* B. *Selvedge at right.*

		A	B
1	Design No. 5, Spitfire & Lancaster	4.00	4.00
2	Design No. 6, Lightning & Vulcan (18.3.81)	4.00	4.00

Nos. FI1/2 are inscribed "January 1981".

£1.15
Royal Mail Stamps
Ten at 11½p

Type FI3
(Des R. Maddox)

981 (6 May–30 Sept). *Museums Series. Blue and turquoise-green cover as Type FI3 (90 × 49 mm). Containing ten 11½p. (No. X893).*
A. *Selvedge at left.* B. *Selvedge at right.*

		A	B
I3	Design No. 1, Natural History Museum (British Museum), London	4.00	4.00
I4	Design No. 2, National Museum of Antiquities of Scotland (30.9.81)	4.00	4.00

Nos. FI3/4 are inscribed "January 1981".

£1.20 Booklets

980 (4 Feb–24 Sept). *Industrial Archaeology Series continued. Red and green cover as Type FH1 (90 × 49 mm). Containing ten 12p. (No. X943).* A. *Selvedge at left.* B. *Selvedge at right.*

		A	B
1	Design No. 2, Beetle Mill, Ireland	4.00	4.00
2	Design No. 3, Tin mines, Cornwall (25.6.80)	4.00	5.00
3	Design No. 4, Bottle Kilns, Gladstone, Stoke-on-Trent (24.9.80)	4.00	4.00

No. FJ1 is inscribed "January 1980", No. FJ2 "May 1980" and No. FJ3 "July 1980".

986 (14 Jan). *Pillar box "Write Now" cover as Type FB31 (90 × 49mm), printed in yellow-green and pale red. Containing ten 12p. (No. X896).* A. *Selvedge at left.* B. *Selvedge at right.*

		A	B
J4	"Write Now" (Pillar box design) (no imprint date)	5.00	5.00

£1.20
Royal Mail Stamps
Ten at 12p

Special Offer
See inside back cover for details

Type FJ5

(Des R. Maddox)

1986 (29 Apr). *National Gallery cover as Type FJ5 (90 × 49 mm), printed in magenta and blue-green. Containing ten 12p. (No. X896).*
A. *Selvedge at left.* B. *Selvedge at right.*

		A	B
FJ5	National Gallery design	5.00	5.00

No. FJ5 is inscribed "November 1985".

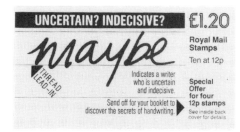

UNCERTAIN? INDECISIVE?
maybe
THREAD LEAD-IN
Indicates a writer who is uncertain and indecisive.
Send off for your booklet to discover the secrets of handwriting.

£1.20
Royal Mail Stamps
Ten at 12p
Special Offer for four 12p stamps
See inside back cover for details

Type FJ6
(Des Trickett and Webb Ltd)

1986 (29 July). *Handwriting cover as Type FJ6 (90 × 49 mm), printed in bright orange and bright blue. Containing ten 12p. (No. X896).*
A. *Selvedge at left.* B. *Selvedge at right.*

		A	B
FJ6	"Maybe"	5.00	5.00

No. FJ6 is inscribed "November 1985".

£1.25 Booklets

1982 (1 Feb–6 Oct). *Museums Series continued. Blue and turquoise-green cover as Type FI3 (90 × 49 mm). Containing ten 12½p. (No. X898).* A. *Selvedge at left.* B. *Selvedge at right.*

		A	B
FK1	Design No. 3, Ashmolean Museum, Oxford	4.00	4.00
FK2	Design No. 4, National Museum of Wales, Cardiff (6.5.82)	4.00	4.00
FK3	Design No. 5, Ulster Museum, Belfast (11.8.82)	4.00	4.00
FK4	Design No. 6, Castle Museum, York (6.10.82)	4.00	4.00

Nos. FK1/4 are inscribed "February 1982".

£1.25
Royal Mail Stamps
Ten at 12½p

Type FK5
(Des S. Paine)

1983 (16 Feb–26 Oct). *Railway Engines Series. Red and blue-green covers as Type FK5 (90 × 49 mm). Containing ten 12½p. (No. X898).* A. *Selvedge at left.* B. *Selvedge at right.*

		A	B
FK5	Design No. 1, GWR Isambard Kingdom Brunel	6.00	6.00
FK6	Design No. 2, LMS Class 4P Passenger Tank Engine (5.4.83)	8.00	8.00
	a. Corrected rate	30.00	30.00

FK7   Design No. 3, L.N.E.R. *Mallard* (27.7.83) 6.00 6.00
FK8   Design No. 4, SR/BR *Clan Line* (26.10.83) 6.00 6.00
No. FK5 is inscribed "February 1982" and Nos. FK6/8 "April 1983".
The corrected rate reads, "36p. for 200g" instead of "37p. for 200g".

£1.30 Booklets

Type FL1

(Des J. Gibbs)

1981 (6 May–30 Sept). *Postal History Series. Cover as Type* FL1
(90 × 49 mm). *Containing No.* X894l. A. *Selvedge at left.* B. *Selvedge at right.*

		A	B
FL1	Design No. 1, Penny Black (red & black cover) ..	5.00	4.00
FL2	Design No. 2, The Downey Head, 1911 (red & green cover) (20.9.81)	7.00	19.00

No. FL1 is inscribed "April 1981" and No. FL2 "September 1981".

Type FL3

(Des J. Thirsk)

1984 (3 Sept)–**85**. *Trams Series. Yellow-orange and purple cover as
Type* FL3 (90 × 49 mm). *Containing ten* 13p. (No. X900). A. *Selvedge
at left.* B. *Selvedge at right.*

		A	B
FL3	Design No. 1, Swansea/Mumbles Railway Car No. 3	5.00	5.00
FL4	Design No. 2, Glasgow Car No. 927 & Car No. 1194 (15.1.85)	5.00	5.00
FL5	Design No. 3, Car No. 717, Blackpool (23.4.85) .	5.00	5.00
FL6	Design No. 4, Car No. 120 & "D" Class Car, London (23.7.85)	5.00	5.00

Nos. FL3/6 are inscribed "September 1984".

Type FL7

(Des Anne Morrow)

1986 (20 Oct). *Books for Children. Cover as Type* FL7 (90 × 49 mm)
printed in rose-red and lemon. Containing ten 13p. (No. X900).
A. *Selvedge at left.* B. *Selvedge at right.*

		A	B
FL7	Teddy bears design	5.00	5.00

Type FL8

(Des Trickett and Webb Ltd)

1987 (27 Jan). *"Keep in Touch" cover as Type* FL8 (90 × 49 mm),
printed in light green and bright blue. Containing ten 13p. (No.
X900). A. *Selvedge at left.* B. *Selvedge at right.*

		A	B
FL8	Handclasp and envelope design	5.00	5.00

No. FL8 is inscribed "October 1986".

Type FL9

(Des Hannah Firmin)

1987 (14 Apr). *"Ideas for your Garden". Cover as Type* FL9
(90 × 49 mm) *printed in bistre and orange-brown. Containing ten*
13p. *stamps* (No. X900). A. *Selvedge at left.* B. *Selvedge at right.*

		A	B
FL9	Conservatory design	5.00	5.00

No. FL9 is inscribed "October 1986".

Type FL10

(Des Trickett and Webb Ltd)

87 (14 July). *"Brighter Writer". Cover as Type FL10 (90 × 49 mm) printed in orange and bright reddish violet. Containing ten 13p. stamps (No. X900). A. Selvedge at left. B. Selvedge at right.*

	A	B
10 Flower design	5.00	5.00

No. FL10 is inscribed "October 1986".

Type FL11

(Des E. Stemp)

87 (29 Sept). *"Jolly Postman". Cover as Type FL11 (90 × 49 mm) printed in pale blue and deep blue. Containing ten 13p. stamps (No. X900). A. Selvedge at left. B. Selvedge at right.*

	A	B
.11 Boy drawing design	5.00	5.00

No. FL11 is inscribed "October 1986".

Type FL12

(Des E. Hughes)

1988 (26 Jan). *Bicentenary of Linnean Society. Cover as Type FL12 (90 × 49 mm) printed in blue and claret. Containing ten 13p. stamps (No. X900). A. Selvedge at left. B. Selvedge at right.*

	A	B
FL12 Mermaid, fish and insect (from "Hortus Sanibatis", 1497)	5.00	5.00

No. FL12 is inscribed "October 1986".

Type FL13

(Des Hannah Firmin)

1988 (12 Apr). *Recipe Cards. Cover as Type FL13 (90 × 49 mm) printed in brown and green. Containing ten 13p. stamps (No. X900). A. Selvedge at left. B. Selvedge at right.*

	A	B
FL13 Vegetables design	5.00	5.00

No. FL13 is inscribed "October 1986".

Type FL14

(Des Trickett and Webb Ltd)

1988 (5 July). *"Children's Parties". Cover as Type FL14 (90 × 49 mm) printed in blue-green and bright purple. Containing ten 13p. stamps (No. X900). A. Selvedge at left. B. Selvedge at right.*

	A	B
FL14 Balloons and streamers design	5.00	5.00

No. FL14 is inscribed "October 1986".

£1.40 Booklets

1981 (26 Jan–18 Mar). *Industrial Archaeology Series continued. Red and green cover as Type FH1 (90 × 49 mm). Containing ten 14p. (No. X946). A. Selvedge at left. B. Selvedge at right.*

	A	B
FM1 Design No. 5, Preston Mill, Scotland	5.00	5.00
FM2 Design No. 6, Talyllyn Railway, Tywyn (18.3.81)	5.00	5.00

Nos. FM1/2 are inscribed "January 1981".

Type FM3

(Des E. Stemp)

1981 (6 May–30 Sept). *19th-century Women's Costume Series. Claret and blue covers as Type* FM3 *(90 × 49 mm). Containing ten 14p. (No.* X946). A. *Selvedge at left.* B. *Selvedge at right.*

		A	B
FM3	Design No. 1, Costume, 1800–15	5.00	5.00
FM4	Design No. 2, Costume, 1815–30 (30.9.81)	5.00	5.00
	Nos. FM3/4 are inscribed "January 1981".		

Type FM5

(Des A. Drummond)

1988 (5 Sept). *"Pocket Planner". Cover as Type* FM5 *(90 × 49 mm) printed in grey-black and yellow. Containing ten 14p. stamps (No.* X903). A. *Selvedge at left.* B. *Selvedge at right.*

		A	B
FM5	"Legal Charge" design	5.00	5.00

Type FM6

(Des Debbie Cook)

1989 (24 Jan). *150th Anniv. of Fox Talbot's Report on the Photographic Process to Royal Society. Cover as Type* FM6 *(90 × 49 mm) printed in reddish orange and black. Containing ten 14p. stamps (No.* X903). A. *Selvedge at left.* B. *Selvedge at right.*

		A	B
FM6	Photographs and darkroom equipment	5.00	5.00
	No. FM6 is inscribed "September 1988".		

£1.43 Booklets

1982 (1 Feb–6 May). *Postal History Series continued. Cover as Type* FL1 *(90 × 49 mm). Containing No.* X899l. A. *Selvedge at left.* B. *Selvedge at right.*

		A	B
FN1	Design No. 3, James Chalmers (postal reformer) (orange & turquoise-blue cover)	5.00	5.00
FN2	Design No. 4, Edmund Dulac (stamp designer) (brown & red cover) (6.5.82)	5.00	5.00

Type FN3

(Des J. Gardner)

1982 (12 July). *"Holiday Postcard Stamp Book". Purple and turquoise-blue cover as Type* FN3 *(90 × 49 mm). Containing No.* X899l. A. *Selvedge at left.* B. *Selvedge at right.*

		A	B
FN3	*Golden Hinde* on front, postcard voucher on back	5.50	5.50

1982 (21 July)–**83**. *Postal History Series continued. Cover as Type* FL1 *(90 × 49 mm). Containing No.* X899l. A. *Selvedge at left.* B. *Selvedge at right.*

		A	B
FN4	Design No. 5, "Forces Postal Service" (grey & violet cover)	5.50	5.50
FN5	Design No. 6, The £5 Orange (orange & black cover) (6.10.82)	5.50	5.50
FN6	Design No. 7, Postmark History (brt scarlet & dp dull blue cover) (16.2.83)	5.50	5.50

No. FN1 is inscribed "February 1982", No. FN2/3 "May 1982", FN4 "July 1982", FN5 "October 1982", FN6 "November 1982".

For booklet No. FS2 with cover price of £1.45, see £1.60 booklets.

£1.46 Booklets

1983 (5 Apr–26 Oct). *Postal History Series continued. Cover as Type* FL1 *(90 × 49 mm).* A. *Containing No.* X899n. B. *Containing No.* X899na.

		A	B
FO1	Design No. 8, Seahorse High Values (blue & green cover)	8.00	8.00
	a. Corrected rate	16.00	12.00
FO2	Design No. 9, Parcel Post Centenary (turquoise-blue & carmine cover) (27.7.83)	8.00	8.00
FO3	Design No. 10, Silver Jubilee of Regional Stamps (dull green & reddish violet cover) (26.10.83).	8.00	8.00

No. FO1 is inscribed "March 1983", No. FO2 "May 1983" and No. FO3 "June 1983".

The corrected rate reads, "36p. for 200g" instead of "37p. for 200g".

£1.50 Booklets

1986 (14 Jan). *Pillar box "Write Now" cover as Type* FB31 *(90 × 49mm), printed in ultramarine and red.* A. *Containing No.* X897l. B. *Containing No.* X897la.

		A	B
FP1	"Write Now" (Pillar box design)	6.00	6.00
	No. FP1 shows no imprint date.		

986 (29 Apr). *National Gallery cover as Type FJ5 (90 × 49mm), printed in violet and vermilion. A. Containing No. X897l. B. Containing No. X897la.*

	A	B
P2 National Gallery design	6.00	6.00

No. FP2 is inscribed "November 1985".

986 (29 July). *Handwriting cover as Type FJ6 (90 × 49 mm), printe in blue-green and bright blue. A. Containing No. X897l. B. Containing No. X897la.*

	A	B
P3 "No"	6.00	6.00

No. FP3 is inscribed "November 1985".

£1.54 Booklets

984 (3 Sept)-**85**. *Postal History Series continued. Reddish purple and pale blue cover as Type FL1 (90 × 49 mm). A. Containing No. X901l. B. Containing No. X901la.*

	A	B
Q1 Design No. 11, Old & new Postage Dues	7.00	7.00
Q2 Design No. 12, Queen Victoria embossed stamps (yellow-green & blue cover) (15.1.85).	7.00	7.00
Q3 Design No. 13, Queen Victoria surface-printed stamps (blue-green & carmine cover) (23.4.85)	7.00	7.00
Q4 Design No. 14, 17th-century mounted & foot messengers (dp brown & orange-red cover) (23.7.85)	7.00	7.00

No. FQ1 is inscribed "July 1984" and Nos. FQ2/4 are inscribed "September 1984".

£1.55 Booklets

1982 (1 Feb–6 Oct). *19th-century Women's Costume Series continued. Claret and blue covers as Type FM3 (90 × 49 mm). Containing ten 15½p. (No. X948). A. Selvedge at left. B. Selvedge at right.*

	A	B
FR1 Design No. 3, Costume, 1830–50	5.00	5.00
FR2 Design No. 4, Costume, 1850–60 (6.5.82)	5.00	5.00
FR3 Design No. 5, Costume, 1860–80 (11.8.82)	5.00	5.00
FR4 Design No. 6, Costume, 1880–1900 (6.10.82)	5.00	5.00

Nos. FR1/4 are inscribed "February 1982".

£1.60 Booklets

Type FS1

(Des Carol Walklin)

983 (5 Apr). *"Birthday Box" Design. Magenta and red-orange cover as Type FS1 (90 × 49 mm). Depicting birthday cake and associated items. A. Selvedge at left. B. Selvedge at right.*

	A	B
S1 Containing ten 16p. (No. X949) (no imprint date)	6.00	6.00
a. Rates altered and "February 1983" imprint date	16.00	30.00

Type FS2

(Des R. Maddox)

1983 (10 Aug). *British Countryside Series. Special Discount Booklet (sold at £1.45). Greenish blue and ultramarine cover as Type FS2 (90 × 49 mm). Containing ten 16p. stamps (No. X949Eu). A. Selvedge at left. B. Selvedge at right.*

	A	B
FS2 Design No. 1, Lyme Regis, Dorset	6.75	6.75

Stamps from No. FS2 show a double-lined "D" printed in blue on the reverse, over the gum.

No. FS2 is inscribed "April 1983".

1983 (21 Sept). *British Countryside Series continued. Dull green on violet cover as Type FS2 (90 × 49 mm). Containing ten 16p. stamps (No. X949). A. Selvedge at left. B. Selvedge at right.*

	A	B
FS3 Design No. 2, Arlington Row, Bibury, Gloucestershire	6.00	6.00

No. FS3 is inscribed "April 1983".

Type FS4

(Des M. Newton)

1984 (14 Feb). *"Write it" Design. Vermilion and ultramarine cover as Type FS4 (90 × 49 mm). Containing ten 16p. stamps (No. X949). A. Selvedge at left. B. Selvedge at right.*

	A	B
FS4 Fountain pen	6.00	6.00

No. FS4 is inscribed "April 1983".

£1.70 Booklets

Type FT1

(Des G. Hardie)

1984 (3 Sept). *Social Letter Writing Series. Rose and deep claret cover as Type* FT1 (90 × 49 mm). *Containing ten 17p. (No. X952). A. Selvedge at left. B. Selvedge at right.*

	A	B
FT1 Design No. 1, "Love Letters"	6.50	6.50

No. FT1 is inscribed "September 1984".

1985 (5 Mar). *Social Letter Writing Series continued. Special Discount Booklet (sold at £1.55). Turquoise-blue and deep claret cover as Type* FT1 (90 × 49 mm). *Containing ten 17p. (No. X952Eu). A. Selvedge at left. B. Selvedge at right.*

	A	B
FT2 Design No. 2, "Letters abroad"	7.00	7.00

Stamps from No. FT2 show a double-lined "D" printed in blue on the reverse, over the gum.
No. FT2 is inscribed "September 1984".

1985 (9 Apr). *Social Letter Writing Series continued. Bright blue and deep claret cover as Type* FT1 (90 × 49 mm). *Containing ten 17p. (No. X952). A. Selvedge at left. B. Selvedge at right.*

	A	B
FT3 Design No. 3, "Fan letters"	6.50	6.50

No. FT3 is inscribed "September 1984".

Type FT4

(Des B. Smith)

1985 (30 July). *350 Years of Royal Mail Public Postal Service. Special Discount Booklet (sold at £1.53). Cover Type* FS4 (90 × 60 mm), *printed in rosine and bright blue. Containing ten 17p. (No. 1290Eu) with selvedge at top.*

FT4 Datapost Service design		7.00

The stamps from this booklet show double-lined letters "D" printed on the reverse over the gum.
No. FT4 is inscribed "September 1984".

1985 (8 Oct)–**86.** *Social Letter Writing Series continued. Black and bright scarlet cover as Type* FT1 (90 × 49 mm). *Containing ten 17p. (No. X952). A. Selvedge at left. B. Selvedge at right.*

	A	B
FT5 Design No. 4, "Write Now" (Pillar box)	6.50	6.50
a. Revised rates (2nd class (60g) 12p.) (1.86)	12.00	10.00

1986 (29 Apr). *National Gallery cover as Type* FJ5 (90 × 49 mm), *printed in blue-green and blue. Containing ten 17p. (No. X952). A. Selvedge at left. B. Selvedge at right.*

	A	B
FT6 National Gallery design	6.50	6.50

No. FT6 is inscribed "November 1985".

1986 (29 July). *Handwriting cover as Type* FJ6 (90 × 49 mm) *printed in red and bright blue. Containing ten 17p. (No. X952). A. Selvedge at left. B. Selvedge at right.*

	A	B
FT7 "Yes"	6.50	6.50

No. FT7 is inscribed "November 1985".

£1.80 Booklets

1986 (20 Oct). *Books for Children. New blue and orange-brown cover as Type* FL7. *Containing ten 18p. (No. X955). A. Selvedge at left. B. Selvedge at right.*

	A	B
FU1 Rabbits design	7.00	7.00

1987 (27 Jan). *"Keep in Touch" cover as Type* FL8 *printed in magenta and bright blue. Containing ten 18p. (No. X955). A. Selvedge at left. B. Selvedge at right.*

	A	B
FU2 Handclasp and envelope design	7.00	7.00

No. FU2 is inscribed "October 1986".

1987 (14 Apr). *"Ideas for your Garden". Claret and brown-olive cover as Type* FL9 (90 × 49 mm). *Containing ten 18p. stamps (No. X955). A. Selvedge at left. B. Selvedge at right.*

	A	B
FU3 Garden path design	7.00	7.00

No. FU3 is inscribed "October 1986".

1987 (14 July). *"Brighter Writer". Turquoise-green and reddish orange cover as Type* FL10 (90 × 49 mm). *Containing ten 18p. stamps (No. X955). A. Selvedge at left. B. Selvedge at right.*

	A	B
FU4 Berries and leaves design	7.00	7.00

No. FU4 is inscribed "October 1986".

1987 (29 Sept). *"Jolly Postman". Cover as Type* FL11 (90 × 49 mm) *printed in deep blue and claret. Containing ten 18p. stamps (No. X955). A. Selvedge at left. B. Selvedge at right.*

	A	B
FU5 Girl drawing design	7.00	7.00

No. FU5 is inscribed "October 1986".

1988 (26 Jan). *Bicentenary of Linnean Society. Cover as Type* FL12 (90 × 49 mm) *printed in dull yellow-green and dull claret. Containing ten 18p. stamps (No. X955). A. Selvedge at left. B. Selvedge at right.*

	A	B
FU6 Wolf and birds (from "Hortus Sanitatis", 1497)	7.00	7.00

1988 (12 Apr). *Recipe Cards. Cover as Type* FL13 (90 × 49 mm) *printed in claret and Indian red. Containing ten 18p. stamps (No. X955). A. Selvedge at left. B. Selvedge at right.*

	A	B
FU7 Fruits, pudding and jam design	7.00	7.00

No. FU7 is inscribed "October 1986".

1988 (5 July). *"Children's Parties". Cover as Type* FL14 (90 × 49 mm) *printed in violet and rosine. Containing ten 18p. stamps (No. X955). A. Selvedge at left. B. Selvedge at right.*

	A	B
FU8 Balloons and party hats design	7.00	7.00

No. FU8 is inscribed "October 1986".

£1.90 Booklets

1988 (5 Sept). *"Pocket Planner". Cover as Type* FM5 (90 × 49 mm) *printed in yellow-green and magenta. Containing ten 19p. stamps. (No. X956). A. Selvedge at left. B. Selvedge at right.*

	A	B
FV1 "Marriage Act" design	7.00	7.00

1989 (24 Jan). *150th Anniv of Fox Talbot's Report on the Photographic Process to Royal Society. Cover as Type FM6 (90 × 49 mm) printed in emerald and black. Containing ten 19p. stamps (No. X956).*
A. *Selvedge at left.* B. *Selvedge at right.*

	A	B
FV2 Fox Talbot with camera and Lacock Abbey	7.00	7.00

No. FV2 is inscribed "September 1988".

£2 Booklets

(Des Debbie Cook)

993 (1 Nov). *Postal Vehicles Series. Dull vermilion and deep blue cover as Type FW1 containing eight 25p. (No. Y1701).*
W1   Design No. 1, Motorised cycle-carrier 3.00

Christmas Booklets

Type FX1

(Des J. Matthews)

1978 (15 Nov). *"Christmas Greetings". Cover Type FX1 (90 × 49 mm). Printed in rose-red and sage-green.*
FX1   £1.60, containing booklet pane No. X875l 4.50
No. FX1 is inscribed "August 1978".

Type FX2

(Des P. Sharland)

1979 (14 Nov). *"Christmas Greetings". Red and green cover as Type FX2 (90 × 49 mm), showing Christmas cracker.*
FX2   £1.80, containing booklet pane No. X879l 5.00
No. FX2 is inscribed "October 1979".

Type FX3

(Des E. Fraser)

1980 (12 Nov). *Christmas. Red and blue cover as Type FX3 (90 × 49 mm), showing Nativity scene.*
FX3   £2.20, containing booklet pane No. X888m 6.00
No. FX3 is inscribed "September 1980".

HAVE YOU READ THE NOTES AT THE BEGINNING OF THIS CATALOGUE?

These often provide answers to the enquiries we receive.

Type FX4

(Des W. Sanderson)

1981 (11 Nov). Christmas. Red and blue cover as Type FX4
(90 × 49 mm), showing skating scene.

FX4   £2.55, containing booklet pane No. X893l 7.00
No. FX4 is inscribed "January 1981".

Type FX5

(Des A. Davidson)

1982 (10 Nov). Christmas. Red and green cover as Type FX5
(90 × 49 mm), showing Christmas Mummers.

FX5   £2.50, containing booklet pane No. X898l 9.00
No. FX5 is inscribed "February 1982" and was sold at a discount of
30p. off the face value of the stamps.

Each stamp in the pane has a blue star printed on the reverse over the
gum.

Type FX6

(Des Barbara Brown)

1983 (9 Nov). Christmas. Brown-lilac and yellow cover as Type FX6
(90 × 49 mm), showing pantomime scenes.

FX6   £2.20, containing twenty 12½p. (No. X898Eua) 8.00
No. FX6 is inscribed "April 1983" and was sold at a discount of 30p. off
the face value of the stamps.

Each stamp in the pane has a double lined blue star printed on the
reverse over the gum.

Type FX7

(Des Yvonne Gilbert)

1984 (20 Nov). Christmas. Light brown and red-orange cover as Type
FX7 (90 × 60 mm), showing Nativity scene.

FX7   £2.30, containing twenty 13p. (No. 1267Eu) 9.00
No. FX7 is inscribed "September 1984" and was sold at a discount of
30p. off the face value of the stamps.

The stamps from this booklet show double-lined blue stars printed
on the reverse over the gum.

Type FX8

(Des Adrian George)

1985 (19 Nov). Christmas. Bright blue and rose cover as Type FX8
(90 × 60 mm), showing The Pantomime.

FX8   £2.40, containing twenty 12p. (No. 1303Eu) 8.00
The stamps from this booklet show double-lined blue stars printed
on the reverse over the gum.

Type FX9

(Des Lynda Gray)

1986 (2 Dec). *Christmas. Red and dull blue-green cover as Type* FX9
(90 × 49 mm), showing Shetland Yule cakes. A. Selvedge at left.
B. *Selvedge at right.*

	A	B
FX9 £1.30, containing ten 13p. (No. X900Eu)	9.00	9.00

No. FX9 is inscribed "October 1986" and was sold at a discount of
10p. off the face value of the stamps.

Each stamp in the pane has a blue star printed on the reverse over
the gum.

For 1990 and later Christmas stamps, see Barcode booklet Section L.

Greetings Booklet

£1.90 Booklet

Type FX10

(Des L. Moberly)

1989 (31 Jan). *Greetings Stamps. Multicoloured cover as Type* FX10
*(89 × 60 mm). Containing booklet pane No. 1423a, including twelve
special greetings labels in a block (3 × 4) at right, attached by the
selvedge.*

FX10 Greetings design 28.00

No. FX10 is inscribed "September 1988".

The cover of No. FX10 shows an overall pattern of elements taken
from the stamp designs. Due to the method of production the
position of these elements varies from cover to cover.

For Greetings stamps in Barcode booklets, see Nos. KX1 onwards.

1988 (11 Oct). *Laminated cover as Type GA1 (75 × 56 mm) printed by Walsall.*
GB2   Containing booklet pane No. X903l 5.00

Barcode Booklets

These booklets are listed in five sections.

SECTION C. G numbers containing Machin stamps

SECTION D. H numbers containing Machin NVI stamps

SECTION E. J numbers containing Machin Penny Black Anniversary stamps

SECTION F. K numbers containing Greetings stamps

SECTION G. L numbers containing Christmas stamps

Type GB3
Large Crown

1988 (11 Oct). *Laminated cover as Type GB3 (75 × 48 mm) with stamp printed on the cover in deep blue.*
GB3   Containing booklet pane No. X903n 6.00
No. GB3 is inscribed "5 September 1988" and has the horizontal edges of the pane imperforate.

1989 (24 Jan). *Laminated cover as Type GB3 (75 × 48 mm) with stamp printed on the cover in deep blue by Walsall.*
GB4   Containing booklet pane No. X903q 16.00
No. GB4 is inscribed "5 September 1988" and has the three edges of the pane imperforate.

C. Barcode Booklets containing Machin stamps with values shown as Type **367**.

These are produced for sale in both post offices and commercial outlets.
COVERS. These are all printed in scarlet, lemon and black with the barcode on the reverse. Type GA1 has a clear "window" to view the contents. Type GB3 is shorter and has a stamp illustration printed on the cover to replace the "window". These illustrations show an oblique white line across the bottom right-hand corner of the "stamp". Unless otherwise stated all covers were printed by Harrison.
NOTE: All panes are attached to the covers by the selvedge.
Barcode booklet covers are illustrated at two-thirds linear size unless otherwise stated.

52p. Booklet

Type GA1

1987 (4 Aug). *Laminated cover Type GA1 (75 × 60 mm).*
GA1   Containing booklet pane No. X900n 3.00
No. GA1 is inscribed "20 October 1986".

56p. Booklets

1988 (23 Aug). *Laminated cover as Type GA1 (75 × 56 mm).*
GB1   Containing booklet pane No. X903l 5.00

72p. Booklet

1987 (4 Aug). *Laminated cover as Type GA1 (75 × 60 mm).*
GC1   Containing booklet pane No. X955m 3.00
No. GC1 is inscribed "20 October 1986".

76p. Booklets

1988 (23 Aug). *Laminated cover as Type GA1 (75 × 56 mm).*
GD1   Containing booklet pane No. X956l 6.00

1988 (11 Oct). *Laminated cover as Type GA1 (75 × 56 mm) printed by Walsall.*
GD2   Containing booklet pane No. X956l 6.00

1988 (11 Oct). *Laminated cover as Type GB3 (75 × 48 mm) with stamp printed on the cover in bright orange-red.*
GD3   Containing booklet pane No. X956n 6.00
No. GD3 is inscribed "5 September 1988" and has the horizontal edges of the pane imperforate.

1989 (24 Jan). *Laminated cover as Type GB3 (75 × 48 mm) with stamp printed on the cover in bright orange-red by Walsall.*
GD4   Containing booklet pane No. X956q 16.00
No. GD4 is inscribed "5 September 1988" and has the three edges of the pane imperforate.

78p. Booklet

GD4a (As Type GL1 but, without "4")

1992 (28 July). *Multicoloured laminated cover as Type GD4a (75 × 49 mm) with stamp printed on cover in bright mauve by Walsall.*
GD4a Containing two 39p. stamps (No. X1058) (pane No. X1058l with right-hand vert pair removed) and pane of 4 air mail labels.. 1.75
Stamps in No. GD4a have top or bottom edge imperforate.
Booklet No. GD4a was produced in connection with a Kellogg's Bran Flakes promotion.

£1.04 Booklet

1987 (4 Aug). *Laminated cover as Type GA1 (75 × 60 mm).*
GE1 Containing booklet pane No. X971al.......................... 15.00
No. GE1 is inscribed "20 October 1986".

£1.08 Booklets

1988 (23 Aug). *Laminated cover as Type GA1 (75 × 56 mm).*
GF1 Containing booklet pane No. X973l.................. 7.00

1988 (11 Oct). *Laminated cover as Type GB3 (75 × 48 mm) with stamp printed on the cover in chestnut.*
GF2 Containing booklet pane No. X973m...................... 22.00
No. GF2 is inscribed "5 September 1988" and has the horizontal edges of the pane imperforate.

£1.16 Booklets

Type GG1
Redrawn Crown

1989 (2 Oct). *Laminated cover as Type GG1 (75 × 48 mm) with stamp printed on the cover in deep mauve by Walsall.*
GG1 Containing booklet pane No. X1054l.......................... 14.00
No. GG1 has three edges of the pane imperforate.

1990 (17 Apr). *Laminated cover as Type GG1 (75 × 48 mm) with stamp printed on the cover in deep mauve by Walsall.*
GG2 Containing booklet pane No. X1055l.......................... 20.00
No. GG2 has three edges of the pane imperforate.

£1.24 Booklet

Type GH1
Crown on white

1990 (17 Sept). *Multicoloured laminated cover as Type GH1 (75 × 49 mm) with stamp printed on the cover in ultramarine by Walsall.*
GH1 Containing booklet pane No. X1056l.......................... 5.50
No. GH1 has the horizontal edges of the pane imperforate.

£1.30 Booklet

1987 (4 Aug). *Laminated cover as Type GA1 (98 × 60 mm).*
GI1 Containing booklet pane No. X900o 6.00
No. GI1 is inscribed "20 October 1986".

£1.32 Booklet

Type GJ1

1991 (16 Sept). *Multicoloured laminated cover as Type GJ1 (75 × 49 mm) with stamp printed on the cover in light emerald by Walsall.*
GJ1 Containing booklet pane No. X1057l and a pane of 4 air mail labels 2.00
No. GJ1 has the horizontal edges of the pane imperforate.

£1.40 Booklets

1988 (23 Aug). *Laminated cover as Type GA1 (97 × 56 mm).*
GK1 Containing booklet pane No. X903m 8.00

1988 (11 Oct). *Laminated cover as Type GA1 (97 × 56 mm) printed by Questa.*
GK2 Containing ten 14p. (No. X1007)................................ 12.00

1988 (11 Oct). *Laminated cover as Type GB3 (75 × 48 mm) with stamp printed on the cover in deep blue.*
GK3 Containing booklet pane No. X903p 8.00
No. GK3 is inscribed "5 September 1988" and has the horizontal edges of the pane imperforate.

1988 (11 Oct). *Laminated cover as Type GB3 (75 × 48 mm) with stamp printed on the cover in deep blue by Questa.*
GK4 Containing ten 14p. (No. X1007)............................ 12.00

1993 (1 Nov). *Laminated cover as Type GJ1 (76 × 50 mm) with stamp printed on the cover in yellow by Walsall.*
GK5   Containing four 35p. (No. Y1751) and a pane of 4 air
         mail labels 2.10

£1.56 Booklet

Type GL1

1991 (16 Sept). *Multicoloured laminated cover as Type GL1 (75 × 49 mm) with stamp printed on cover in bright mauve by Walsall.*
GL1   Containing booklet pane No. X1058l and a pane of 4
         air mail labels 2.40
         No. GL1 has the horizontal edges of the pane imperforate.

£1.64 Booklet

1993 (1 Nov). *Laminated cover as Type GL1 (76 × 50 mm) with stamp printed on cover in drab by Walsall.*
GM1   Containing four 41p. (No. Y1752) and a pane of 4 air
         mail labels 2.40

£1.80 Booklet

1987 (4 Aug). *Laminated cover as Type GA1 (98 × 60 mm).*
GN1   Containing booklet pane No. X955n 6.50
         No. GN1 is inscribed "20 October 1986"

£1.90 Booklets

1988 (23 Aug). *Laminated cover as Type GA1 (97 × 56 mm).*
GO1   Containing booklet pane No. X956m 10.00

1988 (11 Oct). *Laminated cover as Type GA1 (97 × 56 mm) printed by Questa.*
GO2   Containing ten 9p. (No. X1011) 14.00

1988 (11 Oct). *Laminated cover as Type GB3 (75 × 48 mm) with stamp printed on the cover in bright orange-red.*
GO3   Containing booklet pane No. X956o 12.00
         No. GO3 is inscribed "5 September 1988" and has the horizontal
edges of the pane imperforate.

1988 (11 Oct). *Laminated cover as Type GB3 (75 × 48 mm) with stamp printed on the cover in bright orange-red by Questa.*
GO4   Containing ten 19p. (No. X1013).............................. 14.00

D. Barcode Booklets containing No Value Indicated stamps with barcodes on the reverse.

Panes of 4 2nd Class stamps

Type HA1
Redrawn Crown (small)

1989 (22 Aug). *Laminated cover as Type HA1 (75 × 48 mm) with stamp printed on the cover in bright blue by Walsall.*
HA1   Containing booklet pane No. 1449a 3.50
    No. HA1 has three edges of the pane imperforate.
    No. HA1 was initially sold at 56p., which was increased to 60p. from 2.10.89.

1989 (28 Nov). *Laminated cover as Type HA1 (75 × 48 mm) with stamp printed on the cover in bright blue by Walsall containing stamps printed in photo by Harrison.*
HA2   Containing booklet pane No. 1445b 3.50
    No. HA2 has three edges of the pane imperforate and was sold at 60p.

Type HA3
Crown on white

1990 (7 Aug). *Multicoloured laminated cover as Type HA3 (75 × 48 mm) with stamp printed on the cover in deep blue by Walsall.*
HA3   Containing booklet pane No. 1515a 3.00
    No. HA3 has the horizontal edges of the pane imperforate.
    No. HA3 was initially sold at 60p., which was increased to 68p. from 17.9.90.

1991 (6 Aug). *Multicoloured laminated cover as Type HA3 (75 × 48 mm) with stamp printed on the cover in bright blue by Walsall.*
HA4   Containing booklet pane No. 1449b 1.50
    No. HA4 has the horizontal edges of the pane imperforate.
    No. HA4 was initially sold at 68p., which was increased to 72p. from 16.9.91.

Type HA5
Olympic Symbols

1992 (21 Jan). *Multicoloured laminated cover as Type HA5 (75 × 48 mm) with stamp printed on the cover in bright blue by Walsall.*
HA5   Containing booklet pane No. 1449b 1.50
    No. HA5 has the horizontal edges of the pane imperforate and was sold at 72p.

1993 (6 Apr). *Multicoloured laminated cover as Type HA3 (75 × 48 mm) with stamp printed on the cover in bright blue by Walsall.*
HA6   Containing four 2nd Class stamps (No. 1665) 1.10
    No. HA6 has perforations on all edges of the pane and was initially sold at 72p., which was increased to 76p. from 1.11.93.

1993 (7 Sept). *Multicoloured laminated cover as Type HA3 (75 × 48 mm) with stamp printed on the cover in bright blue by Harrison.*
HA7   Containing four 2nd Class stamps (No. 1663a) 1.10
    No. HA7 has perforations on all edges of the pane and was initially sold at 72p., which was increased to 76p. from 1.11.93.

Panes of 4 1st Class stamps

1989 (22 Aug). *Laminated cover as Type HA1 (75 × 48 mm) with stamp printed on the cover in brownish black by Walsall.*
HB1   Containing booklet pane No. 1450a 7.50
    No. HB1 has three edges of the pane imperforate.
    No. HB1 was initially sold at 76p., which was increased to 80p. from 2.10.89.

1989 (5 Dec). *Laminated cover as Type HA1 (75 × 48 mm) with stamp printed on the cover in brownish black by Walsall containing stamps printed in photo by Harrison.*
HB2   Containing booklet pane No. 1447b 9.00
    No. HB2 has three edges of the pane imperforate and was sold at 80p.

1990 (7 Aug). *Multicoloured laminated cover as Type HA3 (75 × 48 mm) with stamp printed on the cover in bright orange-red by Walsall.*
HB3   Containing booklet pane No. 1516a 2.00
    a. Containing pane No. 1516ca 8.00
    No. HB3 has the horizontal edges of the pane imperforate.
    No. HB3 was initially sold at 80p., which was increased to 88p. from 17.9.90 and to 96p. from 16.9.91.

1992 (21 Jan). *Multicoloured laminated cover as Type HA5 (75 × 48 mm) with stamp printed on the cover in bright orange-red by Walsall.*
HB4   Containing booklet pane No. 1516a 2.50
    No. HB4 has the horizontal edges of the pane imperforate and was initially sold at 96p., which was increased to £1 from 1.11.93.

1993 (6 Apr). *Multicoloured laminated cover as Type HA3 (75 × 48 mm) with stamp printed on the cover in bright orange-red by Harrison.*
HB5   Containing four 1st Class stamps (No. 1664) 1.50
No. HB6 has perforations on all edges of the pane and was initially sold at 96p., which was increased to £1 from 1.11.93.

1993 (17 Aug). *Multicoloured laminated cover as Type HA3 (76 × 50 mm) with stamp printed on the cover in bright orange-red by Walsall.*
HB6   Containing four 1st Class stamps (No. 1666) 1.50
No. HB6 has perforations on all edges of the pane and was initially sold at 96p., which was increased to £1 from 1.11.93.

Panes of 10 2nd Class stamps

1989 (22 Aug–2 Oct). *Laminated cover as Type HA1 (75 × 48 mm) with stamp printed on the cover in bright blue by Harrison.*
HC1   Containing booklet pane No. 1445a 6.00
    a. Inside cover with new rates (2 Oct)......................... 6.00
Nos. HC1/a have the horizontal edges of the pane imperforate. No. HC1 was initially sold at £1.40, which was increased to £1.50 from 2.10.89. No. HC1a was sold at £1.50.

1989 (19 Sept). *Laminated cover as Type HA1 (75 × 48 mm) with stamp printed on the cover in bright blue by Questa.*
HC2   Containing ten 2nd class stamps (No. 1451)............... 7.00
No. HC2 was initially sold at £1.40, which was increased to £1.50 from 2.10.89.

1990 (7 Aug). *Multicoloured laminated cover as Type HA3 (75 × 48 mm) with stamp printed on the cover in deep blue by Harrison.*
HC3   Containing booklet pane No. 1511a......................... 6.00
No. HC3 has the horizontal edges of the pane imperforate.
No. HC3 was initially sold at £1.50, which was increased to £1.70 from 17.9.90.

1990 (7 Aug). *Multicoloured laminated cover as Type HA3 (75 × 48 mm) with stamp printed on the cover in deep blue by Questa.*
HC4   Containing ten 2nd class stamps (No. 1513)............... 7.50
No. HC4 was initially sold at £1.50, which was increased to £1.70 from 17.9.90.

1990 (7 Aug). *Multicoloured laminated cover as Type HA3 (75 × 48 mm) with stamp printed on the cover in deep blue by Walsall.*
HC5   Containing booklet pane No. 1515b......................... 6.00
No. HC5 has the horizontal edges of the pane imperforate.
No. HC5 was initially sold at £1.50, which was increased to £1.70 from 17.9.90.

1991 (6 Aug). *Multicoloured laminated cover as Type HA3 (75 × 48 mm) with stamp printed on the cover in bright blue by Questa.*
HC6   Containing ten 2nd class stamps (No. 1451) 3.75
No. HC6 was initially sold at £1.70, which was increased to £1.80 from 16.9.91.

1991 (6 Aug). *Multicoloured laminated cover as Type HA3 (75 × 48 mm) with stamp printed on the cover in bright blue by Walsall.*
HC7   Containing booklet pane No. 1449c......................... 4.00
No. HC7 has the horizontal edges of the pane imperforate.
No. HC7 was initially sold at £1.70, which was increased to £1.80 from 16.9.91.

1992 (21 Jan). *Multicoloured laminated cover as Type HA5 (75 × 48 mm) with stamp printed on the cover in bright blue by Walsall.*
HC8   Containing booklet pane No. 1449c 4.25
No. HC8 has the horizontal edges of the pane imperforate and was initially sold at £1.80, which was increased to £1.84 from 1.11.93.

1992 (31 Mar). *Multicoloured laminated cover as Type HA5 (75 × 48 mm) with stamp printed on the cover in bright blue by Questa.*
HC9   Containing ten 2nd class stamps (No. 1451)................ 2.75
No. HC9 was sold at £1.80.

1992 (22 Sept). *Multicoloured laminated cover as Type HA3 (75 × 48 mm) with stamp printed on the cover in bright blue by Harrison.*
HC10   Containing booklet pane No. 1445a........................... 2.75
No. HC10 has the horizontal edges of the pane imperforate and was sold at £1.80.

1993 (6 Apr). *Multicoloured laminated cover as Type HA3 (75 × 48 mm) with stamp printed on the cover in bright blue by Questa.*
HC11   Containing ten 2nd Class stamps (No. 1665) 2.75
No. HC11 has perforations on all edges of the pane and was initially sold at £1.80, which was increased to £1.90 from 1.11.93.
No. HC11 was re-issued on 17 August 1993 showing changes to the text on the inside of the cover.

1993 (Nov). *Multicoloured laminated cover as Type HA3 (75 × 48 mm) with stamp printed on the cover in bright blue by Walsall.*
HC12   Containing ten 2nd class stamps (No. 1665) 2.75
No. HC12 has perforations on all edges of the pane and was sold at £1.90.

Panes of 10 1st Class stamps

1989 (22 Aug–2 Oct). *Laminated cover as Type HA1 (75 × 48 mm) with stamp printed on the cover in brownish black by Harrison.*
HD1   Containing booklet pane No. 1447a......................... 8.00
    a. Inside cover with new rates (2 Oct)......................... 8.00
Nos. HD1/a have the horizontal edges of the pane imperforate.
No. HD1 was initially sold at £1.90, which was increased to £2 from 2.10.89. No. HD1a was sold at £2.

1989 (19 Sept). *Laminated cover as Type HA1 (75 × 48 mm) with stamp printed on the cover in brownish black by Questa.*
HD2   Containing ten 1st class stamps (No. 1452) 10.00
No. HD2 was initially sold at £1.90, which was increased to £2 from 2.10.89.

1990 (7 Aug). *Multicoloured laminated cover as Type HA3 (75 × 48 mm) with stamp printed on the cover in bright orange-red by Harrison.*
HD3   Containing booklet pane No. 1512a......................... 4.50
No. HD3 has the horizontal edges of the pane imperforate.
No. HD3 was initially sold at £2, which was increased to £2.20 from 17.9.90 and to £2.40 from 16.9.91.

1990 (7 Aug). *Multicoloured laminated cover as Type HA3 (75 × 48 mm) with stamp printed on the cover in bright orange-red by Questa.*
HD4   Containing ten 1st class stamps (No. 1514) 4.25
No. HD4 was initially sold at £2, which was increased to £2.20 from 17.9.90 and to £2.40 from 16.9.91.

1990 (7 Aug). *Multicoloured laminated cover as Type HA3 (75 × 48 mm) with stamp printed on the cover in bright orange-red by Walsall.*
HD5   Containing booklet pane No. 1516b.......................... 4.00
No. HD5 was initially sold at £2, which was increased to £2.20 from 17.9.90 and to £2.40 from 16.9.91.

1992 (21 Jan). *Multicoloured laminated cover as Type HA5 (75 × 48 mm) with stamp printed on the cover in bright orange-red by Harrison.*
HD6   Containing booklet pane No. 1512a.......................... 5.50
No. HD6 has the horizontal edges of the pane imperforate and was sold at £2.40.

1992 (21 Jan). *Multicoloured laminated cover as Type HA5 (75 × 48 mm) with stamp printed on cover in bright orange-red by Walsall.*
HD7   Containing booklet pane No. 1516b.......................... 5.50
No. HD7 has the horizontal edges of the pane imperforate and was sold at £2.40.

1993 (9 Feb). *Multicoloured laminated cover as Type HA3 (77 × 44 mm) with advertisement for Greetings Booklet on reverse showing Rupert Bear as in Type KX5. Stamp printed on cover in bright orange-red by Walsall.*
HD8   Containing booklet pane No. 1516b.......................... 4.00
No. HD8 has the horizontal edges of the pane imperforate and was sold at £2.40.

1993 (6 Apr). *Multicoloured laminated cover as Type HA3 (75 × 48 mm) with stamp printed on the cover in bright orange-red by Harrison.*
HD9   Containing ten 1st Class stamps (No. 1664)................ 3.50
No. HD9 has perforations on all edges of the pane and was initially sold at £2.40., which was increased to £2.50 from 1.11.93.
No. HD9 was re-issued on 17 August 1993 showing changes to the text on the inside of the covers.

1993 (6 Apr). *Multicoloured laminated cover as Type HA3 (75 × 48 mm) with stamp printed on the cover in bright orange-red by Walsall.*
HD10   Containing ten 1st Class stamps (No. 1666)............. 3.50
No. HD10 has perforations on all edges of the pane and was initially sold at £2.40., which was increased to £2.50 from 1.11.93.
No. HD10 was re-issued on 17 August 1993 showing changes to the text on the inside of the covers.

1993 (1 Nov). *Laminated cover as Type HA3 (75 × 50 mm) with stamp printed on cover in bright orange-red by Questa.*
HD11   Containing ten 1st Class stamps (No. 1666)............. 3.75
No. HD11 was sold at £2.50.

1993 (1 Nov). *Laminated cover as Type HA3 (75 × 50 mm) with advertisement for Greetings Booklet on reverse showing Rupert Bear as in Type KX5. Stamp printed on cover in bright orange-red by Walsall.*
HD12   Containing ten 1st Class stamps (No. 1666)............. 3.75
No. HD12 was sold at £2.50.

1994 (22 Feb). *Multicoloured laminated cover as Type HA3 (75 × 48 mm) with stamp printed on the cover in bright orange-red by Walsall. Inscribed "FREE POSTCARDS" on yellow tab at right.*
HD13   Containing ten 1st class stamps (No. 1666) and additional page giving details of Greetings Stamps postcard offer.. 3.75
No. HD13 was sold at £2.50.

Panes of 20 1st Class Stamps

Type HE1

1993 (19 Oct). *Multicoloured cover as Type HE1 (91 × 77 mm).*
HE1   Containing booklet pane No. 1789a........................ 7.25
No. HE1 contains self-adhesive stamps and was initially sold at £4.80., which was increased to £5 from 1.11.93.

E. Barcode Booklets containing Penny Black Anniversary stamps with barcodes on reverse.

60p. Booklet

Type JA1

1990 (30 Jan). *Laminated cover as Type JA1 (75 × 48 mm) showing Penny Black Anniversary stamp in bright blue. Containing booklet pane No. 1475l, printed in litho by Walsall.*
JA1   Containing booklet pane No. 1475l 5.00
No. JA1 has three edges of the pane imperforate.

80p. Booklets

1990 (30 Jan). *Laminated cover as Type JA1 (75 × 48 mm) showing Penny Black Anniversary stamp in brownish black and cream. Containing booklet pane No. 1476m, printed in litho by Walsall.*
JB1   Containing booklet pane No. 1476m 5.00
No. JB1 has three edges of the pane imperforate.

1990 (17 Apr). *Laminated cover as Type JA1 showing Penny Black Anniversary stamp printed on the cover in brownish black by Walsall containing stamps printed in photo by Harrison.*
JB2   Containing booklet pane No. 1469r 4.50
No. JB2 has three edges of the pane imperforate.

£1.50 Booklets

1990 (30 Jan). *Laminated cover as Type JA1 (75 × 48 mm) showing Penny Black Anniversary stamp in bright blue. Containing booklet pane No. 1467l printed in photo by Harrison.*
JC1   Containing booklet pane No. 1467l 5.00
No. JC1 has the horizontal edges of the pane imperforate.

1990 (17 Apr). *Laminated cover as Type JA1 (75 × 48 mm) showing Penny Black Anniversary stamp printed on the cover in bright blue by Questa.*
JC2   Containing ten 15p. (No. 1477) 8.00

1990 (12 June). *Laminated cover as Type JA1 (75 × 48 mm) showing Penny Black Anniversary stamp in bright blue. Containing booklet pane No. 1475m, printed in litho by Walsall.*
JC3   Containing booklet pane No. 1475m 6.00
No. JC3 has three edges of the pane imperforate.

£2 Booklets

1990 (30 Jan). *Laminated cover as Type JA1 (75 × 48 mm) showing Penny Black Anniversary stamp in brownish black and cream. Containing booklet pane No. 1469m printed in photo by Harrison.*
JD1   Containing booklet pane No. 1469m 7.00
No. JD1 has the horizontal edges of the pane imperforate.

1990 (17 Apr). *Laminated cover as Type JA1 showing Penny Black Anniversary stamp printed on the cover in brownish black by Questa.*
JD2   Containing ten 20p. (No. 1478) 10.00

1990 (12 June). *Laminated cover as Type JA1 (75 × 48 mm) showing Penny Black Anniversary stamp in brownish black and cream. Containing booklet pane No. 1476n, printed in litho by Walsall.*
JD3   Containing booklet pane No. 1476n 8.00
No. JD3 has three edges of the pane imperforate.

F. Barcode Booklets containing Greetings stamps with barcodes on the reverse.

£2 Greetings Booklet

Type KX1
(Illustration reduced. Actual size 135 × 85 mm)

(Des Michael Peters and Partners Limited)

1990 (6 Feb). *Greetings Stamps. Cover printed in scarlet, lemon and black as Type KX1 (135 × 85 mm). Containing booklet pane No. 1483a, and a separate sheet of 12 greetings labels.*
KX1   "Smile" design cut-out showing stamps inside 12.00

Greetings Booklets containing No Value Indicated stamps

Type KX2

(Des. Tony Meeuwissen)

1991 (5 Feb). *Greetings Stamps. Multicoloured laminated cover as Type KX2 (95 × 69 mm). Containing booklet pane No. 1536a, including twelve special greetings labels in a block (3 × 4) at right, attached by the selvedge.*
KX2   "Good Luck" charms design 7.00
No. KX2 was initially sold at £2.20, which was increased to £2.40 from 16.9.91.

Type KX3

(Des Michael Peters and Partners Limited)

1991 (26 Mar). *Greetings Stamps. Multicoloured laminated cover as Type KX3 (95 × 69 mm). Containing booklet pane No. 1550a, including twelve special greetings labels in a block (3 × 4) at right, attached by the selvedge.*
KX3   Laughing pillar box design 3.25
    No. KX3 was initially sold at £2.20, which was increased to £2.40 from 16.9.91 and to £2.50 from 1.11.93.

Type KX5

(Des Newell and Sorell)

1993 (2 Feb). *Greetings Stamps. Multicoloured laminated cover as Type KX5 (96 × 60 mm). Containing booklet pane No. 1644a and pane of twenty special greetings labels in a block (5 × 4), both panes attached by a common gutter margin.*
KX5   Children's Characters design .... 3·50
    No. KX5 was initially sold at £2.40, which was increased to £2.50 from 1.11.93.

Type KX4

(Des Trickett and Webb Ltd)

1992 (28 Jan). *Greetings Stamps. Multicoloured laminated cover as Type KX4 (95 × 69 mm). Containing booklet pane No. 1592a, including twelve special greetings labels in a block (3 × 4) at right, attached by selvedge.*
KX4   Pressed Flowers design 3.50
    No. KX4 was initially sold at £2.40, which was increased to £2.50 from 1.11.93.

Type KX6

(Des Newell and Sorell)

1994 (1 Feb). *Greetings Stamps. Multicoloured cover as Type KX6 (96 × 60 mm). Containing booklet pane No. 1800a and pane of twenty special greetings labels in a block (5 × 4), both panes attached by a common gutter margin.*
KX6   Children's Characters design 3.50

G. Barcode Booklets containing Christmas stamps with barcode on the reverse.

Type LX1

(Des A. Davidson)

1990 (13 Nov). *Christmas. Multicoloured laminated cover as Type LX1 (95 × 60 mm). Containing booklet pane No. 1526a, attached by the selvedge.*
LX1   £3.40, Snowman design 9.00

1991 (12 Nov). *Multicoloured laminated cover as Type LX1, but 95 × 70 mm. Containing booklet pane No. 1582b attached by the selvedge.*
LX2   £3.60, Holly design 8.25

Type LX2

(Des Karen Murray)

1992 (10 Nov). *Multicoloured laminated cover as Type LX2 (95 × 70 mm). Containing booklet pane No. 1634a attached by the selvedge.*
LX3   £3.60, Santa Claus and Reindeer design 7.50

1993 (9 Nov). *Multicoloured laminated covers as Type LX2, but 95 × 60 mm, each showing Santa Claus and Reindeer. Panes attached by selvedge.*
LX4   £2.50, containing ten 25p. stamps (No. 1791) 3.75
LX5   £3.80, containing twenty 19p. stamps (No. 1790) 5.75
       No. LX4 was only available from Post Offices in the Central T.V. area and from philatelic outlets.

STANLEY GIBBONS
FOR
ALBUMS
CATALOGUES
HANDBOOKS
ACCESSORIES

The following pages give details
of selected items from the
Stanley Gibbons Publications range

A complete listing with current prices
is available from your local stockist
or direct from

Stanley Gibbons Publications
Unit 5 Parkside,
Christchurch Road,
Ringwood,
Hampshire BH24 3SH.

or telephone 0425 472363

Stanley Gibbons Great Britain
WINDSOR Album

The Windsor's superiority of other Great Britain albums is largely due to the fact that it is based on the GB listing in the Stanley Gibbons 'Part 1' Catalogue.

Popular with collectors since 1925, the four-volume Windsor is our most detailed Great Britain album with spaces for all those special items such as se-tenant strips and panes, side-ways watermarks and shades as well as all the definitives, special issues, postage dues, officials, regionals and Channel Islands Occupation issues.

The superb quality printed leaves provide spaces for every stamp while on the facing page is an illustrated catalogue giving details and SG Catalogue numbers for easy reference.

The Windsor comes in two formats – the traditional Windsor popular, housed in handsome springback binders in a choice of deep green or scarlet and the Windsor Sovereign, a luxury 22-ring binder, bound in tan leather-effect PVC with a matching slip case – the perfect setting for the special GB collection.

All new Windsor Albums come with a free sheet of self-adhesive Album Titles which includes volume numbers for those collections which have already expanded to more than four volumes.

The Windsor Popular

Item 5241　Volume 1 1840-1970
　　　　　　pre-decimal issues
Item 5242　Volume 2 1970-1981
Item 5243　Volume 3 1982–1990
Item 5244　Volume 4 1991–1993

The Windsor Sovereign

Item 5245　Volume 1 1840–1970
　　　　　　pre-decimal issues
Item 5246　Volume 2 1970-1981
Item 5247　Volume 3 1982–1990
Item 5248　Volume 4 1991–1993

Annual Supplements are published in January each year and blank leaves headed 'GREAT BRITAIN', suitable for both Windsor Popular and Sovereign Albums, are available for those 'special' items not provided for on the printed pages.

For further details visit your favourite stamp shop or write to:

**Stanley Gibbons Publications
Parkside, Christchurch Road
Ringwood, Hampshire BH24 3SH**

The
GREAT BRITAIN
Album, Produced in
GREAT BRITAIN
for the
GREAT BRITAIN
Collector

STANLEY GIBBONS

COVER ALBUMS

Safety First!

All Stanley Gibbons cover albums are now supplied with 'Polyprotec' leaves as standard; this offers considerable advantages over traditional materials in that it does not crease or tear easily, does not degrade and gives considerable protection against ultra-violet light.

THE NEW PIONEER COVER ALBUM

A fully padded binder in a choice of black, green or red. Holds up to 40 covers in a high capacity, low priced album, ideal for the beginner.

THE MALVERN COVER ALBUM

Another great value album suitable for collectors at all levels. The 4-ring arch fitting binder contains 19 double-pocket leaves, 1 single pocket leaf and holds up to 78 covers in all. Available in blue, green, black or red. The Malvern binder is now fully padded for extra luxury.

THE NEW CLASSIC COVER ALBUM

A compact de-luxe album with 20 'Polyprotec' leaves offering full protection for up to 40 covers and two clear fly leaves to hold an index of notes. Available in black, red or blue and supplied in a protective slip box.

THE UNIVERSAL COVER ALBUM

The cover album which allows stamps, booklets and presentation packs to be housed all together.

and COLLECTA COVER ALBUMS TOO!

The very popular range of Collecta Albums are also available direct from us. Please write for full details of the Stanley Gibbons cover album range to:

Stanley Gibbons Publications
Parkside, Christchurch Road,
Ringwood, Hampshire BH24 3SH
Telephone: 0425 472363

Warwick & Warwick
Highest obtainable prices for private treaty sales – at no cost to the vendor.

75% Advance and the full balance within three weeks

A big claim. But one that we've proved time and again. What we're offering is a new deal for the seller. The highest obtainable prices for stamps within three weeks – and an immediate 75% advance – all at no cost to the vendor! Here's how we do it. We have a constantly increasing demand from our Private Treaty buyers throughout the world and we, therefore, urgently need to contact sellers of quality material of all types. It could be a good collection, a specialised study, an accumulation of remainders, a few good single items, covers. Postal History lots, a complete stock, a modern mint investment holding – in fact anything to do with philately. We can sell it.

Visits arranged for any property

A unique service, completely free of charge and without obligation. We can arrange to visit sellers within 48 hours anywhere in the country – practically irrespective of the size of value of the property to be sold. All you have to do is get in touch with us.

Free valuation GUARANTEED SALE

It will pay you to sell through Warwick & Warwick's Private Treaty Service because:

1. You obtain the services of professional valuers – each an expert in his field – whose interests are best served by selling your property at the highest obtainable price. It pays to have Warwick & Warwick on your side!

2. We can visit you within 48 hours – anywhere in the country – to arrange the sale of your property, subject to our assessment of its size and value. There's no obligation and no extra charge (although we reserve the right to decline to visit vendors of small properties). Overseas visits can also be arranged.

3. We give you a written valuation telling you exactly how much you will receive for your collection. This valuation is given FREE off any charge or obligation. We maintain a worldwide register of keen buyers covering every type of philatelic property. We have many buyers listed for every unpopular territory and hundreds of buyers for popular countries. We have many buyers capable of spending up to £50,000 and several with over £250,000 available. You can be sure we have a buyer, with money, waiting for your collection.

4. The sale will be completed quickly. As soon as you have approved our valuation, we will advance you – cheque or cash – 75% of the valuation. We GUARANTEE the balance within three weeks. In order to underwrite this guarantee we will even buy, ourselves, at the full valuation with absolutely no deductions. In fact, sales are often completed within two or three days.

5. If you refuse our valuation you owe us nothing except return postage or transport costs. No charge is made prior to sale (except where valuations of samller properties – £100 or less – are refused when a charge of £5 is made to partly cover administrative costs).

6. There is no commission or other charge payable by the vendor. You receive the full amount tendered in the valuation. The buyer will be charged with all commissions and any other costs. And, of course, there is no 'unsold' charge. We haven't failed so far – and we don't intend to start now!

Highest prices obtained

Currently the greatest demand is for older high quality British Commonwealth, particularly Australia & States, B.N.A., New Zealand and Pacifics, Western Europe, Japan, USA and, of course, Great Britain. We can obtain very high prices for specialised collections, postal history material and dealers' stocks. Naturally larger properties are the best sellers as international buyers with unlimited funds will be interested. We can, and do, sell everything. We have hundreds of overseas clients with special requirements and have consistently obtained the highest prices for practically every philatelic holding, even including so-called dead territories like Eastern Europe and South America. We will not refuse to handle any lot because it is unpopular. And we will continue to maintain this unique record for our clients in the future.

What the Vendors say

Thank you for your courteous and efficient service.
Mr. C., Ipswich, Suffo⃫
Thank you for the prompt manner you have handled the valuation and sale of my stamps.   Mr. W., Wimborne, Dorse⃫
I am delighted with your offer.   Prof. G., Hong Kon⃫
I trust that our happy association will continue for many years to come   Mr. B., Londo⃫
Astounded and delighted with such services and appraisals.
Mr. D., New Zealan⃫
Thank you for your kind attention.   Mr. N., Clydeban⃫
Copies of these have been submitted to the Editor.

We have the buyers – do you have the stamps?

What can we sell for you? Almost everyone connected with stamps has something which is no longer required and can be turned into cash. Think about it for a few minutes – then let us know. You can either send your material to us by registered mail, call and see us at our offices, or write giving details. Or telephone Warwick (0926) 499031 and ask for a member of our specialist valuation staff. Remember we can be with you in 48 hours.
Free transit insurance can be arranged which will give you full cover for your stamps the whole time they are out of your possession. Contact us for details.

Warwick & Warwick Limited,   Established 198⃫
Private Treaty Department, Pageant House,
Jury Street, Warwick CV34 4EW.
Telephone: Warwick (0926) 499031.
Telefax: Warwick (0926) 491906.

Overseas vendors should quote our VAT no. 307 5218 76 on the outside of the package